Cyclopedia
of
LITERARY
PLACES

Cyclopedia
of
LITERARY
PLACES

Volume Three
The Plague–Zuleika Dobson
Indexes

Consulting Editor
R. Baird Shuman
University of Illinois at Urbana-Champaign

Editor
R. Kent Rasmussen

Introduction by
Brian Stableford
King Alfred's College

SALEM PRESS, INC.
Pasadena, California   Hackensack, New Jersey

Editor in Chief: Dawn P. Dawson

Editor: R. Kent Rasmussen *Acquisitions Editor:* Mark Rehn
Manuscript Editors: Melanie Watkins *Research Supervisor:* Jeffry Jensen
Christine Steele *Production Editor:* Joyce I. Buchea
Assistant Editor: Andrea E. Miller *Layout:* William Zimmerman

Library of Congress Cataloging-in-Publication Data

Cyclopedia of literary places / editor, R. Kent Rasmussen.
    p.   cm.
Includes bibliographical references and index.
    ISBN 1-58765-094-0 (set : alk. paper) — ISBN 1-58765-095-9 (vol. 1 : alk. paper) —
ISBN 1-58765-096-7 (vol. 2 : alk. paper) — ISBN 1-58765-097-5 (vol. 3 : alk. paper)
    1. Setting (Literature) 2. Literary landmarks. 3. Literature—Encyclopedias
I. Rasmussen, R. Kent.
    PN56.S48C97 2003
    809′.922—dc21

                                                                        2002156159

First Printing

CONTENTS

CONTENTS

CONTENTS

COMPLETE LIST OF CONTENTS

Volume 1

Volume 2

Volume 3

KEY TO PRONUNCIATION

As an aid to users of *Cyclopedia of Literary Places*, guides to English pronunciations of foreign place-names are provided for particularly difficult words. These guides are rendered with easy-to-understand phonetic symbols enclosed in parentheses after boldfaced subheads and use the symbols listed in the table below. Stressed syllables are indicated by capital letters, as in "**Yoknapatawpha County** (YOK-nuh-puh-TAW-fuh)." It should be understood that some of the phonetic pronunciations are merely approximations, as both English and foreign pronunciations of many place-names vary.

Symbols	*Pronounced as in*	*Phonetic spellings*
Vowel sounds		
a	answer, laugh, sample, that	AN-sihr, laf, SAM-pul, that
ah	father, hospital	FAH-thur, HAHS-pih-tul
aw	awful, caught	AW-ful, kawt
ay	blaze, fade, waiter, weigh	blayz, fayd, WAYT-ur, way
eh	bed, head, said	behd, hehd, sehd
ee	believe, cedar, leader, liter	bee-LEEV, SEE-dur, LEED-ur, LEE-tur
ew	boot, lose	bewt, lews
i	buy, height, lie, surprise	bi, hit, li, sur-PRIZ
ih	bitter, pill	BIH-tur, pihl
o	cotton, hot	CO-tuhn, hot
oh	below, coat, note, wholesome	bee-LOH, coht, noht, HOHL-suhm
oo	good, look	good, look
ow	couch, how	kowch, how
oy	boy, coin	boy, koyn
uh	about, butter, enough, other	uh-BOWT, BUH-tur, ee-NUHF, UH-thur
Consonant sounds		
ch	beach, chimp	beech, chihmp
g	beg, disguise, get	behg, dihs-GIZ, geht
j	digit, edge, jet	DIH-jiht, ehj, jeht
k	cat, kitten, hex	kat, KIH-tehn, hehks
s	cellar, save, scent	SEL-ur, sayv, sehnt
sh	champagne, issue, shop	sham-PAYN, IH-shew, shop
ur	birth, disturb, earth, letter	burth, dihs-TURB, urth, LEH-tur
y	useful, young	YEWS-ful, yuhng
z	business, zest	BIHZ-ness, zest
zh	vision	VIH-zhuhn

Cyclopedia

of

LITERARY
PLACES

THE PLAGUE

Author: Albert Camus (1913-1960)
Type of work: Novel
Type of plot: Impressionistic realism

Time of plot: 1940's
First published: La Peste, 1947 (English translation, 1948)

Albert Camus sets the entirety of this novel within Oran, an Algerian port on the Mediterranean coast. The narrator, Bernard Rieux, emphasizes the city's drabness and the confinement that residents feel when quarantine prevents movement into or out of Oran.

*Oran. Algerian port city on the Mediterranean Sea. From its opening paragraphs, *The Plague* calls attention to the banality, even the ugliness, of the Algerian city in which the events that Rieux chronicles take place. Though the real Oran, where Camus, a native of Algeria, lived from 1941-1942, was not nearly so bleak, Rieux's city is an ugly, soulless place devoid of trees, pigeons, and gardens and grimly devoted to commerce. Unlike the historical Oran, Rieux's version is secured by municipal gates, and the official opening of the ramparts at the end of the novel is celebrated by the inhabitants as a kind of liberation.

In the 1940's, before an anticolonial insurrection brought it independence in 1962, Algeria still constituted part of France, and the relatively large percentage of Oranians of European descent regarded their town as a provincial outpost of French culture. Yet Raymond Rambert, a journalist on assignment from a Parisian newspaper, feels particularly frustrated at being stranded by the local epidemic in distant Oran.

Almost all Camus's writing accentuates the presence of the sea, the sun, and the sky. Yet, in *The Plague*, Oran is described as having been built with its back to the sea, without easy access to the cleansing Mediterranean, even under ordinary circumstances. The city's segregation from the sea is reinforced when, as part of the quarantine, residents are prohibited from wandering to the harbor, and it is a particularly dramatic moment of release when, exhausted by their efforts to contain the plague, Rieux and Jean Tarrou defy regulations and sneak off for a brief, exhilarating swim in the sea.

Rieux's description of Oran is not very specific, and its majority Muslim population remains invisible. A desolate city of the existential imagination, the quarantined Oran of *The Plague* functions as an archetype of modern urban anonymity, an arena in which solitary individuals pursue their absurd struggles.

Rieux's residence (ree-YEW). Rooms in which Rieux lives. After his wife departs for a sanatorium out of town, Rieux's mother moves in to help him. Several of the novel's characters, including Tarrou, Cottard, and Rambert, come to speak with Rieux here. Before the plague, which finally kills him, is officially declared, Monsieur Michel, the concierge, spots a dead rat in the building.

Rue Faidherbe (rew fehd-ehrb). House on the third floor in which Cottard, who makes personal profit out of the general misfortune by trading on the black market, lives. It is in the same apartment that, at the beginning of the novel, Cottard attempts to hang himself and at the end dies resisting arrest. Living in a nearby apartment and struggling through numerous revisions of a sentence he composes is the municipal clerk, Joseph Grand.

Football stadium. Makeshift quarantine center in which Oranians who have been diagnosed with the plague are involuntarily assembled and isolated from the rest of the population. In keeping with Camus's own reading of the novel as an allegory of resistance against Nazi occupation, the football stadium has been interpreted as analogous to the European concentration camps.

Cathedral. Prodded into piety by the imminence of death, an unusually large number of Oranians congregate here for High Mass on the Sunday concluding the Week of Prayer proclaimed during the first month of the epidemic. It is in the cathedral that Father Paneloux delivers each of his two crucial sermons, in books 2 and 4 of the novel.

Municipal opera house. Night after night, a touring company, trapped in Oran by the quarantine, performs the same work, Christoph Willibald Gluck's *Orfeo ed Euridice* (1762). On the Friday evening that Rieux and Tarrou happen to go to the opera house together, the singer playing Orfeo dies suddenly, on stage, of the plague.

— Steven G. Kellman

THE PLAIN-DEALER

Author: William Wycherley (1641?-1715)
Type of work: Drama
Type of plot: Comedy of manners

Time of plot: Seventeenth century
First performed: 1676; first published, 1677

This comedy unfolds in several seventeenth century London lodgings, a tavern, and Westminster Hall. The private lodgings serve as venues for the exposition of a major thematic conflict between plain-dealing and hypocrisy.

Olivia's lodging. London home of the mistress of Captain Manly, the "plain-dealer" of the play's title. The play's stage directions do not provide a description of Olivia's rooms, but the actions that occur there distinguish the site as the most important set in the play. William Wycherley's intent in *The Plain-Dealer* is to satirize both hypocrisy and idealism, and his satire becomes blatantly obvious every time the scene switches to Olivia's lodging. It is there that Olivia's true nature, an unfaithful, flirtatious hypocrite, is revealed. The plain-dealing Manly is often seen in the shadows or in darkness while visiting Olivia at her home, and truly, he is, for a while, in the dark about her real character. Likewise, she tries to keep others in the dark about the reality of her moral fiber.

Manly's lodging. London home of the naval captain Manly whose chief interest is finding a new ship after losing his last ship in a battle against the Dutch. Manly's lodgings are meant to be a stark contrast to Olivia's. While untruth and infidelity pervade Olivia's "world," his dwelling is, in his own opinion, a shrine to truth and virtue. He will not allow shallow flatterers or false friends into his home; in fact, he attempts to thwart visitors by placing guards outside his door. Ultimately, his actions and attitude simply reveal that he is an idealist and a bit of a misanthrope, a person who erroneously thinks that he can live a righteous life by alienating himself from humankind, thereby avoiding any falseness.

Cock in Bow Street. London tavern that is a center of intrigue. There, Manly and his page Fidelia, an heiress in disguise, scheme to expose Olivia's promiscuity; Manly's previous trusted friend Vernish exposes his hypocrisy; and the widow Blackacre and two knights talk of past and future forgeries of legal documents. Ultimately, all characters seen at this tavern prove themselves hypocrites, even Manly, who prides himself on his "plain-dealing."

Westminster Hall. This legal arena provides more insight into the character of Widow Blackacre, a woman obsessed with the law, lawsuits, legal briefs, and legal cases. In addition, her courtroom scene there directly links the legal motifs that pervade the play.

— Michele Theriot

PLATERO AND I: An Andalusian Elegy

Author: Juan Ramón Jiménez (1881-1958)   *First published: Platero y yo*, 1914; complete edition,
Type of work: Poetry   1917 (English translation, 1956)

The small village of Moguer in Spain's Andalusia region is central to this collection, in which the poet rediscovers his childhood home with his donkey companion, Platero, and the joyful, sweet companionship between the man and his donkey unfolds. As they amble through the village and explore the countryside, the speaker describes what they see and do, daily life in Moguer, Spain, around 1905, and the heart and perceptions of a particular poet.

*Moguer (moh-ger). Andalusian village home of Juan Ramón Jiménez and the place to which he returns to rediscover as an adult and established poet. The subtitle of the work, *An Andalusian Elegy*, reflects the nostalgic tone of this work, a lament for his vanished youth in Andalusia. The poems present the simple, seemingly changeless quality of the village and its surrounding countryside.

Moguer is both real and idyllic. The southern climate produces tangerines, grapes, figs, almonds, and, especially, pomegranates—a fruit that the speaker identifies as representing the essence of Moguer. The series of poems moves through all of the seasons of the year. Summer is the most vibrant, when the walks of man and donkey are sensual experiences. Honeysuckle, mallows, and sorrel cover their path while overhead looms the intensely blue sky. The scent of oranges, the sound of cicadas and crickets, the sweet flavors of the watermelon that the companions split and share, punctuate their walks with pleasure. Within sight of an easy walk are the ocean, a river, a stream, farmland, and vineyards.

For Jiménez, the loveliness of the village and countryside and the simple beauties of daily life become metaphorical expressions of his interior self and his interpretation of life seen with eyes made perceptive through close and mindful observation of the simple world around him. Their walk, for instance, he compares to "a mild open day in the midst of a complex life." In the garden with Platero, he sees the sparrows as their brothers, expressing the keen fellowship he feels for all creatures. Under the moonlit sky, the water Platero drinks appears to him as starlight.

Village. Maze of white houses with red terraces dominated by the white village church. The village is a place of tedium and activity, celebration and mourning. Inhabitants range from the kindly, toothless Darbon, Platero's doctor, who, like the poet, responds to his environment with sensitivity and melancholy, to the raucous, unfeeling boys who torment a small bird. The village is home to sweet children who love Platero, to the village priest, the vendors, fishermen, gypsies, shepherds, farmers, grape harvesters, threshers, merchants, and beggars, all going about their daily tasks. The tedium of daily life breaks open when the village erupts into the gaiety of a saint's day celebration, a bullfight, or a carnival. When fireworks and dancing draw villagers to the town square, the man and his donkey happily escape to the countryside. At night the village retreats when workers exchange their toil for song, and widows think of the past and their lost loved ones.

*Andalusian countryside. Favorite place of Platero and his owner as they wander among the trees. There, they feel the gentle breeze or enjoy their siestas under a pine tree. They drink from the stream or soothe their feet in its cooling waters. Able to view the horizon, they observe the scarlet landscape of sunset.

La Corona. Hill that is another favorite spot of the sojourners. Beneath a pine tree atop this hill, they replenish their spirits in the shade of its comforting branches. For the poet, the walk from the stream to the big pine at the top of La Corona is like a man's journey in life. Once on this journey and admiring a wayward flower, the speaker reflects on the fleeting loveliness of life. He assures Platero that one day he will bury him here where his donkey can always hear the birds sing. This he does.

— *Bernadette Flynn Low*

THE PLAYBOY OF THE WESTERN WORLD

Author: John Millington Synge (1871-1909)
Type of work: Drama
Type of plot: Comic realism

Time of plot: Early twentieth century
First performed: 1907; first published, 1907

The setting for this play, a public house in an isolated part of County Mayo, in the west of Ireland, highlights the tension in that island nation between urbanized and "civilized" eastern Ireland and the wild, "truly Irish" western Ireland.

Tavern. Unlicensed public house in the wild Mayo County region on the west coast of Ireland in which the play is centered. The location is somewhat north of John Millington Synge's beloved Aran Islands, and thus an apt setting in which to illustrate Synge's repulsion at the ignorance of Ireland's poor. Synge came by this disdain honestly, through his fiercely Protestant family, who owned land in both County Galway and County Wicklow (thereby bracketing the island both east and west).

Within the setting's isolation, there is community. The tavern stands alone but is constantly filled with people. These people have carved an existence out of their remote setting, relying on contact with the larger world both through the post and the gossip at social gatherings. Nevertheless, this is a place beset by evil, both real and imagined. There are strange people out at night, from the madmen of Keel to the ten tinkers in the glen to the thousand militiamen in the countryside. Even the unseen priest, Father Reilly, haunts the action. The people surrounding this public house threaten it with madness, theft, war, or religion. Into this place comes Christy, a boy from eastern Ireland, and therefore one possessing more native wit than the westerners he encounters. He brings the evil of the outer world with him but wins over the local folk. When the truth is found out, they turn against him savagely. However, after he is reprieved from a lynching, he goes forth, returning to the east, a new man, having briefly seen himself as a hero in the eyes of the local people and found out a bit of his true nature.

— *Joe Pellegrino*

THE PLOUGH AND THE STARS

Author: Sean O'Casey (John Casey, 1880-1964)
Type of work: Drama
Type of plot: Social realism

Time of plot: 1916
First performed: 1926; first published, 1926

The setting of this play is a Dublin tenement during Easter week, 1916, that presents a panorama of social types who define Ireland's response to revolutionary idealism.

Clitheroe apartment. Two-room apartment of Jack and Nora Clitheroe in an aging Georgian house in a Dublin slum. The place bears the marks of self-conscious gentility, with lofty windows, a fireplace painted to resemble marble, prints on the walls, and delftware decorations. Together these amenities suggest "an attempt toward a finer expression of domestic life" and represent Nora's aspirations for domestic tranquility.

Public house. Bar in which the tenement's inhabitants encounter Dublin's street life. The place is defined by a large counter, central window, and comfortable booths where patrons engage in barbed conversation. As armchair patriots debate bromides, the voice of an anonymous patriot drifts in from outside. The voice is that of Padraig Pearse, who is delivering an oration on the steps of the General Post Office which proclaimed Ireland's independence and inaugurated the Easter Uprising. These words are a dramatic counterpoint to the vapidities of the bar's customers.

Bessie Burgess's room. Apartment in the Clitheroe building in which another tenant lives. This home, with its "unmistakable air of poverty bordering on destitution," stands in stark contrast to the Clitheroes' place. Burgess is hosting a wake for the dead child of another tenant. Once again the actions on the barricaded streets inform life in the building as soldiers battle and a stray bullet kills Burgess.

Sean O'Casey's Dublin reveals the hard reality of the slums which nurtured him and the desire for national independence. The contrasting idealism of the Clitheroe home and the grimness of Burgess's apartment underscore the author's divided attitudes toward Irish patriotism.

— *David W. Madden*

THE PLUMED SERPENT

Author: D. H. Lawrence (1885-1930)
Type of work: Novel
Type of plot: Psychological realism

Time of plot: Early twentieth century
First published: 1926

This novel's setting in Mexico, away from what D. H. Lawrence saw as the sterility of Europe, allows for a transformation of the central character, Kate Leslie, whose spiritual and sexual awakening accompanies her literal re-creation in the form of a resurrected Aztec goddess. The novel's setting is central to both the plot of the Aztec revival and the theme of rebirth from the deadness of Europe.

*Mexico. Country in which the novel is set. Lawrence visited Mexico shortly before writing the novel looking, simultaneously, for a climate to help his failing health, an escape from the censorship he faced in England for his political views and for the overt sexuality of his novels, and, perhaps most important, an alternative to what he saw as the dead, "mechanistic" quality of European life.

The title *The Plumed Serpent* refers to the Aztec god Quetzalcoatl, who functions in the novel as, among other things, a symbol for Mexico itself. Lawrence describes Mexico as embodying the qualities of both the reptile and the bird. On one hand, Mexico and its people appear as primitive and somewhat sinister; Lawrence repeatedly uses the word "reptilian" to describe them. On the other hand, Mexico offers the protagonist, Kate Leslie, a spiritual transformation akin to soaring. Her transformation occurs through her sexual union with the Mexican general Cipriano Viedma, whose pure Indian blood is undiluted by European corruption. "Plumed serpent" describes not only Cipriano's country but also his penis. The equation of Mexico with powerful male sexuality helps explain the country's appeal for Lawrence.

Lawrence contrasts Mexico with both Europe and the United States. Europe kills the soul and sometimes even the body. Kate's former husband, an Irish revolutionary, ruined his health and died fighting for his own country's freedom. The United States represents pure consumerism and greed.

*Mexico City. Capital city of Mexico in which the novel opens in the midst of a bullfight. The city, especially as represented by the bullfight, appears as a place of utter degradation with an undercurrent of violence. This particular bullfight, however, is not typical of Mexican culture; even its bulls are imported from Spain because they are believed to be livelier than Mexican bulls.

Kate is both fascinated and repelled by the Aztec artifacts she sees in Mexico city. She claims that Aztec objects "oppress" her and refers to the country's ancient gods as "Aztec horrors." However, she stays in Mexico even after her friends leave, wanting to learn more about a movement to revive the Aztec religion.

*Sayula. Sleepy resort town in west-central Mexico's Jalisco state to which Kate is drawn because it is the center of a movement to revive the ancient Aztec gods. At the town's plaza, the men of Quetzalcoatl pass out fliers and sing chants praising the ancient gods. Ramón Carrasco, the leader of the Aztec revival, has a hacienda, Jamil-tepec, near Sayula. There he hosts ceremonies in honor of the gods and plays the role of the living Quetzalcoatl. Cipriano becomes the living Huitzilopochtli, and Kate becomes Malintzi, the bride of Huitzilopochtli.

*Lake of Sayula. Kate's interest in Sayula arises from a newspaper report she reads about women claiming to have seen a great man coming down from Sayula's lake, telling them that the ancient Aztec gods are about to re-turn. Legend holds that the ancient gods are "bone under the water" while they wait to return. On Kate's voyage across the "sperm-like water" of the lake to reach Sayula, her boat is stopped by men demanding tribute to Quet-zalcoatl. The boatman pulls a little pot from the water shaped like a cat or a coyote; such pots were placed in the lake as offerings to the gods below the water.

The spiritual rebirth of Mexico, then, literally arises from this lake. Its water holds the "sperm" to fertilize the rebirth. In addition, the water's comparison to sperm hints that Kate's journey across the water takes her to a place of sexual significance. At Sayula, she falls in love with her new husband, Cipriano.

— *Joan Hope*

POINT COUNTER POINT

Author: Aldous Huxley (1894-1963)
Type of work: Novel
Type of plot: Social realism

Time of plot: 1920's
First published: 1928

The cross-section of contemporary upper- and upper-middle-class English people, whose lifestyles, attitudes, and opinions are skeptically examined and satirically evaluated in this novel, radiates outward from Tanta-mount House in London, tracking the connections and expeditions of the guests at a social occasion held there. London looms large as the core of the novel, with the rest of England, Europe, and the British Empire relegated to the city's fringes.

Tantamount House. Home of the Tantamount fam-ily in one of the most fashionable addresses in London—on Pall Mall Street, between the Reform Club and the Traveller's Club, not far from St. James Palace. De-signed in 1839 in an ostentatious Italianate style by the architect Charles Barry (who also designed London's Houses of Parliament), the house retains most of its orig-inal features—including a statue of Venus by Antonio Canova that decorates the marble staircase. However, part of the top floor has been converted into a biological laboratory by the scientifically inclined Lord Edward Tantamount.

The house became the home of the Tantamounts when their northern England estates, between Leeds and Sheffield, were despoiled by the Industrial Revolution. Unlike the tenants of Crome in Huxley's earlier *Crome Yellow* (1921), who cling to the old custom of entertain-ing on weekends in the country, the thoroughly modern Tantamounts hold social evenings to which represen-tatives of London's intellectual, artistic, and political elites—which are in the process of superseding and dis-placing the aristocratic elite represented by the Tanta-mounts—are generously invited. Tantamount House is thus the nucleus of an extensive web of social relation-ships, whose guests gravitate there from less fashion-able London addresses and maintain significant contacts with elements of the British Empire as far-flung as India and Canada.

Gattenden. Village in the Chiltern hills in Hertford-shire, site of Gattenden Park and Gattenden Hall. The residence of John Bidlake and his family becomes the setting for one of the novel's few dramatic scenes when Philip and Elinor Quarles's child falls dangerously ill there. Gattenden functions throughout the plot as the primary rural counterpoint to the metropolitan city of London.

*London. The districts of England's greatest city that are principally featured in this novel are, in descending order of fashionability: Mayfair, Chelsea, Belgravia, and Chalk Farm. Lucy Tantamount's flat—a magnet to her many admirers—is on Bruton Street, in the heart of Mayfair. Mark and Mary Campion live in an unpretentious house in Chelsea, whose cultural salubriousness is contrasted with Mary's memories of their first meeting in Stanton-in-Teesdale and subsequent sojourn in Sheffield. On their return to England, Philip and Elinor Quarles take up residence in a mews house (one built on a site previously occupied by stables) in Belgravia. Walter Bidlake lives with Marjorie Carling in Chalk Farm, whose suburban mediocrity is contrasted with his nostalgic memories of growing up in Gattenden.

Other famous London locations featured in the story include Fleet Street, where the national newspapers and many periodicals were based in the 1920's. It is here that Walter Bidlake and his spiritually challenged editor, Burlap, work on the *Literary World*. At Speakers' Corner at Hyde Park, on the eastern boundary of Mayfair, the ill-fated fascist Everard Webley addresses the British Freemen from his white horse, Bucephalus.

*Sheffield.** Industrial city in the north of England, characterized in the novel by its smoky air. The Campions' former hometown, it is the residence of Everard Webley. At the time Aldous Huxley wrote this novel, England's heavily industrialized northern cities had not yet been devastated by the Great Depression. Thus, Sheffield functions in the novel as a fountainhead of ill-bred upstarts.

*Paris.** Capital of France that is the source of many costumes worn by the novel's female characters and a useful place of refuge for Lucy Tantamount, who sends tantalizing letters to Walter Bidlake from Paris's quai Voltaire.

*India.** Subcontinent of Asia from which Philip and Elinor Quarles depart in order to return to English society. They embark for their long voyage home to Bombay, having previously spent time in Udaipur and Lahore. Their only intermediate port of call of any significance is Port Said in Egypt. Readers are informed that India is hot and odorous, that large toads are apt to walk across verandas in its sordid suburbs, and that its exotic inhabitants speak English with accents even more peculiar than those manifested by the elder Mr. Quarles and the assassin Spandrell.

— *Brian Stableford*

POLYEUCTE

Author: Pierre Corneille (1606-1684)
Type of work: Drama
Type of plot: Tragedy

Time of plot: 250 C.E.
First performed: 1642; first published, 1643 (English translation, 1655)

All the action in this play takes place in the palace of the Roman governor of Armenia. Pierre Corneille contrasts the elegance of the formal upstairs residence with the brutality of religious persecution taking place downstairs, where the palace contains a prison. The closed space in which this tragedy takes place adds to the emotional intensity as audiences realize that beneath the outward elegance of a palace there may well be places for torture and execution.

Governor's palace. The fictional Armenia in this play is indistinguishable from any other Roman colony in which individual rights are ignored. This entire tragedy takes place in the palace of Félix, a Roman senator who has recently been appointed governor of Armenia. His residence seems to be comfortable, but its cellar houses a prison in which people are tortured and executed. From the very beginning of this play, Corneille effectively contrasts the elegant upstairs rooms of the rulers with the horrible downstairs prisons in which opponents of Roman rule suffer. Those who submit to Roman rule are welcome in the elegant rooms on the palace's main floor, but below the surface there is much unnecessary suffering.

Governor Félix's daughter Pauline, who is Polyeucte's wife, moves between the upper and lower floors of the palace freely. She loves both her father and her husband, who has recently converted to Christianity, a religion that she does not yet understand. She believes that it should be possible for Rome to tolerate this new religion, but she soon recognizes her father's brutality.

In an offstage scene, Félix makes his son-in-law watch in the palace's basement the martyrdom of Néarque, who converted Polyeucte to Christianity. Far from persuading Polyeucte to abandon his new faith, it inspires in him a greater commitment to Christianity, so Polyeucte chooses to remain downstairs. The most powerful scene in this tragedy takes place in Polyeucte's cell, when his wife implores him to save his life, but he persuades her to embrace Christianity to save her own soul. In act 5, Polyeucte's martyrdom is announced onstage on the upper floor. His courage in accepting death provokes the conversions of both his wife and father-in-law, who come to realize that they can no longer justify brutal violations of individual rights.

— Edmund J. Campion

THE PONDER HEART

Author: Eudora Welty (1909-2001)
Type of work: Novella
Type of plot: Regional

Time of plot: Early 1950's
First published: 1954

The fictional Mississippi town of Clay and its environs provide more than a backdrop for Edna Earle Ponder's story of Uncle Daniel and his Ponder heart. Clay, a town that never amounted to much, reflects the Ponders, a family once rich by Clay standards and now on the decline in number, wealth, and status. Within the microcosm of Clay, the story's action moves between the Ponders' Beulah Hotel and their isolated home at Ponder Hill.

Clay. Small county-seat town fifty miles north of Jackson in Mississippi that has at its heart that requisite of all southern towns, the courthouse square. Across the street is the Beulah Hotel, which only fills when court convenes and brings the town to life. Next door is the movie theater, with offices on the second floor for Ponder family friend, Judge Tip Clanahan. The Presbyterian church, spiritual home to the town's elite, faces the more bourgeois Baptist church. Nearby are the post office and the ten-cent store where Uncle Daniel finds his child bride, Bonnie Dee Peacock.

Beulah Hotel. Of a type that once graced the center of nearly every southern town, hotel boasting twelve bedrooms, two baths, two staircases, five porches, a lobby, a dining room, and a kitchen with a pantry. The once-bustling Beulah now hosts only the occasional overnight guest: Mr. Springer, the traveling drug salesman who comes and goes with the seasons, and the unnamed hearer of Edna Earle's tale. When court is in session, though, the Beulah's table feeds everyone from judge to defendant. It is the Beulah to which Uncle Daniel comes for companionship during and after his stormy marriage to Bonnie Dee.

Ponder Hill. Home of the Ponder family. In contrast to the Beulah at the heart of Clay, the Ponders' home is isolated and empty. It sits three miles out of town in woods full of hoot owls, bordered by fields worked by tenant farmers. When Daniel's father, Mr. Sam, built Ponder Hill, he tried to outdo the hotel owned by his bride's parents. He built on a high hill a house as big as the Beulah itself, loaded with trim and brightly painted, its rooms stuffed with furniture and its roof overloaded with lightning rods. Over the years, however, death has emptied Ponder Hill, until only Daniel and the old cook Narciss remain. It is to Ponder Hill that Daniel takes both the wife of his short-lived first marriage, the widow Miss Teacake Magee, and the child bride of his second marriage, the ill-fated Bonnie Dee.

Clay courthouse. County courthouse that is the scene of Daniel's trial for the murder of his wife, Bonnie Dee. Like Clay, the courthouse is in a state of decline. Filled with onlookers on a hot southern day, it offers a ceiling fan inadequate to the heat generated by a packed gallery, a broken water fountain filled with cement mounded over and painted blue, a porch for the overflow crowd, and a cake of public ice on the courthouse steps.

*Jackson. State capital of Mississippi that is the benchmark Eudora Welty provides for the geographical placement of her story. With a population of more than ninety-eight thousand in 1950, Jackson seems metropolitan to the inhabitants of Clay. A branch line train links Clay with Jackson and the state asylum nearby, to which Mr. Sam commits Uncle Daniel. It takes only an hour to make the drive in Mr. Sam's big Studebaker. It is another world, however, a world where even the richest man in Clay, Sam Ponder, is an unknown who can mistakenly be held at the asylum. Its distant presence in the story juxtaposes the dangers of the outside world with the provincialism of Clay.

*Memphis. Tennessee city near the northern border of Mississippi. Even farther than Jackson lies the bigger and more anonymous city of Memphis, three hours and forty-five minutes north of Clay. Memphis is where Mr. Springer reports seeing the missing Bonnie Dee; Memphis is where the Ponders believe she has run to escape the isolation of Ponder Hill.

Silver City. Mississippi town that is near enough to Clay to encourage trade, yet far enough away to be a separate world, Silver City offers what Clay cannot. For Miss Teacake Magee, it is where she buys the hair coloring she applies herself. For Uncle Daniel and Bonnie Dee, it is where the Ponders are so unknown that no one will call Edna Earle to prevent their impromptu marriage. While Jackson symbolizes the danger in venturing beyond the place where one finds identity and Memphis symbolizes a place so remote that one can lose oneself in it, Silver City is not so much dangerous as merely troublesome, a place to obtain what one ought not desire, in Edna Earle's worldview.

Polk. Once a Mississippi town but now merely a place at the end of a gravel road, Polk is off the map literally and figuratively. The Peacock place out from Polk has tin on the roof, a mirror on the front porch, and more old tires than grass in the yard. The daily passing of the local train is such an event that the Peacocks wave when it passes. The local church in Polk is a burned-out shell, so Bonnie Dee's funeral is held in the little front room of the Peacocks' house.

— *Diane L. Chapman*

POOR FOLK

Author: Fyodor Dostoevski (1821-1881)
Type of work: Novel
Type of plot: Impressionistic realism

Time of plot: Early nineteenth century
First published: Bednye Lyudi, 1846 (English translation, 1887)

Setting his novel in Russia's capital, the city of St. Petersburg, Dostoevski expands upon some basic themes that had already been established in Russian literature in connection with the city. Chief among these is the vision of St. Petersburg as a large metropolis that has a demoralizing and even dehumanizing effect on its inhabitants.

*St. Petersburg. Capital of Russia at the time in which the novel is set. The main characters of the novel, the poor clerk Makar Dievushkin and the seamstress Barbara (Varvara) Dobroselova with whom he corresponds, are denizens of one of the shabbier districts of the large city. As a consequence, the story provides only limited views of other sections of the capital. Makar's letters to Barbara are filled with descriptions of the grubby, impoverished areas of the city, and it becomes

clear that this gloomy cityscape has a woeful impact on the psyche of those who dwell in it. Makar's presentation of city life focuses on three sites: his apartment, the streets through which he walks, and the office in which he works. His entire life seems circumscribed by these three realms.

In his descriptions of the people he encounters on the streets of the city, Makar again singles out the poor and the downtrodden. He finds the faces of the artisans and tradesmen frightening and depressing. In a long passage reminiscent of passages from Honoré de Balzac and Charles Dickens, Makar describes the pitiful sight of a young boy begging those passing by for help for himself and his dying mother. The boy is constantly rebuffed, and Makar foresees a grim future for him. Over the course of the novel, as the seasons change from spring to autumn, growing cold and darkness heighten the somberness of the St. Petersburg scenes that Makar describes.

Makar's apartment. Makar's home is a crowded St. Petersburg apartment building, most of whose lodgers are nearly as impoverished as Makar is. Makar mourns the fact that he lives in what is essentially a slum, and that he is surrounded by noise, shouting, and a constant uproar. He lives in a tiny corner behind a partition in the kitchen, yet in an attempt to bolster his image in Barbara's eyes, he tries to convince her that he is quite comfortable there. Other inhabitants, he points out, are even worse off, and entire families are squeezed into even smaller rooms.

In a particularly telling passage, Makar contrasts the building's main entrance, which is clean and spacious, with the back entrance, a dark staircase with greasy walls. The back staircase is littered with filth and rubbish that emit an unbearable odor. In fact, the stench is so bad in the building that pet birds die when they are exposed to it. Through these descriptions, Fyodor Dostoevski reveals to readers a grim reality about the lives of the poor in St. Petersburg. Indeed, in one letter Makar declares that well-to-do people need someone to wake them up and make them realize that there are other things in life besides their comfortable material possessions.

Makar's office. As a lowly clerk in a large, impersonal bureaucracy, Makar seldom comes to the attention of his superiors. However, in one of the most striking scenes in the novel, Makar is summoned to explain a mistake to the head of his department. His description of walking through room after room to get to his superior's room has a nightmarish quality to it.

Barbara's childhood home. Contrasting with the grim conditions of her St. Petersburg existence are Barbara's recollections of her happy childhood in the country. Her evocations of pleasant moments spent out of doors and in the company of her family are brief moments of light amid the relentless series of descriptions of the hardships she has suffered since moving to the city. These positive recollections of country life can also be contrasted with the unpleasant prospects of a future life that awaits her as she marries the caddish Mr. Bwikov and is carried off to a home somewhere in the remote steppes of Russia.

— *Julian W. Connolly*

POOR WHITE

Author: Sherwood Anderson (1876-1941)
Type of work: Novel
Type of plot: Psychological realism

Time of plot: 1866-1900
First published: 1920

By dramatizing the development of a lazy, "poor white" southerner, Hugh McVey, from his origins as the son of the town drunk in Mudcat Landing, Missouri, to his regeneration via exposure to New England industriousness into the inventive, pragmatic mind-set that fuels American industry, and finally to his rebirth with a conscience and morality that are skeptical of America's technology-driven economic exploitation, Sherwood Anderson expresses his contempt for the industrial America born in the late nineteenth century.

Mudcat Landing. Missouri town in which Hugh McVey was born, Mudcat Landing is a place where life without drinking is unbearable, where slavery has left poor whites with a deep aversion to physical labor. However, it is in Mudcat Landing that Hugh is exposed to New England pragmatic industrialism when he lives with the railroad stationmaster and his wife, the latter an energetic woman who cures him of his slothfulness and gives him a good education. She also instills in him a sense of a "glorious future." Hugh departs for parts North and East, eventually bringing his pragmatic, inventive energy to Bidwell, Ohio.

Bidwell. Fictitious Ohio town in which the novel is centered. Surrounded by small farms devoted to fruit, berry, cabbage, corn, and wheat raising, Bidwell initially represents pre-industrial America. It is a place in which everyone knows everyone else, and life is slow and predictable. However, Hugh's agricultural inventions are seized upon by greedy businessmen, factories begin to rise up, and the impersonality and the frantic lifestyle of industrial mass production begin to erode the old values.

However, as greedy capitalists exploit the new labor force, labor unrest begins, mirroring actual American history, and the new system begins to break down. Eventually, Hugh disavows his dedication to inventing in favor of his family. At the novel's end, he symbolically returns to the earlier way of life and values by turning his back on Bidwell's factories by going up the steps and to the farmhouse door of his rural home.

*****Sandusky.** Ohio city where Hugh's epiphany about the flaws of American urban, industrial life begins. There, Hugh walks along the shore of Lake Erie and reflects on the disturbances in Bidwell. As he plays with colored stones in his hands, he notices how their colors blend and separate and realizes that one "could look at the stones and get relief from thoughts." Then, he thinks of industrial towns and "grimy streets of workers' houses clustered closely about huge mills," and realizes that the "gods have thrown the towns like stones over the flat country, but the stones have no color. They do not burn and change in the light." As symbols of beauty and pleasure, Sandusky and Lake Erie move Hugh to reflect on the lack of beauty and pleasure in American industrial and technological life.

— John L. Grigsby

THE POORHOUSE FAIR

Author: John Updike (1932-   )
Type of work: Novel
Type of plot: Social satire

Time of plot: Mid-twentieth century
First published: 1959

John Updike wrote this novel as a recollective tribute to the community in the town of Shillington, Pennsylvania, in which he grew up. While all of the places named in the novel are fictional, they are generally patterned on the actual town and the topography of the countryside surrounding Shillington. Updike's intention is to capture the ethos of a place and a way of living that he felt was in danger of vanishing in the rapid industrialization of the northeastern corridor from Washington, D.C., through New York, and on to Boston.

Diamond County Home for the Aged. Home for elderly people in which the novel is primarily set. A converted mansion that once belonged to a prominent member of the jurisdiction (the local term for county), it has resident rooms, a passageway, and four acres of land that constitute the literal world (or "constricted community") of its residents. John Updike placed it in New Jersey to avoid a too-specific autobiographical equivalence to the Pennsylvania community on which the community is based, and also because his father's family was from Trenton, New Jersey, and he wanted to include that aspect of his background in the book. The land surrounding the home is described as "shallowy concave farms," and the distant horizon dotted with "small hills typical of New Jersey."

Diamond County. Once-rural region of New Jersey that is being transformed by the forces of the mid-twentieth century that Updike recognizes as inevitable but which he regrets to an extent. John Hook, the central narrative consciousness, remembers how as a boy he could go to the top of a hill and not see a house in any direction, whereas now there does not seem to be any space east of the Alleghenies where a person can stand and not be in hailing distance of a house. This motif is emphasized by Hook's references to his boyhood, his life work as a teacher in a village school near the river, and the relative isolation of the families there. Especially significant is his view of the state of Pennsylvania across the river, which he once thought of as "westerly wilderness."

*Delaware River. River forming part of the New York-New Jersey and New Jersey-Pennsylvania borders. At a later stage of his life, after his retirement but before he moves into the Home, Hook lives with his daughter in a house outside the town beside the Delaware. The river functions in the novel as an emblem of passage and as a barrier that separates and isolates individual communities. Hook recalls that a road passed near the house, and that on a bend in the road, a modest store, little more than a shack, served passing motorists. When the "combine" (a petroleum corporation) closes the store, the older winding road is replaced by an interstate highway; the transition from river to country road to limited-access turnpike signifies the change in the countryside.

Andrews. New Jersey town whose residents visit the Diamond County Home during its the annual fair. There,

Updike draws on his detailed sense of Shillington, although his presentation is fragmented so that aspects of the town appear in brief vignettes in accordance with his intention to use some techniques of the "new novel" in *The Poorhouse Fair*. The perspective shifts, as a boy walking with his grandfather first sees the wall surrounding the home. Hook calls the town a "backwater," most of whose inhabitants are only a few generations removed from farm owners. People at the fair talk about the past, about roads and schools and old houses that give an impression of the town's substance and heritage.

Sky. The weather is a noteworthy element of the novel and plays an important part in the ways its characters respond to events of the day. Updike uses reactions to the skyscape as a method to reveal and illuminate character, as in Hook's observation that the sky is "savage red" in the morning, a portent of the coming storm, his exultation when rain lifts, and the way residents of the home join together in "raucous, cruel exhilaration" when the west wing of their building receives the benefit of the setting sun.

— *Leon Lewis*

PORGY

Author: DuBose Heyward (1885-1940)
Type of work: Novel
Type of plot: Regional

Time of plot: Early twentieth century
First published: 1925

Set in and around Charleston, South Carolina, where DuBose Heyward was born and spent a large part of his life, this novel captures the strong African American atmosphere that Heyward associates with the city.

Catfish Row. Fictitious section of Charleston in which a disabled beggar, Porgy, and other black characters in the novel live. Most of the time, Catfish Row is full of life and energy, but whenever a white person enters the neighborhood, every resident leaves its central square for the indoors. Porgy himself usually sits in the square in front of his room and watches what happens, except when he gambles. Aside from one brief summer, when Bess joins him in his dwelling, Porgy participates in the life of the Row and enjoys living.

Opposite Porgy's room is the cookshop run by Clara, who constantly struggles to impose order on Catfish Row. The Row is near the wharf and the bay. When a hurricane comes, its residents flee to upper stories of their buildings to escape the rising waters.

*Charleston. South Carolina port city. Some critics have said that one of the central ideas behind *Porgy* involves the conflict between the recently emancipated black residents of Catfish Row and the modern city in which they live. When members of the African American organization called "Sons and Daughters of Repent Ye Saith the Lord" parade through the "reticent, old Anglo-Saxon town" on their way to greet a steamer, the white residents of Charleston laugh at them. The African Americans appear sadly out of place in the city. Porgy does his begging in the white section of the city, on the corner of King Charles Street and Meeting House Road. When he is presented with a summons to appear in Coroner's Court to identify Crown—whom he has killed when the latter tried to break into his room—he flees up Meeting House Road toward the forests, in which he hopes to hide. A police patrol wagon catches him after he gets beyond the big buildings to where the bungalows stand.

Wharf. Pier adjacent to Catfish Row where stevedores, including Crown, find work and the base for the **"Mosquito Fleet"**—a flotilla of small fishing boats owned and manned by African Americans. During the hurricane, the entire fleet is destroyed. During a lull in the storm, when Clara sees her husband Jake's half-submerged boat approaching the wharf, she runs into the water and drowns, leaving Bess behind to care for her baby. When the full fury of the storm returns, a lumber schooner breaks loose and destroys the wharf itself.

Jail. Charleston jail in which both Bess and Porgy spend time. It is has a small exercise yard where prisoners spend their days trying to keep in the shade. At night, prisoners are locked in what appears to be a steel cage. The jail is damp; moisture clings to its ceilings, runs down its walls, and forms small streams that run across its floor. The jail smells terrible and breeds disease.

Kittiwar Island. Fictional island off Charleston on which Crown is hiding out and to which a steamer transports members of the Sons and Daughters of Repent Ye Saith the Lord for a picnic. When Bess wanders into the island's jungle, Crown finds her and takes her deeper into the interior, where he has his way with her.

*Savannah. Georgia coastal city to which Crown promises to take Bess when he leaves Kittiwar Island and the place to which Bess goes while Porgy is in jail.

— *Richard Tuerk*

PORTNOY'S COMPLAINT

Author: Philip Roth (1933-   )
Type of work: Novel
Type of plot: Bildungsroman

Time of plot: Mid-twentieth century
First published: 1969

This entire novel unfolds within the office of a Manhattan psychoanalyst, Dr. O. Spielvogel, whom Alexander Portnoy visits for treatment. However, the story Portnoy tells Spielvogel ranges through New Jersey, New York, Europe, and Israel. At the end of the book, Philip Roth reminds readers that the setting has all along been Spielvogel's office by having the doctor speak for the first time. As one would expect in a story told in a psychoanalytic setting, place has deep meaning for Portnoy.

*Newark. New Jersey city in which Portnoy grows up. At the time he is born, his family lives in Jersey City in a building inhabited entirely by Jews but surrounded by non-Jews whom Portnoy's parents view as anti-Semitic. Just before World War II, at the urging of Portnoy's uncle, the family moves into what they consider the much safer environment of Newark, in the almost entirely Jewish Weequahic neighborhood, where Roth himself grew up. There, Portnoy, like Roth, attends the almost entirely Jewish Weequahic High School and eventually feels suffocated by his family, especially his mother, as well as by the Jewishness of the milieu in which he lives.

*Manhattan. New York City borough, across the Hudson River from Newark, to which Portnoy moves after finishing college. New York's mayor appoints him assistant commissioner for the city's Commission on Human Opportunity. To Portnoy, Manhattan represents an opportunity to escape from his Newark past, to escape his family, and to live his own life. Part of the escape from Jewish Newark involves a series of affairs he has with non-Jewish women, beginning in college and culminating in an affair with a woman he calls the Monkey, whom he meets as she enters a taxicab in front of his Manhattan apartment. In his sexual escapades with her, he seeks a complete escape from the Jewishness of his childhood that he associates with the Weequahic neighborhood. Nevertheless, the area in and around Manhattan proves to be for Portnoy much too close, physically, to Newark. His parents visit him too easily and too often, and he visits them.

*Europe. Portnoy goes to Europe to escape from his middle-class Jewish background, as well as from his parents. When he and the Monkey depart for Europe, he refuses to tell his parents his itinerary. In Rome, he and the Monkey join an Italian prostitute in a sexual threesome. Thus, Europe, Portnoy thinks, finally provides him with an escape from Newark. After the escapades in Rome, however, the Monkey becomes upset, so irritating Portnoy that he deserts her in Greece. He eventually discovers that not even Europe provides him with the freedom from convention and responsibility that he hoped it would.

*Israel. Jewish-ruled Middle Eastern country to which Portnoy goes after deserting the Monkey. As his airplane lands in Israel's capital, Tel Aviv, he is overcome by the memory of Sunday mornings in Newark, when neighborhood men got together to play softball. In a sense, in coming to Israel, he is, he feels, coming home again.

Ironically, the last chapter in the book—the one that treats Portnoy's adventures in Israel—is titled "In Exile." Through his memories of Newark and his experiences in Israel, Portnoy discovers that unlike the Jews who consider themselves at home in the Land of Israel, no longer living in exile, he still feels that he is in exile, at home no place. Although through memory he may be able to return temporarily to the Newark of his youth, he can find no solace there. To him, Israel, also, is like a dream, a place like his childhood Weequahic neighborhood inhabited almost entirely by Jews. For a moment, Portnoy hopes that Israel will provide him with relief from his feelings of alienation, that it will enable him to return to his Newark childhood to which he thinks he belonged and in which he found at least a kind of happiness. Instead, he finds himself unable to function sexually in Israel although he tries desperately to do so. Thus, he discovers that for him, geographical location provides no solace. Even in Israel, he is still in exile, alienated from his childhood and himself.

— *Richard Tuerk*

THE PORTRAIT OF A LADY

Author: Henry James (1843-1916)
Type of work: Novel
Type of plot: Psychological realism

Time of plot: c. 1875
First published: serial, 1880-1881; book, 1881

In this novel, Isabel Archer, a young, unsophisticated American woman, is eager to travel to Europe to immerse herself in the beauty and culture of the Continent, but once there, she is crushed by the oppressive weight of Europe's past and by the betrayal and deceit that is part of Italian history and that is embodied in Gilbert Osmond. Of the numerous European settings in the novel, the most important is Rome, the site of Isabel's defeat and the setting for half of the novel. Drawing from his many visits to Rome, Henry James creates a setting that suggests the city's twin heritages of art and treachery.

*Rome. Capital of Italy and major center of Western art and culture that provides the novel's primary setting. Isabel Archer's initial response to Rome is similar to that expressed by James himself on his first visit there in 1869: "She went about in a repressed ecstasy of contemplation." Isabel's state of mind is suggested by her lodgings, the Hôtel de Paris on Via St. Sebastiano, a sunny Roman street lined with trees on one side and a hill covered in greenery on the other. The hotel, a short walk from the Pincian Gardens, is located near the Spanish Steps and the Piazzo de Spagna, a popular gathering place for English tourists during the nineteenth century and the neighborhood in which James himself often stayed. Isabel visits many of the famous Roman sites—the Forum, the Palazzo Doria Pamphili, the gallery of the Capitol with its Hall of the Dying Gladiator, and St. Peter's Basilica—all suggestive of a historical tradition so deeply entrenched it can become an oppressive force.

After rejecting several offers of marriage because she fears they will interfere with her desire to experience life, Isabel ironically accepts Gilbert Osmond's proposal. Her marriage transforms her from a passionate, independent woman to an *objet d'art*, another item in Osmond's art collection. The change is symbolized by the change in her residence. The darkness of the Palazzo Roccanero is in sharp contrast to the airiness of the Hôtel de Paris.

Palazzo Roccanero. Isabel's home in Rome after her marriage to Osmond. James modeled Roccanero after Rome's Palazzo Mattei, which was built on the site of the ancient Circus Flaminius in the early seventeenth century. Situated on one of the many "tortuous, tragic streets of Rome," Roccanero is a "dark and massive structure." Even the "damp" interior courtyard receives very little direct sunlight. The palazzo contains both "frescoes by Caravaggio" and "mutilated statues and dusty urns," indicating both the positive and negative aspects of tradition and culture. Representing Osmond's oppressive hold over Isabel, the palazzo, a "domestic fortress," seems to imprison her.

Gardencourt. English country estate by the River Thames, near London, that is the residence of Isabel's cousin, Ralph Touchett. Gardencourt appeals to Isabel's imagination that has been stimulated by her reading and daydreaming in her grandmother's house in Albany. As the word "garden" implies, the setting is idyllic, but Isabel soon encounters a snake in the garden in the personage of Madame Merle, Osmond's former mistress.

After leaving England, Isabel travels with Mrs. Touchett to Paris, then to Florence, where Madame Merle introduces her to Gilbert Osmond, whose elegance and sophisticated taste impress her, and finally Rome. At the end of the novel, she returns to Gardencourt, against Osmond's objection, to tend to the dying Ralph. Gardencourt thus frames the novel, highlighting the change in Isabel; no longer innocent and naïve, she has acquired the wisdom that comes from disappointment and suffering.

*Albany. Capital of New York State that is Isabel's hometown, a prosaic place suggesting that Isabel will be unprepared for the sophistication of Madame Merle and Gilbert Osmond. Upon the death of her father, Isabel leaves Albany, embarking on a tour of Europe with her aunt, Mrs. Touchett.

— *Barbara Wiedemann*

PORTRAIT OF THE ARTIST AS A YOUNG DOG

Author: Dylan Thomas (1914-1953)
Type of work: Short fiction

First published: 1940

These early Dylan Thomas stories blend fiction and autobiography to recall the Welsh town in which he grew up. Each story celebrates a visit or excursion, either within the town or just beyond it. The town and its environs become a character in the book, elaborated in the names of houses, shops and pubs, and local weather, which ranges from the warmth of summer evenings on the beach to wet wintry nights. The locales, like the seasons of the year, change from story to story and help create the image of the region as a setting for the gallery of minor characters who dominate each story.

*Swansea (SWAHN-see). Industrial seaport in southern Wales in which Thomas was born and raised. Wales's second largest town, Swansea stands at the mouth of the River Tawe, from which it takes the Welsh name Abertawe, which Thomas's stories use for it. Stories set within Swansea include "Patricia, Edith and Arnold," which describes two servant girls taking a young boy (Thomas himself) to the park in winter, so that they can meet a young man who is two-timing them. "The Fight" features a school that is based on Swansea Grammar School, which Thomas attended and where his father taught English. This story also features the home of a cultured middle-class family, whose twelve-year-old son writes novels and classical music. His friend, the narrator, writes poems. Later stories include one about a young man taking shelter under a railway arch at night. Another concerns the young man having a literary discussion with friends, working in the offices of a news-

paper, and visiting public houses. All the pub and street names in the stories are real places in Swansea.

*Rhossilli Sands** (rah-see-lee; now spelled Rhossili). Bay at the western end of the Gower Peninsula that runs about fifteen miles southwest from Swansea and is a popular day-trip destination for the town's inhabitants. In "Extraordinary Little Cough," a group of teenage boys travel there by lorry to camp for a fortnight. In "Who Do You Wish Was with Us?" an older narrator and a friend set out to walk to Rhossilli Sands but end up traveling most of the way by bus.

— *Chris Morgan*

A PORTRAIT OF THE ARTIST AS A YOUNG MAN

Author: James Joyce (1882-1941)
Type of work: Novel
Type of plot: Bildungsroman

Time of plot: 1882-1903
First published: serial, 1914-1915; book, 1916

Ireland, with its rich spiritual and cultural heritage, which contrasts sharply with its poverty and political oppression, is the setting for this coming-of-age novel of a sensitive young man who aspires to be an artist. The power of the Roman Catholic Church and of conventional Irish morality is embedded in the very settings of the book.

*University College.** Roman Catholic university in Dublin, as opposed to Trinity College, which was reserved for the Protestant elite. This is the site where Stephen Dedalus and his friends have long, involved discussions and arguments about topics such as art, politics, and the Catholic Church.

As at his earlier schools, Stephen is at odds, intellectually, philosophically, and religiously, with most of his fellows; however, at University College he is much better able to articulate his positions. It is here that Stephen finally renounces his Catholic faith, with his statement that he will refuse to make his Easter duty as his ailing mother has asked. In the physics theater of University College, Stephen and an elderly Jesuit priest discuss the powerful differences in language—particularly differences between English and Gaelic—that are powerful impulses in Stephen's aspirations and actions. During this conversation, Stephen realizes the great potency words have in his life and senses that the artist who can transform reality through words is equivalent to the

priest who can transmute the bread and wine during mass.

Dedalus homes. The large family of Simon and May Dedalus occupy a variety of houses and apartments in Dublin during the course of the novel. The steady decline in the richness and quality of these residences charts the descent of the Dedalus family from relative affluence to harsh poverty. In the first home, an elaborate Christmas dinner presented by servants is the scene of a dramatic political argument between Stephen's father Simon and his aunt, Dante Riordan, over Irish politics, especially the fate of the Nationalist leader, Charles Stewart Parnell. Successive homes and their meals are smaller and less satisfying, until the family is living in less-than-genteel poverty. The decline in material richness is juxtaposed to Stephen's growing intellectual and artistic richness and resources.

*Clongowes College.** Exclusive school, run by Jesuits in County Kildare. Simon Dedalus respects the Jesuits for their ability to help their students achieve material and professional success in life. Clongowes combines classrooms, dormitories, playgrounds, and chapel. There, Stephen first experiences his artistic impulses. It is also here that he is the victim of larger, more powerful boys who mock and bully him for his physical weakness and intellectual inclinations.

***Belvedere College.** More modest Catholic school to which Stephen is sent as the family's fortunes decline. At Belvedere, Stephen attends a retreat where a visiting priest summons up terrifying visions of the eternal damnation and suffering of the tortured souls in Hell. Following these services, and after a night filled with horrible dreams, Stephen hurries to confession and dedicates himself to the Church, to the point where he seriously wonders if he has a vocation for the priesthood.

Bridge. Structure spanning a tidal river on the coast near Dublin. While walking in this vicinity, Stephen watches a company of Christian Brothers, an order of the Catholic Church, march over the bridge. Immediately afterward, he beholds a lovely young girl, birdlike in her appearance, wading in the water. As is often the case in James Joyce's work, water, especially the sea, symbolizes art and freedom. There, the choice clearly is between the Church and art, and Stephen's decision to renounce the Church in favor of art is made the moment he responds to the beauty of the girl.

***Dublin.** Capital of Ireland, although at the time of the novel the nation was not independent but part of the British Empire. Dublin forms a backdrop for much of *Portrait of the Artist*, especially in the scene where young Stephen wanders the streets seeking a prostitute, both to release his sexual longings and to "embrace life" in defiance of the Church and Irish morality.

— *Michael Witkoski*

THE POSSESSED

Author: Fyodor Dostoevski (1821-1881)
Type of work: Novel
Type of plot: Psychological realism

Time of plot: Mid-nineteenth century
First published: Besy, 1871-1872 (English translation, 1913)

Fyodor Dostoevski focuses on a provincial town in Russia to show the dangerous effects of radical political ideas unleashed upon the rural populace in the 1860's. He presents a range of settings to show how these pernicious ideas can spread across the social spectrum from the lower classes to the aristocracy.

Provincial capital. Unnamed town that Dostoevski modeled on the city of Tver (located approximately one hundred miles northwest of Moscow), where he spent five months in 1859. The town is the site of much of the novel's activity, which tends to cluster in one of the following locations: a drawing room in the house of Mrs. Stavrogin (the mother of the novel's central figure, Nikolai Stavrogin); the rooms inhabited by Stepan Verkhovensky, Nikolai Stavrogin's childhood tutor and a longtime friend of Mrs. Stavrogin's; the residence of the provincial governor Von Lembke, an ineffectual bureaucrat who is easily manipulated by the novel's villain, the radical activist Peter Verkhovensky; and a house on Bogoyavlenskaya Street (the Russian name means "epiphany"). This last location is the residence of several of the novel's secondary characters: Shatov, Kirillov, and Captain Lebyadkin and his sister Marya. When Nikolai Stavrogin pays a visit to each of these individuals one night, he symbolically revisits his past, for they each reflect one aspect of Nikolai's futile search for meaning in life. Across the river is a working-class district into which the Lebyadkins move shortly before they are murdered.

Skvoreshniki. Summer estate of Mrs. Stavrogin that is the scene of several dramatic incidents, including a tryst between the married Nikolai Stavrogin and Lisa Tushin, the headstrong woman who loves him desperately. Shatov is murdered in a remote part of the estate, and his body is flung into a pond. Nikolai Stavrogin hangs himself in the attic of the house.

Ustyevo. Small village where Stepan Verkhovensky spends time with a woman who distributes the New Testament. There he renounces atheism and accepts religion before his death.

*St. Petersburg. Russia's capital city, where Nikolai Stavrogin spends several years of dissipation and where he apparently seduces a young girl, committing a crime that would haunt him for the rest of his life.

Yefimyev Mother of God Monastery. Site of the cell of Bishop Tikhon, a monk who is visited by Nikolai with a confession of his crimes in St. Petersburg.

— *Julian W. Connolly*

THE POSTMAN ALWAYS RINGS TWICE

Author: James M. Cain (1892-1977)
Type of work: Novel
Type of plot: Psychological realism

Time of plot: 1933
First published: 1934

A diner located on an isolated stretch of road outside Los Angeles serves as the primary setting for this tale of a drifter, Frank Chambers, and Cora Papadakis, the beautiful young wife of the diner's owner, who conspire to murder her husband. The Depression-era atmosphere portrayed by the author accentuates the loneliness, passion, and desperation driving the two conspirators.

Twin Oaks Tavern. Described by Cain as a "roadside sandwich joint, like a million others in California." The diner also includes living quarters for the husband and wife, a filling station set off to one side, and a grouping of a half dozen shacks referred to as an auto court. The lodgings, in particular, add to the sense of confinement experienced by the two lovers, as they attempt to free themselves from their suffocating lives through a brief and impulsive affair. As portrayed by Cain, this is drifter country, a land of passersby, passing fancies, and passing relationships. It is a place where people are always headed elsewhere. For Frank, it is a place from which to escape. For Cora, it becomes a test of Frank's commitment to her. By agreeing to stay, he would be signaling that he was no longer a vagabond and, more important, that he was no longer trying to make her into one.

Culinary and carnal appetites are closely intertwined in Cain's two main characters, beginning with their first sexual encounter in the diner's kitchen. It is a scene brimming with irony, in that it is the place where Cora's husband has sharply rebuked her for not adequately gauging the size of Frank's appetite. In fact, Frank's desire for the man's wife serves to diminish thoughts of food to the extent that it sickens his stomach.

Roads. The many roads that cover Cain's grim Southern California landscape. The first vision the reader has of Frank is that of him wandering along a road leading to the diner, after having been thrown off a hay truck on which he caught a ride. The open highway symbolizes for Frank the freedom to cross boundaries and to journey into other worlds, where individuals are not bound by stringent social and moral codes. It also acts as a narcotic to undo inhibitions. Accordingly, it is on a mountain road that the two lovers murder Cora's husband and alongside which the two then make love. Yet the road also serves to separate Twin Oaks from the constraints of the communities that lie beyond it, specifically the specter of the Los Angeles urban industrial complex, which threatens to overwhelm it. In Cain's world the road is always there, an ever-present enticement to those who seek escape from their emotional and physical confinement.

*Pacific Ocean. On two occasions in the novel, once before their marriage and once after, Frank and Cora take a trip to the beach, which represents a refuge from the mounting pressures of their unfulfilled lives. "All the devilment, and meanness, and shiftlessness, and no-account stuff in my life had been pressed out and washed off," Frank says to himself on one of these visits. However, the notion of rebirth is not as authentic as the two characters believe it to be. Their rendezvous with the ocean are but brief interludes in their desperate search for fulfillment. The geography of the ocean only magnifies the dislocation of their lives once they return to the diner.

*Los Angeles. Sprawling city in Southern California that acts as a magnet for the hordes of drifters, itinerants, and gypsies who headed west during the Depression era of the 1930's. The city's giant shadow looms over Cain's landscape as a symbol of the broken dreams of those who were seeking a better life but wound up finding just another dead end. The recognition that they may have reached their final destination with nothing to show for it only serves to intensify their desperation and alienation from the rest of society.

— *William Hoffman*

POWER

Author: Lion Feuchtwanger (1884-1958)
Type of work: Novel
Type of plot: Historical

Time of plot: Mid-eighteenth century
First published: Jud Süss, 1925 (English translation, 1926)

The contrast between scenes of magnificent wealth and those of squalid deprivation generate dramatic effect in this novel. Brightly lit palaces are filled with colorful uniforms and sumptuous furnishings, financed by exploiting the populace. Unbearable taxes and forced military service are required to sustain court carousing. As the product of historical oppression and blind prejudice, the Jewish ghetto and the fortresses are dark, spartan, and cramped. The only possible spaces for purity and virtue in the novel are a country house near Hirsau and the mountain landscapes frequented by Rabbi Gabriel.

*Duchy of Württemberg** (WUR-tehm-bayrg). German principality in what is now southwestern Germany. Bisected by the Neckar River, the duchy has hilly green country with cultivated river valleys, and mountains of the Swabian Alps and part of the Black Forest. During the eighteenth century, bumpy roads were frequented by peddlers and others on foot who competed with the carriages and horses of the nobility. Stuttgart and the newer ducal residence in Ludwigsburg were headquarters of courtly life, whereas Wildbad, a Black Forest spa, was for their recreation. Free cities such as Esslingen, islands within the duchy not controlled by the duke, dotted the landscape. The naturally prosperous duchy was impoverished by the wasteful misrule of Karl Alexander, the duke who employs the protagonist, Josef Süss Oppenheimer, as his privy financial councillor.

*Oppenheimer's palace.** Stuttgart residence of the duchy's finance minister, Oppenheimer, who uses his office—a typical role for court Jews at the time in which the novel is set—to amass a fortune. His palace displays expensive tapestries, cabinets of jewels, and busts of sages that signal his worldly success. Decorated with Leda and the Swan on the ceiling, his bedroom is the scene of many amorous conquests. Exotic tokens such as an Arabian steed and a parrot in a gilded cage represent his cultural sophistication and power. Everything in the palace advertises his exquisite taste and high fashion, in marked contrast to his origins in Frankfurt's Jewish ghetto.

*Frankfurt.** German city from whose Jewish ghetto Oppenheimer comes. The novel's description of the ghetto is so general that it could apply to almost any city in Germany or Eastern Europe. Gates separating the ghetto from the rest of the city are locked every evening. Narrow streets and crowded quarters leave no room for vegetation and provide little fresh air. Jews are forbidden from practicing most trades, and Jewish men are forced to grow beards and wear caftans. Frequently afflicted by pogroms, the Jews are pictured cowering in fear in narrow alleys and crooked houses. Having escaped the ghetto, a symbol of all the disadvantages of adhering to the Jewish faith, Oppenheimer triumphs without renouncing his faith.

Rabbi Gabriel's house. Cottage near Hirsau, a German town in the northeastern part of the Black Forest, where Rabbi Gabriel is raising his niece, Naemi, who is Oppenheimer's daughter. Enclosed by a high fence and surrounded by terraces of flowers, the white house looks like a vision. It also harbors Gabriel's library of cabalist writings. Like the innocent and lovely Naemi, the house symbolizes spiritualized virtue, here presented as a flower of Jewish mystical learning. When the duke's party violates the house, it is a sign of the hopeless degeneracy of the times.

Gabriel frequently wanders alone in the stern landscape of stone pines, glaciers, and granite rock around his home, where he cultivates divine meditation. In this setting, he feels especially keenly the grooves on his forehead forming the letter Shin, the first letter in the Divine Name Shaddai, which signals his mystical spirituality.

*****Ludwigsburg Palace** (LEWD-viks-boorg). The more magnificent of Duke Karl Alexander's two residences. Ludwigsburg mirrors the duke's obsession with sexual prowess and ostentation. During his lavish parties, courtiers gamble, drink, and are entertained with music. There, the duke flaunts his wealth and cavorts with mistresses. Fittingly, it is the scene of the final escapade that kills him after his attempted coup fails, following an overly potent dose of an aphrodisiac.

*****Hohenasperg Fortress** (HOH-ehn-AHS-payrg). Historical German fortress containing a notorious prison in which Oppenheimer is kept before being hanged. His cell is a small, damp, rat-infested hole in the ground with scanty light and fetid air. Continually shackled, his body is unkempt and broken by starvation, but his spirit remains strong. The contrast between Oppenheimer's cell and his palace could not be more vivid. However, his stoicism and continued dignity in the face of this adversity help redeem the compromises with virtue he previously made in order to pursue and maintain the life of power and elegance so exceptional for a European Jew of this era.

— *Julie D. Prandi*

THE POWER AND THE GLORY

Author: Graham Greene (1904-1991)
Type of work: Novel
Type of plot: Psychological realism

Time of plot: 1930's
First published: 1940

In this novel, Graham Greene places faith and vision for the future at the center of a violent landscape in which the national government is suppressing the Roman Catholic Church and its priests. The protagonist is an unnamed priest being hunted by police.

*****Mexico.** Country in which the entire novel is set. The novel uses psychological realism to depict the corruption and violence associated with the government's revolutionary vision. That vision is portrayed by an unnamed police lieutenant, who considers himself the champion of hope and betterment and says that "life will never be the same" for the next generation as he pursues a fugitive priest.

In contrast, the priest is engaged in a survival struggle to bring continuity into the spiritual lives of Mexicans who are eager to extend their vision beyond their physical and material needs. Since the Mexican police have advertised a reward for the priest, Greene shows how the theme of trustworthy relationships can sustain hope in a corrupt and threatened environment.

Plaza. Central square of an unnamed Mexican city where a bust of a former president serves as a reminder of Mexican Revolution and the nation's independence. The plaza leads to the river port that offers the priest an opportunity to escape to Vera Cruz on the coast. However, the priest's decision to share a drink with Mr. Tench, then a child's summons to his mother's deathbed, supersede his original plan of escape. In the conclusion, the plaza becomes the site of the priest's execution after the Mexican police arrest him.

Hotel. Hotel beside the river to which a beggar leads the disguised priest for a secret drinking party with a high government official and the governor's cousin. The government officer is clearly corrupt; he violates the prohibition law and symbolizes the internal corruption of a regime that is claiming reform through a revolutionary vision. For his part, the priest himself does not mirror the traditional acts of martyrs or saints whose stories are passed on to the Mexican children. He is an alcoholic who has violated his vow of celibacy and has an illegitimate daughter; however, he manages to dodge the authorities and continue to perform the religious rites that strengthen the Catholic population's hope in the future.

Prison. Unsanitary and overpopulated prison in the city to which the priest is taken when he is arrested for possessing alcohol. The next morning he meets the lieutenant, who does not know his clerical status. The lieutenant discharges him and gives him money as a compassionate gesture for having cleaned up the filthy prison cells. Ironically, while the priest is in the prison, the half-caste recognizes him as a priest but conceals the discovery, so he can acquire the reward without having to share it with the prison authorities.

Plantation. Banana farm owned by an American where the priest finds a shelter and food. There, the planter's daughter Coral secretly brings the priest brandy and keeps him hidden when the police lieutenant comes looking for him. However, when the priest returns to the plantation a second time, he finds that it has been ransacked, apparently by revolutionaries known as the Red Shirts.

Rural church. Whitewashed village church where the exhausted priest passes out and is rescued by German American missionaries, who prepare him for a journey to a safer destination, Las Casas. Before his departure the priest holds a mass for the parish, who also request baptisms and confessions. Apparently, the villagers are so poor that they bargain with the priest over the price of religious ceremonies, yet none seems interested in the reward money for handing over the priest.

— *Mabel Khawaja*

THE POWER OF DARKNESS

Author: Leo Tolstoy (1828-1910)
Type of work: Drama
Type of plot: Domestic tragedy
Time of plot: Nineteenth century

First published: Vlast tmy: Ili, "Kogotok uvyaz, vsey ptichke propast," 1887 (English translation, 1890); first performed, 1888

This, Leo Tolstoy's best play, uses two of his favorite themes in his later writings: the need to improve life in Russia's villages and the need for stricter adherence to Christian morality in everyday life.

Russian village. The setting of the play is an unnamed, large Russian village, in which peasants live and behave in a manner disrespectful of common decency. They mistreat each other whenever the opportunity arises, tolerate immoral marriages, steal from each other, and even murder one another when it serves their purposes. Himself a Russian count, Tolstoy underwent a profound religious conversion late in life and preached in his works a faithful following of Christian virtues and morality. Having lived most of his life in the Russian provinces, he was also keenly aware of the backwardness of the peasants and of their wont to follow their impulses regardless of the consequences.

Although Russia's serfs were freed from virtual slavery in 1861 and expected to show great improvement in their life, there had been little progress when Tolstoy wrote his play. In the character of Akim, a simple, illiterate, inarticulate, and humble villager, who keeps reminding everyone that a man should have a soul and follow God's laws, Tolstoy presents a model to be emulated. Akim's insistence on righting the wrong brings his son, Nikita, who had committed several crimes, including the murder of his newborn baby, to a sincere confession and repentance at the climax of the play. What saves *The Power of Darkness* from being merely a preachy and moralistic exercise is Tolstoy's flair for dramatic action, compact plot, and creation of distinctive characters. He presents his Christian message indirectly and dramatically, as a depiction of universal human tragedy.

— *Vasa D. Mihailovich*

THE PRAIRIE: A Tale

Author: James Fenimore Cooper (1789-1851)
Type of work: Novel
Type of plot: Adventure

Time of plot: 1804
First published: 1827

This novel traces Natty Bumppo, hero of James Fenimore Cooper's Leatherstocking series, in old age. Cooper uses as his setting for the novel the vast grasslands west of the Mississippi, the area of American expansion in 1804 as his hero, now well into his eighties, once again articulates the weaknesses and the strengths of Native American and pioneer attitudes and ideals, with special emphasis on questions of justice and how best to relate to nature and the land.

Prairie. Set just after the Louisiana Purchase, the novel's events occur in a vague area of the prairie, about five hundred miles west of the Mississippi River. Cooper had not traveled in these western regions and was dependent on published accounts of others for his descriptions of the prairie areas. Thus, the places in the plot's development are mostly imagined and generally not tied to identifiable spots on the map. Rather, it is the qualities of the prairie that interest Cooper: its vastness, wildness, emptiness, and sameness. Against this desertlike landscape, even a hero like Natty Bumppo is made to seem less sure and in charge than in the novels which place him in the eastern forests. Here, human efforts appear almost swallowed up by the land itself.

*****La Platte.** Platte River, whose main branch originates in central Wyoming, flows east, through all of Nebraska, before emptying into the Misssouri River just south of Omaha. The novel's references to this river, and its suggestion that the action occurs in this river's vicinity some five hundred miles west of the Mississippi River, lead one to believe that western Nebraska is the likely real-life equivalent of the geographical area Cooper imagined for his narrative. Although Natty Bumppo and his threatened friends, the Bush clan, and the Sioux and Pawnees in the novel are aware of this river and its importance, Cooper never really makes clear that any of the action actually occurs along its banks, preferring instead to rely on unnamed rivers and streams.

First camping area. The Bush clan and Natty meet in the desert waste with Natty pictured against the western sunset as a "colossal," larger-than-life figure, dramatically underscoring his key role in opening up the frontier. The Bushes strip the prairie of its vegetation as they set up camp, thus underscoring their heartless and ruthless disregard for the environment.

Bush fortress. About three miles from the first camping spot, the Bush clan sets up a more permanent home on a hilly prominence which features "a single naked and ragged rock," a natural lookout spot to watch for marauders while at the same time being easy to defend. Cooper uses this touchstone spot throughout the first half of the novel as the various parties vie back and forth over the kidnapped Inez, the stolen flocks, and the murder of Ishmael Bush's son, Asa. Some twenty miles away from this rock, Bumppo manages to set a backfire which saves the day when the Sioux and the Bush clan attempt to eliminate the novel's "good" characters by means of a prairie fire.

Sioux camp (sew). Temporary Sioux encampment near a river, to which Bumppo and his friends are taken after being captured by the Sioux. The site is some days away from the rocky fortress. It is here that the warriors of the Sioux and the Pawnee tribes fight, with Hard Heart, the good Pawnee, the winner (good because he seems to recognize and honor certain "white" values). It is also here that Cooper complicates Ishmael Bush's character by having him mete out prairie justice according to Old Testament principles, freeing Natty and his friends.

Rocky ledge. Located on a small hill above the prairie emptiness, this is the spot Ishmael Bush chooses for the final scene of prairie justice. Not trusting civilization's handling of justice, he determines to execute Abiram, his son's killer, relying on Old Testament texts as his guide. Unwilling to shoot Abiram, he fetters him on the rocky ledge with a rope placed around his neck for either starvation or a self-hanging from the willow, which in its lifelessness seems an appropriately stark symbol for this death scene. Upon hearing what sounds like a death scream after they leave, Ishmael and his wife, showing some degree of mercy, return to bury the dead, at which point Ishmael pronounces a sort of Old Testament forgiveness over the corpse.

Pawnee village. Located close to the Missouri River, this village of supportive Native Americans is the spot where Natty Bumppo and his friends separate. The latter return to civilization, while Bumppo remains in the frontier wastes of the prairie. It is also here, about a year later, that Cooper pictures Bumppo's death, with his hero facing west toward his beloved frontier, gazing into the sunset, the best of human beings, honored by Native Americans and pioneers alike. Bumppo greets his death on his feet with the word "Here!"

— *Delmer Davis*

PRIDE AND PREJUDICE

Author: Jane Austen (1775-1817)
Type of work: Novel
Type of plot: Domestic realism

Time of plot: Early nineteenth century
First published: 1813

Settings in this novel are limited to elegant English homes and country estates, each of which Jane Austen uses to comment on the foolish, class-based prejudices of her characters and the social class differences inherent in early nineteenth century England.

Longbourn Estate. Home of the Bennet family in southeastern England's Hertfordshire. The estate is "entailed," meaning that it can be passed down only through male heirs. Austen uses the estate to point up the condition of single women in early nineteenth century England, demonstrating why they have an intense need to marry. The Longbourn estate is to pass to Mr. Collins, a pretentious young clergyman who stands to inherit Mr. Bennet's property. After the heroine Elizabeth Bennet turns down Collins's proposal of marriage, her best friend, Charlotte Lucas, accepts his proposal because she is poor and needs to marry.

Netherfield Park. Estate rented by Mr. Bingley, the neighborhood's new eligible bachelor, in which Austen sets up the novel's action. The Bennets have five unmarried daughters, and their silly mother is anxious to see them all married. Mr. Bingley soon falls for Jane, the oldest, and it is through him that Elizabeth meets the arrogant Fitzwilliam Darcy, Bingley's best friend. The complex social goings-on at Netherfield illuminate a society in which women scramble to find husbands amid financial snobbery and class prejudice.

Rosings. Home of Mr. Collins's arrogant patron, Lady Catherine de Bourgh, who is also Darcy's aunt. After Charlotte marries Mr. Collins, she moves to the cleric's cottage near the Rosings estate.

Pemberley. Darcy's well-ordered home, in which he and Elizabeth come to view themselves as they truly are: Elizabeth recognizes her own prejudice, and Darcy recognizes his own pride. Pemberley is the perfect setting for the ultimate triumph of romantic love. After Elizabeth spurns Darcy, she eventually begins to regard her decision as a mistake, especially as she realizes that she might have been the mistress of Pemberley, in whose miles and miles of grounds she takes great delight.

— *M. Casey Diana*

THE PRINCE AND THE PAUPER

Author: Mark Twain (Samuel Langhorne Clemens, 1835-1910)

Type of work: Novel

Type of plot: Social satire

Time of plot: Sixteenth century

First published: 1881

A historical fantasy about boyish wish fulfillment, this novel has a dark undertone. When an English pauper boy who dreams of becoming a prince and a real prince who longs for freedom outside his palace playfully switch places, they accidentally become trapped in each other's lives; unable to convince anyone else of who they really are, each finds his new existence a prison from which he struggles to escape.

***England.** The novel can be read as an attack on England's monarchical institutions and hereditary privilege. The book depicts mid-sixteenth century England as a grim place in which most people live hard lives under cruel and unjust laws and heedless rulers. The novel forces Edward, Prince of Wales, to live among his meanest subjects; after he is restored to rightful position, he is moved to liberalize England's laws.

***London.** The principal setting for about half the novel, England's capital city is depicted as existing in two worlds: the unending want of life in places such as Offal Court and the unlimited plenty of the royal court. The pauper boy, Tom Canty, though wise beyond his years, knows nothing about the London outside his slum until the day he wanders to Westminster Palace. Meanwhile, Prince Edward is equally ignorant of the London outside his palace until the accident that causes him to switch placcs with Tom.

***London Bridge.** A hive of shops, inns, and homes, the oldest bridge across the Thames is a microcosm of London whose denizens include some people who have never even set foot ashore. Touching the river's north bank near Offal Court, the bridge is the place where John Canty instructs his family to gather after he kills a priest and has to flee London. Prince Edward's champion, Miles Hendon, takes lodgings on the bridge, which is also the place where he and Edward become separated by a mob after they return from Hendon Hall.

***River Thames** (tehmz). River that winds through London. It is introduced early as a playground of Tom Canty and his friends—much like the Mississippi River is a playground to Tom Sawyer and Huckleberry Finn in other novels by Mark Twain. When Tom Canty tells Prince Edward about the games he plays in the river's mudbanks, the prince declares he would "forego the crown" if he

could but "revel in the mud once." To Edward, the river represents freedom, but to Tom it becomes a pathway to imprisonment. After he is entrapped in the palace and accepted as the prince, he is reluctantly carried on the river on barges, first to a state occasion at the Guildhall and later on the first stage of his procession to his coronation.

Offal Court. Shabby London neighborhood where Tom Canty, his parents, twin sisters, and an abusive grandmother live in a single upstairs room, in which they sleep on straw on the floor. Though Offal Court is a "foul little pocket," Tom is reasonably happy—so long as he is not hungry and his father forces him only to beg, not to steal. Taking ideas from romantic books, Tom finds time to join friends in games, which include holding mock royal courts and pretending to be a prince—training that later serves him well.

To the real prince, Offal Court is one of many prisons he endures outside his palace. He goes there hoping to find help to get back to the palace; instead, he is seized by Tom's father—who thinks he is his son—and is taken to the family lodging, where he is beaten and left to sleep on the floor. Much of the narrative from that moment concerns Edward's struggle to escape from John Canty's control after Canty joins up with a band of thieves in the countryside, and Edward goes from one form of imprisonment to another.

***Westminster Palace.** Royal palace of King Henry VIII (now home to the Houses of Parliament), located upriver from Offal Court. One day, Tom Canty wanders to the palace and is thrilled to glimpse Prince Edward through a gate. When Edward sees Tom being struck by a guard, he invites him into the palace, feeds him, and asks him about his carefree life in Offal Court. On a whim, the prince suggests they swap clothes, and the boys discover that they could be twins. Mistaken for the beggar boy, the prince is tossed out of the palace, leaving Tom alone inside, deathly afraid of being discovered and executed. Tom's dream of being a prince is now a nightmare. Even after he ceases to fear exposure, he finds the palace a weary prison and longs to be restored to his rags and rightful place in Offal Court. However, the power and wealth that surround Tom eventually corrupt him. Whereas he is initially appalled by the wasteful expenses of the royal household, he later doubles the number of his servants.

*Tower of London. Historic castle famous as a prison for traitors and political prisoners. Though not a setting in the novel, the Tower is frequently mentioned as the place where King Henry's enemy, the duke of Norfolk, awaits execution. In the coronation scene at the climax of the novel, when Edward is finally acknowledged as king, the lord protector suggests flinging Tom Canty "into the Tower."

*Christ's Hospital. Government-run home in London for orphans and children of indigent parents. When the displaced prince applies for help there, he experiences his first major rebuff. Instead of being recognized as the prince, he is mocked for his pretensions. Despite his disappointment, he vows that when he becomes king, the inmates of the home will be properly educated. He later keeps his pledge when he makes Tom Canty the school's chief governor.

Peasant barn. Place in which the prince is accidentally imprisoned. After wandering alone in the woods, Edward is relieved to find shelter inside this barn but is dismayed when its doors are locked behind him. Inside the pitch-black barn, he has a terrifying encounter with an unknown creature that brushes against him but relaxes when he realizes it is merely a calf's tail. In the morning he awakens to find a rat sleeping on his chest. He regards this as a good omen that means he can fall no lower.

Hermit's hut. Woodland home of a former priest who takes Edward in, accepts his claim to be king, feeds him, and tucks him into bed. Relieved to escape his pursuers and find shelter, Edward thinks that he has found safety until the priest reveals himself as a madman, a self-styled "archangel" who believes that he would be the pope, had not King Henry abolished England's Roman Catholic monasteries, destroying his religious vocation. Edwards awakens from his sleep to find himself tied to the bed, with the priest about to stab him with a butcher knife, when Miles Hendon suddenly appears at the hut's door. The hermit's hut thus proves to be yet another prison, instead of a sanctuary. "Would God I were with the outlaws again," says the prince, "for lo, now am I the prisoner of a madman!"

Courtroom. Court of a justice of the peace before whom Edward is taken after being arrested for stealing a pig. Innocent of the charge, Edward is inclined to resist arrest until Hendon challenges him to show the same respect for the law that he, as king, would expect from his subjects. Edward's brief trial is an eye-opener for him when he learns that the penalty for theft could be death. The kindly judge manages to reduce the charge, and Edward escapes formal imprisonment only through a trick Hendon plays on the constable leading him to jail.

*Hendon Hall. Ancestral home of Miles Hendon, near Monk's Holm, in southeastern England's Kent region. Getting back to the home from which he has been away for many years is Hendon's supreme goal, and he expects to dazzle Edward with his family's wealth and hospitality. However, after overcoming many obstacles to reach Hendon Hall, his fondest hopes are dashed: His beloved father and older brother are dead; his true love, Edith, is married to his greedy and cruel younger brother, Hugh; and all the faithful family servants are gone. Like Edward, Hendon can find no one who will acknowledge who he is. Instead of the warm welcome and comfort he expects, he and Edward are thrown into a dungeon. For Edward, Hendon Hall proves to be yet another false sanctuary that leads to another prison, this time a true prison and one in which he is indelibly scarred when he witnesses women who have befriended him being burned at the stake for the crime of being Anabaptists.

*Westminster Abbey. Historic church, nearly adjacent to the palace, in which England's monarchs are traditionally crowned. The night before Tom's coronation, Edward sneaks into the abbey and hides in Edward the Confessor's tomb. The next day, at the moment Tom is about to be crowned, Edward appears, proclaims himself the rightful king, and throws the coronation officials and assemblage into total confusion. The assemblage's uncertainty about which boy is the true king is manifested in the physical movements of people being careful not to make a move that might be interpreted as disloyalty to whichever boy proves to be the rightful king.

— *R. Kent Rasmussen*

THE PRINCE OF HOMBURG

Author: Heinrich von Kleist (1777-1811)
Type of work: Drama
Type of plot: Historical

Time of plot: 1675
First published: Prinz Friedrich von Homburg, 1821
(English translation, 1875); first performed, 1821

Heinrich von Kleist, a Prussian nobleman who had served in the army, wrote this play as a tribute to the ruling house of Brandenburg. The cities of Fehrbellin and Berlin, which alternate as the backdrop in the play, reflect this focus. A famous battle that takes place on stage in which the Great Elector defeated Swedish troops marks the beginning of Brandenburg-Prussia as a militarily strong state in Europe. In contrast to the confusion and harsh reality of battle, the peaceful garden of Fehrbellin Palace, which is in the realm of dreams and ideals, frames the play as a whole.

*Fehrbellin Palace. Located forty miles northwest of Berlin, this palace was the Prussian headquarters for the campaign against Sweden. For the prince of Homburg however, the palace gardens become a place to dream of becoming a war hero and marrying the Elector's niece Natalie. In a prearranged pantomime with Homburg half asleep, Natalie removes the victory wreath Homburg has fashioned for himself; it is returned to him unexpectedly only in the final scene. The wreath symbolizes both Homburg's promise as an officer and his tendency to take precipitous action, for which he must do bitter penance in the course of the play. The sweet garden scents and the moonlit night point to Homburg's dream of love.

*Old Palace. Prussian palace in Berlin in whose garden the people of Brandenburg join the Elector to honor the war dead and celebrate victory. As the seat of the Great Elector in his capital, this palace is a proper place in which to hand down a death sentence against Homburg for disobedience in battle. The Elector also hears the petition of his niece and his generals to spare Homburg, since his disobedient action secured the Prussian victory. The setting underscores the duty of the Elector to his country, which must outweigh the promptings of the heart and the wishes of his niece. The key position of the Prussian army for the success of Brandenburg means that obedience to the state is a cardinal virtue.

*Fehrbellin. Site of the decisive Prussian victory over the Swedes in 1675, which provides the setting for the play's second act. This scene helps show the dreamy prince of act 1 as a man of action. Resisting the officer who tries to restrain him, he rides out with his troops decisively despite the crash of cannons, the rain of musket bullets, and a nearby fire.

— *Julie D. Prandi*

THE PRINCESS CASAMASSIMA

Author: Henry James (1843-1916)
Type of work: Novel
Type of plot: Social realism

Time of plot: Late nineteenth century
First published: serial, 1885-1886; book, 1886

The central theme of this novel set in London is relationships between place and socioeconomic class. As the character of Hyacinth Robinson attests, the tension between the two can in fact lead to self-destruction. The novel's point of view is primarily that of the lower class. The difficulty that Hyacinth has in finding a position between the upper and lower classes suggests both the absence of a clearly defined middle class and the impossibility of such a class existing in any real way.

*Lomax Place. Working-class section of Pentonville in north London that is home to Amanda Pynsent, the foster mother of Hyacinth Robinson, who is ostensibly the bastard child of an English lord. In spite of their lowly social position, Pynsent raises Hyacinth to be a gentleman, not only because she believes that in fact he is one, but also because of her reverence for the upper class. Prior even to Hyacinth's own recognition of his "mixed blood," there is already a tension between his social status and his upbringing.

*Millbank. Prison on the River Thames in which Hyacinth's birth mother, Florentine Vivier, has been imprisoned for murdering the man she claims is Hyacinth's father, Lord Fredericks. The prison is the setting for one of the most important scenes in the novel, in which the young Hyacinth meets his dying mother and thus confronts his own mixed origins. This encounter sets up the tension between the two sides of Hyacinth's character that struggle with each other throughout the novel.

James himself visited Millbank in 1884, and Miss Pynsent's commentary on the prison may be seen as James's own reflections on the subject.

*Audley Court. Neighborhood in Camberwell, a lower-class section in south London, in which Paul Muniment, the chemist who leads Hyacinth into revolutionary work, and his wife, Rose, live. Rose has a debilitating illness, but is strong enough to voice her protests against a working-class revolution, making Audley Court another setting for the mounting tension within Hyacinth Robinson.

The Sun and Moon. Small tavern in Bloomsbury in whose rear room secret meetings of the "revolutionaries" take place. The tavern's name is significant, as the Sun and Moon are antithetical bodies that cannot appear together in the night sky, just as Hyacinth's sympathies must either be for or against the existing order, but not both at the same time.

*Pimlico (PIHM-lih-koh). District of London that is home to some of the "petit bourgeois." Considered a step up from Pentonville, Pimlico is home to Millicent Henning, Hyacinth Robinson's childhood friend, who represents the middle road, the middle class, between Hyacinth's conflicting sympathies. Although Millicent's level would seem to be the most logical and comfortable position for Hyacinth, Millicent and the class she represents cannot be faithful.

*Belgrave Square. Upper-class London district in which Lady Aurora has a house that undergoes a transformation corresponding to a transformation taking place within Lady Aurora herself. When her house is introduced, it described as a "magnificent mausoleum," but in the end it is bright and alive, as is Lady Aurora, both acceding to their "noble" constitutions.

Medley Hall. Country home at which Hyacinth Robinson briefly visits with the Princess Casamassima. While the princess's rooms on London's South Street provide him with a glimpse of expensive ornaments, Medley Hall serves as Hyacinth's first taste of the true grandeur of the upper-class life.

*Paris. Hyacinth visits the capital of France after inheriting money from Amanda Pynsent. The art, architecture, and culture of Paris, which he sees as the result of the struggles between the dominant and the oppressed, cause him to reconsider his revolutionary beliefs. He comes to similar conclusions during a visit to Venice.

Madeira Crescent. Dreary London neighborhood to which the princess moves after selling all her beautiful furnishings to live in a tawdry, lower-middle-class house in order to be closer to Paul Muniment and support his "cause." The noble sacrifice she makes is muted by the fact that she continues to use only the most expensive tea and keeps her servants.

Westminster. Working-class London neighborhood in which Hyacinth settles after Amanda Pynsent's death. There he again faces the degrading conditions of working-class life, but with a new respect for the upper classes, which requires the maintenance of the different class levels.

— *Kimberly Jackson*

THE PRINCESS OF CLÈVES

Author: Madame Marie de La Fayette (Marie-
Madeleine Pioche de la Vergne, 1634-1693)
Type of work: Novel
Type of plot: Psychological

Time of plot: Mid-sixteenth century
First published: La Princesse de Clèves, 1678 (English
translation, 1679)

This novel's primary setting is the French royal court, a highly public sphere immersed in political and amorous intrigues. Changes of scene from this glittering worldliness to various private locales beyond Paris reflect the newly married princess's retreat from adulterous passion into dutiful peace of mind.

*Louvre (lew-vruh). Parisian palace that is the mid-sixteenth century site of the royal court of King Henri II in which the novel unfolds during the last years of the king's reign. Madame de La Fayette opens her novel with an account of the king's twenty-year relationship with his mistress, quickly establishing the public nature of romance in this glamorous, pleasure-oriented environment.

Most of the novel's court scenes take place in the Louvre, the royal French residence until King Louis XIV moved to establish a new palace at Versailles in 1682. Giving almost no physical descriptions of the palace, the novel concentrates instead on its moral-social ambience, summed up at one point as "a sort of ordered agitation" that makes "it all quite pleasant, but also precarious, for a young lady." So important are decorum, masks, and dissembling at court that "appearances seldom lead to truth." After King Henri's accidental death at a tournament, the growing estrangement between the princess and her husband plays out against a court destabilized by major power shifts.

*England. Under Queen Elizabeth I, England is an ally of France during the period in which the novel is set, and the country figures into the novel as the source of a prestigious marriage for the duke de Nemours. De La Fayette establishes her fictional hero's extraordinary worth by having him court the new English queen, with every chance of success, before falling in love with the French princess.

One of several stories embedded in the novel recounts the romance of Queen Elizabeth's father, King Henry VIII, with her mother, Anne Boleyn. Boleyn had lived at the French court before becoming Henry's second wife in 1533. This episode not only roots her Protestantism in her French life but also uses the political and sexual intrigues of Henry's reign to mirror the scheming at the Louvre.

*Brussels. Belgian city that is the duke's base for his courtship of Queen Elizabeth. His residence here during princess of Clèves's first arrival at the French court means that he meets and pursues her only after her marriage.

*Spain. Roman Catholic country that is France's enemy at the beginning of the novel and that becomes its ally. In Book 3, the French court celebrates the wedding of King Henri's daughter, Elizabeth of Valois, to Philip II of Spain (by proxy). The widower of Mary I of England, who died in 1558, Philip chooses Elizabeth as his third wife to commemorate a treaty he signed earlier with France. As political alliances, such marriages in the novel contrast not only with the duke's passion for the princess but also with her husband's unusual marital love.

Coulommiers (kew-lom-YAY). Estate of the prince and princess of Clèves, located a day's journey from Paris. As a country retreat, Coulommiers enables the princess to obey her mother's dying wish that she leave the court to protect her virtue and reputation. Twice the duke invades her refuge, his secret presence suggesting the danger his forceful eroticism poses to the princess's integrity. From an alcove in a pavilion in the château's gardens, he eavesdrops on the princess's confession to her husband that she is resisting her love for another man.

Later, when the princess again adjourns from the court to preserve her honor, the duke returns to Coulommiers at night and—while being observed by the prince's servant—watches the princess sitting in an alcove, knotting ribbons on his former walking stick. After rejecting the duke's proposal of marriage, the widowed princess retreats entirely from court, first withdrawing to her estate in the Pyrenees, then dividing her time between Coulommiers and a convent.

Merchant shops. Early in the novel, the prince first sees the princess—still Mademoiselle de Chartres—in an Italian jeweler's shop. At the end of book 4, the duke rents a strategically situated room from a silk merchant for spying on the princess in Paris. In both scenes, valuable merchandise serves as a backdrop for intrusive male appreciation of female beauty.

— *Margaret Bozenna Goscilo*

THE PRISONER OF ZENDA

Author: Anthony Hope (Sir Anthony Hope Hawkins, 1863-1933)
Type of work: Novel

Type of plot: Adventure
Time of plot: 1880's
First published: 1894

The fictional setting of this novel, the central European principality of Ruritania, represents a remote pocket of the world where chivalric culture still survives. Through the creation of this setting, Anthony Hope is able to step back in time without resorting to the techniques of the historical novel. Yet, in many ways, he had to observe the rigors of the historical novelist since the nation he created had to be self-consistent, with its own plausible history and politics.

Ruritania. Imagnary country in central Europe whose name suggests isolation, as in the word "rural." The country is presented as a real place because the novel's protagonist, Rudolph Rassendyl, reaches it via the Dresden train. Dresden would represent, to Hope's European audience, the eastern border of Germany, the territory of the Austro-Hungarian Empire where Germanic and Slavic cultures intermingle. It is the region of Germany once known as Bohemia, which would connote to the late Victorian reader a wild, artistic sense of life. The Dresden train is the last vestige of the civilized nineteenth century; once the hero leaves it, he is plunged into the feudal world of Ruritania. Outside the capital city of Strelsau, Ruritania is a mass of forests and villages. The protagonist Rassendyl speaks of being enchanted by the beauty of the forest outside Zenda, and that elvish word invokes the same fairy-tale sentiment as does the name of the Ruritanian king's family, the House of Elphberg. References to religious ceremonies during the coronation of the Ruritanian king indicate that Ruritania is a Catholic country, though there is no discernible religious significance to the Catholic references. They are merely a part of the overall sense of medievalism in Ruritania.

Zenda. Small town located fifty miles from the Ruritanian capital of Strelsau. Zenda boasts scenic hills, beautiful forests, and an ancient castle which served as the country residence of the Duke of Strelsau, the king's half brother. The castle itself serves as an emblem of the odd marriage of realism and romance in Hope's novel: It is a medieval stone edifice attached to a modern-style villa added by the duke. However, the villa is the only modern thing in Zenda and is associated with the evil duke. There are modern hotels in Strelsau, but in Zenda all the narrator can find is a homey inn as described in medieval romances. A train brings him to Zenda, but once there, all his travel is by foot or by horse. After the castle of Zenda is turned into a prison for Prince Rudolph, to keep him from accepting the crown that the duke covets, the modern villa is not mentioned again, and the gothic gloom of the ancient castle pervades the story.

Strelsau. Capital city of Ruritania represents the home of the would-be king Rudolph, who enjoys the high life of the city and avoids the Ruritanian heartland. Strelsau appears only in the background of the novel, as the only inroad of the modern world in Ruritania. None of the action occurs in the city, though it is frequently mentioned.

— *John R. Holmes*

PRIVATE LIVES

Author: Noël Coward (1899-1973)
Type of work: Drama
Type of plot: Comedy of manners

Time of plot: 1929
First performed: 1930; first published, 1930

A light romantic comedy about misdirected love and incompatible marital partners, this three-act play uses its Parisian settings to fuel or retard romance, to serve as haven or hell in a farce of partners who are unable to live with or without each other.

French hotel. Unnamed Parisian hotel in which the play is set. Noël Coward's stage directions describe the terrace of a French hotel as the setting of the first act, which begins with a mood of honeymoon romance. He calls for two French windows at the back of the terrace to open onto two separate suites. In addition to the small trees in tubs and awnings shading the windows, a low stone balustrade separates the balconies. This simple division serves the action well, for the mechanics of the plot depend on the unexpected meeting of former spouses Elyot and Amanda, who are both on honeymoons with their new partners. The terrace setting, with an orchestra playing nearby, sets the scene for romance, but the coincidental meeting leads to amusing tensions.

*__Avenue Montaigne__ (av-new moh[n]-ten). Parisian street on which Amanda's flat is located. The flat is supposed to be her urban retreat and blends well with Coward's suggestion of characters who hunger for new adventures in exotic settings. Amanda and Elyot talk about their separate travels around the world, without really realizing that physical flight is not always the solution to one's problems. Swapped partners lead to swapped settings, but things go awry here as well. While the piano helps the pair rediscover an intense romantic pull beneath their often-clashing dialogue, some of the other furniture and props (especially the uncomfortable sofa, gramophone, and records) suffer in the comedic farce that results from the inevitable quarrels between Elyot and Amanda and later those of Sibyl and Victor, who reappear on the scene.

— *Keith Garebian*

THE PROFESSOR'S HOUSE

Author: Willa Cather (1873-1947)
Type of work: Novel
Type of plot: Psychological realism

Time of plot: A few years after World War I
First published: 1925

Houses in the Midwest and the Southwest form the primary symbolic keys to Professor St. Peter's midlife crisis. He clings tenaciously to his old, midwestern home, while family members move to homes that mirror the change, selfishness, materialism, and gaudiness of modern life.

Professor's old house. Located adjacent to the college campus at which the professor teaches, the old, oddly built but simple house of Professor St. Peter has for more than two decades been the site of his marital, family, scholarly, and artistic happiness. It is here that he tends his French-influenced garden, a testimony to his preference for the aesthetic superiority of long-established cultures. In this old house, also, is the attic room, spartan in furnishings and unheated, but the location of the professor's work on his great scholarly and artistic efforts, his multivolume history of the great Spanish explorers of the Americas. Even though, as the novel opens, the family's belongings have been moved to a new house, the professor continues over many months to come back to his old house and his old attic room to think and to write. It is here in the old house that he reconsiders his life's efforts and his link to Tom Outland. It is also here that in some despair he nearly gives in to "accidental" death by gas fumes from a faulty heater. His rescue by the faithful seamstress Augusta provides the professor the opportunity to recognize that he would have "to live without delight" in the future.

Professor's new house. Built with funds from the prize money the professor has won because of his distinguished contributions to history, this house has all the modern conveniences possible, but it also is the site of growing family dissension, perhaps best indicated by the separate rooms and baths for the professor and his wife, Lillian, and by the increasing materialistic competition between his daughters and their husbands, as revealed in family social occasions held at the house.

Outland. Large "Norwegian manor house" erected on the shores of Lake Michigan as the Marsellus country retreat; named as a memorial to Tom Outland and his invention, which has revolutionized airplane engines, thus bringing a fortune to Louie Marsellus and the professor's oldest daughter, Rosamund. The professor scorns the extravagance and aesthetic inappropriateness of this mansion, but he particularly objects to the home as a desecration of the memory of Tom Outland, who stands throughout the novel for the values of intellectual integrity and aesthetic simplicity.

Cliff City. The middle part of the novel, told from the perspective of Tom Outland in the memory of Professor St. Peter, centers on Outland's discovery of some fabulous cliff dwellings, presumably never seen before by non-Native Americans. Based on the discoveries of similar remains in what is today Mesa Verde National Park in southwestern Colorado, "Tom Outland's Story" emphasizes the superiority of this ancient culture to the values of twentieth century America. That superiority is mirrored in the buildings themselves, which when first seen by Tom are compared to "sculpture." A tower in the midst of the houses provides a center around which the dwellings cluster to form a compositional aesthetic having to do with peace and eternity.

Tom's excavation of the buildings and his discoveries of archaeological and artistic artifacts, together with the purity of the location, result in an imaginative and almost religious experience. He leaves the mesa a changed man. When he arrives in Hamilton to go to college and meets the professor, he brings with him an intelligence and values sparked by his discoveries. His relationship with the professor is mutually productive. Both of their imaginations are fed by Outland's youthful explorations of the cliff houses. The professor's writing of history becomes more insightful and lyrical, while Outland himself succeeds with his inventive scientific breakthroughs. It is Outland's untimely death in World War I, the professor's completion of his life's scholarly historical works, and his growing alienation from his family that force the dislocated professor to reevaluate his future and realize that happiness and joy may well be behind him.

— *Delmer Davis*

PROMETHEUS BOUND

Author: Aeschylus (525/524-456/455 B.C.E.)
Type of work: Drama
Type of plot: Tragedy

Time of plot: Antiquity
First performed: Prometheus desmōtes, date unknown (English translation, 1777)

The geographic range of this play parallels its cosmic dramatic plot dealing with the world order and conflict between the gods. The story line encompasses the entire known world as well as the underworld and the realm of the gods.

Scythian mountaintop. All the action of this play takes place atop an unnamed mountain on the edge of the Greek world—probably in the Caucasus mountains in what is now Armenia. The remote location emphasizes the isolation of the Titan Prometheus, who is bound to this mountain as punishment for his crimes against the chief god, Zeus, as the ruler of the universe.

Ocean. Mythical great sea that the ancient Greeks believed surrounded a saucer-shaped world. In this play, Ocean is personified in the god Ocean(os), who visits Prometheus on his mountaintop but refuses to ally himself with his fellow Titan. As the daughters of Ocean, the chorus of Oceanids are also identified with this body of water. Unlike their father, the Oceanids decide to cast their fate with that of Prometheus.

*Argos.** Ancient Greek city located in the northeastern part of the Peloponnesian Peninsula, in which the play's only mortal character, Io, was born. Aeschylus's references to this unfortunate woman's homeland provided his Greek audience with a geographical and human framework for this otherwise exotic play. Through Io and her Greek heritage, the audience may not only sympathize more strongly with Prometheus, who, like Io, is a victim of Zeus, but they can also take pride in the play's prediction that Io's descendants will eventually return to Greece and that one of them, Heracles, will eventually free Prometheus from his bondage.

Tartarus. Greek underworld, to which Prometheus and the chorus descend at the end of the play. The location is intended by Zeus as further punishment of the recalcitrant Titan and the completion of his isolation from the world.

— *Thomas J. Sienkewicz*

PROMETHEUS UNBOUND: A Lyrical Drama in Four Acts

Author: Percy Bysshe Shelley (1792-1822)
Type of work: Drama
Type of plot: Allegory

Time of plot: Antiquity
First published: 1820

Inspired by Aeschylus's plays, John Milton's Paradise Lost *(1667), and the beauties of springtime,* Prometheus Unbound *is initially set in the Caucasus region; however, the action resulting from Prometheus's pity united with the Oceanid Panthea's hope and Asia's love spreads throughout the entire world, reflected in the change of seasons from winter to spring. The setting is apt in its sublimity, breadth, and grandeur to reflect the immeasurability of the titan's and humankind's selfless love and endurance in the face of misery.*

*Caucasus.** Mountain range between the Black and Caspian Seas. The mountain to which Prometheus is chained may be seen as an image of permanence, similar to Mont Blanc in Shelley's poem of the same name, externally symbolizing the Titan Prometheus's unalterable refusal to give in to tyranny while he is being punished for having befriended humankind. Even as the mountains endure the extremes of wind and cold, so too does Prometheus endure extremes in torment that include Zeus's eagle, the icy weather, thoughts of unending pain, and the Furies. Paradoxically, however, the mountains alter in appearance over the passage of time.

Prometheus also changes his attitude toward Jove. Suffering over a long period of time leads him from curses and hatred of Jove to wisdom and feelings of pity for the tyrant god. From this pity, hope and love are renewed, echoed in the landscape's alteration from winter to spring and in his wife, Asia's, alteration from passive sleep to active journey through a forest and up to a mountain pinnacle where she enters **Demogorgon's cave**, the seat of the spirit of revolution. Asia's passionate dialogue with the supreme god Demogorgon ends with the latter's trip to Heaven, where he dethrones his father, Jove. Thus the play comes to the conclusion that Shelley came to after experimenting with other forms of revolution: changing the world through love.

— *Daryl Holmes*

THE PROMISED LAND

Author: Henrik Pontoppidan (1857-1943)
Type of work: Novel
Type of plot: Social criticism

Time of plot: Late nineteenth century
First published: Det forjættede land, 1891-1895
   (English translation, 1896)

This novel documents the failure of Emanuel Hansted's Tolstoyan dream of living as a self-sufficient preacher among poor rural folk. The history of his ambition is mapped out in the changes that overtake his parsonage and its surroundings—but it proves in the end that although the man can take himself out of the luxurious city, he cannot take the luxurious city out of himself.

Skibberup. One of two rival villages in rural Denmark that make up Emanuel's parish, the other being **Veilby.** Skibberup is the poorer of the two villages because the three hills on which it stands are almost an island, surrounded by bog land. It has a red-tiled meeting house, two church towers, and three windmills. The fields of the parish have been enlivened by a new system of fertilization, which involves spreading manure immediately rather than letting it fester in the dunghills that are dismissed by the novelist as symbolic relics of serfdom.

The land ripens brightly in summer, when Emanuel looks out upon it from the shade of a mountain ash tree at a high point on the road connecting Skibberup and Veilby. He sees, ominously, that his own harvest will be meager by comparison with those of his neighbors, partly because of his lack of native skill and partly because of the demoralizing aftereffects of Laddie's death.

Veilby parsonage. Once-palatial building situated on high ground between Veilby and Skibberup whose red roof and high poplar avenues rise above the slate roofs of the peasant farmhouses. It has an arched gateway and big courtyard, but the latter is now full of agricultural equipment and stores, with chickens foraging among the litter. The parsonage's rooms have been stripped of all the finery with which they were decorated by the former tenant, Archdeacon Tönnesen. The former "salon" is now empty of furniture, save for benches running around its walls, and is lit by a single petroleum lamp; the other rooms are unused, except for the former day room, which is now the family bedroom. The bookshelves in the archdeacon's former study are dusty and neglected. The whole house is dirty, until it is cleaned for Laddie's funeral.

The parsonage is surrounded by a small park, which the archdeacon once equipped with a wooden bridge in the Chinese style, but the bridge has been lost to sight as the park, overgrown by blackthorn bushes, has reverted to primeval forest.

Kyndlöse. Skibberup's prosperous neighboring village, where Dr. Hassing lives in a luxurious "villa." Strongly contrasted with Veilby Parsonage, the doctor's house has carpeted floors, carved furniture, velvet armchairs, large mirrors, and numerous paintings and statues of male and female nudes. Its dining room is decorated in a hybrid style, half "Pompeian" and half modern. Its drawing room has a piano and French windows leading to a glass-covered veranda.

The lawn beyond the veranda has beds of rose bushes, a honeysuckle arbor, and a vast stone vase. At first Emanuel is profoundly uncomfortable there, but he is seduced by Ragnhild's playing of Frédéric Chopin's funeral march. When he sees the house again from a distance, it is juxtaposed, in his contemplation, with Fen cottages, a cluster of miserable earthen hovels with rags instead of window panes, inhabited by drunkards, whose wretchedness has remained obdurate in the face of all his reformist endeavors.

*Copenhagen. Capital of Denmark from which Emanuel originally comes and to which Ragnhild Tönnesen goes when Veilby Parsonage changes hands. After his dream dies, Emanuel returns there with his children, even though his wife, Hansine, tells him that she cannot go with him. He looks forward to moving back into his old rooms, overlooking the canal and the Kristiansburg Palace, but Hansine feels that her own destiny lies in the remote fishing community into which her sister has married.

Sandinge. Town nearest to Skibberup, where Hansine was educated and where she and Emanuel met. Its high school is a significant motif within the story; a framed photograph of it hangs in the room behind the parsonage's stable where the servant Niels lives. Emanuel visits Sandinge to attend the funeral of the school's old director; there he sees the unnamed "great Norwegian writer" (Henrik Ibsen), whose influence, along with Leo Tolstoy's, helped inspire his dream; after the writer's departure, Hansen the weaver makes the speech that convinces Emanuel of his failure to make the dream come true.

— *Brian Stableford*

PSEUDOLUS

Author: Plautus (c. 254-184 B.C.E.)
Type of work: Drama
Type of plot: Comedy

Time of plot: Late third century B.C.E.
First performed: 191 B.C.E. (English translation, 1774)

Although the setting of the play is ostensibly a street in ancient Athens, the residents of that street represent recognizable Roman types. Roman audiences enjoyed the spectacle of a young man flouting his father's authority and a slave making a fool of his master, despite the fact that such behaviors were impermissible in Roman society, by accepting the playwright's transparent defense that his characters were Greeks, not Romans.

*Athens. Ancient Greek city that was the center of Greek culture. Although Athens provides the setting for the play, the play might have been set in any Greek city or Rome itself. Plautus adapts—and adds elements to—the New Comedy, as represented by the work of the Greek poet Menander. At the turn of the second century B.C.E., Rome was militarily and economically powerful, in transition from city-state to world empire. Plautus's models are Greek, but he uses them comically to reflect the social and cultural changes that are producing strains in traditional Roman life.

House of Simo (SIH-moh). Middle of three adjacent houses in Athens that is the residence of the stern old father of Calidorus, a teenager madly in love with the young courtesan Phoenicium. Pseudolus, the protagonist, is Simo's quick-witted, crafty slave. In Plautine comedy, raised stages generally represented city streets with temporary wooden scenery supplying the background facades of several houses.

House of Ballio (BA-lee-oh). Residence of a slave dealer and pimp. Ballio owns Phoenicium and has sold her to a Macedonian captain. However, before he can complete the deal, Pseudolus swindles him out of both the girl and his fee. Ballio's house is stage left of Simo's. His proximity to his very proper neighbors illustrates the intrusion of sordid materialism into respectable Roman life.

House of Callipho (KAL-lee-foh). Residence of a tolerant old man, who is a foil to the inflexible Simo. His house is stage right of Simo's.

— *Patrick Adcock*

PURGATORY

Author: William Butler Yeats (1865-1939)
Type of work: Drama
Type of plot: Fantasy

Time of plot: Early twentieth century
First performed: 1938; first published, 1939

William Butler Yeats uses a highly symbolic setting in this play—an empty stage with a ruined house and a bare tree in the background—to explore his central theme: the consequences of a tragic misalliance of an aristocratic woman and a groomsman who worked in her family's stables. The play suggests that this mixing of blood has broken the lineage of a noble family, destroying a graceful, ordered way of life.

Ruined house. Charred and derelict building before which the play's only two characters, an Old Man and a Boy (his son), stand throughout the play. The Old Man explains to his disinterested son that he was born in the house and that it was occupied for generations before him by magistrates, colonels, members of Parliament, captains, and governors—great people who loved the house and its intricate passages and magnificent library. However, the house is now a ruin, burned nearly to the ground by the drunken groomsman who inherited it from his wife, the Old Man's mother. All that now remains is a ghostly facade, a ruin without floors, windows, or a roof. For Yeats, the ruined house represents the disordered, democratic present, which he measures unfavorably against the ordered, aristocratic past, symbolized by the house in its original, bygone splendor.

Bare tree. Tree standing behind the house that provides the second key element of the play's setting, while further symbolizing the loss of familial and social order that resulted from the marriage of the Old Man's mother and her groomsman. The Old Man recalls that in his boyhood, the tree had had ripe leaves as thick as butter. Once a sign of life, it is now bare, a symbol of sterility and death. The Old Man also remembers other trees that once surrounded the great house, but these were cut down by the groomsman, leaving the estate the barren, lifeless place that it now is.

Purgatory. Place imagined and described by the Old Man. The souls in Purgatory, he says, return to habitations and familiar spots. Thus, his mother is forced, again and again, to relive her "transgression"—the sexual act that mixed her blood with that of the inferior groomsman. The Old Man witnesses this act in the lit window of the ruined house. His mother's soul must live through everything in exact detail, driven by remorse, just as the Old Man himself must live with the consequences of his mother's and his own actions.

— *Michael Hennessy*

PURPLE DUST

Author: Sean O'Casey (John Casey, 1880-1964)
Type of work: Drama
Type of plot: Satire

Time of plot: 1940's
First published: 1940; first performed, 1944

Although the action of this play is confined to the main room of an old mansion in rural Ireland that is being renovated by two wealthy Englishmen, the language of its characters contains colorful descriptions of the world outside, so that the Irish landscape becomes a vivid presence in the play. At the end, the natural world of Ireland seems to be embodied at last in the unnamed figure who prophesies a disastrous flood that will doom the effort to renovate the house.

Ormond manor. Aging Tudor mansion in Ireland that the English expatriates Basil Stoke and Cyril Poges are renovating. The house is represented by its "great room" which, massive and venerable, becomes progressively more battered as the play progresses. It has a hole in the ceiling, through which a yellow-bearded workman sticks his head at a comic moment. At another moment, a cow causes havoc when it tries to enter through the front door. However, the workmen have difficulty getting an antique bureau through the same door, damaging both it and the bureau in the process. Meanwhile, Poges knocks a hole in the wall with a large garden roller. The deterioration of the great hall is an obvious metaphor for the collapse of the foolish dreams of the house's English owners.

Clune na Geera (cloon naw GEAR-ah). Irish parish in which Ormand Manor is located. Clune na Geera is a provincial region with a strong personality of its own, which is expressed in its residents' skeptical attitude toward outsiders. Though offering a backdrop of natural beauty where the work party's foreman, Jack O'Killigain, and Avril can go on romantic horseback rides, its workmen are individualists who cannot be rushed and often seem perversely determined to ignore instructions. Its parish priest is harshly antimodern but pragmatically willing to accept generous donations from men like Stoke, whose lavish way of living flouts his puritanical standards.

*****Ireland.** The play's Irish setting is the scene of a clash of cultural myths. Exploited by Great Britain in the days of the British Empire, Ireland was long dominated by a Protestant "ascendancy" class of gentlemen land-lords, who gradually lost their power after the coming of Ireland's independence. Nevertheless, to nostalgic English imperialists and Anglo-Irish writers, Ireland has been a land of pastoral enchantment, except for her stubborn people, who obstinately refuse to cooperate with English attitudes and myths about the past. Nevertheless, O'Casey's two pitiable English businessmen, Stoke and Poges, imagine they can recapture this romance in a fantasy life in a mansion of the "ascendancy" or "great house" days, which they will restore with their wealth. For the Irish workmen hired to do the restoration, however, their country's landscape has different associations. For some, Ireland is a stubborn land that grudgingly yields a meager living. However, for O'Killigain, the foreman who has returned from the Spanish Civil War, it is a homeland to be reformed and redeemed from poverty and priestcraft. For Philip O'Dempsey, the visionary second workman, Ireland is a land haunted by ancient Celtic myths and by the legends of the great Irish patriots Wolfe Tone and Charles Stewart Parnell.

— *Edgar L. Chapman*

PYGMALION

Author: George Bernard Shaw (1856-1950)
Type of work: Drama
Type of plot: Comedy

Time of plot: c. 1900
First published: 1912; first performed, 1913 (in German), 1914 (in English)

This play is set in three London locales: Covent Garden; the home of Henry Higgins, on Wimpole Street; and the home of Higgins's mother, in Chelsea. These locales and others mentioned in the play are important in this work about the rigid English class system.

*****London.** In the early twentieth century, London was the center of world commerce and the leading city of the democratic societies. However, for all its importance to world democracies, London was home to the British Empire and organized into a rigid class system, which permitted no crossing of boundaries. One of the chief means of enforcing such a system was categorizing people according to their language patterns. *Pygmalion* is about how a guttersnipe, Eliza Doolittle, overcomes the English class system by exchanging her Cockney accent for an upper-class English one with the help of linguistics expert Henry Higgins. During the course of the lessons, they fall in love with each other, but Higgins is never able to escape his own class sufficiently to reciprocate Eliza's love.

*****St. Paul's Cathedral.** Magnificent late seventeenth century church located located in Covent Garden, London's entertainment and market district. St. Paul's portico, at the entrance to the building, is a place where the different classes are permitted to mingle. There, Eliza encounters Higgins and decides to accept the challenge of changing her speech patterns.

27A Wimpole Street. Address of Henry Higgins's Covent Garden home and speech laboratory, located in an upscale area. It comes to represent the place of learning where Eliza is reborn as a "lady," with an entirely new habit of speech. Higgins assumes that Eliza will never leave Wimpole Street, but to his surprise she does leave him to marry a young man from fashionable Earls Court, the final proof of her transformation.

Mrs. Higgins's home. As a test of her new social skills, Higgins brings Eliza to his mother's home in exclusive Chelsea. There, Eliza meets the Eynsford Hills, who, although poor, are nevertheless members of the upper crust residing in Earl's Court. Freddy Eynsford Hill falls in love with her almost immediately. Mrs. Higgins's home is also where Eliza passes her first test in a new social setting and where she ultimately rejects Higgins.

— August W. Staub

QUENTIN DURWARD

Author: Sir Walter Scott (1771-1832)
Type of work: Novel
Type of plot: Historical

Time of plot: 1468
First published: 1823

The geographical centerpiece of this novel is the city and episcopality of Liege, which at the time in which the story is set were under the Holy Roman Empire, although they were surrounded by the northern territories of the duchy of Burgundy. The Burgundians made several attempts during the fifteenth century to subjugate Liege, while also attempting to distance themselves from the ailing French crown. As a member of the French king's Scottish guard, Quentin Durward represents chivalric principles that were then in decay throughout Europe.

Castle of Plessis-les-Tours (pleh-SEE-lay-TEWR). Royal French stronghold situated two miles south of the ancient capital of Touraine, in and around which the early phases of the story take place. Quentin makes his first appearance at a treacherous ford on a fast-running brook, a tributary of the Cher River, after which he reposes briefly at Saint Hubert's Chapel before going to the castle. Important settings within the castle include the Hall of Roland and its surrounding gallery, where Quentin secretly observes Princess Joan and her attendants; the tower where the astrologer Galeotti Marti, or Martivalle, is lodged in richly furnished apartments, with his library of Hermetic Philosophy and his silver astrolabe; and the Dauphin's tower, where the two countesses of Croye are lodged.

Namur (NAH-mewr). Town in Flanders (now the capital of a Belgian province) where Quentin and the countesses obtain lodgings at a Franciscan convent while they are traveling to Liege. When their guide Hayraddin is expelled from the convent for licentious behavior, Quentin follows him into the nearby woods and discovers his apparent treachery.

Liege (leej). Region of the Low Countries that is now a province of Belgium; its capital city is situated at the junction of the Ourthe and Meuse ("Maes" in the novel) Rivers. The castle of Schonwaldt, the residence of the bishop of Liege at the time of the novel, was situated a mile outside the town; it is one of the most important settings of the novel before and after it is stormed and taken by the robber baron William de la Marck. However, it is destroyed before Charles the Bold's Burgundian troops arrive to retake the city.

The most important settings within the city featured in advance of the climactic battle are the church of Saint Lambert, where Quentin hears mass before being accosted by the burghers, and the house of the Syndic Pavillon, where he takes refuge before returning to the bishop's palace. After the victory, mass is celebrated in the Roman Cathedral church, but the ending of the story is so hurried that Scott does not bother to specify exactly where it is that Quentin and his uncle confront and kill William de la Marck, or where they display his severed head to the satisfied gazes of Louis and Charles.

Péronne (peh-rohn). Town and fortress on the banks of the Somme River, thirty miles east of Amiens in northern France. Quentin's southward journey to Péronne after leaving Liege takes him through Charleroi and across the Lowlands of Hainault, with a brief pause

in the town of Landrecy. The castle of Péronne had a well-deserved reputation throughout the Middle Ages for invincibility—it was never broached until the duke of Wellington's English army captured it in 1815—and was therefore known as Péronne la Pucelle ("the maiden"). The imprisonment there of Louis XI by Charles the Bold is the principal historical incident around which Scott's plot is organized, and the plot makes much of the fearsome "donjon" in Earl Herbert's Tower, where the king is confined with his astrologer and advisers. Scott represents Charles the Bold as a belated embodiment of the dying ideals of chivalry, and the fact that his armies are camped around the virgin citadel when Quentin first encounters him thus has a certain symbolic significance.

Château de Hautlieu (sha-TOH deh oh-LEW). Castle on the banks of the Loire River in France in whose picture-gallery and library the novel's ostensible narrator finds the inspiration for the story. Its name means "high place," echoing the long-lost high ideals of chivalry.

— *Brian Stableford*

THE QUEST OF THE HOLY GRAIL

Author: Unknown
Type of work: Fiction
Type of plot: Arthurian romance

Time of plot: Early eighth century
First published: c. 1300

The lands of the Holy Grail are largely a mythical Britain that is sparsely populated but with hermitages, abbeys and chapels scattered throughout the countryside. Outside Camelot, the only significant centers of population are castles. Many crossroads have crosses bearing messages or are sites of revelations. Most places provide adventures of a spiritual nature for the questing knights, and their landscapes are allegorical.

Camelot. Castle home of the legendary English king Arthur and the base from which the knights of his Round Table ride out on adventures, including quests for the Holy Grail—the chalice that Christ used at the Last Supper. Camelot's palace and chapel are separate buildings within the castle walls. There is a courtyard outside the palace, and the upper hall, where the Round Table may be found, is within the palace. A floating stone bearing Galahad's sword is discovered on the bank of a river running below the castle's outside wall. Below the castle hill is a town.

Logres. Wasteland where corn does not sprout, trees bear no fruit, and in whose waters fish do not swim. Logres represents a Briton whose sins can be healed only by water from the Holy Grail. On a lonely heath is a stone cross beside which is a block of marble stone. Nearby stands an ancient, abandoned chapel. In the porch is an iron grill through which Lancelot sees an altar covered with silk cloths, illuminated by a silver candlestick bearing six candles. It is from this chapel that Lancelot sees the Holy Grail emerge to heal a knight.

Logres also contains the **Perilous Forest**, in which a spring seethes with giant bubbles.

Median River. Deep and dangerous stream that flows through the wasteland, dividing it in two, symbolically separating the earthly from the spiritual. When Lancelot reaches the river, he is hemmed in on both sides by steep cliffs.

Churches. Scattered throughout the landscape are hermitages, chapels, and abbeys, typically inhabited by hermits and recluses who interpret the adventures of the questing knights in spiritual terms. Most of these places have dwellings and chapels and are in remote places, such as deep forests and mountainsides. A woman recluse (anchoress) whom Lancelot encounters sees the world only through a small embrasure facing the altar of her church.

Abbeys, such as the one at which Percival stays, typically have guest houses, chapels, and stables within and encircling walls and deep moats without.

Abbeys, such as one near Castle Vagan, where Galahad finds his shield, are often close to the castles. Castle

Tubele, at which Bors quarrels with Lionel, has a hermitage close by.

Castles. Strongholds of kings and knights that usually have stout outer walls and central palaces (keeps) that are often approached up hills. Their main halls are usually on upper floors, which contains guest rooms. Dungeons are also usually part of these strongholds. The castles have courtyards in front and stables nearby and always have chapels. They tend to be situated in valleys, surrounded by meadows on which tournaments are held when questers such as Lancelot arrive. **Towers**, such as the one at which Bors fights for the heiress of King Love, usually resemble the central structures of castles but lack nearby towns and surrounding walls.

Corbenic Castle. King Pellés's castle in Logres. Its rear wall has a gate opening seaward that is never shut; instead, it is guarded by two lions. A road leads up to its central fortress, and steps lead up to its great hall. Within its palace is the chamber in which Lancelot sees the Holy Grail, which is standing on a silver table and covered by a red silk cloth interwoven with gold. Galahad and his men remove the Grail to Sarras.

Percival's Island. High crag surrounded by sea, out of sight of the shore, where Percival is tempted. It shows no signs of human habitation but is populated with such wild beasts as lions and bears.

Sarras. Heavenly Jerusalem to which Galahad takes the Holy Grail. The road from the shore to the spiritual palace rises to the location where the throne of Josephus is situated.

— Pauline Morgan

QUICKSAND

Author: Nella Larsen (1891-1964)
Type of work: Novel
Type of plot: Psychological realism

Time of plot: Late 1920's
First published: 1928

The several major geographic settings not only correspond to Helga Crane's intensifying search for a place of sanctuary, but they also chart her gradual decline from a free-spirited professional woman to a pathetic, overburdened wife and mother who derives no joy from living.

Naxos. School for African Americans in rural Alabama patterned on Tuskegee Institute. Helga Crane, a native of Chicago and educated in Nashville, Tennessee, teaches literature at Naxos but feels completely out of place in its rural surroundings. She also feels out of sync with the Naxos mold: She despises the school's regimentation, rigidity, and conformity. As she sits in her room in the teachers' quarters, she surrounds herself with expressions of exquisite taste and style, bold colors, fashionable clothes and furnishings, and excellent choices in books. This display is in direct contrast to the starkness and stylelessness that characterize Naxos generally. As Helga contemplates her situation, she resolves to resign her position and leave Naxos at once. Where she will go and how she will live are of no consequence to her, and this impulsiveness is soon revealed as her most damning trait. In addition, her leaving also means the breaking of her marriage engagement to James Vayle, scion of an upper-class African American family from Georgia that has always looked down on her.

Naxos takes its name from the largest Greek island in the Cyclades, which was famed in ancient times as a center of the worship of Dionysus, the god of wine.

*Chicago. Great midwestern city in which Helga grew up and to which she flees after leaving Naxos. However, to her dismay, she finds no comfort there on her return. The grayness and coldness of the city only underscore her sad remembrances of the miserable childhood that she spent as a mixed-race child in a white family. This misery is compounded by the fact that her black father abandoned her and that she had been sent to school at Nashville so that she would learn how to live with her "own kind." Moreover, Helga has difficulty finding a job that suits her training and expectations and is rebuffed by her maternal uncle's white wife, who wants nothing to do with his half-black niece. Fortunately for Helga, she soon lands a job as an assistant with Mrs. Jeanette Hayes-Rore, a well-to-do black matron with whom she travels to New York.

*Harlem.** African American neighborhood of the northern portion of New York City's Manhattan Island. There, Helga finds herself among African Americans of all walks of life, from prosperous socialites and those concerned with "Negro Uplift," to the club and cabaret set, and to the poor and downtrodden masses. She is alternately pleased to be among such a vibrant group and repulsed by the vulgarity of some. Soon the old feelings of ambivalence and discontent engulf her, and she resolves to flee New York in favor of some other place. The arrival of a check for five thousand dollars from her Uncle Peter in Chicago, accompanied by the suggestion that she visit her mother's sister in Denmark provides her with the wherewithal for another escape, which she undertakes at once.

After returning to New York later, Helga discovers that she is still not satisfied. After an encounter with Dr. Robert Anderson, her former boss and now her best friend's husband, Helga has what amounts to an emotional crisis and finds herself in a storefront church where she is rescued, spiritually and sexually, by the Reverend Mr. Pleasant Green.

*Copenhagen.** Capital city of Denmark, where Helga arrives with great relief after escaping the tawdriness of Harlem and the insult of being considered a member of African American classes to which she feels she does not belong. Although her initial stay with her Aunt Katrina and Uncle Poul in Copenhagen is pleasant, she soon develops a distaste for being constantly on display as a dark object in the midst of a predominantly blonde-haired white society. She is particularly offended by the advances of the painter Axel Olsen, whom she dismisses angrily. Interestingly, Helga realizes that not only does she miss America, but she misses being among other African Americans—her people—and she resolves to flee Denmark for Harlem so that she can re-embrace her own.

*Alabama.** With her minister husband, Helga moves to a tiny town in rural Alabama to do the Lord's work, but ultimately finds it as unfulfilling as everything else she has attempted. Unfortunately, Helga finds herself trapped by the marriage, by motherhood, and by the finality of the realization that there is nowhere else for her to go.

— *Warren J. Carson*

THE QUIET AMERICAN

Author: Graham Greene (1904-1991)
Type of work: Novel
Type of plot: Tragedy

Time of plot: Early 1950's
First published: 1955

Set in Vietnam during the final phase of European colonialism in Asia, this novel details the Vietnamese struggle for independence from the French and covert American intervention. The novel provides glimpses into the minds of both the colonizers and their subjects, as well as a context for understanding the large-scale American involvement in the civil war that was to come.

*Vietnam.** Country in Southeast Asia that was colonized by France during the late nineteenth century. The novel is set in Vietnam in the early 1950's at a time when the Vietnamese people believe they have earned their independence, but the French still refuse to withdraw. From their ostensibly secure base in Saigon, the French rule an uneasy country, one whose countryside and northern districts are controlled by nationalist forces known as the Viet Minh. Into a complex atmosphere of political intrigue and violence, Graham Greene interweaves a psychological study of a murdered American espionage agent and a British journalist.

The novel is a partly autobiographical account of Greene's own time in Vietnam, where he was a journalist in 1951 to 1952. His narrator, Thomas Fowler, is also a war correspondent stationed in Saigon through whose eyes readers learn of the murky political situation developing with the increasing American presence in Southeast Asia.

***Saigon** (SI-gahn; now Ho Chi Minh City). Capital of colonial Cochin China. A French stronghold, Saigon is the site for much of the action in *The Quiet American*. The fact that terrorist attacks and bombings occur in the midst of this urbane and sophisticated center of French colonial culture provides strong evidence for the disintegration of French control. The novel depicts Saigon as the center of a culture degraded by colonialism, one in which drug trafficking, opium smoking, and prostitution run rampant.

***Continental Hotel.** Large hotel in central Saigon frequented by foreign correspondents that is the site of much of the novel's dialogue. At this hotel Fowler meets Alden Pyle, the "quiet American" of the title, and Pyle meets Phuong, a beautiful young Vietnamese woman who is living with Fowler. Greene's descriptions of the Continental are realistic and based in fact. The Continental is a real hotel that served as the base for European and American correspondents until the fall of Saigon in the 1970's.

***Tanyin** (tan-YIHN). City about fifty miles northwest of Saigon where Fowler goes to attend a celebration of the Caodists, who are attempting to synthesize Roman Catholicism, Buddhism, and Confucianism. The novel uses Fowler's trip to illustrate what is going on in the countryside outside Saigon. At Tanyin, Fowler runs into Pyle, whose car has broken down, and the two men return to Saigon together. Along the way, Fowler's own car runs out of gas, leaving the men dangerously isolated within disputed territory. Although the French maintain watchtowers every kilometer along the road, the towers often change hands during the night. The episode underscores how the relative peace of Saigon camouflages the instability of the rest of the country.

***Tonkin** (TAHN-kihn). Northernmost district of Vietnam. In both the novel and reality, Tonkin is the location of many battles between the Viet Minh and the French, including the decisive great battle at Dien Bien Phu. Hanoi, the capital, and the important port of Haiphong are located in Tonkin as well.

***Phat Diem** (fat-dee-ehm). Town about eighty miles south of Hanoi that is the site of an important Catholic cathedral. Phat Diem is also the site of a battle that leads to the most gruesome scene in the novel: a canal filled with human bodies.

— *Diane Andrews Henningfeld*

QUO VADIS: A Narrative of the Time of Nero

Author: Henryk Sienkiewicz (1846-1916)
Type of work: Novel
Type of plot: Historical

Time of plot: c. 64 C.E.
First published: Quo vadis, 1896 (English translation, 1896)

The primary setting for this novel is the Rome of Emperor Nero, which serves as the central arena for the conflict between paganism and Christianity. The death of the former and the triumph of the latter pave the way for the transformation of the "city of Caesar" into the "city of Christ."

***Rome.** Capital of the vast Roman Empire, which ruled over perhaps fifty million people in Nero's time, most of Europe and the Middle East. All the subjects of the empire are represented in *Quo Vadis*, from Germans to Egyptians, giving Rome a cosmopolitan quality unmatched until the twentieth century. This great ancient city of more than one million people (half of whom are slaves) provides Henryk Sienkiewicz with a stage on which to present a vast morality play. Two Romes are shown in competition. One, that of Caesar, is dying. The other, that of Christ, is being born.

The novel reaches its climax when Nero starts a fire that consumes much of the city. Fire is a symbol of both destruction and perfection. Christians preach that the world will perish in fire, and Christ promised to cast fire upon the earth. Christianity itself is said to have begun with flames of fire at Pentecost. In this symbol Sienkiewicz illustrates both the death and coming rebirth of Rome.

Nero's palace. The novel repeatedly contrasts houses. Nero's Roman palace is the home of a beast who "devours." Evenings, the palace is the site of excessively lavish and wasteful meals, lascivious sexuality, mediocre artistic performances, superstition, malicious court intrigue, militant atheism, and savage brutality. (Christians are occasionally used as human torches to illuminate evening garden parties). The ultimate waste is Nero's order to burn Rome so that its destruction may inspire his poetry.

Christian houses. Homes of Roman Christians, who typically live in the labyrinthine alleys of cheap Roman apartment complexes. Their houses are places of labor, not leisure, of poverty, not luxury. Nevertheless, these homes are characterized by true equality, simplicity, joy, hope, trust, and love. They radiate compassion, as when a Christian physician tends his would-be murderer.

Sand pits and tombs. Forbidding and forlorn places in Rome where Christians gather in secrecy at night to find fellowship and encouragement. In these places, the Christians perform baptisms and the Eucharist, preach, and pray at the same hours during which Nero's orgies take place—a study in the marked contrast of two philosophies.

Amphitheater. Public area that Nero has had built for the brutal games in which Christian and pagan Rome meet. There, day after day, Christians are fed to wild beasts, killed by gladiators, and burned in fires to amuse the populace and to avenge their alleged responsibility for burning Rome. In contrast to the pagan blood-lust of the crowd is the symbolic blood-sacrifice of the Christians, through whose innocent lives Rome will ultimately be redeemed.

Appian Way (Via Appia). Royal road outside Rome that is the site of the incident that gives the novel its title. While fleeing the Neronian persecution in Rome, Peter encounters Christ, who asks him, "Quo vadis?" (where are you going?). When Peter learns that Christ is going to Rome to be crucified anew, he retraces his steps to experience his own martyrdom. In addition to giving the novel its title. the road symbolizes the choice between the way of Caesar and the way of Christ.

— C. George Fry

R

RABBIT ANGSTROM NOVELS

Author: John Updike (1932-   )
Type of work: Novels
Type of plot: Domestic realism

Time of plot: 1950's-1980's
First published: Rabbit, Run, 1960; *Rabbit Redux,*
   1971; *Rabbit Is Rich*, 1981; *Rabbit at Rest*, 1990

These novels, set in a typical eastern middle-class American town, achieve such a strong sense of realism with believable portraits of the homes and haunts of the protagonist that John Updike has earned a reputation as the novelist of middle-class America.

Brewer. Pennsylvania town in which the novels are centered. Updike's fictionalized version of Reading, Pennsylvania, serves as the principal location for much of the action of the Rabbit novels. Rabbit's family lives in and around the city, a manufacturing town whose glory days have passed by the time Rabbit reaches adulthood. Updike takes great pains to describe the cityscape in meticulous detail, allowing readers to develop a clear sense of the place that seems to Rabbit to be both a magnet and a trap: He is constantly drawn to the city as "home" and concurrently repelled by it, feeling as if he is unable to reach his full human potential as a result of his imprisonment in this middle-class community. As Rabbit grows older, however, he comes to accept the fact that he can survive in this city; perhaps this feeling is reinforced by his promotion within his father-in-law's automobile dealership to a position that allows him to become modestly wealthy. Like so many middle-class Americans, however, as soon as Rabbit earns enough, he leaves the aging northeastern city for the land of eternal youth, Florida.

Mount Judge. Suburb of Brewer in which Rabbit Angstrom and his wife, Janice, live in a tiny row house. Rabbit feels trapped here, and the novel describes the rooms and the streets outside as confining. While much of the action of the novel involves Rabbit fleeing his home, the symbolic significance of this location makes it essential to understanding the novel. Within the Angstrom home occurs one of the central ironic actions of the novel: the death by drowning of Rabbit and Janice's baby daughter. Hence, the home is seen as a place not where life is fostered but rather where it is snuffed out prematurely.

Penn Villas. The second home Rabbit and his wife own is a typical American suburban villa. Living in what might be called a version of Levittown, Rabbit is transformed from a man on the run into someone to whom things happen. Most of the action of *Rabbit Redux* takes place in his home. There he admits a wandering "hippie," Jill Pendleton, and she in turn brings into the home Skeeter, an African American radical. By having these social misfits invade Rabbit's house, Updike is able to contrast the ordinariness of middle-class American life with the turbulent activities that were tearing apart the United States in the 1960's.

Springer home. Because the Angstrom's lose their home in a fire, they are forced to live for a time with Janice's parents. Updike takes this opportunity to show how relationships among parents, children, and in-laws create anxieties in middle-class Americans and also how loving parents like the Springers see themselves as providers for their children and grandchildren. Rabbit often suffers anxiety stemming from Mr. Springer's generously bringing him into the automobile dealership.

These feelings conflict with the resentment he feels regarding his dependence on his in-laws. Living in their home is a tangible sign of that dependence.

Springer Motors. Automobile dealership owned by Rabbit's father-in-law, Fred Springer. The dealership is significant in all the Rabbit novels. Fred Springer is a typical middle-class American pursuing the American Dream. His automobile dealership provides not only financial comfort but also employment for others, including Charlie Stavros, at times Rabbit's friend but at other times Janice's lover. Eventually the dealership becomes the source of Rabbit's income, allowing him to establish a retirement home in Florida.

Deleon. Florida town that is the principal setting of the final novel in the tetralogy, *Rabbit at Rest*. Deleon is the place at which Rabbit goes into semiretirement. His relocation to Florida, Updike suggests subtly, is a metaphor for all America: Constantly at odds with the fact of their aging, Americans seek a land of eternal youth. Further irony is created by the choice of retirement communities: Valhalla, the name of the hall of the gods in Norse mythology.

Basketball courts. Scenes of the opening and closing scenes in the tetralogy. The opening scene of *Rabbit, Run* takes place on a basketball court, where Rabbit, in his twenties, plays a pickup basketball game to demonstrate his youthful prowess. The action is significant and symbolic: Throughout the four novels, Rabbit continually struggles with the fact of his own aging. With skillful irony, Updike repeats the scene at the end of *Rabbit at Rest*. On a basketball court in Florida, Rabbit collapses and dies of a heart attack while playing a pickup basketball game. The symmetry of setting suggests the sense of closure that Updike wishes to achieve in his four-volume saga of middle-class America.

— *Laurence W. Mazzeno*

RABBIT BOSS

Author: Thomas Sanchez (1944-　　　)
Type of work: Novel
Type of plot: Historical realism

Time of plot: 1846-1950's
First published: 1973

Set primarily in the Sierra Nevada near Lake Tahoe and communities to the north and east, this novel depicts the displacement of Washo Indians from their ancestral land after the arrival of whites, who exploit and despoil both the environment and its native peoples. The story focuses on four generations of Washo leaders—the "Rabbit Bosses"—and their mistreatment by settlers, developers, and legal authorities.

*****Lake Tahoe.** Large lake straddling the California-Nevada border in the Sierra Nevada. A deep lake with cold, clear water and surrounded by snow-capped peaks, Tahoe is a place of great natural beauty and abundant wildlife. The lake is also the center of the ancestral homeland of the Washo Indians, to whom land is sacred. The Washo see their land as populated by the power and spirits of animals who guide the people and provide them with food, especially antelope, fish, and deer. Before the coming of white people, the Washo live in harmony with nature at Tahoe, taking only what they need to survive. Their homeland encompasses an oval-shaped region approximately fifty miles east and south of the lake, twenty miles to the west, and one hundred to the north. However, after white hunters, prospectors, railroad builders, and settlers begin arriving in the late 1840's, the Washo are gradually driven from their lands. In contrast, the new masters of the land strip areas of trees for towns and mines, fish out the lake, nearly exterminate the wildlife, and regard the area primarily as a means to wealth and recreation.

*****Donner Pass.** Sierra Nevada mountain pass (now on Interstate 80) at which the novel opens when Gayabuc, a young Washo, witnesses murder and cannibalism among members of the stranded Donner Party in 1847. The cannibalism episode and the migrants' desperate, incompetent misuse of forest resources profoundly shock Gayabuc and convince him that all whites are cannibals who defile the land. Much later, at nearby Donner Lake, the last Rabbit Boss of the novel's four generations, Gayabuc's great grandnephew Joe Birdsong, dies while trying to live in accordance with the traditional Washo hunter-gatherer methods. He is in hiding after being unjustly accused of murdering a rancher. His failure to survive symbolizes the fate of Washo culture.

*Sattley. Small ranching community in California's Sierra Valley, north of Donner Pass where Joe Birdsong lives and works as a part-time ranch hand and hunting guide. He is especially adept at hunting rabbits, a nuisance to farmers. But even this modest accommodation to modern American culture ends when developers start buying up land to build a tourist trailer park near a hot springs in the early 1960's. Birdsong refuses to sell his acreage, even though most of his white neighbors sell out eagerly to make quick profits. Eventually, the greedy developers use a legal ploy to deny Birdsong title to his land, which they confiscate.

*Truckee. California town on the western approach to Donner Pass that is the mountain headquarters of a railroad building crew. Captain Rex, the second generation of Rabbit Bosses, sells the services of his band of Washo men as laborers. He then squanders their earnings on gambling and whiskey in the town, losing much of the money to dishonest card sharps. Meanwhile, his people sicken with tuberculosis and die. Standing in the center of traditional Washo lands, Truckee stands as the epitome of white greed, moral corruption, and exploitation.

*Reno. Nevada desert city thirty miles northeast of Lake Tahoe that is also the site of a Washo reservation. Renown for its casino gambling and wild nightlife, Reno introduces Hallelujah Bob and his son Joe Birdsong to modern American vices in their most concentrated, commercialized, and garish forms. Both Indians reject the city's allures. On the reservation, however, their contemporaries live marginalized lives, dependent upon, but not fully part of, mainstream culture. Poverty, disease, alcoholism, and loss of traditions estrange members of the tribe from one another and their homeland.

— *Roger Smith*

THE RAINBOW

Author: D. H. Lawrence (1885-1930)
Type of work: Novel
Type of plot: Psychological realism

Time of plot: Nineteenth and early twentieth centuries
First published: 1915

This novel draws extensively on D. H. Lawrence's experiences in England's Midlands counties, where he grew up. Amid Nottinghamshire's farms, forests, and fields of wildflowers, the novel traces the lives of three generations of the Brangwen family. A central theme of the novel is the manner in which the natural world invigorates the souls and spirits of the characters, in contrast to numbing effects of the dreary local towns, mines, and factories.

Cossethay. Tiny Midlands village in which the Brangwens are living when the novel opens. The village is the center of a circle about two miles in diameter that provides all the important settings for the entire novel. The Marsh farmhouse, in which the Brangwens lived prior to the novel's opening, is next to what was probably the path of the old Nottingham Canal on the embankment at Cossall Marsh, a real place that has been significantly altered by the development of coal mines, roads, and water passages.

West of Cossethay is Ilkeston, a town that Ursula sees as a place with a small, mean, wet street and grimy and horrible buildings. The journey that she takes to get to the school in which she works as an apprentice teacher is based on Lawrence's tram rides to the Gladstone School where he taught.

Beldover. Town north of Cossethay to which the Brangwens move; closely based on Lawrence's birthplace, Eastwood. Ursula sees Beldover as a stupid, artificial, and "exaggerated town." However, the omniscient narrator describes it more objectively as a sprawling colliery village, a "pleasant walk-round for the colliers." Ursula's grandfather Will Brangwen measures his financial success by his ability to buy a large house in a new redbrick Beldover neighborhood. Ursula, however, would prefer to live in nearby Willey Green, which she thinks is "lovely and romantic."

After Ursula and her husband have a sojourn in London, and Ursula attends Nottingham College for a year, the final scene occurs near Beldover. There, she is "reborn" from a flux of primordial chaos on the northern perimeter of the circle within which the novel takes place.

*English Midlands. Central region of England that became increasingly industrialized during the nineteenth century. The novel benefits from Lawrence's skills as a poet to evoke the ethos of the natural world that he cherished as a youth growing up in the Midlands and carried in memory throughout his life. The novel's most intense passages describing the romantic relationship between Ursula and Anton Skrebensky are largely instigated by, and clearly invigorated by, what functions as a vibrant, organic landscape, whose features seem to echo and reinforce the passions of the protagonists.

The novel has numerous instances in which features of pleasant landscapes and details about weather reflect the psychological moods of the characters. On the first page, for example, the Brangwen family are introduced as being content in a place where they feel the "rush of the rising sap in the spring." Because of real and self-imposed restrictions on literary works at the time Lawrence wrote, he used metaphors linking sensual imagery in the natural world to human action. Hence, Ursula's emotional condition is often expressed in terms of her response to the environment.

Coal mines. Lawrence uses the Midlands coal mines as symbols of industrial devastation and the region's coal towns as proof of the mines' insidious influence. The Brangwens become aware of change after gathering in a harvest, when the west wind brings a "faint, sulphurous smell of pit-refuse burning."

— *Leon Lewis*

RAINTREE COUNTY

Author: Ross Lockridge, Jr. (1914-1948)
Type of work: Novel
Type of plot: Historical realism

Time of plot: Late nineteenth century
First published: 1948

This ambitious novel takes in a broad sweep of nineteenth century American history, placing its protagonist near the center of a number of epochal events. However, its basic theme is an exploration of the American republic in the microcosm of the fictional Indiana county that gives the book its title.

Raintree County. Imaginary Indiana county in which the novel focuses on the small town of **Waycross**. Located on the National Road and near the tracks of the Pennsylvania Railroad, Waycross is the scene of a Fourth of July celebration in 1892. The novel chronicles the events of that date, from dawn until midnight, while weaving in fifty-two flashbacks—not in chronological order—of past events, ranging from national Election Day in 1844 to a day in 1892. Other important sites in the county are Freehaven, the county seat, and Danwebster, a tiny community near protagonist John Wickliff

Shawnessy's home, and a graveyard that plays a significant role in the narrative.

The novel is highly metaphorical, and its fictional places are often clearly symbolic. For example, not only is the aptly named Waycross situated on a major road running from east to west, but it is also the place where Johnny Shawnessy's path crosses and recrosses those of three lifelong friends: Jerusalem Webster Stiles, a cynical professor-newspaperman; Garwood B. Jones, a clever, unscrupulous, and successful politician; and a local merchant, who eventually becomes a railroad baron.

These three recognizable American types are foils for Johnny, the dreamer and poet, throughout the novel.

Shawmucky River. Meandering stream that transects Raintree County from northeast to southwest. The bends of the Upper Shawmucky, as shown in one of the maps accompanying the text, are shaped like the letters "JWS"—the initials of the protagonist, who believes he is destined to become the hero of the county.

Lake Paradise. Body of water formed by the Upper Shawmucky River, northwest of Freehaven. Adjacent to the lake is the Great Swamp, beyond which is an idyllic island. In a flashback scene, Johnny, slightly drunk from Fourth of July celebrations, swims to the lake's island with Susanna Drake, a visitor from New Orleans, Louisiana, with whom he makes love. The island in Lake Paradise becomes an Indiana Garden of Eden in which Johnny tastes the forbidden fruit and pays a price: He marries Susanna who, believing she is a child of miscegenation, later goes mad and burns down their house.

"Raintree." Semimagical tree that gives Raintree County its name. It is located somewhere beyond the swamp, on a remote grassy mound. The tree's yellow flowers shed a dust on young lovers and children, the only types of humans who during the course of the novel are led to the tree. As a symbol of the Tree of Life, it places Raintree County not only at the center of the Republic but also at the center of the universe.

*Indianapolis. Capital and largest city of Indiana, to which Susanna Shawnessy flees shortly before setting a fire that claims the life of her young son. As a result of this tragedy, Johnny returns to Indianapolis in 1863 to join the Union Army. There, as in other real places in the novel, Johnny seems not to leave Raintree County far behind. As he enlists, Johnny encounters Flash Perkins, a boyhood friend with whom he serves in the Civil War until the latter is killed. Also in Indianapolis are Garwood Jones and Johnny's first love, Nell Gaither.

Other cities. The pattern of chance encounters between Johnny and other people from Raintree County is repeated throughout the novel. For example, while he is encamped in Chattanooga, Tennessee, during the Civil War, he is reunited with Jerusalem Webster Stiles, who has given up teaching to become a war correspondent. Later, he meets Stiles again in Washington, D.C., and they are in the audience at Ford's Theatre on the night that Abraham Lincoln is assassinated. He is again with Stiles in Philadelphia on July 4, 1876—the national Centennial Day. While spending a year in New York City, John has an intellectual romance with Laura Golden.

These and other real cities, depicted in realistic detail, ground a poetic novel which is also often experimental in structure. However, just as John Shawnessy abandons life in the big city, returning home to the life of a simple, though intellectual, schoolmaster, the narrative always returns to Raintree County, the romantic heart of the story.

*Chickamauga Creek. Georgia stream near Chattanooga, Tennessee, that is the site of a major Civil War battle in which Johnny Shawnessy experiences his baptism by fire as a Union soldier. Later, he participates in the occupation of Chattanooga, the nearby Battle of Missionary Ridge, the fall of Atlanta, and General William T. Sherman's march through Georgia from Atlanta to Savannah on the Atlantic coast. He is wounded near Columbia, South Carolina, in the same skirmish in which Flash Perkins is killed. Johnny is then sent to Washington to convalesce. This is a very ambitious novel, probably a worthy attempt to write the Great American Novel. The account of Johnny's two-year campaign, beginning in camp in Kentucky and ending in the nation's capital, gives the novel an epic sweep. However, despite Johnny's long wartime march and his journeys to Indianapolis and east to Philadelphia and New York, the themes of the novel are mostly developed back in Raintree County. The author tackles the role of the poet, the meaning of the American Republic, and ultimately the meaning of life. His most overtly philosophical passages appear and are developed in the portion of the narrative set on the soil of Raintree County on July 4, 1892. The middle-aged John Shawnessy has come to realize that to be the poet of Raintree County, Indiana, is to be America's poet.

— *Patrick Adcock*

A RAISIN IN THE SUN

Author: Lorraine Hansberry (1930-1965)
Type of work: Drama
Type of plot: Family

Time of plot: 1950's
First performed: 1959; first published, 1959

This play is set in an apartment in Chicago's Southside, an inner-city ghetto that reflects the limited housing options available to African Americans in the 1950's. However, as the play concludes, the Younger family closes the door of the small apartment for the last time in anticipation of a move to a house in Clybourne Park, the move suggesting that the dreams that had been deferred might not be so any longer.

*Chicago's Southside. Primarily African American neighborhood of Chicago in which members of three generations of the Younger family struggle against poverty and racism. Recently widowed Lena Younger, her children Beneatha and Walter Lee, and Walter's wife Ruth and son, Travis, occupy a three-room apartment with a bathroom down the hall that they share with other tenants. With its worn furniture and limited natural light, the apartment reflects the disappointment and growing despair of the family.

An expected insurance check has Walter Lee planning a business venture, but the scheme involves disreputable characters and the sale of liquor. Realizing that the cramped quarters of the apartment is detrimental to her family in much the same way that it is harmful to a houseplant that she is trying to nurture, Lena uses half the insurance money as a down payment on a three-bedroom house in Clybourne Park with a yard large enough for a garden.

Clybourne Park. White residential area of Chicago in which Lena makes a down payment on a house. Not considering the potential racial problems her family may face, she chooses the neighborhood because she wants "the nicest place for the least amount of money" for her family. After she makes the down payment, however, the Youngers are visited by a man representing Clybourne Park's white residents, who offers to buy the house back at a price that will give them a profit. Walter Lee, who has squandered half the insurance payment in a bad investment, considers the offer but ultimately decides that his family has earned the right to live in a better neighborhood. As Lena leaves the family's South Side apartment, she takes her plant, suggesting that it and her family will thrive in the sunlight of the new house. (When Lorraine Hansberry was a child, her father tried to move his family into a white neighborhood and had to win a court case to do so.)

— *Barbara Wiedemann*

RALPH ROISTER DOISTER

Author: Nicholas Udall (1505?-1556)
Type of work: Drama
Type of plot: Farce

Time of plot: Sixteenth century
First performed: c. 1552; first published, 1566?

Although the action in Nicholas Udall's adaptation of the ancient Roman playwright Plautus's The Braggart Soldier *takes place on only one set, a street with houses on each side, the inhabitants of two of those houses provide the conflict in the play, and the resolution of their conflict marks the triumph of love and logic over pomposity and presumption.*

Street. Udall's play calls for a set comprising canvas stretched over wooden frames to represent houses with a street running between them. There are entrances to the stage from the end of the street and from two houses, one belonging to Dame Christian Custance, a wealthy widow betrothed to Gawin Goodlucke, and the other belonging to Ralph Roister Doister, a braggart who is determined to win Custance's hand. Custance's house is wholly populated by women; Ralph's contains men.

Urged on by Mathewe Merygreeke, a prankster who regularly bilks Ralph of his cash, Ralph writes letters and serenades Custance, who angrily spurns him. The conflict develops into a farcical battle between the two houses as Ralph and his men attempt to invade Custance's house. In the light of the combatants and Ralph's suit, the attempted invasion seems sexual, but the threat is easily overcome as the women, armed with kitchen utensils, easily rout the invaders, including Ralph, who wears a kitchen pot for a helmet. When Gawin, the merchantman who has been away at sea, returns, all is resolved as the adventurous outsider is reunited with Custance, and the townsman admits defeat. In the true spirit of comedy, however, all are reconciled at the end of the play.

— *Thomas L. Erskine*

THE RAMAYANA

Author: Valmiki (fl. fourth century B.C.E.)
Type of work: Poetry
Type of plot: Epic

Time of plot: Antiquity
First transcribed: Rāmāyana, c. 350 B.C.E. (English translation, 1870-1874)

This classical Indian epic poem is set mainly in the kingdom of Ayodhya, in an Indian forest, and in the kingdom of Lanka, usually identified as the modern island of Sri Lanka. Ayodhya, home to Prince (later King) Sita is a center of ancient Indian civilization. The forest is a place outside of society, home to wild animals and to hermits with supernatural wisdom. Lanka is the opposite of Ayodhya. Ruled by the demon king Ravana, Lanka is the place of evil that threatens the ancient Indian kingdom.

*****Ayodhya** (ah-YOH-dyah). Mythical Indian kingdom that may be the same place as the historical ancient kingdom of Ayodhya, in the far north of India between the Ganges River and the Himalaya Mountains, in which is now India's Uttar Pradesh state. Ayodhya is both the birthplace of the epic's hero, Prince Rama, and the place to which he ultimately returns as king with his queen, Sita.

Forest. Wooded region between holy Ayodhya and its evil counterpart, Lanka, in which Rama undergoes his most important transformations. In Hindu mythology, forests are magical places that represent the nonhuman, supernatural world. They are typically home to wise hermits, as well as to wild animals. Rama leaves Ayodhya in response to a plea from the hermit Visva-mitra, who is threatened by demons. Rama spends thirteen years in the forest, fighting demons and learning from Visvamitra. There he also meets King Janak and wins the hand of Janak's half-divine daughter, Sita.

*****Lanka.** Mythical kingdom that may be the same as the island of Sri Lanka (Ceylon), which lies off the southern tip of India. The struggle between Ayodhya and Lanka begins in earnest when Lanka's demon king, Ravana, kidnaps Sita. With the help of the monkey king Hanuman, the bear king Hambavan, and an army of monkeys, bears, and vultures, Rama finds Sita, invades, and conquers Lanka. Afterward, he returns to Ayodhya with Sita, where they become king and queen once more.

— *Carl L. Bankston III*

RAMEAU'S NEPHEW

Author: Denis Diderot (1713-1784)
Type of work: Novel
Type of plot: Philosophical
Time of plot: 1761

First published: German translation, 1805; French original, 1821 as *Le Neveu de Rameau* (English translation, 1897)

Paris and the many real places in Paris that abound in this book anchor the work in reality, as Denis Diderot considers a philosophical problem within the confines of his own time in the form of a conversation between himself and a contemporary. The mention of real places is essential to create the ambiance of reality that was valued by novelists of the period.

***Paris.** France's capital city was the center of all the nation's social and intellectual activity in the eighteenth century. Paris was also where Diderot spent the majority of his working life. Throughout his novel, Diderot mentions familiar places in Paris—places that he and his friends and acquaintances frequented. Diderot wrote *Rameau's Nephew* not for publication, but rather for his own use and to share with a few close friends. For this reason, the Paris in which his book is set is the Paris that he experienced and shared with his friends. For example, he provides very realistic details about the Palais Royal gardens in which he often walked and relaxed on evenings when the weather was fine. He even mentions the banc d'Argenson, an actual bench located in the Allée d'Argenson where he often sat.

***Café de la Régence** (kah-fay deh lah ray-gahns). Café located in the Palais Royal Square that Diderot frequented when the weather was bad. This café was renowned for the men who played chess there, and Diderot was often among the spectators. The café serves as a catalyst to the novel's action, for it is at the café that Diderot encounters Rameau's nephew, Jean-François Rameau, the "He" of the dialogue (to Diderot's "Myself").

Parisian homes. Rameau's nephew finds sustenance in the fine homes of the nobility and upper bourgeoisie, in which he gives music lessons to family daughters and earns himself places at their tables through fawning. His parasitic nature is established by the places he frequents. His own home is a rented loft, which reinforces his social status and parasitic nature. Because his rent is almost always unpaid, he must return to his home without being seen or find other accommodations. On occasions when he cannot enter his loft and the weather is fair, he spends the nights on the Champs Élysées, a broad avenue.

On other occasions, Rameau's nephew sleeps in stables of the nobility, such as that of the Hôtel de Soubise. Discussion of these stables emphasizes his adaptability, lack of social position, and general willingness to profit from whatever and whomever he can.

***Opera.** Center of social life in eighteenth century Paris. It is appropriate that Rameau's nephew terminates his conversation with Diderot in order to get to the opera, as he is a musician by profession. Moreover, the opera is an excellent place for him to socialize with the nobility and possibly get a supper invitation.

— *Shawncey Webb*

RASSELAS

Author: Samuel Johnson (1709-1784)
Type of work: Novel
Type of plot: Philosophical

Time of plot: Eighteenth century
First published: The Prince of Abissinia: A Tale, 1759

The locations in this philosophic narrative are contrived to represent the range of all general and universal nature even though they actually cover no more ground than two countries in North Africa. From these, he deduces general principles of human existence, and while he does include details, or in the language of one of the characters, "number the streaks of the tulip," it is the overall human condition that is the main theme of the story.

Happy Valley. Imaginary place in Africa, vaguely located in the mountains of Abyssinia (now Ethiopia), a country that interested Samuel Johnson because his first published work had been a translation of a travel book about it. This fantastical and ideal location contains flora, fauna, human government, and even architecture that are all meant to represent nature as it should be. The valley is an advanced and highly civilized Eden. A key feature in the valley is a palace, or huge house, of many mysterious rooms; the valley also contains rugged and various natural phenomena. Despite its complexity and variety, however, the valley is boring to the main characters who decide they must move on in order to see the rest of the world. Once they have done this traveling, most of them return to the valley.

*Cairo. Egyptian city that for Johnson is meant to represent the actual metropolis but is far from a realistic depiction. Rather it represents the exotic and wise East. This is a key theme in the literature of the European Enlightenment. For Johnson's readers, stories set in the Middle East or the far East carry with them wise and reliable philosophic information. The underlying principle seems to have been that since the dominant religions came from the East and since the institution of self-confident monarchy seemed to be so strong in the lush and exotic courts of the East, fiction set in the East could be particularly didactic and meaningful. In any case, much of the wise information in this story is expressed when the characters travel to Cairo.

Catacombs. Large vaulted underground tombs near the Nile River that are visited near the conclusion of the tale and provide a properly sublime and mysterious setting for some of the most advanced ideas on the nature of the soul and on the possibilities for immortality, key themes for Johnson.

*Pyramids. Ancient landmarks near Cairo that provide the location for a bit of melodrama in the otherwise highly intellectual narrative. Arabs kidnap two of the women when the group of travelers, who are eager to see the world, venture out of the city to these monuments.

Convent of St. Anthony. Religious community on a remote island in the middle of the Nile to which the Arabs take their victims. When the Arabs decide to give them back, they do so at a Roman Catholic convent. At the end of the story, one of the victimized women chooses to return to the convent rather than to the valley. These locations and plot complications represent Johnson's effort to convey the various religious and political options in the real world of his reader.

*Constantinople. Capital city of Turkey that provides another exotic location in the East, where one of the political thinkers, who is replete with wise ideas, is taken in chains. Johnson seems to want to hint at just enough detail to suggest that the thinking conveyed in the narrative is one of universal coverage of the entire human world.

— Donald M. Hassler

THE RAZOR'S EDGE

Author: W. Somerset Maugham (1874-1965)
Type of work: Novel
Type of plot: Psychological realism

Time of plot: Early twentieth century
First published: 1944

This novel about a young man's search for wisdom and meaning takes him from Chicago to Europe and South Asia. Each location has a symbolic function and represents a vastly different spiritual approach to life. The characters' physical travels are thus also spiritual journeys. The central character follows a circular path that leads him from his ordinary material life through spiritual awakenings that ultimately return him to his starting place, which is infused with a new kind of meaning that brings together East and West.

*Chicago. Illinois's largest city, which in the early twentieth century was one of the most prosperous of midwestern cities and a major center of the rapidly expanding industrial economy of the United States. In W. Somerset Maugham's novel, Chicago symbolizes rising American materialism. By setting the novel's opening scenes there, Maugham emphasizes the materialism that his young seeker, Lawrence Darrell, seeks to leave behind him. The narrator—Maugham himself—first meets Darrell at the Chicago home of Mrs. Bradley and her daughter Isabel, to whom Darrell is engaged. The Bradley home is located on Lake Shore Drive, in a wealthy section of Chicago near the Lake.

*Paris. France's capital city and an old center of European civilization contrasts with the newness of Chicago. Long associated with high society and the arts, the Paris of this novel is two very different places. On one hand, it is the socially elite city loved by Elliott Templeton, Maugham's friend and Mrs. Bradley's brother, where fashionable and aristocratic people gather. On the other hand, it is home to artists and intellectuals, many of whom live unconventional, bohemian lives. Paris thus offers two kinds of alternatives to the materialistic American Midwest. Elliott's apartment is in the elegant Left Bank. Lawrence Darrell, on the other hand, takes a dingy room in the Latin Quarter, a section of Paris near the Sorbonne, the famous French university, and home to students and nonconformist artists. Paris and the other places in Europe suggest the bohemian alternative to materialism and elegant but dying Old World tradition and sophistication.

*London. Great Britain's capital city is not the setting for any significant episodes in *The Razor's Edge*, but it is always in the background, as Maugham himself is English, and his novel is the story of his encounters with other peoples and places. As the narrator, Maugham continually refers to his own return trips to London, and Templeton and Darrell also visit London briefly several times. In a sense, London is the vantage point from which all other locations in the novel are viewed.

*Lens. Mining town in the northern region of France known as Nord-Pas-de-Calais, near Belgium. It occupies an important place in the novel because it is there that Darrell begins the wanderings that detach him from his social roots, introduce him to religious mysticism, and ultimately lead him to South Asia. After studying in Paris, Darrell goes to Lens to work as a miner. In the company of a disgraced former Polish cavalry officer named Kosti, he leaves the mine and travels through Belgium and into southern Germany, where he and Kosti work for a time at a small farm near the city of Darmstadt.

Germany. Center of medieval Christian mystical tradition that is the place where Darrell makes the decisive turn from bohemianism to religious mysticism when he leaves the farm alone and goes to Bonn. There he meets the Benedictine monk Father Ensheim, who introduces him to the writings of the medieval German mystic Meister Eckhart. Ensheim invites him to stay at his monastery in Alsace, a region then in France near Germany.

*French Riviera. Strip of southern France's Mediterranean coast, near Italy, that is a fashionable and expensive resort region. Here, the prosperous and socially ambitious Elliott Templeton builds a home and spends his last years. While India is the geographical symbol of Darrell's quest for wisdom, the Riviera is the symbol of Templeton's quest for social standing.

*India. South Asian country to which Darrell goes after meeting an Indian swami, a wise man, aboard a cruise ship on which he is working as a deckhand while returning to America. The Indian persuades Darrell to disembark at Bombay. Under his guidance, Darrell visits Indian religious centers and is drawn ever more deeply into Indian culture. Eventually, he develops insights into himself that make him decide to return home, by way of France, to lead the life of an ordinary mechanic.

— *Carl L. Bankston III*

THE REAL LIFE OF SEBASTIAN KNIGHT

Author: Vladimir Nabokov (1899-1977)
Type of work: Novel
Type of plot: Parody
Time of plot: Early twentieth century
First published: 1941

Although the locations of this parodic biography follow the itinerary of Vladimir Nabokov's own early life in Russia, England, France, and Germany, none of their external details is as significant as the internal quests of both the fictional biographer V. and his subject, his elusive half-brother Sebastian, whose inner life and its exfoliations in his fiction are products not of place or time, but of the imagination.

***St. Petersburg.** Capital of Imperial Russia that is the birthplace of both Sebastian and V. The novel initially depicts the city in winter in poetic terms, down to the shade that horse dung colors the snow. V.'s description, which compares his own memories of the city with a view of it on a postcard, introduces the theme of the disparity between "reality" and memory, with neither privileged at any one time. This theme is reinforced when V. visits their old governess, who, although her personal experience of living in Russia is minimal, has turned it in her memory into "a lost paradise." Her recollections, according to V., are equally inaccurate.

***Russia.** St. Petersburg also introduces the idea of being Russian. V., who is half English, sees Sebastian as fully Russian. Goodman, Sebastian's spurious biographer, sees Sebastian as repudiating his Russian heritage. Since the novel itself is, in a sense, Nabokov's working out of his own emotions over abandoning his rich Russian language for what he initially thought was the poor substitute of English, the reader cannot be sure how correct V. is. At any rate, Russia remains a "dreamland" for both brothers, more overtly so for V. This becomes more apparent later in the novel when V. learns the identity of the girl whom Sebastian loved in his youth, Natasha Rosanov. Admitting that by now his quest for the secrets of his brother's identity had grown into a "dream," V. constructs out of his imagination (there is no evidence he witnesses any of this) a scene between Sebastian and this girl in a "Russian summer landscape." The first scene includes the obligatory river, aspen and fir trees, flowers, and grass. The deflationary transformation of what at first seems to be a naked girl emerging from the river into a Russian priest blowing his nose after a swim is a clue to the thumbprint of the ultimate author, Nabokov himself, as is the presence in the second scene of a Camberwell beauty butterfly as Sebastian and Natasha meet for the last time. Russia remains only attainable by art.

Roquebrune (ROHK-brewn). French village near the Riviera where Sebastian's mother supposedly has died. Sebastian seeks it out, finds the pension in which she died, symbolically named "Les Violettes" (symbolically because she had given him a pack of violet sweets at their last meeting), and meditates on the surroundings so intently that he has a vision of her. Later he learns that the village he visited was the wrong Roquebrune—another case of imagination triumphing over reality. The appearance of a naked old man on a balcony of "Les Violettes" (similar to the later appearance of the naked priest) alerts sensitive readers to the fact that Sebastian's vision emerges not from the landscape around, but from the mind, as does V.'s vision of Sebastian and his young sweetheart.

***Cambridge** and ***London.** English cities that, for the most part, are described in stereotypical terms of fog and rain. Sebastian writes about an exile's vision of a landscape "with its unofficial rose," a phrase from English poet Rupert Brooke's poem of a nostalgic expatriate, "The Old Vicarage, Grantchester" (1912), and V. talks about his own "Rupert Brooke moods." However, several details indicate a deeper pattern, including Sebastian's address in London, 36 Oak Park Gardens—a number and location that reappear throughout the work.

Blauberg (BLAW-berg). Small French town in Alsace, where Sebastian goes to recuperate for his heart ailment. There, at the Beaumont Hotel, he meets the last love of his life, whose identity V. is so anxious to learn. The hotel is minimally described, but its grounds mark a garden motif that begins in the account of Sebastian's vision at "Les Violettes" and concludes with V.'s realization in Madame Lecerf's garden. That this repetition is intentional is shown when V. elsewhere mentions Sebastian's liking for an otherwise mediocre film, *The Enchanted Garden*, which he sees three times.

*Lescaux (LEHZ-coh). French town in which Madame Lecerf lives. V. eventually comes to believe that Madame Lecerf is Sebastian's last, and unwisely chosen, lover. Although her house seems run down and old, it has been built relatively recently; its garden, in which V. has an epiphany about her identity, is a mixture of signs of life—green leaves on black branches—and death—a pile of earth that reminds V. of a grave.

St. Damier (sahn DAH-mee-ay). French town in whose hospital Sebastian dies. Guided to Sebastian's supposed location in the significantly numbered Room 36, V. feels that before his brother dies he will impart to him the ultimate secret of life and death. However, V. finds himself in the wrong room, and Sebastian has died the day before. Nevertheless, V. feels that he has learned from his erratic, often mistaken quest. His biography is written partly to counter Goodman's erroneous life—erroneous because it reduces Sebastian's life to the mere product of his environment and times, against which his achievement is weighed and often found wanting.

V.'s search, although perhaps equally doomed to viewing Sebastian from the outside, at least recognizes and acknowledges the patterns and symbols of another's life, which, in Sebastian's butterfly image, "unfurl eyed wings." Indeed, the nature of the secret that V. is so close to attaining is described by Sebastian in one of his novels as the realization that "the wild country" around a traveler is not really a landscape but "a page in a book." Certainly, this is what Sebastian and V. ultimately are, creations in the pages of Nabokov's book, but what echoes beyond the covers of this novel is the possibility that perhaps everyone is.

— *William Laskowski*

REBECCA

Author: Daphne du Maurier (1907-1989)
Type of work: Novel
Type of plot: Gothic

Time of plot: 1930's
First published: 1938

Intrigued with the magic and mystery of southwestern England's Cornwall, Daphne du Maurier uses a fictional mansion to epitomize the beauty, the mystery, the secrecy, and the tragedy at the heart of human life. Her tale of jealousy plays out against a dark, primal setting that enhances the novel in Hardyesque fashion. Cornwall and the mansion are both backdrop to and participant in a dramatic tale that could only be set in a wild and romantic region filled with a sense of the past.

Manderley. Estate in Cornwall to which Max de Winter brings his new bride, the second Mrs. de Winter. There, he earlier lived with his first wife, Rebecca. From the blood-red rhododendrons surrounding this house of secrets to its iron gates holding in its past when Max and his second wife arrive in early May, Manderley is a forceful, menacing, and even malignant presence. The house itself seems to cause the events of the plot by acting upon the characters. As willful and capricious as the spirit of the dead Rebecca herself, the house symbolizes her tomb; her spirit infuses the place. In this ghostly personification, *Rebecca* actually seems to transcend the gothic form.

Manderley is based on two distinctive houses, one a house du Maurier visited as a child, and the other, Menabilly, a house in which she herself lived for more than twenty-five years. The houses merged in the landscape of her imagination to become Manderley, which inspired one of the most famous opening lines of twentieth century literature: "Last night I dreamt I went to Manderley again." As potent as a presence, as moody as a person, Manderley has a living aura and is as much a character in the novel as any man or woman. In fact, the house figures in the sensibilities of both of Max de Winter's wives more than any living presence by being imbued with the spirit of his first wife, Rebecca.

According to a published memoir, du Maurier visited a family friend's home, Milton, in 1917, and her memory of that house created the seed for Manderley. Struck by Milton's portraits of four centuries of family ancestors, du Maurier wondered if the ancestors' presences still haunted the house—with menace. For her the past is clearly a destructive force, destroying the present, just as the past wreaks havoc on present lives in *Rebecca*.

*Cornwall. Historic region of southwestern England to which du Maurier felt a passionate attachment. Her sense of Cornwall's atmosphere is integral to each of the novels she set there. Remote, distant from the rest of England, full of antiquities from prehistoric times to Arthurian legend, Cornwall infuses the imagination with history in a setting in which the ghosts of the past intrude upon the present. Dramatic things happen in such settings. For example, a shipwreck that du Maurier witnessed off the Cornish coast in 1930 became transposed as a symbol of the tragedy haunting Manderley in *Rebecca*. Indeed, the novel itself, originated in du Maurier's memory of place. While she was living in Alexandria, Egypt, she became so homesick for the woods and shores of Cornwall that she was moved to write a novel about it, and that novel became *Rebecca*.

— Holly Dworken Cooley

THE RECRUITING OFFICER

Author: George Farquhar (1678?-1707)
Type of work: Drama
Type of plot: Comedy

Time of plot: Early eighteenth century
First performed: 1706; first published, 1706

By setting this play in a provincial English town, Farquhar is able to present an entertaining satirical portrayal of army recruiters who play on the gullibility of rustic yokels. Moreover, as in his masterpiece, The Beaux' Stratagem *(1707), Farquhar's setting provides a comic contrast between the attitudes of urban rakes such as Plume and country authority figures.*

*Shrewsbury. Midlands market town on the Severn River in the county of Shropshire, near England's Welsh border, in which the play is set. For knowledgeable members of George Farquhar's eighteenth century audiences, Shrewsbury evoked memories of William Shakespeare's *Henry IV, Part I* (1597-1598), as it was the site of the climactic battle in that play. His audiences probably also recalled with amusement Falstaff's shameless recruiting tactics in *Henry IV*, in which he enlists the lame, the old, and the blind into the king's army. In Farquhar's own comedy, Shrewsbury furnishes its share of naïve rustics to be conned by Captain Plume and Sergeant Kite; these include the country wench Rose and her stupid brother Bullock. Sergeant Kite's masquerade as a fortune-teller associates military recruiting tactics with charlatanry in general.

Shrewsbury's marketplace is the center of Kite's and Plume's outrageous recruiting tactics. Village marketplaces were notorious venues for traveling mountebanks. A village path by the River Severn is the scene of romantic encounters—a setting enhanced by poetic associations given to the Severn by John Milton and other writers.

Courtroom. A judicial hearing in the play's fourth act, in which Justice Balance reviews Kite's dubious enlistments, is a satirical gem, ridiculing both the recruiting process and the often farcical nature of country justice, especially when the scene culminates in the absurdity of Balance sentencing his disguised daughter to be a recruit.

Balance's house. Home of Justice Balance that is a setting in the play's first two acts for Melinda's and Sylvia's intrigues. Balance's mansion also provides a dignified social location for the fifth act's resolution of conflicts and establishes the formal engagement of Sylvia and Plume, giving their union the stamp of social approval.

— Edgar L. Chapman

THE RED AND THE BLACK

Author: Stendhal (Marie-Henri Beyle, 1783-1842)
Type of work: Novel
Type of plot: Psychological realism

Time of plot: Early nineteenth century
First published: Le Rouge et le noir, 1830 (English translation, 1898)

This novel uses three main settings to trace the hero's progress from his provincial origins to the fulfillment of his grandest ambitions in the capital. Wherever he goes, however, this passionate liberal who worships Napoleon finds himself an anachronism in the France of Louis-Philippe's bourgeois monarchy.

Verrières. (vehr-ee-YER). One of the prettiest little towns in the Franche-Comté, a province in eastern France, located south of Lorraine and north of Switzerland. Both the province's main river, the Doubs, and its mountain range, the Jura, figure in Stendhal's initial description of setting. The Verrières he presents, however, does not actually correspond to any of the towns by that name in the Doubs valley; instead, it seems a fictionalized version of Stendhal's own hometown, Grenoble—south of the Franche-Comté—which he detested as parochial and repressive. The novel's counterpart to Grenoble stagnates in bourgeois moneymaking, vanity, and hypocrisy. Verrières's many walls, its clipped trees, and finally the prison cell to which Julien is confined at the end of the novel symbolize the repressiveness of society and especially of such petit-bourgeois towns; by contrast, the several episodes throughout the novel in which he contentedly views the world from above—the mountains outside Verrières, the top of a cathedral tower—mark not only his solitary contentment in nature but also his moral elevation.

*****Besançon** (buh-zohn-SOHN). Capital city of the Franche-Comté, nestled beneath a hillside fortress. This locale marks a movement for Julien into the broader world in the last third of book 1. As a key nineteenth century military center where Julien enters not the army but a seminary, Besançon offers scope for both his red (soldierly) and his black (clerical) aspirations. In the Besançon seminary, as in Verrières, Julien is alienated from his peers by his finer values.

*****Paris.** Capital of France. Book 2 shifts the action to Paris, where Julien takes up residence in his employer's sumptuous home, the Hôtel de la Mole, situated in the fashionable Faubourg Saint-Germain. Having imagined the city both as the theater of the world, where he can achieve success, and as the center of intrigue and hypocrisy, Julien appreciates his new patron's kindness alongside the greater political stimulation, breeding, and sophistication of the capital. Even so, in this aristocratic milieu he suffers no less than before from the mediocrity and conventionality that Stendhal consistently attributes to postrestoration French society at all levels. Two historical locations in particular emphasize the gulf between the heroic passion and vigor of the past and the anemic lives of the de la Moles: Malmaison, the only site Julien visits on his arrival, formerly Napoleon's home outside Paris, and the Place de Grève, where the lover of Queen Marguerite de Navarre, Boniface de la Mole, written into the novel as the fictional family's ancestor, was unjustly beheaded.

*****Vergy** (vehr-ZHEE). Small French town near Dijon named after a thirteenth century heroine of romance who committed suicide because of love rivalry. It is here that Stendhal locates the country home of Verrières's philistine mayor, Monsieur de Rênal. The author describes these surroundings in terms evoking the countryside outside Grenoble, where he himself spent happy childhood days with his sister. In the novel, Vergy becomes the quintessential pastoral retreat from social corruption: In its garden, its woods, and its closeness to nature, Julien attains some peace of mind, falls in love with Madame de Rênal, and wins her love as well as her children's. In the last chapter of the novel, he recalls Vergy as an idyll from which he foolishly let his ambitions lure him.

Bray-le-Haut (BRAY-luh-oh). Fictional abbey outside Verrières, possibly modeled on the St. Marie d'en Haut church and convent outside Grenoble. Here Julien, dazzled by the glamorous power of a young bishop officiating at ceremonies for a visiting king, participates in celebrations first as a guard of honor, then as a subdeacon—his cassock and the spurs showing beneath it symbolic of his two possible career choices.

***Strasbourg.** Northeastern French city where Julien stays as a courier, taking the opportunity to visit nearby Kehl, a town where two of Napoleon's generals won a glorious victory in 1796. Once again, Stendhal suggests that contemporary France is a lackluster shadow of its revolutionary past.

— *Margaret Bozenna Goscilo*

THE RED BADGE OF COURAGE: An Episode of the American Civil War

Author: Stephen Crane (1871-1900)
Type of work: Novel
Type of plot: Psychological realism

Time of plot: 1861-1865
First published: 1895

This novel about the American Civil War offers no specific information about the location of the battle described in its pages; the whole point of the story is that it might be any battle. It is only in passing that readers even learn that the Union soldier Henry's surname is Fleming and that his unit is the 304th New York, but throughout the story's most hectic phases he is simply "the youth," and his companions are "the regiment."

Camp. Encampment of Henry's regiment where the novel opens. Although the regiment has only been lodged there for a few months, the novel's initial location seems to Henry to be "sort of eternal camp." In the opening paragraph, as a fog clears to display the awakening army, roads "grow" in the distance from "long troughs of liquid mud." The shore of a nearby river is occupied by the enemy, whose campfires glow by night on the ridges of low hills. Sometimes pickets posted as sentries on opposite banks shoot at one another; however, at other times they converse peaceably, their enmity set aside.

The regiment's lodgings are log-walled huts roofed with folded tents. Cracker boxes serve as furniture, grouped around fireplaces whose chimneys—crudely compounded out of clay and sticks—are inefficient, with the effect that the atmosphere inside each hut is foul with smoke: an omen of the battlefield to come.

Henry's home. Henry remembers life on his widowed mother's dairy farm as an endless round of trudging between the house, the barn, and the fields. He recalls that after enlisting he went to say good-bye to his admiring schoolmates, and that as he walked away from the seminary, along a path between two rows of oaks, a girl watched him from a window; his subsequent journey by railroad to Washington, D.C., seemed to be a hero's triumph because of the manner in which the troops were greeted at every station. Immediately before the battle, Henry remembers his local village on the day of a circus parade: an exquisitely detailed image that serves as a counterpoint to his chaotic awareness of the battlefield.

Battlefield. Images of the battlefield are compounded from a patchwork series of briefly glimpsed microcosms, each one narrowly confined by the undulations of the ground and the sprawling pine forests that girdle every little cluster of fields. When Henry first sees skirmishers running back and forth across clear ground, continually ducking into and out of trees, while a dark battle line extends across a sunstruck clearing, it seems to him to be entirely the wrong place to fight a battle. The forest appears to him at times to be an ambush-laden trap and at other times a protective haven. Eventually, however, it becomes a mere blur as his regiment is marched through it, emerging periodically into open land chaotically and cacophonously hazed by gunfire and smoke before moving back again.

When Henry hears that his companions have held the position from which he has run away, the forest creepers begin to catch his legs, as if protesting against his movement; he nearly wanders into a swamp before finding a corpse in a quiet "chapel" of pines. The forest remains resistant, brambles impeding his journey back to the battlefield as the creepers had earlier hindered his retreat, until he joins the procession of wounded men. Reunited with his battered regiment, Henry finds the scene initially reminiscent of the aftermath of an orgy, then of a slaughterhouse.

The landscape becomes increasingly hallucinatory thereafter, and it is while searching for an illusory stream that the youth overhears a general giving the order to send the regiment into a suicidal charge. From then on the almost-monochrome landscape is dominated by two flags: the one that the youth takes over from his own color sergeant and the one flying over the position where the retreating enemy leaves behind a pocket of desperate resistance. Between these two encounters the youth looks back in astonishment at the triviality of distances he has covered; it is because his companions are accused of "not going far enough" that they charge with sufficient resolution to capture the enemy flag.

On leaving the battlefield, the youth and the remnant of his regiment pass a "stolid white house": a symbolic reminder of everything for which they are supposed to be fighting. Although the marching men return to troughs of mud identical to those from which they emerged, they now seem to the youth to be heading toward "prospects of clover": a vision of the meadowy paradise awaiting them on the far side of the river.

— *Brian Stableford*

REDBURN: His First Voyage

Author: Herman Melville (1819-1891)
Type of work: Novel
Type of plot: Bildungsroman

Time of plot: c. 1839
First published: 1849

Herman Melville's descriptions in this novel allow him to develop several themes: the gap between fantasy and reality, the impermanence of life, and the appalling social conditions of his day in Great Britain.

Highlander. Ship on which the young sailor Wellingborough Redburn travels between Liverpool and New York City; based on the actual ship, the *St. Lawrence*, in which Melville made a similar trip in 1839. As with his depiction of Liverpool, Melville's description of the ship serves different purposes at different times. At first the ship is simply a dose of reality counteracting Redburn's fantasies. Before actually going to sea, Redburn has an idealized notion of sailor life. Once aboard ship, he discovers the hardships of being a sailor but also finds things to enjoy, such as the thrill of the ship plunging through the waves and the mastery he feels in fixing the sails. Like life ashore, life aboard the ship is a mixture of good and bad.

On Redburn's return voyage, Melville switches the focus to emphasize the horrible conditions of the Irish emigrants in the ship's unsanitary steerage quarters, which contrast markedly with the much better conditions of the rich cabin passengers, who seem selfishly intent on keeping the poor away by means of ropes rather than providing them with any assistance.

*Liverpool. Major seaport of western England. Redburn, who likes to indulge in fantasy, tries to imagine what Liverpool will be like before he gets there, but instead of the marvels he expects, all he finds are disappointingly dingy warehouses—a demonstration of how a young boy's idealized fantasies about the world may have nothing to do with reality. As Redburn explores Liverpool using an old guidebook, Melville introduces a second, related theme: that life does not stand still. Redburn expects Liverpool to look as it does in the guidebook, but his father's book is fifty years out of date. For example, the city's old fort has disappeared and been replaced by the Old Fort Tavern; Riddough's Hotel, where his father stayed, has been torn down; and the Old Dock in the center of town has been covered over and turned into the customs house.

As Redburn continues to explore the city, another, somewhat different theme emerges: that Liverpool is in some ways horrifying. Redburn encounters numerous beggars and other poor people, most notably a family starving to death in a cellar on a street called

Launcelott's-Hey. He also notes the crime, vice, pestilence, and sooty buildings in the city. The point here seems to be to indict the new industrial age for producing a society full of starving beggars, criminals, and quacks, along with uncaring people who simply ignore the misery around them.

*Bedloe's Island.** Island in New York Harbor whose fort the *Highlander* passes on the way out to sea. Redburn's sight of the fort causes him to remember his visit there and how he had stumbled in its dark vaults but eventually had emerged into sunshine to see cows grazing and calves frolicking. He remembers being happy then and wishes he could live there.

*Nelson Memorial.** Memorial to the great British naval hero Horatio Nelson in Liverpool that Redburn visits. Redburn is moved by the four bronze statues of chained captives in the memorial. Although the figures are supposed to represent Nelson's victories, their despondent appearance reminds Redburn of the former African slave trade. The memorial also contains statues depicting Victory and Death, and Nelson himself is shown

dying. This scene enables Melville to denounce the slave trade and praise those who fought to abolish it, while contributing to the melancholy atmosphere pervading the novel that reflects Redburn's mood.

*Ireland.** First European land that Redburn encounters. It disappoints him because it seems an ordinary sight, not the place of wonders he expects.

*Wales.** Region of western Britain that the *Highlander* passes immediately before reaching Liverpool. Its purple mountains at first make Redburn think, characteristically, of the Prince of Wales. However, he then realizes that they do not look different from the Catskill Mountains back home.

*America.** Though disillusioned with Europe, Redburn is not cured of his tendency to fantasize when he reaches Liverpool, where he rhapsodizes about the Paradise that is to come in America as a result of the equality of nationalities there. Later, however, he notes how much more equality there is in Liverpool among black and white people than there is in America.

— Sheldon Goldfarb

REFLECTIONS IN A GOLDEN EYE

Author: Carson McCullers (1917-1967)
Type of work: Novel
Type of plot: Psychological realism

Time of plot: 1930's
First published: 1941

Although the novel's setting is not specified, indications that it is set in the American South abound throughout the text. Although the army post setting might appear more crucial to the plot than does the geographical location of the post, the southern setting is always embedded in the events that unfold and in the attitudes, habits, and beliefs of the characters.

Army post. Unnamed military installation in the South that is the novel's main setting. Because the novel is set during peacetime, the atmosphere is described as dull, one in which mundane events recur repeatedly. The layout of the army post parallels the routine events that occur on its premises. The post contains rows of officers' tract houses, a gym, a chapel, a golf course, and swimming pools. The structure of the army post is as rigid as the rules imposed on its inhabitants. Within the boundaries of the isolated army post, a subculture emerges. This insular, dull setting makes the action that unfolds in

the novel depart from routine and seem even more dramatic than if it had occurred outside the subculture that exists within the army post. The army post setting is important because it shows how the characters who live within it do not conform to socially acceptable rules, even though they reside in a very rule-oriented, regimented environment. The army post setting also provides an environment in which characters have hierarchical ranks. This situation is imperative to illustrate the complicated relationships between Captain Penderton, Private Williams, and Major Langdon. Amid structured and ordered physical surroundings and clearly defined professional ranks, the characters are all emotionally and psychologically distressed and unstable.

*American South. The narrator points out that the army post is in the South. Readers are also informed that although Leonora was not originally from the South, she has cultivated habits that define her as southern. Moreover, Captain Penderton's aunts never let him forget that he was a southerner. The southern setting, the characterization, the pessimistic outcome, the violence, and the oddity of the circumstances and events that are portrayed place the novel in the southern gothic tradition, a perspective from which many modern southern writers such as William Faulkner, Flannery O'Connor, and Truman Capote wrote.

Penderton home. House Captain Penderton and his wife, Leonora, share on the outskirts of the army post. It is a new two-story stucco house with eight rooms and exactly like every other house in the neighborhood. A large mass of uncleared land faces the Penderton's house. The Captain spends much of his time in the study inside his house. Private Williams stands between the outside of the window in Captain Penderton's study and a row of evergreen trees and peers through the window. Also, Williams routinely sneaks inside the house and sits in Leonora Penderton's bedroom, while she sleeps.

Woods. Fifteen square miles of country that surrounds the army post. The woods are filled with pine trees, flowers, and wild animals. Captain Penderton gets lost in the woods, which symbolizes his search for inner peace. In the woods, Penderton becomes consumed with hatred for Williams.

— *Laurie Champion*

THE REIVERS: A Reminiscence

Author: William Faulkner (1897-1962)
Type of work: Novel
Type of plot: Psychological realism

Time of plot: May, 1905
First published: 1962

This novel transports young Lucius Priest from his hometown in Mississippi to a house of prostitution in Tennessee, exposing him to corrupting influences that his irresponsible adult companion, Boon Hogganbeck, supposes he is too young to recognize. However, the boy's visit to the brothel and the nearby town of Parsham contrast vividly with his small Mississippi hometown and provide him with challenges that mature him far beyond the level normally expected in an eleven-year-old boy.

Jefferson. Seat of William Faulkner's imaginary Mississippi county of **Yoknapatawpha** that is Lucius's hometown. Jefferson is patterned after Faulkner's own home of Oxford in northern Mississippi. Early in the novel Boon drives Lucius's grandfather and the family past the typical small-town livery stable, which the advent of automobiles would eventually render obsolete, and then proceeds proudly through the town square.

Because the author chose the adult Lucius as retrospective narrator of the events of the novel, readers learn that Lucius's home has since been replaced by a gas station and that his grandfather's house across the street has been divided into apartments. As a result, readers share Lucius's memories of a place and way of life that have been profoundly altered, to a large extent, ironically, by the automobile, the very conveyance that takes Lucius on his illicit trip away from home.

Winton Flyer. Automobile belonging to Lucius's grandfather that Boon appropriates and uses to take Lucius to Tennessee. Ned William McCaslin, the grandfather's black handyman, also becomes an accidental passenger on the trip. One of the earliest cars in Jefferson, the Flyer is an object of great interest to Boon, the huge but childlike man who drives it for Lucius's grandfather. Faulkner provides many examples of riding in automobiles around the turn of the twentieth century, such as a time when the grandfather, sitting in his car's front seat, spits tobacco juice which, because of the great speed at which the car is traveling, strikes his wife sitting behind him. Much of the rich comedy of the novel derives from the three travelers' discomfort in the unreliable Winton Flyer on primitive roads, alternately dusty and muddy, that they must traverse on the eighty-mile trip to Memphis.

Hell Creek Bottom. Stream that is the most formidable obstacle on the travelers' journey to Memphis. Boon, who has made the trip to Memphis before, although not in an automobile, broods on the difficulties of the unbridged stream long before the travelers reach it. After reaching the creek, the car sinks into the mud; comedy flows as the travelers attempt to extricate it and eventually pay a farmer what Boon regards as an exorbitant price to pull out the car with his mules. To Boon, Hell Creek Bottom is the boundary between the rural area to the south and what he calls "civilization" to the north. In reality, the creek is the effective border between the relatively unchallenging way of life Lucius has known and a more urbanized environment with its greater array of possibilities and seductions.

*****Memphis.** Tennessee city that is the largest urban center within reasonable traveling distance of Lucius's northern Mississippi home. Although the novel says little about Memphis, other than its descriptions of Miss Reba's establishment, the city is the magnet that draws restless young men like Boon into temptation and away from their ordinary and generally more wholesome lives in Mississippi.

Miss Reba's house. Brothel on Memphis's Catalpa Street. To Boon, Miss Reba's is a familiar destination. To Lucius, the eleven-year-old grandson of the owner of the automobile that Boon has appropriated, it is initially simply a strange house populated by women whose activities are beyond his comprehension. Gradually, he comes to understand, though vaguely, that the house is a place of pleasure for men like Boon.

In the seventh chapter of the novel, Lucius shares a bed with Otis, the nephew of one of the prostitutes. In this setting, Otis tells Lucius that he not only is a peeping Tom but that he also charges admission for voyeuristic men to spy on his aunt at her work. When the appalled Lucius begins to pummel Otis, the latter cuts him with a knife. Order is soon restored, but the next day, as a result of these experiences, Lucius concludes that his childhood and innocence are over. The Memphis sojourn has given him a new appreciation of the decency of his own home in Mississippi.

Faulkner depicts the brothel realistically but not judgmentally. Its denizens, except for Otis and Miss Reba herself, who is primarily interested in maintaining a profitable business, are ordinary, weak people whose lives are shaped by circumstance. Otis is the only inhabitant of the house with no redeeming qualities; he is the one person who makes Miss Reba's a truly bad place for an eleven-year-old visitor.

Parsham. Small town near the Memphis area called "Possum" by several characters. There, at "Uncle Parsham's" place, Lucius discovers the new responsibility that has devolved on him to recover his grandfather's automobile. The racetrack at Parsham is the setting for Lucius's initiation into the activities of a jockey. After Ned trades the Winton Flyer for a racehorse of dubious value, it falls to Lucius to win several races to make it possible to get the automobile back. In addition to providing excitement, the racetrack gives Lucius a chance to prove his manhood.

— *Robert P. Ellis*

REMEMBRANCE OF THINGS PAST

Author: Marcel Proust (1871-1922)

Type of work: Novel

Type of plot: Psychological realism

Time of plot: Late nineteenth and early twentieth centuries

First published: À la recherche du temps perdu, 1913-1927 (English translation, 1922-1931, 1981): *Du côté de chez Swann*, 1913 (*Swann's Way*, 1922);

À l'ombre des jeunes filles en fleurs, 1919 (*Within a Budding Grove*, 1924); *Le Côté de Guermantes*, 1920-1921 (*The Guermantes Way*, 1925); *Sodome et Gomorrhe*, 1922 (*Cities of the Plain*, 1927); *La Prisonnière*, 1925 (*The Captive*, 1929); *Albertine disparue*, 1925 (*The Sweet Cheat Gone*, 1930); *Le Temps retrouvé*, 1927 (*Time Regained*, 1931)

In these seven novels Proust allows his narrator, Marcel (a semi-autobiographical character), to recollect the story of his life and the lives of his family, friends, and acquaintances from childhood until early old age, and their involvement in the high society of Paris.

*Paris. France's capital city, in which Marcel is reared in an upper-middle-class family within the best part of central Paris. Much of the action of the novels takes place in the apartments, palaces, parks, hotels, and restaurants exclusive to the important members of Paris society. This society is ruled by the remnants of the former French aristocracy, still living with considerable splendor in their elegant apartments in the Faurboug Saint-Germain, an old, fashionable district on the left side of the River Seine in central Paris.

Verdurin salon (VEHR-duhr-ihn). Gathering place hosted by Madame Verdurin, a rich social climber of no consequence who accumulates a dubious group of people in her expensive home for regular soirées. The Verdurins represent the second-rate society world, on the edge of the smartest Paris hierarchy. Madame Verdurin's guests are a mixed bag of the newly rich; young gentlemen looking for a good time, often slumming with people of lesser social position; professional men of some repute but socially unimportant; young artists, musicians, and the occasional fashionable prostitute. Marcel occasionally visits the Verdurins, associating below his station. A silly, vindictive, stupid woman, Madame Verdurin represents in her salon the vulgarity of the bourgeoisie. However, she manages in the long run of life to ascend, because of her wealth (after the death of her equally vulgar husband), and marry an aristocrat, with whom she enters the salons of the nobility.

*Champs-Elysees Garden (shahn-zay-leh-ZAY). Park in the center of Paris where Marcel plays as a child and where he becomes a friend of Gilberte, the daughter of Swann and Odette. This relationship, innocent and natural in its beginning, establishes a pattern of conduct in Marcel which is to be repeated over and over in his involvement with women. The edenic surroundings and the unaffected attraction of the children to each other gradually sours as Marcel becomes obsessively possessive and jealous and finally refuses to have anything more to do with Odette. The park is also a common meeting place for the adult lovers in the novel.

Combray. Small French town, based on Illiers, a real town southwest of Paris, near the cathedral city of Char-tres. (The real town is now known as Illiers-Combray because of the fame of Proust's novel.) *Swann's Way*, the first volume of Proust's series of books, begins with Marcel remembering an incident of childish willfulness that occurred while he was still a young child staying with his parents at his great-aunt Leonie's home in the country, and the ruminative course of the entire novel is set with that story. Combray is a place of childhood pleasure for Marcel, and there is an aura of simple, rural religious belief in the landscape over which the church towers of the town and surrounding villages rise. It is here that Marcel for the first time sees Gilberte, Swann's daughter, who will later become the first love of his life.

The town also represents two of the major social groups in the novel; the paths in the village lead to two separate aspects of French society: the Guermantes Way passes the château of the Duke of Guermantes, Combray's ancient aristocratic family, and Swann's Way passes the great house and park of Swann, a popular Parisian playboy.

Balbec. Fictional version of the summer resorts on France's Normandy coast—such as Dieppe, Trouville, and Cabourg—where Proust spent his summer months during his teens. Here Marcel first responds to the mysteries of sexual desire and watches at close hand the ways in which high society and the remnants of the aristocracy come into sometimes intimate and sometimes improper contact with one another, and occasionally with members of the servant class—another thematic interest in the work.

Also at Balbec, Marcel begins his personal connections with the aristocracy through his grandmother, a familiar of some of the older nobility. Robert de Saint Loup, an aristocrat, becomes his closest friend and is ultimately to marry Swann's daughter, an example of the theme of the crossing relations of high society (here at its most questionable, given that Gilberte's mother was a prostitute and her father a Jew). Two further thematic lines are also developed: Marcel's relations to women start here with a group of young girls whom he admires; one, Albertine, is to become his first adult love.

— *Charles Pullen*

RENÉE MAUPERIN

Authors: Edmond de Goncourt (1822-1896) and Jules
   de Goncourt (1830-1870)
Type of work: Novel

Type of plot: Naturalism
Time of plot: Nineteenth century
First published: 1864 (English translation, 1888)

As in many French novels, the places mapped out in this novel constitute a series of routes to and from the cold heart of Paris, where fervent dreams and noble aspirations are lavishly fed and then—more often than not—cruelly broken.

***Paris.** Capital city of France and, in French eyes, the very definition of civilization. Paris is metaphorically personified in the plot by Monsieur Denoisel, a "true Parisian" who sells the land he inherits and invests the money in the stock exchange, thus rendering his capital theoretical rather than concrete. Various artifices and compromises allow him to live well on a modest income. He lodges in a snug three-room flat close to Boulevard des Italiens, dining at clubs and restaurants. Whenever his income is exhausted, he disappears from Paris and lives more cheaply in a country inn, where tobacco is his only indulgence, or even more cheaply in Florence, Italy.

The first Parisian setting featured in the story is the tastefully decorated house on the rue de Madelaine, where Madame Mauperin visits the fashionable Abbé Blampoix. She moves on from there to Henri's flat in the rue Taitbout, with its ominous pair of swords set atop the bookcase, where he holds solemn parties that are more like academic conferences. It is close to the rue de la Chaussée d'Antin, where Renée was taken as a child, in company with Noémi Bourjot, to the lectures that Henri still attends, sometimes dropping into the Café Bignon on the corner.

Other Parisian settings featured include the auction rooms where Madame Mauperin and Renée go to see Lord Mansbury's art collection; the library in the rue Richelieu where Renée overhears the fateful detail that costs Henri his life: and the Ville d'Avray, beside whose frozen lake Henri exchanges pistol-shots with Boisjorand de Villacourt.

***Bourmont** (bor-MOHNG). Town in the Haut-Marne in which Charles Mauperin settles on his return to France from temporary exile in America. He keeps his farm in the village of Villacourt when he moves on, un-

wittingly laying the groundwork for the chain of misfortunes that destroys his family.

Basigny (bah-seeg-NYEE). Estate in Morimond, not far from Maricourt, bought by Charles Mauperin after leaving Bourmont, where Renée is born and to which she returns to die. Basigny is situated in wild country, uncultivated since the French Revolution, near a ruined abbey. Charles retains the property but has to obtain a house closer to Paris when he is elected as a deputy after the Revolution of 1830.

The description of Renée's journey from Briche to Morimond, as the story nears its conclusion, is highly charged: The landscape comes to signify lost innocence. When Renée relapses after her brief recovery, the authors sum up her life in a lavishly detailed description of the souvenir-laden bedroom in which she dies, making much of the bouquets of corn on the wallpaper, the vessel containing holy water, the mirrors framed in blue velvet, and the miniature portraits of her mother. After Renée's death, her parents become voluntary exiles from France, roaming the world with neither home nor direction.

Briche (breesh). Site of Mauperin's house on the outskirts of Paris, near Chantilly on the banks of the Seine, not far from the Ile Saint Denis. Several key scenes take place in the drawing room, where Renée plays the piano and Madame Bourjot sings; it is converted into the "Briche Theatre" for the fateful productions of *The Caprice* and *Pierrot, Bigamist*, which serve to reveal Henri's love for Noémi.

***Sannois** (sahn-NWAW). Village neighboring Briche in which the Bourjots' house is located. The house is a pretentious one in which everything is calculated to intimidate visitors with ostentatious displays of wealth and strict etiquette. It contains no paintings, except for a portrait of Madame Bourjot signed by Jean Auguste Dominique Ingres, but Bourjot owns a fine collection of gemstones. The house becomes an important locus of opposition politics, although Bourjot's past political affiliations have been mixed.

Motte-Noire (moht-nwahr). Miserable collection of hovels in the Croix-du-Soldat woods, situated about nine miles from Saint-Mihiel in Lorraine. Motte-Noire is the current residence of the last of the Villacourts, who have come down in the world since the scion of the family was wounded in the head at Oberkamlach in 1796. The authors' account of the family's history since 1303 dovetails with other synopses of French history which contrast strongly with the depiction of the rootless "true Parisian" Denoisel.

— *Brian Stableford*

REQUIEM FOR A NUN

Author: William Faulkner (1897-1962)
Type of work: Novel
Type of plot: Psychological realism

Time of plot: 1930's
First published: 1951

This is the twelfth novel set in William Faulkner's mythical Yoknapatawpha County. The three acts of its drama alternate among three narrative sections in which Faulkner traces the histories of Mississippi, Yoknapatawpha County, and the town of Jefferson. Faulkner carefully delineates the settings of the various scenes of the play-within-the-novel.

Jefferson. Fictional town based on Faulkner's hometown of Oxford, in the northeastern part of Mississippi. In several novels and stories, he created his own microcosm, his own "little postage stamp of native soil." Although his mythical county bears considerable resemblance to the real locale, he altered certain details involving chronology and individual characters. Recurrent locales and characters, such as Temple Drake and Gavin and Gowan Stevens, link this to other **Yoknapatawpha** fiction, especially the earlier novel *Sanctuary* (1931). By tracing the history of the town and its buildings in the narratives between the acts, Faulkner makes it clear how significant place is in his fiction, particularly in this novel. Both the courthouse and the jail figure in *Sanctuary* and are again employed as settings here.

Courthouse. Act 1 of the play is introduced by a prose narrative titled "The Courthouse (A Name for the City)" that is designed to establish the significance of the place as more than a mere backdrop for the story. In this section, Faulkner traces the history of Jefferson, Mississippi, from its founding, near the beginning of the nineteenth century, to the time of the narrative. The court-house was constructed some thirty years after the town was founded. The narrative sets the stage for the first scene of the play, which occurs in the courtroom in which Nancy Mannigoe, Temple and Gowan's servant, has been tried and condemned to death for the murder of their child. The second and third scenes of the act take place in the modern living room of Temple and Gowan's apartment in an antebellum home in Jefferson.

*Jackson. Capital of Mississippi. The narrative section that introduces act 2, titled "The Golden Dome (Beginning Was the Word)," is devoted to the history of Mississippi in general and the capital, Jackson, in particular. "The Golden Dome" is a reference to the state capitol building. Scenes 1 and 3 are set in the governor's office in the capitol. Faulkner's stage directions describe the set as suspended above the stage, since it symbolizes "the still higher, the last, the ultimate seat of judgment." The second scene, a flashback to a time before the murder, occurs in Temple's private rooms in the apartment she shares with Gowan.

Jefferson jail. The opening narrative of act 3 is "The Jail (Nor Even Yet Quite Relinquish—)," in which Faulkner continues the history of his fictional town of

Jefferson. He uses the jail as a symbol not only for the growth of the community but also for the changes in the United States during the nineteenth century and the first half of the twentieth. The third act's one scene takes place in the common room of the jail on the day before

Nancy Mannigoe is to be hanged for the murder of Temple and Gowan's child. The almost medieval appearance of the jail serves as an ideal backdrop for the tragic story of Nancy, the child, and his parents.

— *W. Kenneth Holditch*

RESURRECTION

Author: Leo Tolstoy (1828-1910)
Type of work: Novel
Type of plot: Social realism

Time of plot: Late nineteenth century
First published: Voskreseniye, 1899 (English translation, 1899)

After experiencing a profound spiritual crisis, Leo Tolstoy turned his formidable literary prowess to an examination of the imperial Russian criminal justice system in this novel. He takes the reader along with his principal characters, Prince Dmitri Nekhludoff and the prostitute Katusha Maslova, on a guided tour of czarist Russia's courts, prisons, and penal camps, examining the sorts of people who are found there and the social wrongs he perceives as having put them there.

Law court. Government court in which the prostitute Katusha is tried and sentenced for murder. When Prince Nekhludoff, acting as an officer of the court, first sees Katusha, he does not recognize her, since she is using the name Lyubov (which in Russian literally means "love"). When the judge demands to know her baptismal name, her patronymic, and her surname, Nekhludoff is horrified to realize that this is the same peasant girl he seduced and then abandoned many years earlier.

While many authors use the courtroom setting as a symbol of justice, Tolstoy makes it a seat of the miscarriage of justice. Katusha is found guilty of the murder of the merchant and sentenced to hard labor in Siberia, although she believed the poison she used on the merchant was in fact a harmless sleep drug. Nekhludoff is stricken with guilt at the knowledge that his seduction and abandonment of her has led to this.

Prison. Institution in which Katusha is detained while awaiting transportation to a Siberian penal camp. Here she meets a large number of other women sentenced for various crimes. Many of these people are not guilty of the crimes for which they are charged, and many of the others have committed crimes that should not be considered crimes at all.

*Moscow. Russia's largest city, in which Katusha is tried and convicted for murder. Tolstoy pays little attention to the emblems for which Moscow is most famous, such as the Kremlin and Red Square, as his focus remains firmly upon the ordinary working people, their markets, cheap pubs, and neighborhoods in which they live in squalor.

*St. Petersburg. Imperial capital of Russia to which Nekhludoff travels to have Katusha's case reviewed by a state council. If that fails, he plans to petition the czar himself to pardon Katusha or commute her sentence from penal servitude to simple exile. Tolstoy portrays St. Petersburg as a place of elegant and subtle corruption, where men with perfect manners who speak perfect French make unethical deals.

Panovo. Estate on which Nekhludoff first meets Katusha. At the time of their first encounter, the estate belonged to Nekhludoff's aunts. In his youth, he was capable of a pure affection for the young Katusha; however, after he became acquainted with the world's corruption, he in turn corrupted her and helped drive her toward prostitution. However, after seeing her unjustly condemned, Nekhludoff arranges for Panovo and his other estates to be managed by trustees so he will be free to follow Katusha to her Siberian exile.

***Siberia.** Vast wasteland of eastern Russia that is the involuntary destination of the exiled Katusha. The wide expanses of the Russian empire east of the Ural Mountains were used for penal camps and internal exile by the Russian government almost as soon as these regions were incorporated into the realm. Even in the days of the czars, Siberia was strongly associated with the exile of prisoners, both criminals and political prisoners, al-

though the conditions that Tolstoy so harshly criticizes in this novel would prove mild compared to the brutality of the Soviet gulag system in the twentieth century. In Siberia Nekhludoff finally makes things right with Katusha. While reading the Bible, he discovers the rules by which God means humans to live, neither harming others nor imposing harmful punishments on them, but loving and caring for one another.

— *Leigh Husband Kimmel*

THE RETURN

Author: Walter de la Mare (1873-1956)
Type of work: Novel
Type of plot: Ghost

Time of plot: Nineteenth century
First published: 1910

Ostensibly concerned with an experience of apparently supernatural possession in a small town in the early twentieth century, this novel uses its different settings and characters as tools for exploring the geography of the human psyche.

Herbert home. Ramshackle house in the English countryside, home to Herbert Herbert and his sister Grisel. Herbert describes the residence as a "queer old shanty," but Arthur Lawford finds it a pleasing refuge from the problems his psychic possession causes at home. Peculiarities of the house mirror Arthur's predicament. The house is situated at a point where the rushing River Widder washes against its lower walls. Similarly, it is purportedly haunted by a ghost which insinuates itself into living beings, and this is how Arthur becomes possessed. The spirit of Nicholas Sabathier has come rushing from the past to fill the susceptible vessel that the convalescing Arthur represents.

Herbert describes the ghost in the house as one who looks into shelves and drawers that no longer exist. Like the ghost, Arthur is someone searching for a past that no longer exists. When he returns to his own home physically transformed by the spirit of Sabathier after his sojourn in the Widderstone churchyard, he discovers that the domestic values that have kept his household and marriage together for seventeen years are a fragile illusion that become strained and eventually broken.

Inevitably, Arthur comes to realize that the spirit of Sabathier, which, though out of place in the modern age,

hungers for life as he himself hungered for life while a young man. Sabathier haunts Arthur much the way the ghost haunts the Herbert residence, and both represent incarnations of the past trying to reassert themselves.

The Herbert residence is imbued with a strong sense of the past. It seems much older than the nearby Widderstone churchyard, arising from its surroundings like a natural part of the landscape, and it is filled with antiquarian books on all manner of subjects. Herbert is a scholarly man knowledgeable about history, including the history of Sabathier. Grisel offers Arthur a type of consolation that he compares to the love his mother showed him as a child. It is no wonder that Arthur comes to a sense of the man he once was during his stay there.

Widderstone. Centuries-old churchyard, a short walk from the Lawford residence. Its unconsecrated ground is the site of Nicholas Sabathier's grave, where Arthur Lawford's possession occurs. Though the vicar of the parish describes it as a beautiful spot, Lawford's family and friends consider it an improper place for Arthur to take a walk; they view his decline following his experience in the churchyard as his just deserts for this transgression. Arthur's attraction to the site is solid evidence of his difference from those around him.

Lawford home. Comfortable middle-class home in suburban England. Arthur Lawford, his wife Sheila, and his daughter Alice have lived unremarkable lives in the house until Arthur's takeover by the spirit of Sabathier, after which Arthur feels himself an intruder and an outsider. The house represents a past from which Arthur becomes an outcast, never to return. Eventually, he refers to it as a "great barn of faded interests."

— *Stefan Dziemianowicz*

THE RETURN OF THE KING

Author: J. R. R. Tolkien (1892-1973)
Type of work: Novel
Type of plot: Epic

Time of plot: Third Age in a remote legendary past
First published: 1955

In this final volume of the Lord of the Rings *trilogy, Aragorn fights for Gondor, to whose throne he is the true heir; Sam and Frodo destroy Sauron's One Ring; and social order is restored. The companions return to their homelands profoundly changed by their travels.*

Paths of the Dead. Accompanied by Gimli, Legolas, and his kinsmen Rangers of the North, Aragorn leads his forces south to the coast, passing through a forbidden door into a haunted passage beneath the Dwimorberg. There he calls upon the Army of the Dead, Numenoreans who once broke a vow to fight against Sauron and now have one last chance to prove their loyalty and rest in peace. The Dead follow, while even Gimli, used to the deep places of the earth, quakes in horror. Meanwhile Merry joins Theoden's troops on a more conventional road to **Gondor**.

Minas Tirith. Chief city of Gondor that occupies a series of circles on Mount Mindolluin. Its ancient culture and people have declined, and many houses stand empty while childless lords brood about death. The White Tree has withered, but the Houses of the Dead are honored. Even this diminished Gondor awes Pippin of the Shire when he and Gandalf arrive. A series of sorties and battles ensues, both within the walled city and outside its gates; the timely arrival of Aragorn's forces temporarily beats back a wing of Sauron's army. The Defenders of the West march to the Black Gate, outnumbered but hoping to draw Sauron's attention away from **Mount Doom** in case Frodo and Sam reach the central plain of Mordor, heading for the fiery volcanic chamber where the One Ring might be destroyed.

Mordor. The Dark Lord's realm. Polluted, arid, and rocky, the plain of Gorgoroth (a name that suggests biblical Golgotha) offers little cover to the exhausted Hobbits once Sam has rescued Frodo and gotten them out of the Orc tower on the border. However, as Sauron focuses his gaze on the Black Gate, they elude capture and approach Mount Doom. Sam, desperately weary and thirsty, dreams of green Shire landscapes—willow trees, cool mud, streams, and pools—but reminds himself, "The way back, if there is one, goes past the Mountain." He carries Frodo, who, being near the heart of Sauron's power, has no individual will left. However, Gollum, who has been stalking the Hobbits, emerges from the shadows, bites off Frodo's ring finger, and falls with it into the volcanic fires.

Road home. The monarchy is restored under Aragorn, and a new vigor is born in Gondor. The other companions begin their journeys homeward, Gimli and Legolas agreeing to visit the Glittering Caves of Aglarond and Fangorn Forest together in a future marked by dwarf and elf friendship. A rest stop at Rivendell reveals Bilbo, who had carried the One Ring for many years, to be very old and frail.

Shire. Homeland of the Hobbits. Saruman and some of his Orcs have occupied the Shire, where naïve and sheltered Hobbits have proved easy prey. Trees have been wantonly cut and rivers fouled. Led by Merry, Pippin, and Sam, the Shire folk are awakened to action and the invaders are killed or driven off. However, it will take generations for new trees to grow, and the Shire may never regain its old innocence or complacency.

Gray Havens. Gimli and Legolas have formed bonds of brotherhood; Aragon has revitalized Gondor; Merry and Pippin will lead long and happy lives in the Shire and make periodic trips back to Rohan and Minas Tirith; and Sam will marry, sire a large family, and reign as Mayor of the Shire for years to come. However, Frodo has been too damaged by his long journey and heavy burden to enjoy Middle-earth any longer. Two years after the Hobbits return, Frodo joins a party of Elrond, Galadriel, Bilbo, Gandalf (whose task is finished), and a number of Elf lords who are riding one last road to the Grey Havens in the Northwest, where an Elven ship has been readied to take them to the Undying Lands beyond the circles of Middle-earth. There is a hint that Sam, who also carried the Ring for a short time, will make this final journey one day.

— Nan C. L. Scott

THE RETURN OF THE NATIVE

Author: Thomas Hardy (1840-1928)
Type of work: Novel
Type of plot: Tragedy

Time of plot: Mid-nineteenth century
First published: 1878

One of Thomas Hardy's earliest novels, this story is set in the fictional region called Egdon Heath, a microcosmic world, whose primitive people cling steadfastly to ancient methods, beliefs, and ritual myths. Hardy's somber legend dramatizes the complete or partial ruin of people whose provincial culture has been intruded upon by spiritual and economic invaders, who represent possible changes in their rural life resulting from England's Industrial Revolution.

Wessex. Imaginary English region that was the setting for Hardy's major fiction. Born in Dorsetshire, one of five counties in southern England, Hardy re-created this region in his novels as "Wessex." This unsophisticated rural area is never entirely absent in his fiction or poetry. Late in his life, Hardy returned to Dorset and a new home for himself and his wife.

Egdon Heath. Gloomy wasteland in southern England. Against this majestic but solemn, brooding background a small group of people work out their tragic drama in the impersonal presence of nature. The heath's grim face, its twisted topography—hills, valleys, rivers, ponds, paths, and open wasteland, a composite of several heaths—is a dominant symbol of primitive, timeless, and uncultivated nature. In this untamed place, nature's four basic elements—earth, air, fire, and water—control this microcosm of a completely indifferent land. Earth is unalterable. Humans grow nothing; they only harvest the land's natural furze. At times, even humans appear no more distinguishable from the landscape than "the green caterpillar from the leaf it feeds on."

To the heath itself, people seem to be just another crop growth. Earthen paths serve as roads for constant travel around and back and forth over the nearly circular heath. Air, in the form of constantly blowing winds, whirls and buffets humans and assaults their ears with eerie sounds. Fire, a symbol of human passion, appears in ceremonial bonfires, signal fires, a black magic fire, and the summer sun's fiery blazes. Rains flooding Shadwater Weir reveal the dual life/death aspects of the water symbol for humans or other creatures caught in the rapidly revolving whirlpool.

In death, humans finally become part of the heath, as the ancient tumulus or burial mounds testify. These elements, humans, and heath creatures share Egdon's alternating faces of fall, winter, spring, and summer. Here, nature seems impervious to human or animal conflicts; only seasonal changes matter.

Rainbarrow. Hill that is the symbolic center and heart of Egdon Heath. Its name suggestively foreshadows water deaths. Near the beginning, a rebellious figure stands, ironically, "like an organic part" of the ancient grave mound at the hill's apex. At the novel's equally ironic ending, the returned native, surviving tragedy, stands harmoniously and indifferently on top of the same mound, symbolically almost as indistinguishable as an erect furze bush, surrounded by heathmen and women.

Quiet Woman. Inn on Egdon Heath that is the home of Damon Wildeve and his bride Thomasin. Hardy took the inn's name, along with its sign and legend of a headless woman carrying her head, from a real inn northwest of the fictional one. Moreover, the inn's name projects a contrasting view of the two young women in the tale, who symbolize the conflict between two value systems: the narrow provincial rules versus the new city freedoms and moralities. The victims of Shadwater Weir are brought to the inn along with the rescuers.

Blooms-End. The Yeobright house is filled with a lifetime of things, treasured objects and furniture, which the unsophisticated culture of the area accepts as a social birthright. The home's place name, however, suggests that value systems and lifestyles are undergoing changes; the blooms of tradition are ending.

Alderworth. Temporary first home for Clym and his wife, six miles from Blooms-End, that is the setting for the crucial blunder that sets the final actions in motion.

East Egdon. Village near Alderworth which has a local festival with games and dancing. Eustacia watches the dancers moving in a rapidly rotating, whirling circular motion from the outer edge to the center of the circle. She realizes that the circular, whirling movement of the dance repeats the premonition of disaster that she has dreamed. This circular movement also repeats the winds' circular efforts on Egdon Heath and foreshadows the final whirlpool deaths in Shadwater Weir.

Shadwater Weir. Pool of water formed by a small dam where, on a windy night, the final struggle in this conflict of value systems occurs. The circular, rotational action of the weir's whirlpool repeats again the foreshadowed movements at the dance and the winds buffeting of walkers on the heath.

Mistover Knap. Home of retired Captain Vye, which resembles a ship in harbor. Unlike any other house in the area, it stands as a symbol of the differences between local practices and values and outside codes and values that have appeared in Egdon Heath.

— *Betsy P. Harfst*

THE REVENGER'S TRAGEDY

Author: Cyril Tourneur (c. 1575-1626)
Type of work: Drama
Type of plot: Tragedy

Time of plot: Renaissance
First performed: 1606-1607; first published, 1607

A depraved Italian court serves as a microcosm of the fallen world in this play that is attributed to Cyril Tourneur.

Italian dukedom. Unspecified Italian principality in which the play unfolds. Although the location is clearly Italian, the play provides not a single place name. By depicting a court in Italy as a hotbed of vice, the playwright follows the English Renaissance tradition of demonizing the unethical Niccolò Machiavelli's birthplace. Simultaneously, the play's geographical vagueness invites audiences to identify "this villainous dukedom vexed with sin" as a distorted mirror of the intrigue in King James I's English court.

Ducal palace. Setting for almost half of the play's twenty scenes. As seen through the revenger Vindice's eyes, this site of the ducal family's routine indulgence in rape, incest, adultery, betrayal, and murder is a living hell of damned souls. The drama's centerpiece is Vindice's revenge in the "unsunned lodge/ Wherein 'tis night at noon"—a palace locale symbolizing the moral darkness of both the duke's sins and Vindice's brutal punishment.

Court of law. The setting of the second scene, in which the royal court undermines the legal one by extenuating rape and delaying the rapist's punishment. Such failure of the law provides context for Vindice's blood revenge, although the heaven that Vindice himself invokes so often as the source of true justice seems to hover just above the stage.

Prison. Scene of two sons' incarceration for sexual crimes, where worldly corruption, rather than justice, again dictates villains' fates.

Countryside. Although no scenes are explicitly set outside the ducal capital, the play's dialogue opposes Christian values beyond the town against those in the "accursed palace." Vindice, living with his family "not far from Court," comments, "Let blushes dwell i' the country," and equates chastity with a "foolish country girl." Nevertheless, the court's poisonous evil spreads to the country to contaminate Vindice's mother, Gratiana (Grace), if not his sister, Castiza (Chastity).

— *Margaret Bozenna Goscilo*

REYNARD THE FOX

Author: Unknown
Type of work: Short fiction
Type of plot: Satire

Time of plot: Middle Ages
First transcribed: c. 1175-1250 (English translation, 1481)

These stories about animals were written to amuse. When their animal characters are found in human settings, contemporary institutions and manners are the target of parody and satire. The episodes which place the animals in their own habitat draw their humor from farce.

Noble the Lion's court. Imaginary court meant to represent the court of the French king. The animals present their grievances to Noble the king, whose weakness and indecision are the targets of satire. The rapacious demands for vengeance by the courtiers and the sophistry of those pleading their cases re-create an important institution of the time but cast it in a ridiculous light. A fictitious court run by animals provides the authors with a certain immunity and poetic license. The world they present is a world turned upside down, and the absurd conduct of the characters is part of that world. Reynard's trial at the court enables the authors to indulge in a lengthy satire on women and their sexual appetites and to poke fun at cuckolded husbands.

Ysangrin the wolf's den. Scene of the adultery of Reynard and Hersent, a dark and private place that provides an ideal setting for animals to imitate the conduct of humans. Courtly love and its rules of privacy and secrecy are satirized in this episode.

Reynard the fox's den. Place with the characteristics of an actual fox's den. It has openings large enough for a fox to enter and exit but not big enough to accommodate a larger animal. Its size and shape enable the author to write a farcical scene in which Hersent, caught at the entrance, is raped by Reynard, who insists he was trying to extricate her.

Maupertuis (moh-pehr-TWEE). Reynard's dwelling tends to have features of both castle and den. It appears to be a castle, but sometimes means of entry and exit are more those of a den. Maupertuis is strong and impenetrable. Here Noble lays siege to Reynard after the fox escapes punishment at his trial. Maupertuis is surrounded by forest. Noble, who has brought his queen, Fière, with him, has encamped his army amid the trees. By combining animal and human attributes of his characters, the author creates an amusing scene in which Reynard ties Noble and his courtiers by their tails to the trees and then rapes Fière in full view.

Battlefield. This setting occasions the parody of the Chanson de Geste. The field is soon strewn with mutilated bodies. The exploits of Noble and his warriors are described with the exaggeration and excess characteristic of the heroic poems of the period.

Well. Typical well from which water is drawn by the use of buckets. In this tale Reynard saves himself and makes a fool of Ysangrin by using the bucket mechanism. The humor of the episode is derived from the two animals mistaking their reflections in the well for real creatures and consequently becoming trapped.

Barnyards. The various barnyards containing hen houses and guard dogs instigate several episodes of trickery and pursuit. Although the animals speak in these tales, they remain animals.

Forests. Places for hunting in which predators and prey meet, and characters consistently try to do each other harm. The humor of the episodes is created by the ill that befalls the animals as they encounter traps, human hunters, and other predators.

— *Shawncey Webb*

RHINOCEROS

Author: Eugène Ionesco (1912-1994)
Type of work: Drama
Type of plot: Absurdist
Time of plot: Mid-twentieth century

First performed: 1959, in German; 1960, in French; first published, 1959 as *Rhinocéros* (English translation, 1959)

After the tranquillity of a small French town is destroyed by a rhinoceros running along its main street, townsfolk argue about whether the animal is of African or Asian origin. Over the next few days most townsfolk change into rhinoceroses. Only Berenger, a young man, manages to resist. One interpretation is that this is a surreal portrayal of the French public's reaction to the German occupation that occurred twenty years before the play was first produced, when playwright Eugène Ionesco was Berenger's age.

Town square. Typical small French town, perhaps close to Paris, in which the play opens shortly before noon on a sunny summer Sunday. The grocer's is open, as is the café-bar with chairs and tables outside. Although the time period is not made clear, it is probably a couple of decades earlier than the time of writing.

Office. Place where Berenger works, in which the play's second act opens. It may or may not be a government office; it has an old-fashioned air, with pens and an inkwell mentioned, as well as typewriters, chairs, tables, and desks, and an inner office for its chief. The main office is reached by climbing up a set of wooden stairs and is thus beyond the reach of a charging rhinoceros.

Jean's home. Two rooms of an apartment house in which Berenger's friend Jean lives and in which the second scene of act 2 is set. Jean is in bed in his bed-sitting room when Berenger calls; the other room is his offstage bathroom. The apartment's furnishings are simple and sparse. It is still Monday morning, because Berenger has been forced out of his office by the rhinoceros attack. Jean's metamorphosis to rhinoceros occurs during the second scene of act 2.

Berenger's room. This is as simple as Jean's with a bed and a chair, but it also contains a telephone and a radio. The day is unspecified but is probably Tuesday. Outside the building, many of the townsfolk are now rhinoceroses, charging up and down the street in large herds, which grow larger as Berenger is visited by his colleagues, first Dudard and then Daisy the typist, to whom he desperately declares his love. The telephone rings, but only rhinoceroses are on the line. They turn on the radio but it broadcasts only the musical trumpetings of rhinoceroses. There is no hope.

— *Chris Morgan*

RICEYMAN STEPS

Author: Arnold Bennett (1867-1931)
Type of work: Novel
Type of plot: Social realism

Time of plot: 1919
First published: 1923

This story of a late-flowering love affair and marriage destroyed by miserliness is set in London's Clerkenwell district, whose shabby quaintness figures prominently in the novel.

Riceyman Steps. Public staircase leading from London's Kings Cross Road to Riceyman Square, directly over the Underground Railway, which throbs with the passage of trains, in the middle of Clerkenwell, a shabby neighborhood. Adjacent to the steps is a small open space, lined with a mixture of private housing, two business yards, a confectioner's shop, an abandoned mission hall, and a bookseller's. Clerkenwell is a real London neighborhood; the Riceyman Steps are fictional but based on a genuine location, known to English children as Plum Pudding Steps and to adults as Gwynne Place, formerly Granville Place. Arnold Bennett, although best known for his novels about England's Potteries region, thoroughly explored the Clerkenwell area of London. He was attracted by the area's Victorian domestic architecture, which remained beautiful even under the soot from coal smoke and untidiness that then blighted the district. The novel places great emphasis on the decaying nature of the area: a "hell of noise and dust and dirt."

The neighborhood is much loved by old T. T. Riceyman, who never tires of reciting how the original tunnel near Clerkenwell Green collapsed, in the spring of 1862. The three opening chapters that sketch this history set the stage for the drama that ensues.

Riceyman's bookshop. Business currently owned by Henry Earlforward, whose uncle is the Riceyman of the title. The shop is small, with its entrance on Riceyman Steps and a window overlooking King's Cross Road. Although seemingly out of place in a neighborhood characterized as sordid and dingy, the shop does well because both it and Riceyman Steps are picturesque, despite the shabbiness and decay.

Full of bays formed by protruding bookshelves, the shop becomes progressively more gloomy the farther into it one ventures. Its floor is covered with piles of books, everything is dusty, and many electric lights do not work. At the very back of the shop is Earlforward's den, also littered with books and dust and poorly lit—especially since its broken window blinds cannot be raised. The miserly Earlforward is obliged to use electric lighting but prefers candles.

When Mrs. Arb marries Earlforward, her wedding gift to him is to have his entire bookshop cleaned by an industrial vacuum-cleaning system to remove the dust. The idea appalls Earlforward—as much for its cost as for what the cleaning will do to his shop—and he strenuously resists his new wife's attempts to tidy his books. However, his wife eventually manages to move some of the books out of his bedroom and bathroom but cannot make the house cleaner or introduce such improvements as proper cooking facilities, electric lighting, and lamp shades. However, she does grow flowers on the front windowsills.

Mrs. Arb's shop. Small shop on King's Cross Road. Its stock comprises "universally recognizable packets" and many other goods, all cluttered together. Although Mrs. Arb is well-spoken and clearly better off than many, her shop is dirty and unwelcoming. Bennett describes it as a poor little shop, with no sense of enterprise or imagination. Indeed, although Mrs. Arb has only recently bought the shop, she is determined to sell it. After she marries Earlforward, she sells her shop to the Belroses, who turn it into a going concern.

Elsie's home. Home of the woman who does cleaning work for both Earlforward and Mrs. Arb who later becomes their live-in servant, with a small room of her own. Initially, however, she is living with a family with two children, with whom she shares three rooms. On the ground floor lives a meat salesman, his wife, and three children. On the second floor lives a dressmaker on her own. All the frustrations of the building's households are focused on the narrow and crowded ground-floor hall of the house, which itself is in a poor state of repair.

— *Maureen Speller*

RICHARD II

Author: William Shakespeare (1564-1616)
Type of work: Drama
Type of plot: Historical

Time of plot: Late fourteenth century
First performed: c. 1595-1596; first published, 1600

This play, the first in William Shakespeare's so-called Henriad tetralogy, explores the theme of what it means to be a king and finds an answer in the monarchy's sacred bond with the land. When England's King Richard II betrays this trust, he loses his kingdom. Without the support of the land, a king cannot rule; without a king, the land cannot thrive.

*England. Set during the late fourteenth century reign of the historical English king Richard II, the play does much to offer audiences a variety of English locales, encompassed by a sense of national identity. This emphasis is not merely a mark of Shakespeare's English patriotism, but a recognition of the crucial link between a king and his land. When John of Gaunt curses his nephew King Richard for exiling his (John's) son, he calls on the land to reject its sovereign and prophesies that the land will suffer from the blood of the countrymen who will die as a result of Richard's mismanagement.

Battlefields. After King Richard goes to Ireland to prosecute a war, he returns to find Henry Bolingbroke, whom he had earlier exiled, back in his lands and supported by a considerable army. Although armed conflicts in the play are minimal, they take place on the field of contention, and much of the play's middle action transpires over clashes of armed men.

Royal palace. The first and last scenes of the play are set at England's royal court, whose throne and altar of kingship project the cold power inherent in the royal court. Richard's confrontation with his uncle John of Gaunt and his conversation with his queen are set in secluded private rooms, which project a palpable sense of the division between the king's public persona and his private person.

In the palace's garden, an odd and seemingly irrelevant scene occurs involving a discussion between the queen and the palace gardeners. However, their conversation about the garden provides a key to understanding Richard's problem: Having allowed too many weeds to grow unchecked, he has failed to exert sufficient care for his land.

*Tower of London. Historic prison to which Richard is sent after Bolingbroke makes himself King Henry IV. Richard's incarceration and death in the tower represent the reduction of the kingdom's mightiest personage to its lowliest. The prison is a state of mind as well as a physical restraint, for without his land, the king is no more than a slave to others.

— *Scott D. Vander Ploeg*

RICHARD III

Author: William Shakespeare (1564-1616)
Type of work: Drama
Type of plot: Historical

Time of plot: Fifteenth century
First performed: c. 1592-1593; first published, 1597; revised, 1623

This play's action is set in related historical places—palaces, battlefields, and the looming Tower of London—where the usurper Richard of Gloucester attains and loses the kingship of England during the last stages of England's War of the Roses. The metaphorical houses of Lancaster and York are the source of the internecine conflict, but it is the space of kingship, located in the royal palace at Westminster, that attracts, enables, and warps the protagonist. Repeated references within the play compare this site of power to the womb that delivered Richard to "this breathing world," misshapen, embittered, and hungry for power.

*Westminster Palace. London residence of the rulers of England from the eleventh through sixteenth centuries (later used for the Houses of Parliament), alongside the River Thames, near Westminster Abbey. Built by William the Conqueror, the palace was long the central locus of both the home of the royal family and the royal court. In this play its dynamics are volatile, given the presence of the Yorkist king Edward IV and his kin, victorious but internally divided, and the widows of the defeated Lancastrian king Henry VI and his Prince of Wales. The palace as crucible of Richard's power is compared metaphorically to his mother's womb, which she herself calls "The bed of death" for nurturing her "damned son," and to the womb of the Princess Elizabeth, where Richard expects to legitimize his reign.

*Tower of London. Ancient, fearful edifice where King Henry VI, the last Lancastrian king, was imprisoned and killed. The prison threatens everyone who may stand in the way of Richard's kingship. It sees the confinement and murder of Richard's brother Clarence, the queen's relatives and supporters (killed at Pomfret Castle), King Edward's sons and heirs, and Lord Chamberlain Hastings, who calls the tower a "slaughterhouse."

*Tewkesbury (TEWKS-behr-ee). Town on the Severn River in west-central England, north-northeast of Gloucester, near which the Lancastrian army was defeated by Yorkist forces in 1471. The battlefield is continually referred to in the play, as the characters relive scenes of the murders of the Lancastrian prince of Wales and Richard's father and youngest brother. The battle is a monument to the families' hatred.

*Bosworth Field. Place in central England near Leicester that was the site of the most famous battle of the War of the Roses, in 1485, that is the setting for the last battle in William Shakespeare's play. Here Richard is defeated and killed, ending his evil rule afoot and alone, speaking his most famous words, "A horse! A horse! My kingdom for a horse!" The victor is the earl of Richmond, who is crowned King Henry VII. He became the first Tudor king and was grandfather to Queen Elizabeth I, during whose reign this play was written.

— *Martha J. Craig*

RIDERS IN THE CHARIOT

Author: Patrick White (1912-1990)
Type of work: Novel
Type of plot: Parable

Time of plot: After World War II
First published: 1961

This sprawling narrative satirizes and condemns what Patrick White sees as a lack of meaning in modern life, and it incorporates the settings into this parable of human failure. The fictional Sydney suburbs of Sarsaparilla and Paradise East embody the emptiness that some of the characters embrace and others reject.

Sarsaparilla. Fictional suburb west of Sydney in which most of the action unfolds. It is probably based on Castle Hill, the actual Sydney suburb where White lived from 1946, when he returned to Australia after serving in World War II, until 1963, when he moved into the city. Although White had previously set plays in Sarsaparilla, this is the first time he used it in his fiction.

While inner Sydney offers spectacular views as it stretches gracefully around the magnificent harbor and along the ocean cliffs, the landscape changes dramatically once the harbor and sea disappear. Sarsaparilla is situated in this colorless, flat, and dusty expanse. Once a rural area of small farms, it gradually became more thickly settled as working-class families moved out of the city into housing developments in their search for a better life. Their cheap, poorly built houses, each with a well-tended yard, may represent security and happiness for their inhabitants, but White unmasks this supposedly ideal community. His version of Sarsaparilla is dominated by hypocrisy, ignorance, cruelty, rigid conformity, and just plain bad taste. Another suburb, **Paradise East**, may be more upscale, but underneath its pretentious exterior it resembles Sarsaparilla.

In spite of the physical ugliness and personal emptiness of these suburbs, four of the characters conquer the environs, discover their potential, and become "riders in the chariot." Mrs. Godbold, a laundress; Himmelfarb, a Jewish immigrant from Germany; Alf Dubbo, an aboriginal artist; and the half-mad Mary Hare are the seekers who find truth even in their squalid surroundings. Others remain in the void of Sarsaparilla and Paradise East, altogether satisfied with their meaningless existence.

Xanadu (ZAN-ah-dew). Decaying estate near Sarsaparilla. The name Xanadu implies an idyllic, beautiful place and came into common use through Samuel Taylor Coleridge's poem *Kubla Khan* (1816). Marco Polo's description of the actual Xanadu in China forever marked it as an exotic, luxurious, and magnificent setting. The Xanadu inhabited by Mary Hare, however, who inher-

ited it from her dreamer of a father, subverts the romantic name and its ramifications. The once-great house has fallen into disrepair, and the formal gardens have grown into a jungle. While Mary feels ill at ease in the house itself, she finds refuge and peace in the tangled gardens, which provide the stimulus for her vision. At the novel's end, Xanadu is destroyed and another shoddy suburb is built on its grounds.

*Sydney. Port city in southeastern Australia. While Australian literature usually celebrates what is often called the "Emerald City," White represents Sydney as a kind of psychedelic hell when the characters venture into its depths: "The train was easing through the city which knives had sliced open to serve up with all the juices running—red, and green and purple." Unlike its outlying communities, the city has a beautiful natural setting, sophistication, and fine buildings, yet in White's hands it too suffers from the spiritual malaise that affects Sarsaparilla and Paradise East. In Sydney's affluent neighborhoods, the characters confront the same vacuum that characterizes the suburbs. Neither the city nor its outlying areas need be set in Australia, for the smugness of most of the characters and the visionary quest of the chariot riders are universal, whatever the place.

— *Robert L. Ross*

RIDERS TO THE SEA

Author: John Millington Synge (1871-1909)
Type of work: Drama
Type of plot: Tragedy

Time of plot: Late nineteenth century
First published: 1903; first performed, 1904

Set on an island off the west coast of Ireland that was one of the most primitive parts of Europe during the time in which it is set, this play pits the members of a poor Irish family against the brutality of the sea that surrounds them.

Cottage. Island home within sight of the sea that is the home of the play's main characters. The play's entire action takes place in a single room that serves as a kitchen, workroom, and storage area. The room is sparsely furnished; its most essential features are its fireplace, a spinning wheel, and its front door. The fireplace provides immediate evidence of the simplicity of the family's existence; it serves both as a cooking oven and

as the cottage's sole source of heat. The fireplace's fuel is turf, which is stored in a loft beside the fireplace. The primitiveness of these arrangements is crude, even by the standards of the late nineteenth century, when turf-burning ovens were found only in places of extreme isolation and poverty.

The room's spinning wheel is clearly not decorative since Cathleen begins working at it immediately. The fact that some pieces of clothing are handmade is important in the identification of Michael's belongings. John Millington Synge makes strong use of the door, through which each drowned member of the house has come, with seawater dripping a trail to the door.

*Aran Islands.** Group of small islands off the west coast of Ireland, near the entrance to Galway Bay, on one of whose islands the cottage stands. Exposed to the full fury of the open North Atlantic Ocean, the waters around these islands are extremely dangerous, and the constantly changing weather is unpredictable. The play emphasizes the danger of life on the sea with references to the numbers of men who have drowned in it—including five members of the family. However, sea travel is also essential to the family's survival—a fact made clear by repeated references to Galway and Connemara on the mainland. Aside from items brought by traveling salesmen, everything the family cannot make must come across the sea.

— *Glenn Patterson*

RIGHT YOU ARE (IF YOU THINK SO)

Author: Luigi Pirandello (1867-1936)
Type of work: Drama
Type of plot: Parable

Time of plot: Early twentieth century
First performed: Così è (se vi pare), 1917; first
   published, 1918 (English translation, 1922)

This play's principal setting is the drawing room of the apartment of a provincial official in an unnamed central Italian town. There busybody villagers gather to discover the truth about a family newly arrived from a village that has suffered an earthquake. The villagers are confronted with two disparate "realities" concerning the identity of a man's wife, one version from the man, Signor Ponza, and another from his mother-in-law, Signora Frola. The villagers find that the truth is relative and subjective, depending on which person they believe.

Agazzi's drawing room (ah-GATZ-ee). Comfortable apartment of an unnamed central Italian town's major official, the middle-class bureaucrat Commendatore Agazzi, that is the play's main setting. Agazzi's family and townspeople complain that his clerk Signor Ponza cruelly does not allow his wife and his mother-in-law, Signora Frola, to see each other. Agazzi opens his home to the meddling townspeople to question the clerk and mother-in-law separately, each of whom gives conflicting versions of the truth about the wife's identity. Is she Ponza's first wife or a second wife following the terrible earthquake in Marsica? The citizens take sides and cannot arrive at one truth because all family records have been destroyed by the earthquake. When summoned, the wife testifies that she is whomever one thinks her to be.

As the playing field of the action, Agazzi's drawing room reveals a family of pained sufferers with a secret sorrow surrounded by busybody townspeople and ineffectual provincial politicians who find that the "truth" cannot be known.

*Marsica.** District of central Italy's Abruzzi region, which borders the Adriatic Sea, that is mentioned in the play as the place from which the Ponza and Frola families come. In January, 1915, the real Marsica was, in fact, ravaged by a devastating earthquake that killed more than thirty thousand people and destroyed several villages in the region. The region's history makes the suffering of the Ponza-Frola family and total loss of their identification papers plausible.

Although the play appears to be set in central Italy, its allusions to crowded villages, petty middle-class society, government bureaucracy, and passionate persons who have undergone suffering were probably inspired by the Sicily in which Pirandello grew up.

— *Christian H. Moe*

THE RIME OF THE ANCIENT MARINER

Author: Samuel Taylor Coleridge (1772-1834)
Type of work: Poetry
Type of plot: Allegory

Time of plot: Late medieval period
First published: 1798

This poem begins and ends with references to the native land in which its unnamed mariner lives, but the vast and limitless high seas are the poem's primary location. The sea provides a site for the learning and change of heart that the Ancient Mariner experiences. Indeed, place names are absent from this poem, although the poet uses the idea of place to reflect the emotional striving of his character.

Kirk. Unnamed church at which the poem opens and closes. This church, as well as other sites to which the Mariner alludes—such as a lighthouse, a hill, and a harbor bay—are evidently located in the Mariner's native country. ("Kirk" is an old and once commonly used word for church in the British Isles, especially in Scotland.) The Mariner comes to understand his place within the universe as one of many creatures that deserve honor and respect, and the church imputes a moral tone to these ideas. Indeed, the Mariner is not simply a relativist, believing that whatever he wants to do is correct for a particular situation. His killing of the harmless albatross emerges from such an incorrect assessment. The church calls this assumption into question. Consequently, the Mariner is compelled to repeat his story to the Wedding-Guest, whom the Mariner believes to be in need of such a lesson.

Ship. Unnamed vessel on which the Mariner rides the waves of the sea, beginning in the third stanza of part 1. As his ship continues its voyage, the sea itself reflects the mood, the emotional intensity, of the ship's sailors. The men have nowhere else to go so long as they remain at sea, and their ship thus becomes both home and prison to them. When the wind drops, and the ship is becalmed, the Mariner is reminded how confining the ship is. When the ship is trapped among ice floes, the Mariner allows himself to kill the albatross for sport. The Mariner's ship becomes the stage for his great sin, as well as for the beginning of his redemption.

Other ships also play important parts in this poem. For example, the skeleton ship approaching from the direction of the westward sky, on a still sea where no wind blows, provides a stage for a dialogue that occurs between Specter-Woman and her Deathmate who cast dice for the lives of the sailors.

*South Pole. The southern tip of Earth's axis is not mentioned by name in the poem, but it is the clear direction in which the Mariner is sent by a storm-blast that drives his ship toward certain judgment in the frigid south. The ice of the southern polar region seems alive, as its movements make noise that sound like wild beasts, frightening the Mariner. The Spirit from the pole embodies these characteristics in the mind of the Mariner, as the Spirit makes the becalmed ship move at the behest of an angelic troupe who still seek vengeance for the albatross.

High seas. Primary location through the poem. Two forms of water trap the ship—ice and water—thereby becoming its primary locus. Sailors learn to read the moods of the sea, based on the winds that propel its waves. The moon, as well, is reflected in the sea's surface. Coleridge uses the sea, as well as other natural forms, as tools to instruct the Mariner on his moral lapse and lack of respect for all creation. The sun rises and sets several times in the poem, not simply to indicate the passage of time. When the sea gives back the sun's face in reflection, the Mariner reacts as if all creation were watching and judging him.

— *Martha Modena Vertreace-Doody*

RIP VAN WINKLE

Author: Washington Irving (1783-1859)
Type of work: Short fiction
Type of plot: Tall tale

Time of plot: Eighteenth century
First published: 1819

This story uses Washington Irving's familiar Catskill Mountains settings and the Dutch settlers of New York to replicate an earlier German folktale. Irving also uses the unnamed village's changes over the twenty years to comment on the changing culture and American identity.

Dutch village. Unnamed village of Dutch settlers in New York that is the home of Rip Van Winkle, who sleeps in the woods for twenty years and then returns to the village. Rip's twenty-year absence from the village gives Irving a chance to reflect and comment on changes that occurred in the United States between the period shortly before the American Revolution and the early years of the independent republic.

Irving first describes the village as one of "great antiquity," founded by the original Dutch colonists who settled in New York. The village rests at the foot of the Catskill Mountains and seems to be a charming and quaint place. Its people are friendly and—except for the henpecked Rip—happy. When Rip escapes from his wife's nagging, he plays with the children of the village and runs errands for all the goodwives. All the village dogs know him and greet him. The familiarity and friendliness of the village before Rip's sleep is shown so that Irving can contrast it with Rip's return from the mountain. When Rip returns from his long nap, children stare at him and mock him, and dogs bark at him.

Before Rip's sleep, the village had a "busy, bustling, disputatious tone about it, instead of the accustomed phlegm and drowsy tranquillity." Rip returns when an election is taking place, and villagers want to know for whom he is voting. The town's former tranquillity has been usurped by the new politics. Rip eventually comes to grip with these changes, even if he does not quite understand them. He even takes his place as a patriarch of the village on the bench. He settles into place and his new role, much like the new country he encounters.

Village inn. Besides moving the plot along, the changes in the village after Rip's sleep also provide a pointed look at the changes in the new republic. Before Rip's twenty year absence, the center of town was an old inn sporting a portrait of England's King George III. On a bench in front of the inn, the elders and idle of the village would gather and discuss events. The innkeeper, Nicholas Vedder, presided over the gatherings and let his feelings on the discussions be known by how he smoked his pipe. Outside the inn stood a great tree that shaded the building. When Rip returns, the inn has changed, and definitely for the worse. Its great tree is gone, replaced by "a tall naked pole" from which hangs a strange flag. The old inn itself has been replaced by a "large rickety wooded building . . . with great gaping windows, some of them broken and mended with old hats and petticoats." It is no longer the old country inn, but the Union Hotel. King George's portrait has been painted over with one of George Washington.

*Kaatskill (Catskill) Mountains. New York range bordering the village. From the beginning of the story, Irving describes the beauty of the mountains and gives them a magical air as he describes them as "fairy mountains." Rip goes up on a mountain to hunt and avoid his nagging wife. The mountain is also the home of the somber Henrik Hudson and his men who play at ninepins. In a hidden amphitheater, the strange little men drink wine and play their game. Rip also helps himself to the wine which leads to his twenty-year sleep. He awakens outside the amphitheater only to find the scenery changed. The use of the Catskills, a chain familiar to American readers of Irving's time, helped to Americanize the German folktale.

— *P. Andrew Miller*

THE RISE OF SILAS LAPHAM

Author: William Dean Howells (1837-1920)
Type of work: Novel
Type of plot: Domestic realism

Time of plot: Late nineteenth century
First published: 1885

Using actual places in Boston, this novel situates the Lapham family in Nankeen Square in the South End. To reflect the Laphams' desire to climb socially, it also has them building a house in the more fashionable Back Bay area on Beacon Street. The Coreys, representing the patrician class, live on Beacon Hill, at Bellingham Place, a once-fashionable street for the elite of Boston.

*Boston. Massachusetts city in which the action of the novel unfolds. Having lived in Boston, Howells was familiar with the city and deftly portrays the social divide that existed there in the late eighteenth century between America's aristocratic patricians, represented by the Coreys, who inherited their wealth and do not have to work for a living, and the rising tide of the newly rich, represented by the Laphams, particularly Silas, the self-made man. In the post-Civil War America Howells portrays, as industrialization increases and people like the Laphams move from farms to cities, the patrician class of Boston is being physically displaced. Along with this physical displacement comes the possibility of the displacement of spiritual and moral values brought about by excessive materialism. With its Puritan background and position as America's cultural center, Boston is the perfect setting for this clash of values.

South End house. Home in which the Laphams have lived in an unfashionable South End neighborhood for twelve years. The furnishings of the house reflect the garish taste of the uncultured Laphams, and this bad taste signifies the possibility of a deficiency of character because it reveals values generated by excessive materialism. Silas is particularly materialistic. Ambitious to move up in society, Silas wants to live in the Beacon Hill neighborhood to display his monetary worth. While he is not a bad person, moral questions are raised about his earlier treatment of Rogers. His quest for wealth and position leads him to seriously consider saving himself financially by engaging in the shady land deal Rogers suggests later in the novel.

Corey house. Home of the Corey family in Bellingham Place. Reflecting the Coreys as members of a dying class, the house is elegantly and tastefully furnished, in contrast with the Laphams', and it is one of several "stately" dwellings of classical simplicity on the street where the upper classes of Boston once lived. However, the houses on the street are gradually being converted into boardinghouses as the working classes displace the patrician families. In contrast to the Laphams (Silas especially), the Coreys are not materialistic but instead value their leisure to invest in cultural affairs. Bromfield Corey and his wife Anna do not need to work for a living, but they must increasingly live frugally as their inheritance is dwindling. It is clear that Tom Corey will have to work and will thus be forced to bridge the social gap.

*Beacon Street. Street in a prosperous Boston neighborhood on which Silas builds a house to show his social equality with, if not superiority to, the Bostonian patricians. It represents Silas's ambition and materialism and thus his misplaced values. The burning of this house represents the reversal of Silas's material ambitions and of his moral values as he comes to recognize at the end of the novel what is truly important in life.

Lapham farm. Farm in Vermont on which Silas grew up—the place where his commercial and materialistic aspirations began and to which he returns at the end of the novel. As people left farms to seek their fortunes in big cities at the end of the eighteenth century, they also left behind so-called rural values. Silas returns to those values in what is the true "rise of Silas Lapham."

— *Michael A. Benzel*

THE RISING OF THE MOON

Author: Lady Augusta Gregory (1852-1932)
Type of work: Drama
Type of plot: Protest

Time of plot: Early twentieth century
First published: 1905; first performed, 1907

Early twentieth century Irish audiences of this play would have immediately related to its seaport setting and contemporary issues of national identity and aspirations for political freedom.

*Ireland. Island nation west of Great Britain that is under unwelcome British rule at the time this play is set. The play's backdrop is the Ireland of rebel Republican organizations that sought the end of British rule. Violent resistance was uncommon in the first decade of the twentieth century, but Irish nationalism was active and assumed many other forms. Lady Gregory's characters assume that great popular sentiment supported the cause, even to sympathy with actions deemed illegal by the British regime. This attitude likely sets the scene in the south or southwest regions of the island, rather than in the Protestant- and Loyalist-dominated north and east regions. The police are native Irish, though hired to protect British interests and capture leaders of the cause, such as the unnamed felon. Ultimately the fugitive uses this commonality of Irish identity to dissuade the sergeant from arresting him.

Quay (kee). Wharf where ships are loaded and unloaded in an unnamed Irish port; the play's stage directions merely indicate "a seaport town." Such places were indeed doorways through which wanted men escaped authorities and aid to the rebels of several generations was provided. The quay on which the action takes place is situated between the nearby town and its jail (gaol), and the freedom of the open water below. It, too, serves specifically as a doorway that the sergeant initially guards and blocks, and that, in the end, he opens by sending off the other Irish policemen. In addition, it is the setting for his own self-realization, prompted by the "ragged man," that he, as an Irishman, might easily have been in the unseen boat on the sea of freedom and resistance to authority. However, he is attached to the police corps, jail, and British authority, located symbolically in the opposite direction.

— *Joseph P. Byrne*

THE RIVALS

Author: Richard Brinsley Sheridan (1751-1816)
Type of work: Drama
Type of plot: Comedy of manners

Time of plot: Eighteenth century
First performed: 1775; first published, 1775

Unlike many seventeenth and eighteenth century English comedies of manners, this play is not set in London. It is, however, set in the fashionable town of Bath. Richard Brinsley Sheridan uses the play's setting to satirize the affected manners of the day.

Bath. Resort town in western England; it and its surrounding area would have been as familiar to London theater audiences as similar well-known resort areas would be to modern readers, and Sheridan capitalizes on well-known facts of the leisure lifestyles of the fashionable in Bath. For example, it was well known that duel-

ing was forbidden in the city yet there were convenient places outside the city where duels were common. Sheridan refers to familiar places in the city such as the North Promenade and the New Rooms. Especially does he laugh at the well-known fashion of circulating libraries in the town. So, in order to do the play justice, audiences must see the world of the play as that of fashionable, leisure society removed for the summer to Bath.

North Parade. Fashionable promenade in Bath that is a place of leisurely walks and fashionable encounters between lovers.

King's-Mead-Fields. Location of the duel, a place well known for its duels outside the town walls on the Avon River.

— *Paul Varner*

ROB ROY

Author: Sir Walter Scott (1771-1832)
Type of work: Novel
Type of plot: Historical

Time of plot: 1715
First published: 1817

This novel of thrilling and melodramatic romance is set against the backdrop of the economic and social history of Britain in the early eighteenth century. All its important places symbolize the social and economic forces that lie behind the novel's conflicts, and several of its places contribute substantially to the novel's powerful atmosphere of mystery and foreboding.

*****Scottish Highlands.** Mountainous area of northern Scotland that was home to the historical Rob Roy. The Highlands are the romantic setting for Scottish clan life in the novel. Several of Walter Scott's works deal with the Scottish Highlands, but *Rob Roy* treats this area with special fullness and complexity. On one hand, the Highlands are beautiful, sublime, poetic, and impressive. On the other hand, they are dark, dangerous, primitive, and lawless. The Scottish clans of the Highlands are brave, daring, resourceful, and, at their best, heroic. They have a strong sense of honor and absolute loyalty to clan leaders like Rob Roy, but their way of life is often violent, disorderly, fearsome, and unproductive. For Scott, both the virtues and the vices of the Highlanders are closely associated with their country and its combination of wild sublimity and desolate barrenness. Scott's descriptions of the Scottish Highlands in this novel are among the book's greatest beauties, and such a scene as the horrific death of Morris and such characters as Rob Roy and Helen MacGregor seem to grow directly out of the soil of the Highlands. In broadly symbolic terms, Scott sees the Scottish Highlands as representing a romantic but doomed culture which belongs to the past. The poetry, feudalism, heroism, and concepts of honor associated with the Highlands must give way to the mercantile and rational values represented by Glasgow and London.

Osbaldistone Hall. Northumbrian country mansion of Sir Hildebrand Osbaldistone and his six sons. Osbaldistone Hall is called "cub castle" by its neighbors and is a large, antiquated country place dedicated mainly to eating, drinking, hunting, and the generally rustic and rude behavior of Sir Hildebrand and his sons. In broad terms, Osbaldistone Hall is the novel's symbol of the old-fashioned English country squire's way of life, which in the novel has become decadent, wasteful, and notably unintelligent. Like the Scottish Highlands, Osbaldistone Hall represents an antiquated way of life that must give way to modernity and mercantilism. Osbaldistone Hall is also used in the novel to lend atmosphere to the characters of Rashleigh Osbaldistone and Diana Vernon and to the mysteries that surround them. In this respect, the Gothic antiquity and the secret rooms, doors, and passages of Osbaldistone Hall provide the perfect setting for the villainies and machinations of Rashleigh and the secret fears and hopes of Diana.

*****Glasgow.** Mercantile metropolis of western Scotland and the home of Nicol Jarvie, perhaps the novel's greatest character. Generally speaking, Glasgow functions in *Rob Roy* as a Scottish symbol for the modern, mercantile, rational world represented by London. Glasgow is a city of law, learning, order, and business. Nicol Jarvie, who is virtually Glasgow incarnate, is both a magistrate and a merchant. Like Glasgow itself, Jarvie stands for practicality, reason, mercantilism, and civil order. The world of Glasgow and Nicol Jarvie may seem a bit prosaic, but it is the world of the future, and in its natural opposition to the wild irregularities and colorful violence of the Scottish Highlands, it will be victorious. Scott also describes Glasgow Cathedral with great power and in doing so creates both a memorable symbol for Scottish Presbyterianism and an effective setting for one of the novel's most thrilling and frightening moments, the whispered warning to Frank Osbaldistone that he is in danger in Glasgow.

*London. Capital of Great Britain that is the home of the great commercial house of Osbaldistone and Tres-

ham. Although Scott never really describes London in the novel, it is symbolically one of the most important places in the novel. London is where the novel begins and where it ends. Throughout *Rob Roy*, the values of poetry, romance, heroism, and feudalism are opposed to the London values of commercialism and rationality. At the beginning of the novel, Frank Osbaldistone leaves London because he rejects what London represents. At the end of the book, Frank has returned to his father's London firm, and the values of London are triumphant.

— *Phillip B. Anderson*

ROBERT ELSMERE

Author: Mary Augusta Ward (Mrs. Humphry Ward, 1851-1920)
Type of work: Novel

Type of plot: Social realism
Time of plot: 1882-1886
First published: 1888

This best-selling Victorian novel about the spiritual crisis of a devoted clergyman follows his career from his promising beginning as an Anglican parish pastor in England's Lake District to his work as the leader of a secular church in one of London's poorest areas.

*Westmoreland. Secluded section of the Lake District in northeastern England. While on a holiday in the region, the young clergyman Robert Elsmere meets Catherine Leyburn, a serious and pious young woman who, like most inhabitants of the region, exhibits a simple faith based on time-tested rituals. She accepts without question the miraculous nature of Christianity and shows little tolerance for more intellectual approaches to religion.

Burwood. Home of the Leyburns, where Catherine, the eldest daughter of a deceased clergyman, sees herself as responsible for managing household affairs. Elsmere's proposal of marriage causes Catherine great consternation because marriage to Elsmere would force her to leave her mother and sisters, who may not be able to get along without her.

Murewell Parish. Anglican parish in which Robert Elsmere is established as pastor. In a fashion similar to many clergymen of his time, Elsmere inherits his position from a relative who has controlled it for some

time. Typical of the makeup of many English country parishes of the nineteenth century, Murewell's parishioners include a small number of gentlemen and ladies and hundreds of working-class families who are employed within the region in farming or various trades.

Murewell Hall. Home of Squire Wendover. Like many historical English estates, Murewell encompasses not only the squire's mansion but also the parish and several villages in which estate workers live. At Murewell Hall, Elsmere becomes a friend of the squire, a religious freethinker and scholar who embraces the skeptical views of those who practice Higher Criticism, a form of theological inquiry that emerged in Europe during the nineteenth century. Wendover has built a library that is a monument to human learning, and he makes it available to Robert to help him investigate the tenets of his faith. As he falls under the influence of the squire, Robert comes to reject the teachings of traditional Christianity and eventually abandons his position in the Church of England.

Mile End. Village near Murewell Hall whose inhabitants live in squalor, victims of an unscrupulous steward who relies on the squire's inattention to his parishioners to enrich himself at the expense of the villagers. As Robert and Catherine become acquainted with residents of Mile End, Robert's shock at their living conditions drives him to seek an audience with Squire Wendover to demand improvements. Robert's efforts to improve conditions there makes him amenable to suggestions from friends that he take up similar work in London after he abandons his ministry in Murewell.

*Oxford. Town that is home to one of England's great universities. Although few scenes in the novel are set at the university, Elsmere's attachment to Oxford is a catalyst for much of the action of the novel. The university was the location for great religious controversy during the mid-nineteenth century. Debates over religion and science at Oxford led Elsmere's tutor Thomas Grey to doubt the truth of Christianity. Under his influence, Elsmere begins to question the truths of his faith even before he falls under the influence of Squire Wendover.

*London. England's greatest city is portrayed as a melting pot for people and ideas in the country. Robert goes there after giving up his living at Murewell. Catherine accompanies him, but their relationship is strained because she refuses to accept his conversion to secularism. In London the two are introduced into high society. For a time Robert is taken in by the favor shown to him by various members of the upper classes. Catherine, on the other hand, rejects their pretensions and values. In the city, however, Robert finds his calling among the lower classes of the East End, where, with the help of friends, he sets up a secular church to assist working-class men and women improve both their material and spiritual lives.

*Algiers. City on North Africa's Mediterranean coast to which Robert goes for his health after he is diagnosed with tuberculosis. There, he and Catherine achieve a final reconciliation, which is brought on both by their isolation from England and Robert's impending death.

— *Laurence W. Mazzeno*

ROBIN HOOD'S ADVENTURES

Author: Unknown
Type of work: Fiction
Type of plot: Adventure

Time of plot: Thirteenth century
First published: c. 1490

Sherwood Forest and Nottingham, located in central England, together form the locale for most tales of Robin Hood's adventures. The stories are often structured so that Sherwood Forest represents a place of freedom and refuge for ordinary men, while Nottingham is a city in which oppression prevails under the rule of a corrupt sheriff.

*Sherwood Forest. Large forested park stretching across the center of England that offers plentiful opportunities for social and dramatic conflict. As a land preserve, the forest represents a rich source of resources for medieval peasants, who lived much closer to the land than people do today. Wood for fuel, building, and weapons; plentiful game; and various plants and herbs for healing were free for the taking. Also, for the experienced, the forest provided safe hiding places from enemies. When the Earl of Huntingdon finds himself without land or title, Sherwood Forest becomes a fine choice

for his base of operations; other outlaws already live there. The natural features make it a prime locale for the sort of guerrilla campaign in which he enlists outlaws. Within the forest, the bow and arrow and the element of surprise can overcome the sheriff's superior armaments.

The way in which Robin and his band of Merry Men use the forest, a royal preserve, enrages the sheriff. If every peasant in England felt entitled to kill the preserve's deer for food, their numbers would surely dwindle. The road cutting through the center of the forest is used by business travelers, government messengers, religious pilgrims, and ordinary people. Sometimes these travelers are robbed by outlaws, who represent a threat to civil order and commerce, much as train robbers did in the Old West. Land rights and issues of social justice emerge in Sherwood Forest in complex form.

Because so many changes have taken place over the centuries, it is hard to tell how much the Sherwood Forest of the ballads and folktales departs from historical reality.

*Nottingham. Midsize market town and seat of local government in northern England, with Nottingham Cas-

tle close by. Public proclamations were read in the town square; archery and other contests were held either there or in the castle's courtyard or tower. Executions and the mustering of men to track down the outlaws also took place at Nottingham. To Robin Hood and his band, the town meant danger and oppression, yet it provided a marvelous public stage for tricking the sheriff. It was their best locale for embarrassing and taunting corrupt officials and building support for their own efforts and for the absent King Richard.

— *Emily Alward*

ROBINSON CRUSOE

Author: Daniel Defoe (1660-1731)
Type of work: Novel
Type of plot: Adventure

Time of plot: 1651-1705
First published: 1719

In this adventure masterpiece, which many literary scholars call the first true novel, a young Englishman ignores the advice of his father to work hard and stay in the middle class and instead goes off in search of adventure and fortune and becomes marooned on an uninhabited island. During his twenty-eight years on the island, he eventually finds redemption through religious conversion.

*England. Home of Robinson Crusoe. When the novel opens, England is being ruled by Oliver Cromwell during the Puritan Revolution, and the middle class to which the young Crusoe belongs is expanding rapidly. To Crusoe, England promises a future of hard, monotonous work and strict Puritanism, so he takes passage on a ship looking for adventure elsewhere. Years later, he returns to England, made prosperous by his long years of work and struggle, and embraces the faith of his father.

*Sallee (sahl-LAY; now known as Salé). North African seaport in what is now known as Morocco that is the base of pirates who attack Crusoe's ship and make him a slave. After two years in captivity in Sallee, Crusoe is rescued by a Portuguese captain, who advises him to return to England. However, Crusoe, still young and defiant, ignores the advice by continuing his travels.

*Brazil. Portuguese colony to which the Portuguese captain takes Crusoe. There, Crusoe sets up a sugar and tobacco plantation. After a few years, the plantation begins to show a profit, but Crusoe remains restless. Intent on making a fortune, and in need of labor, he leads a

slaving expedition to West Africa. Shipwrecked before he reaches Africa, he is marooned on an uninhabited island.

Crusoe's island. Island on which Crusoe is marooned by himself, located somewhere off the northern coast of South America. With only the clothes on his back and odds and ends he salvages from the wrecked ship, Crusoe spends the next twenty-eight years of his life on the island. During his stay, Crusoe works diligently, building not only a serviceable home, but also almost every convenience to which he was accustomed in England. He thereby ironically ends up following the very Puritan dictates that he originally left England to escape.

On the island, Crusoe develops a sense of wholehearted inventiveness, precisely in keeping with Puritan dictates and, most important, returns to the Protestant religion he spurned by going to sea. With the help of his slave Friday, whom he rescues from cannibalism after twenty-four years completely alone, he builds a home, grows his food, makes clothes from animal skins, keeps animals, and builds a boat. By the end of the novel, when he is rescued and returned safely to England, he has amassed a fortune and becomes a gentleman. Thus, the island provides a means for him to move up the social ladder and climb out of his middle-class beginnings.

Although Crusoe spurns his father's Protestant religion by going to sea, the deserted island is instrumental in his return to his father's faith. As in the Bible's prodigal son narrative and many Puritan-conversion narratives of Defoe's era, Crusoe is lost in the wilderness but returns after a period of intense suffering, becomes repentant, and finds forgiveness.

— *M. Casey Diana*

RODERICK HUDSON

Author: Henry James (1843-1916)
Type of work: Novel
Type of plot: Psychological realism

Time of plot: 1870's
First published: 1876

This, Henry James's first fully realized novel, experiments with evoking settings in a fashion akin to that of the Impressionist painters: through the significant but telling stroke, rather than through lengthy descriptions, in the manner of the older Victorian novelists. Although nearly all of the places James uses are real, and although his extensive European travels gave him the knowledge to provide accurate and finely rendered details, the most important locales are also meant to be understood symbolically.

*Rome. Capital city of Italy after 1871 and one of the world's art capitals, in which most of the novel takes place. Rowland Mallet, a man of inherited wealth and cultivated tastes, offers to accompany Roderick Hudson, a young and talented American sculptor, to Europe. Mallet sponsors him during their sojourn, undertaken to refine Hudson's sensibilities through the study of art and general exposure to European culture. They visit Paris, Genoa, Milan, Venice, Florence, and other great cities, but it is Rome that most deeply captures Roderick's imagination. His first fortnight in Rome is an "aesthetic revel," and he declares that Rome makes him feel and understand more things than he can, as he is sure that life there must give all one's senses an "incomparable fineness." Indeed, Roderick's art does impress many people in Rome, especially those connected with the local colony of American artists; however, his successes are short-lived. Soon, his passion for Christina Light, a beauty of vague American origins but a distinctly European social and moral sense, consumes him, and he loses his will to create.

James evokes the romantically charged air of Rome throughout the novel, with lush language that conveys the intoxicating sense of the city. He also sets scenes at places his American readers may have visited or longed to visit: the Colosseum ("Coliseum" in the novel), St. Peter's Basilica, the church of St. Cecilia—all famous sites he word-paints with an unerring eye. However, Rome, for all its beauty, is as much a symbol as a realistically drawn city: It comes to stand for corruption. As with a fine wine, the pleasures of Rome can be deep, but drunk without moderation—or taken in great draughts by an innocent such as Roderick, whose "tolerance" has not been gradually built up—excesses are tragically debilitating.

*Northampton. Roderick's Massachusetts hometown and the home of Rowland's cousin Cecilia. If Rome is dangerous because of its excesses—of beauty, of history, of social complexity—Northampton is deadly dull. Cecilia, who arranges Rowland and Roderick's initial meeting, has three misfortunes: She has lost her husband, she has lost her money, and she lives at Northampton. Rowland's concern that Roderick's raw artistic abilities, prodigious but underdeveloped, will wither unless he has the opportunity to refine them in Europe, seems correct. Readers should remember that James himself, arguably the most important American novelist of his era, spent nearly all of his creative life abroad, believing that it would be impossible for him to create art in what he regarded as the stultifying cultural climate of the United States. Rome is a great delight to Roderick because it is only there that he finds what he has been looking for: a "complete contradiction of Northampton."

Northampton, which might easily be any small town in America, is crude and boring, certainly, but it also nourishes Roderick in his early years. If the land and culture is raw, as is Roderick's talent, there is nevertheless undeniable power there. This power accounts for the strength of Roderick's imagination and the originality of his vision. The charms of Northampton are real, and even the sophisticated Rowland is not immune to them. He falls in love with Mary Garland, even though she is engaged to his friend Roderick. Mary is a distinct Northampton "type" and finally a much more sympathetic character than the European Christina.

If Rome is the old world, Northampton is the new world. If Rome represents corruption, Northampton represents innocence; if Rome represents excess, North-ampton represents deprivation. Roderick's problem is what James saw as the problem of the American artist: How should he hold on to the innocence, originality, and energy of his native land if he is to avail himself of the depth of experience and refinement that only immersion in the great European tradition can afford?

Englethal. Tiny Swiss village near Lucerne in central Switzerland near which Roderick's life ends when he jumps or slips from an Alpine cliff. Whether Roderick commits suicide or falls accidentally is not entirely clear, but it does not much matter. Roderick's cruelties to Mary, just before his death, and his complete absorption in his own deluded passions for Christina, have rendered him morally dead already. The ordinariness of Englethal—a place that appears not actually to exist—mirrors, in a way, the person Roderick, his art by now a glory from his past, has become.

— *Douglas Branch*

THE ROMANCE OF THE FOREST

Author: Ann Radcliffe (1764-1823)
Type of work: Novel
Type of plot: Gothic

Time of plot: Seventeenth century
First published: 1791

Abandoned by her family and forced into the company of self-exiled Pierre de la Motte, virtuous Adeline de St. Pierre, the quintessential gothic heroine, endures a series of imprisonments and escapes in settings whose association with persons of both good and evil character map a moral as well as geographic landscape.

Forest of Fontanville (fon-tan-veel). Imaginary forest in the south of France, where the disgraced aristocrat Pierre de la Motte sets up temporary residence after fleeing with his wife and servants from Paris. Remote and unpopulated, the luxuriant forest is cause for apprehension to de la Motte, who initially worries that it may hide bandits, or that his entourage may stray from the overrun and ill-defined track that traverses it. When his coach breaks down, de la Motte is forced to put up in abandoned St. Clair's abbey, in the heart of the forest. When he decides that the secluded abbey will make a good refuge from his pursuers, the forest becomes part of his self-created prison.

A man of infirm moral character, de la Motte sees the forest only in terms of how it serves his self-interest. However, Adeline de St. Pierre, a young woman traveling with him, finds the forest a source of spiritual refreshment. Sensitive to its vivid colors and varied plant and animal life, Adeline responds wholesomely to the setting, which for her stirs feelings of exaltation and reverence. When the innocent Adeline looks on nature, she is compelled to think of "the great Author of Nature."

The forest is one of several settings in the novel that equate nature with holiness and the sublime. Adeline, who is pure of heart, flourishes in the natural environment, whereas dwellings built by men generally become her prison.

Saint Clair's abbey. Abandoned abbey in the forest of Fontanville that de la Motte converts into his personal sanctuary. At several points, the author describes the castle as "Gothic," which is to say that it embodies attributes associated with the gothic in fiction: it is gloomy, forebidding, and chaotic. De la Motte observes that "the greater part of the pile appeared to be sinking into ruins, and that, which had withstood the ravages of time, shewed the remaining fabric more awful in decay." If the natural world surrounding the abbey suggests the permanence and pervasiveness of the holy, then the abbey suggests the transience and impermanence of man and his works.

Typically, in gothic fiction, crumbling edifices and collapsing architecture incarnate the moral and spiritual decline of their residents. Just as Adeline is in sympathy with nature, so does de la Motte identify with the ruined abbey. "The comparison between himself and the gradation of decay, which these columns exhibited, was but too obvious and affecting." Many different aspects of the abbey find correlatives in parts of de la Motte's character: The abbey, a former place of reverence, is in ruins, just as de la Motte's moral character is infirm. The abbey is supposedly haunted by a ghost from the past, much as de la Motte is haunted by his past indiscretions. It is honeycombed with labyrinthine passages and secret apertures, just as de la Motte is a participant in elaborate, twisted intrigues. The abbey is also a property owned by the marquis de Montalt, and de la Motte's stay in it is equivalent to his entrapment in de Montalt's evil schemes.

De Montalt's villa. Gaudy residence on the outskirts of the forest to which Adeline is abducted by the marquis' henchmen. The villa is magnificently outfitted in "airy and elegant taste," and its fixtures, furniture, and decorations so splendidly arranged that the "whole seemed the works of enchantment, and rather resembled the palace of a fairy than anything of human conformation." Adeline responds positively to the beauty of the villa and outlying gardens but cannot separate them from the marquis, who represents a threat to her virtue. Eventually, she realizes that the voluptuous and provocative character of the furnishings "seemed designed to fascinate the imagination, and to seduce the heart." Their beauty notwithstanding, they are tools the marquis uses in the hope of coercing Adeline into marriage. This marriage, like the villa, would be no more than a fancy prison. The artificiality of the villa contradicts the simple, unaffected natural world to which Adeline is drawn.

Leloncourt (leh-LON-koor). Village at the foot of the Savoy Alps, to which Adeline flees in the company of de la Motte's servant Peter, whose hometown it is. Leloncourt represents an ideal setting that is spiritually superior to all others in the tale. It is regal in natural beauty. Its people, who are entirely uncorrupted by the city life known to most of the book's characters, function as a compassionate community. Adeline finds a surrogate family in the La Luc household, which takes her in and treats her like a daughter. She spends her days free of the concerns that have hitherto oppressed her, and finds that the natural scenery awakens "sensations truly sublime." The idyllic interlude she spends at Leloncourt rejuvenates her soul and the "romantic simplicity" of the environment inspires her to near-religious adoration.

— *Stefan Dziemianowicz*

ROMANCE OF THE THREE KINGDOMS

Author: Lo Kuan-chung (c. 1320-c. 1380)
Type of work: Novel
Type of plot: Historical

Time of plot: c. 180-c. 280
First published: San kuo chih yen-i, fourteenth century (English translation, 1925)

This historical novel covers a one hundred year period in the second and third centuries. Its landscape is mostly innumerable battlefields in the three kingdoms of its title—the Shu Han, the Wei, and the Wu. This most popular of Asian novels ends when the three kingdoms are united to form the land of Chin.

Wei kingdom. First among the three kingdoms in northern China, under the control of Ts'ao Ts'ao. The first sections of the work are narratives that chronicle various battles as Ts'ao Ts'ao conquers, then eliminates, numerous political rivals. The most important conquest is that of the Han empire.

Shu Han kingdom. Kingdom in which Liu Pei eventually succeeds in ruling from his throne in Szechwan and in which a second thread of narratives interwoven in the novel is set.

*****Wu kingdom.** Third and most wealthy kingdom, located south of the other two kingdoms, along the banks of the Yangtze River. This kingdom is controlled by Sun Ch'uan, who joins forces with Liu Pei to defeat Ts'ao Ts'ao. Thus the three kingdoms are for a while at peace. Later chapters in the work tell of military imbroglios between Kuan Yu, governor of a territory known as Hupeh, and Sun Ch'uan. Ultimately, Liu Pei conquers both Kuan Yu and Sun Ch'uan. However, the peace is unstable and various power struggles continue for another two generations until Ssu-ma Yen establishes control over the various kingdoms to make them into one nation.

As a novel that is both "historic" and "romantic," *Romance of the Three Kingdoms* is not always necessarily given to geographic accuracy; moreover, the novel was written more than one thousand years after the events it purports to record. Therefore, while most of the main characters are historical figures whose lives can otherwise be validated, many of the geographical settings cannot. Dozens of villages and cities, several rivers, numerous mountain ranges and lakes provide the backdrop for battles or other activities of the plot. In writing the story, Lo Kuan-chung generally sets these events in cities of his own time. Generally, these correspond to names of places that were in use a millennium earlier.

Wen-te Hall. Residence of Emperor Ling, in the period immediately preceding the beginning of the narrative. This residence is the scene of supernatural occurrences, such as monstrous black snakes floating down from the heavens as a warning that the divine powers are displeased and that changes will occur in the royal family, and provides the setting for the opening chapter of the novel.

Wuch'ang palace. Residence of the evil emperor Sun Hao and the location of his wicked life and corrupt management of government affairs. Given to every kind of debauchery, it is Sun Hao who is finally overthrown. Ssu-ma Yen then takes over the throne at Wu to complete unification of the Chins into one country; that is, it becomes the country of China as it has continued to be known since that time.

— *Carl Singleton*

THE ROMANTIC COMEDIANS

Author: Ellen Glasgow (1873-1945)
Type of work: Novel
Type of plot: Fiction of manners

Time of plot: 1920's
First published: 1926

Place does not play a central role in this novel. The novel's Virginia setting serves merely as a backdrop against which it examines changes taking place in America's "New South," where members of the older generation resist the passing of the old ways, while younger people struggle to assert new views. The novel's fictional town of Queenborough, like a nearby coal mine, is becoming a dying memory of the way life used to be.

Queenborough. Virginia town in which the novel is set; modeled after Richmond, Virginia. Queenborough is known for its beautiful women, who define the mood of the town and its inhabitants during each generation. The older, more refined members of Queenborough society are embodied in Amanda Lightfoot, a woman in her fifties. During the late 1880's, Amanda was a much sought-after beauty. Her beauty, like Queenborough's, has endured, but her ability to charm Judge Gamaliel Honeywell, her former fiancé, has faded. He finds her more mature beauty less appealing than her earlier charm and her voice, which he describes as monotonous, lacking in its former allure. The new Queenborough is symbolized by Amanda's current successor as the town beauty, Annabel Upchurch.

Like many of its residents, Queenborough has also lost its ability of self-criticism and has become old and complacent. The never-ending cycle of dinners and balls that the newly married Judge Gamaliel and Annabel Honeywell attend are symptoms of the malaise of an entire community that refuses to face the realities of a changing world. These social rites represent both a society that has never matured and one that has remained mired in tradition. The judge attends these events only so that his much younger bride Annabel can enjoy herself with friends and dancing. Forever reminding himself of what life was like during the 1880's in Queenborough, the judge can never enjoy these gatherings of Queenborough's elite.

Washington Street. Main thoroughfare running through Queenborough. The new attitudes of Queenborough society are evident even in the naming of the town's streets. The more forward-looking members of the town's older, more practical society do not want to live on the common "streets" and "roads" of the old town. Instead they prefer the more pretentious terms such as "avenue" and "boulevard."

Washington Street was once the aristocratic center of town activity. With the coming of the twentieth century and the New South, that street merges into what is considered a more appropriately named road **Granite Boulevard**. The latter name is appropriate because the new Queenborough is both physically and psychologically harder than the old Queenborough. "Boulevard" is nothing more than a pretentious renaming of the simpler and more aptly named Washington Street.

Judge Honeywell's house. Home originally shared by Judge Honeywell and his first wife, Cordelia, and later by the judge and his much younger second wife, Annabel. The home is a staid brownstone in which the judge takes much pride; the house symbolizes for him both his past with Cordelia and the old way of life—both of which he pretends not to miss. In reality, he wishes to return to both. Mirroring the complacency of Queenborough, he has grown accustomed to his routine and to living alone in his home. Even before Cordelia's death, the judge had become comfortable, though not happy.

Into this home the judge brings Annabel and her modern views and tastes. Just as the older citizens of Queenborough still remember the young Amanda Lightfoot's beauty and charm and keep her on a pedestal, never allowing her to change, the judge refuses to accept even the hint of a change in his home. One of the first things that Annabel wants to do upon arriving at their home after their honeymoon is to replace Cordelia's old lace draperies with what she considers more modern and attractive window dressings. Without even consulting the judge, she removes a favorite piece of furniture in his dressing room to make room for a newer piece that she has commissioned, copied from a piece he admired on their European honeymoon. Gently but firmly, the judge demands his old cabinet back, thus quietly and firmly holding onto the past. The home of Gamaliel and Annabel Honeywell, then, becomes a genteel battleground between the Old South and the New.

— *Kimberley H. Kidd*

ROMEO AND JULIET

Author: William Shakespeare (1564-1616)
Type of work: Drama
Type of plot: Tragedy

Time of plot: Fifteenth century
First performed: c. 1595-1596; first published, 1597

Though acquainted with the geography of northern Italy, William Shakespeare uses the place-names Verona and Mantua in this play merely as labels to suggest to English ears a truthful union and a divided self, respectively. The playwright sets twenty-three scenes in ten different places, indoors and out, public and private, sacred and profane, to accommodate the characters' antithetical needs for violence and peace, love and hate, domestic accord and wayward willfulness.

Capulets' orchard. Walled orchard overlooked by Juliet's window. A place where domestic comfort meets wild nature, the orchard is the place where the play's star-crossed lovers pledge their troth, and through which Romeo enters Juliet's chamber to consummate their secret marriage. There, too, the higher and lower aspects of love are contrasted: Juliet, above, representing true romance; and the lane by the wall, below, where Mercutio taunts Romeo with lewd jests.

Friar Laurence's cell. Sacred place where the lovers repair from the cruel world to find solace and intimate counsel from their sympathetic priest. There the lovers privately confide in the friar their determination to commit suicide. There too the crucial elements of the tragedy's plot are devised: plans for the secret marriage, the sleeping potion Juliet takes to avoid marrying Paris, and the miscarried letter to bring Romeo back from banishment in Mantua.

Capulets' tomb. Place where love and death conjoin in a double suicide on holy ground. Seeming to be dead, Juliet is placed in the tomb, there to awake and find that Romeo has dealt Paris a bloody death and poisoned himself, thinking she is dead. When his lips afford her none of the poison, she plunges his dagger into her bosom. Significantly, the play ends there, not with their deaths, but with the families and townspeople crowding into the holy place to end their feud and honor the dead lovers.

— *John L. McLean*

ROMOLA

Author: George Eliot (Mary Ann Evans, 1819-1880)
Type of work: Novel
Type of plot: Historical realism

Time of plot: 1492-1498
First published: 1862-1863

This novel's historical setting conveys a strong sense of place that is an appropriate backdrop for a mythos that George Eliot develops through both fictional characters and fictionalized historical figures. Her fictional Romola is an epic heroine who grows from the pagan and Stoic influence of her father, Bardo de' Bardi, through the Bacchic period with her husband, Tito Melema, to the evangelical Christian influence of Girolamo Savonarola and, finally, to moral autonomy. Along the way, she experiences her own inferno, purgatory, and paradise.

***Florence.** Italian center of art, philosophy, scholarship, and religious and political intrigue that made the city famous as the cradle of the Renaissance. Eliot's novel is filled with allusions to Florence's history, from 200 B.C.E. through the late fifteenth century; the stages of its growth parallel the psychological and moral growth of her fifteenth century heroine, Romola de' Bardi. Eliot's concern is for both the individual and the larger human community. Many of her Victorian readers who were interested in the contemporary Italian unification movement—the Risorgimento—would have noted contemporary parallels with the historical issues Eliot re-created as a milieu for Romola's development.

Bardo's library. Library of Romola's father, Bardo de' Bardi, a famous scholar. Filled with manuscripts and antiquaries, this colorless, rather cold room represents Bardo's classical Stoic values: a noble integrity that demands justice and truth. Significantly, the competence in classical languages shown by Romola's future husband, the young Greek adventurer Tito Melema, gets Tito admitted to Bardo's presence in the library, where Romola first meets him. Both Bardo and Tito deride the evangelical Christian movement of Florentine religious leader Savonarola as fanatical. Tito's later betrayal of Bardo and Romola by selling the library causes their first major marital rift.

Salotto (sah-LAT-toh). Tito's reception room. Frescoed with nymphs, vines, figures of Eros, flowers, birds, and images of the Roman god Bacchus, this room has been designed by Tito to represent his role as the Care-Dispeller who plans that his marriage to Romola will alleviate the anxious concern and somberness of her life with her father.

*Duomo (DWOH-moh). Florence's cathedral of Santa Maria del Fiore, in which Romola hears Savonarola preach. Later, Tito denies his adoptive father, Baldassarre Calvo, on the Duomo's outer steps. The Duomo was completed around 1434. A year or two before writing *Romola*, Eliot heard a powerful preacher speak in the Duomo who may have been the inspiration behind her description of Savonarola's preaching there.

*Piazza della Signoria. Florence's Square of the Council, a large outdoor meeting place that is the center of Florentine political life and the place where Savonarola staged his infamous "Bonfire of the Vanities," in which Florentines burned objectionable books and art objects. After the political tide turned against him, Savonarola himself was burned at the stake on the Piazza. Eliot captures the struggle for power, especially for restoration of popular government and of the medieval tradition of Florentine liberty, after the death of Lorenzo the Magnificent ended several decades of Medicean dominance.

*Monastery of San Marco. Monastery home of both Savonarola and Romola's brother, Dino, who renounces his home and father to live as a monk. When Romola visits the monastery during a deathbed scene with her brother, Savonarola first identifies her, and Dino reports to her his frightening vision for her future.

— *Carolyn Dickinson*

ROOM AT THE TOP

Author: John Braine (1922-1986)
Type of work: Novel
Type of plot: Social realism

Time of plot: 1947
First published: 1957

John Braine's first novel is rich in its vivid description of the local color of his native Yorkshire, England. Set primarily in Warley, shortly after World War II, this novel treats the efforts of a young man, Joe Lampton, to climb the social ladder to success and acceptance. Throughout the novel, Warley epitomizes the world of social and economic possibilities for Joe, while his hometown of Dufton represents his grimy and forgettable past. Both Warley and Dufton are based on Bradford, Yorkshire, the author's place of birth and his hometown.

Warley. Town in Yorkshire's West Riding district that is the center of a prosperous woolen mill industry. Not many years after World War II, people who have been made rich by the war are beginning to find ways to spend their wealth on grand homes, expensive cars, and other luxuries that were scarce during the war. Warley's Cyprus Avenue, named after the trees that line it, symbolizes for Joe Lampton the grandeur of Warley as a prosperous community. Joe takes up lodging with Mr. Cedric and Mrs. Joan Thompson on Eagle Road at T'Top, a place symbolic of the heights to which Joe hopes soon to climb.

Merton River loops through Warley and is clear enough for children to use safely for swimming, another symbol of the promise of a new and better life for Joe in this community. Into this peaceful world bursting with good fortune the protagonist enters as "General Joe Lampton" who plans his attack carefully for acquiring his share of postwar wealth and position that he sees Warley's elite enjoying in this world of theater, fancy cars, and elegant homes.

Little Theatre. Amateur theatrical organization that Joe joins in order to make social contacts. The theater is the meeting place and performance stage for the Warley Thespians. There, Joe meets both of the women who become his lovers, Alice Aisgill and Susan Brown, as he plans his campaign to reach the upper levels of Warley society. His participation in the play *The Lady's Not for Burning* at the Little Theatre introduces him to many of the upper-middle-class members of his community.

Sparrow Hill. Area on the periphery of Warley that was once planned for development but abandoned. There, Joe and Alice first make love, and there Alice later commits suicide by crashing her car after Joe tells her that he is leaving her for Susan. Sparrow Hill is thus symbolic of incomplete dreams and abandoned relationships. Joe's attack on Warley's upper middle class proves successful, with Alice being the major casualty, one for which Joe feels an enduring sense of guilt even ten years after her gruesome death.

Dufton. Yorkshire mill town that was Joe's original home. To Joe, Dufton is the antithesis of Warley. The prosperous owners of Dufton's mills do not live in Dufton. Dufton's streets, such as Oak Crescent where Joe has lived with his Aunt Emily, are boringly straight and unadorned even by bushes. The houses are small and utilitarian. Even pictures have a strictly functional purpose and are not to be enjoyed aesthetically.

Dufton has numerous mills, a chemical factory, a cinema and fourteen pubs. The river that passes through it changes colors each day, and people often drown in its putrid waters. Even the beautiful snow of the Christmas season seems to be fouled in this grimy town. Joe and his close friend Charles Lufford refer to the town as Dead Dufton and call its residents "zombies," the walking dead.

During the war, Joe's parents were killed in their sleep by a stray German rocket that hit Dufton, and the shattered remains of their house remind Joe of a past to which he can never return.

Cumley. Village on the coast of Dorset to which Joe takes Alice for a short holiday during which they seem to behave as husband and wife. Charles Lufford arrives after Alice leaves and advises Joe to continue pursuing the young and rich Susan. Cumley's region, in which Thomas Hardy set *Tess of the D'Urbervilles* (1891) reminds Alice of a play in which she had the role of Tess. Her thoughts about the tragic Tess foreshadow the tragedy that soon will strike her.

Stalag 1000. German prison camp in which Joe spent three years during World War II. Rather than trying to escape and return to service flying in the Royal Air Force, Joe spent his time studying for the qualifying exams in accounting. The camp thus symbolizes his tendency to think primarily of his own interests.

— *Daven M. Kari*

A ROOM WITH A VIEW

Author: E. M. Forster (1879-1970)
Type of work: Novel
Type of plot: Social realism

Time of plot: Early twentieth century
First published: 1908

The primary settings of this novel are the English countryside and Italy, specifically in and around Florence. England here stands for the safety of home, and Italy is the dangerous yet seductive other, essentially that which is "un-English."

Windy Corner. Home of Lucy Honeychurch and her mother and brother. Windy Corner is located near Summer Street, in the Surrey hills. The Honeychurches live in suburbia, as did E. M. Forster for much of his life, close to London but outside it. Surrey is famous as a recreation destination. As he indicates in the title, Forster considered rooms within houses to be symbolically important places: The rooms in the boxy Honeychurch house are protected from the outside by heavy curtains and filled with solid Victorian furniture. They do not have views. Views are to be had outside on the grounds, or, for those ready to look, within.

Pension Bertolini (pan-see-OHN ber-TOH-lee-nee). Tourist lodge on the River Arno, in Florence, which caters to an English clientele. The Bertolini is based on a real pension in which Forster stayed with his mother on his first trip to Italy in 1901-1902. The pension is run by a Cockney woman, and, with its drawing room and pictures of Queen Victoria and Alfred, Lord Tennyson, on the walls, the hostel is calculated to make the English tourist feel at home. As in Forster's other novels, it is abroad that members of various levels of English society, in particular the middle classes, seem to meet. The room to which Lucy is eventually assigned has a beautiful view of the river and the hills beyond. This view entices her out of the pension and into the dangers and possibilities of the city.

*Florence.** City in northern Italy that was historically a center of culture and political power. For many English writers, Italy figured prominently as a romantically idealized, open, earthy society in stark opposition to closed, ascetic Victorian England. This was true of Forster, who felt that Italy had an awakening effect on him. It was both the seat of the Renaissance and an erotic ideal. As in England, however, Italy has both city and country attractions. Florence's busy Piazza Signoria is the scene of Lucy's first sexual awakening, as she witnesses an altercation between two Italian men. That is followed by her journey out of the city to the hills at Fiesole, where the novel engages the spirit of the place. In a scene, reminiscent of an early Forster work, "The Story of a Panic," Lucy and the Whitmanesque hero George Emerson are overcome by passion and share their first kiss.

*London.** Great Britain's capital city, in which Cecil Vyse lives with his mother. London figures very briefly in the novel and is important in just two scenes. In the first, Lucy plays piano for a children's party, in the chapter titled, "In Mrs. Vyse's Well-Appointed Flat." Lucy tires of everything in London, including her family and her suburban home. In the second scene, the cosmopolitan Cecil meets George and his father at the National Gallery. Cecil plays a joke on the suburban snobs in Summer Street by enticing the Emersons to take a lease on Cissy Villa. Contrasted to Surrey, London is dark, dank, and deserted. While it is the English center of sophistication, art, and culture, London lacks scenic views.

— *James J. Berg*

ROOTS: The Saga of an American Family

Author: Alex Haley (1921-1992)
Type of work: Novel
Type of plot: Historical realism

Time of plot: 1750-the twentieth century
First published: 1976

In this monumental historical novel, Alex Haley traces the history of one line of his family from a West African kidnapped into slavery in the eighteenth century, through generations of slaves and free African Americans, to his own lifetime, finally bringing the story full circle when he visits the village of his uprooted ancestor. His book has provided a sense of origin for all African Americans.

*Juffure** (jew-FUR-ee). Village on West Africa's Gambia River in which Haley's ancestor Kunta Kinte was born and raised. Two centuries after Kunta was forcibly taken from this village, Haley visited Juffure and met many of his African cousins, descendants of Kunta's brothers. Drawing on his experiences in modern Juffure and his historical research, Haley produced a fascinating literary re-creation of the village as it was around 1750, as Kunta Kinte was growing up.

Through the eyes of young Kunta, readers see a village of round thatched huts surrounded by enclosing walls, pierced by the village gates, as well as the traveler's tree, at which travelers are greeted by village children; fields on which men grow groundnuts and women grow rice; and the forest in which boys take goats to browse. Well removed from the main village of Juffure is the manhood-training village to which the boys on the threshold of manhood are taken to learn the skills and secrets of men.

In Haley's novel, Juffure is a place rich in the history of a culture that knows its heritage and has reason to be proud of it. It is a place where each person is known to everyone else, where every action is rich with meaning and tradition, a place where Kunta belongs. However, Kunta does not remain there long, as one day he is ambushed while chopping wood in the forest and sold to slavers.

*Lord Ligonier.** Slave ship on which Kunta Kinte is transported to North America. In an effort to understand what Kunta and the other transportees suffered, Haley booked passage on a modern freighter and slept on a bare plank shelf in the hold each night of the journey. However, his experience only approximated the horrifying conditions experienced by enslaved Africans, chained amid their own filth in the hold of a wooden sailing ship.

*Spotsylvania. Virginia county that is the location of the two plantations on which Kunta Kinte is held as a slave after his arrival in America. On the first, owned by John Waller, the regimen is brutish and conditions harsh. Its slaves live in tumbledown shacks, barely sufficient to shelter them from the elements. Beatings are regular and violent. Kunta repeatedly tries to escape, but each time is tracked down and subjected to even harsher treatment. The plantation of Dr. William Waller, a relative of John, is somewhat more humane, although the physician still regards his slaves as tools of production, not as persons. The slaves live in clean, whitewashed cabins and are treated with gentle firmness instead of violence, but Waller is always ready to sell troublemakers to plantations with harsher conditions and tells his slaves this to keep them in line.

*Caswell. North Carolina county that is home of the gamecock-fighter to whom Kunta's daughter Kizzy is sold. After the high-class respectability of Dr. Waller's plantation, the poor-white brutality of Tom Lea comes as a shock. His fortune is based upon gambling on cockfights, and he retains the crude habits of his impoverished upbringing. He forces himself upon Kizzy, and as a result she bears a son, whom Massa Tom names George. The lad proves to have such talent with the fighting birds that he gains the sobriquet of "Chicken George" and is ultimately given his freedom. That grant does not extend to his wife and children, who remain in bondage until the Emancipation Proclamation during the American Civil War.

*Henning. Tennessee town in which George and his family settle as free blacks after the Civil War. It is a community strictly divided by race, where the former masters of one branch of the family are shunned by the other white people for being too friendly to their former property. Nevertheless, it is a place where George's family can establish a footing as tradesmen and even own a lumber business. It is also the place in which author Alex Haley would be born, where he would hear the stories about his family's past that would ultimately lead him to search for the truth behind the fragmented oral traditions.

— *Leigh Husband Kimmel*

THE ROPE

Author: Plautus (c. 254-184 B.C.E.)
Type of work: Drama
Type of plot: Comedy

Time of plot: Late third century B.C.E.
First performed: Rudens, late third or early second century B.C.E. (English translation, 1694)

Unique among Plautus's plays, this work is set on a North African seashore, near the city of Cyrene. Onstage the sea is framed by a temple of Venus and the house of a slave-owning refugee from Athens.

*Mediterranean Sea. Seaway on which the slave-dealer Labrax tries to abscond with Daemones' daughter Palaestra to Sicily in order to sell her for a better price and cheat Plesidippus, a young man who loves Palaestra. A storm conjured by the gods shipwrecks Labrax's vessel, ends his scheme, and temporarily separates four of the characters, while also separating Labrax from his money and Palaestra from proof of her true identity. Just as the goddess Venus emerged in birth from the sea in ancient myths, first Palaestra and then her identity emerge from the sea, allowing a rebirth of sorts, in her recognition by Daemones.

Cyrene (SI-ree-nee). Also known as Cyrenaica. North African town in what is now Libya and home to the

Greek exile Daemones. The same storm that blows the roof off Daemones' seaside cottage reunites him and his wife with their daughter in the home they have made in this foreign land. The home serves as a backdrop and symbol of the reconstituted family.

Temple of Venus. Temple to the Roman goddess located near Cyrene. The temple and the woman who tends it provide temporary shelter for the shipwrecked women. Labrax's madness and impiety are demonstrated in his assault on them as they cling to the tem-

ple's altar. The temple serves as a witness to the divine source of the storm, and to the familial and erotic love that the storm allows to blossom (Venus as goddess of love). Divinity unites what human actions have geographically torn asunder.

*Athens. Original home to the exiled Daemones, his wife, and Palaestra, it is also the city from which Plesidippus hails.

— *Joseph P. Byrne*

ROSENCRANTZ AND GUILDENSTERN ARE DEAD

Author: Tom Stoppard (Tomas Straussler, 1937-   )
Type of work: Drama
Type of plot: Existential

Time of plot: 1600
First performed: 1966; first published, 1967

This comedy involves two minor characters from William Shakespeare's play Hamlet *who engage in puzzled philosophical dialogue over their predicament. Hamlet appears as a minor character in the play. Part of the play's essence is the uncertainty of its setting.*

Elsinore Castle. Apparent location of the play's first act. Tom Stoppard's stage directions for act 1 describe the scene as "Two Elizabethans passing the time in a place without any visible character." The location seems to be a featureless place, neither indoors nor out, where the courtiers Rosencrantz and Guildenstern discourse and toss coins. At length it becomes clear that this is an outdoor location close to the castle of Elsinore, because the traveling players approach them en route to the castle. However, Hamlet himself appears at the end of the act, so the setting may be within the castle itself. This anomaly is intentional, for the setting of the whole play is more one of "inner space" (inside the mind) than any physical place.

The second act makes use of some of Shakespeare's original lines in *Hamlet*, with which it soon becomes obvious Stoppard's play is dovetailing. However, Stoppard never makes the location clear (just as Shakespeare,

with minimal stage directions, never makes his locations clear for *Hamlet*).

Ship. Apparent setting for act 3. Even more curious than the first two acts, this act is apparently set on a ship at sea—an inference the audience draws from the sound effects suggested by Stoppard, such as "soft sea sounds" and "ship timbers, wind in the rigging." There are three large barrels on the deck (sufficient to hold one or two actors), and a few steps lead to an upper deck. Rosencrantz and Guildenstern are taking Hamlet to England after the death of Polonius, perhaps. But at one point all the traveling players emerge from one of the barrels, and at the end of the play it is clear that the setting is, magically, not a ship but the Danish court.

Perhaps one is meant to assume (from the title) that the play is posthumous, with all the characters dead throughout, not just killed at the end of act 3.

— *Chris Morgan*

ROSMERSHOLM

Author: Henrik Ibsen (1828-1906)
Type of work: Drama
Type of plot: Social realism

Time of plot: Mid-nineteenth century
First published: 1886; first performed, 1887 (English translation, 1889)

This play is concerned with the conflict between traditional conservatism and the liberalism that was becoming prevalent in the nineteenth century, which it dramatizes in the struggle of Johannes Rosmer, a prominent figure in his Norwegian village, to persuade his neighbors to become "emancipated." As Henrik Ibsen does in many other plays, here he uses physical setting symbolically, suggesting that conservative values are embodied in the Rosmer family home, Rosmersholm, which the villagers view as a place where tradition must be respected and innovation should be frowned upon.

Rosmersholm. Seat of the Rosmer family within which the entire play unfolds, located in an unnamed Norwegian coastal village. Rosmersholm is literally the home of Johannes Rosmer, but in keeping with the temper of the play, the title actually signifies his spiritual homecoming. His life, both personal and political, is stormy. Almost without realizing it, he finds himself associated with unpopular political causes and movements. His decision to abandon the beliefs of his ancestors for the freethinking ideals being promoted by modern philosophers and social reformers is an affront to the "house." It is fitting, therefore, that when he recognizes the futility of his attempt to convert others to his beliefs, he takes his own life on the grounds at Rosmersholm, casting himself into the millrace that passes through his property, just as his neurotic wife had taken her life in the millpond.

Ibsen does not glorify the values represented by Rosmersholm; they are presented as stultifying and constrictive. Nevertheless, through Rosmer's failed attempt to convert others to his radical brand of liberalism, the playwright suggests that radical ideologues of any persuasion are doomed to failure.

— *Laurence W. Mazzeno*

ROXANA

Author: Daniel Defoe (1660-1731)
Type of work: Novel
Type of plot: Picaresque

Time of plot: Seventeenth century
First published: 1724

Set during the time of England's King Charles II—which is associated with excess and vice—this novel describes Roxana's descent from middle-class respectability to whoredom and her subsequent accumulation of a vast fortune by the sale of her body and wise management of her money. Each geographical locale represents a stage in her moral decline.

*****London.** During the late seventeenth century, early capitalist London was the trade capital of the world, and Daniel Defoe's own obsession with commerce carries over into *Roxana*. Indeed, money, upon which London's capitalist society is built, is the only true love object throughout the novel. After Roxana's husband leaves her with five children, she herself abandons her children and becomes her landlord's mistress, beginning a pattern of selling herself to the highest bidders, typically signing contracts with her lovers, as if she were a merchant selling goods. Love plays no part in these exchanges.

In her efforts to transform herself and her place in society, Roxana amasses great wealth in London, lodging in Pall Mall, an area well known for housing royal mistresses. There, she entertains members of the city's high society with lavish masquerade parties. During one period in London, she spends seven years with an anonymous aristocrat—possibly the king himself. Her fortune grows with each affair in London.

***Paris.** By setting much of the novel in Paris, Defoe removed much of Roxana's wickedness from his own home city of London. This ploy also allowed Defoe to represent Paris money as dishonest money, accumulated by crime. In Paris, Roxana is intoxicated by dreams of money, high social rank, and the delusion that she can run away from her past.

Roxana's English landlord and lover, a wealthy jewel merchant, takes her to Paris where he is murdered. After she learns that the jewels she removes from her dead lover were stolen, she orders her servant, Amy, to sell all her possessions in London and join her in Paris. Through lying and cheating Roxana amasses an even more sizable fortune and sets herself up as a "she-merchant," who becomes increasingly intoxicated by accumulating wealth. After Roxana meets the French prince to whom the jeweler had intended to sell the jewels, she soon becomes his mistress. For eight years, she lives with the unnamed prince in close proximity to Paris.

Defoe utilizes Parisian settings to criticize how members of the French aristocracy, unlike London's bourgeois merchants, lavishly spend their wealth, saving little. Paris is thus represented as a place of vice and excess. It is in Paris, also, that Roxana discovers her previous husband and, fearing discovery, flees to Amsterdam.

***Amsterdam.** While it is evident that Defoe views Roman Catholic Paris as a prime place of debauchery, he views Holland in a positive light. For him, Holland, long a base of world exploration and commerce, represents strong Protestant values. In Amsterdam, money is earned cleanly and honestly. There, Roxana encounters an honest Dutch merchant who saves her from jail after her jewels are discovered to be stolen property. He helps her escape and attempts to marry her. Intent on maintaining her financial independence, however, Roxana becomes his lover but refuses marriage.

Throughout the novel, Roxana treasures her money and the freedom it gives her. Also, Roxana refuses the merchant because she dreams of achieving a higher social status than he can offer. In Amsterdam, Roxana often vacillates between profit and spirituality. After she returns to London, her Dutch merchant continues to accumulate wealth through hard work and honest trade. He eventually buys a noble title and marries Roxana after her servant sends word that her legal husband has died.

— *M. Casey Diana*

RUBÁIYÁT OF OMAR KHAYYÁM

Author: Edward FitzGerald (1809-1883)
Type of work: Poetry

First published: 1859

Locales of this poem range from a tavern, where the poet reflects on the benefits of wine, on the limits of human reason, and on the afterlife, to a garden beside a river, where the poet feels at one with the flowers, birds, and trees as he reflects on romantic love, the fate of heroes, and death, and to a pottery shop, where clay figures discuss the futility of trying to understand the purpose of human existence.

Tavern. Public inn in which the poet finds momentary relief from life's woes as he contemplates the fate of all humans: a brief life filled with cares and misfortune and followed by eternal oblivion. He counsels readers to devote themselves to a life of blissful forgetfulness, aided by wine, and to nurture a stoic acceptance of life's uncertainties and struggles. The poet searches his imagi-

nation to find apt metaphors to express his vision of life: Earthly existence is a meaningless series of nights and days, and humans are the pawns of destiny; they are moved about randomly like a ball on a playing field kicked by a celestial player. One's life on earth is like a moving finger, indelibly writing out human destiny, while heaven watches impassively through an impenetrable veil or remains enclosed behind a locked door which human reason cannot penetrate. The tavern is better than the temple for helping the individual endure, for its wine offers a glimpse of higher truths. He ponders the fate of heroic warriors of the past, long dead and quite forgotten. The sultan on his throne is in the end no better, and no better off, than the slave, for death equalizes all mortals for eternity.

In the tavern, one of the poem's major symbols predominates: wine. It symbolizes above all merriment, an escape from human cares into a world of pleasing speculations on the meaning of existence and the nature of the universe. Even the nightingale cries to the rose for wine, red wine. The nightingale symbolizes the poet, the melancholy singer, and the rose symbolizes the beloved who beckons him. The poet is drawn to his beloved, but wine is the more potent lure, for humans are like children lost in darkness and burdened by weak reasoning powers, and wine is the best, if not the only, escape from earthly woes and barren reason; wine gives one the power to confute the philosophers and to see beyond ordinary appearances into the spiritual world, beyond time and place into the realm of eternal truth.

Garden. Site on the bank of a river that symbolizes edenic serenity, harmony, beauty, and romantic love. There, the poet finds the rose, symbol of female beauty as well as the human spirit. In the garden, he finds temporary respite by the river, symbol of flowing time, and enjoys moments of pleasure with his beloved. The garden brings together many of the poem's principal symbols such as the bird, symbol of time and of the beauty of melody; it represents the earth, out of which humans are made and which houses them for eternity; it represents the great leveling force of nature, which reduces the mighty and the heroic figures of the past to the level of ordinary humans. The garden represents the spring of youth and the winter of old age; in the garden grow grapes and flowers, symbols of fertility and beauty. This garden wilderness opposes the dry logic of cold reason and the darkness of ignorance. Although it is subject to the passage of time, as humans are, this verdant world of beauty and light renews itself in the seasons and in night and day. It represents all of nature, the harvest, the water, and the wind that, like the human spirit, passes swiftly.

Potter's shop. Place in which a chorus of earthenware pots, speaking as humans, discuss the purpose of their existence. One of them finds it difficult to believe that the Creator would take the trouble to fashion him into an exquisite shape then crush him to common Earth. Another wonders why the Creator would make a misshapen pot, and yet another, unable to fathom the riddle of his existence, says that he could endure his fate better if he were filled with wine. The pottery symbolizes the fate of humans, who are molded by a Creator in varied shapes that ultimately crumble back into clay, unlike the rose, the grape, and all natural elements, which are renewed with the seasons.

— *Bernard E. Morris*

RUBYFRUIT JUNGLE

Author: Rita Mae Brown (1944-   )
Type of work: Novel
Type of plot: Social realism

Time of plot: Early 1950's through late 1960's
First published: 1973

As this novel's protagonist, Molly Bolt, narrates events from the time she is seven years old, in a rural area near York, Pennsylvania, through the family's move to Florida and her own move to New York City, it is clear that prejudice against homosexuality is without geographical boundaries.

*New York City. Largest and most cosmopolitan city in the United States that has long symbolized the highest challenge for American artists and entrepreneurs and the ultimate "escape" destination for individuals disaffected by the prejudices and limitations of their hometowns. Expelled from the University of Florida in Gainesville because she refused to renounce her lesbianism and denied a home with her mother for the same reason, Molly

Bolt hitchhikes to Manhattan, determined to succeed there on her own terms. Although liberating in its anonymity, in many ways the city is a hell for Molly because she has so little money. She meets other women with her sexual orientation and shares part of her life with some of them, but has no intention of settling down with a man.

The other film students at New York University are all men, and neither they nor the professor say a word to Molly when she shows her film of Carrie talking about her life. She graduates with academic honors, yet the film companies, even the underground filmmakers, stereotype her as someone who could only be hired as a secretary or in some other traditionally female capacity. Molly notes that there is a new women's movement beginning to protest such patriarchal attitudes, but she knows that some of those same women would expel her from the movement for being a lesbian. She does stay in New York, however, and remains determined to make movies her way.

Coffee Hollow. Molly's childhood home. She describes it as "a rural dot outside of York, Pennsylvania." York is mentioned again when Molly, age twenty-four, returns to the area for a brief visit. Her childhood friend and first love, Leota, is now conventionally married to a local body-shop owner, pretending to herself to be happy with him and her children. Leota claims not to remember her time with Molly, yet even as she denounces Molly's life as perverted and sick, she clearly envies her.

Although there is some love and support, especially from Molly's sad and defeated stepfather Carl, the dominant image of the Coffee Hollow area, representative of small-town America, is that of closed-minded busybodies intolerant of anyone different from them.

*****Florida.** Molly's and her cousin Leroy's families move from Coffee Hollow to Ft. Lauderdale to escape poverty but find little economic improvement there. Molly is bright and figures out that the wealthier students who control the social scene will like her if she is bold and witty and makes them laugh. She goes to the University of Florida because it offers her the largest scholarship, but she is expelled because of a sexual relationship with her roommate, Faye. Her roommate disappears, leaving a note saying that she lacks Molly's courage and must acquiesce to the rigid wishes of her parents.

Six years later, when Molly returns to Florida to make a film of her mother for her senior project, Carrie denies that she ever refused to take Molly in after she was expelled from the university. Molly also sees Leroy, who has begun an affair with a gay man but is now somewhat resigned to being married. He confides that he dreams of getting away, maybe to get a job as a crew member and sail around the world.

— *Lois A. Marchino*

R.U.R.

Author: Karel Čapek (1890-1938)
Type of work: Drama
Type of plot: Social satire

Time of plot: The future
First published: 1920 (English translation, 1923); first performed, 1921

On a remote island, sometime in the future, R.U.R, or Rossman's Universal Robots, creates an automated workforce to free human beings from the drudgery of labor. When a new formula is used that allows the robots to feel emotions, including hate, they revolt and take over the world, exterminating all human beings, including their makers, and create a new world that restores qualities that human society has lost.

Island. Unnamed island in an unspecified remote location that is the initial launching ground for the robot revolt. By the end of the play, the island becomes a kind of Eden, where the last human man witnesses the birth of love between a young robot couple that holds the promise of a new kind of humanity, albeit a robot one.

Rossman's Universal Robots office. Central office of R.U.R., in which Harry Domin, the general manager, meet Helena Glory, who has come to tour the factory. Harry eventually proposes marriage in a manner that suggests a business transaction. It is fitting that such a proposal takes place in his office.

Helena's drawing room. Ten years after Helena and Harry marry, their drawing room is neatly appointed, revealing the humanizing and feminine influence that Helena brings to the otherwise sterile environment of the robot factory.

Laboratory. Workplace where Alquist—the last human still alive—experiments on robots, hoping to rediscover the formula for their manufacture. He fails but confronts a young robot couple who exhibit signs of romantic love. They have already transcended Alquist's ability to propagate their race and reveal a humanity that all human beings in the play—except Helena—ironically lack.

— *Philip Bader*

RUSLAN AND LYUDMILA

Author: Alexander Pushkin (1799-1837)
Type of work: Poetry
Type of plot: Mock-heroic

Time of plot: Late tenth century
First published: Ruslan i Lyudmila, 1820 (English translation, 1936)

This poem, Alexander Pushkin's first major work, blends the themes of several Russian fairy tales to create a story of an abducted bride who must be rescued by her beloved. It includes references to both historical and imaginary places. With his light tone Pushkin makes a story line that is often deadly serious into a humorous work. Lyudmila plays pranks upon her captor and endeavors to escape. Even the narrator laughs and jokes to the reader.

*****Kiev** (kyehv). Russian city (now part of Ukraine) that is the home of the knight Ruslan and the princess Lyudmila; located in a steppe (similar to the American prairie). The characters of the poem are loosely based upon historical figures of the period, but there is little sense of that history in Pushkin's treatment of it. Instead, Kiev is here a fairy-tale city, home of a fairy-tale king and his many sons.

*****Dnieper** (DNYEH-pehr). Major river of the steppe, upon the western bank of which Kiev is built, where Ruslan fights his rival Rogdai, whom he defeats and throws into the water to drown and be taken by the river-maiden, a Russian folk spirit.

Midnight Mountains. Fictional stronghold of the evil wizard Chornomor. Perhaps inspired by travelers' stories of the Caucasus Mountains and their proud tribes, these fairy-tale mountains are full of perils, including a deadly dragon and a magical dwarf with superhuman strength. The tower of the sorcerer Chernomor is filled with magical delights, but the people within are slaves, whom he has captured through guile.

— *Leigh Husband Kimmel*

S

THE SACRED FOUNT

Author: Henry James (1843-1916)
Type of work: Novel
Type of plot: Psychological realism

Time of plot: 1890's
First published: 1901

The primary setting for this strange novella is an English country house to which several people come from London for a weekend retreat. During the course of the weekend the unnamed narrator, who may be mad, becomes convinced that the apparently innocent diversions of his fellow guests conceal lurid, exploitative sexual relationships, grand sacrifices, and silent suffering.

Newmarch. House in the English countryside, somewhere between London and Birmingham. Because of the "detective" angle to the story, Newmarch bears a faint resemblance to a remote Gothic estate. However, while the Gothic heroines of literature are usually isolated from civilization and friends, Henry James's unidentified narrator is in Newmarch for a social occasion—indeed, a familiar social ritual.

Newmarch represents the height of British civilization: A place in which wit and appearances are the supreme values. It is seemingly the superficiality of the social gathering that makes the narrator imagine all kinds of "horrors" beneath the too-perfect surface, after he detects what seems to him to be a "flaw." In typical Jamesian irony, this "flaw" is a mysterious "improvement" in the wit of one of the guests, which actually makes him "fit in" to Newmarch better than before. Newmarch provides precisely the kind of atmosphere in which a subtle narrator may be expected to flourish. It is "the great asylum of the finer wit," in which people meet to do nothing but talk brilliantly—unless the narrator is correct and they also meet to conduct shadowy love affairs. The narrator's theory of the hidden depths of Newmarch may be the finest flower of its superficiality and idleness.

During an apparently perfectly innocent scene in which guests at Newmarch gather in the evening to hear a pianist that the narrator, in a moment of epiphany, makes a connection between the inhuman beauty and order and cold composure of the kind of society represented by Newmarch and its capacity for cruelty, as though by its refusal to acknowledge certain aspects of reality it victimizes the people who represent them. High society forces one to wear a mask that betrays no emotion. The ugliness of truth and suffering would destroy the serene beauty of what the narrator calls "our civilized state." The beauty of Newmarch is predicated on repression and denial.

The disjunction between masklike appearances and a horrifying reality at Newmarch is most explicitly brought out in a grotesque painting in the gallery of a man holding a mask. One of the characters offers the interpretation that the figure is holding a mask of Death, but the narrator objects that it is the man's real face that is a death-mask, which makes the hard, inhuman, object of art into a mask of Life. Thus, the inhabitants of Newmarch, in the narrator's opinion, conceal the horrifying truth of the immanence of death by wearing inhumanly perfect masks while living a kind of death-in-life that denies profound emotion along with everything else unpleasant.

— *Elise Moore*

THE SAGA OF GRETTIR THE STRONG

Author: Unknown
Type of work: Folklore
Type of plot: Adventure

Time of plot: Eleventh century
First transcribed: Grettis Saga, c. 1300 (English translation, 1869)

Although Iceland figures prominently in this saga, the places and landscapes of the narrative span the entire Scandinavian world and beyond. Each setting—whether hall, forest, mountain, or broad sea—is, in a style typical of sagas, sparsely described. Nevertheless, place is of paramount importance to the saga. Grettir's status as outlaw places him beyond the protection and constraints of society, thus each locale holds great narrative tension as each contains the promise of peril and adventure.

*Iceland. Northern Atlantic island nation, populated mainly by farmers and ruled by chieftains, that is Grettir's homeland. Much of the saga's actions occur in its farmsteads built from turf, timber, and stone or in its icy wastes, sparse woods, rugged mountains, and remote smaller islands. Amid these settings, the saga writer pits the world of community, social interaction, and protection under the law against the harshness of the wilds. Grettir, as an outlaw, must continually navigate the threats and dangers of both. Often enough, these places are under the control of powerful, malevolent, fantastic beings and creatures, as the hero finds himself battling trolls, revenants (people who have returned from the dead), and evil spells.

*Biarg** (by-AHRG). Icelandic birthplace of Grettir. It is here that the hero's stubbornness, strength, and irascible attitude first manifests itself in his interactions with his father, Asmund Longhair. After his father's death, Grettir's mother remains there to bear the loss of her husband and the outlawry and deaths of her children. Grettir's occasional secretive visits are constant reminders of his alienation from his kinsmen.

*Drangey** (DRANG-ay). Remote island in a fjord along the northern coast of Iceland. After years, of outlawry, Grettir, his younger brother Illugi, and a servant withdraw here and are able to defend themselves easily because the island, having no inlet, is only accessible by rope ladders. After succumbing to evil spells, Grettir is given his deathblow there by Thorbjorn Angle, who seeks to regain control of the island. In many ways Drangey's rugged landscape and remoteness are apt metaphors for the hero's own strength and isolation.

*Norway.** Northern European Scandinavian land that was the ancestral home of most Icelanders and a destination for the outlawed Grettir. For most saga heroes, one's reputation at home is enhanced by adventures abroad. Grettir's raiding of a haunted tomb as well as slaying of berserkers and a ravenous bear there ensure his fame and reputation throughout Scandinavia. These initial heroic acts are later juxtaposed with the bad luck he encounters on his second trip abroad. Grettir's bungled attempt to obtain fire from the occupants of an inn cause the burning death of all those inside and brings down upon the hero contempt and banishment by the king of Norway. This event illustrates that Grettir's ill luck, predicted in Iceland after the death of the revenant Glam, is not linked to place and is therefore inescapable.

*Constantinople.** Capital of the Byzantine Empire, in which is now Turkey, and home of the Varangian guard, a troop of Viking warriors who serve the emperor. After his outlawry for the slaying of Grettir, Thorbjorn Angle flees to this capital and enlists in the emperor's guard. His later death there at the hands of Grettir's half brother, Thorsteinn Dromund, is remarkable for the great distance traveled, essentially spanning the entire known world, in order to reap revenge. Moreover, the setting of this act of revenge, amid a throng of people in a city known for its size, culture, and law, stands in contrast to the culturally and physical remote scene of Grettir's death on Drangey.

— *Joseph R. Carroll*

THE SAILOR WHO FELL FROM GRACE WITH THE SEA

Author: Yukio Mishima (Kimitake Hiraoka, 1925-
1970)
Type of work: Novel
Type of plot: Psychological realism

Time of plot: After World War II
First published: Gogo no eikō, 1963 (English
translation, 1965)

The main locations of this novel are the major Japanese seaport of Yokohama, the home of the Kuroda family, and the clothing store operated by the mother. Images of the land and sea are central to the development of the story's darkly perverted plot and nihilistic theme.

*Yokohama. Major Japanese seaport that represents the symbolic place where the land or human culture meets the sea or untamed nature. Noboru, like many boys, is fascinated by the dark call of dangerous foreign seas and the apparently unfettered life of a sailor. This fascination represents an adolescent and romanticized vision of life that is the opposite of the land-bound bourgeois existence he and his friends detest in the adult world they see in Yokohama. Noboru shares this view of the authentic life with Ryuji Tsukazaki who, when he was a young man, had become a sailor for similar reasons. Tsukazaki's plan to marry Noboru's mother and abandon his sailor's life to become a manager in the Kuroda clothing shop in Yokohama is a large element in what the boy and his friends see as a betrayal of their romantic vision. It is also what gives the psychological impetus to the imminent act of terrible violence planned by the group of boys that looms at the novel's conclusion.

Kuroda home. Stately home built by Noboru's now-deceased father. From its hilltop location, it commands a beautiful view of Yokohama Bay. The family bedrooms are on the second floor, and Noboru is locked in his room every night by his overprotective mother, Fusako.

Bedrooms often serve as literary topos, or themes, in which the subjective and irrational sides of the human personality are prominent: Bedrooms are both places where people sleep (the subjective world of dreams) and places where sexual relations occur (the irrational world of sexuality). From a secret peephole in his own bedroom, Noboru regularly watches his mother undress and is filled with feelings of the utter emptiness and ugliness of existence. In this clearly Oedipal situation, the adolescent Noboru feels no arousal and seemingly denies any feelings. The author himself, a highly intelligent and sensitive person with his own deeply conflicted sensuality (married to a woman but also actively homosexual), seems, in his descriptions of Noboru in his bedroom, to portray his own difficulties with human sexuality.

From the bedroom, Noboru also dispassionately observes his mother's love affair with Tsukazaki, whom she intends to marry. Noboru's lack of all emotion at what he sees in his mother's bedroom is the product of his involvement with a group of fellow students—all convinced, in typically adolescent bravado, of their own genius—who follow a philosophy of total nihilism and strive to view everything with dispassionate objectivity. The novel's conclusion—in which the boys lure Tsukazaki to his execution—offers a chilling look into a nihilistic world devoid of human warmth, an irrational vision that begins symbolically, at the novel's opening, in the boy's bedroom with its secret peephole.

Kuroda clothing shop. Clothes shop located in Yokohama that was founded by Noboru's father and is now operated by the mother. The shop deals with expensive fashion imported from Europe and America and serves the wealthy clientele of nearby Tokyo who include a number of famous movie actors and actresses. Yukio Mishima uses the shop as a vehicle to criticize the shallow world of the rich elite of postwar Japanese society, especially in the figure of the attractive, but superficial and insecure, actress with whom Fusako has lunch. The clothing shop is representative of the nonauthentic bourgeois life that Noboru and the other boys so violently reject.

— *Thomas F. Barry*

SAINT JOAN

Author: George Bernard Shaw (1856-1950)
Type of work: Drama
Type of plot: Historical

Time of plot: Early fifteenth century
First performed: 1923; first published, 1924

Although this play uses the actual historical locations of events in Joan of Arc's brief career as the commander of the French army against the occupying English, the great castles and cathedrals provide a humorously ironic contrast to the matter-of-fact earthiness of George Bernard Shaw's Joan, who, though a simple country girl, is intimidated by neither high social rank nor the grandeur of the sites.

*Vaucouleurs castle (voh-kew-lewr). Castle of Robert de Baudricourt in which the play opens. A historical place, the castle stands near the Meuse River, between Lorraine and Champagne, not far from Joan's home village of Domremy. The castle represents the first stage of Joan's odyssey to fulfill her Lord's commands; she must convince Robert to supply her with a horse and an escort to Chinon, where she wants to see the Dauphin, the heir presumptive to the French throne.

The seeming invulnerability of the Vaucouleurs stronghold is indicated by the furnishings of the first-floor room where Robert sits: a "plain strong oak table," a "stout four-legged stool," and a wooden chest. His position on a floor above Joan, which allows him to look down upon her in the lower courtyard, indicates his social superiority. A doorway leads to a winding stair to the courtyard, where Joan waits impatiently for an audience with Robert. When Robert's knight Bertrand de Poulengy enters the castle, he places the stool between the table and the window, just as he acts as an intermediary between Joan and Robert.

Although he is weak-willed, Robert tries to be as imposing as his castle when he finally admits Joan, who easily deflects his arguments with her presumption that her miraculous mission and her logical reasons will enlighten him. This scene represents the triumph of human reason over class snobbery, and identifies Joan as the herald of democracy.

*Chinon (sheeh-NON). Town in Touraine where Joan meets the Dauphin. The curtain that separates the antechamber in which the second scene takes place from the Chinon throne room hints at the curtains that screen the realities of power from ostensible ones. Immature and perhaps illegitimate, the Dauphin is ignored by the real powers in France—his government ministers and

the leaders of the Church. To test Joan's claims that she has been sent by God, the Dauphin and Bluebeard exchange their clothing and their places in the ceremonial order. By immediately recognizing the disguised Dauphin, Joan inspires courage in him, and he gives her charge of the French army. Joan thus demonstrates that common sense may prevail over pretensions, and that places, even the throne room, fail to intimidate her, armed as she is with the sword of God.

*Battlefields. In battles between the French and English on the banks of the Loire River, at Orleans, Joan demonstrates that her conception of warfare makes more sense than the prevailing view of war as a kind of game. The wind that changes direction in the favor of the French not only suggests Joan's divine mission, but hints at a change in Joan's fortune. Indeed, Joan is reported wounded in these scenes. In spite of her wound, she continues to fight, firming the resolve of her army, and firming the resolve of the Church's leaders to burn her, as she places her own private judgments above the dictates of the Church.

*Rheims (reemz; now spelled Reims). Historic city in northeastern France whose cathedral was the traditional site of royal coronations. The play's fifth scene is set in an ambulatory near the foot of the cathedral's vestry, where Joan prays beneath a cross while the Dauphin is crowned King Charles VII. This ancient site of the crowning of kings parallels Joan's fortunes, as she is at the height of her powers, the point at which her fortunes are about to change because she has incurred the indignation of the Church.

*Rouen castle (REW-ahn). Normandy city on the lower Seine, west of Paris, where Joan is tried for heresy in the stone hall of the city's great castle. In scene 6, the elevated seating of the many ecclesiastical judges is juxtaposed with the plain wooden stool below on which she sits, indicating the extent to which the odds are stacked against Joan. Despite her good sense, the political intrigues and subtle theological sophistries of the Church overwhelm Joan's youthful and unschooled naïveté, and she is condemned to be burnt in the adjoining courtyard, indicated by the reddening of the window of the castle.

King's château. The epilogue occurs on a restless night in 1456, the year Joan was officially rehabilitated. Now king for many years, Charles dreams of Joan and the other participants in the drama that had occurred some twenty-five years earlier. His bed is raised, and the canopy bears the royal arms, but other than that, nothing distinguishes this room from an ordinary bedroom, just as nothing inherent indicates the superiority of the man himself. A sudden darkness in the room indicates that, while Joan accomplished her goals with regard to Charles, neither he nor anyone else wants her to return, as saints are easier to tolerate dead than alive.

— *Jo N. Farrar*

ST. PETER'S UMBRELLA

Author: Kálmán Mikszáth (1847-1910)
Type of work: Novel
Type of plot: Comic realism

Time of plot: Late nineteenth century
First published: Szent Péter Esernyöje, 1895 (English translation, 1900)

This novel is an account of a seemingly miraculous transformation that affects both the principal character of the story, Gyury Wibra, and its chief setting, the village of Glogova, with each aspect mirroring and amplifying the other.

Glogova (glog-AH-vah). Small Hungarian village (now part of Slovakia), between Selmecbánya and Besztercebánya, located in a narrow valley between barren mountain slopes. The stream that flows through the valley, the Biela Voda, can be dangerous when swollen by sudden rain. Glogova has a small thatched schoolhouse, the majority of whose pupils bear a suspicious resemblance to the schoolmaster, who is the only man who remains in the village during the summer months, when other men go down to the plain to work as laborers.

When the village is first described—in advance of the arrival of its new priest, János Bélyi—it is a miserable place, its clay soil being full of pebbles, unable to lend much support to any crops but oats and potatoes. The pale feathergrass that grows in abundance resembles grey hair, giving the impression that the land is old and decrepit. However, giant rocks looming over the valley lend a certain dignity to the peasant hovels. Although no flowers grow there, save mallow in the villagers' gardens, the air is perfumed by elder and juniper. The village has no proper land registry, having lost its records in a fire, so all the villagers till as much land as they can and leave the remainder to the Church—a circumstance that embodies an allegory of the villagers' attitude to spiritual matters.

When the new priest arrives, he inherits nothing from his predecessor but a bad dog, but his fortunes are transformed when his orphaned infant sister is brought to him and is saved from exposure to a storm by the unexplained appearance of an umbrella over her basket—the first of several apparent miracles associated with the umbrella.

When the story returns to Glogova in its last chapters, the valley has been transformed by the wealth imported as a consequence of outsiders who come to the village wishing to be married under the miraculous umbrella. When Gyury pursues Veronica, having discovered that he cares more for her than for his lost fortune, the chase takes him across Magát's cloverfield, Srankóas' maize fields, Szlávik's corn fields to Gongoly's meadow—a sequence redolent of the valley's new prosperity, whose symbolism is further extended by the rediscovery of Veronica's discarded ring when grass in the meadow is cut to make hay.

Besztercebánya (behs-tehrt-seh-BAHN-ya; now Banská Bystrica). Town on the Garam River, where the wealthy bachelor Pál Gregorics lives in an ugly stone house. The town is a model of bourgeois conformity; all its drawing rooms are furnished in exactly the same style, and all are equipped with cherrywood pianos. Behind Pál's house is a smaller one, set in an orchard known as the "**Lebanon**," that he buys to house his cook and mistress; it becomes the subject of a bizarre auction when the old man's would-be heirs hear about a potentially valuable caldron walled up inside. Gyury returns to the old Gregorics house when he becomes György Wibra, attorney-at-law. The Jewish merchant Jónás Müncz's shop is on Wheat Street.

Bábaszék (behb-ah-TSHEK). Mountain village near Zólyom, where Müncz's widow takes up residence, summoned to open a shop there because the inhabitants wish to sustain the illusion that their village is really a town and they have been told that no town is worthy of the name unless it has a resident Jew. Gyury first meets Veronica in the so-called town hall. but the most significant setting featured in the story is the Mravuscáns' house. When Gyury and his traveling companions dine and spend a night there, Gyury has a dream about Saint Peter. His subsequent journey from Bábaszék to Glogova, through the Liskovina Woods full of birch trees, ferns, and anthoxantum flowers. past the old castle of Szlatina and the Brána mountain, is described in loving detail.

Haláp. Village in which Veronica Bélyi was born and orphaned at the age of two, when her widowed mother died. The local judge ordered that she should rotate her residence among all the families in the village—an arrangement that lasted only ten days.

*Pest (pesht). City (now part of Hungary's capital, Budapest) in which Gyury attends university. He lives at a lodginghouse called "Seven Owls" and dines at a cheap restaurant called the "First of April."

*Szeged (SEDJ-ed). City on the Danube River where the precious umbrella falls into water, causing the commotion that reveals its true value.

— *Brian Stableford*

ŚAKUNTALĀ

Author: Kālidāsa (c. 100 B.C.E. or 340 C.E.-c. 40 B.C.E. or 400 C.E.)
Type of work: Drama
Type of plot: Love

Time of plot: Golden Age of India
First performed: Abhijñānaśākuntala, c. 45 B.C.E. or c. 395 C.E. (English translation, 1789)

In this ancient Indian drama, Kalidasa, influenced by the Hindu idea of the natural world as a manifestation of god, contrasts the idealized forest settings of the play's opening scenes with a town and a royal palace to underscore the characters' journey from ignorance to love.

Sacred forest. Site where King Dushyanta is hunting as the play opens and where he meets and falls in love with Śakuntalā. He is an intruder in the forest, in contrast to Śakuntalā, who considers animals and plants her kin. Local religious devotees ask Dushyanta, who is devout, not to kill any animals in the vicinity; he assents, but his presence nonetheless upsets the balance of life in the forest, much as Śakuntalā's visit to his palace later in the play upsets the established order there.

King Dushyanta's palace. Here Śakuntalā comes to plead her case with the king, who, due to a curse, has no memory of their love. Courtiers declaim elaborate, somewhat artificial poetry whose nature imagery ironically echoes earlier, happier scenes. Significantly, it is only when Dushyanta retreats to his garden, where he has been attempting to paint a picture of Śakuntalā's forest home—another artificial reach toward nature's authenticity—that deliverance from his troubles comes: a summons from Indra, chief of the gods. He requests Dushyanta's help in defeating a powerful demon.

Sacred grove of Kashyapa (KAWSH-yuh-puh). After triumph in battle, Dushyanta comes here to worship. His faith and his service to Indra are rewarded: He is reunited with Śakuntalā and meets, for the first time, their son, who shows signs of future valor. As in act 1, the action is set in a sacred wood, but now both Dushyanta and Śakuntalā have been brought into harmony with the setting through their devotion and selfless service.

— *Hayes Hampton*

SALAMMBÔ

Author: Gustave Flaubert (1821-1880)
Type of work: Novel
Type of plot: Historical

Time of plot: Third century B.C.E.
First published: 1862 (English translation, 1886)

Gustave Flaubert's purpose in this novel is to make the dead past live again in a literary medium. Flaubert chose to reanimate Carthage precisely because it had vanished more completely than Rome or Athens. He made every possible effort to remain faithful to what was known about the history and geography of the ancient city, but modern archaeology has exposed the inaccuracy of some of his inventions.

*Carthage.** Ancient North African city, whose ruins can now be found in the marshland northeast of Tunis. In classical times Carthage stood on a peninsula (the modern coastline has been much altered by wind-driven sand). It was originally a Phoenician colony founded in the ninth century B.C.E., but it grew to become Rome's greatest rival, the conflicts between the two imperially ambitious city-states being known as the Punic Wars. The great Carthaginian hero of the first Punic War (264-241 B.C.E.), Hamilcar Barca, is one of the principal characters of *Salammbô*.

Flaubert imagines Carthage protected on its landward side by a moat, a rampart of turf, and a two-story wall thirty cubits (about 45 feet) high. This would make Carthage virtually impregnable, although the aqueduct carrying the city's water supply, which runs obliquely across the narrowest part of the peninsula, would be an obvious point of vulnerability. Within the outer wall is Malqua, a quarter inhabited by seamen and dyers. The inner city is laid out in tiers, like an amphitheater, blurred boundaries still delineating three ancient quarters, each one studded with temples. The hill of the Acropolis is a confused mass of monuments and temples. Megara is the newest part of the city, extending to a cliff where a huge lighthouse stands. The suburb of Mouloya clings to the slope behind the lighthouse, with the Teveste gate at its further edge; it is by this route that Salammbô leaves the city when she goes to the barbarian camp.

Megara's palace. The tallest building in the city, constructed from yellow-flecked Numidian marble; the home of Hamilcar Barca. Salammbô, his daughter and a priestess of Tanit, lives in the topmost of its four terraced stories. The adjoining grounds enclose numerous subsidiary structures, including winepresses, bakeries, warehouses, arsenals, lion pits, a prison, and an elephant enclosure. Also enclosed is a garden, which is the site of an opulent feast celebrating the end of the war. Here Hamilcar entertains the mercenaries who helped him withstand the might of Rome.

*Utica** and *Hippo Zarytus.** Small cities neighboring Carthage, independent but allied with her. Both are attacked in the novel by the mercenary army, and the territory between them, which includes several smaller towns and the Pass of the Battle-Axe, where the crucial battle is fought, is hotly disputed in the war between Hamilcar's forces and the rebellious forces.

Temple of Tanit. A sprawling edifice with abundant grounds arranged in three enclosures, situated at the foot of the Acropolis. A rectangular tower, flanked by two long porticoes, contains an inner sanctum where only priests may go. The principal idol of Tanit is encircled by twelve blue crystal globes mounted on monstrous statues in such a manner that they can be rotated. Behind the chariot on which the idol stands is a covert containing the sacred Zaïmph: the veil of Tanit, symbolic of the city's fortunes, whose theft by Mâtho is of tremendous significance.

The accounts of Phoenician mythology current in Flaubert's day imagined Tanit as one element in a supreme triad whose other elements were Baal-Ammon and Eschmoûn. Flaubert presumed, as many of his contemporaries did, that the fearsome and bloodthirsty pagan god named Moloch in the Old Testament was Baal-Ammon, so the other temples featured in the plot as significant locations are the Temple of Moloch and the Temple of Eschmoûn, both close neighbors of the Temple of Tanit in Flaubert's city plan. In the sacrificial ceremony featured in chapter 13, Moloch's brazen idol and effigies, representing many other aspects of Baal, are brought through the streets to the square in front of the Temple of Eschmoûn, their gathering symbolizing a city in crisis.

— *Brian Stableford*

SAMSON AGONISTES

Author: John Milton (1608-1674)
Type of work: Drama
Type of plot: Tragedy

Time of plot: c. 1100 B.C.E.
First published: 1671

Based on the Old Testament account of Samson, this play is set outside a prison and later at a theater in Gaza on a festival day honoring the Philistine god Dagon. The place and day are integral to the themes of betrayal, faith, self-sacrifice, and redemption.

*Gaza. Philistine city. The prison is at once a literal punishment by the Philistines for the Nazarite Samson's Hebraic faith and fight against the Philistines and a metaphorical punishment for Samson's betrayal of himself and his God. Once metaphorically blind to Dalila's treachery, Samson has been physically blinded by the enemy to whom his wife has betrayed him. As the heart of Philistine power, Gaza marks first the nadir and later the zenith of Samson's faith and power. Each of his visitors, the chorus, his father (Manoa), Dalila, and the giant from Gath, Harapha, allows him to show moral strength, revealing to him the strength of his faith and the use to which God plans to put his restored physical strength.

Theater. Site where Philistines from Gaza and the surrounding cities gathered for the festival. The theater becomes the focal point of irony and divine justice when Samson turns a potentially degrading spectacle of enslaved strength into a triumphant act of faith, self-sacrifice, redemption, and the power of his God.

— *Daryl Holmes*

SANCTUARY

Author: William Faulkner (1897-1962)
Type of work: Novel
Type of plot: Melodrama

Time of plot: 1929
First published: 1931

In this novel, as in his other works, William Faulkner employs his native state of Mississippi, his home county and town in a fictional transformation resulting in the county of Yoknapatawpha.

Yoknapatawpha County (YOK-nuh-puh-TAW-fuh). Faulkner's mythical county, which is a setting in several of his works. The **Old Frenchman's Place** is an abandoned plantation house deep in the county, which has been taken over by bootleggers. The violent actions that set the plot of the novel in motion—arguments, fights, a rape, and a murder—occur in and around the old house and barn. Faulkner contrasts this violence and the unsavory nature of most of the characters with the beauty of the natural surroundings, to which the bootleggers are insensitive. Thus, place becomes an integral part of the plot, especially in the contrast between the natural world and what mankind has made of the environment. Characters in the novel associated with the city of Memphis tend to be evil, or at least amoral, while those closer to nature (Horace Benbow, for example) tend to be virtuous—or at least to make an attempt to be. Old abandoned houses are recurrent elements in gothic fiction, and the plantation house, now put to a new purpose, serves as the setting for the events of the plot.

*Memphis. Tennessee city across the state line from Mississippi that is portrayed as something of a "sin city" in *Sanctuary*, and it is true that there was considerable crime in that city at the time of the story. Mulberry Street reflects a real downtown thoroughfare in Memphis, in which the red-light district was located. Such houses are another standard trapping of gothic fiction. Significantly, it is in this house on Mulberry Street that Horace Benbow confronts the fact that evil exists as a real force in his world.

Jefferson. Town in the northwestern corner of the state of Mississippi. Faulkner drew many details from Oxford, his hometown, for his portrayal of Jefferson, although he altered it to suit his needs. Both towns are set in the hills of northeastern Mississippi, which was settled in the first half of the nineteenth century by British, Scottish, and Welsh immigrants who had migrated from Virginia or the Carolinas. Faulkner makes much of the parallels between Jefferson and the real Oxford, but he also draws details from other northern Mississippi towns to round out his creation. He employs specific locations within the town, the courthouse and jail, which also figure in the sequel to this novel, *Requiem for a Nun* (1951).

Sartoris plantation. Farm on the outskirts of Jefferson built by Colonel John Sartoris and inhabited during the time of the events in *Sanctuary* by his sister, elderly Virginia DuPre; Narcissa, the widow of the colonel's great-grandson; Benbow, the child of Bayard and Narcissa; and several black servants. The old house represents the Old South and is a decided contrast to the house in which the bootleggers have established their business. The Sartoris plantation is no longer active, as it was in Faulkner's *Sartoris* (1929), and it may be on the way to being abandoned, just as the Old Frenchman's Place has been.

*Oxford. Town in northeastern Mississippi in which the University of Mississippi ("Ole Miss") is located. Temple Drake is a coed there, and although the town is not named in the novel, its description and the physical details resemble Oxford. It is a decided irony that Faulkner uses both Oxford and Jefferson in this novel, since his mythical Jefferson is actually based on Oxford, his hometown.

*Taylor. Small village, still in existence, south of Oxford, where Temple goes by train for her tryst with Gowan Stevens, an illicit act that is the impetus for the subsequent violence of the novel.

— *W. Kenneth Holditch*

SANINE

Author: Mikhail Artsybashev (1878-1927)
Type of work: Novel
Type of plot: Philosophical

Time of plot: 1906
First published: Sanin, 1907 (English translation, 1915)

Set in Russia in an unnamed provincial town, this philosophical novel of ideas portrays an alienated younger generation at odds with the oppressive environment of early twentieth century Russia. The dull, almost moribund community depicted here is unable to satisfy or even interest its young members, who wander the streets in search of excitement; there is simply no place where they can feel at home in a backwater devoid of either purpose or pleasure for those who yearn to escape to the urban delights of St. Petersburg or Moscow.

Provincial town. Unnamed Russian community in which almost the entire novel takes place. The town is characterized as being unremarkable and thoroughly typical, an example of Russian society in microcosm. Nothing within the town either deserves or receives extensive depiction, and even characters who are new to the town traverse its streets without seeing anything that captures their attention. Against this backdrop of the mundane and the conventional, the violent disruption of the community's social life by Vladimir Petrovitch Sanine seems particularly shocking. Sanine is a cynic, anarchist, and apostle of complete sexual freedom who exhorts his young and impressionable followers to act on impulse rather than with regard to moral conventions. What follows is an epidemic of seductions and suicides, as his ideas prove to be much more difficult to act on in reality than they appear to be in theory.

Sanine house. Residence of the novel's principal character, Sanine, and his mother, Maria, and sister Lidia. A once-proud edifice on the main street of the unnamed town, this ancient mansion is in poor repair and much too large for its few inhabitants. Sanine's lack of interest in maintaining the family home or fulfilling the traditional responsibilities of a prominent citizen is one of many ways that the narrative conveys his disaffection from conventional society.

Svarogitsch house. Residence of Sanine's most effective opponent among the townsfolk, Yourii Svarogitsch, and his father and his sister, Lialia. Ranking among the town's leading families, the Svarogitsches support their son's liberal political views and artistic aspirations. Initially portrayed as a place of beauty and enlightenment, their household is shattered by Yourii's suicide when he fails to reconcile his idealistic beliefs with the realities of sexual passion. The consequent paralysis of Yourii's father, Colonel Svarogitsch, is an apt symbol of the failure of the community's traditional leaders to adjust to contemporary conditions.

Sarudine's rooms. Home of Vladimir Sarudine, an army officer and the seducer of Sanine's sister, Lidia. A center of masculine camaraderie in a military establishment, Sarudine's smoke-filled rooms are a place in which the town's wilder young men plot the seduction of their intended female victims.

Convent and monastery. Communities of religious orders in the town that are centers of social, rather than religious, activity. Although spatially separated, both the convent and the monastery are depicted as picturesque and quaintly old-fashioned excursion destinations for the town's middle- and upper-class youths. Several impassioned love scenes are played out against these congenial but spiritually irrelevant institutions, which appear to offer nothing more than convenient trysting places for the younger generation and thus further represent the decay of traditional values that is a major theme of the novel.

Steam mill. Part of a factory outside the town where occasional political meetings are held by progressive political activists. The gray, gloomy atmosphere of the mill is echoed by the dull, pointless political discussions conducted there, where sectarian bickering and class differences sabotage any possibility of useful action.

*St. Petersburg. Russia's capital city at the time in which the novel is set and the center of national cultural life. St. Petersburg is frequently mentioned as the city in which a meaningful life can be lived, but it is also feared as a place that may reject provincials who do not measure up to its standards.

Train. Conveyance on which Sanine travels in the novel's concluding scene. Unable to tolerate the coarse behavior of his fellow travelers, Sanine leaps off in a deserted stretch of countryside, and then sets out to discover a more hopeful future. The physical context of his action, in which he severs all ties with organized society, implies that he must travel this road by himself, with no assurance of success.

— *Paul Stuewe*

SAPPHO

Author: Alphonse Daudet (1840-1897)
Type of work: Novel
Type of plot: Naturalism

Time of plot: Nineteenth century
First published: Sapho, 1884 (English translation, 1886)

This novel's portraits of French life, both in the provinces and in Paris, provide a vivid, highly descriptive contrast between the gentle country people whose struggles to save their ancestral vines are steeped in natural, wholesome goodness, and the fast life of Paris society, mired in corruption, indolence, and vice. Into the latter world the student Jean Gaussin is drawn by the seductive power of his alliance with Fanny Legrande, otherwise known as Sappho.

Paris. Capital of France in which the novel opens in the midst of a costume ball at the home of the wealthy engineer Déchelette on the rue de Rome. Alphonse Daudet's detailed description of the event and its illustrious personages, as seen through the eyes of the twenty-one-year-old student Gaussin, who has recently come to Paris from the south of France, reveals that the elegant lifestyle of the wealthy and famous socialites is but a facade. The gay masks behind which they hide foreshadow the revelations of hypocrisy and duplicity to follow.

While the grand hall appears like a fairy tale to Gaussin, he is uncomfortable and about to leave the ball when the courtesan Fanny Legrand, in the guise of an Egyptian woman, entices him with conversation, accompanying him to his student lodging in the rue Jacob. There, Gaussin chivalrously offers to carry Fanny up the four steep landings of the narrow stairway, but, in one of the funnier visual moments of the book, he is soon panting like a piano carrier despite his youth and enthusiasm for the task. Afterward, Fanny reappears frequently at his door for uninvited trysts; they walk about Paris, visiting cafés and bumping into once-famous artists who are now tarnished by time and dissipation, but whom Fanny always seems to know.

Eventually, Fanny entices Gaussin to come to her house on the rue de l'Arcade. It, too, appears opulent and luxurious on the surface, but the noisy arrival of a dejected suitor, whom Fanny berates in a low and vulgar fashion, quickly destroys the image of comfort and ease. Gaussin returns to his spartan student quarters, where he repeatedly turns away Fanny's visits and prepares for his exams. When Gaussin becomes ill, Fanny seizes the opportunity to entrench herself in his life. They set up housekeeping on the rue d'Amsterdam, amid all the uproar of a nearly railway terminus. Eventually, however, Gaussin learns of Fanny's checkered past. He loses his respect for her and returns to his family's country estate.

Castelet estate (kast-eh-lay). Once-renowned vineyard in southern France to which Gaussin returns. The estate brought prosperity to Gaussin's family in the past, but it has been brought close to run by his uncle's weakness of character and a series of agricultural disasters. Gaussin's mother, an invalid, and his aunt, the selfless Divonne, as well as his two saintly sisters Martha and Mary, serve as dramatic moral contrasts to the corrupted Fanny, whom Gaussin often thinks derisively of as Sappho, as she was called by her former lovers: the artists, writers, and poets. Gaussin writes to her that all is over, but she sidesteps his dismissal, manipulating him into living with her again, this time in the country.

Chatville (SHAT-veel). Village outside Paris where Gaussin and Fanny settle in order to economize and be near prior neighbors whose company they enjoyed on the rue d'Amsterdam. They live in an old hunting lodge at the entrance to a wood, near the old forest road that is called the Pave des Gardes. This is a more idyllic setting than those in which Gaussin lives earlier in the story. He and Fanny enjoy the silent green space, the surrounding gardens, and a clump of trees sloping to the bottom of a hill.

— *Kathleen M. Bartlett*

SAPPHO

Author: Franz Grillparzer (1791-1872)
Type of work: Drama
Type of plot: Tragedy

Time of plot: Sixth century B.C.E.
First performed: 1818; first published, 1819 (English translation, 1928)

The idea of place as home is of central importance in this play. The Greek island of Lesbos, where the play is set, is the beloved home of Sappho, who holds the affection and veneration of its citizens by virtue of her fame as a poet and her kindness and generosity toward them. On the other hand, Lesbos feels more like a jail to Sappho's youthful lover, Phaon, and her slave girl Melitta, who miss their own homes and feel alienated at Lesbos.

*Lesbos** (lehz-bos). Greek island in the eastern Aegean Sea, off the coast to the east of what is now Turkey. The play calls for a highly romanticized re-creation of the place. At the rear of its stage setting, the sea surrounding the island is meant to be visible, and the sea is bordered on the left by rising rocks. On the right, there are steps and a colonnade leading into Sappho's home, which itself is imagined offstage. The center is occupied by an altar to the Greek goddess of love, Aphrodite (equivalent to the Roman Venus). A grotto, or small cave, overgrown with vegetation, lies at the front, to the right; it provides a convenient hiding place for characters to sneak in and overhear and watch the actions of others. To the left is a rose bush and a grass-covered bench. Many characters reveal their innermost thoughts on this bench, which is designed to lend itself to romantic musings with its blend of the natural and the human.

As re-created in the play, Lesbos is a romantically idealized place. The comfortable attraction it holds to Sappho is clear to see. The people of its capital, Mytilene (Mitilini in modern Greek), add to Sappho's sense of safety, an important aspect of a good home, because they love and protect her.

Phaon's and **Melitta's homes** (FAY-on; meh-LIH-tuh). Unnamed and offstage, these places are described and evoked in the lines of these characters, who speak with romantic longing for their faraway homes. Phaon's strong attachment to his own home reflects the rise of European nationalism during the Napoleonic Wars of the early nineteenth century, shortly after which Franz Grillparzer wrote this play. Invited to Lesbos by Sappho as her young lover, Phaon also utilizes his longing for his native place as an excuse for leaving Sappho, who is too powerful for him in her own home. The playwright's

yearning for his own Germanic homeland is involuntarily revealed when Phaon, a Greek youth, speaks of the linden trees shading his parents' home; however, while linden trees grow in northern Europe, they do not grow in Greece.

Melitta's longings for the place of her birth overwhelm Sappho's love for her, although Melitta spent only the first two years of her life there, before pirates raided her village, enslaved her, and sold her at Lesbos. Melitta asks the gods either to bring her home or to take her life. However, when Phaon contemplates asking Sappho to allow Melitta to go home, Melitta reveals that she cannot even remember the name of her native country, which lies somewhere in Asia. This lapse of memory enables Phaon to promise Melitta to marry her and take her to his own home—a plan that will allow them to leave Sappho on Lesbos and escape from the place that she rules.

*Chios** (KEE-as). Greek island immediately south of Lesbos to which Sappho plans to send Melitta to live with a friend, after she learns of Melitta's love for Phaon. Sappho hopes that the separation will cause Melitta to stop loving Phaon and thereby make it safe for Melitta to return to Lesbos.

*Aegean Sea.** The waters surrounding Lesbos are used both metaphorically and literally. The sea is a powerful symbol for fear, loneliness, and desolation, when characters consider how the sea separates them from their families. In typical German Romantic fashion, characters find insight and resolve from contemplating nature, including the sea. For example, while Sappho is gazing at the moonlit ocean, she feels inspired to send Melitta into exile. After her plan backfires, and Phaon and Melitta try to escape from Lesbos together, their boat is chased, captured, and brought back to shore by Sappho's loyal islanders. This action is narrated as it takes place off-stage, but its drama is highlighted by the visual presence of the sea at the rear of the stage. When she finally realizes that Phaon is lost to her, Sappho decides to commit suicide by throwing herself from the rocks in the background into the raging sea. That place, the characters believe, will bring her into the presence of the gods.

Olympia. Plain in southern Greece's Peloponnesus region that was a center devoted to the worship of Zeus and the site of the original Olympic games. Sappho meets Phaon at the games. The beginning of their love affair at such an important Greek place is told by other characters as Sappho returns home to Lesbos.

— *R. C. Lutz*

SARTORIS

Author: William Faulkner (1897-1962)
Type of work: Novel
Type of plot: Psychological realism

Time of plot: Immediately following World War I
First published: 1929

As William Faulkner's first novel set in Yoknapatawpha County, in the hills of northern Mississippi, this novel launched a series of books written over the next thirty-five years, in which the author created and populated his own microcosmic, mythical world. He drew his inspiration from the town and county in which he grew up.

Jefferson. Fictional town in the northwest corner of the state of Mississippi. Faulkner drew many details from his hometown of Oxford for his portrayal of Jefferson, although he changed details to suit his needs. Both towns are set in the hills of northern Mississippi, which was settled in the first half of the nineteenth century by families of English, Scottish, and Welsh descent, who had immigrated from Britain and settled first in the Carolinas or Virginia, then drifted south toward Mississippi. Faulkner makes much of the parallels between his created Jefferson and the real Oxford, but he also draws details from other northern Mississippi towns to round out his microcosm.

For the inhabitants of Jefferson in the 1910's and 1920's, the events of the Civil War, fought half a century earlier, remain very real, embodied in sites around town. This is particularly true for the elderly Bayard Sartoris and his aunt, Jenny DuPre, both of whom yearn for the past. Bayard's grandson, young Bayard, on the other hand, has just returned from World War I and has a fascination with airplanes and death. Thus he is an alien in this environment, in which he was born and grew up, and is unable to adjust to civilian life in this quiet community, which is still stuck in the nineteenth century.

Sartoris plantation. On the outskirts of Jefferson is the Sartoris plantation, built by Colonel John Sartoris and inhabited during the time of the novel by John's sister Virginia DuPre; his son Bayard, now an old man; his great-grandson, also named Bayard; and Narcissa, the wife of young Bayard. With its retinue of African American servants, the house and land represent a microcosm of the Old South. Faulkner carefully describes the old house and the way in which each room represents some aspect of the past of the family. The house, indeed, seems very much an embodiment of that past, surrounded by an aura of the violent history of the region. In addition, the author includes careful descriptions of the fields and the process whereby cotton, when it was the main crop of the South, was picked by black laborers, ginned, and bound into bales.

Sartoris bank. Major financial institution of Jefferson. It was founded by Colonel John Sartoris and is still controlled by the Sartoris family. Many characters of the novel are somehow related through the bank, and here some of the story lines are developed and given direction.

Yoknapatawpha County (YOK-nuh-puh-TAW-fuh). Fictional county that Faulkner uses in many different works. Several scenes are set in the rural areas of his mythical kingdom, including a foxhunt at the Mac-Callum farm. There is also a Christmas scene at the shack of an impoverished black family, where Bayard hides when, after the death of his grandfather, he is fleeing the world represented by the Sartoris family. The shack and the touchingly simple life of the family underscore the levels of society in Yoknapatawpha County. The places with which the classes are associated demonstrate the differences between them. With these two settings, Faulkner completes the social portrait of the people of his world: the aristocrats, represented by the Sartoris family; rural farmers and hunters, represented by the MacCallums, themselves descended from the gentry that migrated from the Eastern Seaboard during the nineteenth century and the descendants of slaves who made up a large part of the population of the area.

Virginia. Southern state about 450 miles northeast of Mississippi. A set narrative piece in the novel is the story told by Virginia DuPre about an episode that occurred in Virginia during the Civil War. Her story demonstrates the close connection between Mississippi and the southern states on the Eastern Seaboard. The scene and the locale of the story she tells also reflect significantly on the setting and action of the novel.

— *W. Kenneth Holditch*

THE SATANIC VERSES

Author: Salman Rushdie (1947-   )
Type of work: Novel
Type of plot: Fantasy

Time of plot: Late twentieth and early seventh centuries
First published: 1988

With its focus on the plight of the late twentieth century postcolonial migrant, this novel has two primary settings, London and Bombay, representing the two cultural realities between which the main characters, Chamcha and Gibreel, find themselves torn. As a reflection of the disorientation and racism experienced by immigrants, London as depicted in the novel is a phantasmagoric region in which ghosts from the past appear and people metamorphose into mythological beasts and divine beings.

Bostan. Fictional Air India flight from Bombay to London that is blown up by Sikh terrorists over the English coastline. This airplane, named after one of the Islamic gardens of paradise, is the novel's opening setting, acting as a metaphor for the migrants' movement between cultures. With the onset of the hijacking, the flight gradually loses its empirical reality, launching Gibreel and Chamcha into a world of illusion. The journey initiates their metamorphoses into their angelic and demoniac incarnations, which solidify in the home of Rosa Diamond, an octogenarian Englishwoman who repeatedly sees the specters of Norman invaders from nine hundred years earlier. These two locations mark the main characters' entry into England in their metamorphosed states as desirable and undesirable immigrants.

London. Great Britain's capital city has two distinct faces in the novel. Superficially, it is the capital of British culture and civilization, the dream destination of immigrants from former colonies. As an educated, financially secure immigrant, Chamcha sees London as prosperous and accommodating, a place where he is accepted as a proper Englishman with an English wife, a successful career in television, and a mansion in Notting Hill. This rosy veneer, however, belies the city's dark underside, characterized by racial discrimination and police brutality.

When Chamcha lands in England following the plane explosion, penniless and unable to prove his British citizenship, he finds the nation transformed into a horrible fantasy, "some counterfeit zone, rotten borough, altered state." In this negative aspect of London, immigrants are literally transformed into animals and demons, tortured by officials, incarcerated, and forced to flee at night into a hellish underworld. The immigrant community, centered in the racially diverse neighborhood called **Brickhall**, modeled on the real London suburb of Brixton, lives with fear, intimidation, and poverty. The **Shandaar Café** in Brickhall, where Chamcha is concealed after his metamorphosis into a devil, symbolizes both the vitality of the immigrant community and its exploitation by outsiders and by its own members. In the Brickhall disco **Club Hot Wax**, immigrants vent their frustration against their oppressors by melting wax effigies of English politicians, especially Prime Minister Margaret Thatcher.

While Gibreel does not experience the immigrant's nightmare version of London, his perception of the city mirrors his disintegrating sense of reality as he struggles with the divine visions that cast him as the archangel in search of his adversary, Shaitan (Satan). In Gibreel's view, the city becomes a hallucinatory labyrinth that constantly changes shape, a cosmological battlefield populated with ghosts and monstrous creatures. He alters the city's temperature with his will, turning it into a tropical hothouse primed for racial conflagration.

*Bombay** (now called Mumbai). Large city on the west coast of India. As it also does in Salman Rushdie's other works, Bombay in this novel symbolizes both the best and worst of modern Indian society. A creation of British colonial power, the city prides itself on its European sophistication and eclectic multiculturalism. While the city's diversity is celebrated in the novel, it is also made clear that disasters such as the Assam massacre result from interneccine racial and religious tensions. Like London, Bombay in the novel is divided between rich and poor, between the luxurious lifestyles of those at Scandal Point and the high-rise Everest Villas and the poverty of Gibreel's childhood as a tiffin, or lunch, carrier. Unlike London, Bombay is depicted largely in realistic terms, though it too is suffused with questions of illusion and identity, as suggested by the dominance of the "Bollywood," or Indian, film industry.

For both Gibreel and Chamcha, Bombay is the home that they are trying to put behind them by going to England. In Gibreel's case, the city is associated with the Islamic heritage he wants to deny; for Chamcha, it is the crystallization of a culture he deems uncivilized and a father he rejects. At the end of the novel, though, Chamcha's return trip to Bombay represents his successful integration of his past and present and Indian and English selves.

Jahilia (jah-HEEL-ee-ah). Fictional depiction of the city of Mecca, birthplace of the Islamic religion, in the early seventh century. This city, which appears only in Gibreel's dream sequences, is presented in somewhat caricatured, ultimately controversial terms, which underscore the novel's interrogation of the viability of faith based on literal interpretation. Jahilia, which refers to the period of ignorance that preceded the Islamic religion, is also believed to be the name of the desert location where Ibrahim (Abraham) heeded God's command to abandon his wife Hagar and child Ismail, who were then saved by the archangel Gibreel's (Gabriel's) revelation of the Spring of Zamzam. The word thus connotes both devotion and doubt, the latter of which is symbolized by the city's total construction from sand, "the very stuff of inconstancy."

With its temples devoted to 360 different deities, Jahilia is a favored destination for pilgrims, and its citizens benefit financially from markets and festivals attended by the faithful. Mahound, the novel's parodic depiction of the prophet Muhammad, opposes his new religion of submission (Islam), with its one god (Allah), to the city's polytheistic decadence. On nearby Mount Cone, he wrestles with the archangel Gibreel while receiving the Recitation (the Qur'an), whose divine authority is presented as questionable. Although Mahound is driven out by his enemies, his eventual return marks a new period of austerity in Jahilia, which is temporarily undermined by the creation of a town brothel, **The Curtain**, in which prostitutes masquerade as the prophet's twelve wives.

Titlipur. Fictional twentieth century Muslim Indian village. This village, whose name derives from the butterflies that proliferate in the area, serves as the starting point for Gibreel's second dream sequence, also dealing with questions of absolute faith. The impoverished inhabitants of the village are persuaded by Ayesha, a local girl with miraculous qualities, that the archangel has commanded them to make a foot pilgrimage to Mecca. They are joined by Mishal, the fatally ill wife of the local zamindar, or wealthy landowner, Mirza Saeed, a secularist, who lives nearby in a colonial mansion called Peristan (Fairyland). This test of faith terminates in a parting of the Arabian Sea, perceptible only to believers, which results in the drowning deaths of the pilgrims.

— *Lynn Wells*

THE SATYRICON

Author: Petronius (Gaius Petronius Arbiter, c. 20- c. 66 C.E.)

Type of work: Short fiction

Type of plot: Satire

Time of plot: First century C.E.

First transcribed: c. 60 (English translation, 1694)

This surviving fragment of a much larger work follows the narrator Encolpius, a young student, through a series of ribald adventures in southern Italy that include a perilous maritime voyage. The southern Italian provincial settings, rife with the heavy cultural scent of their Greek origins and influence, and fettered by their positions as relative cultural and social backwaters, provided satisfying counterpoints to the relatively sophisticated conditions in which lived Petronius's urban Roman audience.

*Southern Italy. Region in which most of *The Satyricon* is set. Until the Pyrrhic and Second Punic Wars of the third century B.C.E., much of southern Italy—especially its seaports—was controlled by Greek colonists. Writing in the first century C.E., Petronius used the continuing presence of Greek influence, and the stereotyping by urban Romans of Greek greed, dishonesty, homosexuality, and overblown philosophizing to create scenes of life in southern Italian towns that are both caricatures of Greek stereotypes and assaults on traditional Roman sensibilities.

*Puteoli (poo-CHOH-lee; now Pozzuoli). Southern Italian port city, west of Naples, that Petronius portrays as suffering from high prices, food shortages, and bad gladiatorial games. According to Petronius, Puteoli lacks any real sense of high culture. Despite being a Greek town in origin, it has no room for poetry, and both its philosophy and its art are decadent. Petronius is, however, actually, critiquing Roman culture as a whole, a dangerous thing to do during the age of Emperor Nero.

Puteoli's role as a major port for eastern goods meant that it had both a prevalence of Easterners and a general ethic focused on money, as embodied in Trimalchio. Encolpius himself, however, is truly an outsider to this ethic, a beggar and an exile, and is thus easily lost in Puteoli's maze of streets.

The city's shrine to Priapus, into which Encolpius and Ascyltus stumble, sets the sexual tone of the work. The prevalent homosexuality that is taken for granted throughout Puteoli seems the one characteristic binding Encolpius to the town's society. That a man such as Trimalchio should serve as the apex of local society marks the city as a poor place indeed.

Trimalchio's house (trih-MAHL-kee-oh). Puteoli home of Trimalchio, a former slave who is now rich. Unused to wealth, he is vulgar and makes great shows of his riches to impress other people. Petronius's swipe at the pretensions of provincial people who are newly rich and lack any genuine sense of taste is focused on Trimalchio's house. Its mural of the freedman's deeds recalls similar domestic murals in patrician houses depicting celebrated ancestors—rather than the owners themselves. Trimalchio's crude personal habits and banal, if ostentatious, banquet reflect both on the economic successes of his class and its inability to do more than mimic the established families of Roman society. His home is the meeting place for the mediocre and fawning, ne'er-do-wells and toadies who value and praise Trimalchio for his money and little else.

Lichas's ship. Vessel on which Encolpius and Eumolpus escape from Puteoli, that evolves into a trap in itself after Encolpius discovers that an old nemesis is a fellow passenger. The deck of the ship becomes a battlefield and then a court for negotiation as the parties dispose of their differences. Their voyage to Tarentum is spoiled, however, by a shipwreck in which Lichas is drowned. Encolpius and Eumolpus make their way ashore at Croton.

*Croton. Southern Italian city where Eumolpus poses as a rich landowner, while Encolpius and Gito pose as his slaves. By cleverly deluding the inhabitants, they live luxuriously as guests of the town. After a year, however, the local people grow suspicious about Eumolpus's alleged wealth. Encoplius and Gito escape just in time, but the angry townspeople deck out Eumolpus with boughs and sacred vestments, lead him through the city, and hurl him down a cliff.

Croton's distance from Rome, in the very "toe" of the Italian peninsula, allows Petronius to make it appear even less Roman than Puteoli. Petronius's depiction of Croton and its society is not as well developed as that of Puteoli, as Croton may have been less well known to him. His emphasis is on fortunes and on fortune hunting: Encolpius and his party claim the former, while pursuing the latter. Stereotypes of Greek greed and dissimulation again come to the fore. The association of magic with charlatans and shysters in Croton goes well with Croton's depiction as a den of legacy-chasers.

— *Joseph P. Byrne*

THE SCARLET LETTER

Author: Nathaniel Hawthorne (1804-1864)
Type of work: Novel
Type of plot: Psychological realism

Time of plot: Seventeenth or eighteenth century
First published: 1850

In this novel, as in many of his other works, Nathaniel Hawthorne establishes a story inexorably linked to the time and the place in which the characters find themselves. Although Hester Prynne's story of alienation and ridicule by hypocritical countrymen is universal, the form these injustices take could only have been concocted by the early American Puritan society of New England in which she lives.

*Massachusetts Bay Colony. Early American New England colony established by British Puritans who were seeking religious freedom. This is the primary setting of the novel in which all the other places to be mentioned are found. While ostensibly seeking a place of freedom, the Puritans had created a society more repressive than America has ever known through the present day. Beauty and creativity in the surroundings the Puritans themselves created were not valued. A premium was instead placed on utilitarianism and frugality.

While there must surely have been sunshine and beautiful landscapes in the actual area, Hawthorne focuses on the starker, gray quality of New England as those qualities seem to reflect the personalities of its citizens. Hester has been jailed, then ostracized, for her crime of committing adultery and having a child out of wedlock. As a result, there are very few bright spots in her world. The hard, dark landscape with its cleared fields and minimalist human-made structures mirrors the rigid mindset which represses her.

Prison and courtyard. Colony's jail, in which readers first encounter Hester and her daughter, Pearl. The jail cell where Hester spends the days of her imprisonment is presented as small and gloomy. It is in the prison's courtyard, also plain and cheerless, where Hester is dragged in front of the townspeople to parade her shame on the scaffold.

Interestingly, there is a spot of color in the prison yard. In the midst of the weeds and ugliness, a rosebush blooms. This can be seen as the landscape yielding up some hope for relief in all the surrounding bleakness.

Forest. Wilderness area surrounding the township. The forest is the scene of a meeting between Hester and Reverend Arthur Dimmesdale. It is a place of nature, beauty, and freedom from inhibitions. The sensual quality of the untamed land is a perfect backdrop for the forbidden lovers and the complete opposite of the repression of the settled areas of the colony. It is also in the covering of the forest that Hester is able to shed her shame, physically (by removal of the "A") as well as mentally, and be a more free-spirited woman.

King's Chapel Church. Church at which Arthur Dimmesdale is the pastor. The church is a typical New England building of worship—square and boxy—suggesting that something is pent in by its shape. It is within the cloak of the church that Dimmesdale hides from his part of the guilt of the adultery and where Hester's sin is condemned in the name of God; it does not project an image of love or forgiveness.

Scaffold. Platform in the center of town, near the prison, where prisoners are brought for public viewing. The scaffold is the scene of Hester's initial shame as well as the novel's climax. Although it is under darkness of night that Dimmesdale stands on the platform with Hester to finally accept his shame, it is its openness that is important. It is elevated and open, a place for the revelation of secrets.

— *Emma Sue Harris*

THE SCHOOL FOR HUSBANDS

Author: Molière (Jean-Baptiste Poquelin, 1622-1673)
Type of work: Drama
Type of plot: Comedy of manners

Time of plot: 1660's
First performed: 1661; first published, 1661 as
    L'École des maris (English translation, 1732)

Molière set this early comedy about women's liberation in Paris because that city was the center for the most innovative ideas and fashions of his day. His primary setting is a bourgeois neighborhood in which the Aristotelian unity of place makes it necessary to show two houses in close proximity.

*****Paris.** France's capital and leading city whose liberating influence on the naïve, obedient, exploited Isabelle makes place essential to the play's plot. Since using minimalistic props made it impossible to show where the play's action takes place, the dialogue establishes the location. For example, Valère tells Sganarelle, "Paris really is unique; / Its pleasures elsewhere you may vainly seek." Elaborate costumes worn by Ariste, Valère, and especially by Léonor, as well as the rich assortment of activities and amusements these characters describe, also establish Paris as the only possible location for this play.

Within the strict limitations of the Aristotelian unities of place, time, and action, Moliere creates the illusion of a whole exciting city exerting its intoxicating and liberating influence on a young newcomer who escapes an aging tyrant to find freedom, love, and happiness. Much of the laughter is evoked by showing the self-important gentleman Sganarelle used as a go-between by his ward, Isabelle, and her lover, Valère.

Houses. The exigencies of the Aristotelian unity of place required that the set represent two houses separated by an open space, all within the confines of approximately thirty feet. Valère lives in one, and Isabelle is imprisoned in the other. Sganarelle has good reason to fear the dangerous proximity of his sophisticated, fashionable young rival in this glamorous city and for wishing to marry his young ward and spirit her away to the country as quickly as possible. Only a small portion of Sganarelle's own house and only a wall and window of Valère's house could be shown in the seventeenth century productions. When Sganarelle confronts Valère, they happen to meet outdoors. Valère invites Sganarelle to come inside, but the older man replies, "There is no need." Valère then calls his servant to bring the older gentleman a chair. Through such contrivances, most of the action takes place in the open area between the two dwellings, and unity of place is preserved.

— *Bill Delaney*

THE SCHOOL FOR SCANDAL

Author: Richard Brinsley Sheridan (1751-1816)
Type of work: Drama
Type of plot: Comedy of manners

Time of plot: Eighteenth century
First performed: 1777; first published, 1780

This play, with its tightly constructed plot, grand comedy, and polished wit, has delighted audiences since its debut. In addition to being called a comedy of manners, this type of play is often called a drawing-room comedy because so much of its action takes place in the formal rooms of fashionable London town homes.

Lady Sneerwell's dressing room. Despite the fact that the stage direction indicates that the first scene of the play takes place at Lady Sneerwell's dressing table, the room in which the scene takes place is a large room used by fashionable ladies for waiting on their most confidential guests. Thus Lady Sneerwell uses her dressing room to converse with Snake in much the same way the men of the house would use the library.

Drawing room. Other scenes in Lady Sneerwell's house are set in the typical drawing room of a fashionable house. For example, in act 2, scene 2, Sheridan presents the famous school for scandal in attendance in the drawing room. Drawing rooms were used purely for public purposes. It was here that a hostess would receive guests or where guests would gather before and after dinner. Usually they were among the larger rooms of the house and certainly the room in Lady Sneerwell's house is big enough to handle her rather large group of scandalmongers.

Library. Joseph Surface's library, in which the play's most famous scene is set. Like women's dressing rooms, libraries were places where men met their friends for personal visits. Usually, however, it was where they met their male friends, so the scene in which Joseph meets intimately with Lady Teazle has a special significance in its being set in the library.

— *Paul Varner*

THE SCHOOL FOR WIVES

Author: Molière (Jean-Baptiste Poquelin, 1622-1673)
Type of work: Drama
Type of plot: Comedy of manners

Time of plot: Seventeenth century
First performed: 1662; first published, 1663 as
    L'École des femmes (English translation, 1732)

Molière set this love-triangle story in Paris because, as Arnolphe tells Horace, there is pleasure for every taste, the town is full of womanizers seeking romantic adventure, and every woman is a coquette who enjoys the game of love as much as the gallants who woo them. Adhering to the Aristotelian unity of place, Moliere adroitly confines all five acts to a single place—an open square. All meetings between Horace and Arnolphe must occur outdoors because the plot revolves around Horace's confiding the details of his blossoming romance while unaware that Arnolphe is Monsieur de la Souche.

*Parisian public square. The play's setting—an open square in a city full of coquettes and seducers—is integral to the comedy, as well as essential to adherence to the Aristotelian unity of place, which was essential in seventeenth century French drama. Arnolphe's silly vanity induces him to change his name to "Monsieur de la Souche," which allows the newly arrived young Horace to believe that Agnes is the ward of a different man and makes it necessary for Molière to stage his frequent encounters with Arnolphe outdoors. The information obtained from Horace by the increasingly horrified Arnolphe motivates the middle-aged man to decide to marry his ward immediately, thus enabling Molière to adhere to another Aristotelian unity—that of time. Most of the laughter the play evokes is a function of Horace's and Arnolphe's talking at cross purposes. Horace is a newcomer, a friendly, trusting young man who does not realize he is confiding in the Monsieur de la Souche, who is the strict and jealous guardian of the sweet, innocent, and desirable Agnes, a seventeen-year-old ingénue fresh from the convent.

— Bill Delaney

SEA GARDEN

Author: H. D. (Hilda Doolittle, 1886-1961)
Type of work: Poetry

First published: 1916

Settings in this collection of poems are the interfaces of sea, shore, and mountains associated with much of classical Greek literature. The landscapes of most of the poems are not named, however particularly they are described. As a result, the scenes have a timeless quality well suited to the poet's attempt to locate and define her emotional reaction to whatever moves her. As in Greek literature generally, the sense of place in these poems is sometimes heightened by the invocation or appearance of gods and goddesses such as Apollo, Hermes, and Artemis, who are seen primarily as tutelary spirits.

Sea. The basic symbolic contrast in the poems is between the sea and the land, the sea being treated as both nurturer and destroyer. Several of the collection's most successful poems—such as "Sea Poppies" and "Sea Violet"—are set where the sea and the land intersect, among the pebbles, shells, and sandbanks of the shore. At times this struggle of beauty to survive at the borderline of elemental forces yields a brilliant metaphor, as in "Sea Violet," in which a blossom catching the light on the edge of a sandhill is described as frost that a "star edges with its fire."

Gardens. The poem "Sheltered Garden" laments the lack of a bracing environment in a garden that is too orderly and predictable: "there is no scent of resin/ in this place/ no taste of bark, of coarse weeds,/ aromatic, astringent—." The pastoral landscape and tenor of most of the poems are echoed more than contrasted by the collection's final poem, "Cities," in which H. D. imagines "the maker of cities" and sees the process of urban growth and decay in organic terms, as stages in the life of a beehive.

Dictaeus. Mountain cave on the Mediterranean island of Crete where the infant god Zeus was reared by nymphs. The cave, along with the places that follow below, is mentioned in the poem "Acon."

River Erymanthus (ir-a-MAN-thahs). Location of Heracles' capture of the Erymanthian boar—one of his famous twelve labors.

*Arcadia. Region of Greece's central Peloponnesian Peninsula that is traditionally associated with idyllic pastoral life. The speaker in "Acon" enjoins the dryads, nereids, and Pales (Roman divinity of shepherds and herdsmen) to bring offerings of the highest quality to the stricken Hyella: fruit from Arcadia, wine from Assyria, fine cloth from Phoenicia, and irises from Illyria.

— Roy Scheele

THE SEA OF GRASS

Author: Conrad Richter (1890-1968)
Type of work: Novel
Type of plot: Regional

Time of plot: 1885-1910
First published: 1936

Throughout this, Conrad Richter's first full-length novel, place parallels character, and changing locales preface major changes in the main characters, both physically and psychologically. Over a twenty-year period, the novel explores in three parts relationships of the past to the present, relationships shaped and often destroyed by the consuming realities of place.

Salt Fork. Fictional New Mexico frontier town that embodies characteristics of historically real places on the Western frontier. Vividly displaying the shifting boundaries of a newly settled prairie land, Salt Fork plays a central role in *The Sea of Grass*. Borrowing from folklore, the wild frontier of this place helps readers understand the types of people who migrate to the West, the promise and hopes that draw them there, and the realities and dangers they encounter at their journeys' ends.

Rich men, like Colonel Jim Brewton, seeking more wealth, claim this frontier and its luxurious prairie as their own, building empires of cattle and grasslands. They created the first settlements, developed the first city governments, and became the "law of the land." These cattle barons, not unlike kings in their prairie kingdoms, viewed new migrants to the area, often referred to as "nesters" or "grangers," as destructive interlopers who understood neither the value of the grasslands they hoped to plow nor the environment and climate that would foil their success as farmers. It is the ongoing struggle for ownership, the battle between cattle barons and would-be settlers, that introduces the initial conflict between Colonel Jim and the new district attorney, Brice Chamberlain.

As the backdrop for yet another type of frontier relationship, Salt Fork becomes the stark, violent behavioral and environmental canvas onto which is juxtaposed the fragile qualities of eastern socialite, Lutie Cameron, who travels from St. Louis, Missouri, to New Mexico to join her future husband, Jim Brewton, who owns the **Cross B Ranch** outside Salt Fork. The very qualities of this Western territory magnify Lutie's sensitivity—her overprotected, eastern-bred persona—as she struggles to adapt to her new life in the Southwest. It is finally the harshness of the land and of the men who draw their identities from the land that forces Lutie to leave, to seek the comfort of a more familiar place.

In his mother's absence, Brock Brewton, the son of Lutie and her lover, Chamberlain, remains in Salt Fork only to become a romantic desperado, challenging any authority who dares to tame him or the untamed territory of his youth. Brock's destiny, however, is the destiny of all frontiersmen who hold to the violent past of the West, and he dies the victim of his own rebellion, a rebellion appropriately cast in this place of adventure and irreverence.

"East." References to the "East" are frequent in *Sea of Grass*, which portrays the East as a world of non-Mormon "gentile" society and culture, of beautiful women, and of all that is domesticated, proper, and law-abiding. However, from the perspective of the people of Salt Fork, the "East" is centered in Missouri, in such cities as St. Louis, Lutie's original home; Kansas City, which Colonel Jim frequents when he goes east to sell cattle; and Lexington, the location first feared then hated by Hal Brewton, the colonel's nephew, who is "banished" to school there at Lutie's suggestion. Lutie Cameron and Brice Chamberlain are characters designed with eastern qualities and temperaments, characteristics less laudable in Salt Fork, whose frontier mentality honors power and the right of eminent domain over moral or legal correctness.

*Denver. Colorado city that boasts amenities of eastern society while reveling in its wild, frontier-town legend. Denver represents a city on the edge, the boundary edge that marks the end of the East and the beginning of the West, the end of safety and diplomacy and the beginning of unrestrained power and violence. It is through Denver, a symbol of her coming of age, that Lutie passes on her way to her new life with Colonel Jim in the Southwest. After her humiliation in Salt Fork and her abandonment by Brice Chamberlain, Lutie returns to Denver, then a symbol of her resignation, but a safer haven. Ironically, Lutie never revisits the East of her youth and eventually returns after a fifteen-year absence, unapologetic and unexplained, to Salt Fork from Denver to resume her life on what remains of the Cross B Ranch. In this last part of the story, Denver metaphorically encompasses both Lutie's emergence from her self-assigned banishment and her reconciliation with her past.

— *Linda E. Smith*

THE SEA-WOLF

Author: Jack London (1876-1916) *Time of plot:* 1904
Type of work: Novel *First published:* 1904
Type of plot: Adventure

The story of an involuntary sea voyage by a wealthy amateur writer, this novel throws what Jack London called a "super-civilized" man into a "primitive sea-environment" to see how he would cope. After becoming a virtual prisoner aboard a rugged seal-hunting ship in the Pacific Ocean, the writer gradually discovers his own strength of character and eventually challenges the ship's tyrannical captain and masters the harsh new environment into which he is thrust.

***San Francisco Bay.** California's great natural harbor, in which the novel opens with the protagonist, Humphrey Van Weyden, crossing the bay on a ferryboat. In the midst of a dense fog, the ferry collides with another ship, and Van Weyden is washed out to sea by strong currents, leaving behind the soft and comfortable life that civilized San Francisco represents. Near the Farallon Islands, about thirty miles west of the coast, he is rescued by the schooner *Ghost*.

Ghost. Seal-hunting schooner bound for Japan on which most of the novel takes place after Van Weyden is forced into joining the ship's crew. Much of the novel consists of philosophical conversations between Van Weyden and the ship's self-educated and brutal captain, Wolf Larsen, as the *Ghost* makes its way through the Pacific. Eventually, each man earns the other's respect, and having to cope with the conditions aboard the ship makes Van Weyden strong enough to master what he initially regards as an impossibly brutal environment in which might makes right.

***Pacific Ocean.** To take advantage of wind currents, the *Ghost* sails southwest across the Pacific before turning northwest toward Japan, following a route resembling the letter *V*. Although the story takes place aboard the ship, the ocean itself is the harsh world that surrounds the tiny, savage society dominated by Larsen. A turning point occurs immediately after the *Ghost* reaches the southernmost point of its voyage, when two crew members throw Larsen and his first mate overboard, only to see Larsen climb back on board. On a whim, Larsen promotes Van Weyden from cabin boy to mate. The southern apex of the journey's *V* is thus the point at which the originally soft Van Weyden begins to realize his own power and potential. It is also the point where Larsen's power begins to be challenged by the crew and by Van Weyden himself.

***Yokohama** (yoh-koh-HAH-mah). Major port city on the eastern coast of Japan that marks another twist in the plot. When the *Ghost* is five hundred miles southeast of Yokohama, two crew members take a boat, hoping to reach Yokohama. Larsen changes course to pursue them. On this new course, the *Ghost* rescues five survivors of a ship that has sunk in a storm. One of these people is Maude Brewster, a poet whose work Van Weyden knows well. Brewster's coming aboard the *Ghost* complicates the relationship between Larsen and Van Weyden, as the two men become rivals for her attention after Larsen insists on sailing north, rather than continuing to Yokohama to put Brewster ashore.

***Siberia.** Desolate region of eastern Russia, north of Japan. As the *Ghost* passes the Siberian coast, Larsen's control of events slips out of his hands when he encounters the steam-powered **Macedonia**, a seal-hunting ship under the command of his brother and enemy, Death Larsen. His brother's ship beats the *Ghost* to the best seal areas and takes members from its crew. Meanwhile, Van Weyden and Brewster manage to steal a boat and provisions, and set sail to the southwest, hoping to reach Japan.

Endeavor Island. Desolate northern Pacific island on which Van Weyden and Brewster are marooned after being swept north on the boat on which they escape from the *Ghost*. The island is inhabited by seals, which leads Van Weyden to hope that human beings are near, but it soon becomes apparent that he and Brewster are alone. Drawing on his new-found skills and strengths, Van Weyden conquers this harsh new environment, from which he and Brewster are fortuitously rescued when the almost derelict *Ghost* appears after Larsen has lost the rest of his crew.

— *Carl L. Bankston III*

THE SEAGULL

Author: Anton Chekhov (1860-1904)
Type of work: Drama
Type of plot: Impressionistic realism

Time of plot: Nineteenth century
First performed: 1896; revised, 1898; first published, 1904 as *Chayka*, (English translation, 1909)

Anton Chekhov stages this entire play in and around a house on a small Russian farm owned by a family of the gentry named Sorin. One effect of this compressed setting is to underscore the fundamental stasis or lack of movement in the lives of some of the play's main characters.

Sorin farm. Setting for the entire play. Chekhov carefully crafts the setting of his play so that the action of the work gradually moves from the outside into the confined spaces of an interior room. The play begins on the back lawn of the Sorin farm. A small stage has been set up in the middle of a path leading down to a lake. The curtain is drawn so that the lake cannot be seen.

During the first act, a young aspiring writer named Konstantin puts on an avant-garde play which confuses the audience (particularly his mother, Irina Arkadina, a famous actress). He uses the natural setting of the moon rising over the lake to add a dramatic touch to the arid, overly intellectual verbiage of the play itself. A young woman named Nina Zarechnaya (her surname means "beyond the river") delivers Konstantin's words. She has spent her whole life by the lake and now yearns to become an actress.

In the second act, Konstantin presents her with the body of a seagull he has just killed, and this bird becomes an emblem of Nina's future destiny. She is drawn to Arkadina's lover, the writer Trigorin. He too finds Nina attractive, and he makes a note to write a story about a girl who loves the lake like a seagull, when along comes a man with nothing better to do but to destroy her life, just as the seagull was destroyed. Trigorin subsequently seduces Nina, but abandons her to remain with Arkadina.

The final act takes place in a parlor which Konstantin has converted into a study. Two years have passed, and the main characters have reassembled. Konstantin, however, has never left the farm. Nina arrives unannounced, drenched by a cold autumn rain. After she describes to Konstantin her difficulties, her nostalgia for her simple life by the lake, and her renewed determination to continue her acting career, she leaves him, and the young man kills himself out of despair. It is characteristic of Chekhov that the suicide occurs offstage while the other characters are engaged in mundane pursuits such as playing lotto.

— *Julian W. Connolly*

A SEASON IN HELL

Author: Arthur Rimbaud (1854-1891)
Type of work: Poetry

First published: Une Saison en enfer, 1873 (English translation, 1932)

In this confessional farewell to his poetic career, Arthur Rimbaud portrays himself addressing his readers from hell. The work rapidly shifts settings between the speaker's place in hell and the paradise from which he has been ejected and between Western civilization and other, more "primitive" cultures.

Hell. Place of damned souls. As in the traditional story of Lucifer, the narrator has, for the sin of pride, been cast out of paradise—here represented as the licentiousness and naïve arrogance of his earlier poetic career. Rimbaud's hell, however, seems to represent temporary confinement within one's own selfish desires rather than eternal punishment. Indeed, the narrator relates that he has purged himself of desire and thus is ready to depart.

*Europe.** The narrator's home, whose drab, restricted way of life incited the rebellion that placed him in hell. The narrator repeatedly asserts that he is more of an uncivilized savage than a European and that he envies non-European cultures their ignorance of sin and salvation. He realizes, however, that although he finds Western civilization distasteful, his literary aspirations enmesh him in that civilization. Trapped in a maze of sin he compares to the mythological Cimmerian land, the narrator cannot escape until he renounces his pretensions to the artistic life. Rimbaud includes several of his earlier poems in *A Season in Hell*; their idyllic rural settings contrast ironically with the narrator's present torment, and their catalogs of natural beauty mock his attempts to imprison in words the chaos of creation.

Paradise. Like the poem's hell, paradise is understood not as a fixed location but a state of mind. Rimbaud's paradise is a state one must earn over and over again. As his narrator, near the end of the poem, renounces poetry, he is able to envision a new Christ and a new form of salvation. The new heaven will be provisional; Rimbaud hints that the narrator will one day outgrow it and be cast into hell again, beginning the cycle anew.

— *Hayes Hampton*

A SEASON IN RIHATA

Author: Maryse Condé (1937-   )
Type of work: Novel
Type of plot: Psychological realism

Time of plot: Late twentieth century
First published: Une Saison à Rihata, 1981 (English translation, 1988)

Whether it is describing the West Indies or West Africa, this novel shows how public places and private places interconnect and become shared through a kind of contagion. For author Maryse Condé, place becomes a collective state of mind.

Rihata. Sleepy, impoverished African town standing at the bend of an unidentified river in an unnamed country. Rihata is home to people who have been forced by hard times to leave the bush country, moving from family compounds on the river's banks, where cooperation was a way of life, to the dubious modernity of isolated, rickety colonial-style buildings in town. Like the bush dwellers, the Guadeloupan mulatto Marie-Hélène moves to Rihata. When she first comes to this country, she and her bank-manager husband, Zek, live in the capital city of N'Daru. After she has an affair with Zek's brother, Madou, Zek asks for a transfer to Rihata, where nothing ever happens. To the people in Rihata, Marie-Hélène is an outsider—almost a white woman. Living in a kind of mental no-man's-land, she watches her life disintegrate as she waits for her brother-in-law to come to Rihata to celebrate the anniversary of the coup d'état that brought to power the country's brutal dictator.

Farokodoba. Town in which Madou, a high-level minister in the unpopular government, is assassinated by rebels. Farokodoba and its neighboring town of Bafing are, if possible, even more claustrophobic and isolating than Rihata. Illuminated only by the lights of peanut sellers, the town is almost pitch dark at night, casting dark shadows on Madou's attempts to reconcile with his brother and negotiate an alliance with the socialist government of the neighboring country to the north.

Marie-Hélène's bedroom. Site both of Marie-Hélène's imprisonment and of the means of her escape. As a place of imprisonment, her bedroom is the place where she surrenders to sexual needs and thus seals the contract of her unhappy marriage. However, the dreams she has while sleeping there offer her release from both time and space, allowing her escape from a life in which she feels uprooted and homeless.

N'Daru. Capital city of the unnamed African country and the most corrupt of the three urban centers described in the novel. Possibly modeled, in part, on Kinshasa, the capital city of the Democratic Republic of the Congo (formerly Zaire), N'Daru is divided unequally between rich and poor. The most important job in the city is that of chief of police.

Here Madou is popular with citizens and beloved by President Toumany; he lives a charmed life in N'Daru. Before he is to return there, however, he is assassinated by a guerrilla fighter from the north intent on avenging Madou's arrest of a popular leader. The murder sabo-

tages Zek's and Marie-Hélène's chances for a better life and also plays into Toumany's hands.

The dictator receives the news of Madou's death in his magnificent, heavily guarded palace, surrounded by a 250-acre park. He privately boasts that he fooled Madou into believing an alliance with the neighboring socialist country would help liberalize his own regime, and he capitalizes on Madou's death by making him honorary prime minister in death, thereby ensuring that he will never need to appoint another person to that position. Madou's removal thus makes possible Toumany's elimination of all potential rivals and the isolation of his country from the rest of the world.

— *Susan Tetlow Harrington*

THE SEASONS

Author: James Thomson (1700-1748)
Type of work: Poetry

First published: 1730; final version, 1746

Place in James Thomson's poems is usually elusive. His descriptions of the natural world typically use generalized language, naming no specific places, although the descriptions of the natural scenes themselves may be composed of vivid and realistic details. The sources of Thomson's best natural descriptions are his potent memories of the border landscapes of southern Scotland, a varied landscape of remarkable and dramatic extremes where he grew up, and he developed a striking ability to portray the sublimity and power of nature. Thomson uses wild nature and English landscape gardens to present the politics of place.

*****Scotland.** Thomson's native country, which he left in 1725 in order to pursue a literary career in England. In a letter home, he compared the natural landscapes of the two countries, ruing England's lack of living streams, airy mountains, hanging rocks, and other features characteristic of Scotland. A Scottish influence pervades his descriptions in *The Seasons*, working on many levels, both general and particular, conscious and unconscious.

*****England.** Thomson's dramatic descriptive skills and political commitments emerge in descriptions of the cultivated landscapes of his three patrons, at Hagley Park,

Eastbury, and Stowe. Landscapes in *The Seasons* are imagined as political places. Thomson sees wild landscapes as bastions of natural British freedom, and he presents cultivated landscapes as indexes of the virtues of the patrons whose political commitments he shared. The poet perceives this wild native freedom and cultivated virtues of British landscapes as threatened by the spreading corruption of Prime Minister Robert Walpole's government of abusive power. This corruption is literally covering the landscape, attacking both natural freedom and the civil freedoms of a just society.

— *Robert Eddy*

THE SECOND SHEPHERDS' PLAY

Author: The Wakefield Master (c. 1420-c. 1450)
Type of work: Drama
Type of plot: Mystery and miracle play

Time of plot: c. 4 B.C.E.
First transcribed: Secunda Pastorum, fifteenth century

This play was inspired by a biblical passage about shepherds in the field at the time of Jesus' birth in Bethlehem, but most of the play is set in fifteenth century northern England. Only at the end does the play switch to ancient Bethlehem. The play's anonymous author, known as the Wakefield Master, points up the relevance of Jesus' birth to contemporary issues by his choice of English setting.

*Yorkshire. Northern England moors on which shepherds are watching over their flocks by night. In contrast with biblical shepherds, however, these shepherds complain about typical problems of the fifteenth century rural poor. The shepherds are dispossessed tenant farmers who suffer from the bone-chilling Yorkshire winter, from hunger, and from oppressive landowners. They represent the poor, meek, and downtrodden for whom Jesus is a symbol of hope and social justice, even across the centuries.

Mak and Gill's home. Hovel in which Mak and Gill hide the sheep that Mak steals from the shepherds. Gill, pretending she has given birth once again, wraps the sheep in swaddling clothes and lays it in a cradle. The three are a comic if not blasphemous version of Joseph, Mary, and baby Jesus. The setting again connects the contemporary poor to Jesus, the lamb of God, who was born in a stable, wrapped in swaddling clothes, and laid in a manger.

*Bethlehem. The play's final brief scene is set in the stable in Bethlehem in which Jesus was born. Returning to biblical text, this scene shows the shepherds bringing gifts to the Christ Child, thereby merging ancient and contemporary time and clinching the universal relevance of Jesus' message.

— *Harold Branam*

THE SECRET AGENT: A Simple Tale

Author: Joseph Conrad (Jósef Teodor Konrad Nałęcz
  Korzeniowski, 1857-1924)
Type of work: Novel

Type of plot: Psychological realism
Time of plot: 1880's
First published: 1907

Late nineteenth century London is the setting for this tale of sinister revolutionaries secretly employed by foreign governments and the British police who pursue them. Adolph Verloc, one of those revolutionaries, owns a small stationery shop which helps serve as a cover-up for his criminal activities.

*London. Center of the British Empire and home to exiled revolutionaries and refugees from throughout Europe. During the time of the novel, the great latitude and freedom extended by the British government to these exiles was a perpetual source of irritation and concern for more repressive governments on the continent of Europe, especially the unnamed country represented by Mr. Vladimir.

Verloc's shop. Shabby establishment at 32 Brett Street in the Soho section of London. As a cover to his activities as a secret agent for a foreign government (probably Russian), Adolf Verloc operates a small shop where he sells stationery, inks, and questionable publications, most of them of a vaguely revolutionary or quasi-pornographic nature. During business hours, the shop's door is left open and the coming and going of customers is signaled by a small, loud bell. Faded magazines, obscure newspapers, a few shabby bottles of ink, and other writing materials are displayed in the glass front of the shop and ranged along the shelves behind the counter. During much of the time, Verloc sits on a stool at the counter, hardly moving.

Verloc's home. Behind the shop live Verloc and his wife, Winnie, along with Winnie's aged mother and mentally deficient brother, Stevie. The home is furnished with what furniture remains with Winnie's mother from earlier, more prosperous days of her own marriage. Together, the shop and home present a thoroughly unremarkable appearance; the business is adequate but hardly prosperous. In a similar fashion, Verloc's secret life is only marginally successful. The parlor of the Verloc home is the meeting place of anarchists, socialists, and revolutionaries from throughout Europe, but these conspirators are merely ineffectual talkers, incapable of true action. Verloc's establishment is an appropriate physical setting for his secret but sordid activities.

Assistant commissioner's office. Office in the headquarters of the London police charged with investigating crimes such as Verloc's and the site of a lengthy discussion between the assistant commissioner and the chief inspector on the Verloc case. The assistant commissioner's office, barely described by Conrad, is a lean, functional place, much like the assistant commissioner

himself. Its function defines its appearance: It is a place where solid, honest work is performed.

London embassy. Typical diplomatic establishment of an unnamed European government. From the hints given by the narrative, the unnamed government is most probably the Russian Empire, although it might possibly be the Austrian-Hungarian Empire, both of which were highly fearful of international revolutionaries and employed secret agents such as Verloc against them. It is in these highly polished surroundings that Mr. Vladimir gives Verloc his instructions that lead to the bombing incident at the Greenwich Observatory.

Sir Ethelred's chambers. Official chambers located near the Houses of Parliament in London. As the office of the secretary of state, a high-ranking ministry in the British government, Sir Ethelred's dignified, solemn chambers represent the stability and solidity of Britain and its society. When the assistant commissioner reports to Sir Ethelred about the progress of the Verloc case, he does so in this setting.

Drawing room of a "great lady." Highly decorated site of social events which draw together characters from all ranks of society, including the assistant commissioner, revolutionary friends of Verloc, and foreign diplomats such as Mr. Vladimir. In a sense, the drawing room is a microcosm of London society.

— *Michael Witkoski*

SEEING THINGS

Author: Seamus Heaney (1939-   )   *First published:* 1991
Type of work: Poetry

The settings of this collection include the poet's childhood haunts in rural Northern Ireland, European capitals, and locations found in Irish or classical mythology. Such settings allow Seamus Heaney to demonstrate his belief in poetry's unique power "to credit marvels" while still "seeing things" as they are.

*Cumae (KYU-mee). Ancient town in Italy, believed to be the seat of an oracle whom the hero Aeneas is addressing in Heaney's opening poem, "The Golden Bough," translated loosely from a passage in Vergil's *Aeneid* (c. 29-19 B.C.E.; English translation, 1553). The references to the Greek underworld—Avernus, Tartarus, the River Acheron—find their counterparts in Heaney's closing poem in the volume. In this way, Heaney places

Seeing Things—with its many elegies—within the realm of the spirits.

*Inishbofin. One of many small islands off the west coast of Ireland, the site of medieval monastic settlements. The speaker in the book's title poem imaginatively likens the boat that travels to the island to that of Charon, the ferryman who carries souls across the mythical River Styx.

***Glanmore.** Location in County Wicklow, south of Dublin. The sonnet sequence "Glanmore Revisited" updates the "Glanmore Sonnets" which appeared in Heaney's 1976 collection *Field Work*. Heaney derives renewal from the quiet, natural setting, moving from feelings of being under siege in the first sonnet to the lifting of spirits in "Lustral Sonnet" and "The Skylight."

***Dungannon.** Town in County Tyrone, Northern Ireland. In "A Retrospect," a character points out nearby Glenshane Pass, quoting a seventeenth century British military dispatch comparing the local inhabitants to "Virgil's ghosts."

***Clonmacnoise** (klahn-mak-NOYZ). Monastery established in the sixth century south of Athlone along the River Shannon in central Ireland. For centuries the monks here produced or preserved various illuminated manuscripts and also kept records of daily life, from which Heaney amplifies the anecdote related in "Squarings."

***Lough Neagh** (lock nay). Largest lake in the British Isles, located in Northern Ireland, a place of fascination and reminiscence for Heaney.

***Giant's Causeway.** Natural rock formation on the Antrim coast in Northern Ireland, where massive hexagonal pillars of stone appear to have been placed or fitted in conjunction with each other, as if by some "giant."

***Coleraine** (kole-RAYN). Township on the River Bann in Northern Ireland. Heaney uses the place as a landmark for personal and poetic revelation in "Squarings."

— *James Scruton*

SEIZE THE DAY

Author: Saul Bellow (1915-   )
Type of work: Novel
Type of plot: Domestic realism

Time of plot: 1950's
First published: 1956

Setting is essential to this short novel, whose urban world crushes but finally cleanses Tommy Wilhelm on his one day of reckoning. The setting is richly realistic at the same time that the story is highly symbolic.

***Manhattan.** Borough of New York City in which most of the novella's action takes place, particularly among the fashionable neighborhoods near Broadway in Manhattan's Upper West Side. During a single day, Tommy Wilhelm remembers growing up in his family home on West End Avenue, visits the brokerage house where his commodities are losing value, eats lunch with Dr. Tamkin in a nearby cafeteria, takes old Mr. Rappaport to a cigar store—all familiar locations on the Upper West Side in the 1950's.

Gloriana. Aging Manhattan hotel. The major characters here, Tommy, his father (Dr. Adler), and his enigmatic advisor (Tamkin), all live at the Gloriana. Tommy spends time talking with Rubin at his newsstand in the lobby, eating breakfast with his father and then Tamkin in the dining room, and finally chasing Dr. Adler into the subterranean massage room where the father rejects his son. Housing mostly retired Jewish men and women, the Gloriana is contrasted with the Ansonia,

a hotel built by turn-of-the-century architect Stanford White.

***Brooklyn.** New York City borough that is home to Wilky's family, his former wife and two sons. While it has been a site of much of Wilky's suffering, it is also the location of Ebbets Field, where Wilky has taken his boys on happier days to watch the Dodgers play baseball.

***Los Angeles.** Southern California home of Hollywood and the scene of Tommy's first failure, in the 1930's, when, lured by the idea of easy money, he goes to the West Coast hoping for a career as an actor, and there changes his name from Wilhelm Adler to Tommy Wilhelm.

Funeral parlor. Scene of Tommy's final epiphany. At the end of the novel, searching for the elusive Tamkin, Tommy is pushed by a crowd into a funeral parlor, observes the corpse, and sobs. In Saul Bellow's symbolic prose, Tommy achieves some kind of catharsis.

— *David Peck*

SEJANUS HIS FALL

Author: Ben Jonson (1573-1637)
Type of work: Drama
Type of plot: Tragedy

Time of plot: First century C.E.
First performed: 1603; first published, 1605

A devoted classicist, Ben Jonson remains faithful to his sources in presenting both character and setting in this play. His principal aim is to give both readers and playgoers a sense of the historical Sejanus, a man who rose to favor with Emperor Tiberius, only to fall from his lofty position when Tiberius perceived him as a threat.

*Rome. Center of the ancient Roman Empire, which is under the rule of the emperor Tiberius at the time in which the play is set. The sense of intrigue that surrounds the machinations of Sejanus to discredit the legitimate heirs to the throne of the Roman Empire is captured in the careful juxtaposition of settings within the capital city. Factions supporting Sejanus and those opposed to him meet in the chambers of the emperor's palace, at Sejanus's home, in various gardens, on city streets, and at the home of his principal rival, the widow Agrippina, mother to three sons who stand in line to inherit the throne. In a key scene at the center of the play, the parties clash inside the Senate.

*Temple of Apollo. Roman temple dedicated to the god of wisdom, where Tiberius calls the Senate into session in order to humiliate and discredit Sejanus publicly. Tiberius's choice of a temple dedicated to the god of wisdom can be seen as an act of wisdom on his part, although many readers may see a certain irony in having such a politically calculated decision masked as a move that is officially declared to be in the best interests of the empire.

— *Laurence W. Mazzeno*

EL SEÑOR PRESIDENTE

Author: Miguel Ángel Asturias (1899-1974)
Type of work: Novel
Type of plot: Historical realism

Time of plot: Early twentieth century
First published: 1946 (English translation, 1963)

This novel generalizes the concept of the cycle of ruthlessness eventually visited upon enemy and friend alike by a dictator of an unnamed Latin American country struggling to maintain his power. Arbitrary and senseless violence characterizes every level of society and reaches almost every place—even those places normally regarded as sanctuaries of safety, protection, and comfort. Although the setting appears to be a Central American nation, this story of opposites plays upon the fears of every person, everywhere, that no one is safe anywhere.

Cathedral. Unnamed cathedral in whose shadow the novel opens as the sleep of several homeless men is disturbed by a police officer who starts to taunt a mentally disturbed man, who in turn inadvertently kills him. In medieval Europe, cathedrals were once places where those pursued for any reason could take refuge without fear of reprisal. However, this is decidedly not true in this unnamed country, where everyone from the rejects of society to the one-time elite may suffer arbitrary and senseless violence in any location, including a church.

Presidential palace. Home of the dictator of the unnamed country, "el presidente" of the novel's title. There, the ruthless president and his henchmen make arbitrary decisions about life and death, based upon their own selfish and greedy motives. Opposites abound in the palace. The beautiful—such as the president's aide Angel Face—are evil, the powerful are duplicitous, and friendship and personal loyalty cannot be trusted.

General Canales's house. Home of General Eusebio Canales, a once-trusted ally of the president, whom the president falsely suspects of involvement in the death of the colonel killed at the cathedral. The general's home is invaded and destroyed by officials, and he and his daughter, Camila, must flee. The president's own aide, Angel Face, later falls in love with Camila and takes her under his protection in his own home, but even his house proves to be unsafe.

Two-Step Tavern. Public house where Camila, a fugitive general's daughter, is nursed back to health and protected. Drinking places are ordinarily associated with society's excesses and sins and are not regarded as places of safety. In the novel, however, the Two-Step Tavern is just the opposite: a true sanctuary. In this regard, it contrasts sharply with police headquarters, where a woman named Fedina is detained by the police, who prevent her from feeding her baby until it dies, while demanding that she provide information about a situation she knows nothing about.

— *Debra D. Andrist*

SENSE AND SENSIBILITY

Author: Jane Austen (1775-1817)
Type of work: Novel
Type of plot: Domestic realism

Time of plot: Early nineteenth century
First published: 1811

This novel treats the need, in the search for marriage partners, to adapt tastes, manners, and affections, to the realities of predictable incomes. Its opening signals the importance of place, as the widowed Mrs. Henry Dashwood and her daughters are dislodged from the sizable estate that is their home until Henry Dashwood dies, leaving the estate to a son whose only obligation to his stepmother and stepsisters is a deathbed promise to his father. Where Henry's widow and her daughters are to live will play a major role in the daughters' opportunities for marriage.

Barton cottage. Home of Mrs. Dashwood and her three daughters, near Barton Park in Devonshire, three days' journey from London in southwest England, that is under the control of a distant relative. Mrs. Dashwood and her daughters move into the cottage after her stepson, John Dashwood, marries and his new wife makes it clear that they are no longer welcome in the home that she now manages. The women make the cottage comfortable and are resigned to the social gaucheries of Sir John Middleton and his mother-in-law, Mrs. Jennings, who apparently are to be their main social resources.

The novel's central romantic entanglements are introduced at the cottage, where the daughters begin receiving gentleman callers who represent prospective husbands. One caller, Edward Ferrars, who gives Elinor hope that her affection for him may be returned, is partial toward the cottage because he prefers the seclusion and quiet of country life to the social bustle of London.

Eventually the two older daughters find happiness with the lovers of their choice.

Norland Park. Sussex home of the widowed Mrs. Dashwood and her daughters that is inherited by her stepson, John Dashwood. Mrs. Dashwood fondly remembers it as her former home, Marianne remembers it for its elegance, and Elinor remembers it as the place where she and Edward became fond of each other.

Berkeley Street. Exclusive London neighborhood where Elinor and Marianne are the guests of Mrs. Jennings, Lady Middleton's mother, for an extended winter visit. At a party there, Marianne is stunned by the appearance of her former lover, Willoughby, and his efforts to snub her.

Cleveland. Somersetshire home of Mr. and Mrs. Palmer, Mrs. Jennings's other daughter, that serves as a convenient stopover for Elinor and Marianne on their return from London to Barton Cottage. Here, primarily from self-neglect, Marianne contracts an infectious fever, giving Colonel Brandon the chance to serve her by going after her mother. A drunken Willoughby appears, having heard that Marianne is dying, to beg her forgiveness for his marrying for money and to insist that he loves only her. Marianne recovers and comes to appreciate Colonel Brandon's devotion.

— *Carolyn Dickinson*

A SENTIMENTAL EDUCATION

Author: Gustave Flaubert (1821-1880)
Type of work: Novel
Type of plot: Realism

Time of plot: Nineteenth century
First published: L'Éducation sentimentale, 1869
(English translation, 1898)

This novel is set mostly in Paris during the 1840's, a period of political ferment and revolution. Seen through the eyes of the young student Frédéric Moreau, the setting provides a backdrop for his life and loves, and at the same time, the descriptions of the city reflect his fluctuating emotional states.

*Paris. France's leading city functions as the setting for the novel on several levels. First, it exists on the purely physical level. Gustave Flaubert—who was once, like Frédéric early in the novel, a young law student in Paris—uses realistic details and names of streets, boulevards, monuments, and other landmarks to describe Frédéric's life in Paris, meticulously reproducing the city of the pre-Haussmann 1840's. Readers can map out Frédéric's walks or carriage rides through Paris to the Latin Quarter, where he studies law; the Seine River, which runs through the heart of Paris; the Champs-Élysées; the Bois de Boulogne, where Frédéric engages in a duel; and Montmartre, where Madame Arnoux lives.

These physical descriptions of Paris are filtered through Frédéric's mind and colored by his imagination and emotional states. For example, when he walks through the streets with Madame Arnoux, the great love of his life, the chilly, foggy, wet day is for him delightful. When his mood is downcast, descriptions of the city darken. A walk through the Jardin des Plantes, a botanical garden with a museum of natural history, located on the Left Bank, serves as a catalyst for Frédéric's imagination, and the actual scene disappears as he envisions Madame Arnoux and himself traveling to faraway lands. In fact, at times, everything he sees in Paris reminds him of her.

Other elements of the Parisian setting include cafés, drawing rooms, boudoirs, apartments, and gardens. As Frédéric visits these places, descriptions indicate not only what he sees but also how he feels about what he sees.

Paris is, in addition, a city of politics and revolution during the 1840's. Flaubert carefully researched each political event and its location before integrating it into the novel. Descriptions of barricades in the streets or of the attack on the Palais Royal, in the heart of Paris, are based on contemporary sources. These events, though they are recounted in the novel, are often on the edge of Frédéric's awareness. While Frédéric is planning a tryst with Madame Arnoux in February of 1848, a revolution is breaking out in Paris and King Louis-Philippe abdicates; however, Frédéric is too preoccupied with his personal life to take much note of it. During June, 1848, when fighting fills the streets of Paris, Frédéric is out of town and only afterward reads reports of the upheaval. Thus, the life of the city often pulses forward while Frédéric is either only a spectator to the events or even oblivious to them as they occur.

On occasion, the city itself and its elements take on a life of their own, as when the pavement of a Parisian street appears to speed Frédéric along toward Madame Arnoux, a door opens "almost by itself," and its handle seems "as gentle and sensitive as a hand in his own." In peace time, Frédéric hears in the sounds of the morning the "great voice of Paris awakening," whereas in time of conflict, a friend of Frédéric's describes Paris as "bristling with bayonets."

Flaubert admitted that because his novel's setting crowded its pages, he had to make room for his characters to live by relegating the setting—both places and history—to the background. Even so, Paris of the 1840's is a major force in the novel.

Nogent-sur-Seine (noh-ZHAWN-syur-sehn). Small provincial bourgeois town southeast of Paris where Flaubert's father was born and spent his early childhood. Years later, Flaubert regularly visited cousins in Nogent and in the novel re-created its small-town atmosphere, which contrasts with the cosmopolitan atmosphere of Paris. The family house in Nogent is the prototype for Frédéric's mother's house, to which Frédéric returns several times, only to escape back to Paris.

Fontainebleau (fawn-tehn-BLOH). Town southeast of Paris that is the location of one of the palaces of the kings of France and of the Forest of Franchard. Both the palace and the forest were tourist attractions, even in the nineteenth century. Frédéric and Rosanette, one of his mistresses, leave Paris just as the city is being barricaded and as fighting is breaking out in the streets. Absorbed with each other, they visit the palace and forest, awed by the grandeur of past monarchies and nature, peacefully exchanging confidences, unconcerned about the revolutionary events of the present, until Frédéric sees the name of a friend in a list of the wounded and insists on returning to Paris. Again, Frédéric's focus on his personal life blinds him to momentous national events in Paris.

— *Elizabeth A. Hait*

A SENTIMENTAL JOURNEY

Author: Laurence Sterne (1713-1768)
Type of work: Novel
Type of plot: Sentimental

Time of plot: 1760's
First published: A Sentimental Journey Through France and Italy, 1768

This book's original title, "A Sentimental Journey Through France and Italy," is misleading in that its fictional traveler, Mr. Yorick, sees little of the former country and absolutely nothing of the latter. Satirizing real travel books of his day, Laurence Sterne generally ignores places in favor of people. His protagonist, Yorick, rarely remarks on his surroundings, choosing instead to focus on the hearts and minds of those he meets.

Calais (ka-LAY). French port town on the English Channel, where Yorick lands after crossing from England. The author places travelers in various categories such as "Inquisitive" and "Splenetic." Yorick himself wishes to be a "sentimental traveller." He will experience the world without a jaundiced eye, and thereby learn more about himself than about the places he visits. It hardly concerns this type of traveler where he goes; it is the journey that matters.

Yorick has not entirely slipped into the sentimental mode when he first arrives in Calais. While dining at a local inn, he rudely dismisses a poor monk seeking alms. He quickly repents of his harsh treatment, however, and, through the rest of the novel treats people, from noble-

men to beggars, with great interest and compassion. This is particularly true of the many women he encounters. Though Calais is Yorick's first experience in a foreign country, he spends his entire time there flirting with a woman from Brussels. Time is largely irrelevant to the sentimental traveler. If one looks at everything around him with interest in his heart, he muses, "what a large volume of adventures may be grasped" within a single hour.

Paris. French capital and obligatory stop on the grand tour of Europe. On the way to the great city, Yorick employs a manservant named La Fleur, a young Frenchman who is a sentimental traveler in his own right and who sees the world through his heart. When they arrive in Paris, Yorick makes a point of avoiding famous sites such as the Louvre, the Palais Royal, and galleries and churches. He believes that the "originals" of art are humankind and that all people are temples unto themselves. Sterne himself was a cleric, and Christian love for one's neighbor, both charitable and physical, suffuses his traveler's universe.

Eschewing the city's traditional tourist spots, Yorick explores bookstores, millinery shops, and the comic opera. While his adventures routinely involve pretty young shop girls and chambermaids, he engages a wide variety of characters from all rungs of the social ladder. He is particularly taken by an old French military officer, who declares that the great advantage of a journey is that through seeing a great deal of human nature, one is taught mutual tolerance, and, by extension, mutual love. This is contrary to most eighteenth century travelogues, in which excessive description of locality is the norm.

After gaining entry into Parisian society, and establishing himself as a popular house guest, Yorick soon tires of the artificial milieu. He longs to return to people whose behavior is guided more by nature than by etiquette. Here, Sterne touches on the common literary dichotomy of city/artifice in opposition to country/nature. But, importantly, he shies away from overly simplistic qualitative judgments. The sentimental traveler sees both the good and the bad wherever he wanders.

*Versailles (ver-SI). Town on the outskirts of Paris that was the royal seat of France's government during the eighteenth century. Tired of high society, Yorick decides to leave Paris. He is obliged, however, to get a passport or possibly face the unpleasantness of the great prison, the Bastille. He ponders the unhappy fate of cap-

tives and immediately sets out for Versailles to lobby a government official. Along the way, he pointedly remarks that there was nothing on the trip which interested him. Instead, he tells a story about a bird in a cage that is never able to gain its freedom, possibly referencing the barbarity of slavery. Imprisonment, then, is especially horrible because it deprives one of social interaction, not freedom of movement.

*Bourbonnois (bor-bo-NWAW). Historic rural region in central France, also called Bourbonnais. Having acquired a passport, Yorick journeys into the countryside. He describes the Bourbonnois as one of the "sweetest" regions in France. It is harvest time, and the laughter and singing of workers in the field complete a bucolic picture of happiness. There, he meets a poor, country girl named Maria who has gone mad with grief over her father's death. Yorick, in turn, is overcome with emotion for the girl, and thereby unable to enjoy his lovely surroundings. Again, there is no environment or location that affects the sentimental traveler more than the human condition he finds there.

Later, Yorick takes refuge at a peasant farmhouse where he is treated with great hospitality. Among these generous folk, he has found a home, if just for a few hours, because he has found hearts full of sentiment and goodness.

The novel abruptly ends in the middle of a delicate situation involving a chambermaid at a country inn. Ostensibly, Sterne died before he could complete the book. Alas, poor Yorick never reaches Italy. However, to a sentimental traveler, this failing scarcely matters.

— *John Slocum*

SET THIS HOUSE ON FIRE

Author: William Styron (1925-   )
Type of work: Novel
Type of plot: Psychological realism

Time of plot: Mid-twentieth century
First published: 1960

Two persistent geographical dichotomies in this novel's settings help underscore the parallels established between the United States and post-World War II Europe. New York (representing the demoralizing North) and Virginia (representing southern morality) are set in opposition to each other, as are the United States and

Europe, Italy in particular. In trying to show these settings to be geographically and morally distinct from one another, the characters and plot end up emphasizing how alike and how similarly demoralizing they actually are, though in the end they prove to be similarly healing.

Sambuco. Fictional village on Italy's west-central coast, not far from Salerno—a six-hour drive south from Rome and one hour from Naples. It sits atop imposing cliffs and looks downward into deep gorges, one of which Cass Kinsolving nearly falls into and another in which American millionaire Mason Flagg's body is eventually found.

Built in the ninth century, Sambuco enjoyed its greatest prosperity in the thirteenth century. In World War II, it escaped destruction because of its physical isolation. However, beneath Sambuco's facade of longevity and bucolic peacefulness lies a village being gradually demoralized by postwar poverty and despair. Mason Flagg's arrival and subsequent "Americanization" of his Sambuco experience, despite his expatriate posings, set events in motion. Sambuco's remoteness, its geographical aloofness toward the rest of Italy, and the village's uninvolvement in the war's violence and destruction all stand in ironic contrast to the violence that occurs in the novel.

New York City. Before the departure of the novel's narrator, Peter Leverett, for Europe, he and Mason Flagg reconnect in a Greenwich Village bar. Mason introduces Peter to his version of New York City—a new and eye-opening world of sex, excess, self-indulgence, and alcohol. At first, Peter marvels at both Mason's and the city's fearsome duality: gentleman by day, nihilist by night. However, following ten days of debauchery and excess in New York City with Mason, Peter is relieved finally to leave behind the city's depravity as he sets sail for Europe. To Peter, New York represents America and Mason represents New York, and he is ultimately horrified and mesmerized by them both.

Port Warwick. Virginia city of Peter Leverett's youth and, for a time, Mason Flagg's. Mason and Peter both attend St. Andrew's School in Port Warwick until Mason is expelled for allegedly raping a female classmate. While growing up at Merryoaks, a palatial colonial plantation manor, Mason is surrounded by the wealth, parties, celebrities, flash, and glamour that he later surrounds himself with in the Sambuco version of his home.

(Although "Port Warwick" was a fictional place when William Styron wrote this novel, it is now the name of an experimental village in Newport News, Virginia. In tribute to the novel, the community's three-acre town square has been named Styron Square, and Styron himself was accorded the honor of naming most of Port Warwick's streets and squares.)

Europe and **North America.** These two continents are treated metaphorically as two parts of the same place, divided by an ocean. From the beginning, a generalized parallelism exists between them despite their obvious differences. Additionally, Mason, who represents much that is objectionable about America, merely transports his own "America" to Italy. In Sambuco, the three expatriates' purported disdain for America is contradicted by their apparent embrace of things American, such as Mason's Cadillac, Hollywood houseguests, and flashy wealth, all of which are surprisingly evident in postwar France, Italy, and presumably other parts of Europe. At various points in the novel, Europe and America are both decried as artistically, morally, and spiritually "dead."

— *Cherie Castillo*

SEVEN AGAINST THEBES

Author: Aeschylus (525/524-456/455 B.C.E.)
Type of work: Drama
Type of plot: Tragedy

Time of plot: Antiquity
First performed: Hepta epi Thēbas, 467 B.C.E. (English translation, 1777)

This play describes the attack on Thebes and its king Eteocles by his brother Polyneices and six other warriors from various Greek towns. Action takes place in an open area of the city, the agora, and centers on the fighting between warriors at each of the seven gates of Thebes.

*Thebes (theebz). Largest city in the ancient Greek region of Boeotia. In Greek mythology, Thebes is a central location in tales of Oedipus, Antigone, Pentheus, and Teiresias and is particularly important as a location of meetings connecting mortals and the gods. Thebes had unusual connections with the East, as its founder, Cadmus, was believed to have come from Phoenicia. In drama, Thebes is often marked by archetypal conflicts between gods and humans, young and older generations, brothers, and, most notably, between self and other, inside and outside.

Throughout *Seven Against Thebes*, Thebes is presented as a ship buffeted by a storm at sea, despite its actual physical distance from the sea. Eteocles strives to retain control of the ship of state but ultimately fails in the face of more powerful forces. As in most plays by Athenian poets, such as Aeschylus, the city of Thebes is on many levels a substitute for Athens, and the drama presents issues of philosophical and intellectual concern to citizens of the Athenian democracy.

*Agora. Greek term for a city's central business and meeting area. The agora of Thebes is the place where King Eteocles plans the defense of his city and explains his actions to the citizens. In this play, the agora is the site of battle-planning, an unusual activity for a place normally associated with ordinary business matters.

*Seven Gates. Entrances to Thebes. In ancient culture, the number seven had ritual and religious significance and the seven gates of Thebes represent the portals to power. It is only when Eteocles and Polyneices clash at the seventh gate that the royal House of Laius finally falls. The gates are like holes in the ship of state, as more are opened, the doom of Eteocles and his city is assured.

— *David Larmour*

THE SEVEN WHO WERE HANGED

Author: Leonid Andreyev (1871-1919)
Type of work: Novel
Type of plot: Social realism

Time of plot: Early twentieth century
First published: Rasskaz o semi poveshannykh, 1908 (English translation, 1909)

Set in Imperial Russia's capital city, this story about early twentieth century Russian revolutionaries condemned to death for trying to assassinate a prominent minister offers a fine psychological portrayal of the thoughts and feelings of people facing death by hanging and conveys a dreary depiction of Russia's criminal justice system.

*St. Petersburg. Capital of Russia at the time this novel is set. The entire story takes place in this city; Leonid Andreyev never mentions it by name, but its identity is obvious. There are no glimpses of the city itself. Andreyev uses it simply because it was the capital and nerve center of the country. He also implies that the Russian government was unjust in its treatment of those who disagreed with it. Andreyev does not take political sides; as a matter of fact, political issues are hardly mentioned. It is clear, however, that he portrays the revolutionaries with sympathy. Other locations are mentioned in passing, such as the unnamed villages where two of the condemned men committed their crimes.

At the beginning of the twentieth century, Russia was troubled by the unrest of workers who demanded better living conditions. This was manifested in the revolutions of 1905 and 1917. *The Seven Who Were Hanged* depicts the death sentences and hangings of five revolutionaries and two common criminals in St. Petersburg. The revolutionaries are branded terrorists by the authorities, though there is no proof of their crime.

Prison. Fortress building in which the accused prisoners are held. Their alleged crime was not Andreyev's main concern. Rather, he wanted to show the behavior of the unjustly condemned facing death. The prisoners languish in their cells in a fortress, where they can only sense that spring is coming and everything is ready to burst to life except for them. The only external sound they hear is the striking of a steeple clock, especially at night. The ticking is symbolical of their lives literally eroding by the minute. The final scene is placed in a forest, where the hanging takes place. Amid the soft snow and the balmy forest the lives of seven young people are snuffed away.

Courtroom. Nondescript government building in St. Petersburg which seems to have one purpose only—to convict people and sentence them to death. The novel's action takes place mainly in this room.

— *Vasa D. Mihailovich*

SEVENTEEN

Author: Booth Tarkington (1869-1946)
Type of work: Novel
Type of plot: Comic realism

Time of plot: Early twentieth century
First published: 1916

This novel's setting is tightly focused, confined to a single neighborhood. Most of the action, in fact, takes place in or near only two of the houses in this neighborhood. One of the charms of this novel is indeed its evocation of the physical details of times past and of the innocence of Middle America before the terrible trauma of World War I, the Great Depression, and World War II.

Midland city. Unnamed midwestern city that provides the novel neighborhood setting; Booth Tarkington calls it simply a "middle-sized midland city." However, Tarkington based it on Indianapolis, Indiana, his birthplace and hometown. (Readers will note that, in the novel's first paragraph, its protagonist, William "Willie" Baxter, appears at the corner of Washington Street and Central Avenue. Washington Street was and is a major thoroughfare of Indianapolis, running east to west through the city and into surrounding counties.)

Tarkington's city serves as an icon of nostalgia, a kind of literary museum of the way things once were, culturally and morally, in small cities and villages across America. Readers of the twenty-first century will perhaps be surprised to note some of the physical features of the city: one can easily walk from its center to its residential neighborhoods. Automobiles are mentioned but seldom seen, and are not at all something that every family has. The story's characters move from one place to another on foot or on the trolley. One scene, near the middle of the novel, is staged on a "streetcar." Travel outside the city is by train (one of the last scenes in the novel takes place in the city's railway station).

The novel's first scene is set in an old-fashioned drugstore. Such family-owned businesses served as popular meeting places for young people. The adolescents in *Seventeen* are remarkably conscious of decorum and proper dress. Even a stroll down the streets of the residential areas calls for suits and hats for the teenage boys, and dresses, elegant shoes, and hats for the girls.

The novel's "midland city" is racially divided. It is plain that African American characters are only a generation or two removed from slavery; their speech patterns and customs seem southern rather than midwestern. Moreover, their relationship to such families as the Baxters is ambiguous. The African American Genesis, for example, is regularly employed by the Baxters and other neighborhood families as a handyman and waiter. He is always on call, and Tarkington depicts him as grateful to earn what he can to support a very modest lifestyle.

Avynoo. African American neighborhood in the unnamed city—where all the "colored" people live, as one of the novel's African American characters puts it. Again, this fictional section of *Seventeen*'s nameless city has its origin in fact. The "avynoo" is a transparent allusion to Indianapolis's Indiana Avenue, which has been known for many years as "the avenue," the heart of the city's African American culture.

While the neighborhood where the Baxter family and their friends live is white middle-class America, the avynoo refers to urban American ghettos. The tranquil milieu of *Seventeen*, however, does not belie any racial tension; neither the novel's whites nor its African Americans seem to regret that the races are sharply segregated in their neighborhoods and opportunities.

— *Gordon Walters*

SHADOWS ON THE ROCK

Author: Willa Cather (1873-1947)
Type of work: Novel
Type of plot: Historical

Time of plot: Late seventeenth century
First published: 1931

This novel is set in French Canada in the late seventeenth century. Willa Cather makes effective use of its remote location to convey to her readers both the isolation of French emigrants from their native land and their efforts to cope with the harsh climate in their new land.

*Quebec City. French settlement on the St. Lawrence River, in what is now Canada's province of Quebec, that is the novel's principal setting. The oldest section of the city is enclosed within walls. The lower city is at the level of the river, and the upper city stands on palisades several hundred feet higher. Steep steps connect the two parts.

As the novel opens, Euclide Auclair, a pharmacist, watches a ship depart for France, thinking that the river's building ice floes will prevent any new ships from arriving from France for at least six months. He is not depressed by the physical isolation of the French immigrants from their native land. He and other colonists have attempted to recreate French culture in the harsh climate of Quebec and have also tried to coexist with Native Canadians, whom they do not truly understand. Missionaries, including the real historical figures of Bishop Laval and Sister Marie of the Incarnation, have built French schools and churches in Quebec. They have also introduced innovations that do not exist in France. In the quiet isolation of Quebec City, these two missionaries are adapting to their new country and introducing changes that enable French immigrants and Native Canadians to respect each other's cultures.

As the French immigrants adapt to life in Canada, they eventually come to realize that they will never return to France. With Bishop's Laval's blessing, Father Hector takes a vow of perpetual stability. This means that he will spend the rest of his life in Canada and will never return to a comfortable life in France.

The physical isolation of French immigrants from their homeland and their need to accept a multicultural society make the characters change. While the French immigrants maintain their strong commitment to Roman Catholicism, they eventually realize that Catholicism and ethnocentrism are incompatible. Bishop Laval gives all of his earthly possessions to charity and lives a simple life. Even the count of Frontanec, the French governor of Canada, considers religion to be more important than politics. He attends mass daily and willingly sacrifices his career in France so that he can help devout missionaries to meet the spiritual needs of immigrants and Native Canadians alike. The harsh climate and the simple residences in which even such influential characters as Bishop Laval and Governor Frontenac live help Cather's readers to realize that the true reality for these characters is not this life but rather the eternal life in heaven.

Auclair house (oh-KLAYR). Quebec home of Euclide Auclair and his twelve-year-old daughter Cécile. Auclair initially strives to maintain the daily customs of his native France and obtain most of their goods and furnishings from France. He also tries to have a proper French garden with French flowers and plants. Inside his house and garden, he and his daughter try, but in vain, to give the impression to visitors that they are more French than Canadian. Gradually, they come to understand the artificiality of their pretense. Differences in climate and people make it impossible to replicate France in Canada.

— *Edmund J. Campion*

SHE

Author: H. Rider Haggard (1856-1925)
Type of work: Novel
Type of plot: Adventure

Time of plot: Late nineteenth century
First published: 1887

This adventure novel, set in a wholly imaginary part of Central Africa, creates a sense of place that appealed to the willingness of late nineteenth century readers to believe that Africa was a land of mystery containing "lost" civilizations and supernatural phenomena. The novel leaves readers thinking of Africa as a dark and terrible place.

***Cambridge University.** Great English university in which the novel begins and ends. The university represents the staid, rational, and traditional patterns of British thought and learning. Against this familiar background of scientific knowledge and reason, a highly implausible tale unfolds. The juxtaposition of the university's prosaic surroundings with the horrifying story found in an ancient chest of Egyptian origin makes for an atmosphere of eerie disbelief.

Within the Spiritualist movement that was popular at the time *She* was written, stories of reincarnation and previous lives spent in ancient Egypt were capturing the imagination of the British public. Rider Haggard combined a Spiritualist theme with elements of thrilling adventure in an imaginary Africa of lost tribes ruled by white queens and secrets of eternal life to add to the atmosphere of foreboding and death.

Central Africa. Region in which the main action of the novel is ostensibly set. The novel's two English protagonists, Ludwig Horace Holly and his ward, Leo Vincey, approach the east coast of Central Africa on an Arab boat that is sunk by a sudden violent storm. The storm, which represents the savagery and mutability of the African continent, deposits the adventurers in a bay along a rugged coastline. There, they find a gigantic stone, shaped like a human, marking the mouth of a river that proves to be part of a system of quays and canals built by some ancient civilization. These ancient remains lend a sense of mystery and foreboding to the novel. Haggard also describes some of the region's exotic animals, including species that have never been cataloged before, thereby adding to the sense of mystery.

Amahagger caves (ah-muh-HAH-ger). Large underground complex that is part of an ancient stone city, to which the castaways are taken by a tribe of light-skinned men. Carved within the crater of an extinct inland volcano, the caves are inhabited by the stone-age Amahagger people, who prefer living in the catacombs, amid ancient mummies, to living in the stone ruins of the city itself. The mummies suggest a connection with Egypt, and the whole setting creates an atmosphere soaked in morbidity combined with a sense of dread.

The novel is filled with images of decay and death that include brutal executions and torture, caverns in which people sleep on burial slabs, embalmed figures of long-dead people, heaps of human bones, a wild dance illuminated by burning corpses, and, finally, the image of the queen Ayesha disintegrating before the eyes of her appalled comrades.

Kôr. Hidden city, deeper in the interior, to which the Englishmen are taken. The route from the caves leads through deep swamps that eventually give way to an open plain that in turn leads to a tunneled mountain, through which the men are taken, blindfolded, to another plain and then to apartments cut into solid rock. There, they are introduced to the white queen Ayesha, "She-who-must-be-obeyed." The Englishmen learn that the ruins of Kôr have remained in exactly the same condition for more than two thousand years, since the city's people were destroyed by a plague.

Cave of Fire. Another terrible and dangerous journey faces the travelers as they discover the cavern of the fire of eternal life in which Ayesha renews her vitality.

— *H. Alan Pickrell*

SHE STOOPS TO CONQUER: Or, The Mistakes of a Night

Author: Oliver Goldsmith (1728 or 1730-1774)
Type of work: Drama
Type of plot: Comedy of manners

Time of plot: Eighteenth century
First performed: 1773; first published, 1773

Oliver Goldsmith sets this comedy in an English village, which he says is about a day's carriage ride from London. Late action includes a bumpy carriage ride through muddy lanes which ends in an artificial pond for watering stock. All this comes to represent the bumpy changes in British society from the old to the new.

Hardcastle Mansion. This village dwelling is a substantially built house, which nevertheless must have been timbered and devoid of the familiar medieval stone turrets and towers that marked the castles of the nobility and the upper class. The mansion can be easily mistaken for a country inn. This mistaken identity of place represents the major theme of the play. The Englishman, especially the male, is a modern person for whom identity is always a question; a satisfactory resolution of identity depends on a wise marriage of the old and the new, in which both the man and the woman are strong characters. The complex nature of the house in the play symbolizes this theme.

Three Pigeons Inn. Tavern whose taproom is the location where the plot of mistaken identity is planned by Tony Lumpkin, who is even more innovative in his notions of identity than the marrying couple of the play. Drinking and the carefree life of the tavern may represent future social change for Goldsmith, or at least his mockery of it in the play.

Feather-bed Lane. Bumpy road on which the wild roundabout ride in the final act of the play begins only to end in the pond. The comic chase represents again how revolutionary Goldsmith is with his suggestions of a changing British society, in which town and country values are tossed together.

— *Donald M. Hassler*

THE SHELTERED LIFE

Author: Ellen Glasgow (1873-1945)
Type of work: Novel
Type of plot: Psychological realism

Time of plot: 1906-1914
First published: 1932

In this novel that examines the struggle between the "Old South" and the "New South," place is a vital component. The fictional town of Queenborough itself almost takes on the role of a character, for it is a place that is at once sheltering and deceiving. Even the odor from its chemical factory symbolizes the struggle between the old and the new, between the past and the present.

Queenborough. Fictionalized version of Virginia's capital city, Richmond, during the early twentieth century. In the years following the Civil War, Queenborough is sharply divided into three distinct geographical areas: Washington Avenue, Granite Boulevard, and Canal Street. Queenborough society is divided by these physical delineations as well. Granite Boulevard is the neighborhood where the most expensive and elegant homes are located. Only those families who are secure financially and socially live in this neighborhood.

Washington Street houses the older families, those who lack the financial means to move to Granite Boulevard or are determined to maintain the status quo. The Archbald family, headed by General David Archbald, and the Birdsong family, consisting only of the comparatively impoverished George and Eva, are the mainstays of the upper end of Washington Street.

On the opposite end of town lies Canal Street, where only the poor families and those on the fringes of society make their homes. Though Canal Street is physically only three blocks distant from Washington Street, socially it is much farther removed.

Penitentiary Bottom. Section of Queenborough near the penitentiary, where the lower classes of society live. Penitentiary Bottom is located at the lower end of Canal Street on the opposite end of town from the Archbalds and the Birdsongs. Nine-year-old Jenny Blair Archbald, curious to see where a bad smell comes from, decides to go to this place to see for herself what it is like. The chemical factory that is the source of the odor is also located here, and it symbolizes change, progress, and the New South. When Jenny returns, she asks her grandfather, General Archbald, if only bad people live there. He assures her that there are good people everywhere, even in Penitentiary Bottom.

Archbald garden. Property of the Archbald family on Washington Street. Jenny Blair sees her family garden as a place where time moves at the same steady pace it always has. The beauty and serenity of the walled garden are occasionally marred, however, by the odor from the chemical factory on the other side of town. Even within the walls of the family garden, the "stench" of progress is beginning to take over. The world outside the Archbald home and garden is a place of factories, steam whistles, bad smells, and modern "touring cars." In direct opposition to the outside world, inside the Archbald property is a place of sounds from the stable, piano playing, and hushed voices discussing private family matters.

Birdsong garden. Property of George and Eva Birdsong on Washington Street. Unlike the Archbald property, the Birdsong home and garden seem to be succumbing to the ravages of passing time. The gardener, Uncle Abednego, fights a losing battle to keep the house and garden in good repair. But for Jenny Blair, the Birdsong property has taken on the beauty of Eva Birdsong, the embodiment of the Old South for Queenborough. The Birdsong property symbolizes the dying values and ideals of the Old South. No matter how much work is put into trying to return the property to its days of former glory, time and change are slowly taking their toll. Even the name of the resident bullfrog, Old Mortality, conveys a feeling of the passage of time and the passing away of the old way of life once lived on Washington Street and indeed in all of Queenborough.

Curlew. Country home of the Peyton family. This home is a place reminiscent of the kinds of balls and parties attended by the important Queenborough families in the years just before and after the Civil War. Even in 1906, the wealthy families gather at Curlew for a ball, symbolizing their attempt to reclaim the past. However, progress is unrelenting, and even the presence of Eva Birdsong is unable to restore the past to Queenborough.

— *Kimberley H. Kidd*

THE SHELTERING SKY

Author: Paul Bowles (1910-1999)
Type of work: Novel
Type of plot: Psychological realism

Time of plot: After World War II
First published: 1949

This novel chronicles a young American couple's journey deep into North Africa's Sahara Desert, with which the husband, an avid map-reader, is so mesmerized that he keeps warnings about the desert's dangers to himself. He intends to merge himself with the desert in order to experience a psychological unity that he cannot attain at home.

*Northwestern Africa. Vast arid region overlapping modern Algeria and Mali in which the novel is set and where author Paul Bowles spent a year touring before writing this, his first novel. He later traveled extensively through the Sahara and eventually settled in North Africa, the scene of most of his later fiction.

*Oran. Algerian port city on the Mediterranean coast in which the novel opens. The freighter on which the Port and Kit Moresby arrive spews them out onto hot docks and into a cluttered and disorganized city. When the husband, Port, awakens from an afternoon nap, he is initially aware only of being "somewhere" after experiencing a vast "nowhere." This duality of his mental landscape makes place essential to the novel. Port considers himself a "traveler" and not a "tourist," one who lives by moving from place to place; however, he also seems foolishly unaware of the dangers of the North African climate and alien culture ahead.

Port walks alone in the native Algerian section of the French-ruled city, wandering toward the outskirts of town, observing crowds of impoverished people, whom he finds merely repetitive, spiritless beings. He passes through dark, narrow streets lined with increasingly dilapidated shacks. At the city's edge, he slides down a hillside dump through a litter of fish bones and similar garbage. From there he sees the glistening salt beds ("sebkas") stretching out into the desert below, illuminated by a "giant rift" in the sky—the Milky Way, from which a filtered white light emanates.

*Sahara. Great desert expanse that stretches from the northwestern coast of Africa to the Red Sea and across the Arabian Peninsula. As the Americans venture ever deeper into the desert, both societal and natural conditions steadily worsen; hotels grow shabbier and travel more difficult. The people they meet—other travelers, French military officers, and Algerians alike—regard them with a mixture of tolerance, indifference, and hostility. The desert itself becomes increasingly fierce, barren, and oppressive.

Boussif. Desert town in which Port, Kit, and their American companion, Tunner, find a treeless, modern collection of square blocks, mud-filled streets, and inhabitants shielded from the violent sun by tightened burnouses or cloaks that cover their heads. A wasteland surrounds the town, its emptiness stretching to mountains of "raw, savage rock without vegetation." In spite of tension in their marriage, Port and Kit enjoy observing a sunset together, though it reveals to each of them their extreme differences: The vast emptiness and silence of the desert fulfills Port's expectations but simply terrifies Kit.

Aïn Krorfa. Algerian desert town, the approach to which is verdant, thanks to plentiful "seguias" or watercourses. However, the air is clotted with flies and the Grand Hotel's courtyard has a dried-up fountain filled with garbage, children with bursting sores, hairless pink dogs, and a dead fig tree whose branches are looped with barbed wire. Kit complains about the heat and squalor, and even Port is experiencing nervousness, bad dreams, and chills. Hoping to improve his relations with Kit, he persuades Tunner to continue on to Messad with other travelers.

*Bou Noura. Algerian fortress town in which Port and Kit stay in the second segment of the novel, "The Earth's Sharp Edge," when Port becomes ill. From there, they travel on to El Ga'a, where, despite Port's weakened condition, they cannot find lodging. Arriving in Sbâ, they are given a room in a fortress where Port, expecting in his last moments to achieve the repose he envisions beyond "the sheltering sky," dies of fever.

*French Sudan. West African colony that became independent as Mali in 1960. In the final section of the novel, "The Sky," Kit flees from Bou Noura by joining two men in a camel caravan. Forced to travel as a sexual slave through the Sahara to the French Sudan, she is placed in a harem and loses her sanity.

— *Margaret A. Dodson*

SHIP OF FOOLS

Author: Katherine Anne Porter (1890-1980)
Type of work: Novel
Type of plot: Allegory

Time of plot: August 22-September 17, 1931
First published: 1962

This allegorical novel consists of three parts, with the majority of the action occurring within the confines and levels of a German passenger ship sailing from Mexico to Germany in 1931. The first part of the novel describes the Mexican port city, Veracruz, from which the ship initiates its voyage, while the third part mostly refers to the final German destination.

***Veracruz.** Port city in Mexico from which the German ship *Vera* departs. Most of its passengers are Germans returning to their homeland after visiting Mexico for various reasons and lengths of stay. Passengers from other European nations, the United States, and Cuba also board the ship.

The novel opens with a French epigram meaning, "When are we setting forth toward happiness?" It suggests the allegorical nature of the voyage that is to come. The notion of human happiness is set forth as a destination, that is, a place, or a stasis, that the travelers desire to reach. Thus, the literal geographical references introduced in the novel parallel the great variety of human culture across the globe, yet these various places represent the particular and universal longings of passengers who inevitably mistake place for purpose, who confuse national identity for authenticity. The localizing of the passengers at Vera Cruz anticipates what will occur on the ship once the passengers are on board en route for Europe.

In addition to Vera Cruz, the novelist refers to numerous cities and countries in her work. Since the story is an allegory, it uses these places literally; on one level the book is about a great variety of peoples coming together to travel on a ship. Each passenger has a special reason for traveling to a specific destination. On other levels, however, the work is a moral commentary on the political climate, class distinctions, and social displacement of humans in the 1930's. Porter comments in a preface to the novel that she is "a passenger on that ship" and implies that the readers are as well.

Vera. German passenger liner on which the bulk of the novel's action occurs. Passengers interact with one another and reflect on various matters as they are united in the controlled environment of this ship. Attitudes of superiority, suspicion, and animosity that exist among people the world over are accentuated when viewed in the controlled space of the ship. Attitudes that might otherwise be dissipated or obscured by political and geographical boundaries are centrally focused because of the confines of the ship.

The second section of the novel opens with a German epigram that translates as "No house, no home." It suggests the existential displacement of the passengers. Although most passengers are literally returning to their own homes (or continuing points of destination for the tourists on board), the allegory suggests a disconnect between place and value.

As the ship crosses the Atlantic Ocean, its passengers are located in distinct places on board that suggest their social position. On the lowest level—literally near the bottom decks of the ship—in steerage, more than eight hundred dislocated migrant field hands are uncomfortably bunched together. At the other end of the spectrum, the German captain has the freedom to wander throughout the ship, though he does not want to enter the lowest part of the ship, and other people are not allowed to enter his domain. He routinely interacts socially with the fifty or so passengers who are traveling on the high, first-class deck. The places of the characters on the ship thus parallel their places of social privilege and assumed value in the larger world.

***Bremerhaven.** German port that is the final destination of the ship and most of its bourgeois passengers.

***Canary Islands.** Islands off the western bulge of Africa that are the destination of the Cuban field workers traveling in the ship's steerage level.

— *Kenneth Hada*

THE SHOEMAKER'S HOLIDAY: Or, The Gentle Craft

Author: Thomas Dekker (c. 1572-1632)
Type of work: Drama
Type of plot: Comedy

Time of plot: c. 1413-1422
First performed: 1600; first published, 1600

Most of the action in this play involves members of England's shoemakers' guild, practitioners of the "gentle craft," and focuses on the areas in which they work and play. Looming behind the play's comic setting is the darker sphere of King Henry V's wars in France that contrast, sometimes tragically, with otherwise happy city scenes.

Tower Street. London residence and workshop of Simon Eyre, who rises from master shoemaker to become lord mayor of London. A chaotic place populated by Eyre, his wife, his apprentices, and numerous hangers-on, it sees thwarted romances, the comic social-climbing of Mrs. Eyre, and street brawls as the apprentices try to avenge the wrongs inflicted on their fellow Rafe, who has been conscripted to fight in England's wars in France. The setting reflects the unruliness and uncertainty of the era in which Dekker's characters live.

*****Old Ford.** Country house belonging to Sir Roger Oteley, lord mayor of London at the outset of the play. Oteley has sent his daughter Rose to the country to separate her from Sir Rowland Lacy who, like Lacy's uncle, opposes a match between the two young people because of their unequal status. Bucolic and beautiful, Old Ford also holds sadness and danger. There, Rose is separated from her lover and falls prey to Hammon, her father's choice as her husband. When Simon Eyre is elevated to alderman, he visits Old Ford, which he declares the perfect residence. Eyre's admiration for Old Ford indicates that his increasing status has caused him to forget his origins in the rowdy streets of London.

*****France.** None of the play's action takes place here, but England's wars with the French affect all the play's characters. Simon's assistant, Rafe, for example returns from the wars a cripple whose wife has been duped into believing he is dead.

*****Leadenhall.** Enormous new London guildhall built to celebrate Eyres's rise to lord mayor of London. However, even its one hundred tables accommodate less than a fourth of the guests at the Shoemakers' Shrove Tuesday feast. The holiday atmosphere provides the opportunity for the king to pardon Lacy and Rose for defying their elders and to unite them in marriage. This marriage, the reunion of Rafe and Jane, and the expulsion of Hammon symbolize the return of order after the disorders inflicted by interfering parents and disruptive foreign wars.

— *Mary Anne Hutchinson*

A SHROPSHIRE LAD

Author: A. E. Housman (1859-1936)
Type of work: Poetry

First published: 1896

This collection of sixty-three of A. E. Housman's lyric poems is set in Shropshire, England, a remote, rural county on the border with Wales. The poet celebrates farm and country life and links the brevity of youth with the passing of seasons in familiar Shropshire landmarks and towns.

*****Shropshire.** The sheep farming county of Shropshire provides the backdrop for Housman's poems and functions as the nurturing mother country of the personas depicted in his verses. While bucolic and peaceful in many respects, the harsher aspects of farm life, which include theft and fratricide, are also evoked. Many natural features of the landscape, which include rivers such as the Severn, Teme, and Clun, and mountains such as Bredon Hill, Wenlock Edge, and Titterstone Clee, are woven into the poems. These natural elements contribute to a feeling of homesickness and the longing for friends and youth, which permeate Housman's work.

*Ludlow. Small Shropshire town. Ludlow, and to a lesser extent Shrewsbury, provide urban touches to Housman's poems; but these were very small towns in 1896, when the collection was first published. Ludlow, a market town, is the site of fairs and taverns where Housman's lads can drink beer and socialize with one another, thereby providing the congenial memories looked back on with fondness in the poetry.

*London. Great Britain's capital city is depicted as a bustling metropolis with values different from those in the country. Here country lads may get lost, sometimes never returning to the solace of Shropshire.

Remote foreign lands. Exotic places such as the Nile River, where Shropshire soldiers are serving the British Empire, are occasionally used to evoke homesickness for Shropshire.

— *Isabel Bonnyman Stanley*

SIDDHARTHA

Author: Hermann Hesse (1877-1962)
Type of work: Novella
Type of plot: Bildungsroman

Time of plot: 563?-483? B.C.E.
First published: 1922 (English translation, 1951)

The setting of this novel is integral to everything that transpires in it, as it represents stages in the development of the title's character, Siddhartha, whose spiritual progress is united with the space in which it occurs.

*India. Asian country in which the young Siddhartha, a tall and handsome Brahman's son, lives and travels in his search for fulfillment. His quest for enlightenment parallels the Buddha's legendary journeys in India: He departs his father's house to join the Samana ascetics; after forsaking them, he goes to the city, and eventually abandons the city to become a ferryman on the river.

India, where Herman Hesse traveled in 1911 to study Eastern religions and philosophies, is the birthplace of Buddhism and its promise of enlightenment, as well as Hesse's conscious opposition to it. Whereas Buddhism attempts to prescribe an established pattern of development, Hesse attempts to show, through Siddhartha's journey through India, that quests for spiritual fulfillment are voyages of discovery in which each person finds his or her own path to absolute peace. The setting of India, with its nameless features, incorporates the Buddha's legendary journeys and their accumulated wisdom, through which Siddhartha pursues his own quest for universal oneness.

River. Unnamed river that is the central natural element in the novel. The river functions symbolically, marking Siddhartha's evolution. Siddhartha's early years in his father's house are spent on the river's bank in a state of innocence. At the age of eighteen, Siddhartha hopes to find truth by joining the Samanas, whose prescribed truth stirs his doubts. He then crosses the river and goes to the city. Representing boundaries of time and development, the river symbolizes Siddhartha's passage from the realm of spirit to sense and back again.

When Siddhartha returns to the river, twenty years after his first crossing, he suffers from sickness of the soul and desires death. He listens to the river's characteristic *om* murmuring—a sound that is the sacred syllable of the Hindu priestly Brahmin caste—for the unity of all being. The same *om* wells up within his soul and forms a bond between him and the river. The river's murmuring lulls Siddhartha into a trancelike sleep. Eventually he awakens, refreshed, and begins the process of restoration to his former state of innocence.

The river proves to be the agent through which Siddhartha finds fulfillment. He assists Vasudeva, the wise old ferryman who transported him across the river twenty years earlier. He learns that the river represents the natural synthesis of sense and spirit; he also realizes that life is a river and that the past, present, and future are all one. The river embodies all creation, all layers of consciousness, memories and impulses common to humankind as a whole; the eternal *om* brings them to the surface, awakening in Siddhartha knowledge of the essential unity of being.

The river has one last lesson to teach Siddhartha—love. Many years later, Kamala, Siddhartha's love from the city, arrives at the river with the son she has borne him and soon dies of snakebite. Little Siddhartha runs away to the city, leaving his father stricken with grief. Once again, the river speaks the sacred syllable *om* and heals the wound produced by his grief.

City. The projection of feeling into abstract geographical places continues with the unnamed city, Siddhartha's destination after leaving the Samanas—a move signifying a progression from the spirit to the senses. There he meets the beautiful courtesan Kamala, through whose assistance he becomes prosperous and comes to lead a life of luxury. At length, sickened by his own degeneracy and intent on suicide, he quits the city, unwittingly abandoning Kamala, who is pregnant with his son. The city represents the second step in Siddhartha's development, which cancels out the earlier excursion into the spirit and leads to his return to the river and his state of innocence.

— *Mary Hurd*

THE SIGN OF FOUR

Author: Sir Arthur Conan Doyle (1859-1930)
Type of work: Novel
Type of plot: Detective and mystery

Time of plot: 1888
First published: 1890

The second of only four novel-length adventures featuring the consulting detective Sherlock Holmes, this story is set in and around Victorian London. Places not directly involved with Holmes's deductive processes are usually sketchily described or accorded only a cursory description. Places and events are described by Dr. John Watson, who chronicles all of Holmes's cases.

***Baker Street.** London street on which Sherlock Holmes and Dr. John Watson share upstairs ("first floor" in British terminology) lodgings at the fictional address of 221B. Their landlady, Mrs. Hudson, lives on the ground floor and provides meals and services for her lodgers, including answering the door and showing visitors up to Watson and Holmes's flat. A large, airy room, cheerfully furnished and illuminated by two broad windows looking down into the street, their sitting room is the place where most of Holmes's cases begin and where Holmes later explains to Watson how he has arrived at his solutions.

Sholto's house. Residence of the art collector Thaddeus Sholto, near Coldharbour Lane, in south London. Holmes, Watson, and Miss Morstan, Holmes's client, go there in a horse-drawn cab. Although a route is given, it is not possible to trace it on a modern map. Although some London streets mentioned in the novel—such as

the Strand, Wandsworth Road, and Coldharbour Lane—do still exist, others are either invented or misnamed, or have names that have been changed. Enough real London street names are provided, however, to give a sense of traveling some distance through dark London streets. Sholto's house, the third in a newly built terrace, is in an unfashionable part of London characterized by streets of brick houses and rows of two-story villas with tiny front gardens. The house's entryway is ill-lit and poorly furnished, a great contrast to Sholto's own apartments, which are richly furnished. Curtains and tapestries drape the walls and are hooked back to reveal paintings and oriental vases. The soft, amber and black carpet, the two tiger skin rugs and a silver lamp suspended from the ceiling by gold wire all give an impression of great wealth.

Pondicherry Lodge. Upper Norwood home of Thaddeus Sholto's twin brother, Bartholomew Sholto. Located about eight miles south of central London, the house is surrounded by a high stone wall topped with broken glass and is approached along a gravel drive that winds through grounds greatly disturbed by Sholto's diggings in search of a treasure he believes has been buried by his father, Major Sholto. The house itself is square built and has only one entrance—a narrow, iron-clamped door, securely fastened by many bolts and locks, as Sholto's father had feared break-ins. The most important room in the house is on the top floor, up three flights of stairs that end in a long, tapestry-lined corridor. Situated at the front of the house, Sholto's workroom is filled with chemistry apparatuses, including carboys of acid. A hole cut in the plaster-and-lathe ceiling exposes a hidden garret in which the father's treasure was hidden; the hole also provides an escape route, through a skylight, for the Andaman islander who kills Bartholomew in the room. Other parts of the house are filled with Indian curiosities, a clue to the source of the Sholtos' wealth. An Indian servant has a garret room in the roof, next to the sealed one, and the housekeeper has rooms on the ground floor.

Pinchin Lane. Street in London's Lambeth district on which the taxidermist Sherman lives. Sherman owns the odd-looking dog Toby, which possesses the keenest nose in London. Located near the edge of the River Thames, the lane contains a row of shabby, two-story brick houses. The window cases of Sherman's No. 3 location contain stuffed animals; inside the house are live animals—a badger, a stoat, and various fowl perched among the rafters.

*River Thames (tehmz). England's largest river, which runs through London and forms the backdrop for the novel's final chase and capture of Jonathan Small, who is behind the murder of Bartholomew Sholto. During Victorian times, the Thames was an important commercial waterway for barges, steamers, and merchant vessels. Boat repairers, such as Jacobson's Yard—at which the launch *Aurora* is hidden by Small in the novel—were common, as were wharves, such as that at which Small hires the *Aurora*.

— Pauline Morgan

SILAS MARNER: The Weaver of Raveloe

Author: George Eliot (Mary Ann Evans, 1819-1880)
Type of work: Novel
Type of plot: Domestic realism

Time of plot: Early nineteenth century
First published: 1861

This parabolic novel shows how love and sincere communal interaction bring about the moral and psychic regeneration of Silas Marner, a wronged man, delivering him from the alienation of his self-imposed spiritual death of isolation and despair. His place of salvation is a rural English village, untouched by the Industrial Revolution, in which he ravels an "O," or circle of community, from the charitable fellowship offered to him when he finally reaches out to appeal for help in a crisis.

Raveloe. Village in central England to which Marner moves after his best friend's false accusations of dishonesty force him to leave an unnamed industrial city in northern England. During his first fifteen years in Raveloe, he lives an almost wholly solitary life; his work is all that he has; he virtually lives within his loom, reduced to the stooped and malformed life of a spinning insect. After he takes a foster child into his home, he finally begins to connect with the community.

Marner's cottage. Former home of a stone cutter in which Silas Marner lives in Raveloe. The cottage is located at the edge of an abandoned quarry. Within his cottage, Marner quietly amasses a hoard of gold coins, which he earns through years of painstaking weaving work. After his gold is stolen, his literal and figurative myopia—accentuated by his cataleptic trances—causes him to mistake for his returned coins the golden hair of an orphaned infant girl, Eppie, who wanders into his cottage on a dark, cold night, seeking light and warmth. Marner's loving care of Eppie for sixteen years, shored up by the kindness of the villagers, awakens in him an imaginative sympathy that renews and expands his formerly dead sensibilities. Through the influence of the child, Eppie, the bare, stone cottage and its surroundings are transformed into a place of a growing garden that promises to keep flowering at the end of the story, with the help of the young man whom Eppie marries.

Rainbow Inn. Village gathering place in which the character of the community is revealed through the vivid dialogue of those who come to socialize. Marner comes to the inn to seek help after he discovers his gold has been stolen because it is the place where important village decisions are made, such as what to do about the robbery. The narrator reveals that the unaccustomed human interaction that Marner experiences here precipitates his growth of social consciousness. The suggestion of hopeful promise connoted by the inn's name culminates with its serving as the location of Eppie and Aaron's wedding feast.

Red House. Home of Squire Cass, the village landlord, which provides a background for developing the character of his two sons, Godfrey, who refuses for sixteen years to acknowledge that he is Eppie's natural father, and Dunstan, whose thievery of Marner's gold goes

undiscovered through the same period. The motherless home is seen as loveless until Godfrey marries Nancy, when feminine touches begin to add warmth.

Lantern Yard. Gathering place for Dissenters of a narrow religious sect with whom Marner attended chapel when he lived in an unnamed northern industrial city before moving to Raveloe. The Lantern Yard is associated with impersonal and mechanical ways, represented in part by the drawing of lots to determine guilt or innocence. At the beginning of the novel, Marner is victimized here, falsely accused by William Dane, whom he has regarded as his best friend. Although he is innocent, the drawing of lots makes him appear guilty. After being cast out by his Calvinist-influenced religious group, he arrives in Raveloe feeling abandoned and betrayed by God and man.

Through the influence of Dolly Winthrop, Marner becomes open to fellowship through the traditional church of Raveloe. At the end of the novel, he and Eppie go in search of Lantern Yard because Marner hopes to find explanations for the earlier events in his life. However, they find only a factory where the chapel stood before. Eppie's repulsion at the crowded and dirty scene reinforces Eliot's presentation of place as all-important to the nurturing of community fellow-feeling.

— *Carolyn Dickinson*

SILENCE

Author: Shūsaku Endō (1923-1996)
Type of work: Novel
Type of plot: Historical realism

Time of plot: 1632-1644
First published: Chimmoku, 1966 (English translation, 1969)

In this haunting look at the introduction of Christianity to Japan in the seventeenth century, the island nation itself is a central character. As Portuguese missionaries seek to bring their god to Japan, they encounter what one eventually calls "this swamp of Japan," in which Christianity can never take root. One scholar has compared the "austere terrain" of the novel to a Japanese Golgotha, "stubborn and brutal, yet empty and soundless."

*Kyushu (kyew-shew). Southernmost island of the Japanese chain, where the Portuguese missionaries land. Their entry at the foot of the nation suggests an interesting geographic resonance with the importance of feet

and faces in this text. The island's coastal villages are places where Christianity survived, but the faith of the local people is not one that many Europeans would recognize as Christian. Only such an isolated area could support this life. Far removed from the seat of governmental and indigenous religious power, the villagers use their landscape to hide their religious activities.

Their faith is at once simple and complex—a mixture of native folk beliefs and Western Christianity that is the cause of death (and perhaps eternal life) for many villagers and their missionaries. This duality is also manifested in the landscape, as the bounty of the seacoast itself becomes the setting for their hand-to-mouth existence, and the presence of such an immensity of water gives way to many instances of dire thirst throughout the text.

The villages are also places of trust and betrayal. While the missionaries trust the peasants and are trusted by them, Kichijiro, one of the peasants closest to the missionaries, eventually betrays them. When the lone surviving Portuguese missionary is led to Nagasaki, Kichijiro remains with him throughout his captivity, attempting to explain and justify his actions as he begs for forgiveness. The isolation of the villages allows Kichijiro his life: News does not travel fast, so he can remain, in effect, a double agent, professing his Christianity while subverting its spread in his nation.

*Nagasaki (nah-gah-sah-kee). City on the northern half of Kyushu, which can be seen as the "head" of the island to which the missionaries must travel after landing at the foot. In the seventeenth century, Japan closed itself off almost entirely from the outside word, leaving only Nagasaki open to foreigners. The missionary Rodrigues seeks his teacher, Ferreira, there, where both are *gaijin* (outsiders), in Japan's city of *gaijin*.

Nagasaki is a center of civic and religious power where the formerly great missionary Ferreira has been sucked into the Japanese bureaucracy. He has turned his back on his faith but can still make himself useful as a translator for the government. Here, Western religious power has met the East and lost. Nagasaki represents not the triumph of Buddhism or Shinto, but the ultimate failure of Christianity. In this urban environment, the crypto-Christians of the villages are spared by the apostasy of their missionaries. Shūsaku Endō suggests that the relative isolation of the rural villages may make it easier to persevere in one's faith. When one's faith must rub shoulders with faiths of those who do not believe, or indeed who are actively opposed, as in Nagasaki, the faith may quaver.

— *Joe Pellegrino*

SIMPLICISSIMUS THE VAGABOND

Author: Hans Jakob Christoffel von Grimmelshausen (1621-1676)
Type of work: Novel
Type of plot: Picaresque

Time of plot: Early seventeenth century
First published: Der abenteuerliche Simplicissimus, 1669 (English translation, 1912; also known as *The Adventurous Simplicissimus*)

This novel ranges far and wide across Europe, initially concentrating on the regions afflicted by the Thirty Years' War of 1618-1648 (whose disorders blighted Hans Jakob Christoffel von Grimmelshausen's own early life), gradually widening its scope as its narrative pace increases to take in the major cities of continental Europe, even accommodating a brief excursion to the center of the earth.

*Spessart. Town in a mountainous region of Germany, not far from which is located the earthen hut where Simplicissimus lives until the age of ten, when the town is looted and destroyed by marauding soldiers. He returns to Spessart much later, having discovered his true parentage, to obtain documentary evidence of his real identity.

Hermit's hut. Mean refuge in the forest that Simplicissimus finds after the destruction of his first home, where he is educated in piety and poverty; this existence too is interrupted by marauding soldiers.

*Hanau. Fortified town where Simplicissimus is conscripted into domestic service in the governor's house, where he progresses to the role of professional fool.

Hirschfeld Abbey. Quarters of the Croats who capture Simplicissimus from Hanau, where he acquires a new master; after fleeing therefrom he becomes embroiled in a witches' Sabbath.

***Magdeburg.** German city in which Simplicissimus arrives—apparently having flown there—after the witches' Sabbath, to be conscripted yet again. It is there that he first meets Herzbruder and is charged with treason before being delivered into the service of another military master.

***Soest** (sewst). Westphalian town where—after a brief interval of calm and comfort in a convent called Paradise—Simplicissimus begins to rise through the ranks of the dragoons, leading something of a double life as the "Huntsman." His ambition to become an ensign is briefly advanced by his military exploits and his discovery of a treasure but is ended when he is captured by the Swedes.

Werl. Residence of the outlaw who duplicates Simplicissimus's role as the Huntsman before becoming his friend and—in his secondary role as the god Jupiter—advisor on the complications of earthly current events.

***Lippstadt.** Fortified town, two miles from Soest, where Simplicissimus is installed after his capture, and where he eventually rises to the rank of lieutenant colonel in the Swedish army. It is there, much later, that he misguidedly sends his wife for safety's sake.

***Cologne** (ka-LOHN). German city where the merchant who keeps Simplicissimus's treasure in trust resides. Simplicissimus later returns to find that the merchant has been declared bankrupt. He returns again briefly, after returning to Germany from Vienna in search of a palliative for Herzbruder's injuries.

***Paris.** France's capital city, to which Simplicissimus journeys after the collapse of his prospects in Cologne. There he becomes the successful comedian and gigolo Beau Alman (a contraction of "Allemand," the French word for German). He never learns to love Paris, which seems to him to be a rather dirty city, and he contracts a venereal disease there, so he longs to return to his native land, although he has to make his way on foot, supporting himself as a dealer in quack medicines.

***Philippsburg.** Town to which Simplicissimus is taken after being captured on his re-entry into Germany, where he becomes a common soldier again, undertaking further campaigns in that capacity before becoming a fugitive yet again.

***Vienna.** Austrian imperial capital, to which Simplicissimus journeys after making a pilgrimage with Herzbruder to Einsiedeln, a shrine in Switzerland; he also convalesces in Vienna after receiving a leg wound in battle, having been conscripted yet again.

***Griesbach** (grees-BAHK). Spa in Germany's Black Forest, not far from Ulm, which becomes Simplicissimus's base of operations when he takes Herzbruder there in search of a cure.

***Mummelsee.** Lake from which Simplicissimus travels to the center of the earth, whose king shows him the floor of the Pacific Ocean and acquaints him with other marvels.

***Moscow.** Russian city that is the objective of Simplicissimus's final campaign, which interrupts the quiet life of scholarship to which he devotes his later years.

— *Brian Stableford*

SIR CHARLES GRANDISON

Author: Samuel Richardson (1689-1761)
Type of work: Novel
Type of plot: Fiction of manners

Time of plot: Eighteenth century
First published: 1753-1754

Grandison Hall epitomizes the social and moral values of Georgian England. It is near London and its political, social, and economic opportunities, but it is also in the country, and free from the corruptions of the city. The Europe of Sir Charles's grand tour presents temptations of a different sort: a misguided sense of honor, Roman Catholicism, unreasonable passions, desertion of Great Britain—all of which are epitomized in Bologna. At the end of the novel, the Porrettas, representatives of the European temptations, ultimately recognize and submit to the domestic ideals embodied by Harriet, Sir Charles, and Grandison Hall.

Grandison Hall. Family home of Sir Charles Grandison in the Essex suburbs of London. Located just outside London, Grandison Hall represents a level of remove from the city even as it permits active engagement in the great city's social, political, economic, and cultural spheres. However, the hall is close enough to the city to be tainted by urban vices, such as Sir Charles's father's having a mistress, whom Sir Charles tactfully removes to a London home upon returning from his tour. Reinforcing the hall's role in virtue, an Anglican clergyman friend of Sir Charles administers charitable support from Grandison Hall. Sir Charles also restores the beauty of the parks of the estate, as well as the health of the estate as a whole. Doing so satisfies two ideals: the contemporary Georgian obsession with landscaping estates and having the wealth to afford to do so. Finally, as the home of the now-married Sir Charles and Harriet, Grandison Hall facilitates the reconciliation for the Porretta family and thus the international triumph of the Georgian domestic ideal.

*London. Capital and leading city of Great Britain, that demonstrates both the social and moral sensibilities of the 1750's. Sir Charles lives in a town house on St. James's Square, an exclusive neighborhood built around a carefully landscaped park. During the mid-eighteenth century, the square's town houses were considered extremely fashionable; the fact that Sir Charles lives there demonstrates his high social status.

Grosvenor Street is another fashionable London neighborhood; its homes are not as exclusive as town houses on a square, but appropriate for a well-to-do Northamptonshire family, such as the virtuous young Harriet Byron and her aunt and uncle.

The extraordinary cultural opportunities that London offers, such as playhouses, recreational gardens, and opera houses make it an exciting destination. However, it also crowds together opportunities for vice—such as gambling and usury—and vapid entertainments. The novel conveys the impression that living in London too long coarsens one's social and moral sensibilities. Minor women characters who have lived for a time in London have attitudes opposed to successful domestic lives: they become either too witty, too ignorant, or too fashionable. Likewise, the male characters who reside there tend to prefer silly women and dissipated entertainments.

*Northamptonshire. County in northern England that is several hours' travel by carriage from London, in which Harriet has grown up under the care of relatives. Sir Charles goes to Northamptonshire to court Harriet and to marry her, so it offers a background for domestic virtuousness. However, that background is tainted by rural enthusiasm, symbolized by the Methodist Sunday services. Because Anglicanism is part of the domestic ideal, Grandison Hall is superior to Northamptonshire. However, Northamptonshire is more remote from the moral ambiguities of London. It is therefore an appropriate place for young women like Harriet and her cousin Lucy to mature, which is why Emily Jervois spends time there at the close of the novel.

*Bologna (boh-LOH-nyah). North-central Italian city that was favored as a travel destination for English gentlemen on their grand tours because of the opportunities it offered for fine music and for acquiring art objects. Sir Charles spends most of his time in Italy there with the Porretta family. Bologna also represents the temptations available to British gentleman on tour, and Sir Charles faces his ultimate temptation in Lady Clementina, a woman at once noble, beautiful, virtuous, conversant in English, and in love with him. However, in order for him to marry her, she insists that he convert to Roman Catholicism and take up permanent residence in Bologna. Sir Charles rejects the offer and offers a compromise that will allow him to maintain his British identity, but that, in turn, is rejected, and he returns to England, where he encounters Harriet.

Lady Clementina is also delicate of health. When Sir Charles returns to Bologna, he comes equipped with English physicians and their suggestions to assist in curing her and her brother, thereby symbolically bringing British superiority in medicine. After he is satisfied that Clementina and her brother are cured, he returns to England. When the Porretta family unexpectedly arrives in England, bringing European instability to his doorstep, Sir Charles once again facilitates a "cure" by demonstrating the British domestic ideal through his life with Harriet at Grandison Hall.

— *Clare Callaghan*

SIR GAWAIN AND THE GREEN KNIGHT

Author: Pearl-Poet (fl. late fourteenth century)
Type of work: Poetry
Type of plot: Arthurian romance

Time of plot: Sixth century
First transcribed: Fourteenth century

This epic is set in Wales and England but begins and ends by stressing connections between Britain of King Arthur's time and the ancient world. The poet sees Britain as having been settled by refugees from ancient Troy and thus implicitly connects Arthur's court at Camelot with both failure and renewal. The poet also contrasts wilderness scenes with the comfortable amenities of Arthur's court and Bercilak's castle.

Camelot. Site of **King Arthur's court**. As the poem begins, attractive young lords and ladies celebrate the Christmas season at Camelot. Dressed in their best, the courtiers frolic in a charming atmosphere. Laughter and mirth prevail while a lovely Guenevere and a boyish Arthur sit on an attractive raised platform. The poem hints that the court, despite its superficial attractiveness, may be naïve and untried.

*Wirral (weh-REL). Forest in Cheshire, England, that Gawain enters from northern Wales during his quest through the wilderness. The weather is cold, and the woods are dark and full of wild men, giants, and monsters. The Wirral may symbolize the forces of nature as opposed to the civilized atmosphere of Camelot and Bercilak's castle. The geographical closeness of castles and the forests surrounding them suggests that civilization is fragile and that the primitive forces of the forests are always ready to destroy what human beings have built.

Bercilak's castle (BUR-ceh-lack). Castle of Sir Bercilak de Hautdesert, the good-humored knight who is Gawain's host and who is disguised as the Green Knight by the arts of Morgan le Fay. Like Arthur's court, Bercilak's castle is a pleasant place. From a distance, its white silhouette looks as if it were cut from paper. The castle and its moat are set on a hill, near the Green Chapel. Gawain's private bedroom and luxurious bed emphasize that the castle is one of the finest of its era. However, the poet contrasts this luxury with Bercilak's hunt in the forest. By graphically describing the death and disemboweling of the deer, the boar, and the fox, the poet creates a realistic picture of the brutality of a medieval hunt.

Green Chapel. Moundlike chapel of the Green Knight, which Gawain approaches on New Year's Day. The frightening-looking chapel stands in a wasteland; it is hollowed out, like a cave, and symbolic. It seems to connect with the tree worship of the pre-Christian Celts. On one hand, the castle seems like a tomb; on the other hand, because it is a chapel it reminds medieval readers that Christ left his cave-tomb and entered into everlasting life. Like many of the places described in the poem, the Green Chapel is rich with ambiguity.

— *Charles S. Pierce, Jr.*

THE SIRENS OF TITAN

Author: Kurt Vonnegut (1922-   )
Type of work: Novel
Type of plot: Science fiction

Time of plot: Nightmare Ages, between World War II and the Third Great Depression
First published: 1959

This novel is driven by a bizarre theme: That all human history has been manipulated by beings of a distant planet for the sole purpose of delivering a replacement part to a space messenger whose disabled ship has left him stranded on Saturn's moon Titan for hundreds of thousands of years. The story follows several characters who are sent hither and thither through the solar system as unknowing pawns in that scheme. When the content of the traveler's message is finally divulged and found to be meaningless, both the lives of the novel's characters and all human history are exposed as equally meaningless.

Chrono-synclastic infundibula. Vaguely defined phenomena in space that serve as something like space and time portals through which living creatures and objects can be simultaneously scattered everywhere between the Sun and Betelgeuse. The first discovery of a chrono-synclastic infundibulum in Earth's solar system prompted the shutting down of the U.S. space program because of the danger it posed to astronauts. However, the existence of chrono-synclastic infundibula drives the plot. As Wilson Niles Rumfoord explains, when he flew his own spaceship into a chrono-synclastic infundibulum, "it came to me in a flash that everything that ever has been always will be, and everything that ever will be always has been." Thanks to chrono-synclastic infundibulation, Rumfoord and his dog, Kazak, travel through the solar system and through time effortlessly, while manipulating the lives of Malachi Constant and other characters.

Tralfamadore (trahl-fahm-ah-DOHR). Imaginary planet in a star system many thousands of light years distant from Earth's solar system from which the space traveler Salo was long ago sent to carry a message across space. Unbeknownst to earthlings—and apparently to Salo himself—Tralfamadorians have manipulated Earth's history for hundreds of thousands of years to direct events leading to the eventual delivery of a replacement part to Titan for Salo's disabled spaceship. Tralfamadorians are responsible for all the technology used to colonize Mars and build a fleet of spaceships.

In their remote role as manipulators of human history, the unseen Tralfamadorians have godlike attributes— both in their power and in their indifference to human suffering. The novel's central character is named Malachi Constant—an appropriate name for the role he fills. A Greek name, "Malachi" means "faithful messenger"— a description reinforced by his surname, "Constant." Throughout the novel, Constant is the unknowing dupe of the Tralfamadorians and ultimately becomes the messenger who helps deliver the replacement part to Titan.

Wilburhampton Hotel. Shabby Los Angeles hotel in which Malachi Constant's father, Noel Constant, lives out the last decades of his life. Voluntarily spending virtually all of his time alone in Room 223, he builds a massive fortune on the stock market by following a brainless scheme that involves using biblical texts to select his investments. Unbeknownst to him and his son, who inherits his wealth and continues the scheme after his death, his fabulous success is made possible by Tralfamadorian manipulation. Under the direction of a former Internal Revenue Service agent, Ransom K. Fern, Constant channels his wealth into Magnum Opus, Inc., a giant industrial conglomerate whose thirty-one-story headquarters are built across the street from the hotel.

Rumfoord mansion. Large house in Newport, Rhode Island, in which Rumfoord's estranged wife, Beatrice, lives alone. Rumfoord himself periodically rematerializes there, and it is there, during one of his materializations that Malachi Constant first meets him. Built like a fortress, the mansion's only entrance is a tiny "Alice-in-Wonderland door," through which Constant must crawl to enter and leave. Beatrice eventually loses the mansion in her efforts to divest her holdings in everything that might link her future to that of Constant.

Later, when Constant returns to Earth after long years on Mars and Mercury, Rumfoord takes him to the estate, where Constant is greeted by a large crowd as the "Space Wanderer." Still bewildered by all that has happened to him, Constant is directed to board yet another spaceship, with Beatrice and their son, that takes them all to Titan.

*Mars. Planet that earthlings colonize under the indirect supervision of Rumfoord, whose agents implant electronic devices in recruits' brains in order to control them with radio signals. Using technology supplied by the Tralfamadorian Salo, who is marooned on Titan, the Martians—who are all transplanted earthlings—build a vast fleet of spaceships and train for an invasion of Earth. Despite their advanced space technology, the Martian forces have primitive weaponry and lack the numbers to pose a serious threat to Earth. Their invasion is an unmitigated disaster in which almost all the Martians are easily killed. Afterward, however, the people of Earth feel great shame for what they have done to the Martians—a reaction that Rumfoord eventually reveals to have been the only objective of the hopeless invasion.

Among the people whom Rumfoord draws into his Martian scheme are his wife, Beatrice, and Malachi Constant (Unk), who together have a son who proves to be the carrier of the replacement part that all three of them transport to Titan.

*Mercury. Planet nearest to the Sun to which Unk and Boaz are taken from Mars by an automatically piloted spaceship, which lands in a labyrinthine cave complex more than one hundred miles below the surface of Mercury's perpetually dark side. During the three Earth years that Unk remains there, he tries to figure out how to escape, while he and Boaz lead increasingly separate lives. Boaz becomes enamored of the cave's eerie harmonium creatures—the only lifeforms on the planet—which are nourished solely by vibrations. With the help of clues left by Rumfoord, Unk eventually leaves the planet by turning the spaceship upside down, so the sensors on its bottom side can find a way out of the caves. The only ostensible reason for Unk's time on Mercury is to keep him safe from the slaughter of Martians taking place on Earth.

Whale. Rocket ship left from the abandoned U.S. space program that is renamed the *Rumfoord* when the United States begins a new age of space exploration. Malachi Constant initially owns the ship—the last one on earth capable of going into space after the discovery of chrono-synclastic infundibula causes the government space programs to shut down. After Rumfoord tells Constant that his future holds travel to Mars, Mercury, and Titan, Constant unloads the company that owns the ship so he will not have any way to reach Mars. However, both he and Beatrice Rumfoord are later tricked into boarding the ship, which carries them to Mars.

*Titan. Largest moon of the planet Saturn and one of the few moons known to have an atmosphere. While the real Titan is known to be a cold and dark place with a poisonous atmosphere, the Titan of the novel is an edenic world with a perfect climate. There, the Tralfamadorian robot Salo, an apparently immortal space traveler, has been stranded for hundreds of thousands of years. To get a replacement part to Salo's ships, creatures on the planet Tralfamadore manipulate human history so that earthlings will eventually produce and deliver to Titan a simple spare part that will enable the robot to repair his spacecraft and continue his journey.

— *R. Kent Rasmussen*

SISTER CARRIE

Author: Theodore Dreiser (1871-1945)
Type of work: Novel
Type of plot: Naturalism

Time of plot: 1889
First published: 1900

While also a novel of characters, this story is considered to be a great novel of the American city, taking place almost exclusively in Chicago and New York. While Theodore Dreiser depicts the two cities as quite different from each other, he convincingly portrays both as places of great opportunity as well as dangerous pitfalls.

*Chicago. Great Midwestern American city for which Caroline Meeber, or Carrie, boards a train as the novel opens. When Carrie arrives in Chicago, she is both nervous and youthfully optimistic about her opportunities in this vibrant new place. In depicting this place, with which he was intimately familiar, Dreiser describes an energetic young city of over 500,000 people, full of opportunity for those lucky enough to find and take advantage of it. He depicts the bustling factory and wholesale districts in which Carrie seeks work, the crowded tenements where her sister lives with a husband and baby, and the lovely new mansions erected along Lake Shore Drive, the viewing of which contributes to Carrie's restless discontent with her lack of money. In spite of the vast opportunities for the industrious, however, the fact that Carrie becomes a mistress to first one man and then another indicates that Dreiser also wished to portray the big city as a place offering moral temptations for young unmarried women, especially those without money. Many of the events that unfold in the first half of *Sister Carrie* could only happen in a big city, and some of them only in a young, growing city such as Chicago.

Interestingly, Dreiser also briefly depicts a sense of Chicago's inadequacy and lack of sophistication when Carrie attempts to work as an actress and is told that New York City is the only place in which to begin a stage career. In addition, late in the novel, Carrie's lover Hurstwood reflects upon the fact that his prior position of some influence in Chicago means nothing in the larger, more sophisticated East Coast city.

*New York City. Great eastern city to which Hurstwood ultimately takes Carrie when he must flee Chicago after stealing money from his employer. To Hurstwood, New York at first represents anonymity and the opportunity to start anew, although he is soon discouraged to find that the social barriers between the rich and the poor are not as easy to navigate as those in Chicago. This less forgiving nature of New York City ultimately contributes to Hurstwood's downfall.

Her Chicago dreams of the stage temporarily forgotten, Carrie initially does not care for New York. Ensconced in the small flat that is the best Hurstwood can afford, Carrie is simultaneously fascinated and desperately envious of the city's opulence, far above that which she saw in Chicago. In particular, Dreiser describes the lavish fashion parade that regularly occurs along the famous Broadway in the theater district and serves to reawaken Carrie's vague ambitions for money and social status.

As Hurstwood's fortunes continue to decline, Carrie resolves once again to find work on the stage, and she achieves fairly quick success, leaving Hurstwood in the process. For Carrie, then, New York ultimately represents a place of unparalleled opportunity, where things can happen overnight; it is also the first place where she is able to support herself without a man's help. To Hurstwood, on the other hand, New York is a city so unfeeling that he is forced to turn to panhandling and ultimately to suicide. The opulence and poverty that exist side by side in New York make Carrie and Hurstwood's opposite destinies quite believable, yet Dreiser also makes apparent the role that luck plays in the big city, suggesting perhaps that Carrie's and Hurstwood's fates could perhaps just as easily have been reversed.

*Montreal. Canadian city to which Hurstwood initially flees with Carrie in order to escape arrest following his theft from his employer. At first Hurstwood intends to stay there to get his bearings; therefore, Montreal serves as a temporary sanctuary from the American authorities. However, when he immediately runs into a business acquaintance from Chicago, Hurstwood realizes that Montreal cannot offer him the fresh start he needs; he therefore returns most of the stolen money and leaves immediately for New York with Carrie.

Columbia City. Fictional Wisconsin town from which Carrie begins her journey to Chicago. To Carrie, Columbia City is a stifling place with no opportunities, and she believes that to return there would be an admission of defeat.

— *Amy Sisson*

SISTER PHILOMÈNE

Authors: Edmond de Goncourt (1822-1896) and Jules de Goncourt (1830-1870)
Type of work: Novel
Type of plot: Psychological

Time of plot: Nineteenth century
First published: Sœur Philomène, 1861 (English translation, 1890)

Although this novel is clearly set in Paris, that great city is conspicuous in the plot by its near-absence. Philomène remembers certain aspects of it from her youth, but the hospital in which she serves as a Sister of Mercy insulates her completely from its life—as perhaps befits an institution that serves, in effect, as the threshold of the tomb.

Sainte-Thérèse Ward (sant-tay-REHZ). Hospital ward committed to Sister Philomène's charge that eventually becomes her entire world. The hospital in which the ward is situated is never identified, although it is likened at one point to the Hospital de la Pitié in Paris's rue du Fer-à-Moulin. The novel opens with a description of Philomène doing her rounds, emphasizing the limited nature of her daily and nightly routines.

The vocation that brings Philomène to the ward is a trifle arbitrary. She is meekly following in the footsteps of her friend and role-model, Céline; however, she is no less powerful for that. The neatness, cleanliness, and discipline of the wards, brightened by a copious display of frequently laundered white linen, are carefully contrasted with the disorder of the resident doctors' room: a vaulted hall whose stone walls ooze damp, equipped with a pipe-rack, a slate board on which the surgeons scrawl memoranda, and their untidy pigeonholes. Philomène is glad to have the suffering in the wards carefully veiled and curtained but still must work hard to suppress the vivid imagination that informs her of what happens in the consulting rooms and—most horrifically of all—the dissecting room.

Her inability to recognize the sexual nature of her feelings for the young doctor Barnier, the surgeon responsible for her patients, is symbolized by the delight she takes in the news he brings her of the great city that she could experience for herself if she would only allow herself to step out into its streets.

Madame de Viry's house. Town house in the rue Chaussée d'Antin, into which the infant Marie Gaucher—later renamed Philomène—is received after being taken in by her aunt, who is a servant there. It is because Marie is indulgently received by Madame de Viry that she gets ideas above her station that lead to her being packed off to an orphanage. By the time she returns to Madame de Viry's house, it has become Monsieur Henry's house, an unendurable den of iniquity.

Orphanage. Establishment run by the nuns of a calculatedly unnamed order, situated in Paris's Faubourg Saint-Denis, where Philomène (renamed because the orphanage already numbers another "Marie" among its charges) grows up. She adapts as readily to its disciplined passivity and her work as a seamstress as she earlier adapted—inappropriately—to life in Madame de Viry's house. The children leave the convent once a week to walk along the Canal Saint Martin, and once a year visit the country, usually the park at Saint-Cloud, walking from Sèvres to Suresnes. The convent's inmates also visit the house of their benefactress, Madame Mareuil, at Lagny. Philomène receives her first communion at the shabby local parish church, Saint Laurent, at the end of the boulevard de Strasbourg.

Mother House of the Sisters of Saint Augustine. Convent to which Philomène's friend Céline is sent to serve her novitiate, once she has fully absorbed the piety and religious fervor of the orphanage, leaving a void in Philomène's life that the latter cannot fill. Philomène eventually follows Céline to the convent, after failing to adjust to the requirements of Monsieur Henry's establishment.

*Marne. Provincial French department—named for its major river—where the unnamed village in which Barnier grew up is situated. There, his father kept horses that towed barges along the Meaux Canal. His first love, Romaine, whose suffering and death in Sainte-Thérèse Ward sets him on the road to ruin, follows him to Paris from the village.

Notre-Dame-des-Victoires. Church at the end of the rue de la Banque to which Philomène goes, on one of her rare excursions outside the hospital, to pray for Barnier. Her modest foray outside the hospital is, however, far too little and far too late. She cannot save Barnier from himself.

— *Brian Stableford*

SIX CHARACTERS IN SEARCH OF AN AUTHOR

Author: Luigi Pirandello (1867-1936)
Type of work: Drama
Type of plot: Comedy
Time of plot: Early twentieth century

First performed: Sei personaggi in cerca d'autore:
Commedia da fare, 1921; first published, 1921
(English translation, 1922)

In this play-within-a-play, an empty and minimally furnished Italian stage for theatrical productions suggests an impromptu, in-process drama about to unfold. The play's universal location represents the conflict between non-fictional and fictional characters, the audience and readers perceiving the drama in their own lives, and Luigi Pirandello's own creative play on traditional theatrical forms.

Theater stage. The primary setting of the stage play is itself a theater stage. On this naked, darkened protruding platform in a theater, actors are rehearsing another Pirandello play, *Mixing It Up*, until they are interrupted by six people claiming to be dramatic characters hoping to be realized by an author. These six people (Father, Mother, Step-daughter, Son, Boy, and Child) are mystically enshrouded in light, suggesting further the theme of tension between art or illusion and life or reality. These six real personages dressed in black and wishing to relay their tragic stories are contrasted to the stage actors and the play's manager, who listen to the tale of the Mother who "ran off" with the Father's secretary and started a new family, only to be left a destitute widow of three offspring and of the Step-daughter, who is fixated in time by a near-incestuous encounter with the Father at Madame Pace's brothel.

Madame Pace's shop. Attractive women's shop with a table, racks of women's cloaks, and hats that in act 2 is a front for procurement. The play's stage becomes a mental platform on which the Step-daughter and Father insist on reliving their true feelings and actions, much to the chagrin of Leading Lady and Leading Man, who perceive, as artists, their own interpretation as more valid. Audiences must decipher which is more "real"—the never-changing illusion or the universal human tragedy. Readers, too, must examine their own selves in the process and must question their own philosophical-moral-aesthetic beliefs.

Out-of-doors. Location of the third act, which is a naturalistic one with a backdrop of trees with one or two wings and a fountain basin. It can be any time or place. The Child is found drowned in the fountain; the Boy, hiding behind the trees, fires a revolver. The play's manager-author, like Pirandello the dramatist himself, becomes agitated with conventions and closure and with the uncertainty of reality, shouting: "To hell with it all! Never in my life has such a thing happened to me. I've lost a whole day over these people, a whole day!"

— *Connie Pedoto*

THE SKIN OF OUR TEETH

Author: Thornton Wilder (1897-1975)
Type of work: Drama
Type of plot: Phantasmagoric

Time of plot: All human history
First performed: 1942; first published, 1942

The settings of this drama symbolically underscore the tendency of history to repeat itself, and they dramatize the ways both nature and the follies of human beings repeatedly push the human race to the edge of extinction.

Excelsior. Fictional New Jersey city, whose very name implies upward striving, that is the home of the novel's Antrobus family. Mother, daughter, son, maid, and pets await the return of the father, who is at his office. Mrs. Antrobus berates the maid, Sabina, for letting the fire go out in the suburban living room as the Ice Age is dawning. When Mr. Antrobus comes home, he brings along refugees whose talents he hopes to save, among them Moses, Homer, and several of the Muses. As the room fills up, a baby dinosaur and a little mammoth are ordered out into the cold. Nature is not humanity's only enemy; viewers learn that the Antrobus son Henry has another name: Cain. As the ice grinds nearer, Sabina, the maid, includes the audience in the setting, asking them to contribute their chairs for firewood.

*Atlantic City.** New Jersey resort city. Thornton Wilder's Atlantic City offers that image of it well known to popular culture: the Boardwalk, the ocean, the beauty contests. A fortune-teller's tent spotlights the chancy nature of survival. Sabina, now a pageant winner, confers with the gypsy about seducing George Antrobus, present as a conventioneer. The crone laughs darkly and predicts rain and the destruction of every living thing except two animals of every kind. Nature and tawdry humanity are again complicit in the erosion of civilization, which once more teeters on the brink. Suddenly the seafront playland has become an embarking stage for a modern ark. Storm warnings hang on the pier, and the family and the pairs of animals board the ship as the waters rise.

Antrobus house. Having survived the flood, Sabina and Mrs. Antrobus crawl out of the wreckage of the Excelsior house. Walls tilt drunkenly, and fire burns in the distance. The daughter emerges from a trapdoor carrying a baby, and Henry, now identified as the enemy, staggers into the battered home to fall asleep, forgiven one more time. The back wall disappears to reveal an arching path across which actors parade, speaking words of wisdom. There is a blackout; then lights come up to show Sabina repeating her act 1 opening speech in a restored house as the cycle of renewal begins again.

— *Nan C. L. Scott*

SLAUGHTERHOUSE-FIVE

Author: Kurt Vonnegut (1922-   )
Type of work: Novel
Type of plot: Historical realism, science fiction, black comedy

Time of plot: 1922-1976
First published: 1969

With its unusual mixture of historical realism and often bizarre science fiction, this novel often transcends both space and time. Its primary settings are upstate New York in the late 1960's, the European theater of World War II during the early 1940's, and the fictional planet Tralfamadore through eternity.

*Cape Cod.** Massachusetts setting of the novel's present-time autobiographical frame in the first and last chapters, Cape Cod is where author Kurt Vonnegut lived while writing the novel during the 1960's.

Ilium. Fictional New York city where the main action unfolds. Modeled on New York's upstate city of Schenectady, where Vonnegut once worked for General Electric, Ilium (after the Greek name for ancient Troy) is the place where protagonist Billy Pilgrim grows up, returns after serving in World War II, marries the daughter of the founder of his optometry college, and has a successful career as an optometrist.

The novel's present-day setting of the late 1960's is heavily middle-class and suburban and, in Vonnegut's satirical prose, is revealed to be empty of such important American values as compassion and diversity. The novel's loose plot turns on Billy's waning enthusiasm for living. His sudden and inexplicable weeping episodes suggest that he is a victim of delayed stress syndrome, due to his horrific wartime experiences. His stress is manifested by his claim that in 1944 he became "unstuck in time." Since then, he has traveled back and forth throughout time and interstellar space.

Vonnegut's frame makes clear that the novel's larger meaning applies to the late 1960's, when Robert Kennedy and Martin Luther King, Jr. were assassinated, riots were tearing cities apart, "and every day my Government gives me a count of corpses created by military science in Vietnam." Scenes set in Ilium—such as Billy's speaking at the Lions Club or driving through a black ghetto in his Cadillac with the windows rolled up tight—reveal an American city whose leading citizens seem oblivious to the country's real problems.

*Dresden. German city destroyed by Allied bombing toward the end of World War II. The novel's most intense action takes place during the war, in which Billy is captured by Germans and taken to Dresden and housed with other American prisoners in an abandoned slaughterhouse (which gives the novel its title)—a real place in which Vonnegut himself had been kept as a prisoner of war. While the city is leveled by an Allied firebomb attack that kills 135,000 inhabitants, both the prisoners and their guards are safely sheltered in a deep underground meat locker, which is "hollowed in living rock under the slaughterhouse." The novel ends with Billy being freed. While the setting is the historical Germany of World War II, its action is clearly meant to remind readers of the war in Vietnam, where U.S. forces rained napalm firebombs on suspected enemies during the late 1960's.

Tralfamadore (trahl-fahm-ah-DOHR). Imaginary distant planet that provides a setting for this and other Vonnegut novels. On the night of his daughter's wedding in 1967, Billy is kidnapped by aliens and flown on a flying saucer to Tralfamadore. He is not missed on Earth, he explains, because the Tralfamadorians take him through a time warp that permits him to spend years on their planet, while being away from Earth "for only a microsecond."

In contrast to his bland suburban life in Ilium and his horrific experiences in Dresden, Billy's life on Tralfamadore is pleasant. The Tralfamadorians display him naked in a zoo they have built for him, and there he lives contentedly with another earthling, beautiful film star Montana Wildhack. On Tralfamadore Billy learns that "all moments, past, present, and future, always have existed, always will exist." This relativistic philosophy apparently allows him to live perpetually in the present. His uncontrollable weeping, however, suggests that something is amiss beneath his surface. Perhaps the controlled "zoo" setting and human free will—which Tralfamadorians say is a notion that exists only on Earth—are incompatible.

— *David Peck*

SLOW HOMECOMING

Author: Peter Handke (1942-   )
Type of work: Novel
Type of plot: Philosophical realism
Time of plot: Late 1970's and early 1980's
First published: Langsame Heimkehr, 1979 (*The Long Way Around*); *Die Lehre der Sainte-Victoire*, 1980

(*The Lesson of Mont-Sainte-Victoire*); *Kindergeschichte*, 1981 (*Child Story*) (English translation, 1985 as *Slow Homecoming*); conceived together with the drama *Über die Dörfer* (beyond the villages), 1981

In this story of geologist Valentin Sorger's journey across North America during his return to his native Austria, the changing American landscape and Sorger's reflections upon it play a central symbolic function as reflections of the character's spiritual healing.

*Alaska. Northern wilderness country where Sorger, a deeply alienated person seeking some kind of personal salvation or healing, is conducting geological surveys. In a clearly existential quest to find forms or patterns that will guide or give meaning to his life, he sketches the landscape. His sketching—making marks on paper with a pencil—becomes a literary symbol for author Peter Handke's own philosophically self-conscious (and yet highly personal) activity of writing: the imaginative creation of aesthetic forms by which can he can somehow orient his own existence.

For Handke, the fictional images of otherness that human beings generate in and through language (and the human imagination)—artistic visions not of what is but of what might possibly be—circumscribe the domain of human freedom in that they establish a world in which choice is possible. Sorger hopes that his clearly mystical sketches of the vast geological forces at work in the Alaskan wilderness may yield some kind of inner natural law by which he can know himself, a "geology," as it were, of his own soul. He comes to realize, however, that his union with the natural forms of the wilderness landscape is dangerously egocentric and that he must slowly begin his return to both his child and his native home in Europe.

*San Francisco Bay Area.** Northern California region visited by Sorger after he leaves Alaska. The natural landscape unspoiled by human contact in Alaska gives way to the inhabited landscapes of the Berkeley area, and the latter serve to illustrate the importance and the reality of human relationships and community. The European married couple Sorger meets in the Berkeley area show him the meaning of caring for others, and he is forced to contemplate the self-centeredness of his mystical vision of nature in Alaska. Handke seems to suggest that his own philosophical self-absorption in his solitary, "ivory-tower" world of literature represents a personal dead end in his own journey toward self-understanding and spiritual healing. It is also in Northern California that Sorger sees the power of the earthquakes that have upended the landscape there and compares them in his sketches to the frequent shocks or jolts to his own consciousness that he has experienced throughout his life. He again undergoes a similar dislocation in the Bay Area. He loses all sense of spatial orientation and becomes speechless, the loss of language being a singular moment, a nadir of the personality in Handke's fiction, when the existential self is utterly sundered from the world. He again affirms the power of his writing to establish some kind of connection and orientation to existence. For Handke, language is the primary point of connection between consciousness and the world. As literary or imaginative language, it becomes the major source of personal liberation.

*Denver.** Capital and chief city of Colorado where Sorger goes to see an old friend, an Austrian ski instructor, whom he learns has died. This discovery becomes the occasion for his reflections on loss and separation and for his memories, namely those of his brother and sister in Austria. It is in Denver that he firmly decides to return home. He regains here his sense of spatial orientation and continues to seek some kind of spiritual law or guideline by which he can live his life, and he believes this law can be found in the fictions and images, a language of aesthetic forms, generated by the creative imagination.

*New York City.** Sorger's last stop before his flight back to Europe, where his process of healing continues as he meets a countryman named Esch, a stranger whom he had encountered on the plane, in a Manhattan coffee shop. As Esch talks, Sorger realizes the power of narration, the simple telling of a story, as a means of creating coherence and unity—a sense of form—out of the chaos of his own myriad experiences. The densely populated urban landscape of New York with its buildings and crowds serves as the symbolic counterpoint to the isolation of the Alaskan wilderness with its natural forms; as such, it represents Sorger's reintegration into human society.

— *Thomas F. Barry*

THE SMALL HOUSE AT ALLINGTON

Author: Anthony Trollope (1815-1882)
Type of work: Novel
Type of plot: Domestic realism

Time of plot: Mid-nineteenth century
First published: serial, 1862-1864; book, 1864

The Allington house and its lovely lawn and gardens provide a home for widowed Mrs. Dale and her daughters, Lily and Bell. Here there are courtships, proposals, refusals, a jilting, and a marriage. This cottage also serves as a setting for visits from gruff Squire Dale of the manor house, or the Great House of Allington, and from his nephew Bernard. Nearby Courcy Castle contrasts with this vital and loving family at the Small House, as do the scenes in London offices, clubs, and boardinghouses that add social commentary, satire, and comedy.

Allington. Estate of Squire Christopher Dale in Anthony Trollope's fictional district of **Barsetshire** in southern England. The squire lives in the estate's **Great House** and his widowed sister-in-law, Mrs. Mary Dale, and her daughters, Bell and Lily Dale, live in its **Small House**, which is connected to the Great House by adjoining gardens and lawns. The gardens are the setting for Lily's and Bell's walks, games, and talks with friends and lovers. Their lively and loving household is also the scene of disappointment and sadness; it is here that Bell refuses to please her uncle by marrying his nephew Bernard, which would ultimately make her mistress of the Great House. Here Lily is joyously pledged to Adolphus Crosbie, hears with pain that he has jilted her, and refuses John Eames's subsequent offer of marriage.

The Small House represents the dependency of the widow Dale on her brother-in-law, who has provided this dwelling so that she and her daughters might have a comfortable and socially suitable residence. However, when the squire seeks to pressure Bell into marrying his nephew, Mrs. Dale announces that she will leave the comforts of the Small House and their dependency on the squire, for inexpensive lodgings in nearby Guestwick. In the end, tempers cool, Bell is happily married, and Lily and her mother decide to remain in the Small House, near enough to cheer the old squire, who also relents and generously offers to have the whole house freshly painted.

Courcy Castle. Home of the dysfunctional family of the Earl de Courcy, that provides Trollope with occasions to expose the small-mindedness, greed, and malice of the nobility. At a showy Christmas reception given at the castle, social criticism is leveled at both the earl's family and their guests, who are shallow snobs, social climbers, and gossips. Adolphus Crosbie knows that he was much happier in his stay at the Small House in Allington, which the countess ridicules as "primitive" and "rural." She mocks Crosbie, accusing him of going about with a crook among the country bumpkins of Allington. Expecting social advantages, he proposes to Lady Alexandrina de Courcy. She does not fool herself that they wed for love, but rather knows that her motive is to get a house of her own, one that is less dull and less embittered by torment.

*London. Great Britain's capital city is the scene of social, political, and economic satire, as Trollope introduces Crosbie's workplace in the General Committee Office at Whitehall and John Eames's Income Tax Office. Several scenes are set at Seabright's, the private club to which Crosbie belongs, and Trollope develops a subplot at John's London lodgings—Mrs. Roper's Somerset House. Trollope's depiction of this boardinghouse is based on his own London experiences as a young man, when he saw his share of sleazy accommodations, tawdry romances, and rowdy confrontations. When John's finances improve, he escapes the clutches of the designing Amelia Roper and the other residents to seek new lodgings. These shabby boardinghouse scenes contrast with both the loveless flirtations at Courcy Castle and the genuine affections of the Dale women's Small House.

*Paddington Station. London train station that provides John with an opportunity to punish the jilting Crosbie, whom he recognizes on a train to London. Although the encounter is not a heroic duel, he manages to give Crosbie an embarrassing black eye.

Albert Villa. Home of Crosbie's future sister-in-law, Lady Amelia, in Hamilton Terrace of London's St. John's Wood district. Lady Amelia promises her sister that she will keep an eye on Crosbie until the Valentine's Day wedding. Crosbie comes to hate the very street lamps and even the geraniums on his way to this house, which gives him an unpleasant taste of the de Courcy coldness and bossiness. While visiting at Albert Villa, his lively, optimistic nature withers.

Princess Royal Crescent. Fashionable, but new and expensive area of London in which Crosbie and Lady Alexandrina build a house. It is labeled quite a "correct locality" because from one end, the corner of Hyde Park is visible. Crosbie would prefer a place near Vauxhall Bridge, but Lady Alexandrina puts her foot down. After an expensive wedding on Valentine's Day, an inexpensive honeymoon in Folkestone, and a dull and cold ten weeks of married life together, she decides to stay indefinitely with her mother and sister in Baden-Baden, Germany. The London house is dismantled, and Crosbie returns to his rooms in Mount Street where he lived as a bachelor.

— *Marie J. K. Brenner*

SMOKE

Author: Ivan Turgenev (1818-1883)
Type of work: Novel
Type of plot: Social realism

Time of plot: 1862-1865
First published: Dym, 1867 (English translation, 1868)

This novel is set primarily in Baden-Baden, Germany; however, Ivan Turgenev uses the German setting as a stage on which to present a love story about Russians traveling abroad and to address Russian issues that preoccupy him in many other works. Thus, although basically a love story, the novel is also a political and social satire.

*Baden-Baden. Popular spa in Germany's Black Forest area in which the novel is set. A Russian student and the son of a civil servant, Grigóry Litvinov, visits Baden-Baden, as was the wont of well-to-do Russians. Baden is a typical European spa of the mid-nineteenth century; it is pleasant, festive, with luscious green trees, pastel-colored houses, and orchestras playing in its gardens. This festiveness contrasts with Litvinov's sadness, as he tries to drown his sorrows in foreign travel (a typical refuge of Turgenev's failing characters) after an unsuccessful love affair with Irina, a daughter of an impoverished aristocratic family Osinin. However, just when Litvinov is ready to marry his new fiancé, Tatyana, Irina appears in Baden-Baden with her husband and professes still to love Litvinov.

Turgenev uses Baden-Baden because he himself was a frequent visitor to it and other European localities and therefore quite familiar with Western European spas, but also because the deep split among the Russian intellectuals made it natural to set the novel in a Western European location. He probably chose a German location because German philosophers and writers had a considerable influence on Russian thinkers and writers in the nineteenth century.

*Russia. Russia is often alluded to through the presence of Russian characters in Baden-Baden and by way of their arguments. Inevitably, Russia is prominently mentioned, but without dwelling on specific localities. Indeed, although this love story is one of the best written by Turgenev, it is overshadowed by endless discussions and tirades among the Russian visitors about Russian problems, centering on the relationship between Russia and the West and the attitudes of various Russians concerning that issue.

In the three years depicted in the novel, two kinds of Russian visitors to European cities, mostly spas, parade, as depicted by Turgenev: reactionary aristocrats—nobility, generals, and other well-to-do members of society—and the radical liberals. Russian intellectuals are also deeply divided into Slavophiles and Westerners. Turgenev, himself a Westerner, suggests through Potugin that his radical compatriots not look down on the West and idolize uncritically the Russian *muzhik* (peasant) and "the Russian spirit," but, instead, learn from the West and adopt those features that are beneficial to Russia. Most important, they should apply themselves to honest and serious work, rather than wasting time and efforts in pursuing revolutionary and unrealistic goals.

*Moscow. In a flashback, Turgenev relates how Litvinov, then a student at Moscow University, meets and falls in love with Irina, who lives near Dogs' Square, in a wooden house with a front porch, green lions on the gate, and other pretensions of nobility. The house resembles the wooden structures of Moscow that played an important part in the burning of the city before Napoleon's invasion in 1812.

Train. Heart-broken and utterly disillusioned, Litvinov eventually returns to Russia to forget and to make something of his studies for the benefit of his people. While riding a train through Germany, he looks at the smoke emitted from its steam engine, and everything seems to him to be as ephemeral and transparent as the train's smoke.

— *Vasa D. Mihailovich*

THE SNAKE PIT

Author: Sigrid Undset (1882-1949)
Type of work: Novel
Type of plot: Historical
Time of plot: Late thirteenth and early fourteenth
 centuries

First published: Olav Audunssøn i Hestviken and *Olav Audunssøn og hans børn*, 1925-1927 (*The Master of Hestviken*, 1928-1930, 1934; includes *The Axe*, 1928; *The Snake Pit*, 1929; *In the Wilderness*, 1929; *The Son Avenger*, 1930)

Medieval Norway provides a harsh setting in this novel about a family's struggle to stay together. The northern land's long, cold winters and isolation provide the backdrop for many scenes of personal revelation.

Hestviken. Home of Olav Audunsson's family, that is the primary setting of the novel. The estate is near an icy fjord, where ocean waves throw up spray against sheer cliffs and rock promontories, which, with fog, block the view in many directions. Physical features of Hestviken symbolize the moods of Olav and his wife, Ingunn. When they begin their life together there, both are optimistic, their feelings buoyed by the beautiful sights and smells of the summer farm. The fragrance of lime trees reminds Olav of his childhood. Ingunn feels healthy and beautiful as she surveys the pleasant scene. However, she soon notices other things that reinforce her downward spiral into depression, such as the monotonous booming of the ocean's waves in the fjord and the seemingly endless rains.

Manor house. Ancestral dwelling at Hestviken that has replaced an earlier and finer house that burned down. The rustic replacement is dark and sparsely furnished. Undset uses her extensive knowledge of medieval home furnishings to give a historically accurate depiction of the home layout and contents. In the dark rooms of the house, the lonely Ingunn torments herself over having borne an illegitimate child, leaving the child with strangers, and failing to be a strong helpmate for the morose Olav. Her plight reflects the difficult lives led by most women in the Middle Ages, lives made up of endless toil with few diversions, frequent pregnancies, and total dependence upon men.

A powerful symbol of Olav's struggles is an old plank that has been carved to depict a snake pit. A relic from the former manor house, it forms the doorpost of the rebuilt home's bedchamber. Its carving shows a man surrounded by serpents, one of which is biting his heart.

Like the figure entangled in snakes, Olav is entangled in many problems, including feelings of guilt, Ingunn's illness, and his disappointment with his stepson, Eirik.

Outbuildings. In addition to its manor house, Hestviken has turf-roofed sheds, storehouses, and stables. Hestviken's mundane structures are the settings for many scenes in which characters experience important personal revelations. For example, an old longboat shed is the location of Olav's discovery that Eirik cannot distinguish truth from falsehood. A cow barn under construction is the locale for cavorting workers and Ingunn's jealous reaction to Una, the servant girl.

Church. Unfinished church between Oslo and Hestviken at which Olav, on the night before Ingunn's death, stops to rest. Inside the cold, desolate place, he studies a piece of artwork depicting Christ's Crucifixion, a sight that makes him realize that he himself should seek forgiveness.

Foster home. Home of a poor family in which Ingunn's five-year-old son has been placed. In the cluttered, dark environment, Eirik spends his formative years in the company of a disorderly pack of ragged children. This bleak setting highlights the dreary lives of the common people of the time and helps explain Eirik's arrested intellectual development.

Galley ship. A break in the story's dark mood comes during a summer that Olav spends captaining a galley ship under Duke Haakon. At sea, the horizons in view in every direction provide a great contrast to Olav's enclosed life along the fjord, and his time at sea liberates him from the circumscribed life in his troubled household.

— *Nancy Conn Terjesen*

SO BIG

Author: Edna Ferber (1885-1968)
Type of work: Novel
Type of plot: Social realism

Time of plot: Early twentieth century
First published: 1924

Edna Ferber's Pulitzer Prize-winning novel is set primarily in Illinois, which was a magnet for thousands of European immigrants in the late nineteenth century. Chicago's ethnic neighborhoods were becoming "cities within the city," and many immigrants settled on fertile agricultural lands to its south and west, retaining their Old World languages and customs.

High Prairie. Dutch farming community southwest of Chicago where Ferber's protagonist, Selina Peake, goes to teach in a primitive one-room schoolhouse after her gambler father is shot to death. There she lives with a farming family named Pool and experiences an environment as different from that of her life with her peripatetic father as the fine finishing school she attended in Chicago is different from the tiny schoolhouse in which she teaches. Selina's school opens its sessions in November after the fall harvest. During the cold winters, students huddle at their pine desks, arranged close to the school's pot-bellied stove. They write their assignments in chalk on slates, bring their own lunches, drink water from the well, and use the privy outside.

At the town's Dutch Reformed Church, sunlight penetrating the red and yellow windows makes the faces of the solemn Calvinist worshipers look jaundiced. For recreation, families attend a dance and box supper held upstairs at Adam Oom's general store.

Pool farm. Home of the Pool family, with whom Selina lives while beginning her teaching job in High Prairie. Thrifty, hard-working farmers, the Pools raise hogs and cabbages. The Pools' life, she finds, is not a game but an unending job in which they devote every possible minute to making their livelihood from the soil: plowing and reaping, repairing farm tools, cooking, and mending clothes. The most striking aspect of life at the Pools', so far as Selina is concerned, is the fact that there is no time to appreciate and seek beauty. Up to this point in her life, Selina has devoted much of her time and energy to searching for beauty; now she, too, must devote herself to the problems of farming life and to teaching children whose parents are more concerned with their children's abilities in the fields than their abilities in the classroom.

A cast iron wood stove dominates the Pool's clean but cluttered kitchen that smells of pork grease, manure, and damp wool. The house has no indoor plumbing, and family members spend considerable time cutting wood and hauling water. Their parlor walls display pictures of their ancestors; a narrow stairway leads to Selina's unheated room, which is furnished with a huge walnut-frame bed.

DeJong farm. Home of Pervus DeJong, a poor but handsome farmer whom Selina eventually marries. Its dark, damp farmhouse has a leaky mansard roof and peeling paint. From May to October, DeJong cultivates vegetables on twenty-five acres of unproductive lowland. Other farmers improve their productivity by draining their marshy fields, but Pervus refuses to change. After he dies, Selina studies horticulture books to improve the farm's productivity and her marketing of its crops. She buys twenty-five additional acres, drains and fertilizes the land, raises hogs, and eventually sells the farm's increasing produce to an exclusive Chicago clientele.

*Haymarket. Chicago market center to which farmers travel by night to arrive before it opens at dawn, when hundreds of wagons line Haymarket Street. The market is a male-dominated environment in which the predominantly male farmers and buyers resent Selina's intrusion and make it difficult for her sell her produce.

— *Martha E. Rhynes*

SOHRAB AND RUSTUM

Author: Matthew Arnold (1822-1888)
Type of work: Poetry
Type of plot: Historical

Time of plot: Antiquity
First published: 1853

By setting this entire poem in Central Asia, Matthew Arnold removes the action to a place where it can be contemplated with stoic acceptance and without Romantic emotionalism. Central Asia also provides a wealth of exotic and grand materials, which Arnold works into the many epic similes in the poem. The main action of the poem takes place along the ancient Oxus River in Central Asia, and this river is used symbolically to comment on that action.

Central Asia. Scene of the battle between the forces of Persia and their Tartar enemies. Arnold wrote this poem in part to illustrate his theories concerning the superiority of the classical, objective, and affirmative epic over the Romantic, lyric, and melancholy poetry of his own time. By placing his poem in Central Asia, among Persians and Tartars, he achieves an emotional distance and objectivity that removes the poem from the Romantic intensity and lyrical sadness of the typical poetry of his age. Set in a distant and ancient place, the tragic tale of a warrior father who unwittingly kills his warrior son can be treated not as an occasion for sentimental tears but as an illustration of fate and its inevitability. Moreover, Arnold uses the places, landscapes, and customs of Central Asia as materials for the complex epic similes that are crucial to the poem's epic style.

*Oxus River. River upon whose plain Sohrab and Rustum fight. When Rustum slays Sohrab on the banks of the Oxus, Arnold ends with an elaborate and symbolic account of the Oxus, describing its origins, its troubled but continuous flow, and its final absorption into the tranquil Aral Sea. In this way, Arnold allows the setting of the action to comment on that action. Rustum's killing of Sohrab is only one event in human destiny, which itself flows like a river. Human life persists, and every human life ends in the quiet Aral Sea of death.

— *Phillip B. Anderson*

SOLARIS

Author: Stanisław Lem (1921-   )
Type of work: Novel
Type of plot: Science fiction

Time of plot: The future
First published: 1961 (English translation, 1970)

This, the best-known novel of Polish author Stanisław Lem to English-speaking readers, is a work in which place actually becomes a character. The planet Solaris, with its mysterious life-forms that interact with the human protagonists, is not merely a setting, but a puzzle the protagonists strive, and ultimately fail, to solve.

Solaris. Fictional planet in a distant star system on which the entire novel is set. A planet in a binary stellar system (one with two suns), Solaris has a highly unstable orbit that may be related to the complex gravitational forces of a binary star but which also seems to be effected by the mysterious living ocean that covers most of the planet. In the future period in which the novel is set, humans have reached this mysterious world and established a small experimental base on it. On the planet, the humans come under the influence of Solaris's living ocean.

The name "Solaris" invokes the name of the sun that is the source of life-giving warmth to Earth. As such, it can also be seen as a pun on "son," since much of the novel's action is psychological in nature, dealing as it does with human sexual drives and erotic guilt, albeit in complex, symbolic ways. Thus, the planet Solaris can be seen as a place where humanity is forced to confront the dark side of its own psychology.

Solarian ocean. Body of water that covers the entire surface of Solaris. This mysterious body of colloidal fluid is both a geographical feature and a major character of the novel. It is apparently intelligent at some level, and is believed by some humans to cause the peculiar perturbations in the planet's orbit, rather like an extreme version of the "Gaia hypothesis," which suggests that the totality of life on Earth works together to preserve conditions suitable for life to continue.

This living ocean is also the probable source of the mysterious Phi-creatures, beings that resemble their human counterparts so closely that only microscopic examination can distinguish them. The Phi-creatures appear to be intermediaries, an attempt by the ocean to create an interface through which it can communicate with the humans that have come to its planet. However, there is no known communication channel between the Phi-creatures and the ocean, so these attempts at communication ultimately prove fruitless.

Prometheus. Spaceship on which protagonist Kris Kelvin arrives on Solaris. While most American science fiction writers of the 1960's would have lavished upon readers detailed descriptions of the physical hardware of their spaceships, Lem keeps the technological details spare, a minimum necessary to create the impression of an interstellar vessel. As in the rest of the novel, the thrust is primarily philosophical, and the classical reference of the ship's name is significant. In Greek mythology, the Titan Prometheus was renowned for stealing fire from the gods and giving it to humans, who had been denied such natural defenses as sharp teeth and claws. However, that act led to Prometheus's being chained to a rock, where his liver was gnawed by a vulture as punishment. Thus Prometheus was an ambivalent figure, symbolizing both enlightenment and condemnation, civilization and punishment. Similarly, the spaceship *Prometheus* is both a technological triumph and the instrument by which Kelvin is delivered to psychological torment.

Research station. Human research base on Solaris that floats at an altitude of from five yards to nearly a mile above the ocean. It is maintained by gravitors, a kind of gravity-control device. The station can be thrust well into the planet's stratosphere at the first hint of upheavals in the planetary ocean, such as one that took the lives of 106 people some years earlier.

The station is a bit of earthly environment brought to this alien world, within which the human researchers live. As such it can be seen as a sort of womb, even a mother figure. At the same time, it is also symbolic of the idea that the explorers come to a distant world thinking that they are trying to learn about an alien world, when in fact they are attempting to impose upon it earthly certainties and expectations.

— Leigh Husband Kimmel

THE SONG OF HIAWATHA

Author: Henry Wadsworth Longfellow (1807-1882)
Type of work: Poetry
Type of plot: Folklore

Time of plot: Aboriginal period
First published: 1855

This poem, Henry Wadsworth Longfellow's attempt to create an epic of Native American mythology, depends not only on its geographical setting in the Ojibwa Great Lakes region but also on its historical setting in the distant mythological past.

Ojibway land (oh-JIHB-way; also spelled Ojibwa). Area inhabited by the Algonquian-speaking peoples of the Upper Great Lakes—a region encompassing much of what is now Ontario, Manitoba, Saskatchewan, North Dakota, Minnesota, Michigan, Wisconsin, Indiana, and Ohio. Longfellow never visited this area and he relied heavily on books by John Tanner and Henry Rowe Schoolcraft to write his poem. He was probably also influenced by engravings by George Catlin to create his mental visualization of Ojibway life in the Great Lakes region. At the time when *The Song of Hiawatha* was published, Ojibway land was still remote and mysterious to many eastern Americans. At the same time, however, the Upper Great Lakes region was one of the first parts of the North American interior in which Europeans and Native Americans began their uneasy coexistence. Longfellow ends his poem with the incursion of white men into the "Land of the Ojibway" and the departure of Hiawatha.

Longfellow's Great Lakes region can be seen as the mythic and Edenic vanished land of the Ojibwa, as well as a place in which Europeans were settling in ever greater numbers, encouraged by the region's rich ore deposits. Thus, for Longfellow's readers, the location of the poem presents a paradox: On one hand, it depicts the romantic notion of the "noble savage" living at one with nature; on the other hand, it depicts the contemporary reality of logging camps and copper and iron mines. It does so, however, without blaming the intrusive white population for the destruction of a way of life; rather, there is an air of inevitability in the poem, which suggests that the Ojibway land must fade from existence as states such as Michigan and Minnesota are taking shape.

Vale of Tawasentha (tah-wah-SEHN-thah). Located somewhere in Ojibway land, the Vale of Tawasentha is the location of Longfellow's mythic singer, Nawahada, who tells the story of Hiawatha. The description of the vale suggests a golden, prehistoric paradise where Native Americans lived in harmony with nature. Further, Longfellow attempts to connect his poem with the oral traditions of the Native American singer by inventing Nawahada.

Red Pipestone Quarry. Place where Gitche Manito, the Master of Life, calls the tribes of men to gather, entreats them to make peace with each other, and teaches them to make peace pipes. While it is not possible to identify accurately this location geographically, it is likely that Longfellow was thinking about the pipestone quarries of southern Minnesota where native peoples have long gathered to collect the precious pipestone for fashioning into sacred relics and pipes. One such Minnesota quarry is the Pipestone National Monument. By using this location as the site for the important ritual meeting of the tribes, Longfellow ties his poem to actual Native American customs as well as to contemporary American geography, all while preserving the sense of a prehistoric, mythic past.

Gitche Gumee (GIT-chee GEW-mee). Indian name for **Lake Superior**—which is also called Big-Sea-Water—by which Hiawatha grows up. The largest of all the Great Lakes, Superior is also the Great Lake that extends farthest north and west. Lands surrounding the lake include Ontario, Minnesota, Wisconsin, and Michigan. As one of the largest bodies of fresh water in the world, Superior is of suitable size and grandeur to be associated with Longfellow's vision.

*****Dakota land.** Area west of Ojibway land, including parts of present-day Canada, North Dakota, South Dakota, Wyoming, and Montana that was the traditional home of the Dakota peoples. The "Dakotahs" to whom Longfellow refers are probably Sioux. Their land plays an important role, because it is here that the young Hiawatha finds his beloved, Minnehaha, the daughter of an arrow maker. Traditionally, the Falls of Minnehaha are associated with waterfalls in present-day Minneapolis. Structurally, it is important for the poem as a journey quest that Hiawatha leaves his own people and goes to the land of the enemy to find his mate. Moreover, this union produces peace among the Ojibway and the Dakotah.

— *Diane Andrews Henningfeld*

THE SONG OF ROLAND

Author: Unknown
Type of work: Poetry
Type of plot: Chivalric romance

Time of plot: c. 778
First published: Chanson de Roland, twelfth century

Although the events that happen to King Charlemagne and his court in this oldest of all extant French epic poems are fictional, they are based on certain historical occurrences. Scribes in the thirteenth century appropriately categorized this work with other epic poems as one of those in the Cycle of the King. Its unnamed author presents what transpires in a way that permits readers to see how this particular account of the battles of Charlemagne and Roland transcends time through the various localities discussed.

*Roncesvalles (rahn-SEHS-val-yay). Pass in northern Spain's Pyrenees mountain range where Roland, King Charlemagne's nephew, is believed to have been ambushed and massacred by Basques while Charlemagne was leading his army back to France after his campaigns in Spain. According to *The Song of Roland*—which was written during the time of the First Crusades, approximately three hundred years after the events it describes took place—Roland's forces fought the Muslims (Moors or Saracens), rather than the Basques (or Gascons). The unnamed author may have wished to elevate the battle at "Roncevaux" into a struggle between Christians and pagans as a result of the contemporary views of the struggles between the two groups at that time. In addition, Roland is presented as a Frank from France, not the Breton from Brittany that he actually was. Roncesvalles may also symbolize the border between destruction and death and honor and everlasting life.

*Saragossa. City in northeastern Spain located on the south bank of the Ebro River (now the capital of Aragon). One of its towns, Salduba, which is of Celtic and Iberian origin, was made a colony by the Romans during the first century B.C.E., and called "Caesaraugusta," from which "Saragossa" is adapted. In this epic, Saragossa is the only Spanish city that is not yet under King Charlemagne's control. Its pagan king Marsile is persuaded by Ganelon to kill Roland (Charlemagne's nephew and Ganelon's own stepson), because of the strength that the young man represents for Charlemagne. This locale signifies that which is foreign, pagan, or other; it is also symbolic of treachery and betrayal, especially in the case of Ganelon, one of Charlemagne's own kinsmen.

*Aix-la-Chapelle (aks-lah-shah-pel). Now Aachen, Germany, a well-known town of historic importance, known especially as having become the permanent residence and burial place of King Charlemagne, In this poem, certain details are altered, such as the origin of those with whom Charlemagne and Roland do battle. For example, Aix-la-Chapelle is described as a place in France, when in fact it is a region in Germany. What is consistent with factual information, however, is that the king is described as living and supporting a chapel there. This setting represents the domain of Charlemagne: that which is Christian, and according to the text, that which is just, right, proper, and honorable.

— *Adriana C. Tomasino*

SONG OF SOLOMON

Author: Toni Morrison (1931-   )
Type of work: Novel
Type of plot: Bildungsroman

Time of plot: 1869-1963
First published: 1977

This novel chronicles the coming of age of Macon (Milkman) Dead in 1963 in urban north and rural Virginia, while connecting his personal history to the history of his ancestors, and tying their familial and cultural history to the land. As African slaves wandered in an unfamiliar land in search of meaningful roots, so Milkman travels from place to place hoping to find his people and his personal truth.

Shalimar (SHAL-ee-mahr). The ancestral home of Solomon and Ryna, Jake (Macon Dead), and Sing (Singing Bird). According to legend, Solomon could fly.

Close by are Ryna's Gulch and Solomon's Leap. The mysteries of Pilate's behavior, and Macon's, are found here, and memorialized in a children's song. Here Milkman finds his truth. Pilate finds peace as they bury their father's bones in the land of his birth. She discards the burden symbolized by the earring she has worn all her life. As Milkman jumps from Solomon's Leap, he knows he can soar. He has found truth, a connection through time and place that is forever unbroken by earthly bonds.

Dead home. Michigan home of the well-off family of Macon Dead, his wife, Ruth Foster Dead, and their two daughters, Magdalene, called Lena, and First Corinthians, located at 12 Not Doctor Street in a large city. It is a home filled with nice things, including a polished mahogany table and fresh flowers. They have a certain social status. Ruth is the daughter of the late Doctor Foster. Her husband Macon is a man of property and pride. His self-worth is tied to what he owns. Yet their home is truly a "dead" house. There is no life, no love within its walls. The Dead home is haunted by past secrets. Ruth is sad and loveless. Macon is angry and dissatisfied; he equates money with freedom. The daughters are troubled and frustrated, and Milkman is puzzled and angry at the rigid structure, and at his lack of personal peace and contentment in the constantly changing world of the 1960's. The Dead home has a history, but it lacks roots.

Pilate's house. Home of Pilate, her daughter Reba, and Reba's daughter Hagar; a small house backed by pines, without gas or electricity. The house has no modern conveniences and smells of wine and spices, and sometimes peaches. It is disorganized, not well kept, and lacking status; yet this house on Darling Street is rich with music, love, and history. Here one finds connections to the land in the trees, the grapes, the earthy attitude of Pilate, and the thread of affection and loyalty that binds the three generations of women together. There is mystery here as well, in the green tarp hanging from the ceiling. Pilate calls the contents her "inheritance." She speaks of personal and spiritual substance. She has much though she lacks wealth. Her home embraces her physical and emotional history. Her music and her joy connect her to people and places beyond the confines of her meager walls. She has found peace.

Hunter's Cave. Scene of what Pilate and Macon believed was a murder. In fact, the bones Pilate retrieves and carries with her, literally and figuratively through the years, are those of her own father. Her history is always with her no matter where she travels.

Lincoln's Heaven. Homestead of the original Macon Dead located outside of Danville, Pennsylvania, a town 240 miles northeast of Pittsburgh. For Macon Dead, land ownership was a tangible symbol of his freedom. His farm is small, with room for crops and fruit trees, a pond, and a rich forest of mahogany and pine. To a hardworking man, a former slave, unable to read, stripped of his dignity and even his given name by the oppression of slavery, this rural setting in Montour County was his own personal heaven on Earth.

Literacy was not required to work the land. He could provide for his family and put down roots. He owned this land and would protect this emblem of freedom to the death. His love for his land would be passed on to his son and grandson, but their understanding of this inheritance would be tarnished by the money, the grit and greed of the cold, and often heartless, city skyline. As the generations progressed, ownership became for Macon and Milkman not a sense of pride, but an occasion for greed and profit. The spirit of Macon (Jake is his given name) will speak to Milkman and to Pilate until they understand their connections to the land, to their heritage, and to one another.

— *Kathleen Schongar*

THE SONG OF THE LARK

Author: Willa Cather (1873-1947)
Type of work: Novel
Type of plot: Impressionistic realism

Time of plot: Late nineteenth and early twentieth centuries
First published: 1915

Always important in Willa Cather's fiction, the settings in this novel help to underscore the various phases in the growth of the vocal artist Thea Kronborg from her raw, frontier-town beginnings to her eventual operatic triumphs in Europe and New York City.

Moonstone. Fictional town set in the sand hills of Colorado, closely modeled on Red Cloud, Nebraska, where Willa Cather spent her late elementary school and high school years. Her parents lived in this town for the rest of their lives, providing her with numerous opportunities to revisit and refresh her memory about the people and places that appear continuously in her fiction.

Thea Kronborg, the central character in *The Song of the Lark*, starts her artistic journey in Moonstone as the daughter of a Scandinavian Methodist minister. She is somewhat inhibited by her family's small-town religious values and the routine nineteenth century expectations of women. Although Cather herself was frustrated by similar small-town conventions, she recognized that key persons in Red Cloud had helped her in her education and her eventual success as a writer, and she created similar characters in Moonstone to provide Thea with recognition of her unusual personality and talents. These include Professor Wunsch, a wandering and dissolute musician who teaches Thea to play the piano; Dr. Archie, a lifelong friend and mentor, who provides wisdom, insight, and fatherly concern; and Ray Kennedy, a brakeman on the railroad, who bequeaths Thea enough money to allow her to go to Chicago to study music.

Even her father and mother recognize her talent and do not prevent her from doing formal study far away in a big city. Her participation in the church choir, in local talent shows, and in the somewhat questionable festivities of Moonstone's Mexican town provide opportunities to display her musical talent and for town recognition as a promising musician. By age fifteen, she has quit high school to become the main piano teacher in the small town but is frustrated by what appears to be a future clouded by frontier cultural limitations.

*****Chicago.** The largest city in the Midwest, where Thea pursues her musical education in the 1890's, at the same time that Chicago itself is experiencing a renaissance in the arts. Thea's Chicago piano teacher, Andor Harsanyi, soon recognizes that Thea's real future is

in singing and arranges for another mentor, Madison Bowers, to give her vocal lessons. Thea's artist self is also awakened by hearing the Chicago Symphony perform and by visiting the Chicago Art Institute, where she sees the painting by French artist Jules Breton (1827-1906) of a young peasant girl's awakening to the possibilities of life. The title of Breton's painting, *The Song of the Lark*, provides the title of both the novel and its second section. In Chicago, Thea begins to have success as a singer and meets the wealthy Fred Ottenburg, who is drawn to Thea both as an artist and as a woman.

Panther Canyon. Arizona ranch of the Ottenburgs, a wealthy family of brewers, to which Fred Ottenburg sends Thea to recuperate when he realizes that overwork has put her on the verge of a breakdown. There, she is revitalized by a summer in the hot sun and dry air. Based on Walnut Canyon in north-central Arizona, Panther Canyon is the site of Native American cliff dwellings that become an important inspiration to Thea's continued maturation as an artist. Among houses carved out of the cliffs, Thea realizes the true nature of art and renews her commitment to live the life of an artist. However, it is also here that she falls openly in love with the married Fred and starts an affair that complicates her artistic life.

*****New York City.** Artistic center of American culture to which Dr. Archie comes and agrees to provide money for Thea to go abroad to Germany and study with the best teachers in order to become a successful operatic artist. Although Fred Ottenburg has enough money easily to subsidize Thea, she cannot accept his support because she believes it would come with obligations with which a true artist cannot coexist. Dr. Archie, she feels, can provide funds without such ties. It is also in New York City, when, after ten years, Thea returns from her musical study and successes in Europe, that Andor Harsanyi, Dr. Archie, and Fred Ottenburg hear Thea triumph over fatigue and hoarseness, winning over audiences and critics alike.

— *Delmer Davis*

THE SONG OF THE WORLD

Author: Jean Giono (1895-1970)
Type of work: Novel
Type of plot: Impressionistic realism

Time of plot: Early twentieth century
First published: Le Chant du monde, 1934 (English translation, 1937)

Although set in a specific and lyrically described region of southeastern France, Alpes-de-Haute-Provence, this novel seems to take place in a timeless, epic landscape, a world of wild rivers and towering peaks in which Jean Giono's primal characters play out an age-old story of love, revenge, and death. The author's evocation of autumn, winter, and spring in the novel's three sections reinforces its elemental quality.

River. Unnamed stream that is the thread on which most of the events in *The Song of the World* are strung, portrayed as an animate being. It is up the river that Danis sets out to cut fir trees that he plans to fashion into a raft that will carry him back downstream. Asked by Danis's father, Sailor, to help search for the youth when he does not reappear, Antonio knows the river intimately and is able to "read" its character at any given time. He lives on the isle of jays in the middle of the river and can sense when its channels and fords have shifted. Swimming in the river's icy currents, he knows that it has rained in the mountains and that he and Sailor must pass through the river's gorges before they become impassable.

***Nibles Forest** (nee-blah). Woodland in which the woodcutter Sailor lives with his family. Like the river, the forest is portrayed as a living entity composed of innumerable sensate plants and animals. Its trees breathe, and Sailor recognizes the individual smells of pine and willow, allowing him to lead Antonio through the darkened forest at night. Both Antonio and Sailor are aware of the comings and goings of wolves and foxes, and can identify the sounds of shepherds' horns and church bells ringing in belfries high up in the mountains. Sailor's camp in the forest consists of a simple cottage, a low hut, and a long shed.

Rebeillard country (reh-bay-YARD). Rich, more densely populated, but dangerous region upriver, past the gorges and higher in the mountains. The Rebeillard country is the site of Puberclaire, the great estate of tyrannical bull-raiser Maudru that Antonio and Danis set afire in revenge for the murder of Sailor, and of Maladrerie, the estate of Maudru's daughter Gina.

***Villevielle** (veel-vee-el). Medieval French village of tanneries, covered alleys, and interconnecting cellars in the upper Rebeillard country. Although they are town-dwellers, Villevielle's inhabitants are governed by the seasons just as inexorably as Antonio and Sailor, and they joyfully celebrate the approach of spring. The village is also the home of Jérôme, a hunchbacked almanac vendor and herbalist, as well as Sailor's brother-in-law. Jérôme's house becomes the refuge of Danis, who hides his raft in a nearby creek, and of Danis's lover Gina. The house is a mysterious storehouse of books and gems and dried herbs, a magical abode from which the disabled healer rarely strays.

***Alpes-de-Haute-Provence** (ALP-duh-OHT-pro-VAWNS). Department of southeastern France, known in Giono's day as Basses-Alpes and the scene of many of his works, including *The Song of the World*. Noted for its mountains and rapidly falling rivers, the department lies between the highest peaks of the Alps and the coastal region of Provence. Giono was born and grew up in the town of Manosque near the geographical center of the department.

— *Grove Koger*

SONNETS FROM THE PORTUGUESE

Author: Elizabeth Barrett Browning (1806-1861)   *First published:* 1850
Type of work: Poetry

The most widely read of Elizabeth Barrett Browning's poems, these sonnets in the Italian form were written as a result of her having fallen in love with poet Robert Browning, whom she later married. Many of the sonnets are grounded in a pastoral setting, as if the beauty of creation helps illustrate the love that both poets shared.

Pastoral settings. Elizabeth Barrett Browning's imagery derives from several sources suggestive of place. Often, she does not specifically name the place that she invokes, but a close reading can determine it. Her first sonnet speaks of Theocritus, an ancient Greek poet who developed the pastoral, using bucolic scenes and idylls. Barrett Browning's sonnets reveal her dependency on natural scenes as sources of wisdom. Nature is considered to possess a purity that fallen human nature cannot own. The sonnets are filled with references to owls, bats, crickets, woodland nightingales, bees—all manner of living things.

*Venice. Italian city that is mentioned several times in the sonnets. In contrast to her pastoral references, Barrett Browning's references to European cities add a layer of urban sophistication to the sonnets. For example, she calls a mirror "Venice-glass," alluding to Murano glass, which was manufactured in Venice. In writing about the contents of her soul, she mentions the Rialto, a theatrical district and marketplace that takes its name from an island in Venice. The poet thereby shows her lover that she has the innocence of the pristine countryside, but the sophistication of a city.

Heaven. Perhaps the most mentioned place in the sonnets. The poet longs for her union with her beloved, believing that such love is consistent with her soul's longing for Heaven. Indeed, just as life in Heaven is blessed, so, too, is life on Earth blessed by such a union. The poet beseeches Heaven's blessing and fears the loss of Heaven should her union with her lover not stand the test of time.

— *Martha Modena Vertreace-Doody*

THE SONNETS OF SHAKESPEARE

Author: William Shakespeare (1564-1616)   *First published: Sonnets,* 1609
Type of work: Poetry

Much of the greatness of William Shakespeare's sonnets lies in the poet's ability to find exactly the right images to convey particular ideas or feelings, and many of his images are allusions to places, some specific, but most generic. Many of these allusions reflect the contemporary Elizabethan belief that Earth was the center of the universe and that every star, rock, and species had a fixed place and purpose in a Great Chain of Being.

Cosmos. Natural phenomena of heaven and Earth are compared to human activities. The universe is like a huge stage, on which each natural element performs at its peak of perfection then declines and dies; likewise, a youth experiences a moment of perfection that does not last. An astrologer predicts the future by reading the stars, but the speaker looks into his lover's eyes for truth and beauty. Fate bestows fame on military heroes and the prince's favorites, who will soon wilt like marigolds.

Time and season. Many of Shakespeare's sonnets compare stages of life to time passing from dawn to midday to sunset, and from spring to summer to fall and winter. Youth is like a blazing sunrise, maturing at high noon, declining in old age, and dying at sunset. The rising sun kisses earth's mountaintops, meadows, and streams, but clouds of disgrace sometimes emerge to hide its brilliance. Time turns youthful black curls silver, and green meadows fall to the scythe. Time is a tyrant that drives summer onward to winter and death, leaving behind the fragrance of summer flowers. A lover's absence seems bleak like winter, even though it may be spring, and Nature is reproducing so extravagantly that the gloomy planet Saturn laughs.

Gardens. Several sonnets compare a lover's faults to flaws in nature: thorns on roses, mud in silver fountains, clouds and eclipses that hide the Sun and the Moon, and the worm inside a rosebud. Except for their thorns, wild roses are as colorful and smell as sweet as cultivated roses. Cold, unemotional people are like stones, while lovers are like lilies. If lilies become infected, they smell worse than weeds that choke them out. The speaker accuses flowers (other lovers) of stealing color and scent from the youth's cheeks and breath, white from his hand, gold from his hair, roses from his blush, and white from his low spirits. In retaliation, worms soon steal life from the flowers.

Familiar settings. Familiar Elizabethan settings appear in many sonnets. For example, one speaker compares his stage of life to ruins of a deserted chapel, where trees are bare and no birds sing, to twilight after sunset, and to the dying embers of a once-glowing fire. In another, a family's heritage is like a house needing constant repair—through its heirs—so it can withstand storms of misfortune and death. Lawyers in a courtroom argue over whether a lover belongs to the defendant or to the plaintiff; the jury decides in the defendant's favor.

In another sonnet, two men are imprisoned in the steel cell of a woman's heart; the speaker begs the woman to release his friend and in return promises to remain her prisoner. Elsewhere, a mirror reflects a speaker's aging face; a clock reminds him of time wasted, and blank pages in his journal reflect his lack of creativity. While a woman plays a spinet, admirers wish they were the wooden keys being caressed by her fingers; they kiss her hand, but the speaker wishes to kiss her lips. Although marble monuments may be overturned during wars, and memorial stones in church floors may be effaced, the poet claims his verse will last until Judgment Day.

— *Martha E. Rhynes*

SONS AND LOVERS

Author: D. H. Lawrence (1885-1930)
Type of work: Novel
Type of plot: Psychological realism

Time of plot: Late nineteenth century
First published: 1913

Set in D. H. Lawrence's childhood home of Nottinghamshire, England, this novel has exceptionally strong autobiographical strands. Its characters are shaped and constrained by the town, the countryside, and the coal mine that dominates the region.

Bestwood. English coal-mining town in Nottinghamshire in which the novel is primarily set. Dominated by mine buildings, machinery, and towering slag heaps, Bestwood depends for its existence on the local coal company, Carson, Waite and Company, and its residents are virtually owned by the company store.

D. H. Lawrence modeled Bestwood on the real Nottinghamshire mining town of Eastwood, in which he was born and spent his early years. There, he lived in circumstances very similar to those described in his novel. His father worked for Barber, Walker Coal Company,

on which he modeled his fictional Carson, Waite and Company.

The Bottoms. Bestwood neighborhood in which the Morel family lives. The neighborhood contains six blocks of miners' homes, distributed "like dots on a blank-six domino," with twelve houses to a block. Outwardly, the houses appear substantial and decent. They have pleasant little gardens in front, neat front windows, porches, privet hedges, and dormer windows. However, the insides of the houses tell a different story.

The main rooms of the houses are the kitchen, which is

located at the back of each house, overlooking scrubby little back gardens and garbage dumps. Between the rows of houses and long lines of ash-pits are alleys in which children play, women gossip, and men smoke. Thus, the house that appears to be "so well built and that looked so nice, was quite unsavory because people must live in the kitchen, and the kitchens opened on to that nasty alley of ash-pits."

Willey Farm. Home of Miriam Leivers, Paul Morel's first lover. Located in the countryside outside Bestwood, Willey Farm stands in startling contrast to the Bottoms, where Paul lives, as it represents the natural world.

There, Paul comes to know a family tied to the earth and to nature's cycles—a strong contrast to the mining environment that brutalizes the land, the men who work in the tunnels, and their families. Willey Farm lives in accord with the rhythms and purpose of nature in its unspoiled state. Among its animals and crops, Paul begins to discover his own physical and emotional identity. As an antithesis to Bestwood, Willey Farm offers Paul a pastoral escape from the smothering presence of his domineering mother, his father's drunken rages, and the drabness and dirt of the coal-mining town.

— *Melissa E. Barth*

SOPHIE'S CHOICE

Author: William Styron (1925-   )
Type of work: Novel
Type of plot: Psychological realism

Time of plot: 1947
First published: 1979

Told largely in flashbacks by the title character, this novel is narrated by a callow young American southerner, Stingo, who goes to New York to become a writer and meets Sophie Zawatowska, a beautiful but tormented Polish refugee. Through his acquaintance with her and the Nazi brutality she endured during the recently concluded war, he confronts the depths of humanity's capacity for cruelty and evil and finds parallels between German Nazism and the southern slave system.

**New York City. Great cosmopolitan city in which Stingo meets Sophie. The city has long drawn young people from the hinterland, and Stingo is no exception. Certain that the bright lights of the big city will make New York the perfect place for his writing career to develop, he takes a job with a major publishing firm, only to discover that he does not fit into the corporate culture there. Unwilling to return to his southern home, he uses a tainted legacy of money from a slave-owning ancestor to support himself while he writes his first book. Thus he meets Sophie and becomes entangled in her tormented relationship with Nathan Landau, the mentally ill scion of a wealthy Jewish family.

The city's cosmopolitan and democratic setting functions as a powerful contrast to the story of bigotry and tyranny from her past that Sophie reveals to young Stingo. At first Stingo knows only that Sophie is a European refugee, a survivor of the horrors of the Holocaust who suffered terribly and nearly died in a Nazi concentration camp. Gradually—as though peeling an onion—

Sophie reveals more and more of the specific horrors she endured, as well as her own ambiguous role in those horrors—a role that has left her with strong feelings of guilt. At the same time, the disturbing nature of Nathan's mental illness is revealed. At length the pressure in their tormented relationship drives them apart, and Stingo tries to save Sophie, but at the end the story returns full circle and Sophie goes back to New York, to Nathan and her destruction.

*Auschwitz. Infamous Nazi concentration camp in southern Poland in which Sophie was a prisoner during World War II. The name of Auschwitz has become almost synonymous with the Holocaust, a symbol of the enormity of Adolf Hitler's obsession with exterminating Europe's Jewish population. However, for Sophie, a Polish Roman Catholic, Auschwitz is a more personal horror of death and deprivation, combined with the ambiguity of having had special skills that afforded her a privileged position as a secretary to the camp commandant, Rudolf Höss. Although she was still a prisoner, she

The Sorrows of Young Werther / 1091

was not subjected to the brutalities that worked her fellow prisoners to death and had sufficient food to support life. After the war, however, she carries the constant burden of thinking that she purchased her survival with her complicity in Nazi atrocities. Worst of all, she bears the crushing guilt of knowing that she purchased her own survival and that of her son with the death of her daughter—the choice to which the novel's title alludes.

After Höss was replaced as camp commandant, Sophie returned to the general secretarial pool of the camp, which still provided some protection from the worst brutalities of the camp. However, as the extermination program progressed, Sophie was moved to another part of the prison complex, Birkenau, where she was subjected to destructive labor and contracted diseases that permanently damaged her health. She lay within days of death by starvation when the camp was liberated by the Soviet army.

*Cracow** (KRAH-kow). Polish town in which Sophie grew up as the daughter of a respected professor and wife of her father's protégé. When the Germans invaded Poland, her father and husband were among the educated men rounded up and ultimately executed. However, Sophie's family life was not so genteel as she later tries to portray it, for her father was a virulent anti-Semite who actually praised the Nazis as having a "solution" to Poland's Jewish "problem."

*Warsaw.** Poland's capital, where Sophie found refuge after the German invasion. Although she associated with a number of members of the Polish resistance, she remained unable to commit herself to their cause. At the time she claimed that she could not endanger her children; afterward, however, she wondered if it was not simple cowardice that held her back. When she attempted to smuggle food to her dying mother, she was captured and sent to Auschwitz.

*Washington, D.C.** U.S. capital city, where Sophie makes her final revelation to Stingo. After the last violent breakup with Nathan, Stingo takes Sophie on a train south, intending to set her up as his wife on a farm he inherited in Virginia. Along the way they stop over in the nation's capital, intending to visit national landmarks. Amid the monuments to democracy, Sophie reveals the horrible "choice" she was forced make at Auschwitz: to save one of her children by condemning the other to death.

*Virginia Tidewater.** Coastal region of Virginia from which Stingo comes. At first Stingo is only vaguely uncomfortable about the American South's history of slavery. Although he finds such crude supporters of racism as lynch mobs and Mississippi's Senator Bilbo disgusting, he has no qualms about accepting an inheritance from an ancestor who made his money by selling a slave before the Civil War. However, as Stingo's acquaintance with Sophie progresses, he comes to see the common threads of contempt for the fundamental humanity of the other which binds American southern slavery and the slave labor of the concentration camps, and he resolves to write a book about Nat Turner, a famous leader of a Virginia slave rebellion.

— *Leigh Husband Kimmel*

THE SORROWS OF YOUNG WERTHER

Author: Johann Wolfgang von Goethe (1749-1832)
Type of work: Novel
Type of plot: Bildungsroman

Time of plot: 1770's
First published: Die Leiden des jungen Werthers, 1774
(English translation, 1780)

This epistolary novel revolves around a picturesque German village in which a young man finds great happiness that ultimately proves elusive.

Walheim (vahl-HIM). Small town in Germany's Rhineland-Pfalz region. Near this town is an idyllic country village that enables the novel's young protagonist, Werther, to forget his romantic disappointments. There, he can languish in the hills, amid streams and flowers, and enjoy the Godliness of peasant life, which he extols in the letters that make up this epistolary novel. Werther expresses his passion for nature, his admiration of natural country folk and simplistic living, and his overflowing emotions for his new obsession, Lotte, about whose selfless nature he raves. This edenic setting is, however, spoiled by the entry of a rival for Lotte's affections, Albert—a rational, stable young man, who is the antithesis of Werther, who follows the lovers on walks, reads Ossian's love poetry with Lotte, and weeps for her daily.

When a more melancholic Werther returns to Walheim to renew his pursuit of Lotte after a year's absence, he finds her married to Albert. In this peaceful domain, he makes his ultimate tragic decision to end his life, his misery, and his ties to bourgeois society.

*Weimar (VI-mar). City in Thuringia in central Germany where Werther takes a position in the government civil service. However, his inability to shake off his gloom about his romantic disappointment combines with his repugnance at his superior's class snobbery, and he resigns after only five months.

Werther's hometown. Unnamed town to which Werther returns after leaving Weimar. As he nears the town, he recollects pleasant boyhood experiences in the surrounding mountains, under the linden tree, and over the valley. As Weimar represents conventionality and artificiality, Werther's hometown signifies naturalism and individualism. Werther later wanders to a rich young prince's hunting lodge, where he stays for a short period before deciding to return to Walheim.

— *Connie Pedoto*

THE SOT-WEED FACTOR

Author: John Barth (1930-   )
Type of work: Novel
Type of plot: Picaresque

Time of plot: Late seventeenth and early eighteenth centuries
First published: 1960

The theme of the variability and mutability of human personality is underscored by the contrasting settings of this picaresque novel: the cultivated, civilized London of the late seventeenth century, the lawless high seas racked by pirates, and the almost unexplored wilderness of provincial Maryland.

*London. Capital and leading city of England. The last years of the seventeenth century and first years of the eighteenth were a time of exploration, growth, and enormous vitality. The novel's central character, Ebenezer Cooke, quickly abandons his studies at Cambridge University to live in London, where he pursues his avocation as a poet by frequenting coffeehouses with his fellow versifiers. During his stay in the capital, Ebenezer manages to sample the full range of London life, from the lowest to the highest. On one hand, he meets and falls in love with the whore Joan Toast but cannot convince her to marry him, while on the other he visits Henry Calvert, Lord Baltimore, and persuades that nobleman to make Ebenezer poet laureate of Maryland, even though Baltimore no longer has actual ownership of the colony.

The picturesque locations, the extravagant dialogue of the characters, and the intense vitality of the city of London are essential ingredients of the genre of the picaresque novel, to which *The Sot-Weed Factor* belongs. The extremes of poverty and wealth and the mixture of refined culture and coarse, common life are rendered vividly both to establish a sense of reality and location and to contrast with later scenes in Maryland, a colony which has not yet had time to develop the intricate layers of social custom and history found in the Old World.

*Poseidon. Ship on which Ebenezer sails from England to reclaim his father's plantation of Malden in Maryland. Aboard the ship, Ebenezer and his manservant exchange identities, the first in a series of such masquerades and personal confusions, which form a repeated subtext of the novel. Like London, the *Poseidon* is a microcosm of the society of the day, but it is decidedly skewed to the more coarse and common side of existence. The brutality aboard ship becomes literally unbearable when the vessel is seized by pirates. This first capture is followed by the assault of the *Cyprian*, a vessel full of women bound for the American colonies. The mass rape which follows both horrifies and excites Ebenezer, but before he can resolve his moral confusion he and his fellow travelers are forced to walk the plank. Fortunately the ships are close to the Maryland shore, although, characteristically, Ebenezer is slow to recognize this. The sea-voyage section of the novel again fits well into the picaresque genre and locates the action within a setting (the sailing ship bound for the colonies) popularly associated with this period. Ebenezer has repeated aquatic misadventures. He ends up in the water numerous times for various reasons: ordered to walk the plank, forced overboard at gunpoint, and by the relatively simple expedient of a shipwreck. These can be seen as John Barth's subtle commentary on his main character's plight at being at the mercy of events.

*Chesapeake Bay. Setting for most of Barth's novels and key to the action in *The Sot-Weed Factor*. Focus is particularly on the "Eastern Shore" of Maryland, the inner coast of the Bay which is composed of innumerable small islands, inlets, and tidal rivers, in particular the Choptank River. During the time of the novel Maryland is still largely wilderness, home to American Indians as well as English settlers. The major town of the novel, Cambridge, is a rude, frontier settlement perched between the Choptank River and the vast expanse of forest. Most of the Marylanders in the novel live in even smaller, less civilized hamlets such as Church Creek, a place which boasts nothing more than an inn, a mill, and a few houses. Still others live in even greater isolation, in primitive cabins near the shore or hidden deep in the woods.

Part of the Chesapeake setting is even further removed in time and closer to the first days of European exploration and exploitation. Throughout the novel Ebenezer and the other characters search for a manuscript titled the "Privie Journall of Sir Henry Burlingame," which recounts the "true" history of Captain John Smith's famous adventures in America, including the hidden story of the "true" (and salacious) events regarding the Indian king Powhatan and his daughter the famous Pocohantas.

Malden. Maryland plantation built by Andrew Cooke, Ebenezer's father. The estate consists of a fine manor house on Cooke's Point on the Choptank River and a thousand acres of timber and excellent farmland. Malden is the final destination of all of Ebenezer's travels, and its possession is his ultimate goal throughout the novel. The climactic scene of the book, the improvised hearing called by Maryland Governor Nicholson to unravel the actual identities of the various characters and determine the true owner of the estate, takes place in the front parlor of the manor house at Malden. In the novel, Malden serves both as an actual physical location whose possession provides the motive for many actions by several characters and as a symbolic representation of Ebenezer's desires to claim his inheritance from his father and, at the same time, establish himself as a successful colonial planter. Malden derives further symbolic importance as the site of the graves of both Ebenezer's mother and his wife, the whore Joan Toast, whom he finally marries. It is also the location where Ebenezer and his twin sister Anna are finally reunited and live out their lives in relative peace and prosperity.

— *Michael Witkoski*

THE SOUND AND THE FURY

Author: William Faulkner (1897-1962)
Type of work: Novel
Type of plot: Stream of consciousness

Time of plot: 1900-1928
First published: 1929

This novel presents four viewpoints of the life of the Compson family. Much of the landscape is interior, taking place in the minds of three narrators. The novel uses stream-of-consciousness narration to build this tragic story of the Compson family, deeply rooted in their native Jefferson, Mississippi.

Yoknapatawpha County (YOK-nuh-puh-TAW-fuh). Beginning with his third novel, William Faulkner set a great deal of his fiction in the imaginary Yoknapatawpha County. Faulkner drew this county for a map included in his novel *Absalom, Absalom!* (1936). He included details about plot events and where they occurred. The county is named after a river in Mississippi and the Native American word Yoknapatawpha. The details make it clear that it corresponds to Lafayette County, Mississippi, where Faulkner lived in the town of Oxford, called Jefferson in his fiction. Throughout Faulkner's fiction, he creates a detailed history of the land, its inhabitants, its changes, and its significance. By taking his home, what he called his own "little postage stamp of native soil," and transforming it into the powerful mythical county of his fiction, Faulkner created an enduring literary landscape.

Jefferson. Typical southern town of the period, Jefferson plays a central role in the story. The siblings play on their land and the surrounding area, from Benjy's pasture to neighboring yards, the riverbank, and the creek, where a number of important events take place. The powerful last scene of the novel takes place in the town square, complete with Confederate statue, where Luster upsets Benjy by going the wrong way on a one-way street. The town is also where Jason rushes in and out of the store where he works, in and out of the cotton trading office, back and forth from home, and up streets and alleys looking for the female Quentin. Through comparing the present-day surroundings to the characters' memories of them, the reader sees that great changes have taken place.

Compson home. Once-fashionable house that is the home of the Compsons, a fine family that has fallen on hard times. The family once owned the surrounding land, but so many parcels of it have been sold that now only the house and servants' quarters remain. Benjy spends almost all his time here, watched by a succession of servants. The reader learns that "Benjy's Pasture," as the family calls it, a place where Benjy spent many happy hours with his siblings (especially his sister Caddy), has been sold to send his brother Quentin to college. By the time of the novel, it has been turned into a golf course; Benjy mournfully hopes for his sister's return and mourns her absence every time a golfer yells "Caddy." Mrs. Compson, the children's mother, controls the environment in the house. A proud, bitter, neurotic, and manipulative woman, she reigns through guilt and suffering, creating an environment that first Caddy and then her son Quentin feel they must escape.

*Harvard University. The second section of the novel, Quentin's section, occurs in his dormitory room, the college grounds, and the city of Cambridge, Massachusetts. The narrative follows Quentin on the last day of his life, which begins and ends in his room. During the day, he walks through the town, into stores, and along the river. While physically set in Massachusetts, much of the content of this section plays out in Quentin's memory, back in Yoknapatawpha County, through his memories of his sister, his long talks with his father, and his resulting anguish. At the end of this section, he jumps off the bridge to his death.

— *Caroline Carvill*

THE SOUND OF WAVES

Author: Yukio Mishima (Kimitake Hiraoka, 1925-1970)
Type of work: Novel
Type of plot: Idyll

Time of plot: The 1950's
First published: *Shiosai,* 1954 (English translation, 1956)

This novel is about the romance of a young Japanese fisherman, Shinji Kubo, with Hatsue Miyata, the daughter of the wealthiest man on a remote island. The young lovers must meet in secret until Shinji wins the approval of his prospective father-in-law through his heroic action on a ship caught in a violent storm.

Uta-jima (ew-tah-jee-muh). Japanese island, whose name translates as "Song Island," that provides the novel's central setting. With a coastline of less than three miles, the tiny island is located near the Gulf of Ise, which opens into the Pacific Ocean. The island is rocky, wooded, and not good for agriculture. Its residents' lives are shaped by the patterns of the sea: fishing, shipping, weather, and waves. Most of the islanders are involved in fishing for octopus and squid or diving for abalone, pearls, or seaweed.

Yukio Mishima describes the island as a place of astounding beauty with coastline vistas, ancient pine forests, rocky promontories, and a gorgeous shrine dedicated to the god of the sea. Its residents live in a kind of pastoral serenity. The island itself functions as a character in the novel because of the idyllic peacefulness, isolation, and simplicity of the lives of the people who live there. In many ways, Kerukichi Miyata, the father of Hatsue, represents the values of the island. He is the personification of Uta-jima's toil, ambition, and strength with his uncannily accurate weather predictions, his superior experience in all matters of fishing and navigation, and his great pride in knowing all the history and traditions of island culture.

*Okinawa (oh-kih-naw-wah). Island south of Japan that is part of the Ryukyu chain of islands, where Shinji goes as a crewman on a cargo ship carrying lumber from Japan. During the height of a typhoon, the ship cannot navigate easily through the coral reefs because it has no radio. Shinji must tie a lifeline to his waist and swim out to find a buoy in the thrashing waves of the storm. Shinji nearly drowns, but he saves the ship from being wrecked on the reefs. Because of his heroism, Shinji can now visit the Miyata house openly.

Yashiro Shrine (yah-shee-roh). Shrine dedicated to Watatsumi-no-Mikoto, god of the sea, that sits atop a hill above the island's village. Mothers frequently leave offerings at the shrine in the hope that the god of the sea will protect their children. The shrine includes an icon of sixty-six bronze mirrors, an ancient copy of a Chinese mirror of the Six Dynasties period. Shinji and Hatsue walk to the shrine to give thanks and pray after Shinji's safe return from Okinawa.

*Kyōto (kyoh-toh) and **Osaka** (oh-sah-kah). Important industrial cities on the mainland of Japan that are the sites of an annual school excursion for Shinji's brother Hiroshi, who is twelve years old. His school group travels there on a ferry and spends six days and five nights away from Uta-jima. Most of the children have never previously seen the world outside their island. The difficult cultural transition from the peaceful ways of the island to the streetcars, tall buildings, movies, subways, neon lights, and fast pace of city culture makes a deep impression upon Hiroshi. In many ways, the differences between Kyōto, Osaka, and Uta-jima define the values of the novel because of the idyllic, peaceful quality of the love between Hatsue and Shinji.

— *Jonathan L. Thorndike*

SOUTH WIND

Author: Norman Douglas (1868-1952)
Type of work: Novel
Type of plot: Social satire

Time of plot: Early twentieth century
First published: 1917

More than in most fictional works, the setting of this novel is intrinsic to its plot. Norman Douglas set out to develop in witty terms a serious idea: that place determines character. Having made his home in the Mediterranean world for most of his life, he believed that the region had a benign influence on its people, counteracting the debilitating influence of formal religion. In this novel he illustrates how a Christian bishop, in the liberating atmosphere of such a landscape and under the influence of persuasive characters eager to share their iconoclastic points of view, could countenance murder.

Nepenthe (nih-PEHN-thee). Fictional Italian island in the Tyrrhenian Sea. Nepenthe is noted for its *sirocco* or south wind, upon which the island's inhabitants routinely blame their foibles and shortcomings. From a distance, Nepenthe looks to Mr. (Bishop) Heard like a cloud, its outline "barely suggested through a veil of fog." There is "an air of irreality" about it. Once the morning mists roll away, however, Heard realizes that Nepenthe is a "rambling and craggy sort of place" studded with palms and festooned with green vines. As Mr. Keith, one of Nepenthe's residents, remarks to Heard, "'There are no half-tones in this landscape.'"

Although commentators have routinely identified Nepenthe as Capri, a famous Italian island where Douglas spent many years, he himself pointed out that he had borrowed many of Nepenthe's physical features from other islands such as Ponza, Ischia, and the Lipari Islands. Douglas is careful not to locate Nepenthe too precisely, placing it several hours away by ferry from a busy port yet within sight of the Italian mainland. A clue to the island's real nature is suggested by its name; nepenthe is a drug that helps those taking it forget their woes.

Nepenthe town. Port and only city on the island of Nepenthe. Its courtyards are aglow with oranges, and its precipitous streets are "noisy with rattling carriages and cries of fruit-vendors." Heard finds the effect "almost operatic." By inviolable custom, the town's inhabitants gather every morning in its busy piazza or marketplace, one side of which presents a view of the island's lower slopes and the sea. This custom is viewed as "admirable," as it prevents anyone from getting anything done in the morning. A siesta accomplishes much the same result in the afternoon, at which time several of the novel's male characters may be found slumbering at the tawdry Alpha and Omega Club, often suffering from the effects of the proprietor's house brand of whiskey. Others gather to drink at Luisella's grotto-tavern. On the edge of Nepenthe town, down a narrow lane, is the Villa Khismet (KIHZ-meht, meaning "fate"), where Mr. Keith entertains Mr. Heard.

Old Town. Upper, somewhat inaccessible quarter of Nepenthe town. Unlike the modern settlement on the island's lower slopes, the Old Town is "calm and reposeful," its weather cooler thanks to its elevation and northern exposure. Its shady gardens are watered by the moisture of the south wind. The Old Town was originally built at such heights to preserve it from pirates. Subsequently it was revived by the good Duke Alfred, a feared and revered ruler who painted its buildings pink and enclosed it within a massive wall. The Old Town is the site of Count Caloveglia's villa, where Mr. Heard enjoys many edifying conversations, as well as a villa known as Mon Repos ("My rest"), leased by Mr. Heard's cousin Mrs. Meadows. Near Mon Repos is a dangerous and precipitous cliff, the Devil's Rock, from which many have fallen or jumped to their deaths.

— *Grove Koger*

THE SPANISH TRAGEDY

Author: Thomas Kyd (1558-1594)
Type of work: Drama
Type of plot: Tragedy

Time of plot: Sixteenth century
First performed: c. 1585-1589; first published, c. 1594

Set in Spain and Portugal at a time of mutual hostility between the two countries, this play by an English writer deliberately obliterates differences between the countries' courts to convey a sense of menace for the Spanish General Hieronimo and his family. This is in sharp contrast to the garden where Horatio, the son of Hieronimo, is murdered.

Royal courts. The play opens by alternating scenes between the court of Spain and the court of Portugal— with the only perceptible difference between the two royal courts being the individual people found at each. Typical directorial practice would be to place props on stage to indicate one or the other court. The lack of distinguishing characteristics at these two courts reflects the lack of differences between the two sides in the war that is keeping them apart. Neither Spain nor Portugal occupies a morally superior ground; however, English attitudes toward both Spain and Portugal in the 1580's tended to be negative, as both Roman Catholic countries were at odds with England.

Hieronimo's garden. Outdoor area at the home of the Spanish general Hieronimo. It is a refreshing area, but one warped by envy, lust, and murder. The garden is the play's first outdoor setting, and it is there the crime of Horatio's murder occurs. The tension here resides in differences between the human menace and what would otherwise seem a place of sweetness.

Before stabbing herself to death near the end of the play, Hieronimo's wife, Isabella, hacks at the garden arbor with a sword, unable to bear its promise in the face of her son's death. Hieronimo and his wife make extensive reference to the irony of the garden's symbolization of growth and life, while it is also the place where the crime takes place. Audiences are presumably left to infer that the despoiled garden represents a post-Fall world.

— *Scott D. Vander Ploeg*

SPECULATIONS ABOUT JAKOB

Author: Uwe Johnson (1934-1984)
Type of work: Novel
Type of plot: Psychological realism

Time of plot: 1956
First published: Mutmassungen über Jakob, 1959
 (English translation, 1963)

One of the first novels to portray life in communist East Germany shortly after World War II, this story, set in the fictional Baltic coast town of Jerichow, evokes the dreariness of the region's gray, windswept landscape, while stressing the permanence of place, where life goes on regardless of changing political systems, and the town's inhabitants always have the large sky and fresh smell of the sea.

Jerichow (YEHR-ee-kov). Seaside town in East Germany's Mecklenburg state (not to be confused with the real town of Jerichow in Saxony-Anhalt). Once a rural town, owned mostly by a single noble family, Jerichow has "a thousand and one houses along the Mecklenburg stretch of the Baltic coast, with the wind blowing stark and dark all year round." The town's church dates back to Saxon times, with Romanesque and Gothic architectural features revealing how it was built in stages. Gabled houses surround the marketplace and are relics of the elegance and affluence of earlier times. Now, they are subdivided because of the acute postwar housing shortage and because the First German State of the Workers and Peasants has eradicated the ruling class. The castle that rises from the forest near Jerichow is regarded as a memorial to exploitation and is now used as a home for the elderly. Jöche's young family lives in two sublet rooms separated by a hall, with three parties sharing the kitchen. Many people are still housed in barracks.

Johnson creates a sense of place in Jerichow that transcends the town's present problems. For example, the residents' language does not change overnight, and the novel's original German text contains many remarks in the local Mecklenburg dialect. Similarly, the efficient East German secret police agent Herr Rohlfs uses topographic maps from the discredited fascist German Reich because the "gracefully undulating landscape" remains the same. The fertile region was populated by Germanic settlers a millennium earlier, and waves of people have passed through since then, leaving "round graves, long graves, conic graves." Jakob himself arrived there as a refugee from Pomerania.

Cresspahl's house. Home of the widowed cabinet maker Heinrich Cresspahl. The long one-story house is located at Ziegeleiweg 3-4, at the quarry "behind the old, burned-out tile kilns across from a fenced-in park around the villa of the Soviet Headquarters." It resembles a house that Johnson lived near when he attended school in Güstrow, Mecklenburg, after World War II.

After the war, Cresspahl divided his house into two apartments to accommodate Jakob and his mother when they were refugees. Their half is now registered as a railroader's apartment. Jakob carved the letters "CRESSPAHL HARDWOOD INLAYS" over the workshop door for Cresspahl. The expansive house, garden, and workshop have been Cresspahl's for years; its living-room ceiling is gray with age, and he has no thought of leaving. In the turbulent postwar period, his home represents reassuring continuity. Cresspahl is quietly self-sufficient. He tends the garden, collects firewood for his stove, and likes sitting in his leather armchair smoking his pipe. A seventeenth century map of the coast hangs on the wall. Even Cresspahl's cat has a long Jerichow lineage.

Railway yards. Government railroad facility in a fictitious port city on the Elbe River where Jakob works until he is struck by a train and killed. The railway yards have their own atmosphere, "heavy sooty air between the groaning engines." When fog from the river rolls in, visibility is reduced and the tracks are slippery. From his locked observation tower, Jakob communicates with other dispatchers over the microphone and tries to keep the trains on schedule. The rundown state of the railway makes precision impossible. Tracks torn up by the Red Army's wartime invasion have not been replaced, the trains are old, and there is a shortage of coal.

*Federal Republic of Germany. Commonly known as West Germany, a capitalist country whose fast pace of life is illustrated by Gesine Cresspahl's demonstration of how they play autobahn: You pass me, I pass you. Jakob finds it offensive that the jukebox in the bar still plays the "Badenweiler March," a Nazi song, and is shocked that the Bundesbahn runs express trains with only one employee aboard

— *Jean M. Snook*

THE SPOILS OF POYNTON

Author: Henry James (1843-1916)
Type of work: Novel
Type of plot: Social realism

Time of plot: Late nineteenth century
First published: 1897

At first glance, it is the things of Poynton, not the place itself, that seem most important in this novel. However, those things—the furniture, the art, the decorations, the arrangements—truly belong only to and in the house, Poynton. The last event of the novel, the burning of Poynton and its things, emphasizes the place as the very center of the novel.

Poynton. English home of Mrs. Gereth and her son that is the focus of the novel. Mrs. Gereth lived in the house with her husband until his death and intends to remain there until her son marries. The novel describes the house only in bits and pieces, sometimes in contrast with other places, but these descriptions are all aimed at showing how important the house is to the novel's meanings.

The house and its furnishings appear to be in the very best of taste. For example, the house is wainscoted—an expensive feature, but one that is subdued and not showy. The house has no wallpaper at all, as wallpaper is modern and vaguely commercial. The house gleams with old gold and brass ornamentation and also has "deep, old damasks," a sofa of velvet brocade, a great Italian cabinet, and Louis Seize (sixteenth) French furniture and Oriental china. Especially important is the house's Maltese cross. Although it is relatively small, it becomes almost a symbol of the house. In short, the house is fitted out with the best of the best ages. Equally important, it has neither a billiard room nor a conservatory, as at Waterbath, which are both fads of the moment.

The actual architecture of the house is not given, but it would seem to be an attractive place, whose design sets off its furnishings well. Still, in a hint at the thematic matter of how destructive good taste can be, Fleda Vetch thinks that Poynton, with all its treasures, inhibits artistic creativity.

Waterbath. Family home of Mona Brigstock, the fiancé of Mrs. Gereth's son, Owen. At the beginning of the novel, readers meet Mrs. Gereth and Fleda Vetch, guests at Waterbath who discover that they have tastes in common and that Waterbath reveals no taste at all. Waterbath's central attraction is a billiard room and conservatory, rooms regarded by the Brigstocks as the latest thing, and its walls are at best decorated only by "the family splotches," meaning the bad paintings produced by the Brigstocks themselves. Moreover, it has wallpaper.

Ricks. Small dower house in which Mrs. Gereth is to live after her son's marriage. It has been furnished in bad taste by a distant maiden aunt of the Gereths—and Mrs. Gereth cannot stand it. It has, for example, a "stiff flap of green baize" that Mrs. Gereth, moving there from Poynton, has not yet found time to remove. It has such things as a plastered portico, which Poynton would never have. However, when Mrs. Gereth fills her new home with almost all of the furnishings from Poynton, both she and Fleda admit that the house is transformed. Nevertheless, it is now overcrowded and in the end hardly the place for the "spoils," for they do not really fit. They need their own setting.

Mr. Vetch's house. Home in which Fleda lives with her father. The place jars her. Her father is a collector of odd, tasteless things, and his house becomes a storage place for these "treasures," including old calendars, handbooks, penwipers, and ashtrays. It is unlike Waterbath in being unfashionable, but it is nevertheless ugly.

Maggie's house. Home of the impoverished Maggie and her husband. Their house is obviously small and cluttered and hardly in a fashionable place, with "local puddles," among smelly cottages and "smellier shops," and Fleda notes its soiled tablecloth. There is no taste here because good taste is financially out of reach. At best, Fleda's future, if it were not for Mrs. Gereth, would be at best a similar place and so her sacrifice of Poynton is all the more shocking and yet admirable.

— *L. L. Lee*

SPOON RIVER ANTHOLOGY

Author: Edgar Lee Masters (1868-1950)
Type of work: Poetry

First published: 1915

Place is central in this landmark collection of poetry, whose several hundred voices are all based on actual farmers, lawyers, journalists, craftsmen, and clergymen from the rolling prairie land and farming country of the Midwest, in which Edgar Lee Masters enjoyed a memorable childhood.

Spoon River. Imaginary midwestern town that is probably loosely based on Lewiston, Illinois, where Masters studied law in his father's office and practiced for a year before moving to Chicago. Masters's book is a collection of 243 free verse epitaphs, in which the citizens buried in the Spoon River Cemetery talk about their lives, their failures, their loves, philosophies, triumphs, conflicts, secrets, and crimes. Many of the stories in the collection are related and intertwined, and to read the entire anthology is to experience a panoramic view of human existence and experience, a view filtered through the perspective of a small American town.

Because these people are no longer members of the living community, in which they would have had to preserve facades, please relatives, or impress employers, they have nothing to lose by being honest. Death frees them to show the reader the reality of their lives and their emotions. With this freedom, the audience is granted a visceral and moving portrait of how members of the human family can and do treat one another, how they really behave, what truly motivates them. The secrets Spoon River's dead inhabitants reveal are sometimes shocking—stories of intrigue, corruption, frustration, adultery. On the other hand, the speakers tell their stories with a calmness and simplicity that induce a similar sense in the reader. Because of its very frankness, the anthology provoked protest from some readers who felt that it presented too sordid a picture of American small-town life.

— *Christopher E. Kent*

THE SPORT OF THE GODS

Author: Paul Laurence Dunbar (1872-1906)
Type of work: Novel
Type of plot: Naturalism

Time of plot: Late nineteenth century
First published: serial, 1901; book, 1902

In this most significant of Paul Laurence Dunbar's several novels, the author examines life for African Americans in America a few years before the turn of the twentieth century. By juxtaposing the black experience in a typical southern town with that in pre-Harlem Renaissance New York City, Dunbar shows that there is no place of sanctuary for the black man; that regardless of where he is—in the North or in the South—he suffers at the hand of "some Will infinitely stronger than [his] own."

Southern town. The unnamed southern town is supposed to represent a typical place in the South following the Civil War. While from appearances things appear to be looking up for former slaves remaining in the South, Dunbar shows that once the veneer of gentility and goodwill lifted, the South was the same wretched place it had always been, so far as its black citizens were concerned.

Hamilton cottage. Home of the Hamilton family in the yard of the Oakley family mansion; a play on words that reflects the facade of improved conditions for African Americans. The Hamiltons' "cottage" is a former slave cabin, but as the means and status of the Hamiltons seem to improve, so the cabin takes on a new appearance of its own and becomes a "bower of peace and comfort," furnished mostly with discarded items from the Oakley mansion. Indeed, its edenic appearance is further exemplified by the many blooming flowers in its yard and the profusion of morning glories and Virginia creeper that hang over the entranceway. Also, Berry Hamilton, his wife Fannie, and his children Joe and Kitty appear to have garnered for themselves a life of freedom and high standing. Not only are they gainfully employed, but they have both the time and means for a full complement of social and cultural activities, and they seem to be living quite well in the South that only a few decades earlier was plagued by the evils of slavery. However, Dunbar holds this myth up to ridicule once Berry is wrongly accused of theft of money from the Oakley mansion. Not only does his employer turn against Berry Hamilton, but so do the others of the town, white and black. Berry, though innocent, is imprisoned for ten years at hard labor, and his family is turned out of their jobs and cottage and become virtual outcasts in the small southern town.

*Harlem. African American section of New York City to which the remaining members of the Hamilton family go after Berry is imprisoned in the South. There they hope to begin anew, away from the southern prejudices and backlash. Although Harlem is never mentioned by name, it is clear from signs and markers in the text that Dunbar is portraying it during its pre-Harlem Renaissance days.

Although the Hamiltons find lodgings easily enough and have some money from savings and the sale of household items, their disintegration as a family begins almost immediately upon their arrival. Ill equipped to deal with city life, the Hamiltons are too unsophisticated to avoid being easy prey for crafty Harlemites trying to exploit new arrivals. This is evidenced by the porter Mr. Thomas, who clearly has ulterior motives in recommending Mrs. Jones's rooming house to Fannie Hamilton and her children. Also, while Mrs. Jones appears to run a decent house, it becomes clear that she is not above taking advantage of others whenever opportunities to do so arise.

Most important, what becomes abundantly clear is that the Hamilton's New York is no promised land. Dunbar is even more cynical when he shows time after time that while in the South the Hamiltons are taken advantage of by whites, in the North they are at the mercy of fellow African Americans, who are agents of their destruction at every turn. In the course of their stay in New York, Joe is imprisoned for killing a woman; Kit becomes a stage girl—the very antithesis of the church girl she once was—and Fannie, in order to survive, is forced to marry a man who beats her. Once again, Dunbar shows that appearances are misleading, for the newness, largeness, and sophistication of New York prove to be the downfall of the Hamilton family. Interestingly enough, through the persistence of a white reporter for a New York paper, Berry's innocence is proved and he is pardoned, and after a painful reconciliation with Fannie, the two of them move back to their southern home in the yard of the now mad and deranged former employer Maurice Oakley, a move welcomed and made possible by Mrs. Oakley.

— *Warren J. Carson*

THE SPY: A Tale of the Neutral Ground

Author: James Fenimore Cooper (1789-1851)
Type of work: Novel
Type of plot: Historical

Time of plot: Late eighteenth and early nineteenth centuries
First published: 1821

With the exception of its last chapter, this novel is set entirely within the neck of land that lies to the northeast of New York's Manhattan Island, between the Hudson River and Long Island Sound. This dubious ground, hotly disputed and laid waste by the contending American and British forces, makes an ideal backdrop for a tale of complex deceit and divided loyalties.

*New York City.** At the time in which this story is set, the city that James Fenimore Cooper calls New York is confined to Manhattan Island, whose northern territory is the last major stronghold of the royalist forces.

*Westchester County.** Large tract of land northeast of Manhattan, to which it is connected at the point of narrowest separation by the strategically important King's Bridge. The country between the Hudson and Long Island Sound comprises a vast patchwork of hills and valleys, until it flattens out to the northeast into the plains of Connecticut. The hills are relatively gentle in the eastern part of the county, but they rise more precipitously as they approach the Hudson, into a ribbon of terrain that Cooper calls the Highlands.

Neutral Ground. Land lying to the east of the Highlands that is controlled by neither the British, who command the southern entrance to the Hudson, nor the Revolutionary forces, who hold the Highlands to the north. The effects of the war have left the Neutral Ground abandoned, its fields unplanted, its fences fallen, and its roads in a perilous state. Few of the sites at which the rival armies camp and exchange fire are named, but reference is made to the "hamlet" of White Plains, the heights above Sing Sing and—most significantly—to the village of Fishkill, around which the Revolutionary forces regroup. The most significant setting other than those detailed below is the ledge bearing the log cabin sealed with clay and roofed in bark, where Frances Wharton discovers Harper in hiding and eventually confronts Harvey Birch.

The Locusts. Residence of Henry Wharton's family; one of three key locations within the Neutral Ground. Wharton's grounds are situated in a valley that runs from northwest to southeast, opening on to a view of Long Island Sound. The hills on the eastern side are quite steep. The local graveyard is on Wharton's land, although family members themselves have traditionally been returned to Manhattan—from which the family migrated—for church burial.

The house itself is a long single-story stone building with cellars and a wing at each end. It has a wooden roof and a piazza supported by wooden pillars. Until it is destroyed by fire, it contrives to maintain a certain semblance of grandeur even in the midst of the territory's ruin, with carpeted floors and curtained windows—in which respect it contrasts quite sharply with Harvey Birch's neighboring cottage. Dunwoodie fights his first skirmish against the British in this valley, to the left of a small wood. A good deal of information is given in the course of the text about the effect of the changing seasons on the landscape, with particular reference to the effects of the wind; the advent of the winter snows further emphasizes the desolation of the Neutral Ground.

Four Corners. Abandoned village in which Dunwoodie's Revolutionary troops make camp after the first skirmish. It consists of a half dozen small buildings gathered about a crossroads. The building that plays the most significant role in the story is ironically labeled a "hotel" by the troopers because it is adopted as a temporary residence by the camp follower Elizabeth Flanagan, who serves the troops as a washerwoman and "petticoat doctor." It is to this rude shelter that the Whartons are removed after the destruction of the Locusts.

*****Niagara River.** River in upstate New York that connects Lake Ontario and Lake Erie. The last chapter of the novel, set thirty-three years after the main story, finds another American army in contention with British forces on the Chippewa plains, on the banks of the Niagara. Here the descendants of the chief characters finally discover for which side the eponymous spy was working.

— *Brian Stableford*

STEPPENWOLF

Author: Hermann Hesse (1877-1962)
Type of work: Novel
Type of plot: Psychological

Time of plot: 1920's
First published: Der Steppenwolf, 1927 (English translation, 1929)

This novel has two main physical settings: the rented rooms in which Harry Haller (the Steppenwolf) lives and the Black Eagle pub. Both are located in a small town in central Europe, presumably in Germany or in northern Switzerland. However, the real setting of this classic descent-into-hell story is actually the many compartments, experiences, and attitudes within Harry Haller's mind—here known as the Magic Theater.

Magic Theater. Literally, the hell of Steppenwolf's mind and soul. Although the trip to the Magic Theater does not occur until the end of the novel, it is there that Hesse puts forth his ideas about the fractured soul of modern man manifesting the existential and the suicidal, here represented and embodied by Harry Haller. Hermine, Haller's lover—a prostitute who herself has a death wish—teaches him to dance and takes him to a great ball. When he descends to the basement for a drug-induced experience brought on by laudanum, opium, and cocaine, Hell reveals itself to be a place where one can get anything one wants. Seeing himself repeatedly in a magic mirror that displays his many schizophrenic personalities and selves, Haller can fulfill any want he can imagine, whether real or illusionary. His Magic Theater contains one hundred doors, each of which has a name designed to seduce and satiate, such as "All Girls Are Yours."

Rented rooms. Residence of the Steppenwolf from the beginning of the novel until his suicide at the end. For reasons never explained, Haller arrives in the unnamed town and takes up residence in a private home, in which he meets the initial narrator of the story, a young man who is the nephew of the owner of the house. Haller is attracted to the home because it is, as he repeatedly describes it, "bourgeois." He likes its middle-class cleanliness, the smells from the kitchen, and the lifestyle of the family who own and run the home, as well as the other lodgers.

Haller's rented rooms themselves assume the qualities of this man who fancies himself a wolf from the steppes; they become primarily a study in which he has art works as well as books, and he lives here in a kind of hearth and home environs protected from the howling landscape of modern man outside his windows. Basically, these rented rooms, like the nameless, unidentified small town in which Haller is living, are intentionally nondescript so that they can have universal applicability.

Black Eagle. Most important of three public bars that Haller frequents, a place with food, drink, and other accommodations. It is located in the basement of the business establishment where he experiences the Magic Theater. While apparently decent on its exterior, the

Black Eagle is at its core emblematic of the decadence that pervaded Germany in the period between the two world wars in which the novel is set. Its music is that of American jazz—which in the context of the novel symbolizes wanton abandonment. Drugs are in endless sup-ply, and casual sex is rampant, easy, and multidimensional. Though tame by standards to occur later in the twentieth century, the Black Eagle is intended to be something of a moral pigsty of its day.

— *Carl Singleton*

STEPS

Author: Jerzy Nikodem Kosinski (1933-1991)
Type of work: Novel
Type of plot: Existentialism

Time of plot: Indeterminate
First published: 1968

Jerzy Kosinski's novel never identifies any place by name, but roughly two-thirds of its episodes take place in a country reminiscent of communist Poland. Most of the remaining episodes are set in a location strongly resembling New York City. This deliberate geographic vagueness served as a cover for Kosinski, who worried about retribution from the Polish and Polish American communities for painting a grim picture of life in his native land. It is also a stylistic device to give a sense of global universality to the episodes.

*Central Europe.** Apparent location of most of the novel's episodes. A whitewashed village in an unnamed country appears to indicate backwardness and remoteness from twentieth century city life. From here, the anonymous narrator travels to the unnamed capital city of the country, where he impresses his rustic girlfriend with his credit card. The coexistence of two places in one country, in which life seems a century apart, creates the dramatic tension of the opening episode.

In a landscape characterized by dark, remote forests and isolated, backward villages, the protagonist encounters humans whose meager and harsh surroundings have rendered them particularly vicious. Sexual exploitation and abuse is rampant, as if humans react to a sullen environment with nothing but sexual depravity of their own. Because the places where they dwell appear cut off from the rest of the world, it is as if worldly civility and morality has not reached them there, either.

On the way to an airport to leave his native country to fly to America, the narrator feels a kind of existentialist nausea when he realizes that the place where he has spent twenty-four years of his life means nothing to him. He is saddened by the fact that the landmarks of his native city stir up no emotions in him. Place fails to create nostalgia in the protagonist. He moves from location to location without any attachment to his surroundings.

Volcanic island. Located in what appears to be the Greek Mediterranean, the island is chosen to make the protagonist a complete outsider. The place literally illustrates humanity's essential alienation, which is a key idea of the philosophy of existentialism. Here, the narrator can neither communicate with the world beyond the waves engulfing the island, nor talk to its remote inhabitants.

Sanatorium. Tuberculosis treatment center at a resort in mountains that appear to be based on the Polish Carpathians. The juxtaposition of the mountains' natural splendor and the unhappy fates of patients dying from the ravages of tuberculosis creates a setting in which human beings must confront their mortality in the midst of a stunningly beautiful but finally uncaring landscape. Many of the patients and attendants react to the dark message of the place with sexual escapades.

University. Unnamed institution of higher learning that suffers from the domination of the Communist Party, which has turned it into a sinister location in which the only places in which free thought takes place is the rest rooms. With their university perverted by politics, the students react to the pressures pervading the location by indulging in bizarre acts of revenge against one another.

Airplane. While flying from his native country to America, the protagonist wishes to remain suspended in midair in this unreal nonplace forever. He prefers a fantasy location over any real place, and wishes he could defy both gravity and reality.

American city. Clearly a stand-in for New York City in the 1950's, the place of the narrator's destination is described in bleak and disillusioned terms. The youth hostel where he stays is crowded and inhospitable. His menial work stripping paint off a ship moored in the city's dirty harbor introduces him to the city's seedy underside. The city's alleys become the place for a criminal car game of daring, as the underworld takes over the place at night. Disillusioned by a place which makes him an outsider by virtue of language and economic prospects, the narrator envies the black residents who seem to live free at the margins of the city. Exaggerating his alienation by adopting the guise of a deaf-mute, the narrator plans a secret war on the city, whose features he imagines to be those of a living body that he can oppose and destroy.

The protagonist's arrival in America is anticlimactic. Again, the place fails to stir up any special feelings. It merely appears of mundane and pedestrian nature. Every place fails to enchant the narrator.

Tropical American country. Unnamed country to which the protagonist goes to become part of its political revolution. Behind the tropical facade of palm trees gracing the unnamed capital's airport, there is violence and upheaval. However, the place holds no meaning for the narrator, who embraces an absurd existence.

— *R. C. Lutz*

THE STORY OF AN AFRICAN FARM

Author: Olive Schreiner (1855-1920)

Type of work: Novel

Type of plot: Social realism

Time of plot: 1880's

First published: 1883

This novel is true to its title: almost all its action occurs on an African farm or on the surrounding arid plain, and the effect is a claustrophobic, constricted one, reflecting the restricted lives of the two central characters, Waldo and Lyndall.

*Karroo. Arid, dusty plateau of the southwestern part of what is now the Republic of South Africa and the interior of what was the British Cape Colony during the period in which the novel is set. Most of the action takes place on the plains of the Karroo, a region at once beautiful and oppressive. The blazing summer sun, which makes the earth itself cry for water, oppresses both man and beast, adding to the sense of powerlessness felt by the child characters who are the focus of the story. On the other hand, at night the moon and the stars lend a touch of beauty to the land; and at the end, after seasonal rains again turn the land green, even the sun seems benign, and the landscape becomes lovely—so lovely that Waldo almost melts into it. However, the overall effect of the landscape is that of something oppressively hot and barren, another source of suffering in a novel of suffering. Even Waldo's union with the landscape at the end is achieved only through his death.

Farm. Ostrich and sheep ranch on the Karroo that gives the novel its title. There, Waldo, Lyndall, and Em live under the control of the Boer farm woman Tant' Sannie. The farm is a simple place, with a few plain buildings and corrals (kraals) for animals. It is not a place of prosperity; rafters in its buildings are worm-eaten, and the roof and the bricks of its main house are crumbling, contributing to the sense of gloom that pervades the novel. The farm also projects a feeling of claustrophobia. When Tant' Sannie's stepdaughter, Lyndall, returns from school, she says that she feels suffocated in the farmhouse—a feeling that perhaps symbolizes the way society suffocates her desires because she is a woman.

A room at the top of the farmhouse contains provisions, books, and women's dresses. It is a place where characters learn things. When Waldo, the son of the farm's German overseer, goes there, he discovers books that promise to teach him the meaning of life. When Tant' Sannie goes there, she finds out that her sweetheart is pursuing another woman. When Lyndall's admirer, Gregory Rose, goes there, he discovers that he likes to dress in women's clothes.

Kopje. Stony hill on the Karroo to which Waldo likes to go to think about such things as life, God, and history. The apparently ancient Bushman paintings on the kopje's stones lead Waldo to speculate about the painter and the passage of time. Waldo concludes gloomily that one day he and the other children will be as remotely gone as the unknown ancient painter, and only the stones will remain.

Imaginary places. In a long allegorical aside, a stranger tells Waldo about such places as the Valley of Superstition, where one must abandon conventional religious beliefs in order to find the truth, and the Land of Negation and Denial, a dark place through which one must pass when one rejects religious faith on the way to the real truth that is supposed to be found in the Mountains of Dry-Facts and Realities. However, even in these mountains, truth turns out to be elusive, so the hope the stranger seems to offer Waldo—that there may be some way out of unhappiness—turns out to be illusory.

Waldo again sees the stranger when he goes to the botanic gardens in Grahamstown to hear a concert; however, he suddenly feels that he is too shabbily dressed and unworthy to approach the stranger, who is talking to some fashionably dressed women. Once again, Waldo seems cut off from any possible escape from his unhappy life.

Town. Unnamed town in the Cape Colony to which Waldo first goes after escaping from the farm, and before going to Grahamstown. There, he works as a sales clerk. Although the farm had seemed him a prison, the town is no improvement. He lives in a small room with packing cases for furniture, and the people he meets are either vulgar or hypocritical.

*Bloemfontein (BLEWM-fahn-tayn). Capital of the Orange Free State, an independent Boer republic, to which Lyndall flees before going on to other towns. Her admirer, Gregory, tracks her there and eventually finally finds her in a hotel in another unnamed town in the Free State. She is on her death bed in a dark room containing a massive lion's paw, which perhaps symbolizes the taming or destruction of her dreams.

Oom Muller's farmhouse (ewm MEW-lehr). Site of Tant' Sannie's wedding, a vulgar celebration which Waldo and Lyndall soon leave, as it represents a life utterly alien to them. Indeed, the wedding scene helps demonstrate how alienated the two of them are from the life around them.

— *Sheldon Goldfarb*

THE STORY OF BURNT NJAL

Author: Unknown
Type of work: Fiction
Type of plot: Adventure

Time of plot: Tenth century
First transcribed: Njáls Saga, thirteenth century
(English translation, 1861)

Just as the grim events recounted in this family saga are rooted in medieval Icelandic history, its setting is rooted in the stark and rugged landscape of medieval Iceland. Most of the events occur at or near family farmsteads, which are often the settings for deadly violent assaults and retaliations of internecine feuds. These settings are juxtaposed with the plain at Thingvellir, the site for the annual Althing, a judicial and legal meeting where cases are heard and fragile peaces are brokered. At times, however, the narrative's setting breaks away from the island and moves to Norway, the Orkney Islands, or Ireland. These lands provide interesting contrasts to Iceland.

*Iceland. North Atlantic island on whose southwestern corner most of events of the saga take place. Between the mountain ridges, near the Eyjafell Glacier, are fertile pastures of river valleys that are dotted with the farmsteads inhabited by powerful chieftains and the people—free and slave—who owe them allegiance. These farmsteads with their main halls constructed of sod, wood, and stone, and their open hearths and few interior chambers are the literal and symbolic centers of family life and activity. There, political alliances are forged, and plans of revenge or retaliation are hatched. These halls are also the last refuges for the main characters when cornered by overwhelming adversaries. For the most part, however, it is in Iceland's open spaces, its frozen rivers, sparse woods, or rugged paths, that violent deeds against foe are carried out in surprise attacks or ambush.

*__Bergthorsknoll__ (BERG-thors-nohl). Farmstead of the title character, Njal, and his extended family. It is often frequented by neighboring chieftains, especially Gunnar, who seek Njal's sage advice and legal counsel. Within his hall, Njal and his family grimly accept their fate to be burned alive at the hands of their attackers. Inside the smoking hall, the saga author is able to present the ultimate expression of the fatalistic northern warrior as Skarp-Hedin, Njal's bravest and fiercest son, utters humorous quips amid flaming beams and timbers.

*__Hildarend__ (HILD-ah-rehnd). Farmstead of Gunnar and his family. The beauty of Hildarend, its fields and newly mown hay, move Gunnar to remain where he is, despite his outlawry and exile from the island. Later, from the protection of his hall, Gunnar manages to hold his attackers at bay before finally succumbing.

*__Thingvellir__ (THING-vehl-lihr). Site of the annual open-air judicial and legislative assembly in which feuding factions state their grievances against others in the hopes of winning favorable and honorable settlements. Within and around the temporary stone and turf enclosures at Thingvellir, the various chieftains and their men (perhaps women and children) trade news, make alliances, strike deals, and, most important, administer justice and uphold the law. The Althing and Thingvellir are consistent reminders that despite the numerous violent actions, ultimately Iceland is a nation built upon the foundation of law.

*__Norway.__ Ancestral homeland of most Icelanders. Governed by an aristocratic class, Norway has strong cultural and economic centers that are destinations for many Icelanders who travel abroad in pursuit of adventure or wealth or because of their outlawry. Gunnar's economic, political, and martial successes there and on Norway's surrounding seas elevate his status upon his return to Iceland. The power and authority of Norway's aristocracy, who are the source for the law of the land, contrast greatly with the Icelanders' belief in the law itself as the highest political authority.

*__Orkney__ and __Hebrides.__ Island groups off northern Scotland to which Flosi and his men flee after being declared outlaws for their burning of Njal's hall. The practice of outlawry for the most egregious breaking of the laws of Iceland generally implies banishment from the homeland thus an expulsion from the sphere of the law's authority. With Earl Sigurd Hlodvisson earl of Orkney, some of Flosi's men go on to participate in the Battle of Clontarf in Dublin in 1014. From these islands Flosi begins his pilgrimage to Rome in order to receive absolution from the pope for his role in the burning.

— Joseph R. Carroll

THE STORY OF GÖSTA BERLING

Author: Selma Lagerlöf (1858-1940)
Type of work: Novel
Type of plot: Picaresque

Time of plot: Early nineteenth century
First published: Gösta Berlings Saga, 1891 (English translation, 1898)

This, Selma Lagerlöf's first novel, is frequently described as the saga of a Swedish province, her native Värmland. Although the setting of the novel revolves around places that closely resemble real places in Värmland, its spatial characteristics exemplify, in a fantastically condensed and concentrated form, both animate and inanimate natural features of the whole province, including human types and social relations. The sense of place dominates the narrative to such an extent that the province itself becomes a central character, the element that provides a most compelling sense of stylistic and artistic unity.

Ekeby (EH-keh-BIH). Swedish estate around which the novel is centered. Initially a prosperous estate, it declines nearly to the point of ruin because of neglect after Margareta Samzelius, its capable and resourceful owner, is expelled by her husband when she is exposed as an adulteress. The chaos in the human world finds its manifestation in nature, and an overpowering storm brings near destruction to the whole province. However, rather symbolically, it is the constructive work ethic and love of another woman, Elisabet Dohna, that save both Gösta Berling and Ekeby by restoring communal morality and natural order. The fate of Ekeby gives an unambiguous expression of Lagerlöf's Christian ethics, which seek a balance between joy and work, romantic adventure and doing good.

Ekeby's prototype is Rottneros, situated near the Swedish town of Sunne, at the heart of the province of Värmland. Critics and biographers see in Ekeby an idealized portrayal of Mårbacka, Lagerlöf's place of birth in Värmland. Geographically and culturally, Lagerlöf perceived her native province as a border territory: between Norway and Sweden, man and nature, culture and wilderness, the visible and the invisible, the real and the imaginary.

The world Lagerhof created in *The Story of Gösta Berling* emphasizes the constantly shifting and often indistinguishable boundaries separating the past from the present. Although textual references identify the 1820's as the time frame of the narrative, the novel's temporal as well as spatial characteristics continually contract and expand to include a kaleidoscope of narrative worlds, including those of Icelandic sagas, myth and romance, local folk tales, legends, and superstitions. The result of this act of vivid imagination is a powerful recovery of a sense of place which defies both linear time and traditional notions of the animate and inanimate in nature.

Lake Löven (lewh-ven). Lake around which most of the novel's action concentrates. Modeled on Sweden's Lake Frycken, Löven is introduced in the novel's first chapter; the fairly detailed full-length portrait of the lake is painted by a striking combination of personification and realistic detail. The description of the adjoining landscape also proves significant as it underlines an organic merger between culture and wilderness: The cultivated fields on the lake's shores and the deep forests assume in the distance the harsh, rocky features of mountainous semiwilderness. Human presence is a mere extension of the natural world without dominating it in any way. The lake and the surrounding flora and fauna thus possess a personality of their own and are capable of establishing and sustaining an intimate relationship with man.

— *Miglena I. Ivanova*

THE STRANGE CASE OF DR. JEKYLL AND MR. HYDE

Author: Robert Louis Stevenson (1850-1894)
Type of work: Novella
Type of plot: Gothic

Time of plot: Nineteenth century
First published: 1886

This novella is a gothic story dealing with the dualism of good and evil in the human soul and with the main character's attempt to separate the two sides of human nature into two different beings. Place is used brilliantly in the story to create atmosphere and develop the main themes and symbolic meanings of the narrative. Robert Louis Stevenson's evocation of London provides an unforgettably ominous atmosphere, while the houses of Jekyll, Utterson, Lanyon, and Hyde become symbols of dualism, duplicity, repressive respectability, mystery, and evil.

London. Great Britain's capital and leading city is the general setting for the novella. The story depends for its effect on a suitably gothic atmosphere, and its portrayal of London is one of the great triumphs of the work. However, in the view of many scholars, Stevenson's London is based more on his native Edinburgh, Scotland, than on the actual London of his time.

The story's London is full of ominously empty streets

and glaring lamps; it is silvered by ghostly moonlight or drowned in impenetrable fog. Its streets echo with sinister footsteps, and it is a place of questionable neighborhoods, strange houses, and dubious doors. Fog penetrates the very interiors of houses; biting winds whip sparse trees against railings, and even in the daylight, fog and mist can create ghostly and frightening phantasmagorias. In this story, London is mostly a city of the night, a place in whose darkness or under whose lurid lamps a child can be trampled or a dignified old man be murdered. Stevenson creates the overwhelming sense that just beyond the warm hearths and respectable characters' sitting rooms there lurks a dark and dangerous place.

Jekyll's house. London residence of Dr. Henry Jekyll. Like Jekyll himself, his house is possessed of a dual and bifurcated nature. Indeed, almost every detail of the house reflects symbolically his character and situation. Jekyll's "official" house has a respectable and handsome facade, a door that is opened by an old and decent servant, and an interior that is expressive of wealth, comfort, and security. This house, or the public part of his house, is a perfect expression of the front that the eminently respectable Dr. Jekyll presents to the world.

In his investigations, the lawyer Gabriel John Utterson learns that what he has taken to be Jekyll's house is actually only one part of a larger residence. The respectable house that Utterson first knows is connected through a back door and a small yard to a mysterious and sinister part of the house that is at once attached to, and separate from, its imposing opposite side. Every aspect of this dark side of the residence reveals something about Jekyll's own other side. It is a dingy, secretive, disorderly place that contains a laboratory (once a dissecting room) and a kind of inner sanctum which is referred to as the "doctor's cabinet."

It is also worth noting that the small yard that connects the two sides of Jekyll's residence was once a garden but is so no longer. Finally, the dark side of Jekyll's house has its own front side and door that seem at first unconnected to the other side of the house; they are blank, ugly, sordid, and ominous. It is through the entrance on this side of the house that Mr. Hyde comes and goes. In coming to understand the strange two-sidedness of Dr. Jekyll's house, Utterson approaches and foreshadows an understanding of Jekyll himself.

Utterson's house. London home of Utterson, Jekyll's lawyer. This house is comfortable, safe, respectable, and sterile. It is a place from which everything unconventional, imaginative, or odd has been expelled. It reflects Utterson's dry bachelor ways and his masculine professionalism. Utterson's house is the embodiment of Victorian respectability that Jekyll worships in his Jekyll form but rebels against in his Hyde form.

Lanyon's house. Home of Dr. Hastie Lanyon, Jekyll's friend and medical colleague, in London's Cavendish Square. This fashionable house reflects Lanyon's stature as a physician and his general success. In this comfortable and hospitable home, Lanyon sees to his growing medical practice and entertains his friends. Like Utterson's house and one side of Jekyll's home, Lanyon's residence is a symbol of a repressive but brittle respectability. When Lanyon witnesses Hyde's transformation back to Jekyll within his own home, the sight utterly destroys all that he and his house represent.

Hyde's house. Squalid residence of Mr. Hyde in London's dismal Soho district. When Utterson finds the house, he experiences it and its neighborhood as a kind of dingy nightmare. The house is a dark and wicked place, but it reveals a few hints of Hyde's connection to Jekyll.

— *Phillip B. Anderson*

STRANGE INTERLUDE

Author: Eugene O'Neill (1888-1953)
Type of work: Drama
Type of plot: Psychological realism

Time of plot: After World War I
First performed: 1928; first published, 1928

This nine-act play covers several decades in the life of its heroine, Nina Leeds, and the three men who love her. Eugene O'Neill uses setting as a means of emphasizing themes of repression, despair, commitment, and resignation. He also provides explicit stage directions to ensure that physical settings subtly suggest the psychological states of his characters.

Leeds home. New England home in which the first two acts are set. The location suggests the domination of Nina's puritanical father over her adolescence, and his priggishness is mirrored in his well-ordered study. In the second act, after Leeds dies, his study falls into disarray, suggesting that his values are not perpetuated in the modern world. Once he is gone, Nina is free to marry Sam Evans, a likable figure who, like Nina, worships the memory of Gordon Shaw, the fiancé she lost in World War I.

Evans homestead. Decaying house that is an apt setting for Sam's mother to reveal to the newly married Nina the dark secret of the Evans family—that the unborn child Nina now carries may grow up insane. After aborting her pregnancy, Nina seduces Ned Darrell in the Evans house so that she can bear a child to make her husband happy.

Evans apartment. Well-appointed Park Avenue residence in New York City that suggests the level of affluence the Evans family has achieved. It contrasts, however, with the growing dissolution that Nina feels. Her son is more devoted to Sam Evans, whom he thinks is his natural father, than to her, At the same time, Nina continues to feel deep affection for Ned Darrell. In the apartment, her son sees a physical display of her affection for Darrell; afterward, he forms a hatred for Darrell and disgust for his mother.

Evans's yacht. Aboard their yacht anchored in the Hudson River Nina, her husband, and others watch her son Gordon in a boat race. Seemingly adrift herself, Nina reaches out symbolically to hold on to her son by threatening to reveal the dark secret about the family's past to Gordon's fiancé—even though Gordon is not Sam's biological son. Ned prevents her from doing so, however, and her husband's stroke aboard ship causes her to change her plans and nurse Sam Evans in his final days.

Evans estate. Luxurious, almost decadent, Long Island location at which the play's final act takes place. The material excesses of the Evans home are set in stark contrast to the psychological bankruptcy of the widowed heroine. She turns for solace to the father-figure and longtime admirer Charles Marsden. Ironically, he responds by promising to return her to the refuge of her girlhood home.

— Laurence W. Mazzeno

THE STRANGER

Author: Albert Camus (1913-1960)
Type of work: Novel
Type of plot: Existentialism

Time of plot: Late 1930's to early 1940's
First published: L'Étranger, 1942 (English translation, 1946)

In this novel, a hot and sun-filled Algeria represents an environment of absolutes—a place where behavior is precise and feelings are clear. It also conveys the violent quality of an absurd world intent on destroying man.

*Algiers. Coastal capital of Algeria, a country in North Africa. Although not specifically described, Algiers serves as a general backdrop not only to the main action but above all to Meursault's struggle with the collective forces of nature arrayed against him.

Beach. Outside Algiers, where Raymond, Meursault's friend, has a bungalow. When the sun beats down on Meursault, the reflecting light gouges into his eyes, the lazy sea waves turn him lethargic, the fiery beach presses him forward, and the cloudless sky pours a sheet of flame on him. Under this onslaught, he has no other choice but to react in self-defense, first, by erasing the source of the attack (the Arab and his shining knife) and then by firing four additional shots for the four elements of nature.

Prison. Tiny cell in which Meursault awaits his execution. Only a confined space can allow him to concentrate on the essential and to think philosophical thoughts, unmolested by outside distractions and pointless discussions. After his final metaphysical revolt he is ultimately at peace, as evidenced by the stars shining on his face like a celestial projector, instead of the relentless and punishing sun, and by the heat now being replaced by the refreshingly cool night breeze on his cheeks. This Meursault calls "the benign indifference of the universe."

*Marengo.** Retirement home and cemetery located some fifty miles west of Algiers. Before and during his mother's funeral Meursault shows a strange callousness and lack of sorrow about her death. The unbearable heat and the blinding glare of the sun further aggravate this insensitivity, as he matter-of-factly attends the ceremony. Apparently unmoved by the occasion, he also observes the arid landscape around him, noting the green cypresses, the red soil, the humming insects, the rustling grass, and the various smells.

Swimming pool. Part of the harbor complex. Rather than mourn over his mother's death, he spends the next day with a female former coworker at the pool. The two then go to a movie theater to see a comedy and lastly to his apartment, where they spend the night together.

Detention center. Jail in which Meursault is held before his trial. He and his court-appointed lawyer discuss his defense, which given his general apathy, does not look promising. Progressively, as he understands the purpose of his imprisonment, he adapts to his new environment by killing time and by sleeping.

Courtroom. Room in which Meursault's trial takes place. Again, the heat is stifling, increased by the hour of the day and the large crowd of spectators and reporters. Again he responds and reacts in an all-too-aloof and unconcerned manner. This is why he is considered a "stranger," quickly found guilty, and sentenced to death.

Examining magistrate's office. The first time Meursault is formally interrogated, the nondescript, ordinary room is so hot, with flies buzzing around, that he nods to any statement, from accepting Christ as his personal savior to being vexed over having shot a man.

— *Pierre L. Horn*

STRANGER IN A STRANGE LAND

Author: Robert A. Heinlein (1907-1988)
Type of work: Novel
Type of plot: Science fiction

Time of plot: Early twenty-first century
First published: 1961

Most of this novel's action occurs in a future United States that is part of a world government called the World Federation of Free States. The United States has no military forces or space program of its own. However, Robert A. Heinlein was writing satirically about religious and other cultural practices of his time, many of which persist into the twenty-first century.

*Mars.** Fourth planet from the Sun and the birthplace of Valentine Michael "Mike" Smith, the title character and only survivor of the first human expedition to that planet. All the original members of the expedition die shortly after Mike is born, but native Martians raise him

to physical adulthood. World War III prevents a second expedition until twenty years later. When that expedition returns to Earth, they bring Mike home with them.

When Heinlein finished his juvenile novel *Red Planet* (1949), he felt he had enough unused background material on Mars for another book, which became *Stranger in a Strange Land*. This novel was one of the last major science fiction stories published before the NASA probes of the 1960's. As in the earlier novel, Heinlein incorrectly postulated that there are canals carrying scarce water from the poles to the equatorial region and that the planet is inhabited by a super-intelligent species. A typical Martian household, called a nest, consists of eggs, nestlings, adults, and Old Ones.

Since Heinlein's purpose is satire, the story would be the same whether the planet was Mars or one in a distant galaxy. The main point is that Mike spent the first twenty years of his life on a planet where water was scarce.

*Bethesda Medical Center. U.S. Navy hospital in a Maryland suburb of Washington, D.C. In *Stranger in a Strange Land*, the hospital is affiliated with the Federation, because there is no longer a U.S. Navy. The name Bethesda has connection to both water and religion, because it was the name of a pool in biblical Jerusalem believed to have healing powers.

When Mike arrives on Earth, he is held incommunicado in a hospital suite with no windows supposedly because of Earth's stronger gravity and to protect him from the press. In reality, he is a prisoner. Jill Boardman, the female lead of the novel, is a nurse who brings him water. Unknown to her, the sharing of water is an important bonding ritual on Mars. She and Michael become "water brothers," and Michael trusts her absolutely although they have just met.

Harshaw's home. Fourteen-room house in the Pocono Mountains of Pennsylvania, a rural resort area noted for religious tolerance. The house sits on several acres and is surrounded by an electric fence. One of the world's leading dissidents, Jubal makes a living by writing stories, which he dictates to three beautiful female secretaries who live there. They also cook the meals and clean the house. Heinlein based the setup on the household of mystery writer Erle Stanley Gardner, creator of Perry Mason.

When Jill realizes that Mike's life is in danger, she helps him escape to Jubal's house, where Mike learns to read and write English, dress himself, and eat with a knife and fork. Mike uses Jubal's extensive library of medical and legal textbooks to gain a theoretical knowledge about human beings. After Mike and Jill's arrival,

the household resembles a Martian one, where Mike is the egg, Jill the nestling, the secretaries and other staff adults, and Jubal the Old One.

Harshaw's home has a swimming pool, which Mars-born Mike considers the ultimate in luxury. Everyone who swims with him becomes his "water brother."

Archangel Foster Tabernacle. Headquarters church of a new religion, the Church of the New Revelation, also known as the Fosterites. Supreme Bishop Digby, the head of the church, invites Mike to a service, which he attends with Jubal and Jill. Heinlein uses the visit to satirize all churches, temples, and mosques as forms of entertainment. They enter through the Happiness Room, where they find slot machines and a bar. Then they visit the Happy Thoughts meditation chamber, where they see the preserved corpse of Foster, the religion's founder. For the service itself, they sit in a luxury box, which has adjustable seats, ashtrays, and refreshments. Although hidden from view during the service, they are told there is a giant television screen that allows the church to double as a sports bar. The service itself includes a snake dance, a sermon, and hymns. Each hymn has a different corporate sponsor.

*San Francisco. California city named for Saint Francis, the founder of the Franciscan Order, that stands on a peninsula between the Pacific Ocean and San Francisco Bay. These connections give the city both religious and water connections. While visiting the zoo there, Mike has an epiphany at the Monkey House. When he observes the behavior of the monkeys, he finally grasps the human concepts of comedy and tragedy and, consequently, what it means to be a human being.

Mike's nest. Informal name for Mike's Church of All Worlds in St. Petersburg, Florida. Heinlein chose this city because it literally means "city of Saint Peter," Christ's leading disciple and the first Pope, and, like San Francisco, it lies on a peninsula between two bodies of water, the Gulf of Mexico and Tampa Bay. The church contains an auditorium for public meetings, smaller rooms for invitational meetings, a large library, a swimming pool, and living quarters. Like Harshaw's household, it is organized like a Martian one, in which the beginning disciples are eggs, intermediate ones are nestlings, advanced disciples adults, and Mike is the Old One.

Mike and his disciples have a group marriage and live there until an incendiary bomb forces them to flee to the Sans Souci Hotel, elsewhere in St. Petersburg, which Mike secretly owns. *Sans Souci* is French for "without worry," and they feel safe inside. Mike and his disciples have a kind of Last Supper there.

Heaven. The afterlife. It too is organized like a Martian household. Ordinary humans are eggs, saints are nestlings, angels and archangels are adults, and God is the ultimate Old One. Heinlein's Heaven is an ecumenical one. Mike enters at the Archangel level. Bishop Digby, who died shortly after their meeting, is already there and becomes Mike's assistant, despite the differences in their religions. When they need rest and recreation, they can visit the Muslim Paradise for unlimited food, drink, and sex.

Heinlein describes Heaven in greater detail in *Job: A Comedy of Justice* (1984). However, any similarity is superficial. In *Stranger in a Strange Land*, Heaven is a vigorous place in which the organization has constructive purposes, such as building new universes and saving souls on the Earth and other planets. In the later book, it is a decadent place with a rigid class system for which the abiding principle is "Rank Hath Its Privileges."

— *Thomas R. Feller*

STREET SCENE

Author: Elmer Rice (Elmer Leopold Reizenstein, 1892-1967)
Type of work: Drama

Type of plot: Social realism
Time of plot: 1929
First performed: 1929; first published, 1929

As its title indicates, this play focuses on its realistic outdoor location: the sidewalk and exterior facade of a single brownstone apartment building in Manhattan. Because this is the sole setting of all three acts, the detailed street scene is not merely a backdrop but also an integral part of the play.

Manhattan apartment building. Ordinary brownstone tenement, crowded with roughly a dozen families in New York City's Manhattan borough. Although the stage directions indicate the geographic location only as "a mean quarter of New York," Elmer Rice later revealed in his autobiography that he and designer Jo Mielziner had modeled this particular facade on an actual brownstone located on Sixty-fifth Street. The stage directions further indicate that this is an "ugly brownstone" built in the 1890's, surrounded by a storage warehouse on stage left and a building being demolished on stage right. The most prominent features of this street scene are "a 'stoop' of four shallow stone steps flanked on either side by a curved stone balustrade," the apartment's vestibule just inside the front door (always open) at the top of the steps, the windows of the janitor's basement apartment, and the six narrow windows of the first-floor apartments, through which some of the residents can be seen. The windows of the apartments located on the upper floors are not visible.

As an example of social realism, *Street Scene* relies on its detailed stage setting to evoke an atmosphere of everyday life in New York, not only visually but aurally. According to the stage directions, the sounds of the city should be heard as constant background noise, from the distant roar of elevated trains and rattling trucks, to the barking of dogs and murmurs of New Yorkers at work and play over the course of twenty-four hours on a sweltering June day.

— *James I. Deutsch*

A STREETCAR NAMED DESIRE

Author: Tennessee Williams (Thomas Lanier
   Williams, 1911-1983)
Type of work: Drama

Type of plot: Tragedy
Time of plot: Late 1940's
First performed: 1947; first published, 1947

A sense of place gives meaning and contrast to the characters of this play, and the type of place—a tiny, hot, one-bedroom, inner-city apartment in New Orleans—drives the action. Because there are three very different adults living in a space inadequate for two and because there is no way to alleviate the overcrowding, the inherent tensions between the characters are forced into bitter conflict that leads to tragic consequences.

*New Orleans. Louisiana city in which the Kowalskis live adds to the tensions inside the apartment. New Orleans just after World War II but before air-conditioning was a hot and humid place to live. Windows had to be kept open, which adds to the noise and sense of overcrowding in the Kowalski apartment. The apartment is in the French Quarter, known for incessant activity day and night. Noises of all sorts, from trains to cats to prostitutes to street vendors, constantly intrude upon the tiny space. Rowdy neighbors, also with their windows open, increase the sense of invaded privacy. Furthermore, music and vulgar merrymaking emanate from neighborhood bars. Indeed, the life outside is so much a part of the life inside that Tennessee Williams calls for a transparent wall so that outside images and activities may be seen through the apartment wall at crucial moments. Stanley, whom Williams describes as a "richly feathered male bird . . . a gaudy seed bearer," loves the turbulence, and he contributes to it at every opportunity. Blanche, the essence of cultured southern womanhood, is flabbergasted by the endless clamor of New Orleans. Stella, the bridge between the two, is caught between her attraction to the crude and exciting vigor of Stanley and his New Orleans and her loyalty to Blanche and her background of old South gentility.

Kowalski apartment. The entire action of the play takes place in and around the apartment of Stella and Stanley Kowalski, recent newlyweds. The two are from opposite backgrounds. Stanley is a working-class former army sergeant, who now works for a tool supply company. Stella is from Laurel, Mississippi, where her family for generations owned a large plantation outside town. The days of family wealth have gone, hence

Stella's journey to New Orleans to seek her fortune, where she meets and falls in love with Stanley, a man with little income.

Located ironically on a street called **Elysium Fields** (heaven), the apartment consists of a small kitchen area, a small bedroom area, and a bath. It is located near the railroad tracks in a poor section of the French Quarter. Blanche Dubois, Stella's older sister, comes for a visit and is given a daybed in the kitchen. A curtain is hung between the kitchen and the bedroom area. All three must use the same bath. When it becomes obvious that Blanche's visit will be a long one, tensions erupt, especially over the space occupied by Blanche's luggage, which symbolizes to Stanley Blanche's superior attitude to people with a less privileged background. To worsen matters, Blanche is addicted to taking long baths, especially as an escape when Stanley is at home, much to Stanley's emotional displeasure and genuine physical discomfort.

Desire Street. New Orleans in all its earthiness and quirkiness is so much a motivator in the play that the work's very title comes from a streetcar that ran along Desire Street. Williams also uses two other actual place names when he has Blanche say she was told to "take a streetcar named Desire, transfer to one called Cemeteries and get off on Elysian Fields." This reciting of place names ironically contains the whole story of the play. It is the city of New Orleans, however, with its French Quarter's permissive attitude, that drives Blanche and Stanley to the cultural war that ends in sexual brutality and tragedy.

Belle Reve (bel rev). Blanche and Stella grew up at Belle Reve, a lovely, graceful antebellum plantation, fronted with white columns, whose name means "beautiful dream." Located outside Laurel, Mississippi, it is the antithesis of the brawling, urban French Quarter. The two places serve as emblems of the irreconcilable and tragic conflict between Stanley and Blanche. Blanche comes to tragedy because she cannot give up "Belle Reve," and Stella contributes to Blanche's agony because she chooses Stanley's New Orleans over Belle Reve.

— *August W. Staub*

STUDS LONIGAN: A Trilogy

Author: James T. Farrell (1904-1979)
Type of work: Novel
Type of plot: Naturalism
Time of plot: 1916-1931

First published: 1935: *Young Lonigan: A Boyhood in Chicago Streets*, 1932; *The Young Manhood of Studs Lonigan*, 1934; *Judgment Day*, 1935

The streets of Chicago provide the backdrop of Studs Lonigan's story; as they change, so does he. During the period of this story, Chicago goes through political, economic, and social changes that transform it from familiar turf for Studs and his gang to an unfamiliar, alien environment where Studs feels oddly out of place. The city that initially nurtures his cocky independence becomes at last a confinement that locks him into a hapless life.

*Chicago.** City of the street tough Studs Lonigan's birth, youth, and eventual death. From 1916 to 1931, Chicago goes through significant changes. Once insulated into distinct ethnic neighborhoods with the different racial components seriously "turf" conscious, it gradually becomes more racially, culturally, and politically diversified, and the subsequent changes play havoc with Studs's self-esteem. The political corruption and petty crime that allow Studs to see himself as a self-proclaimed tough guy shift as he grows older. The adult responsibilities he is forced to take on during the Great Depression wreck his confidence in himself. Throughout his life, however, the streets of Chicago remain the one constant in his life even as they evolve; they hold Studs to what he has been and hopes to become.

Fifty-eighth and Indiana Avenue. Chicago neighborhood in which young Studs and his gang hang out. From his early adolescence, this street corner is the place where Studs feels he is a force to be reckoned with; here he establishes his reputation as a tough guy. When Studs is a boy, the mostly Irish Catholic neighborhood has private homes and apartment buildings housing Irish families, and Studs can always walk down its streets and feel true to himself. In later years, when he is in his late twenties, he occasionally returns to the old neighborhood—now filled with Jewish and African American residents and no Irish—and may still be reminded of the "good old days" of his youth.

*Washington Park.** City park near Studs's neighborhood. Full of trees, flowers, shrubbery, grassy lawns, playgrounds, and a lagoon, the park is a veritable Garden of Eden to the young Studs. There he spends one memorable, tender afternoon with Lucy Scanlon, a girl for whom he has strong and lasting feelings. When he is older, he often drifts to this park for less idealistic or romantic reasons; it becomes a place to pick up girls, to play roughhouse prairie football, or to ditch high school classes. In spite of the occasional pedophiles and perverts lurking about, trying to lure youngsters such as Studs, the park is most often a place where Studs allows himself to dream of what he could be and do and to aspire to being a better person.

Lonigan home. Apartment in a building owned by Studs's father. For many years, this well-appointed apartment represents an impressive achievement of Mr. Lonigan, an uneducated man who has pulled himself up by his bootstraps to become a successful painting contractor. The home he provides for his family has everything it needs for his caring wife, two sons, and two daughters to live comfortably. After the neighborhood is "overrun" by people he considers undesirable (Jews and African Americans), the Lonigans sell out and regretfully move to a new building in a new neighborhood. All the while, Studs remains living with his father, mother, and brother even as he nears the age of thirty. (Both sisters marry well and live with their husbands.)

Saloon and poolroom. Places where Studs and his friends most often hang out during their late adolescence and young manhood. At the saloon Studs gets drunk for the first of many times in his life. There, he and his friends talk about all kinds of things, but mostly girls they would like to "make" or to have made, about

people they would like to beat up, about politics and social issues that mostly reveal their racial and political prejudices. Non-Irish outsiders are looked upon with suspicion and often treated with threatening disdain, so much so that strangers rarely venture into these domains. After Prohibition starts, the poolroom becomes almost as popular as the saloon has been, even though it changes ownership and eventually goes out of business altogether.

— *Jane L. Ball*

A STUDY IN SCARLET

Author: Arthur Conan Doyle (1859-1930)
Type of work: Novel
Type of plot: Detective and mystery

Time of plot: Nineteenth century
First published: 1887

This novel, which introduces Sherlock Holmes, history's first "consulting detective," is atypical of Holmes stories in many ways, particularly in its treatment of place. Most Sherlock Holmes stories are closely tied to Holmes's point of view, with Holmes himself either visiting every important location or hearing about it from a crime victim. In this story, however, the third-person narrative follows Jefferson Hope's adventure and tragedy in the American West directly, and displaces Holmes entirely during that section.

***Afghanistan.** Southwest Asian country over whose control Great Britain and Russia clashed in the nineteenth century and in which the novel's narrator, Dr. John Watson, served as a British army physician in the late 1870's, before the period in which his narrative proper begins. Only a few pages of his narrative discuss Afghanistan directly; however, these passages indicate how powerfully place shapes men. Watson's time in Afghanistan transformed him. After he was shot, he contracted enteric fever and returned to London almost an invalid, forever marked by his military service.

The first thing Sherlock Holmes says to Watson when they meet is, "You have been in Afghanistan, I perceive." Able to recognize all types of soil at a glance, Holmes can instantly deduce where people have recently been. He can also recognize other signs of regional origin such as tattoos, spices, or dialects. Doyle based Holmes's ability to make such judgments on the ability of one of his medical school professors, Dr. Joseph Bell, who made similar observations about his medical patients.

This ability also shows Doyle's uneasiness with Britain's role as an imperial power, and his belief that Britain's time in foreign lands would change all those who went, and would return to threaten Britain itself.

***London.** Capital of the British Empire. The London in which Holmes and Watson live is a microcosm of the empire. It contains a population of British citizens who have lived in London their entire lives, peoples whose residential addresses immediately reveal their class origins. However, because of the strict class hierarchy in British society during the period in which the novel is set, London is also a place of separate and distinct cultures, where the poor are largely invisible to the rich. Holmes's London is also a cosmopolitan place in which exotic foreigners may suddenly intrude, bringing violence and strange practices as does the American Jefferson Hope, who brings new poisons and vengeance from home to kill fellow Americans Drebber and Stangerson.

When Watson first returns to London from Afghanistan, he finds it a "great wilderness," rather than the familiar place he expects. Part of Holmes's genius is his ability to communicate with members of all social classes, as he does with the beggar boys who spy for him. Another part of his genius is his ability to read foreign threats correctly. However, Holmes's greatest gift is his ability to restore to London the order that most of its denizens wish for it.

*Baker Street.** London street on which Holmes and Watson share a flat. They live at the imaginary address of 221B, which consists of two bedrooms and a large shared sitting room. Their landlady (Mrs. Hudson) is not given a name until a later story. The Baker Street flat becomes a haven from the threatening confusion of London. Many later Sherlock Holmes stories begin in the sitting room, where police officers, government officials, and private citizens bring their problems to Holmes, who listens to them and then emerges from the flat to solve their problems in the larger world.

*American West.** Mainly frontier region of the United States that stretches from Nebraska to the Rocky Mountains and beyond. In this story, the West serves the role that India serves in such later Sherlock Holmes stories as "The Speckled Band" as a place of wild danger and mystery. However, this land, described as "an arid and repulsive desert," differs in being completely untamed; it tests the character of those like John Ferrier who pass through it. Doyle focuses on the harshness of the land, its dryness and wide open spaces. A major part of the narrative follows the story of Jefferson Hope in the West; he has the ideal character to deal with such a place: brave, physically powerful, and passionate.

*Utah.** Territory of the United States that is dominated by the authoritarian Mormon Church, whose people settled the territory in the late 1840's, when they were fleeing religious persecution in the East and the Midwest. Doyle's descriptions of Utah and Mormon culture highlight the difficult contradictions that the state offers to Anglo-American culture. Doyle praises the rocky beauty of the area and the industry of Mormon communities, but dwarfing these positive attributes is the threat of Mormonism itself. The mysterious authority of Brigham Young, combined with practices such as polygamy, makes Utah seem as alien and dangerous as India.

— *Greg Beatty*

SUDDENLY LAST SUMMER

Author: Tennessee Williams (Thomas Lanier Williams, 1911-1983)
Type of work: Drama

Type of plot: Psychological realism
Time of plot: 1936
First published: 1958

New Orleans was, for Tennessee Williams, one of the last frontiers of "Bohemia." Here he found, as a young man, the freedom from the oppressive life he had led in St. Louis. New Orleans served as the setting for some of his best dramas, and in this one, the contrasts between different parts of the city serve to illustrate the action.

*New Orleans.** Louisiana city at the mouth of the Mississippi, on the Gulf of Mexico. Although for the young Williams, it exerted a liberating influence, nevertheless he was aware of sinister and malign elements in the old French city. One factor contributing to Blanche DuBois's mental collapse in *A Streetcar Named Desire* (pr., pb. 1947) is the casual decadence of the French Quarter, which is almost a living entity in the drama. In this play it is the uptown Garden District of New Orleans, home to wealthy nonbohemian residents, which is a metaphor for oppression. The topography and people of the Garden District stand in sharp contrast to the more easygoing lifestyle of the old Quarter.

Garden District mansion. House in which all the action of this short play occurs. The mansion is described in Williams's stage directions as a house in the Gothic style. The word *gothic* is of particular significance, since the setting, the action, and at least one of the characters put the play in the tradition of Southern gothic literature. Its strange configuration as described by the playwright—a house with a tropical garden—is the perfect setting for the disturbing story and story-within-the-story that unfolds in the drama. There is a decadent and terrifying air about the place, its steamy unworldly atmosphere filled with carnivorous plants such as the Venus flytrap.

This eerie and menacing setting, which according to Williams was inspired by the movie *The Big Sleep* (1946), a *film noir* detective story, is meant to underscore the horror of what has happened to Sebastian Venable and Catherine and what fate may await Catherine. It is also the perfect backdrop for the character Violet Venable, a society matron seemingly lacking in compassion for anyone other than her son and herself and willing to sacrifice her niece to prevent the truth's being told. There are also lengthy references to other sinister locales: the Encantadas, to which Sebastian and his mother traveled; Cabeza de Lobo, where Sebastian died; and Lion's View, the psychiatric hospital where lobotomies are performed.

*Garden District. Section of New Orleans founded by the American settlers early in the nineteenth century after the United States had purchased the Louisiana Territory from France. The area was inhabited mostly by descendants of British immigrants and so was at odds with the old French Quarter, inhabited by Creoles, the descendants of French and Spanish settlers. An immediate animosity between the Creoles and the Americans developed at the time of the Louisiana Purchase, and the two areas were always disparate in architecture and the character of their inhabitants. The name "Garden District" derives from the fact that the American settlers wanted front yards, which were virtually nonexistent in the Quarter. Often they turned those yards into gardens, though probably none like the one in this play.

In later years, the Garden District became the center of the socially elite New Orleanians, and the French Quarter, or Vieux Carre, after an exodus of the Creoles, became more or less a slum before it was taken over by artists and writers in the 1920's and became a bohemian enclave. Thus when Catherine says that she came out in the French Quarter before she made her debut in uptown society, she is identifying herself with that raffish area and its outcast population and distancing herself from the social world of Violet Venable.

The importance of the Garden District in this play is indicated by the fact that *Suddenly Last Summer* was printed with another play, *Something Unspoken*, under the combined title *Garden District* (1959), and the two plays are often performed in tandem.

— *W. Kenneth Holditch*

SULA

Author: Toni Morrison (1931-   )
Type of work: Novel
Type of plot: Psychological realism

Time of plot: 1919-1965
First published: 1973

Set primarily in Medallion, Ohio, primarily in the black neighborhood called the Bottom, the novel tells not only of the friendship of two girls as they grow into women but also the life story of the neighborhood itself. All actions on the part of the characters take place under the scrutiny of the community.

Medallion. Imaginary Ohio town in which the main action of the novel is set. Morrison grew up in the small town of Lorain, Ohio. Bordered by Kentucky to the south but a Northern state in the Civil War with important Underground Railroad sites, Ohio functions in many of Morrison's novels as a place of alternating prejudice and freedom for the black characters.

The fictional Medallion's geography shows the distinctions between black and white characters: The white characters live in the fertile valley, protected from the harshest winds of winter, while the black characters inhabit the rocky, unproductive hillside where the poorly built houses cannot protect their residents from the elements. During a particularly difficult winter, when ice coats the ground and does not melt for days, the black residents lose their jobs in the valley because they cannot get down the steep hill in the ice.

By the end of the novel, the Bottom, the black neighborhood, is disappearing because the wealthy white people have decided the hillside on which it stands is desirable for a golf course and for luxury homes. The new development reflects the town's power structure as did the earlier layout.

The Bottom. African American neighborhood in Medallion. Local legend holds that the neighborhood's first settler was tricked by a white man into taking the rocky hillside land rather than the fertile valley land below. The neighborhood's ironic name refers to the "bottom of heaven." The residents are not consoled that they can "literally look down on the white folks." The neighborhood eventually disappears as the homes of wealthy whites and a golf course are put in on the hillside. A tunnel built by white laborers offers a focus for the rage the Bottom's residents feel at their economic and social privation. In their attempt to destroy it, many are killed when it collapses.

The residents of the Bottom interpret and pass judgment on events and actions of the novel's characters. Morrison's giving a communal voice to a place is reminiscent of a technique of William Faulkner, on whom Morrison wrote a master's thesis. Like Faulkner, Morrison creates characters who seemingly could not exist in different settings.

Train. After Helene's grandmother dies in 1920, Helene and Nel travel to New Orleans on a train. Their ride provides a vivid picture of the unequal treatment that African Americans received in the Deep South during the days of rigid Jim Crow segregation. The train's conductor is extremely nasty when Helene accidentally gets on the coach for white passengers. The train stations do not even have rest rooms for black passengers. Although Helene is disgusted by the way she is treated on the trip and by the cold welcome she receives from her mother, her ten-year-old daughter Nel finds the experience exciting. The new sense of self she develops from her journey makes her feel brave, so that she starts talking to Sula Peace, who will become her best friend.

Helene Wright's home. House in which Nel grows up. Like its mistress, the house is orderly and attractive, to the point that Nel finds it oppressive. Sula, coming from a more chaotic household, loves to visit the house.

Eva Peace's home. House in which Sula grows up, also inhabited by her grandmother Eva, mother Hannah, uncle Plum, three boys all named Dewey, and various others over time. The house was constructed in pieces and contains rooms and stairways in no particular arrangement, in contrast with the orderly Wright home. Nel prefers the Peace home to her own.

— *Joan Hope*

THE SUN ALSO RISES

Author: Ernest Hemingway (1899-1961)
Type of work: Novel
Type of plot: Social realism

Time of plot: 1920's
First published: 1926

Changing settings in this novel play an integral part in the development of the story's major theme: the quest for meaningful values in the moral wasteland of Europe after World War I. As the war-wounded protagonist Jake Barnes travels on vacation from Paris to several Spanish destinations, places accrue thematic significance.

***Paris.** French capital, in which the novel opens. There, American newspaperman Jake Barnes lives and works in the midst of a community of American and British expatriates who find the city a wasteland of values. A question regarding values that arises early in the book is the contrast between work and idleness, and this opposition is reflected in the Parisian locales frequented by Jake and his friends.

Paris is split by the River Seine into two sections: the Right Bank (*Rive Droite*) and the Left Bank (*Rive Gauche*). In the novel, work is associated with the Right Bank. Jake's newspaper office, for example, is on the Right Bank, in the vicinity of the avenue de l'Opéra and the Tuileries garden. On the Right Bank, too, he encounters Georgette, who as a prostitute is a working woman.

When Jake, with Georgette in tow, goes partying with his idle and rich expatriate friends, they go to the Left Bank, near the Panthéon. There they encounter Jake's love, Lady Brett, with an entourage of gay men. The similarity between Georgette and Brett is emphasized by their rhyming names and their promiscuity; the difference between them is that one engages in sex professionally, and the other is an alcoholic amateur in promiscuity.

It is evident that Ernest Hemingway endorses the values of work and the Right Bank, rather than the bohemian idleness of the Left Bank, for those who work are realistic and tough-minded, while those who remain idle are escapist and emotionally untidy. However, both workers and idlers, realists and escapists, all of them are physically or emotionally wounded: Jake is impotent, Brett is an adulterer, Cohn has a broken nose, Georgette has rotten teeth. Hence, both the Right Bank and the Left Bank are like Paris as a whole, wastelands of lost values and denatured love.

*Pyrenees** (pihr-ah-neez). Mountain range running along the border between France and Spain to which Jake takes his newly arrived American friend Bill Gorton on a five-day fishing trip. If Paris is hellish, the Spanish hamlets in which the men stay in the mountains are edenic. Hemingway depicts landscapes of breathtaking natural beauty in which nature and humanity coexist in a blessed ecological union, as when "fields of grapes touched the houses." It is an idyllic and healing experience, contrasting with that of Paris. Whereas Jake suffers from insomnia and cries in the night in Paris; in the Pyrenees, he sleeps soundly and dreamlessly.

*Roncesvalles** (rahn-sihs-VAH-yay; also known as Roncevaux). Spanish town in the Pyrenees whose medieval monastery Jake and Bill visit, along with the Englishman Wilson Harris whom they meet while fishing. The trip becomes almost a pilgrimage. For Roncesvalles is a relic of an epoch when friendship, valor, and combat had meaning. Indeed, it is the site of the French national epic, *The Song of Roland* (twelfth century), an epic that celebrates the true friendship of Roland and Oliver and the prowess of their small band of courageous companions who died fighting against a Moorish invasion, thereby buying time for Charlemagne to redeploy the forces that saved Europe for Christianity. At Roncevaux, even in modern times, Hemingway shows that friendship can have real worth and meaning. As the men part company, Harris gives Jake and Bill some fishing flies that he himself has tied—symbols of friendship valuable beyond anything that can be bought or sold.

*Pamplona** (pam-PLOH-nah). Town in northern Spain in which Jake's vacation with his friends reaches both its high and its low points. The men stay in the town during its famous annual Fiesta de San Fermín, which lasts for a week in July. During this nominally religious fiesta, there are daily bullfights preceded by the running of the bulls through the city streets, followed by spontaneous eruptions of inebriated parties.

Hemingway uses Pamplona's fiesta to highlight contrasts between meaningful and empty values. The bullfighter Pedro Romero represents the best values because, through work and artistry, he creates beauty out of violence, while risking his life in its creation. True fans of bullfighting, including Jake, know and understand this almost as if it were an article of religious faith.

The empty values are emblematized by Brett, who becomes a paganistic Circe-like figure attracting throngs of idle, pleasure-seeking party-goers. When Pedro (the worker-artist) and Brett (the partying idler) fall in love, Jake finds himself in a dilemma; he loves them both, yet knows that Brett's lifestyle will endanger Pedro's talent. However, through loyalty to his (impotent) love for Brett, Jake brings them together, only to be reviled by bullfight aficionados as a pimping traitor, and he is beaten up by Robert Cohn. Thus is the central drama of the novel played out in Pamplona.

*San Sebastian.** Spanish seaside resort town in which Jake recuperates after the debacle in Pamplona, There, he goes for a long swim that is renewing and almost baptismal in effect, making him feel as though he "could never sink." Afterward, he heeds Brett's request to meet her in Madrid after she breaks off from Pedro.

— *C. L. Chua*

THE SUNKEN BELL

Author: Gerhart Hauptmann (1862-1946)
Type of work: Drama
Type of plot: Fantasy

Time of plot: Indeterminate
First performed: 1896; first published, 1896 as *Die versunkene Glocke* (English translation, 1898)

This play is a tale of two incompatible worlds that meet and intersect on a single stage: the Christianized world of human society, symbolized by the village, and the world of the pagan imagination, populated by the elves and elements of German folklore, symbolized by the forested wilderness of the mountain slopes.

Mountains. Wilderness regions, untamed by human culture, where the supernatural still holds sway. Mountains have a dual symbolism in *The Sunken Bell*, as they also represent the heights of human aspiration and ambition. The elves and wood-sprites, who contrive such mischief as luring the vicar, the schoolmaster, and the barber deeper into the woods by calling for help in Heinrich's voice, are trying to preserve the first function and defeat the second. An uneasy amalgam of the two roles is forged by Heinrich's association with Rautendelein, but it cannot last.

Abandoned glassworks. Site of Heinrich's doomed attempt to found a better bell with the aid of dwarf labor supplied by Rautendelein. It is refitted with a smithy and a water-bearing earthenware pipe before being further extended into the body of the mountain.

Heinrich home. Coarse but comfortable domestic setting in which Magda awaits her lost husband, surrounded by cooking apparatus and Christian imagery; the latter includes engravings of work by the sixteenth century artist Adam Kraft.

Lake. Resting-place of Heinrich's first bell—a church bell—that falls into the water when a wood-sprite upsets the cart transporting it. The sunken bell, rung by the jealous Nickelmann, finally awakens Heinrich's conscience by evoking a vision of his children carrying a bucket of his wife's tears.

— *Brian Stableford*

THE SUNLIGHT DIALOGUES

Author: John Gardner (1933-1982)
Type of work: Novel
Type of plot: Psychological realism

Time of plot: Mid-1960's
First published: 1972

Although the cities in this novel are real, the events are not specific to those particular places. The novel contains a progression of locations that represent the downward slide of middle America, from what America was, to what America is becoming: the Indian reservation, last remnant of the continent's original civilization; the farmlands, once the backbone of society but now falling to waste; the small town, run-down and becoming as unsafe as the city. Finally there are the cities themselves, such as Buffalo, a small city that is beginning to experience racial tensions like larger cities, such as Chicago, the setting for the "modern morality" of drinking and orgies.

*Batavia (ba-TAY-vee-uh). Large town in western New York, near the Great Lakes. Author John Gardner was born in Batavia and spent most of his youth there. His novel *The Resurrection* (1966) creates a Batavia that geographically resembles the Batavia he knew. Unlike *The Resurrection*, whose protagonist leaves and returns to Batavia and contrasts his idealized memory of the town with the present reality of its changes, the central characters in *The Sunlight Dialogue* are life-long residents of Batavia. They notice its small changes gradually.

Batavia is a nondescript backdrop, familiar to most people even if they have never been to the town itself; it is a typical town of the mid-1960's. Batavia serves as the typical middle-class American town with typical middle-American virtues and vices, a perfect setting in which to explore the effect of the changing times on individual characters. The marks of the changes that are affecting the rest of the nation at this time become evident: an influx of new residents of different races and nationalities, a rise in violence and drinking, changes in labor and the work ethic. The town cannot cope with these changes; it is dying and decaying, as are many of its citizens in this novel.

Placing the novel's magical, mysterious plot in this realistic setting grounds it and makes it easier to relate to, though not entirely believable. Batavia faces a confusing and brilliant terror that is both new and familiar. The Sunlight Man is a former resident of Batavia whose return after an absence of fifteen years brings new questions to the town and its police chief. He personifies the questions he asks about religion, sex, race, and politics, and police chief Fred Clumly personifies Batavia's reaction to these questions. All those who interact with the Sunlight Man are forced to examine how they look at these important questions. Clumly, the representative of law and order, is unable to keep order, first in his own station, then in his town, and finally in his conception of the universe in general.

The farmlands surrounding Batavia are the last remnant of the agrarian culture that once dominated the country. Ben Hodge is the only main character who actually farms for a living, although many of the characters live, or once lived, on farms. The Hodges' history and downfall as a family is also Batavia's history and downfall.

Buffalo. Upstate New York city that although only a half hour distant from Batavia is, in the eyes of its inhabitants, worlds away. For the small-time crook Walter Benson (alias Walter Boyle), it is impossible to make a living in Buffalo, because its inhabitants are more cautious than those of a small town. He relies on the small-town sense of safety to provide him with the opportunities for stealing cash from people's homes.

While Benson cannot work in Buffalo, Will Hodge, Jr. cannot work in Batavia. He is comforted by the impersonal nature of the city, where it does not matter that he is the grandson of a congressman. Hodge views Batavia as a transitional place. Buffalo is the next evolutionary step beyond Batavia, and Hodge embodies this transition of values from small town to big city.

— *Shalom E. Black*

THE SUPPLIANTS

Author: Aeschylus (525/524-456/455 B.C.E.)
Type of work: Drama
Type of plot: Tragedy

Time of plot: Antiquity
First performed: Hiketides, 463 B.C.E.? (English translation, 1777)

Although the action of this play is set in the Greek city of Argos, the story of the daughters of Danaus and their suitors actually begins in Egypt, whence the "suppliants" have recently arrived, seeking asylum. Argos represents Athens on several levels, as all plays by Athenian dramatists are ultimately concerned with affairs of their own city.

Argos. Ancient Greek town in the eastern Peloponnese, three miles inland from the sea. Historically hostile to Sparta, Argos is allied with the great Greek city of Athens at the time this play is set. In Homeric times, Argos was the home of Diomedes and the center of Agamemnon's kingdom. In this play, it is ruled by King Pelasgus, whose name has maritime connections. The action takes place in the central business area, the agora, or in front of the royal palace, the traditional stage settings in Greek tragedies.

Argos functions in *The Suppliants* as a place of asylum, and, as such, represents Athens, where the concept of asylum was a cherished value of the radical democracy. Like all dramas by Athenian poets, this play transposes subjects of topical concern to suitable locations in mythical sources.

*Egypt.** Although a distant land across the Mediterranean, Egypt had long featured in Greek trade and history. Here, it is the strange "other" realm, where the bizarre story of the daughters of Danaus begins. The fifty suitors whom they are fleeing are the sons of Aegyptus, the hero after whom Egypt is named. In the play, Egypt embodies non-Greek customs and behavior, especially in the matter of marriage between sets of cousins.

— *David Larmour*

THE SURROUNDED

Author: D'Arcy McNickle (1904-1977)
Type of work: Novel
Type of plot: Social realism

Time of plot: Early twentieth century
First published: 1936

The title of this novel is an allusion to Sniél-emen (Mountains of the Surrounded), a reference to the Salish (or Flathead) Indians who live surrounded by mountains and by the encroachment of white settlers. The novel is set primarily on a ranch in western Montana and in a mission town close by. The setting determines the outcome of the novel in a conflict set up between the ranch/town/school and the natural setting of the mountains. Neither setting offers protagonist Archilde Leon any long-lasting refuge, as he is ultimately trapped by a destiny he cannot avoid.

St. Xavier. Mission town in western Montana's Sniél-emen Valley. It is also the name of the church and boarding school where Indian children are trained by Roman Catholic nuns and priests. Like the real Montana mission town of St. Ignatius, in which D'Arcy McNickle was born, St. Xavier is on the Flathead Indian Reservation and was created to convert the Indians to Christianity. Its church has an air of grandeur given to it by the hovels that are set against it. Both the church and the school play important roles in the novel as places in which Indians are educated in Western values, with various levels of success. Mike and Narcisse, nephews of Archilde Leon, run away from the school to hide out in the mountains.

Max Leon's ranch. Ranch built up by Archilde's father, a prosperous Spanish immigrant to Montana. Archilde develops a fondness for the ranch, even as he thinks of leaving it. He would like to be able to take with him its evening sounds and smells. Max's house is as well furnished as any white man's house, but Catherine, his Indian wife, lives apart from him in a nearby dirt-roofed cabin. Contrasts between these two houses reflects the divide between the white world and the Indian world. Although they are still married, Max and Catherine live differently and have different experiences. Max's life revolves around cultivation of his land and the profit he derives from it. Catherine, meanwhile, is undergoing a gradual, inexorable return to the beliefs and rituals of her Salish people.

Mountains. The Sniél-emen Valley is enclosed by the Bitter Root Mountains to the west and the Rocky Mountains to the east. These mountains have unspoiled natural areas that are still not tamed by the white man. Wanted by the law, Archilde's brother Louis escapes to the mountains with his stolen horses. The mountains are deemed outside the law, but the law encroaches even there, thus reinforcing the novel's theme that there is no escape.

Even the beauty of the mountains is described as a "magnificent barricade against the eastern sky." Max, a proud, stubborn man, feels humbled by them. Catherine longs to go hunting in the mountains, regarding them as a great release from the strictures of her life with Max. Archilde has a dimmer view, regarding the mountains as empty of life, meaning game. He is wrong about this, and the shooting of a deer in the mountains leads directly to the tragic killing of Louis by a game warden, who is in turn killed by Louis's mother, Catherine.

The freedom of the mountains is an illusion. Although Mike and Narcisse escape into the most remote reaches of the mountains at the novel's end, there is little hope that they can maintain any sort of long-term residence there.

Buffalo Creek. Indian dancing ground located a mile below St. Xavier, in a grove of willows and cottonwoods. There, Mike is healed of his boarding school-induced fears by leading the blind chief Modeste to the ceremony. Catherine's tepee, although a temporary shelter erected for the Indian dances, provides a sanctuary for Archilde after an encounter with his nemesis, Sheriff Quigley. In his mother's tepee, he finds security. This security, however meaningful, is temporary.

Modeste's ranch. Ranch of the blind Salish chief Modeste. In contrast to Max's ranch, it is a typical Indian homestead, where Archilde finds Modeste living in a ramshackle house. There, he meets Elise, Modeste's granddaughter, who brings joy and chaos into his life.

Badlands. Treeless, grassless, desolate area near the reservation to which Archilde goes to be alone and finds an aged mare and her colt. He tries to feed the mare and trim her mud-caked tail but ends up shooting her instead because she is incurably lame. The futility of good-hearted effort to help is underlined by the desolation of the badlands.

*Portland. Oregon city in which Archilde is attempting to make his living as a fiddle player before he returns to his father's ranch. Archilde regards Portland and other cities as attractive places where he can escape the doomed life of his tribe. When he is in the mountains, he longs for the "gleaming lights" of a city, any city.

— *Claire Keyes*

SWALLOW BARN: Or, A Sojourn in the Old Dominion

Author: John Pendleton Kennedy (1795-1870)
Type of work: Novel
Type of plot: Social realism

Time of plot: Early nineteenth century
First published: 1832

Called by one scholar the first important fictional treatment of Virginia life, this novel uses sketches and folk legends to re-create country life in Virginia in the early nineteenth century. Like Thomas Jefferson, John Pendleton Kennedy here examines how environment determines character and how property and place shape a person's values, expectations, and responsibilities.

Swallow Barn. Frank Meriwether's plantation home on the southern bank of the James River in Virginia's coastal tidewater region. Meriwether's home combines the rustic and the elegant, embodying the hospitality, industry, and self-restraint of its owners through the previous century. The house has ample space without being pretentious. Family and friends visiting the house enjoy riding, fishing, eating, conversation, and song, all influenced by surrounding nature. The house's inhabitants are favorably shaped by a type of environmental determinism similar to that described in the French writer Michel-Guillaume Jean de Crèvecœur's *Letters from an*

American Farmer (1782) and in Thomas Jefferson's *Notes on the State of Virginia* (1785). Frank Meriwether explains that country life prevents people from being hollow-hearted and insincere like people in the city. His wife, Lucretia, exhibits a pattern of industry necessitated by the demands of supervising a large household. The couple's daughters, Lucy and Victorine, make their way to womanhood in happy and guarded ignorance, avoiding ambition, vanity, and overstimulation.

In addition to leading to virtue and self-restraint, the country life also leads to the formation of the distinctive character of the Virginia cavalier. As the patriarch of

Swallow Barn, Frank Meriwether exemplifies the "cavalier" tradition of plantation owner as regent of his estate. By that tradition, a cavalier benignly rules over a hierarchy that descends from family to associates—such as a parson or overseer—to the slaves at the bottom. Meriwether explains that even though slavery is not an ideal institution, his own slaves benefit from kindness and the security of their lives on his estate. The cavalier figure directly stems from the isolation of the plantation and the nature of its labor-intensive economy. Further, the isolation of the plantation intensifies the authority of the patriarch, who is not apt to be contradicted. In one amusing illustration, a visiting cousin, Mark Littleton, describes the "under-talkers" who pick up on the "crumbs of wisdom" falling from a rich man's table and repeat everything Frank says. Generally, Littleton praises the conviviality, spaciousness, and regularity of life at Swallow Barn.

The Brakes. Estate adjoining Swallow Barn that belongs to the Tracys, who are close neighbors and friends of the Meriwethers and the Hazards. *Swallow Barn* partly focuses on the courtship of Ned Hazard and Bel Tracy, but the most significant event involving land concerns a forty-year-old dispute over the property bordering the Apple-Pie Creek. The thirty-acre tract is worthless swampland; however, Isaac Tracy spends considerable time and money fighting to reclaim part of it for the sake of his family's honor, as well as for the sheer sport of it. The dispute does little to tarnish the friendship of the families, but land is land and rights cannot be undermined. Land stands so firmly at the center of a family's honor that even the loss of swampland is important.

Woods. Forested area near Swallow Barn that provides a site for the imagination in Kennedy's exploration of other aspects of Virginia life through an intriguing mix of realism, romance, and folk legend. When Bel Tracy accidentally finds Ned and Mark acting and singing in the woods, the incident embarrasses Ned greatly. The woods also provide the setting for Bel's elaborate medieval fantasy centering on training her hawk to hunt. Ned pursues her escaped hawk throughout the countryside, retrieving the bird and presenting it to Bel as an act of chivalry.

The areas surrounding Swallow Barn also give rise to folk legend. Littleton records the story of blacksmith Mike Brown's encounter with the devil in the Goblin Swamp. In addition to fictional characters, the area seems to be peopled by ghosts of the past, particularly by past generations of family and retainers who have lived at Swallow Barn. These stories preserve the legends and history of tidewater Virginia.

The Quarter. Slave quarters of Swallow Barn. Kennedy's description of the slave hovels as "picturesque" leads into a lengthy discussion of the role of slavery in the South. The extended description of the cottage of elderly slave Lucy and the connected story of her son Abe sentimentalize slave life.

— *Ann M. Cameron*

THE SWISS FAMILY ROBINSON

Authors: Johann David Wyss (1743-1818) and Johann Rudolf Wyss (1782-1830)
Type of work: Novel
Type of plot: Adventure

Time of plot: Late eighteenth century
First published: Der Schweizerische Robinson, 1812-1827 (English translation, 1814, 1818, 1820)

The geography of this novel is hopelessly confused, presumably because it was written by two different people, who may have had different notions about where the story is set. However, the didactic enthusiasm of Johann David Wyss gave the fictional castaways such a cornucopia of natural resources that plausibility had already been sacrificed by the time his son took over. Because the story embodies a religious allegory as well as an argument in favor of an education in natural history, however, it is by no means entirely inappropriate that the castaways' home becomes a microcosm of the entire world.

Ship. Unnamed vessel on which the Robinsons are traveling when the novel opens. Readers are told little about the ship, except that it is a sizable sailing vessel with a substantial and varied cargo; its name and intended destination are carefully unmentioned. Its main function, while it remains stuck on a rock close to the shore of the island on which the Robinsons are marooned, is to provide the castaways with a rich source of useful materials, including food, tools, gunpowder, livestock, and a small boat.

Refuge Bay. Shore on which the family lands. The exact location of this bay is unspecified. It initially appears to be in a subtropical zone off the coast of either Central or South America because its native floras include coconut palms, potatoes, and sugarcane, while its faunas include penguins, agoutis, and margay cats—all species native to that part of the world. However, as the story continues, the varieties of flora and fauna on the island become improbably elaborate and extraordinarily extensive, eventually even including numerous creatures native to Africa, such as ostriches, hyenas, and a hippopotamus.

The Robinsons' decision to name their landfall Refuge Bay sets a pattern echoed in other place-names chosen by the castaway family. For example, the promontory on which they search unsuccessfully for the crew of their ship becomes the Cape of Disappointed Hope (a clear takeoff on Southern Africa's Cape of Good Hope), and the hill on which they make their survey they call the Observatory. Other names are improvised according to circumstance, with a careful simplicity that represents the determined utilitarianism of their approach to life. Thus, the place where they spend their first night becomes Tentbourne, the wetland inland of it Flamingo Swamp, and the stream where they glimpse the eponymous animal, Jackal Brook.

Falconeyrie. Family's principal dwelling, so called because it is constructed around the base and within the branches of a huge tree. Hastily contrived at first, this home-away-from-home and its surrounding estates are steadily improved, despite the occasional intervention of destructive storms.

Kingdom of Truth. Allegory constructed by the narrator on the family's first Sunday ashore (which, as good Calvinists, they observe meticulously). The Kingdom of Truth is also known as the Kingdom of Day, and is contrasted with the Kingdom of Vagueness, or Kingdom of Night. The capital of the Kingdom of Truth is Heaventown, but, in order to be worthy of life in that paradisal location, candidates for citizenship drawn from the Kingdom of Vagueness must serve a probationary period on an uninhabited island called Earthland. Unfortunately, the candidates forget their goal before arriving in Earthland, which results in some of them failing in their duty of diligent labor and many of them fearing the arrival of the fleet that will come to their rescue—whose Admiral Death has an ironclad flagship named *The Grave*. This symbolic description of human life has a particular reference to the family's predicament; their island, too, is a microcosm of the world, and their duty is not merely to survive in the hope of rescue but to cultivate the land and exercise technological mastery of their environment, demonstrating their worthiness with their achievements.

Grotto. Natural cavern lined with mineral salts that is exposed to view when the Robinsons use gunpowder to clear a way through inconvenient rocks near Tentbourne. The Grotto becomes a secondary dwelling during the rainy seasons, one that contains storerooms and a workshop, as well as a source of useful substances.

Highpeak. Hill on which the family's fourth settlement—after Tentbourne, Falconeyrie, and the Grotto—is established. The hut they erect there they name Woodstead. Although the family is not large enough to require four separate dwellings, the steady expansion of their petty realm is a key example of their steadfast commitment to the Protestant work ethic.

Stony Arabia. Casual name that the Robinsons give to the inhospitable region that makes inland journeys difficult for them, even when they have become securely established in the coastal strip. This region is reached via the Causeway, which extends away from Boarsford. Although it is a desolate plain, it is not completely lifeless, as it is more suggestive of South America's Patagonian plain than the exceptionally arid Arabian desert; however, it figures into the story at the moment that geographical confusion rapidly intensifies, presumably because the second author has stepped into the narrator's shoes to replace his predecessor.

Pearl Bay. Destination of the family's most adventurous journey in their "cajak" (although the boat in question does not much resemble a kayak). It takes them past

Nautilus Bay and Cape Snubnose, allowing them to discover Churchcliff, Otter Reef, Bird's-Nest Bay, and—eventually—the Isle of Gladness, where they rescue the young English castaway, Jenny Montrose.

New Switzerland. Name given to the family's little Refuge Bay colony after contact with civilization is reestablished. Its location on the world map remains slightly mysterious, although Jenny Montrose's assertion that she was en route from Batavia (on the north coast of the Indonesian island of Java) to New Guinea when her ship went down moves the novel's apparent setting from Central or South America to the other side of the world. Moreover, an encounter with the British navy confirms that, wherever the Robinsons were to start with, they now seem to be on an island in the Banda Sea, within the Indonesian archipelago. Although the elder Johann Wyss might not have approved of his successor's failure to pick up on all the clues indicating that the family was supposed to be near South America, there is a certain strange symmetry in placing a sea-surrounded New Switzerland on the other side of the world from landlocked Old Switzerland.

— *Brian Stableford*

SYBIL: Or, The Two Nations

Author: Benjamin Disraeli (1804-1881)
Type of work: Novel
Type of plot: Political realism

Time of plot: 1837-1843
First published: 1845

The subtitle of this novel illuminates the centrality of its symbolic geography. England is shown as possessing two separate geographies: one, aristocratic, traditional, well-heeled, and powerful; the other, disorganized, popular, powerless, and disease-ridden. These two geographies exist in both rural and urban settings, particularly in the manufacturing districts of the north of England and in London, the capital and seat of political power.

*London. As in Elizabeth Gaskell's similar novel, *North and South* (1854-1855), the London of *Sybil* is not systematically portrayed. However, a contrast is set up between areas of power and those of powerlessness. The former include the Houses of Parliament, the prime minister's residence, and such politically influential meeting places as men's clubs and the houses of aristocratic women who see themselves as power-brokers. The latter are places where the Chartists, outsiders to London, find temporary residence on the fringes. The Temple, where "Baptist" Hatton has an office, is a sort of middle-ground, a place where power can be transferred in a way that a reactionary Parliament refuses to.

Mowbray Castle. Modern edifice in the Gothic style, built on the newly purchased Mowbray estate by the River Mowe, where it has extensive woods and parklands. The castle is built by the first man to hold the title of Lord Fitz-Warene—a newly created title that is eventually shown to be false, as the castle should belong to Sybil Gerard's family. Meanwhile, the estate's wealth is greatly increased by the prosperity of the nearby town of Mowbray. However, at the end of the novel, the castle is burned down by a mob of disgruntled workers, and the title reverts to its rightful owner.

Mowbray. Town that was originally a village on Mowbray estate before growing rapidly during the Industrial Revolution. Although the town's central parts reflect its new prosperity, it also has wretched slums in its suburbs, and shantytowns beyond. Disraeli symbolically shows the result of the division of rich and poor by contrasting the parish church, administered by the philanthropic Reverend Aubrey St. Lys, himself an aristocrat, with the Cat and Fiddle inn kept by "Chaffing Jack." The latter has a genuine working-class culture but no spiritual values as such.

Mowedale. Peaceful and still rural valley of the Mowe River. Disraeli uses this space between town and castle to show the possibility of a middle way, particularly by showing Mr. Trafford's model factory, whose workers live in a properly built village on site. The benign influence of this environment is able to withstand the rioting mob at the end. Also in this space stands Mowbray Convent, a center of good works and spiritual influence, especially for Sybil. Gerard's cottage, and for a while, Charles Egremont's, also exist in this space of enlightenment.

Marney Abbey. Former church that is now the home of the wealthy landowner Lord Marney, Egremont's older brother. The abbey is located on the side of the county opposite that of Mowbray Castle and represents another aristocratic center, the place where Egremont's family has its ancestral seat. The abbey's lands were originally church lands, but the old abbey lies in ruins. Significantly, this is where Egremont meets Sybil, showing the need to reach back into the past to find a true foundation for future union. The new abbey was built in 1610 and constantly upgraded to become a comfortable house in a well-wooded park. However, Lord Marney shows no concern for his tenants, resisting all change unless personally profitable. He is thus unfit to continue the line, symbolized by an accidental death and the inheriting of the title by Egremont.

Wodgate. Large village in a mining area. Because its land belongs to no one, its inhabitants enjoy squatters' rights. The village is self-regulated, under the leadership of master workmen who rule through fear and brutality. Its center is aptly called Hell-house Yard.

Disraeli sees this village, where labor reigns supreme, as the ugliest spot in England. The leading master becomes the "bishop" of this utterly pagan town. It is from here the mob emerges to hijack the Chartist reform movement.

Mining village. Unnamed village located ten miles closer to Mowbray than Wodgate that has no real organization, typical of the unplanned and unchecked industrial growth of the time. Child labor is rife, as is social injustice, especially in the nonpayment of wages in cash. These malpractices, Disraeli shows, are what is likely to bring revolution to England.

— *David Barratt*

A TALE OF A TUB

Author: Jonathan Swift (1667-1745)

Type of work: Satire

First published: A Tale of a Tub: To Which Is Added

an Account of a Battle Between the Ancient and Modern Books in St. James's Library; and the Mechanical Operation of the Spirit, 1704

The battlefield for this carefully controlled attack on scholarly pedantry, on foolish hack writing, and on empty religious enthusiasm is primarily the mental geography of scholarly controversy over methodology and practice. Nevertheless, Jonathan Swift makes this intellectual battlefield concrete by linking it to London, Oxford, and Protestant Europe of the sixteenth and seventeenth centuries.

Grub Street. Minor district of London near the northwest edge of the old walled city in the vicinity of Moorfields. Daniel Defoe, who was a master of popular writing at the time, lived nearby, and the region became the symbol for the new commercial writing that supported writers who did not have noble patrons. Swift satirizes these writers as Grubaean Sages. Since Covent Garden, as well as the merchant centers of the city, are close by in greater London, these hack writers of Grub Street can also be attacked as prostitutes of literature, associated with the brothels in Covent Garden and as superficially commercial in their work in other ways as well. Although Swift himself created some brilliant hack writing which was very popular, he took great pride in the support he enjoyed from his noble patron Sir William Temple.

Gresham College. Educational institution located in the grand London mansion of Sir Thomas Gresham, who bequeathed the house to the city; a group of practical "Greshamists" started the scientific group that became the Royal Society of London. Partly because of its location in Gresham House and hence its commercial associations with Moorfields and with the city, the new science of the Royal Society comes under attack by Swift for its airy superficiality and its beating of the tub of self-promotion.

Bethlehem Hospital (Bedlam). Government lunatic asylum at Moorfields. Continuing his case for guilt by association of location deep in the center of greater London, Swift can attack both the hack writers and the new scientists as insane Bedlamites. Throughout most of the eighteenth century the public could pay admission to watch the institution's inmates.

Royal Library. Library in St. James Palace in London's West End in which the battle of the books, the appended narrative to the main tale, is fought. Not a great deal of elegance is achieved, however, by moving the action farther out, although Swift does articulate the ancient and modern theme most clearly in this shorter and simpler narrative. Nevertheless, the combatants are insects, so the satiric attacks on small grubbiness in writing continues despite the royal location.

Moor Park. Elegant country estate of Swift's patron Sir William Temple. Swift lived on the estate for a time in the last decade of Temple's life, and he conceived this text as he followed the heated debate over ancient as opposed to modern writing in which Temple played a role as essayist and translator. The universities were the real seat of the debate, and so Swift's move to satirize and to trivialize the debate is effectively done by locating it close to commercial London. The ideal of Moor Park and of genuine intellectual thinking serves

as the measure of the satiric attacks on superficial modernity.

*Leyden (LI-dehn). City in the Netherlands where Swift's attack takes aim at the superficiality of religious enthusiasm, especially that expressed by the sects of Protestant fanatics that were not Anglican. He includes Martin Luther in this group, but his prime whipping boy is an Anabaptist named Jan Buckholdt. He was a tailor and known as "Jack of Leyden" during the religious debates that had become particularly bloody battles by Swift's time. The text makes wonderful use of images of superficial coats sewn by such an enthusiastic tailor that the enemies of Swift suffer from the various characterizations of being airbags, insects, and prostitutes of ideas but also from being located in the grubby low countries of Europe, which were so similar to the commercially tainted centers of London. The many digressions in Swift's text and, perhaps, some of its airiness make locations difficult to pin down. However, that may be a key point of the satire; the ancients possessed a more solid sense of place.

— *Donald M. Hassler*

THE TALE OF GENJI

Author: Murasaki Shikibu (c. 973-c. 1014)
Type of work: Novel
Type of plot: Romance
Time of plot: Tenth century

First published: Genji monogatari, c. 1004 (English translation, 1925-1933; unexpurgated and annotated translation, 2001)

This novel's central focus is Japan's imperial city of Kyōto, to which noble and illustrious characters go to enjoy life and indulge in their various romantic pastimes. Kyōto's elaborately described Imperial Palace dominates the city as much as the emperor dominates his aristocratic society. Nature is appreciated, but mostly in a domesticated form. City residences sport elaborate gardens, and day trips to the countryside are popular.

*Kyōto (kyoh-toh). Japanese city in west-central Hōnshu, northeast of Osaka, that was the imperial capital from 794 through 1869. Protected by forested hills and drawing its drinking water from the clear Kamo River, the city has pleasant surroundings that make it a worthy dwelling place for the imperial household during the novel's medieval Heian period. The aesthetic pleasures of the place are deeply appreciated by the characters, foremost of whom is the refined but illegitimate son of the emperor, Prince Genji. The characters draw inspiration from Kyōto and try to build exquisite dwellings that will add to the city's many splendid residences and grace and stimulate the lives of their magnificent inhabitants. To be fully away from the city, living in other towns or remote rural dwellings, is seen as a form of unfortunate exile.

During the time of the novel, the imperial city was laid out in a strict grid pattern expressing the imposition of human order over a natural location. In line with ancient Chinese prescriptions for an emperor's proper dwelling place, which Japan's aristocracy adopted for its own use, the imperial palace stands at the center of the northern edge of the city. Facing south in his great ceremonial hall, the emperor beholds a city neatly divided into two equal parts. To the east, at his left hand, and symbolized by a cherry tree in the garden outside his hall, is the Left City, Genji's favorite haunting place. At his right hand, to the west and symbolized by an orange tree, is the Right City.

This geographical division extended into society. The imperial government is divided into Left (eastern) and Right (western) factions, and Genji's strongest opponent is the minister of the Right, who manages to have Genji temporarily exiled. The two geographically aligned factions primarily serve the interests of their aristocratic members and do not reflect differing political views.

*Suma. Desolate stretch of coastline west of Kyōto, ringed by mountains to the north and facing Japan's Inland Sea. (Suma is now part of the city of Kobe.) The bleakness of Suma derived from its geographical distance to Kyōto, the absence of societal entertainments, and the acrid smoke from the fires of saltmakers on the shore. Historically, it was a place for exiles who ran afoul of the court, and once Genji has to follow this pattern. After a horrific storm typical of the location, Genji dreams that his dead father wants him to leave the dreadful place, and he gladly acts on this.

*Akashi. City five miles west of Suma, and with similar geographical features, that lies outside the emperor's home provinces and is therefore in a different political world. Genji's spirits revive at Akashi, and he falls in love with a woman who bears him a daughter after he is allowed back to Kyōto.

Rokujo. Fictional mansion of Genji's estate, finished during his thirty-fifth year. It is symbolic of Genji's return to good fortune and high social esteem. The elaborately described compound on the sixth street of Kyōto has always fascinated Japanese readers as the perfect example of a nobleman's appropriate dwelling place. More

beautiful and aesthetically balanced than any real surviving medieval mansion, Rokujo consists of a tastefully built and decorated main house, in two wings of which Genji puts up his primary lovers in grand style, and an exquisite garden. The garden has a fishing pavilion, artificial lake, and a brook—all inviting guests and inhabitants to dwell on the splendid yet transitory beauty of nature and human life, a topic essential to medieval Japanese literature.

*Uji. Typical Japanese provincial town, located south of Kyōto, from which it is reached by a bridge over the Uji River. Provincial towns such as Uji always appear somewhat forlorn and isolated in the intensely metropolitan *The Tale of Genji*, where any place beyond a day trip from Kyōto inspires feelings of loneliness. The fact that the primary romantic activities of Genji's son Niou and his rival Kaoru revolve around three sisters in this town, rather than taking place in the capital, indicates how mundane the world has become with the passing of Genji's generation.

— *R. C. Lutz*

A TALE OF TWO CITIES

Author: Charles Dickens (1812-1870)
Type of work: Novel
Type of plot: Historical

Time of plot: French Revolution
First published: 1859

The narrative in this novel is equally divided between English and French settings, in which common people suffer under the brutal arrogance and irrationality of the Old Regime. The threat from the brewing French Revolution can be heard across the English Channel as footsteps in Soho Square, echoing events that may come to pass in England.

Tellson & Co. English merchant bank with branches in London and Paris. The bank's London office is dark, ugly, and staffed by old-fashioned bankers. Dickens describes the bank as resembling both a prison and a grave. As the oldest bank in England, Tellson's is a symbol not only of English economic dominance but also of resistance to change. The bank's London office is located "in the shadow" of Temple Bar, a large stone gateway which was used until 1780 to display on spikes the heads of executed criminals. The London office becomes a

place of refuge for French aristocrats fleeing the violence of the revolution. In the yard of the bank's Paris branch, the mob sharpens its weapons on a large grindstone, while the blood of already-executed victims drips from their clothes.

For Dickens, England is peaceful only on the exterior. Like France, it suffers from cruelty and widespread oppression of the majority of its population. The Old Regime in Europe comprises an upper class resistant to change and high-handed kings attempting to maintain the status quo. Dickens models Tellson's Bank on Child and Company (founded in the seventeenth century on 1 Fleet Street and Thelusson's Bank in Paris, in which a major financial adviser to King Louis XVI named Jacques Necker once worked).

*Saint Antoine (sah[n]-tahn-twahn). Poor and densely populated district in Paris's eastern suburb, where the attack on the Bastille takes place. It is an emotionally charged setting in which actions of violence and vengeance take place during the revolution. Descriptions of streets and buildings in Saint Antoine take on the character of the residents. It is at the main fountain in St. Antoine that a child is accidentally hit by the speeding coach of the marquis, who offers a few coins as a compensation for the child's life.

Defarge's Wine Shop. Parisian wine shop which for Dickens is the eye of the storm that becomes the French Revolution. The shop serves as a meeting place for the leaders of the revolution. It is in front of the wine shop that one of the most memorable scenes in the novel takes place. A broken casket of wine results in neighborhood people rushing to salvage the precious drops of wine from the casket with their earthenware mugs, thus establishing not only an intoxicating brotherhood of blood but also one of wine.

*Bastille. Massive fortification in Paris that served as an armory and a prison for the four centuries preceding the French Revolution. Although it houses only four prisoners in 1789, the Bastille stands as a gargantuan symbol of the oppression of the Old Regime. In Cell 105, North Tower (a fictional creation), Dr. Manette languishes for eighteen years. As the revolution begins, a great firestorm surrounds the Bastille. Dickens borrows from Thomas Carlyle's history *The French Revolution* (1837) in describing the storming of the Bastille in minute detail. It was at the Bastille that Defarge finds the letter from Dr. Manette that will later be used to condemn Darnay.

Château St. Evrémonde (shah-toh sah[n]-tev-ray-MOHND). Sumptuous but heavily stoned mansion of the marquis. The villagers meet at the fountain at the château, and their rural poverty is stressed by Dickens. The descriptions of the stony home symbolize the coldness and inhumanity of the French aristocracy. The decadence of the marquis' salon, at the château and in Paris, stands in stark contrast to the poverty of the general pop-

ulace. It is the château life that Charles Darnay, the nephew of the marquis, rejects. Ultimately, after the assassination of the marquis, the château is destroyed by fire. Water boils in the fountain, followed by molten lead and iron; fountains symbolized life and also death for Dickens.

*Beauvais (boh-VAY). French province that was the center of the fourteenth century serf revolt against the aristocracy. The revolt was bloodily suppressed. The Defarges originate from Beauvais, and their blood lust is an attempt to gain retribution for historical crimes. Beauvais, which is thirty miles north of Paris, is also the hometown of Dr. Manette. It is in Beauvais, a symbol of the rural violence of the French Revolution, where Darnay is almost killed by an infuriated mob.

*Dover Road. Filled with ruts and clouded with steamy mist and fog, this access road to the ferry leaving Dover for France is a dangerous road to travel. Dickens uses it as a symbol of the rampant lawlessness still a part of England. Shooter's Hill, near the road, is a thickly wooded rise that is the scene of many robberies by highwaymen. The hill was so named because of the many armed robberies that took place in the vicinity. In the novel, Dickens discusses many roads, all of which have metaphorical significance. In short, Dickens attempts to portray England as similar to France in burglaries, highway robberies, and exploitation of the general population by the elite minority.

*Soho Square. London neighborhood that is the site of the Manettes' secure and peaceful household, which is located in a fashionable square laid out in 1681. It is here that Lucie hears footsteps in a rainstorm, a symbol of the threat of revolution within England. For Dickens, although England is just across the English Channel, it is relatively secure compared to events on the Continent.

*La Force. Prison used during the French Revolution for the proceedings of the Revolutionary Tribunal courts. La Force was the scene of the 1792 September Massacres, in which more than 1,100 accused counter-revolutionaries were massacred. The killing of prisoners is meant by Dickens as an ironic contrast to the saving of prisoners at the Bastille, three years earlier. It is at La Force (and three other prisons) that Dr. Manette tends to the medical needs of inmates.

— *Irwin Halfond*

TALES OF ISE

Author: Unknown, attributed to Ariwara no Narihira (825-880)
Type of work: Short fiction
Type of plot: Love

Time of plot: Ninth century
First published: Ise monogatari, tenth century, based on *Narihira kashū*, ninth century (English translation, 1968)

Place defines the emotions which the characters feel and express in more than two hundred poems of this classic text of medieval Japanese literature. City life is joyful, erotic, and charged with a desire to take in as many of life's finer pleasures as possible. The nearby countryside yields inspiring vistas of exquisite natural beauty; yet life in the far provinces reflects cruel exile from the vivacity of urban aristocratic society.

***Ise** (ee-say). City, in province of the same name, that is the site of the great Ise Shrine which dramatically faces the Pacific Ocean at the southern tip of Nagoya Bay, almost in the middle of the Japan's central island of Honshū. According to legend, it was at Ise that the human Amaterasu gave birth to a child conceived with a god, founding Japan's imperial family. An imperial Virgin served as High Priestess at the Inner Shrine. The central episodes of the novel, now placed in the middle of the narrative, tell of Narihira's one legendary night of love with the Virgin of Ise, Princess Tenshi.

Leading a hunting expedition through the rich forests of Ise with the task of returning game birds fit for the table at the nearby imperial capital, the aristocratic poet had been allowed to room at the Virgin's fine residence at Ise, built in the classic wood-and-rice paper style of medieval Japanese architecture. On the second night, while he was resting on his futon atop tatami mats and looking out at the moonlight in the garden before his open screen door, the Virgin appeared with a little girl. Delighted, Narihira led the Princess into his room. Yet she departed at two-thirty in the morning, and his official duties prevented any second meeting. The erotic meets the sacred at Ise, and Narihira's tryst echoes the earlier love between a god and a human at the same location.

***Nara.** Traditional capital surrounded by the picturesque Kasuga Plain and the Kasugayama hills, located southwest of Tokyo, that Emperor Kammu left in 784. Outside the city lay the hunting estates of the noblemen. In the first episode of the novel, an aristocratic hunter spots two beautiful local sisters. Cleverly, he tries to seduce them with a poem inspired by the camouflage pattern of his hunting robe, which uses dyes from local plants. Appealing to the ironic connection of his clothes to their village, he tries to impress the young women.

***Nagaoka** (nah-gah-o-kah). City north of Tokyo, lying below the harsh, wooded, and steep Mikuni Mountains, close to the Sea of Japan, where the emperor settled after leaving Nara. The area around Nagaoka was still relatively rustic. In episode 58, court ladies tease a nobleman for preferring to oversee his rice harvest, rather than wooing them. When the man retreats into his house, the ladies challenge him with a poem attributed to Lady Ise. However, the man does not come outside, even though the ladies imply his house is demon-haunted.

***Heian-kyo (Kyōto).** In 794, the imperial dynasty moved to Heian-kyo, the contemporary Kyōto, which gave its name to their reign. Surrounded to the north and south by the Eastern Hills, in a valley traversed by the Kamo river, the city is site of many episodes. Within the wooden mansions, splendid gardens, far-flung palaces, and crowded streets, the nobles lead an active social life. Here, they conduct secret passionate affairs, host drinking parties and witty poetry competitions, and draw romantic inspiration from the tamed nature of their gardens. In Episode 81, Narihira admires a minister's miniature imitation of scenic Shiogama Bay, in northeastern Japan, built within his private gardens.

***Provinces near the capital.** Trips to scenic spots were popular pastimes of the aristocracy. Nunobiki Falls, with a drop of two hundred feet across fifty feet of rock surface, inspires the travelers to contrast the beauty and power of nature with the vanity of human efforts, in Episode 87.

Harbors and pleasant shorelines, like the beach of Sumiyoshi, situated west of Kyōto facing the Bay of Osaka, in Episode 68, move the poet. Even though he knows that fall will come soon, he enjoys his spring day at the beach. Given the poet's feeling of nature's longevity, it is sadly ironic that his admired beach no longer exists, due to human land reclamation.

Remote provinces. Legend has it that Narihira was banished to the eastern provinces after having abducted an imperial princess. In Episode 9, he is disconsolate at seeing snow-capped Mount Fuji, because the mountain seems indifferent to the poet's plight.

Other episodes tell of husbands and wives tearfully taking leave of each other, when one has to move to a faraway location. For the Heian aristocracy, the splendors of the countryside were best enjoyed in the knowledge that a return to the capital was assured.

— *R. C. Lutz*

THE TALISMAN

Author: Sir Walter Scott (1771-1832)
Type of work: Novel
Type of plot: Historical

Time of plot: Twelfth century
First published: 1825

Much of the romance of this highly romantic tale derives from its setting, the Holy Land during the time of the Crusades. The novel employs all the exotic trappings of the Middle East: the burning sands of Syria, an oasis in the desert, a holy hermit's rock cavern, a voluptuous hidden chapel, and the camps of the European crusaders and the Muslim Saracens—both of whom are romanticized.

Diamond of the Desert. Natural fountain amid solitary groups of palm trees and a bit of verdure, located in the region of the Dead Sea. At this oasis, Kenneth of the Couching Leopard and the Saracen Sheerkohf, the Lion of the Mountain, refresh themselves after confronting each other in an inconclusive duel in the desert that gives them a mutual respect for each other. Sir Kenneth is supposedly a poor Scottish knight, who as a mere adventurer has joined the crusaders in Palestine. Emir Sheerkohf (called Ilderim by the hermit of Engaddi) is supposedly a prince descended from the Seljook family of Kurdistan, the same family that produced the Saracen ruler Saladin. However, in this novel, several characters are not what they initially represent themselves to be. In the final two chapters, the Diamond of the Desert becomes the center of Saladin's encampment.

Cave of Theodorick of Engaddi. Home of the hermit Theodorick, which is hidden among sharp eminences in a range of steep and barren hills near the Dead Sea. Theodorick (called Hamako by Sheerkohf) is a religious recluse who dresses in goatskins. In chapter 18, he reveals his true identity—Alberick Mortemar, of royal blood. He does constant penance for having corrupted a nun and causing her suicide. As the Scottish knight and Saracen spend a night in Theodorick's cave, Theodorick leads Sir Kenneth through a secret door and up a staircase into a magnificent chapel while Sheerkohf sleeps.

Chapel of the Convent of Engaddi. Church hewn from solid rock to which Theodorick takes Sir Kenneth. The structure features six columns and their groined roofs, revealing the work of the ablest architects of the day. Brilliantly lit by silver lamps hanging from silver chains, the chapel is redolent with the scent of the richest perfumes. At its upper and eastern end stands an altar before a gold curtain of Persian silk. The curtain is mysteriously drawn aside to reveal a reliquary of silver and ebony. It is opened and displays a large piece of wood emblazoned with the words "Vera Crux" (true cross). Sir Kenneth hears a choir of female voices singing "Gloria Patri" and the sound of a small silver bell, then sees four beautiful boys serving as acolytes, followed by six Carmelite nuns and six apparent novices. As the procession moves three times around the chapel, one of the novices twice drops rosebuds at the feet of the kneeling Kenneth. The nun is, in truth, Lady Edith Plantagenet, kinswoman of King Richard I of England and Sir Kenneth's courtly lover. She, along with Queen Berengaria, has come to the chapel on a pilgrimage on behalf of the king's health.

Crusader camp. Huge tent city in the wilderness, housing the massed armies of the Christian knights—the English, French, Austrians, and others. Due to constant dissension among the European princes, the Crusade is collapsing, and England's king, Richard coeur de lion, the effective commander in chief of the crusaders, is confined to his pavilion, ill with a potentially fatal fever "peculiar to Asia." Saladin sends a physician, Adonbec el Hakim, to minister to his noble adversary. Hakim administers an apparently magical elixir—the talisman of the title—which cures the King.

Saladin's camp. Saracen army encampment at the once lonely site, the Diamond of the Desert. The large pavilions are vividly colored and bear gilded ornaments and embroidered silken flags. Here, more identities are revealed. Emir Sheerkohf and Adonbec el Hakim, it seems, were but disguises for Saladin himself, King of Egypt and Syria (the Saracens were originally nomadic tribesmen of Syria and nearby regions). Sir Kenneth, earlier disgraced and forced for a time to disguise himself as a Nubian slave, reclaims his honor by vanquishing King Richard's archenemy, Conrade, Marquis of Montserrat. King Richard then announces that Kenneth is actually David Earl of Huntingdon, Prince Royal of Scotland. Thus, he is of high birth and may marry the Lady Edith. Somehow, these twists of plot seem more plausible in twelfth century Palestine than they might in a less exotic setting.

— *Patrick Adcock*

TALLEY FAMILY SAGA

Author: Lanford Wilson (1937-   )
Type of work: Drama
Type of plot: Psychological realism
Time of plot: July 4, 1944, *Talley's Folly* and *Talley and Son*; July 4/5, 1977, *Fifth of July*

First performed: Fifth of July, 1978, first published, 1978, revised, 1982; *Talley's Folly*, 1979, first published, 1979; *Talley and Son*, 1981 (as *A Tale Told*), first published, 1986

The midwestern setting of the Talley plays represents a basic conflict in modern American society. Lanford Wilson cares deeply about family and tradition as is experienced in small midwestern towns like Lebanon, but he is wary of the small-mindedness to which they sometimes lead.

*Lebanon.** Small south-central Missouri town where the Talley family lives and where Lanford Wilson was born. The Talleys have lived and prospered in Lebanon for generations, and their well-being is firmly grounded in tradition and the status quo. As in other Wilson plays, the Midwest in these plays is peopled with somewhat narrow-minded characters who believe in the American dream. An outsider like Matt Friedman in *Talley's Folly* threatens the family's stability, because he brings new ideas, experiences, and expectations that challenge the foundation of their society. Talleys who venture outside

Lebanon also bring danger. Because Timmy is killed in the Pacific during World War II, the family business cannot be handed down as expected in *Talley and Son*. Ken and June, of *Fifth of July*, have attended Berkeley and nearly lost their regard for the family and the family home. It is only when Ken returns to the Talley home, and is reunited with his Aunt Sally, who never left, that he comes to understand the importance of family ties.

Boathouse. Elaborate and whimsical Victorian structure on the Talley property, the "folly" of *Talley's Folly*. The boathouse was built by Sally's Uncle Whistler, who also built the town's bandstand. The folly is not only the setting for Sally and Matt's encounters, but also a representation of what Matt asks Sally to do: to dare to create something unusual and dreamlike in a town that does not understand such things. The fact that Sally is the only member of her family who still visits the boathouse makes it possible for her to meet Matt there undetected, and shows that she is unlike the rest of her family in being able to appreciate the structure's quirky beauty.

— *Cynthia A. Bily*

TAMAR

Author: Robinson Jeffers (1887-1962)
Type of work: Poetry
Type of plot: Psychological

Time of plot: World War I
First published: 1924

This poem is set in the unspoiled coastal region of Big Sur, a forested region along the coast of Northern California whose extreme beauty induces tragic error in human behavior. The narrative events of the poem draw on the biblical story of the ill-fated Tamar.

***Carmel.** Northern California town near Point Lobos, the location of the fictional Cauldwell ranch. Robinson Jeffers lived in Carmel while he wrote this poem. He placed many of his later works in the area, repeatedly emphasizing his belief that its wild environment influenced its inhabitants.

Cauldwell ranch. Pastures and an isolated family residence overlooking the Pacific Ocean. In the first segment of the poem, the drunken son Lee, traveling home in the dark from Monterey, falls from his horse and tumbles down a steep cliff, where he lies unconscious on the beach, nearly drowning in the incoming tide.

***Carmel region.** After his recovery, Lee reforms, but as he rides through the springtime beauty of the high pastures, he sharply misses his sister Tamar. The same earthy senses overcome Tamar, and later, while out riding with Lee, she seduces him. The narrator suggests that the two were driven to incest by the forces of the "wild rock coast" with its "beaten trees" or by the "wing-subduing immense earth-ending water." Tamar soon discovers a family history of incest. Fearing exposure of her relations with Lee, she rides to meet her old suitor Will under the Mal Paso Bridge. Although she seeks help, Tamar is prey to the wild forces that drive her. As the fall season commences and local men set brush and pastures afire in order to cleanse the land, the Cauldwell family moves toward its own fiery destruction.

— *Margaret A. Dodson*

TAMBURLAINE THE GREAT

Author: Christopher Marlowe (1564-1593)
Type of work: Drama
Type of plot: Tragedy

Time of plot: Fourteenth century
First performed: part 1, c. 1587; part 2, 1587; first
    published, 1590

Christopher Marlowe's blank-verse drama about the Scythian shepherd-turned-conqueror Tamburlaine is set in regions that stretch across Asia and encompass the empires of Persia, Turkey, Syria, and North Africa. However, Tamburlaine's military ambitions and fierce cruelty have few boundaries. Marlowe creates a global stage on which Tamburlaine's thirst for power and glory lead him toward an ultimately tragic fate.

Asia. Largest continent on Earth, stretching from the Black Sea in the west to the China Sea in the east, and from the Arctic Circle in the north to the Indian Ocean in the south. *Tamburlaine the Great* dramatizes the rise and fall of the historical conqueror Timur, who reclaimed much of Asia from the Mongols in the late fourteenth century. The location of some of the world's most powerful dynasties, Asia represents the ultimate achievement for Tamburlaine, who is driven to conquer the world.

Royal courts. Marlowe sets most of the action in *Tamburlaine the Great* in the imperial court of Persia, and in the courts of the king of Arabia, the king of Jerusalem, the governor of Damascus, the king of Hungary, and the governor of Babylon, among others. The courts are the scenes of political duplicity, at which characters boast about their strength and plot the overthrow of their enemies. They are also places where the specter of Tamburlaine continually gains substance, as his military conquests bring him closer to controlling all of Asia. Throughout the play, Marlowe uses court settings to reveal the human and political dimensions of his charac-

ters. He does not stage the many battle scenes in the play. Rather, he emphasizes the forces that shape his character's decisions and the consequences of those decisions.

Tamburlaine's camps. As he moves through Asia, conquering Persia, Damascus, Turkey, and North Africa, Tamburlaine is generally depicted throughout the play in his camps near the sites of his many military victories. Marlowe portrays Tamburlaine's valor as a soldier and his vicious cruelty as a tyrant, not on battlefields, but rather in the personal settings of his military camps. There, Tamburlaine gives way to the mitigating influence of Zenocrate, the daughter of the Soldan of Egypt, with whom he is in love.

In the second part of Marlowe's play, the death of Zenocrate removes the last restraints on Tamburlaine's lust for blood and power. He then demonstrates his brutality by humiliating and murdering his enemies, who include his own son Calyphas, whom he kills. As with the imperial courts of the kings of Asia, Tamburlaine's camp provides an intimate portrait of the forces that contribute to his rise and fall as the king of Persia.

— *Glenn Canyon*

THE TAMING OF THE SHREW

Author: William Shakespeare (1564-1616)
Type of work: Drama
Type of plot: Comedy

Time of plot: Sixteenth century
First performed: c. 1593-1594; first published, 1623

The "taming" of this play's title, part of the play-within-the-play, takes place in Padua, while the story is actually staged in an English country house by traveling players. The introductory scenes, laced with thematic motifs of performance and transformations of identity, class status, and gender, firmly entrench the play in the social realities of English rural life in the late sixteenth century.

Warwickshire. County in England's Midlands area, which contains William Shakespeare's hometown of Stratford-upon-Avon. The induction scenes, outside a tavern and within a nameless lord's country house, contain specific references to actual villages such as Greet, Wincot, and Burton Heath. This landscape introduces contemporary sociopolitical issues such as enclosure (the tavern abuts the lord's hunting preserve), vagrancy and sumptuary laws (for example, Sly's list of jobs and his being jokingly dressed as a lord), and the economic

tensions produced by changes in land use (Sly's poverty contrasts with the conspicuous wealth of the lord's house—dogs, servants, food, and erotic art).

Padua. City in northeastern Italy, about twenty miles west of Venice. Shakespeare borrows this setting from the Italian source for his comedy, Ludovico Ariosto's *I suppositi*, complete with disguises and clever manservants. As usual on the fluid, nonrepresentational Elizabethan stage, the action moves effortlessly, without the use of stage directions, from the first street scenes to the reception rooms, where Petruchio woos Kate, to the music room. The impression achieved is of a successful mercantile community, where personal wealth is measured in numbers of ships and household goods. The streets and houses near the home of Baptista Minola provide the fictional displacement from the England portrayed in the introduction, a displacement that parallels the thematic shifts from class anxieties to those of contemporary gender politics.

*Petruchio's farmhouse (peh-TREW-kee-oh). Near Verona, a city in northern Italy, forty miles west of Padua. Petruchio's property, with its muddy roads and bustling servants, provides a material reality in contrast to Padua's nondescript spaces. As signified by the names of the servants, Petruchio's blunt masculinity is construed as characteristically English in contrast with the mannered Italians. Furthermore, Petruchio's house functions as a site of transformations, where the pretensions of wealth and social behavior can be stripped away from Kate by Petruchio's "taming."

— *Nicolas Pullin*

TARTUFFE

Author: Molière (Jean-Baptiste Poquelin, 1622-1673)
Type of work: Drama
Type of plot: Comedy
Time of plot: Seventeenth century

First performed: 1664; revision, 1667; first published, 1669 as *Tartuffe: Ou, L'Imposteur* (English translation, 1732)

The main setting of this play is a wealthy French landlord's home; however, in a broader sense, the setting represents the importance of reason during the Enlightenment period and the evils of extreme or erratic human behavior and false piety. Before the play was first produced in 1664, it required three petitions to the king, after it was falsely denounced as an attack on religion.

Orgon's house. Parisian home of Orgon, a wealthy former officer of the King's Guard, that is the play's principal setting. The class and wealth of Orgon's home exist with the craziness and irrationality found inside. The extravagant house where Orgon, the master, and his new younger bride, Elmire, abide is a place where carriages frequently appear at the door, and footmen and lackeys are kept busy. Orgon's children and loyal maid, Dorine, must share their dwelling with duped Orgon's new houseguest, the religious hypocrite Tartuffe. The house becomes a battleground between Tartuffe's supporters, Orgon and his mother, and the more "enlightened" or reasonable personages of Dorine and Elmire, and especially Cleante—Orgon's wise and temperate brother-in-law.

Closet. Small and well-hidden enclosed space in one of the sitting rooms in Orgon's mansion that represents the pivotal point in the play's plot. In the third act, Orgon's son Damis, while hiding in the closet, overhears the pious Tartuffe attempting to seduce his father's wife, Elmire. The closet also serves to heighten the erratic behavior of Orgon, who refuses to believe the accusations against Tartuffe. Orgon even denounces and disinherits his son, forces Mariane to commit herself to Tartuffe, rather than her lover Valere, and then makes the religious imposter his sole heir.

Table. Heavy, long food-serving table that provides a place of thematic importance in the play: true virtue versus its outward appearance. In the fourth act, Elmire's plan for her husband to hide under a table and to hear the false holy man's lascivious, adulterous remarks enables Orgon to come to his senses and condemn the liar, who now is the owner of the property and money. Again, the location points to the folly of extreme, nonrational behavior as Orgon comically denounces all future interaction with godly men and holds them all in utter abhorrence.

— *Connie Pedoto*

A TASTE OF HONEY

Author: Shelagh Delaney (1939-   )
Type of work: Drama
Type of plot: Psychological realism

Time of plot: 1950's
First performed: 1958; first published, 1959

The tawdriness of the room rented by Helen and her daughter Jo in this play brought an almost unprecedented lower-class realism to the London stage of the 1950's. The play's depiction of an impoverished mother and daughter in a working-class English city was an even more frank and shocking depiction of working-class urban life than John Osborne's Look Back in Anger *(1956) had been two years earlier.*

*Salford.** Town adjacent to Manchester in the industrial Midlands district of England that is the setting for the play and the place in which playwright Shelagh Delaney was born and grew up. The location is identified in a prefatory page of the published text; however, the play's opening stage directions place its location "in Manchester." Having been the center of England's textile industry since the fourteenth century, Manchester is also the country's most densely populated area, though not its largest city. Containing many Port of Manchester docks, Salford became part of the new metropolitan county of Greater Manchester in 1974. Factories dominate the urban landscape, and its population is predominantly working class.

Helen and Jo's flat. Described in Delaney's stage directions as "comfortless," the semifurnished apartment that Helen, an alcoholic "semi-whore," has rented for herself and her teenage daughter, Jo, is the latest in a series of such rooms that they have occupied, each cheaper and tawdrier than the one before. It has only one bed, and Helen acknowledges that "everything in it's falling apart . . . and we've no heating—but there's a lovely view of the gasworks, we share a bathroom with the community and this wallpaper's contemporary." The stage set also includes a portion of the street outside the apartment building, where Jo's boyfriend, "a coloured naval rating," proposes marriage to her.

Jo notes that fifty thousand people live in tenements near the cemetery and a slaughterhouse. Scenes of such urban squalor had rarely been depicted realistically on the English stage before this play. They were in stark contrast to the middle- and upper-class elegance of then-popular plays by Noel Coward and others. This flat is considerably worse than the apartment in John Osborne's *Look Back in Anger*, another working-class drama that premiered in 1956 and was also set in the English Midlands. Like the readers of Émile Zola's novels more than six decades earlier, London theatergoers were shocked but also intrigued by the urban naturalism of Delaney's setting, her lower-class characters, and the grim events that transpire among them.

— *William Hutchings*

THE TEMPEST

Author: William Shakespeare (1564-1616)
Type of work: Drama
Type of plot: Fantasy

Time of plot: Fifteenth century
First performed: 1611; first published, 1623

This play's setting, an unnamed oceanic island, reflects the influence of travel literature about European explorations during the sixteenth and seventeenth centuries. As such, the island is also a microcosm of European colonialism. In addition, the island is a showplace for the superior power of European science and technology.

Enchanted island. Remote home of the rightful duke of Milan, Prospero, as well as his daughter Miranda and his slave Caliban. Presumably the almost deserted island is in the Mediterranean Sea, but it resembles the tropical islands of even more remote seas around the world that European navigators were beginning to discover during William Shakespeare's time. Europeans were coming to expect far-off islands to be home to strange creatures and peoples, such as Prospero's islander slave, Caliban. To the Europeans, remote tropical islands also seemed like earthly paradises, recalling myths of an original Golden Age or a new Utopia.

Such earthly paradises—or any new lands, for that matter—were starting to be occupied by Europeans without much regard for their original inhabitants. A microcosm of this developing colonial mentality exists in *The Tempest*, whose island originally belonged to

Caliban, who is described as a "savage" and "monster." After becoming stranded on the island with his young daughter, Prospero at first coexists peacefully with Caliban. However, when Caliban tries to mate with Miranda, Prospero takes over the island and enslaves Caliban.

What enables Prospero to enslave Caliban so easily is his knowledge gained from books (much superior to the black magic of Caliban's mother, a witch). Through this knowledge, Prospero is able to torture Caliban's joints and give him nightmares. Prospero uses the same knowledge to draw his European enemies to the island, stir up a storm that shipwrecks them, and harass them until they beg forgiveness. Prospero is an archetypal figure of the scientist, and his abilities to play music in the air, control the weather, and call on spirits to do his bidding make the island a science and technology museum.

— *Harold Branam*

THE TEMPLE OF THE GOLDEN PAVILION

Author: Yukio Mishima (Kimitake Hiraoka, 1925-1970)

Type of work: Novel

Type of plot: Psychological realism

Time of plot: Mid-twentieth century

First published: Kinkakuji, 1956 (English translation, 1959)

This novel deals with the psychologically complex and desperate crime of a young Japanese Buddhist monk who deliberately burns the Temple of the Golden Pavilion to the ground. It is based on an actual incident in Japanese history, the story of a young acolyte born with an ugly face and stammering speech who becomes obsessed with the temple because it represents beauty, perfection, and the values of his father, who had been disgraced by his mother.

Kinkakuji (kin-ka-kew-jee). Temple, also known as the **Temple of the Golden Pavilion**, in Kyōto that is a rare masterpiece of Buddhist garden architecture, the central metaphor of the novel. The temple dates back over five centuries to the days of the great Shogun Ashikaga Yoshimitsu, a powerful military leader, appreciator of fine art, and devoted follower of Zen Buddhism. The temple served as a spiritual retreat for this hard-driven military leader because he enjoyed evenings of music and poetry, which took him away from the constant warfare of his dynasty.

The temple dominates the thoughts of the novel's main character, the acolyte priest, Mizoguchi, who reads

about it in books for years before he sees it in person. It is a three-storied tower structure overlooking a pond in a garden. The first two stories are built in traditional style of domestic architecture with folding shutters, but the third story consists of a square room built in pure Zen style. The roof is covered with cypress bark and capped with a copper and gold phoenix.

To Mizoguchi, the temple constantly changes its meaning throughout his life. The temple sometimes represents enduring beauty, envy, and eternal moral authority in contrast to the failings of human beings. Sometimes the temple is comforting, and sometimes it is forbidding and deadly. When Mizoguchi thinks of the temple, he recalls his own personal failings and the immorality of his mother. The memory of the temple makes it impossible for him to make love to a girl when he visits the geisha district of Kyōto. Mizoguchi comes to the conclusion that only by destroying the Temple of the Golden Pavilion can he free himself from his own obsessions.

*Maizuru** (mi-zew-rew). Town west of Kyōto, in which Mizoguchi grows up, knowing the Golden Pavilion only through photographs. Mizoguchi recalls East Maizuru Middle School of his early school years, remembering its spacious grounds, pleasant surrounding hills, and the bright, modern buildings of the school. As a boy, Mizoguchi had a weak constitution, he stuttered frequently, and other children teased him because of his physical differences. He dreamed of seeing the Golden Pavilion in Kyōto for years before his father actually took him there. Though his father was only a simple country priest ignorant of the terminology of architecture, he taught Mizoguchi that the Temple of the Golden Pavilion was the most beautiful thing on earth. After his father's death, Mizoguchi left his village to become an acolyte in Kyōto.

*Kyōto** (kyoh-toh). Japanese city and cultural center, which along with Tokyo, defines Japanese values. Kyōto is a city of great beauty with raked pebble gardens, exotic contours of beautiful temples, and traditional costumes of geishas. The city is filled with more than two thousand shrines and temples, in addition to palaces, gardens, and an abundance of Buddhist artwork.

When Mizoguchi first goes to Kyōto and sees the Golden Pavilion in person, the experience contrasts with the grim news of World War II and the imminent American bombardment of Japan. Speculation abounds about whether the Golden Pavilion will survive Allied bombing. Mizoguchi sees airplanes from the Maizuru squadron flying over the Golden Pavilion, but the eternal beauty of the place is untouched by bombing.

Even when Mizoguchi accepts cigarettes from an American soldier who tries to terminate the pregnancy of a Japanese prostitute in the garden, the Golden Pavilion seems unaffected. Mizoguchi becomes convinced that the temple will be burned down by the American incendiary bombs, and he is "released" by the idea that absolute beauty will not survive. When the Temple is not bombed, he takes matters into his own hands after the war and sets fire to it himself.

— *Jonathan L. Thorndike*

THE TEMPTATION OF SAINT ANTHONY

Author: Gustave Flaubert (1821-1880)
Type of work: Novel
Type of plot: Historical

Time of plot: Fourth century
First published: La Tentation de Saint Antoine, 1874
    (English translation, 1895)

The stage provided by this play for Anthony's temptation is a minimalist one, stripped bare of all but the most basic necessities, reflecting the state of his soul. The visions with which the Devil afflicts him carry him to places he knew as a young man and to those constructed in his imagination.

Saint Anthony's cell. Hermitage in which Anthony lives. It is set on a crescent-shaped platform high on a mountainside in the Thebaid desert, above the Nile. It is constructed from mud and reeds, with a flat roof and no door. Its only furniture, apart from mats on the floor, is a wooden frame supporting a book. A single palm tree grows on the edge of the platform, whose only other embellishment is a wooden cross. The Libyan mountains are visible on the desert horizon.

Anthony has previously dwelt in a pharaoh's tomb and a ruined citadel and has traveled a great deal. Here, his final refuge, is where he makes baskets, mats, and shepherds' crooks, bartering his products to nomads in exchange for bread. This crude stage becomes the arena in which the Devil launches his most powerful temptations as the saint's spirits fall into weary despair. Although Anthony never leaves this place, he is transported in his imagination to several different locations.

*Thebaid. Domain of Thebes in Upper Egypt. The site of Thebes is now occupied by Luxor, but the desert remains as desolate as it was in Anthony's day.

*Alexandria. Egypt's great seaport built by Alexander the Great after his capture of Egypt in 332 B.C.E. Anthony is transported to the Panium, an artificial mound in the city center overlooking Lake Mareotis. When the monks of the Thebaid invade the city to kill the Arian heretics, Anthony joins the slaughter, subsequently enjoying the hospitality of Constantine the Great, but it all disappears when he resists the temptation of power.

Basilica. Vast cathedral in which all the Christian faithful are gathered. Manes (the author of the Manichaean heresy) is preaching from a throne of gold, and his example is followed by many other heretics, who succeed in rousing the entire crowd to murderous violence. Beyond the limits of the basilica, Anthony meets more exotic heretics and representatives of many other religious traditions, in various sketchily described but appropriate settings.

Firmament. Ultimately, the Devil carries Anthony away from Earth. They pass by the Moon, a luminous sphere resembling a ball of ice, into the infinite realm of the stars. This lofty standpoint within an immensity of darkness is supposed to prove to Anthony the utter irrelevance of Earth, and hence of humankind, within the universe. The Devil's plan backfires, however, because this journey into realms of abstraction and scientific imagination provides Anthony with a useful intellectual instrument. When he is returned to his hovel and presented with a parade of bizarre monsters, he is able to convert the vision in his mind's eye into a panorama of life, in which animals become indistinguishable from plants and plants from minerals: an ecological free-for-all in which the fervor of creation is everywhere manifest. It is this vision that facilitates the reaffirmation of his faith.

— *Brian Stableford*

THE TENANT OF WILDFELL HALL

Author: Anne Brontë (1820-1849)
Type of work: Novel
Type of plot: Social realism

Time of plot: Early nineteenth century
First published: 1848

This novel has two narratives: Helen's narrative presents the fashionable world of London, while Gilbert's presents the homey setting of farm life in the north of England. Wildfell Hall stands between the two and forms an appropriate meeting place for them.

Wildfell Hall. Old run-down country house dating back to the Elizabethan era, situated in the north of England, some seven miles from the nearest town and two miles from Gilbert's farm. The house belongs to Frederick Lawrence, Helen's brother, and was the family home until fifteen years earlier, when he removed to a more spacious modern house, Woodford, in the neighboring parish, leaving the hall untenanted. It is described as being built of dark gray stone; having thick stone mullions and narrow, latticed windows; being surrounded by stone walls and an overgrown garden; and being set on the moors and therefore completely isolated. A few rooms have been prepared for Helen, including one room she uses as a studio.

Linden-hope. Family farm of Gilbert Markham, where he lives with his mother, sister, and brother. The farmhouse is portrayed as typical of a gentleman farmer, where good manners and etiquette are combined with open hospitality and unpretentious living. The farmlands are situated in a fertile valley and run up the sides of the moorland. The nearby village is not well described apart from the parish church and its vicarage, where Gilbert's first love lives. The setting corresponds to Yorkshire, the home county of Anne Brontë.

Linden-Car Bay. Nearest seaside place to the village, the overlooking cliffs being five miles away. A group excursion is made here through the summer countryside. The location is probably Scarborough, where Brontë spent several holidays. It is also featured in her earlier novel, *Agnes Grey* (1847).

Staningly Hall. The first place mentioned in Helen's narrative, it is the country residence of her aunt and uncle, with whom she lives. It contains extensive grounds and woods, to which Mr. Maxwell invites a party of Helen's suitors to enjoy the hunting, symbolic of Helen's being hunted, she being heiress to the estate. At the end of the novel, Gilbert and Helen take up residence there, after it has been made clear that class differences and financial inequality are no bar to true love.

Grassdale Manor. Country residence of Arthur Huntingdon, where Helen spends her married life. It is not dissimilar to Staningly in location or architecture, both being vaguely described, and probably both being based on Thorp Hall, Yorkshire, where Brontë was a governess. The contrast is in Helen's treatment at both places. Near Grassdale stands the Grove, another country house belonging to their neighbor, Mr. Hargrave, one of Huntingdon's "friends." Hargrave lives at the Grove, with his mother and sisters, who become friends to Helen. It lies a day's coach ride from Staningly and a similar distance from Wildfell Hall.

*****London.** Capital of Great Britain whose fashionable life is described by Helen and consists of a series of meeting grounds, where young women may find a suitable husband in the presence of chaperones. Such meeting places consist of balls and dinner parties. Brontë's descriptions are necessarily vague and derivative as she had hardly ever left her native Yorkshire village. Another side of fashionable London emerges through the novel: that of dissipation. Arthur retreats to various drinking and gambling haunts with his companions, escaping the domesticity Helen seeks to create for him.

— *David Barratt*

TENDER IS THE NIGHT

Author: F. Scott Fitzgerald (1896-1940)

Type of work: Novel

Type of plot: Social realism

Time of plot: 1920's

First published: 1934

This complex novel deals with wealthy expatriate Americans who seem to be on perpetual holiday in Europe. Contrasts between them and the Old World settings contribute to F. Scott Fitzgerald's continuing examination of the American spirit, character, and ultimate corruption. Protagonist Dick Diver exists as both an individual character and a symbol for the degenerating, self-destructive, and superficial nature of post-World War I America. Much of the story takes place on the French Riviera and Switzerland, but within these foreign settings is the indelible sense of an American mentality and presence that is dissipated by surface glitter and moral decadence. The setting thus signals the ultimate loss of an American idealism and innocence.

*****French Riviera.** Resort area along France's Mediterranean coast that the novel refers to as the "home" of Dick Diver and his wife. The novel opens there, and the Divers periodically return there, and there the novel concludes with Dick blessing the beach from a terrace. As a literary device, the Riviera and its cities represent various aspects of the characters, the lives they lead, and the kinds of people they are becoming. The Riviera is pictured as a playground for the rich and famous, a place where Rosemary attends empty, pretentious parties with the Divers; where Nicole Warren spends money prodigiously—an indication of the relentless materialism of her family; where Dick repeatedly shines as glib host at dinner parties; where Mary North and Lady Caroline Sibly-Biers are arrested for their careless, condescending shenanigans; and where Nicole's infidelity with Tommy Barban occurs.

Gausse's Hôtel des Étrangers (gos-es oh-tel day-say-trahn-jay). Hotel on the French Riviera located somewhere "between Marseilles and the Italian Border" in which the novel opens. The hotel's beach is where the initial infatuation begins between Dick Diver and film star Rosemary Hoyt and is the site of many scenes juxtaposed to indicate both the Divers' charm as a couple and the ultimate disintegration of their marriage.

The hotel is significant as a gathering place for an elite group of wealthy and fashionable people, of whom Dick Diver is the indisputable star. Initially Diver's "talent" is described as an ability to bring out the best in people and make them feel inexplicably satisfied with themselves without too much self-examination. It is his idealism that draws people to him. The hotel also serves as a meeting place for the disparate symbolic elements in *Tender Is the Night* in which an older, worldly, aesthetically and morally bankrupt Europe—which is epitomized in the Hotel, the Riviera, Paris, and Rome—is contrasted with a "diseased" America, epitomized by Nicole Diver's mental illness brought on by a betrayal of her innocence. Although Dick represents all that is vital, charming, hopeful, and best in America, he is unable to save his "home" (an Old World sense of tradition and values) and himself (American idealism). Instead, he sacrifices his own spiritual depth and potential to revitalize his psychologically sick wife (an irrevocably materialistic America).

*Zurich. Swiss city that is the site of the novel's first flashback (to 1917), which delineates how Dick Diver meets and decides to wed—and rehabilitate—Nicole, the mental patient. It is also the site of Nicole's internment after falling ill later in the novel.

Zurich may represent parallels with Fitzgerald's own problems with his wife Zelda, who was hospitalized in a Swiss sanatorium until her death. The novel's book 2 opens in Zurich, where Dick is to complete his studies. Switzerland is described as an "island" and implies isolation from the complications of a more morally bankrupt world. Switzerland is also where the couple finally retreats when Nicole's sister, Baby Warren, finances Dick's interest in a mental clinic. Finally, the city and its country also represent the field of psychoanalysis (Dick's profession), his dedication to his wife, and ultimately his inability to cure himself of his incipient alcoholism.

*Rome. Italy's capital city is the site of Dick Diver's brawl with police, his affair with Rosemary, and a physical representation of his apparent deterioration. A horrific scene of violence in the Italian jail is symptomatic of the morally degenerating Dick—who can be saved only by the influence and money of Baby Warren—evidencing his moral degradation at being "bought" (implied throughout the novel every time Nicole's money is mentioned.) The final irony, foreshadowed by Rome, is that by "consecrating" himself to his marriage, Dick is destroyed, while Nicole is cured. The cure, however, is representative of a prosperous America—robust, powerful, eminently capitalistic—just as Nicole herself has become, and who spends frivolously because she can. This "cure," however, is achieved at a terrible cost, for Dick's idealism and essence are lost.

— *Sherry Morton-Mollo*

TESS OF THE D'URBERVILLES: A Pure Woman Faithfully Presented

Author: Thomas Hardy (1840-1928)
Type of work: Novel
Type of plot: Philosophical realism

Time of plot: Late nineteenth century
First published: 1891

The many journeys of this novel's heroine through village and countryside, often on foot, constitute a rural woman's pilgrimage through life, with her successive environments mirroring her spiritual progress. Although nature offers Tess some refuge from oppressive social and religious laws, ultimately it can protect neither her nor itself from predatory humans, mechanized agriculture, and cosmic indifference to suffering. To emphasize Tess's tragic insignificance in the universal scheme, Thomas Hardy often presents her as a tiny figure against a vast landscape of forces beyond her control.

Wessex. Hardy's fictionalized version of the region around Dorset, a coastal county in southern England, taking its name from the West Saxon kingdom of the sixth to tenth centuries. Hardy introduced Wessex in *Far from the Madding Crowd* (1874). In later fiction, he layered a detailed topography modeled on actual locations with archetypal symbolism. The capital city of Wessex, Casterbridge, mentioned several times in *Tess of the D'Urbervilles*, is Hardy's version of Dorchester.

Marlott. Village in the north of Wessex on a plain called the Vale of Blackmoor (or Blakemore), modeled on Marnhull, that is Tess Durbeyfield's original home. Even before she is forced to leave this "fertile and sheltered tract of country, in which the fields are never brown and the springs never dry," mishaps and catastrophes in its environs indeed seem destined to mar her lot in life.

Trantridge. Town east of Marlott, based on Pentridge, where the Durbyfieldses' supposed D'Urberville relatives live in a redbrick lodge. At the edge of this newly rich estate, Hardy places the Chase, a forest dating back to the time of the Druids that he bases on Cranbourne Chase, once a royal hunting ground. There, primeval shadows and modern corruption collude in Alec D'Urberville's rape of Tess.

Chaseborough. "Decayed market-town," located two or three miles southeast of Trantridge, whose hard-drinking looseness drives Tess into Alec's company.

Talbothays Dairy. Destination of Tess's second journey from home, in the Great Dairies region, which Hardy alternately calls Var Vale and Froom Valley after its double-named river. Lying symbolically in almost the opposite direction from Trantridge, the fertile valley is the scene of Tess's summer healing and rebirth after her rape. At times, Talbothays seems to be Eden after the Fall, at others a pagan pastoral idyll.

Emminster. Little town surrounded by hills in which the religious family of Tess's husband, Angel Clare, lives. A dominant church tower signals the contrast to Talbothays' natural, pagan lushness.

Wellbridge. Village in which Tess and Angel honeymoon in a farmhouse. There her ancestors' looming portraits represent Tess's entrapment by her past, and Angel leaves her after she finally reveals part of her past to him.

*Brazil. South American country to which Angel flees to gain new farming experience after he is disillusioned by Tess's revelation. In addition to reflecting a trend among British agriculturists of the period, Angel's stay in the New World serves to liberate him from England's narrow conventions.

Flintcomb-Ash. Bleak "starve-acre place" about fifteen miles southwest of Marlott where Tess works at swede-hacking during a harsh winter. Hardy explicitly contrasts Flintcomb-Ash, his fictionalized Nettlecombe-Tout, with "Talbothays Dairy, that happy green tract of land where summer had been liberal in her gifts." At Flintcomb-Ash, Tess simultaneously endures seasonal hardship, renewed sexual predation by Alec, and mechanical oppression by a demoniac, black threshing machine.

Kingsbere-sub-Greenhill. Former home of Tess's highborn D'Urberville ancestors, now buried in its churchyard. The migration of Tess's family from Marlott to Kingsbere (modeled on Bere Regis) exemplifies village depopulation caused by seasonal work but also symbolizes how Tess's heritage has a death-grip on her fate.

Sandbourne. Fashionable resort modeled on Bournemouth where Angel finds Tess after returning from Brazil. Hardy uses this "city of detached mansions; a Mediterranean lounging-place on the English Channel" to emphasize his rural heroine's sense of alienation in living as the wife of Alec, whom she kills after she turns away Alec.

New Forest. Setting for Tess and Angel's delayed consummation of their marriage, contrasting with the antiquity of the Chase.

*Stonehenge. Circle of stone monoliths placed in prehistoric times on a plain about eight miles northwest of Salisbury, which Hardy calls "ancient Melchester," in the county of Wiltshire. In this pagan setting, which Angel associates with human sacrifices to the sun, Tess rests on a stone slab before her arrest for Alec's murder. As the police close in around her, the setting makes her not merely the law's victim but also a sacrifice to some unjust, even cruel, universal power beyond natural phenomena.

— *Margaret Bozenna Goscilo*

TEVYE THE DAIRYMAN

Author: Sholom Aleichem (Sholem Rabinowitz, 1859-1916)

Type of work: Short fiction

First published: Tevye der Milkhiger, 1894-1914 (English translation, 1949, 1987)

Although only three communities have a role in the stories in this collection, they represent the dire Jewish situation in Eastern Europe, and from their social and political character it is possible to infer much of the history of Russian Jewry in Sholom Aleichem's time.

Boiberik. Small Russian town, modeled on Boyarka near Kiev, where Tevye travels in his horse-drawn wagon to sell cheese, cream, and butter to the wealthy who eat, drink, and enjoy their leisure in luxury. This is where the rich migrate to relax in their summer *dachas*. Boiberik forms a contrast to the impoverished, unnamed community nearby where Tevye lives with Golde and their unmarried daughters.

In "Tevye Strikes It Rich," which first appeared in 1894 and was revised in 1897, Tevye transports two women to a *dacha* by a pond at the far end of the woods. Tevye fantasizes about starting a grocery store in Boiberik, which he hopes will lead to a dry-goods store, a woodlot, and a tax concession. At the end, he simply buys a milch cow.

Yehupetz. Russian city that is a fictional representation of Kiev and supposedly a place where fortunes thrive. The rich live in mansions with walls to keep out beggars. When not traveling to German health resorts when their wives have even so trivial a complaint as a stomachache, they ride around town in rubber-wheeled *droshkies*. The most famous rich person ironically happens to be Brodsky, a Jew, but his name is invoked simply to demarcate the separation of rich Jews, who are immune to suffering, from poor ones, who experience great dangers inside and outside the Pale of Settlement.

Anatevka. One of the small Russian towns, declared a village, in "Today's Children," so that Jews could be more easily expelled from it. A place unified by Jewish religion and tradition. The richest man is Lazar Wolf, the widower-butcher who asks for Tsaytl's hand in marriage. His house has a cupboard full of copper, two samovars, a brass tray, a set of gilt-edged cups, a pair of silver candlesticks, a cast-iron menorah, a chest for cash, and an attic filled with hides. However, even these emblems of prosperity are not enough for him to win Tsaytl, who goes, instead, to Motl the tailor.

— *Keith Garebian*

THEIR EYES WERE WATCHING GOD

Author: Zora Neale Hurston (1891-1960)

Type of work: Novel

Type of plot: Bildungsroman

Time of plot: Around 1900

First published: 1937

The three different geographic settings of this novel, though confined to the state of Florida, correspond to the stages of protagonist Janie Crawford's heightened search for self-actualization and self-fulfillment.

West Florida. Region in which Janie Crawford spends the early years of her life. The initial part of the novel is set in her maternal grandmother's house and charts Janie's coming into womanhood. Janie has been raised by her maternal grandmother Nanny who fled slavery with her infant daughter and later migrated to West Florida with her employers, the Washburn family. With the Washburns' assistance, Nanny purchases her own home so that she can properly raise and protect Janie from derision following the tragic rape and subsequent disappearance of her mother Leafy. On a particular spring afternoon, Janie experiences her budding sexuality beneath a blooming pear tree as a bee enters the inner sanctum of a pear blossom in the act of pollination.

When Nanny spies Janie kissing the shiftless Johnny Taylor, she immediately arranges for young Janie to marry Logan Killicks, a much older man who owns a house and some property, so that Janie will be protected from men whom Nanny fears will take advantage of her granddaughter. While Janie objects to this marriage, she nevertheless tries to make the best of it for awhile, until it becomes quite clear that she will never be able to live for herself in these circumstances. Thus West Florida becomes associated with her grandmother's dream and Logan Killicks's dream but not her own dream. When Janie meets Joe Starks, a traveler from Georgia, she walks out of her marriage with Killicks and casts her lot with Joe to pursue the far horizon.

*Eatonville. All-black town in central Florida just north of Orlando near Maitland. Janie comes here with her new husband Joe in pursuit of the horizon. When they arrive in Eatonville, Joe is disappointed with the place. Through Joe's energy and foresight Eatonville is soon transformed into a thriving town, but as the years pass Janie discovers once again that this is not the place of her dreams, but of Joe's. She becomes alienated from the townspeople and forbidden to participate in any of the community's rituals. In addition, as a woman in a male-dominated world Janie is oppressed, as evidenced by her being forced to wear her hair tied up and by the brutal way that Joe verbally humiliates her in the presence of the men of the town. When Joe dies of a lingering illness, Janie is liberated. Soon she meets a considerably younger man, Vergible "Tea Cake" Woods. Finally deciding that widowhood and life in Eatonville are too confining, she follows Tea Cake to Jacksonville where they marry.

De muck. Name for the portion of the Florida Everglades south of Lake Okeechobee near Clewiston and Belle Glade. The name is derived from the rich black soil that grew lush vegetation. It represents a certain earthiness, a certain *carpe diem* spirit, as Janie and Tea Cake quit Jacksonville to live and work among the hordes of migrant workers. Like the weeds and vegetables, Janie flourishes in this locale among the folk with a man who loves her for who she is. Thus de muck represents the horizon for Janie, a place where she can finally realize the fullness of life and live out her dreams. Unfortunately this bliss is short-lived, for in the aftermath of a devastating hurricane, Janie is tried and acquitted for killing Tea Cake in a tragic act of self-defense. After she buries him in a lavish ceremony, Janie returns to her home in Eatonville where she intends to grow old.

— *Warren J. Carson*

THÉRÈSE

Author: François Mauriac (1885-1970)
Type of work: Novel
Type of plot: Psychological realism

Time of plot: Twentieth century
First published: Thérèse Desqueyroux, 1927 (English translation, 1928)

François Mauriac was interested in the dark side of human nature and liked to depict life in a world bereft of religion and thus of God's grace. This novel's protagonist, Thérèse, is shown to be a product of such a world, a woman who tries to poison her husband and goes free merely because of false testimony, only to live a life of loneliness, guilt, and self-hatred. The novel is set in southeastern France near Mauriac's home in Bordeaux, and later in Paris, where Thérèse barely survives in a kind of exile.

Argelouse (ahr-geh-LOOZ). Fictional small town in an isolated part of southwestern France, largely abandoned, except for some tenant farmers and two prominent families, the Larroques and the Desqueyroux. Thérèse is from the former family and her husband, Bernard, from the latter. Eventually many members of the two families live a good part of their lives in Saint-Clair, where other former Argelouse families now reside.

Much of Argelouse is falling into a state of disrepair. However, it is a heavily forested region, and resin from its pine trees becomes the source of Thérèse's income. In her late years, Thérèse learns that most of Argelouse's pine trees have been cut down and that the town has become an even more desolate place.

Argelouse becomes Thérèse's "prison" after she is acquitted in her trial for attempting to kill Bernard, who confines her to her room for years. Bernard's main interest in the place derives from its being a good place for duck hunting. He returns there only for duck-hunting season.

Saint-Clair (sah[n]-klehr). Market town six miles from Argelouse, In her younger days, Thérèse often travels between the two towns, which are connected by a neglected road on which nothing more modern than a wagon can travel. However, Saint-Clair is an important stop on the railway and has a station that anyone going to Argelouse finds necessary to traverse. It serves as a milestone in the book.

Because there is no church in Argelouse, Thérèse attends Sunday Mass in Saint-Clair, which she finds a welcome respite. However, Bernard decides that Mass has no meaning for Thérèse, whom he forbids from going to Saint-Clair, which eventually becomes the site of Thérèse's death.

*****Paris.** Capital of France in which Thérèse lives after Bernard permits her to leave Argelouse. Alone in the great city, Thérèse tries to make a new life for herself, but without success. The sense of sin she carries with her perverts all of her attempts to find happiness. As the years pass, she retreats more and more into herself.

During her first years in Paris, she lives on Ile Saint-Louis, a small island in the Seine River. In her declining years, Thérèse lives in an apartment in an old house on the rue du Bac, on the Left Bank of the Seine that crosses the larger boulevard Saint-Germain, where Thérèse feels a temporary relief from the oppression that is usually her lot.

— *Robert W. Small*

THÉRÈSE RAQUIN

Author: Émile Zola (1840-1902)
Type of work: Novel
Type of plot: Naturalism

Time of plot: Early 1860's
First published: 1867 (English translation, 1881)

A work of psychological realism, of nerves and atmosphere, with a minimum of characters and physical action, this book is an interior novel. Much of its drama takes place within the minds of its two main characters, Thérèse and Laurent. The light and atmosphere of the setting are grimy and dismal, reflecting Émile Zola's dark tale of adultery, murder, and revenge. The setting is enclosed and nightmarish, mostly restricted to interior spaces: a shop and two rooms above it, and the damp, murky passage in Paris where the shop is located. This gloomy, limited environment both reflects and influences the psychological drama of the novel. It is significant that the first pages of the novel describe the setting in detail.

Passage du Pont-Neuf (pah-SAHJ dyu POHN-newf). Covered arcade in Paris; a flagstone-floored alley that runs between two streets lined with small shops. The passage is vividly described in the opening lines of the novel. Its strongest characteristic is its darkness and grime, setting the mood of the drama. It exudes a damp odor, and the sun rarely penetrates the grimy glass of its

roofing. Its shops are dusty and dim; passersby are limited to those taking a short cut as they walk rapidly on to their true destination. During the day, the shops are dark caves; at night, the arcade takes on a shadowy, sinister look.

Haberdashery shop. Dry goods store in the dismal Passage du Pont-Neuf belonging to Thérèse Raquin.

The shop sells odds and ends of clothing, such as socks, stockings, muslin collars and caps, as well as buttons, knitting needles, spools of thread, and balls of yarn. All its stock is faded and yellowed, decaying in the dust and damp within the dim shop. Here, Thérèse Raquin spends her days, in the shadows behind the counter. From the shop, a spiral staircase leads to the upstairs rooms.

Bedroom. Room above the shop that is entered from the dining room at the top of the spiral staircase; it has a second door opening onto an exterior staircase that leads outside to the passage. This is the door which Thérèse's lover, Laurent, uses throughout their affair. The bedroom itself is the only element of the setting that changes as the novel progresses. As the novel opens, the room is a cold place to which Thérèse and her sickly, weak husband retire each night. Thérèse refuses to decorate or add cheer to the room in any way. Later, when she and Laurent become lovers, Thérèse becomes filled with excitement and happiness and redecorates the bedroom with pots of flowers, new wallpaper, carpets, and curtains. Even the room is transformed by the relationship. After Laurent and Thérèse drown Camille, Thérèse's personality becomes more relaxed and outgoing. Again the atmosphere of the bedroom changes, from a place of passion to a place of peace and quiet.

The bedroom's transformations and importance in the atmosphere of the novel climax on Thérèse and Laurent's wedding night. On this night, a fire blazes in the fireplace and the heat releases the scent of big bunches of roses. The bedroom is a place of sensuality. But the irony of the marriage of Laurent and Thérèse is that they find no peace. The ghost of the man they have drowned in order to be together haunts and terrifies them as soon as they fall asleep. Formerly the scene of their passion, the bedroom becomes the scene of Thérèse and Laurent's agonies as they struggle to stay awake.

Dining room. Another of the three rooms above the haberdashery shop. This room is the scene of the Raquin family's Thursday evening entertainments, which are dominated by the lamp-lit table on which dominoes are laid out along with the samovar of tea. The lonely people participating in these dull evenings never realize how desperate they are. Much of the plot advancement occurs in this room. Here Thérèse and Laurent meet and carry on their deception in front of the family and friends. After Camille's death, it is the members of the Thursday evening group who encourage Thérèse and Laurent to marry.

The dining room becomes important to Thérèse and Laurent as a place of respite from the nightmares of the bedroom. It is the scene of the terrible quarrels between them while they are alone, yet to the Thursday visitors it reeks of respectability and normality as the couple lives a double life. Finally, the room is the scene of the death of Thérèse and Laurent by double poisoning, a death which by this time they both welcome.

— *Susan Butterworth*

THE THIN MAN

Author: Dashiell Hammett (1894-1961)
Type of work: Novel
Type of plot: Detective and mystery

Time of plot: 1930's
First published: 1934

This novel is a murder mystery with a light tone. Its sleuth, Nick Charles, is a retired private investigator who spends his time in living rooms and bars and never visits an actual crime scene. He solves crimes while drinking and wisecracking his way through life. The Manhattan in which the novel is set is primarily a backdrop providing references to stylish places.

***Manhattan.** New York City borough that is the financial and cultural center of the United States and the primary setting for the novel. Though various plot threads link the investigation to other places—such as Philadelphia and San Francisco—the entire novel unfolds within Manhattan, where Hammett himself lived for several years. His fictional sleuths, Nick and Nora Charles, move from city landmark to landmark and clearly know all stylish elements of the city. They meet with artists and professors in Greenwich Village and move from illegal speakeasies to Harlem, looking for fun. However, the novel offers little description of the city itself; instead Hammett merely drops minimal details into the narrative, contributing to the novel's fast-moving pace, feeling of insider knowledge, and sense that all of Manhattan is merely a stage setting on which important people act with style.

Charles apartment. Nick and Nora's upper-class residence in Manhattan's Normandie Building. The apartment has a bedroom, bathroom, living room, and enough space to have a bar. Its building contains a restaurant and a bellboy, whom the Charleses pay to take care of their pet dog, Asta. However, like the city, the apartment's furnishings are never described. Despite this, the Charleses seem to live in an airy, stylish place. Hammett achieves this impression through witty exchanges among his characters that strongly suggest that the Charleses have an expensive and elegant lifestyle. He reinforces this impression by describing other places in details that create an implied contrast with their apartment.

*Colorado. Mountainous former frontier state in the West that Nick compares to Manhattan. When the young Gilbert Wynant asks Nick about cannibalism, Nick gives him a book with an account about a prospecting party trapped by a blizzard in Montana and makes the point that while violence occurs in both Manhattan and Colorado, the violence in Colorado is more likely to dehumanize the men involved. In contrast, a gunman who bursts into the Charleses' Manhattan apartment is apt to be greeted with a quick witticism and competent action.

Clyde Wynant's laboratory. Place in which the inventor Clyde Wynant (the "Thin Man" of the novel's title) conducts experiments and where his murdered body is found. The novel offers little description of the lab, beyond the fact that it has a heavy concrete floor. Wynant's murder there reinforces the novel's impression that no cultural site is free from the threat of violence in Hammett's Manhattan. Violence occurs in domestic, public, and scientific locations. The lab is also important because only Nick thinks to look there. He does so specifically because murderer Clyde Macauley leaves the place out of the many comments he makes to misdirect investigators. This piece of sleuth work demonstrates Nick's skill as a detective and also underscores the novel's narrative technique of communicating key details through implication. The place that is not named is the most important place of all.

Jorgenson apartment. Upper-class Manhattan residence of Mimi and Christian Jorgenson. While the apartment appears to be virtually interchangeable with the Charleses' apartment, it has a much different atmosphere. The Jorgensons are quick to feel threatened by outsiders and react angrily to anything they do not want to hear.

Nunheim's apartment. Lower-class apartment of the minor thug Arthur Nunheim. When Nick Charles and Guild, the police officer investigating the Wolf murder, interrogate Nunheim at his home, Charles describes its building as dark, damp, smelly, and noisy. This apartment is one of the novel's few settings that is described in sufficient detail to create a vivid, if implicit, contrast with the Charles's apartment.

Pigiron Club. Manhattan speakeasy run by Studsy Burke, a former safecracker whom Nick Charles once arrested. The club has a comfortably shabby look and is full of people, noise, and smoke in the evenings. Dorothy Wynand and Nick's wife Nora are out of place in the Pigiron Club and cannot understand the slang spoken by its criminal patrons.

— *Greg Beatty*

THINGS FALL APART

Author: Chinua Achebe (1930-   )
Type of work: Novel
Type of plot: Tragedy

Time of plot: Late nineteenth century
First published: 1958

As one of the first and most influential great African novels, this book relies heavily on its sense of place. For Okonkwo and his clan, a man is inseparable from his land, while for the Christian missionaries, the things of this earth are temporary and of little value.

Umofia (oo-moh-FEE-uh). Area in southeastern Nigeria, comprising nine villages, where the Umofia clan live. "Umofia" is the Igbo word for "people of the forest." The word "village" is a loose translation of a complicated concept in Igbo society and is used in *Things Fall Apart* to represent both the nine villages and the larger area; thus, the village of Umofia comprises nine villages. In Umofia at the end of the nineteenth century, homes are mud huts set in compounds. Each of the villages is advised by a male elder, and the nine elders meet to make decisions for the clan. The center of village life is the market. Okonkwo is known throughout Umofia for his strength and his success in warfare, unlike his father, who also came from Umofia. He is not an elder and has no official status as a leader, but he is relied upon as a man of action and he hopes one day to become a leader. In his father's village, a male-dominated society, Okonkwo knows his place, and the place of his wives and his children. For him, social order is bound up in tradition and home.

When Okonkwo returns to Umofia after seven years in exile, he finds that the Christian missionaries have made several changes. New buildings—a church, a courthouse—have appeared in the village, representing new ideas and rules. For Okonkwo, the physical changes in the village symbolize the erosion of the Igbo culture—the things that are falling apart.

Okonkwo's compound. The home of Okonkwo and his immediate family. Okonkwo has a hut for himself and one for each of his three wives, a barn, and several yam fields, all enclosed in a red mud wall. None of this was inherited from his father, Unoka, who never prospered. Okonkwo has built up his wealth and his property through his own hard work and the work of his family. When it is determined that Okonkwo must be banished from Umofia, men storm his compound dressed as they would for a war. They burn Okonkwo's buildings, kill his animals, and tear down his red walls. They do not do this out of anger or hatred (in fact, Okonkwo's closest friend is one of them), but simply because a man's land is inseparable from him, and to purify the village they must remove every trace of the offender. Okonkwo understands and accepts his punishment.

Mbanta (m-BON-tuh). Okonkwo's mother's village, just beyond Mbaino, where Okonkwo spends his seven years of exile. In his motherland, he is immediately accepted, and his relatives give him land and fields to begin a new life. As Uchendu the elder explains, "A man belongs to his fatherland when things are good and life is sweet. But when there is sorrow and bitterness he finds refuge in his motherland."

Mbaino (m-BI-no). Village bordering on Umofia. Umofia and Mbaino are traditional enemies. When a woman from Umofia is murdered at the market in Mbaino, Umofia threatens a war of vengeance. Rather than face a war with the stronger Umofia, Mbaino sends a young man (Ikemefuna) and a young virgin girl as payment. Throughout the story, Mbaino is referred to as a place where the people are weaker and less just, and the crops are poorer than in Umofia.

Abame (ah-BAH-may). Neighboring village where the white man on an iron horse is killed. After the people of Abame kill the white man, they are attacked by European soldiers. Many of the Abame clan are killed, and the rest are scattered. Crops and fish die. It is the end of the clan, for without their land the clan cannot endure.

*Great River (Niger River). West Africa's biggest river, rising in Guinea and flowing generally east before turning southward to flow through Nigeria. For Umofia, the Great River represents all that is far away and mysterious, since any travel over large distances would be by water. The missionaries establish their base at **Umaru**, on the Great River, because they are people who are not of the land and who will not stay in one place. They do not value land or land ownership, because they look to Heaven rather than to Earth.

— *Cynthia A. Bily*

THE THIRTY-NINE STEPS

Author: John Buchan (1875-1940)
Type of work: Novel
Type of plot: Spy

Time of plot: 1914
First published: 1915

The setting of this novel emphasizes the theme of secret danger in the midst of a period of ostensible peace, which provides a fitting background for the suspenseful plot. Moreover, the setting allows the novelist to emphasize an obvious contrast between urban flaccidity and rural strength of character.

*Scotland. Numerous rural locations in the lowlands of Scotland, including small towns, farms, country houses, and open fields, figure into this spy story. Through most of the novel, the inhabitants of these locations are shown going about their customary lives, ignorant of the secret assassination plot that drives the action. Thus, the characters complain about self-important railway employees, discuss price fluctuations in the cattle markets, and sleep off hangovers, in ironic contrast to protagonist Richard Hannay, who is trying to hide himself from foreign agents.

Hannay, a moderately wealthy South African, takes an undercover tour of this placid setting and comes to know Scotland as a place of great, though subtle, beauty. The rural people with whom he interacts are distrustful of strangers but generous to a fault, especially to those down on their luck. The positive representations of the Scottish people and of Scotland reflect John Buchan's own Scottish upbringing.

More important from the point of view of the novel, the peaceful country and virtuous inhabitants are used to emphasize the familiar espionage contrast between hidden dangers and surface placidity. Like many other spy novels, this one uses setting as theme, and appearances are deceiving. In fact, the Scottish setting allows for a two-fold incorporation of this theme since both the assassins and Hannay go under cover. The assassins do so in order to carry out their criminal scheme, and Hannay does so in order to save his own life. This irony is not only situational but also dramatic, since Hannay shares his hard-won knowledge with readers. Hence, readers also understand the falsity of appearances.

Seaside housing development. Collection of resort villas on the coast of England, presented as typically En-

glish. This setting is highly significant, although it is presented only in the final chapters of the novel. Close to the end of the work, Hannay convinces various government ministers of the reality of an assassination plot and works with them to arrest the assassins. To do this, Hannay must penetrate the disguises of the villains, who take the covers of middle-class Englishmen.

This coastal setting concludes the novel and provides final emphasis to the theme of deceptive appearances. Only at the very end of the novel are the seemingly English inhabitants revealed as German spies.

*London. Great Britain's capital city provides the novel's opening setting and is sketchily presented as a place of boredom for Hannay. The fashionable sights and sounds of pre-World War I London pale quickly for this man of adventure, who has earned his fortune in the rough and tumble of South Africa's diamond fields. To Hannay and the readers, London quickly turns into a familiar facade, behind which devious operators execute hidden and malicious schemes. This theme is introduced through a secondary character who intrudes himself on the narrator and spins a paranoid and anti-Semitic tale of espionage and assassination. This secondary character impresses Hannay so much that Hannay begins to take on his worldview and perceive the falsity of surfaces. When Hannay flees London into rural Scotland, he takes this learned view with him.

London settings also allow Buchan to introduce a minor theme, that of the contrast between urban flaccidity and rural hardiness. In contrast to the later Scottish setting, the London of the novel is too tame a place in which to live, and Hannay longs for some adventure to revive his flagging spirit.

— Michael R. Meyers

THREE LIVES

Author: Gertrude Stein (1874-1946)
Type of work: Novel
Type of plot: Psychological realism

Time of plot: Late nineteenth and early twentieth centuries
First published: 1909

Gertrude Stein's years in Baltimore provided the background for her constructed southern city of Bridgepoint, the setting for all three parts of this novel, which details the lives and deaths of three humble women—the African American woman Melanctha, and two servant girls from Germany, Anna and Lena.

Bridgepoint. Fictional southern port town in an unspecified state in which the entire novel is set. Created from Stein's memories of Baltimore at the turn of the twentieth century, Bridgepoint contains diverse neighborhoods, from well-appointed row houses erected like dominoes along steep hills, to slum districts near the factories, and the home of fortunetellers and the poor. To the novel's three women, Bridgepoint presents a narrow life that forbids escape.

Part one of the novel, titled "The Good Anna," views Bridgepoint through the eyes of Anna Federner, a hard-working immigrant woman who is generous to all who need help, employers and friends alike. Anna lives in the homes of a series of wealthy families, who benefit from the responsible, frugal servant who can always strike a good bargain with local shopkeepers. Eventually one of her rich employers moves from Bridgepoint to a new, unnamed country and leaves Anna the redbrick house they have shared for many years. To pay the bills, Anna takes in boarders, which allows her no time to visit old friends. The endless work causes Anna to grow tired and thin: Eventually she dies.

Melanctha Herbert, the sad, graceful, central character of part two, lives in the African American community of Bridgepoint. Intelligent and courageous, she loves too hard and too often. When she is young she lives with her pale-yellow, sweet-appearing mother and only rarely sees her black father, who treats her roughly. As Melanctha develops into a young woman, she explores—sometimes alone, sometimes with friends—

other working-class neighborhoods of Bridgepoint, as well as the railroad yards, docks, and construction sites. For her, the exciting stories of the workmen and railroad porters evoke a free and adventurous future, but one that she will never know.

In part three, "The Gentle Lena," Stein introduces Lena Mainz, a patient, sweet servant brought from Germany to Bridgepoint by a cousin. Working for a pleasant mistress and her children, Lena enjoys her peaceful life and the sunny afternoons with other servant girls in the park. After four years, however, her life abruptly changes when she enters into an arranged marriage to Herman Kreder and moves to the house he shares with his mother and father, a thrifty old German tailor who works at home. The Kreders's smelly, dirty, poorly heated house soon overflows with the addition of the couple's three children. The normally clean and happy Lena is transformed into a lifeless shell of her former self. None of her friends visit the Kreder house to see her, and eventually she dies giving birth to their fourth child.

*New York City. Northern city to which Herman Kreder flees to escape his arranged marriage with Lena. He stays in the home of his married sister, but she urges him to take a train back to Bridgepoint to marry the woman his parents have chosen for him. His departure from New York signals his loss of freedom and individual will and ultimately leads to the same loss for his wife, Lena.

— Carol F. Bender

THE THREE MUSKETEERS

Author: Alexandre Dumas, *père* (1802-1870)
Type of work: Novel
Type of plot: Historical

Time of plot: 1626
First published: Les Trois Mousquetaires, 1844
   (English translation, 1846)

Set during the reign of French king Louis XIII, this novel celebrates the heroic exploits of four exceptionally loyal friends at court and in battle. Their adventures originate in an intrigue-filled palace and spread through a panorama of Parisian neighborhoods, country roads and inns, channel crossings, port cities, and small towns in England.

*****Gascony.** Region of southwestern France between the Atlantic coast, the Garonne River, and the western Pyrenees. In making the hero, d'Artagnan, a Gascon, Alexandre Dumas early establishes the region's association with boastfulness and flamboyance. He repeatedly demonstrates that d'Artagnan deserves his Gascon reputation for passion, daring, and astuteness. Characterized as an idealistic outsider first encountering the corruption of the capital and the court, d'Artagnan eventually tells the Englishman Lord Buckingham, "The Gascons are the Scotchmen of France." Other admirable Gascons in the novel include Captain de Treville and Porthos of the king's musketeers.

*****Paris.** France's capital is the scene of much of the action of the novel. Dumas's representation of the seventeenth century capital combines striking historical accuracy with some nineteenth century anachronisms. Most of the court scenes take place in the Louvre, the royal residence before Versailles (begun in 1661). A Romantic-Gothic atmosphere dominates the fictionalized city, which emerges most memorably as a place of ambush, midnight assignation, kidnapping, eavesdropping, and dueling.

Beyond the Louvre, Dumas's detailed naming of streets makes it possible to retrace many of d'Artagnan's movements through Paris on modern maps. Sometimes, however, Dumas calls a seventeenth century street by its nineteenth century name or mentions a building erected years after the story takes place. He also errs by identifying d'Artagnan's lodging on the rue des Fossoyeurs with a number; Parisian houses started using numbers later, in 1775.

*****Meung** (muhn). City located on the Loire River, between Orléans and Tours, in which the novel opens. For d'Artagnan's first appearance en route to the glittering capital where he dreams of making his fortune, Dumas chooses a site resonant with chivalry, his first sentence distinguishing Meung as "the birthplace of the author of the *Romance of the Rose*," a thirteenth century poem by Guillaume de Lorris and Jean de Meung.

*****La Rochelle** (lah roh-shehl). Protestant port on France's Atlantic coast that first rebelled against the Catholic regime in 1622. Dumas devotes seven chapters to the Siege of La Rochelle, which started in July, 1627, when France's last Calvinist bastion and only port open to English ships accepted the duke of Buckingham's help against his countrymen.

In an entirely fictitious episode, d'Artagnan, his three friends and their servants take possession of the equally fictitious Bastion of St. Gervais for a private breakfast and council, in the course of which they casually kill two dozen Huguenots. The port of La Rochelle reluctantly collaborating with Buckingham serves as an appropriate backdrop for the four heroes' private decision to warn their country's English opponent of a murder plot against him.

*****Anjou** (AHN-zhu). Old province in western France near the city of Angers that figures indirectly in the novel as the region producing d'Artagnan's favorite wine. Sending a dozen bottles of poisoned Anjou wine to La Rochelle is one of Lady de Winter's murderous ploys against the heroes.

*****Armentières** (AHR-mohn-tyehr). City north of Lille on the Belgian border. The novel's resolution there suggests the wide net of evil that Lady de Winter has spread, temporally and geographically. Her beheading by the executioner of Lille takes place at a slight remove from the heroes' unchivalric passing of a death sentence on a woman—on the other side of the Lys River, in Belgium.

*England. Although the narrative alludes to England at one point as France's "eternal enemy," its prominent English figures, Buckingham and Lord de Winter, prove quite sympathetic characters, even while the English are supporting La Rochelle. Dumas reduces Buckingham's politics, including his alliance with the Huguenots, to romantic gestures motivated by love for Queen Anne. Once Lady de Winter's plots on behalf of Cardinal Richelieu and herself take her to England, she is clearly the far greater enemy for the French heroes—a satanic femme fatale from whom they would save the dashing English lover.

Whenever Dumas shifts the action to England for several chapters, detailed descriptions of his characters' travels between Paris and the French coast fade into a vague landscape where the most prominent feature seems to be Puritanism.

*Portsmouth. English port that is the point of disembarking for travelers from Boulogne and the scene of Buckingham's murder by the Puritan Felton, seduced into homicide by Lady de Winter. A belated warning at Portsmouth marks the heroes' temporary defeat by their female archenemy and the end to Queen Anne's traitorous weakness for a national enemy.

*Spain. Roman Catholic stronghold on the periphery of the novel. France's uneasy relations with its neighbor Spain, and its distrust of its own Queen Anne—daughter of Philip III of Spain and an Austrian—as a double foreigner mark the Spaniards' potential for turning from allies to foes.

— *Margaret Bozenna Goscilo*

THE THREE SISTERS

Author: Anton Chekhov (1860-1904)
Type of work: Drama
Type of plot: Impressionistic realism

Time of plot: Nineteenth century
First performed: 1901; first published, 1901 as *Tri sestry* (revised, 1904; English translation, 1920)

This, Anton Chekhov's most-frequently performed drama, is set in an unnamed town in provincial Russia. The Prozòrov sisters, Olga, Masha, and Irina, are highly educated and hope for a more exciting life in Moscow. The play chronicles the erosion of this hope as events in the lives of each sister move them ever farther from fulfilling their dream of escaping the provinces.

Provincial town. The drabness of life in provincial Russia grates on the three Prozòrov sisters. Compelled to find some kind of happiness in life, Chekhov's characters settle for professions and marriages that seem to provide some comfort against the tediousness of life, but which ultimately result in despair. Andrey's marriage to Natasha threatens the position of his sisters within the household, and eventually the household itself, when Andrey mortgages the property at Natasha's request.

Prozòrov house. Large provincial house left to the Prozòrov children by their father. The house is their birthright as well as the only possession of value that might provide the means of returning to Moscow. Natasha's marriage to Andrey relegates the sisters to the position of guests in their own home, effectively eliminating any chance of selling the house for their return to Moscow. Once a symbol of hope for the sisters, the Prozòrov house becomes another anchor that keeps the sisters in the provinces.

Garden. As in many of Chekhov's plays, a garden serves an important function in *The Three Sisters* by illustrating how simple and beautiful life should be. Baron Tusenbach articulates this idea just prior to his death in a duel with Solyony in the final act of the play. "What beautiful trees they are!" he says, "And how beautiful the life around them ought to be."

— *Philip Bader*

THREE SOLDIERS

Author: John Dos Passos (1896-1970)
Type of work: Novel
Type of plot: Social realism

Time of plot: 1917-1919
First published: 1921

This novel uses World War I settings—an army training camp in the United States, battlefields in France, streets, houses, and cafés of Paris and the small country towns of France—to underscore the war and the rigidly organized military. In settings reminiscent of the American and French Revolutions, army life grinds away at the humanity of soldiers, while the more subtle manipulative control of society at large further erodes their hopes and dreams.

Army camp. U.S. training camp in which the novel's three soldiers prepare to be sent overseas. In the boring, restrictive confines of army camp life, Andrews, Chrisfield, and Fuselli chafe under the dull monotony of daily training and routine designed to force them to perform their tasks in lock-step automation. Ill-trained for combat, their unit departs by ship to France, where the three young men begin another period of boredom while awaiting their assignment to the war front.

***France.** While waiting for orders to move to the front, the men get their first look at the shell-shocked and wounded men returning from a battle at the Argonne Forest. As they confront the realities of battle injuries and exhaustion, their ardor for fighting the "Huns" begins to cool, and they resent even more the endless routine and orders to march here and there seemingly without purpose. When their orders finally come through, Fuselli's spirits lift. He wants to move up in the ranks to corporal and is eager for the glory that frontline combat will give him a chance to earn. However, his sergeant's promises are false and the promotion he expects goes to another. Fuselli gives up on himself and insults the sergeant, and is arrested for insubordination.

As the troop train moves slowly through the darkness, it passes a hospital train returning from the front, and a rumor spreads that Germans have attacked the hospital train. Finally arriving in an unnamed village, the men spend more hours sitting on their packs, waiting. After they march to the camping area, they visit a local café and are soon bragging about encounters with French wine and women.

As the army unit machine rolls through Dijon, with its clusters of little brick and stucco houses, Chrisfield is reminded of the peacefulness of his home in Indiana. From the train, the soldiers march to the front, sleeping on the ground like animals, covering their fears with grumbling about the rain, the mud, and tasteless food. As they reach the war and finally come under attack, the realities of the noise of battle, the "stinking uniforms," and the smell of death surround them; the men grow frightened and fractious. Chrisfield's hatred for his sergeant builds until he kills him during a battle.

After Andrews is wounded, he is taken to a hospital behind the lines. Before the doctors release him, the war is over. Men are no longer fighting, but they cannot yet go home. The mechanized army sits and rusts, while the terms of the treaty are negotiated.

Andrews is assigned to a school in Paris at which he can continue his studies in music. There, he is befriended by a Parisian family. He travels to the seashore with their daughter, Genevieve. The beauty of the country and sunshine at the seashore refresh his spirit, and he begins to compose music again. However, because he is away from Paris without his papers, he is arrested by military police and placed in a prison camp, where he sees Fuselli. Andrews escapes, discards his uniform, and returns to Paris and Genevieve. However, she scorns him as a deserter. He composes music until his money is gone and his landlady reports him to the police. He is arrested for desertion and faces a long prison term.

— *Marguerite R. Plummer*

THE THREEPENNY OPERA

Author: Bertolt Brecht (1898-1956)
Type of work: Drama
Type of plot: Social satire

Time of plot: 1837
First performed: 1928; first published, 1929 as *Die Dreigroschenoper* (English translation, 1949)

Bertolt Brecht's play examines attitudes and self-deception among the bourgeoisie of London by creating bourgeoisie standards within the lower, criminal classes. The basic philosophy is contrasted against the Victorian concept of family values.

*Soho. District of central London in which all the action of the play is confined. However, locations within Soho change rapidly as the plot moves. Soho historically was infamous as an area devoted to crime, poverty, dissolution, and moral depravity. Interested in criticizing society at large, Brecht chose to set his commentary in a removed place and time, making a point about how little society changes and the universality of his themes.

Dark, dirty, and dingy, Soho is a metaphor for the hypocrisy that exists within all strata of society. Its sordid settings and characters reflect the world around them and add to the sense of depravity and disappointment with a world that allows such hypocrisy to exist. Within the context of the drama, the criminal element proves to be no worse than the middle or upper classes, the major differences being found in economics rather than morality or honor. The rich and powerful can perform illegal and immoral acts and escape detection, while the poor receive a separate justice. Brecht's socialistic idealism is propagated by the play, and the setting enhances his message.

— *H. Alan Pickrell*

THROUGH THE LOOKING-GLASS: And What Alice Found There

Author: Lewis Carroll (Charles Lutwidge Dodgson, 1832-1898)
Type of work: Novel

Type of plot: Fantasy
Time of plot: Nineteenth century
First published: 1871

The Looking-Glass Land of this novel is a huge chess game that the protagonist Alice joins as a white pawn, hoping to cross the board to be made a queen. Each time she enters a new square, however, the world is transformed around her: from train to forest to shop to river to town. In keeping with a world patterned on a game with rigid rules, Looking-Glass Land is filled with characters whose fates are somehow predetermined—by their stories (or nursery rhymes), by their set moves as chess pieces, or even by their names.

Alice's house. The story starts and ends in the overstuffed Victorian parlor of Alice's English home. As in *Wonderland*, a safe, comfortable world surrounds the sometimes threatening dream world.

Looking-Glass Land. World that Alice enters by stepping through the mirror in her home. Because the land is on the other side of the mirror, many things go by opposites. Books are printed in mirror-writing, walking directly toward an object results in leading one away from it, one must run as quickly as possible merely to stay in one place. Time can move both forward and backward, just as some chess pieces—not pawns—can move in either direction.

The world is laid out in a pattern of squares, like a chessboard whose columns are divided by hedges and whose rows are separated by small brooks. As a White

Pawn in the Queen's file, counting from the White side, Alice begins on square Q2 and proceeds to Q4, Q5, Q6, Q7, and Q8. She can see and interact with characters from her square or on adjoining squares. The book signals her chess moves with triple rows of dots.

Train. Alice covers the third square quickly, moving by railway (in chess, pawns may advance two full squares on their first move but only one square at other times). The train rushing forward is a parody of hectic, commerce-driven, modern life, in which not only is time money (a thousand pounds a minute), but also words, and even puffs of smoke.

Wood where things have no name. In the next square, Alice learns about Looking-Glass insects, whose natures seem determined by their (punning) names. Identity is an abiding concern in Looking-Glass Land. Growing up, finding out who one is, can feel like a process of trying on different identities, and in this world especially, identity (what piece one is) determines one's role and actions. Within the wood, Alice cannot remember who or what she is, nor can her companion, a fawn. However, once the fawn leaves the wood and again becomes aware of its name, it becomes a slave to its nature and can do nothing but flee.

Even forking paths give no choice in the wood. Both signposts that Alice follows point the same way, to Tweedledum and Tweedledee. These mirror twins must follow their rhyme and fight, though reluctantly. On an adjacent square Alice encounters the Red King who, according to the Tweedles, is dreaming her, and so may be determining not only her actions, but her existence.

Wool and water shop. Modeled on a shop across the road from Carroll's college at Oxford, this location is perhaps the most dreamlike place in Looking-Glass Land. The shop dissolves in true dreamlike fashion into a rowboat traveling along a river full of dream-rushes. Those Alice picks fade and lose scent almost at once, as dreams do, and youth, and, perhaps, life itself, an idea echoed in the book's closing poem.

Humpty Dumpty's square. Poised atop a thin wall, the giant egg Humpty Dumpty proudly pretends to be the master of language, his usage not determined by prior meanings; yet he cannot change the outcome of his own rhyme. As Alice leaves him, she hears a terrific crash, and all the King's horses and men rush past her through the forest. She then encounters the Lion and the Unicorn, who must do battle, as their rhyme ordains.

Wood. Place where the Red and White Knights engage in stylized combat over Alice, fulfilling their roles as chess pieces.

Banquet hall. In this square, Alice consistently has a Queen on either side of her (White Queen in QB8 and Red in K8). The climactic scene, as at the end of *Alice's Adventures in Wonderland* (1865), is a ceremonial occasion with characters present from throughout the book and royalty presiding. The White Queen moves to QR6 (the soup tureen). Alice "takes" the doll-sized Red Queen, seizing her as she runs around the table, a move to K8. Her move puts the Red King in checkmate, presumably waking him, ending the game and the dream— without our knowing which dreamed it.

— *William Mingin*

THYESTES

Author: Seneca (4 B.C.E.-65 C.E.)
Type of work: Drama
Type of plot: Tragedy

Time of plot: Antiquity
First performed: c. 40-55 C.E. (English translation, 1581)

Seneca locates this play in the traditional Homeric setting of the myth about the Mycenaean king who unknowingly eats the flesh of own sons, but follows his usual practice of adapting the settings of Greek tragic to resemble those of Rome, allowing him to comment covertly upon events in contemporary Rome.

Mycenae (Mi-SEE-nee). Fortified city in southeastern Greece and site of the Bronze Age kingdom ruled by the mythical general who led the Greek alliance in the Trojan War. Seneca follows Homer rather than Aeschylus in locating this dynasty in Mycenae rather than in nearby Argos. Lust to possess the city and the royal power it conveys motivates the chief characters to commit monstrous crimes which are described as polluting not only Mycenae's Argive territory but also neighboring lands, such as the Isthmus of Corinth and Mount Cithaeron to the north and even the entire earth.

The hero describes specific features of Mycenae; its massive, irregular stone walls and cliffside palace site are still visible today, but a hippodrome and huge palace complex are monuments belonging to contemporary Rome. The intra-dynastic atrocities committed at Rome under the reign of Nero recall the events of the play. Seneca's detailed depiction of the Mycenaean palace resembles an imperial Roman villa of a sort that was familiar to him, as he was once the Roman emperor Nero's close advisor and knew Rome and the emperor's palace well.

A messenger in the play luridly describes a shrine deep within the vast wings and porticos of the palace where a gloomy grove shelters a hellish spring, howling ghosts, relics of the dynasty's crimes, and altars which receive human sacrifice. At the play's climax, temple doors open to reveal the sumptuous royal banquet hall where the hero discovers he has unknowingly indulged in cannibalism. However, the play regularly evokes place through vivid rhetorical description rather than by scenic effects.

Hell. Mythical region of punishment for earthly crimes. The ghost of the Mycenaean dynasty's founder and his tormenting fury open the play, summoned from Hell to motivate the action. The ghost describes Hell's tantalizing pool with its elusive fruit tree and the fiery river Phlegethon, features familiar from traditional mythology, and promises that his entire progeny will someday join him in Hell to pay for their crimes.

— *Elizabeth A. Fisher*

TIGER AT THE GATES

Author: Jean Giraudoux (1882-1944)
Type of work: Drama
Type of plot: Mythic
Time of plot: Trojan War era

First performed: 1935; first published, 1935 as *La Guerre de Troie n'aura pas lieu* (English translation, 1955)

Jean Giraudoux designed this play so that it could use a single, minimally defined setting somewhere near the walls of Troy, the ancient city under attack by the Greek army. The bare stage is dominated by a pair of gates, the Gates of War, open when Troy is at war and closed in times of peace, but imagination and references to off-stage events extend the scene in a variety of ways.

Off stage. Characters refer to actions that they can see, but that the audience can only imagine, chiefly for comic effects. In the opening scene, however, these descriptions contrast the personalities of Andromache—who describes a beautiful, sunny day—with soldiers stopping to caress stray cats—and Cassandra—who cynically sees suffering and cats as emblems of tigers and of danger. The ambiguity of the play revolves around the question of whether war will break out and hangs on the conflict between these two visions that the audience can not verify.

Similar offstage observations invoke sexual suggestions for comic purposes. As Helen approaches, for example, her entry teasingly delayed, Cassandra jealously describes how she displays her beauty to the men of Troy.

Battlefield. The serious aspect of war appears with Hector who describes the battle from which he has just come to explain to Andromache why he now opposes war. The vision that begins in beauty with images of nature turns to a portrayal of inflicting death as akin to suicide. By portraying the scene through Hector's narration, Giraudoux can totally transform it.

Paris's ship. Suggestive sexuality returns when the sailors describe the voyage on which Paris takes Helen to Troy as a prisoner. The sailors graphically describe the positions of the bodies they observed on deck to prove that Trojan men are lovers of beautiful women.

— *Dorothy M. Betz*

THE TIME MACHINE: An Invention

Author: H. G. Wells (1866-1946)
Type of work: Novel
Type of plot: Fantasy

Time of plot: Late nineteenth century
First published: 1895

The physical locations in this story of time travel do not change, but the settings differ greatly in each of the three main scenes as the unnamed Time Traveller moves farther and farther into the future.

Time Traveller's home. Although it is reasonable to infer that Wells's unnamed traveler lives in London—and probably southwest London—nothing in the novel locates his home precisely. His home is a large upper-middle-class house typical of homes of its class in the late nineteenth century. Wells takes pains to make the home warm and welcoming, comfortable and convivial. It appears to be popular with visitors, as the two times the house is mentioned in the novel it is the setting of well-attended dinner parties that bring together intelligent and well-connected men. The guests are identified only by their professions, for example, such as the Medical Man and the Editor. There are also servants and other indications that the Time Traveller is wealthy. Thus, the home in which the Time Traveller tells his story is a place of both solid reality and aspiration, the height of ambition for Wells's audience. This is the measure of achievement, the sign that these intelligent and comfortable Victorians really are the peak of evolution.

Eloi world. The Time Traveller's first stop in the remote future. Although it occupies the same space as the Time Traveller's home, the world of the Eloi is separated from it by some 800,000 years. That fact alone expresses Wells's primary Darwinian purpose: to demonstrate that evolution will continue beyond the world he and his readers know. This setting is, at first, a pastoral idyll, a place of green fields, strange flowers, and a curious innocence. Soon, however, a different impression is created, as the Time Traveller notices the decaying buildings, the sense of things running down, and in particular the sense that the inhabitants of this world, the Eloi, are, though pretty and innocent, also in decline. This is emphasized in his visit to the Palace of Green Porcelain, once a great museum though now most of its exhibits have rotted away; the age of human achievement is long passed.

Morlock world. Though visited only once and very briefly, the underground realm of the Morlocks forms a constant counterpoint to the pastoral simplicity of the world of the Eloi. It is a lightless world, a world of dark oppression, and the Morlocks are as much its victims as anyone else. There is a sense of machinery, though the reader never encounters it directly.

Beach. After finally escaping the world of the Eloi and the Morlocks, the Time Traveller flees to a point in the far distant future when the world is coming to an end. In one of the most effective and influential scenes in the whole of science fiction, he describes a tideless sea and desolate shore, all bathed in the dim, red light of a huge and unmoving Sun. Far out across the water one lone, dark shape flops hopelessly. Given the scientific knowledge of Wells's time, it is an accurate portrait of one possible end-of-the-world scenario—with the Moon gone, the Sun's energy failing, Earth pulled from its orbit and losing its rotation, with only the steady approach to the dying sun preventing it being a completely frozen waste. It is also an effective metaphor for the message of evolution: All this must pass.

— *Paul Kincaid*

THE TIME OF YOUR LIFE

Author: William Saroyan (1908-1981)
Type of work: Drama
Type of plot: Psychological realism

Time of plot: 1939
First performed: 1939; first published, 1939

This, William Saroyan's most acclaimed play, is set in San Francisco on the cusp of the Great Depression and World War II. It unfolds entirely inside a tavern focused on conviviality, food, and community, enabling a diverse cast of characters to share their innermost selves.

*San Francisco. Port city in Northern California in which the play is set. Saroyan delighted in setting his tales in his native California. While he often preferred rural locations, he also used urban settings, and although he wrote this play in New York City, his heart was in San Francisco, where he lived and secured a place for his mother to live. It was a city he knew well—and for him it provided daily illustrations of the miracle of life. By 1939, when this play was first produced, San Francisco had approached its peak population and the surrounding Bay Area region contained about a third of California's inhabitants. As a transportation hub, the city drew together people from all over the Americas and the world, who arrived by ship under the Golden Gate Bridge, or by rail over the Union Pacific lines. Nearly destroyed by an earthquake in 1906, the city was constantly reinventing itself. As one character in the play puts it, San Francisco has "no foundation, all the way down." That kind of life on the edge, both physically and socially, appealed to Saroyan and inspired the cast he created to populate a typical Bay Area bar.

Nick's Pacific Street Saloon. San Francisco waterfront bar in which the entire play is set. The saloon is the kind of honky-tonk that Saroyan loved—a place in which drinkers can talk, play music, and dance, while hearing the blare of foghorns from the bay. Its furnishings include card tables, a marble game, a juke box, piano, small dance floor, and a long bar. A uniquely American place, the saloon has characteristics of a church—a place in which confessions are made and heard. It is also a stage on which talent is displayed in talk, by tap, and on the keyboard. It is microcosm of pure democracy in which Thomas Jefferson's philosophy prevails—a place in which no one is the inferior of or superior of anyone else.

Set against the backdrop of the Great Depression, the rise of European fascism, and the beginning of a new world war, Nick's Saloon is also a rehabilitation center, a meeting place, in which perceptions of difference can be transcended by a shared recognition of human value. As Saroyan himself noted, Nick's is committed to the belief that life can be redemptive. Finally, Nick's is a philosopher's club; bartender Harry believes that the world is sorrowful and needs laughter, which he will provide. The power of Nick's Saloon, in the script, on the stage, and in its screen adaptation, is that it possesses the delightful ambiguity of being both ordinary, like any neighborhood tavern, and also extraordinary, a special place in which life can be made whole.

— *C. George Fry*

TIMON OF ATHENS

Author: William Shakespeare (1564-1616)
Type of work: Drama
Type of plot: Tragedy

Time of plot: Fourth century B.C.E.
Written: c. 1607-1608; first published, 1623

Although this play is structured primarily around the character of the Athenian nobleman Timon, the settings of Timon's great hall and cave outside the walls of Athens have dominant roles in its exploration of disillusionment and misanthropy.

Timon's house. Large, richly appointed abode in Athens in which Timon's wealth and good nature win him many false friends and hangers-on, as his vast hall becomes the site of a procession of characters who prey upon his generosity. Loud music, masques, great banquets, and Timon's bestowal of lavish gifts on guests are customary. William Shakespeare's purpose here is to reveal through the setting and ceremonious or formal modes of conduct how the prodigal and ostentatious Timon is exploited. The hall itself is important for the play's second banquet scene, in which Timon somberly parodies religion in his bitter misanthropy by serving lukewarm water and stones to his fellow senators.

Cave. Place near the seashore where Timon lives after rejecting Athens. The senate (a pure fiction on the part of Shakespeare who clearly was thinking of Rome), Lucullus's home, and Sempronius's house are minor settings in short and relatively minor scenes; they take a secondary position to the cave where Timon is alone. Timon's first great soliloquy comes as he looks back at the walls of Athens and ferociously condemns the city and its inhabitants to total ruin.

The surrounding woods are within an otherwise barren coast that is filled with strange noises, wild beasts, and birds of prey. The extreme harshness of this setting accords with the mental and emotional state of Timon, whose character is revealed by misfortune. Starved and ragged, he has to dig for edible roots to survive. However, within the cave he discovers gold that he gives away as his sign of abnegation. His end comes when he disappears into the cave; however, Shakespeare does not reveal whether his death is by suicide or natural causes.

— Keith Garebian

THE TIN DRUM

Author: Günter Grass (1927-   )
Type of work: Novel
Type of plot: Social satire

Time of plot: 1899-1954
First published: Die Blechtrommel, 1959 (English translation, 1961)

This autobiographical novel chronicles Europe's violent history during the first half of the twentieth century. It focuses on Germany's role in that upheaval as the narrator records his experiences, first in a Polish city, then in a German city. The long and turbulent pasts of these cities provide striking backgrounds for the action that unfolds and the social satire that emerges. In this complex novel, locations are always reproduced with exactness, only to be transfigured into places far removed from reality. That the novel is essentially a fictional version of the theater of the absurd demands that the treatment of place be as quirky as the plot and character development.

*Danzig or **Gdansk** (DAN-zik; GEH-danshk). Major Polish port on the Baltic Sea that has a long and colorful history dating from the tenth century. At times through the ages Germany controlled the city, and it was called Danzig. During other periods it was a city-state known as Gdansk. In 1939, when Germany invaded Poland and seized Gdansk, its name was again changed to Danzig. After World War II it became a part of Poland and was again called Gdansk, which has continued to be its name.

Günter Grass was born and grew up in this city, where his parents owned a grocery store. The opening section of *The Tin Drum* outwardly recalls Grass's early years through the voice of his fictional narrator, Oskar Matzerath. Like Grass, Oskar was born in the 1930's. His parents also operate a small grocery store, and much of the first part of the novel takes place in the shop and the family's adjacent living quarters. Oskar succeeds in creating the ambience of a family-run store, bringing the customers to life, as well as making the goods, their texture and smells, tangible. He fully captures the colorful port city with its ancient buildings, narrow streets, and cramped quarters, along with its waterfront and beach areas. He also recounts the lives of his grandparents, who lived on a farm in the Polish province of Kashubia, a rural area that he describes in a distinctive manner.

Like his fictional Oskar, Grass lived through the German invasion of the city in 1939 and its aftermath. These events are turned into a vivid piece of fiction that depicts how the presence of the German occupation force dramatically alters the city's atmosphere. Although Grass certainly drew on his early years to give this part of the novel its rich texture and realistic tone, the narrative itself undermines the authenticity of its setting. Places and objects take on a significance in the novel far removed from reality, as Grass converts ordinary surroundings and objects into extended metaphors and motifs—Oskar's tin drum being the most notable example.

As the narrative progresses, Gdansk, which is accurately drawn in its pre-World War II condition, exemplifies any city transformed from a peaceful state by war. Under its new name of Danzig, the city once called Gdansk turns into a place where barbarity and fear dominate. That its identity as "Gdansk" and "Danzig" has vacillated over the centuries adds to its metaphoric possibilities, which Grass exploits to the fullest.

*Düsseldorf. Industrial city in west-central Germany where Oskar is writing his memoirs in a mental hospital.

After the war, Oskar and his family are forced to emigrate to Düsseldorf. Grass, who served in the German army during World War II, also ended up in Düsseldorf after the war and had experiences there similar to those that Oskar records in his autobiography.

Starting out as a fishing village in the seventh century at the point where the Düssel River flows into the Rhine River, Düsseldorf gained importance during the Industrial Revolution. It became the financial center of the surrounding industrial area known as the Ruhr, whose coal mines produced the energy and whose factories built most of the implements for both world wars. Significantly, during the 1930's the German industrialists met with Hitler in Düsseldorf to offer their support if they could be assured of another war. In the 1940's the Allies bombed the city into rubble, which is what Oskar finds when he arrives there. Düsseldorf's checkered history makes it a suitable place for Grass to carry out his satiric view of Germany during and after the war.

Oskar relates how he and his family survive among the ruins of Düsseldorf and how his mother makes a living on the black market. At first Oskar works as a tombstone engraver, which provides the opportunity for him to describe the cemeteries in detail; cemeteries are another recurring motif in the novel. Later he becomes a model at the newly opened art academy, a venue he pictures with exactness.

As the city starts to rebuild, night clubs and dance halls open in bombed-out buildings, such as the Lion's Den, one of Oskar's favorites. Oskar's jazz trio plays in another club called the Onion Cellar, an appropriate name considering that the owner serves raw onions to make his patrons cry, a response they desire and enjoy. This idiosyncrasy illustrates how Grass extends the meaning of place throughout the novel.

In Düsseldorf the sense of place is remarkably concrete, including its rutted-out streets, its blocks of shattered apartment buildings, its once grand buildings that lay in ruins. Even though this devastated postwar city, like so many in Germany, is described in realistic detail, it is at the same time turned into a succession of metaphors and motifs to depict the senselessness of war.

— *Robert L. Ross*

THE TITAN

Author: Theodore Dreiser (1871-1945)　　　*Time of plot:* 1890's

Type of work: Novel　　　*First published:* 1914

Type of plot: Naturalism

Set in Chicago in the last decade of the nineteenth century, this novel is as much the story of the city as it is of Frank Algernon Cowperwood. Theodore Dreiser was mainly concerned with capturing the look and feel of Chicago as it was in the process of growing into a major world city during the dynamic period in which America was being transformed from an agrarian into an industrial nation.

*Chicago. Dreiser loved and admired Chicago. He wrote about it in many of his novels, including *Sister Carrie* (1900) and *An American Tragedy* (1925). *The Titan* presents a vivid, accurate picture of urban life in America at the turn of the twentieth century, when horses provided almost all the city's transportation, and there were no automobiles, buses, telephones, radios, phonographs, refrigerators, air-conditioning, or other amenities that are now taken for granted. All entertainments were live; social life centered around private homes. Women were largely confined indoors as housewives, mothers, and hostesses. Social classes were rigidly stratified. There were no labor unions, social security, unemployment insurance, or workers' compensation insurance.

The plot of *The Titan* centers on the epic struggle of ruthless men for control of the lucrative streetcar traffic in the city. The evolution of streetcars exemplifies not only Chicago's rapid growth but also the frantic pace of change taking place in the United States, in which millions of native-born citizens and European immigrants are being torn from the soil and drawn into urban centers. The slow, inefficient horse-drawn streetcars are replaced by cable cars, which in turn are quickly replaced with cars powered by electricity. Finally, elevated tracks become the last word in urban transportation. The city expands with the streetcar lines, and the streetcar lines form a larger and larger web around the expanding city.

Michigan Avenue Mansion. Chicago home of the powerful entrepreneur Frank Algernon Cowperwood, for whom social success means as much as financial success. He builds his first mansion near the homes of the Chicago social elite in the hope that he and his wife, Aileen, will be accepted into high society. Their new mansion, built along conventional lines to emulate the homes of their neighbors, is described in detail. After the Cowperwoods are rejected by society, their mansion seems like an empty shell. Aileen has only a few humble visitors to entertain. She feels humiliated, isolated, and lonely. Cowperwood begins spending more and more time away from home, involved in liaisons with other women.

Tunnels. Cowperwood's discovery of two rat-infested abandoned tunnels under the Chicago River is a turning point in his career. He realizes that they can be adapted to alleviate the chronic congestion on the bridges and enable him to provide faster, more dependable streetcar service from the suburbs into the central city. The history of the La Salle Street and Washington Street tunnels illustrates Dreiser's cynical but realistic attitude toward capitalists and politicians generally. After the tunnels had become unprofitable for their original speculators, these men induced the city fathers to pay one million dollars of taxpayer money for them and then board them up. Cowperwood's acquisition of the tunnels displays the superior intelligence and creative imagination that sets him apart from ordinary men.

New York mansion. House that Cowperwood has built on New York City's Fifth Avenue. His conception of this mansion shows the change that has taken place in his character over the years. He builds a gaudy, spectacular palace to flaunt his wealth and declare to the world his indifference to social acceptance by timid, conventional souls: "Only the Italian palaces of medieval or Renaissance origin which he had seen abroad now appealed to him as examples of what a stately residence should be."

Ironically, Cowperwood's fabulous mansion, which is described in newspapers and magazines all over the United States, instills such envy among the common people that his Chicago enemies can turn the masses against him and defeat his scheme to monopolize the streetcar lines there.

Chicago City Hall. Dreiser uses the City Hall in Chicago to dramatize the climax to his novel. The big building—described as a "large, ponderous structure of black granite—erected at the expense of millions and suggesting somewhat the somnolent architecture of ancient Egypt"—is packed with an angry mob, while the surrounding streets are thronged by thousands more. Without microphones, the speakers have to shout to make themselves heard, but they are shouted down by the incensed spectators whose passions have been aroused by the newspapers, the dominant media of the day. The irate citizens intimidate the bought politicians into voting down the proposal to award Cowperwood the long-term streetcar franchises he desperately needs.

— *Bill Delaney*

TITUS ANDRONICUS

Author: William Shakespeare (1564-1616)
Type of work: Drama
Type of plot: Tragedy

Time of plot: Early Christian era
First performed: 1594; first published, 1594

While other historically situated plays of William Shakespeare often attempt some accuracy in describing locale, the settings for Titus Andronicus *offer locales in name only, with the events drawn from a compilation of classical myths, and its characters fictional amalgams of historical figures set within the fourth century, after the Goths sacked Rome. This play only hints at verisimilitude. Shakespeare's stage was analogical; that is, the playhouse set forth an analogy of humanity's place in God's cosmos, with the heavens above (the hut of the theater), Hell below (beneath the stage), and the stage proper representing humankind's earthly journey between the two.*

*Rome. Center of the Roman Empire, where the play opens at Emperor Titus's royal court. The entrance of the emperor's sons through different doors opens the play and denotes the division and divided loyalties that will plague Rome, preparing the audience for the political strife that ravages the court. In contrast, the tribunes and senators of Rome, along with Marcus, the brother of Titus, appear aloft on the balcony, in order to underscore the tradition of a once mighty and proud Rome that remains "above" the fray of petty squabbles and familial strife. Into this contrasting setting appears Titus on the main stage in his triumphal entrance to the city, bringing both prisoners and Roman dead, as he moves to the trapdoor, which functions as the burial site for those slain in battle.

Later in the play, the trapdoor becomes a pit dug in the countryside of Rome, used by the sons of the evil queen to hide a murder and to ensnare two of Titus's sons. Thus the location of the play is less important than the symbolism of where characters perform. In and nearby the court of Rome may be the referenced sites, but the playhouse stage reveals more, offering the medieval concept of *theatrum mundi*, or "world as a stage," which measures all things vertically, from hell below to heaven above, as mankind "frets and struts his hour upon the stage," as Macbeth says in another of Shakespeare's plays.

— *Wayne Narey*

TO KILL A MOCKINGBIRD

Author: Harper Lee (Nelle Harper Lee, 1926-   )   *Time of plot:* Mid-1930's
Type of work: Novel   *First published:* 1960
Type of plot: Bildungsroman

The retrospective narrator, Scout, examines how she learned to understand racial and social prejudices of small-town southern life by seeing the world through others' perspectives.

Maycomb. Seat of Alabama's fictional Maycomb County, located twenty miles east of Finch's Landing. Through its citizens from professional, middle, and lower classes, Harper Lee analyzes the values and problems common in small southern towns during the Great Depression. Scout learns from Atticus to reject the racial and social prejudices of the town without hating its inhabitants. By walking in the shoes of others both before and after the Tom Robinson trial, she respects Mrs. Henry Lafayette Dubose, who is determined to cure her morphine addiction before dying, and she appreciates Judge Taylor, Sheriff Tate, and farmer Link Deas, all of whom try to give Tom Robinson as fair a trial as possible in Maycomb.

Radley place. Home of Arthur (Boo) Radley and his family; located near Atticus Finch's home. Community rumors about the seclusion of Boo in his home and about his violent actions provide mystery and excitement for Scout, Jem, and Dill during their summers. Actually seeing Boo or enticing him to leave his dark, isolated home becomes a goal for the children and a lesson in tolerance and acceptance. Through the gifts they find in the hollow tree in the Radley yard, they learn of Boo's tentative attempts at friendship with them. When Boo saves their lives by killing Bob Ewell in the woods behind the school, they learn to respect his privacy and his desire to remain hidden from the probing eyes of the community.

Schoolhouse. School attended by the Finch children. By having children from the town and from the rural community in the same classes, Lee shows the various social classes in the county and how all have learned to live together. Miss Caroline Fisher, Scout's first-grade teacher, is considered an outsider because she is from Clanton in northern Alabama. She does not understand the social caste system of her students, and her new educational practices appear impractical to her students.

Courthouse. Government building in the town square in which Tom Robinson is tried for murder. The architecture of this building symbolizes the strong ties of the town to the past and its unwillingness to change. After fire destroyed the original classical structure, its massive columns were retained while a Victorian clock tower was added. This symbolizes the town's acceptance of change only as a result of a conflagration and its attempt to preserve the past as completely as possible.

Having the black residents sit in the balcony of the courtroom during the Robinson trial stresses the physical and social segregation of the races. In contrast, having Scout, Jem, and Dill accepted by Reverend Sykes in the balcony also symbolizes the hope that the young generation of white southerners will be able to see both blacks and whites differently as they grow up. On the courthouse grounds during the trial, Scout and Dill learn from Dolphus Raymond that his false drunkenness is only a ruse he assumes in order to provide the community with an excuse for his living with a black wife and fathering children of mixed blood.

Finch's Landing. Town in which Atticus Finch grew up. Located on the banks of the Alabama River, it was begun in the early nineteenth century by Atticus's ancestor, Simon Finch, an immigrant from England, and remained the home of the Finch family until Atticus left to study law in Montgomery, Alabama, and his younger brother, Jack, left to study medicine in Boston. Their sister Alexandra continued to live there with her husband. The small town provides a strong sense of history and family within which Scout and Jem grow up. Although they only visit there, each child understands how their current home is an extension of the values and beliefs in which Atticus, Uncle Jack, and Aunt Alexandra were raised. Neither Atticus nor Jack returns to Finch's Landing to live because the town is too small to support their professions, and each seems to disregard many of the mores espoused there as shown through the actions of Aunt Alexandra.

— *Alan T. Belsches*

TO THE LIGHTHOUSE

Author: Virginia Woolf (1882-1941)
Type of work: Novel
Type of plot: Stream of consciousness

Time of plot: c. 1910-1920
First published: 1927

The primary setting of this novel is based on a seaside house that belonged to Virginia Woolf's family when she was a child, and the novel's main characters are modeled on her parents. Transplanted in her novel from the south of England to a rocky coast off Scotland, the Ramsay summerhouse, the adjacent sea, and the nearby lighthouse are the three major locales of a story that explores life, death, and the passage of time in a world moving from Edwardian times into modernity.

Summerhouse. Ramshackle Victorian house on an island in the Hebrides that accommodates both the large Ramsay family and their friends. It is here that Mrs. Ramsay is in her element, ministering endlessly to the needs of her husband, children, and guests. Whether in her parlor knitting, presiding over the dinner table, or tucking her children into bed, Mrs. Ramsay is the life and soul of the house. However, while the nearby lighthouse seems to endure without change, the summerhouse gradually deteriorates over time. Neglected after a series of family deaths, the house succumbs to the forces of nature and falls into disrepair. While the lighthouse—always a symbol of timeless serenity—can withstand the sea and the weather, the Ramsay house is at the mercy of these elements. Similarly, the members of the Ramsay family themselves are at the mercy of a series of upheavals that devastate their lives, particularly the untimely deaths of Mrs. Ramsay of heart-failure and of one of her sons on the battlefields of World War I. The passage of time wreaks havoc on both the family and their home, marking the end of the Edwardian world in which Virginia Woolf herself had spent her childhood. Eventually, however, after the war, the house is restored to good order, and Mr. Ramsay and his two youngest children, along with Lily Briscoe and an old poet-friend of the family, return to it to try to put their lives back together.

*****Hebrides Islands** (HEH-brah-dees). Island group off the northwest coast of Scotland on which the summerhouse stands. Woolf probably chose this as her novel's setting because of its sense of wilderness and its proximity to an untrammeled sea that suggests the mysterious and the primal. The sea here is associated with danger and disorder and, after Mrs. Ramsay dies, with an existential meaninglessness.

Lighthouse. Coastal edifice near the summerhouse and a constant presence in this novel, beginning with its opening scene, in which the Ramsays debate the idea of making a picnic outing to the lighthouse. Mrs. Ramsay, the wife and mother who presides over the summerhouse and its various guests and children, and who is sure the weather will be fine enough for the trip, has a special connection to the lighthouse. When she sits at her parlor window looking out at the lighthouse while knitting, her spiritual communion with the lighthouse occasions a flood of strong feelings. Later, as she presides over dinner, she still feels the lighthouse's presence, which for her represents a transcendental sense of security and well-being.

Six or seven years after Mrs. Ramsay's sudden death, Mr. Ramsay and his two youngest children return to the summerhouse and finally make the long-awaited trip to the lighthouse. Although all three are lonely and still feel the loss of Mrs. Ramsay, things miraculously begin to go well. The outing to the lighthouse becomes an occasion during which the rift between Mr. Ramsay and his children begins to be healed. Lily Briscoe, a family friend of the Ramsay's, also seems to encounter the lighthouse through a picture she is painting from the shore. As she places a straight, lighthouselike line in her picture, she feels at last a sense of peace and completion similar to that of Mrs. Ramsay before she died.

— *Margaret Boe Birns*

TOBACCO ROAD

Author: Erskine Caldwell (1903-1987)　　　　*Time of plot:* 1920's
Type of work: Novel　　　　　　　　　　　　*First published:* 1932
Type of plot: Naturalism

In this novel, an impoverished region of Georgia has the power to grind down the Lester family to a point at which they are indifferent to one another's pain and suffering. The land, once a source of familial pride, has become an inescapable weight pulling them ever more deeply into a morass of stark poverty and animalism.

Lester farm. Georgia home of Jeeter Lester's family, near the town of Fuller. A three-room ramshackle house with a sagging porch and leaky roof stands in a grassless yard with a few chinaberry trees here and there. The surrounding cotton fields have not been cultivated for several years and are overgrown. Some seventy-five years before, it had been a promising tobacco farm owned by Jeeter's grandfather. Running through the property is a tobacco road nearly fifteen miles long, once used to roll tobacco casks to the steamboats on the distant Savannah River.

Jeeter's inability to produce a reasonable crop from the sandy, depleted soil has left him so heavily in debt that he has turned to sharecropping on what was once his family's plantation. The soil resists Jeeter's increasingly weak, though well-intentioned, efforts to grow a sustainable crop. Its infertility mirrors the impotence that gradually overtakes Jeeter and reduces him to little more than a shadow of a man. By the end of the novel, there remains even less of the farm after a fire destroys the old house, leaving only a "tall brick chimney . . . blackened and tomb-like."

The utter, hopeless poverty so graphically depicted by the Lesters' plight is representative of the rural squalor and degradation faced by many Americans living at the lowest levels of economic and moral debasement.

*Augusta. Georgia city about fifteen miles from the Lester farm. The Lesters go to Augusta naïvely hoping to sell some firewood. The trip, in a brand-new car purchased by Sister Bessie, the new wife of Jeeter's sixteen-year-old son Dude, fails to raise any money to buy food or other necessities. They spend the night in a "hotel," which resembles a brothel or hookers' hotel, and Sister Bessie, in her ignorance, gets shunted about from room to room, encountering various unknown men waiting in beds. When they all head home the next day, they are none the wiser or richer for having had the experience. Furthermore, the load of wood and the lack of oil in the engine have ruined the new car.

Fuller. Town about five miles from the Lester farm and about fifteen miles from Augusta. It is large enough to have a Ford car dealership, at least one church (Baptist), stores, and a courthouse, where Sister Bessie and Dude Lester obtain their marriage license.

The stores in Fuller had at one time extended credit to Jeeter because he raised a fair cotton crop each year. When his debts increased so much that he had no hope of paying them, his farm was bought by Captain John Harmon. Harmon allowed Jeeter to sharecrop for several unprofitable years but finally gave up, sold out, and moved to Augusta. The stores in Fuller, aware they can no longer expect to be paid, refuse Jeeter credit, thus cutting off his last source of sustenance.

Fuller's bounty is close and yet completely out of Jeeter's reach. Just as his wish for a decent crop is ongoing yet unattainable, so Fuller represents the relief that is impossible for Jeeter to obtain.

— Jane L. Ball

THE TOILERS OF THE SEA

Author: Victor Hugo (1802-1885)
Type of work: Novel
Type of plot: Sentimental

Time of plot: 1820's
First published: Les Travailleurs de la mer, 1866
  (English translation, 1866)

Set in the stark maritime environment of the Channel Islands off the coast of France, this novel underlines the isolation of the islands' seagoing inhabitants from both England and the nearby French mainland, as well as from the relatively comfortable green garden villages on the islands themselves.

*Channel Islands. Group of islands off the coast of Normandy (known to the French as the Normand Islands) that alternated between British and French control after the Norman Conquest of England in 1066. Victor Hugo's vignettes of early nineteenth century maritime life are set primarily on Guernsey and Jersey, the two principal islands in the group. Possessing an unusual microclimate, the islands are legendary for their mild winters and frequent light rainfall, which makes them ideal for cultivating vegetables and fruits, but Hugo's novel is more concerned with the lives of the islanders who reap their harvests from the sea. Thus, the moderate comforts that might be reflected in the material life of the islanders who dwell ashore year round are not apparent. Rather, the challenges and dangers of the sea, frequently symbolized by the threatening names of spaces separating the islands from the mainland, shape the vignettes that Hugo chooses for the subjects of his stories.

*Douvres (dew-VRUH). Treacherous rocks that jut out of the sea about fifteen miles south of Guernsey. The arduous ordeal of Hugo's protagonist Gilliatt, who is shipwrecked on one of the rocks, underlines the power of immense forces in nature, such as shattering waves pushed by heavy winds. At the same time, Gilliatt's entry into the struggle of individual creatures at his feet, where crabs devour helpless tidepool victims, helps him restore his own strength as he clings to the rock. Ironically, rocks such as the Douvres and another group, the Hanways, though "guilty of all evil deeds," offer the most solid hopes for survival in the rough seas.

*Cherbourg Peninsula (SHAYR-bewrg). French peninsula immediately east of the Channel Islands that projects into the English Channel. Despite the peninsula's relative closeness to the islands, its long western coastal shores play only a small role in the lives of the island seafarers. The notable absence of safe havens on the peninsula—other than Cherbourg itself, which is inconveniently situated beyond the tip of the peninsula—makes Saint Malo, near the western base of the peninsula, the most practical maritime destination and, for Hugo, the logical setting for extension of his stories and characters to the French mainland.

*Saint Malo (sahn mahl-OH). Normandy port city that to Channel islanders represents a microcosm of mainland France itself. Its importance as a port of call for commerce provides a source of livelihood for many islanders. Hugo does not closely focus on the normal commercial or social life of the port, preferring to depict its lowlife in scenes set in a particular rooming house, the Jacressarde. There, an atmosphere of thieves, prostitutes, and general ne'er-do-wells contrasts markedly with the modest but upstanding lives of Hugo's islanders.

*Weymouth. English port that is closest to the Channel Islands yet seems so distant from the lives of the island seafarers as to be another and unfamiliar world. Because the islanders' lives depend on serving as shipping intermediaries between England and France, they are always alert to news of ship departures from Weymouth.

— *Byron D. Cannon*

TOM BROWN'S SCHOOL DAYS

Author: Thomas Hughes (1822-1896)

Type of work: Novel

Type of plot: Social realism

Time of plot: Early nineteenth century

First published: 1857

This Victorian coming-of-age novel is set almost entirely at Rugby School and its environs in the West Midlands of England. It describes a world of privilege, intended to prepare boys for the universities of Oxford or Cambridge and ultimately for service to the British Empire. Rich with detail, the story presents a clear picture of Rugby as it was in the 1830's.

*Rugby School. One of the great English public schools, founded in 1567. In writing this novel, Thomas Hughes described the world of Rugby School as he knew it when he was a student there in the 1830's. Tom's first sight of the school is of the playing field and a long line of stone buildings, with the chapel at one end and the schoolhouse, containing the headmaster's residence, at the other. Much of the action occurs on the close, or playing field, a large, open space divided into two areas. Between a gravel walk bordering the building and a line of elm trees, the younger boys play their cricket matches, and on the other side of the trees the older boys play theirs. There are goals at the ends of these fields, which are kept in good repair by the school's servants, as are the grassy fields themselves, which are regularly wetted down and smoothed with rollers. At one side is a fives' court for handball players. From his first day, when he throws himself into a cricket match, until his last day, nine years later, when he plays as the respected captain of the school's best team, many of Tom's successes and failures take place on the close.

Schoolhouse hall. Large chamber, thirty feet long and eighteen feet high that is the setting for many of the indoor events in the story. Along one side are two large fireplaces whose blazing fires provide the heat and much of the light. There are two long tables where the boys eat, one in the middle of the room and the other closer to the wall. It is in this room that Tom first sees the august headmaster, Dr. Thomas Arnold, presiding over the main meal, served at midday. This room is the site of mealtime pranks, companionable chats, and school singings. It is also the place where Tom is dangled before one of the great fireplaces by Flashman, the school bully.

Study rooms. The boys' studies are important in the novel. The study rooms are roughly six by four feet assigned to pairs of boys for the preparation of their lessons. Each contains a table, a chair, a sofa and bookcases. The study of Tom and his friend East, adorned with prints of dogs and horses, is the repository for their beloved cricket bats and fishing rods. Later, Tom shares a larger study with George Arthur, a young protégé assigned to him by Dr. Arnold. George's mother provides a fine desk, curtains, and a carpet. These studies are the places in which Tom foments rebellion against the tyranny of the older boys, struggles with his Latin and Greek translations, and has long religious and philosophical discussions with his friends.

Chapel. In the area behind the chapel, traditionally the location for the boys' fights, Tom engages in his only bout of fisticuffs. Within the chapel, Dr. Arnold delivers from the high pulpit sermons which hold the attention of some of the boys, while others fidget in the pews and scratch their initials into the wood. Others stare out at the treetops visible through the large window behind the organ loft. In the book's closing scene, Tom pays his respects to the memory of Dr. Arnold, whose remains lie beneath the altar.

*Rugby. Village located about twelve miles southwest of Coventry. Rugby of the 1830's is a quiet place, lacking street lighting or paving. The boys are in the village almost daily, most especially to visit Sally Harrowell's, a shop where they buy sweets and roast potatoes for their teatime. Throughout the year they roam the nearby farmers' fields and woods and swim and fish in the River Avon, which borders the town.

— *Beverly Haskell Lee*

TOM JONES

Author: Henry Fielding (1707-1754)
Type of work: Novel
Type of plot: Romance

Time of plot: Early eighteenth century
*First published: The History of Tom Jones, a
    Foundling*, 1749

*Settings in this novel span much of western England. The novel's three divisions—country, road, and city—are
realistic and symmetrical backdrops for three pursuit plots: Tom's pursuit of both his identity and his sweetheart, Sophia; Squire Western's pursuit of Sophia, his reluctant daughter, to force her into a marriage of convenience; and Squire Allworthy's pursuit of his true heir, Tom. The epic sweep across England represents pursuits
of happiness love, wealth, and family.*

Paradise Hall. Estate of Squire Allworthy in Glastonbury in southwestern England's county of Somersetshire. Allworthy's estate borders that of Squire Western.
Paradise Hall is just that, an Eden from which Tom Jones,
Allworthy's good-natured ward (later discovered to be
his elder nephew), is banished due to his lack of prudence
and the conniving of Blifil, Allworthy's younger nephew.
Paradise Hall is the allusive setting for Cain versus Abel
and Devil versus Adam parallels in Blifil and Tom.

Western's estate. Home of Squire Western and his
daughter Sophia. This estate is characterized by hunting,
heavy drinking, singing, and an absolutist but loving father. Each estate symbolizes a political opposite: Allworthy is a sober and refined Whig; Western is a sports-
loving and rough-edged Tory. Western England was
dominated by Tories in the eighteenth century, hence the
symbolism of the squire's name.

Little Baddington. Village that is the center of petty
jealousies, vicious gossip, and a mock-epic battle. In the
village the house of Partridge, the schoolmaster, and his
shrewish wife extend the marriage theme. The cottage of
"Black" George Seagrim, the gamekeeper, appropriately is a trap for both Tom and his hypocritical tutor,
Mr. Square, caught there by the wiles of the wanton
Molly, George's daughter. The houses frame recurring
types of the family theme in different social classes: contrasting parents, upbringings, siblings, courtships, and
marriages.

*****Salisbury.** Cathedral town where Squire Allworthy's
sister dies and from which she sends a letter, intercepted
and hidden by Blifil, to her brother that Tom is her son,
not an orphan.

Inns and taverns. Accenting the novel's realism is
the passage of the three groups through many real places

on their chases to London. Among them are Wells,
Coventry, Daventry, Stony Stratford, Dunstable, and
Barnet. However, it is the inns and alehouses along the
way that serve the novel materially. They dramatize a
hospitality theme, satirize dishonest landlords and their
marriages, introduce strangers whose stories deepen the
courtship, marriage, and family themes, and bring complications to the plot that unravel only at its end. These
places are at Hambrook, Cambridge (in Gloucester-
shire, not the university town), Worcester, Gloucester,
Meriden, and St. Alban's.

Upton. Village in which the paths of the three chases
finally meet. In a hilarious scene at the town's **White
Lion Inn**, Tom is seduced; Sophia, arriving later learns
about Tom's indiscretion and leaves angrily. Squire
Western then storms in, too late to capture Sophia, while
Mr. Fitzpatrick storms in, too late to capture his runaway
wife, Sophia's cousin.

Countryside. In addition to country inns, Fielding
uses other places to accent his themes. For example, at a
barn off the road between Meriden and Coventry, Tom
and his companion Partridge encounter a band of gypsies whose society is a political satire on the Jacobite
myth of the good life under an absolute monarchy. At
the house of the Man of the Hill in the Malvern Mountains, Tom hears his cynical host's life story, a parable of
many of the novel's themes: injudicious fathers, contrasting brothers, marriage, imprudent lives, selfishness,
deceit, and misplaced charity. In the same way, Fielding
cites the real country houses or estates of Esher, Stowe,
Wilton, Eastbury, and Prior Park as examples of elegance to contrast with the more rustic estates of Devon,
Dorset, Bagshot Heath, and Stockbridge. The architectural metaphor was a typical eighteenth century phrasing

of the art versus nature theme personified in the artful conniving of Blifil and the natural good will of Tom.

*London. Besides the Bull and Gate Coaching Inn in the neighborhood of Holburn where Tom spends his first night in London, other minor places add to the novel's topographical and sociological realism. These include White's Chocolate House, a fashionable gambling club; Will's and Button's Coffee House; clubs for wits and writers; Broughton's Amphitheater on Oxford Road, a popular site for prizefighting by boxing, cudgels, and broadswords; Lombard Street, a middle-class neighborhood of bankers, merchants, and goldsmiths; the Hedge Tavern near Aldersgate and Deptford, two disreputable, low-class neighborhoods; Hanover and Grosvenor Squares, neighborhoods of the elegant upper classes; Doctors Commons, an ecclesiastical court at which marriage licenses can be obtained; and Goodman's Fields and Drury Lane, theaters whose audiences show cross-sections of the social classes.

Three London scenes are most thematically important. One is Mrs. Miller's house in Bond Street where Tom lodges along with another young boarder, Nightingale, whose father threatens to disown him because he wishes to marry for love rather than money. Another is the masquerade at the Opera House in the Haymarket, where Lady Bellaston begins her seduction of Tom. Considered a sinful and shameful place by Fielding and other authors, a masquerade is the perfect setting to focus themes of appearance versus reality, deceit, and subterfuge that have run through the novel.

Gatehouse. London prison in which Tom is held in a scene that frames character and theme. He is fixed there in despair because he mistakenly thinks that he has shown ingratitude to Squire Allworthy, that he has lost Sophia because of his indiscretions, that he has engaged in incest with his mother, that he has killed Fitzpatrick in a duel, and that he will be hanged for murder. The prison is the setting for Tom's dark night of the soul when his wisdom is born and where his past good will and charity become known and his redemption becomes complete. He can then be happily reborn as the true nephew of Squire Allworthy, marry his Sophia, and return to the country and his inheritance of Paradise Hall.

— *H. George Hahn*

TONO-BUNGAY

Author: H. G. Wells (1866-1946)
Type of work: Novel
Type of plot: Social satire

Time of plot: Late nineteenth and early twentieth centuries
First published: 1909

Looking back on his life, middle-aged George Ponderevo, a marine engineer, charts his self-made progress by the places that have enabled him to view his native England darkly with an outsider's detachment. After a ten-page combined retrospective and announcement of his aims in his "first and certainly last novel," the narrator opens with an account of his boyhood in a country estate called Bladesover, then traces the London "trajectory"—the rise and fall—of a fake do-all elixir.

Bladesover House. Fictional seventeenth century estate nine miles southeast of London. It is modeled on Up Park, a great house near Peterfield, Kent, where H. G. Wells's mother was chief housekeeper, that still stands as a government-owned historic landmark. Bladesover House signifies for George, looking back, the "Gentry, the Quality, by and through whom the rest of the world, the farming folk and the laboring folk, the tradespeople, and the upper servants and the servants of the estate, breathed and lived and were permitted."

Teatime in his mother's room is the below-stairs setting for class-conscious George's earliest fears and hatreds. There he hears the gossipy small talk of pensioned former servants who visit daily. The great house theoretically commands a view of the English Channel southward and the River Thames northeastward, but in the hero's retrospective lens, Bladesover House is London in microcosm.

The estate contains numerous walled gardens, one of which is the setting for young George's first breakthrough of the Victorian class structure. He encounters Beatrice Normandy, a niece of the lady of the house, and his adolescent "crush" leads to several scenes in which Wells uses place to symbolize the hero's place in society. Invariably Beatrice sits prettily astride an arbored wall *above* George, lest he "profane" her. Behind the puppy lovers, "dim and stately, the cornice of the great facade of Bladesover [rose] against the dappled sky."

Chatham. Municipal borough southeast of London. This "squalid" village, seen by George as in complete contrast to Bladesover, is the first of his several stops before he is "rescued" to London. Whereas what he calls the gentrified "Bladesover effect"—that of being England in miniature—strikes him as fatally outmoded, that of Chatham is of a "wilderness of crowded dinginess," a well-packed dustbin.

Wimblehurst. Town in Sussex that is George's second stop. A cut above Chatham, Wimblehurst is significant as the place where he meets a bubbling sprite of an uncle, Teddy Ponderevo and his wife, George's unforgettable Aunt Susan. Uncle Teddy is a pill dispenser in still another dead country town. In Wimblehurst George is introduced to Teddy's do-all pill, Tono-Bungay.

*London. Great Britain's capital and leading city, where George goes after Wimblehurst. From being an unpromising small-town pharmacist's apprentice, George moves upward to London on a science scholarship. From his Bladesover experience, he evolves a "theory of London," in which—like his creator—he combines urban sociology, wit and metaphor, polemics, and prophecy. Having seen Bladesover House as the clue to England's class structure, George also finds in Bladesover the clue to the structure of London. Both are under siege, he believes, "by the presence of great new forces, blind forces of invasion, of [cancerous] growth."

Much of the novel consists of guided tours of London—of "remote" railway termini, of the great port's "dingy immensity," of East End industrial sprawl, and everywhere signs of "some tumourous growth-process."

Tono-Bungay is the earliest English novel to capture the spirit of modern advertising. As George walks along London's Embankment, his eye catches food and drink advertisements. They blend in with London's "new world of vulgar commerce jauntily confront[ing] the old order across the Thames [at Bladesover House] with ads for Tono-Bungay."

Each stage in Tono-Bungay's rise and fall is marked by the progress and retrogress of Teddy Ponderevo's changing domestic environment, conducted in such a way as to provide an ironic comment on the swindle of the fake elixir. These moves from house-to-house are mostly made to emulate Bladesover House. The novel ends in a montage of London maritime landmarks as George, builder of a warship called X2, navigates his destroyer down the Thames. He can now see London "from the outside without illusions. We make and pass . . . striving upon a hidden mission, out to the open sea."

Hardingham Hotel. Residence of George's uncle, Teddy. The hotel's rooms are a string of apartments along a handsome thick-carpeted corridor. Although a bedroom and private sanctum are in view, Teddy maintains what is now called a "suite"—a place, to use his favorite phrase, with lots of "room for enterprise." The burgeoning tycoon has a waiting room, where the thick carpeting has been replaced by gray-green cork linoleum; a workroom with two secretaries but no typewriters—the clacking noise distracts him; and two little rooms where Teddy talks up Tono-Bungay and listens for offers.

After profits from Tono-Bungay begin to roll in, the Ponderevos move to a flat on Gower Street in Wimblehurst. On his first visit, George is taken aback by the chintzy chairs, sofa, and a "remote flavour of Bladesover." Soon Ponderevo buys a villa in Beckenham, with a conservatory, tennis lawn, vegetable garden, and coach house. No sooner does Aunt Susan settle in than she is uprooted to Chislehurst where Teddy acquires a Bladesover of his own, Lady Grove.

Crest Hill. Great house that Teddy has built. Ill at ease among certain ghosts of his past in Lady Grove, Teddy builds himself a twentieth century house. Crest Hill, the new Bladesover House, is to stand as his career's climax—both the epitome and the insolvent end of Uncle Teddy's delusions of grandeur, but it is never completed.

Mordet's Island. Fictional island off the West African coast that is the repository of a rare radioactive substance called quap. This time it is the scientifically minded hero who is taken in by one of the many hucksters who approach his uncle for financial backing. An expedition to the island for the highly valued quap—a bid to pay off Teddy's debts—ends in failure.

Luzon. Fictional village in the south of France where Teddy, a fugitive after his commercial empire collapses, abjectly dies of pneumonia.

— Richard Hauer Costa

TOP GIRLS

Author: Caryl Churchill (1938-   )
Type of work: Drama
Type of plot: Social realism

Time of plot: Early 1980's
First performed: 1982; first published, 1982

Staged primarily in the two competing spaces of two sisters, a "masculine" city office and a "feminine" country home, this play concentrates on the harsh compromises necessary for women to succeed in late twentieth century England. However, the play's social realism is contextualized by an initial fantasy scene, which defies time and place in order to universalize the subject matter.

Restaurant. Fictional space outside time and place with a table set for dinner. Caryl Churchill's realistic dialogue, with overlapping chatter and constant ordering from menus, grounds this surreal scene in naturalistic behavior in order to humanize the five characters who act as the various thematic voices within Marlene's culturally splintered psyche. All six women travel to find adventure or notoriety, filling the scene with "true" tales of exotic globetrotting, all of which contrast with the depressing conditions of the women's home lives within their different social structures. The expressionistic space of the restaurant itself may be seen as symbolizing Marlene's feelings of isolation and loss, emotions she hides in work and drink. The consumption of this sumptuous meal contrasts with the apparent poverty in Joyce's home.

"Top Girls" Employment Agency. Business in London run by Marlene. The spaces themselves are nondescript and colorless, suggesting corporate dehumanization and lack of maternal succor. Churchill staffs them only with upwardly mobile female managers in what would usually be viewed as a masculine field. This gender shift and destabilization is underlined by the ill health of Howard, the one male manager, who, like all men mentioned in the play, remains firmly offstage.

Joyce's kitchen and backyard. Small house in a country village, the childhood home of Joyce and Marlene and their working-class parents, situated near the town of Ipswich in Suffolk, about sixty miles east of London. The damp house, the junk-filled backyard, and the nearby fens provide the play's most detailed environment, to contrast with the smart, tidy London offices. This naturalistic specificity explores the effects that such an environment has on women trapped in social roles, both those who remain and those who attempt to escape. The kitchen, often used to symbolize the female space, is instead the site of a political debate between the sisters and a head-on collision between capitalist individualism and the moral responsibilities of family and class identity.

— Nicolas Pullin

TORCH SONG TRILOGY

Author: Harvey Fierstein (1954-   )
Type of work: Drama
Type of plot: Psychological realism

Time of plot: Mid-1970's
First published: 1979; first performed, 1981

Although this play is clearly set within New York City, the set design and stage directions in each piece of this trilogy—including the positioning of the characters on stage—are meant to concentrate audience attention on the characters themselves. There are no set changes and few props to distract from the story.

*International Stud Bar. Gay men's hangout in New York City's Greenwich Village that contained the most notorious backroom bar of its time. Opened in 1969, it consisted of two rooms, one with a regular bar setup and the other a venue for casual sexual encounters. In Harvey Fierstein's play, it is depicted onstage as a series of platforms with as little scenery as possible. The sparse sets force the audience to focus on the characters and not their surroundings.

Apartments. Both Arnold's apartment and Ed's apartment are merely platforms on stage; each is furnished with only one chair, one table, and one telephone. The chairs themselves are descriptive of their owners: Arnold's is worn and comfortable, hinting at both his experience and his comfort with his sexuality, while Ed's is new and straight, a reference to his prudish and closeted attitude toward his bisexuality.

Vacation house. Farmhouse in upstate New York where Ed and Laurel invite Arnold and his new lover, Alan, to spend the weekend. The set consists of an eight-by-nine-foot bed, heaped with all the props needed in the course of the play. The bed serves as all the rooms in the house. Although both couples are in the bed at the same time, they are illuminated separately so they never appear to be in bed together. The intent is to show the vulnerability of the characters without being offensive. The conversations are orchestrated in the same manner as the musical style of a fugue, and different colored lights are used to indicate the pairings when the conversations become more complex.

Arnold and David's apartment. Two-bedroom apartment overlooking New York City's Central Park. The stage directions describe it as "a realistically represented living/dining room and kitchenette." In scene 3, the sofa doubles as a park bench. The nighttime Central Park setting is produced through the use of lightshields (gobos) and projections. This serves to make the audience aware of the simultaneous events unfolding.

— *Molly M. Dean*

TORTILLA FLAT

Author: John Steinbeck (1902-1968)
Type of work: Novel
Type of plot: Naturalism

Time of plot: Early 1920's
First published: 1935

This short novel is set in an impoverished Latino community in California, to which the protagonist, Danny, returns after World War I to discover he has inherited two houses. This fact sets in motion the events of the novel, most of whose narrative unfolds in one of Danny's houses or is the direct result of the houses' presence in the lives of Danny and his friends.

Tortilla Flat. Impoverished neighborhood outside Monterey, California, in which "paisanos" (people of mixed Spanish, Indian, Mexican, and Anglo heritage) live. It is a barrio neighborhood on a hill where the forest and town "intermingle" above the beauty of nearby Monterey. Its streets are unpaved and its corners are free of street lights.

The subculture of Tortilla Flat provides a striking contrast to the natural beauty of the local region, as well as to the wealth of Monterey. Within this lowest existence, humans live and die, enduring misery and enjoying pleasure. The place demonstrates inequities of life in this region and accentuates human suffering. It also reveals humorous but humble attempts to rectify such inequities through rationalization, insubordination, and above all, fraternization. The intensity seen in the inhabitants of this place generates sympathy and ultimately serves to raise questions about the capitalist assumptions of the privileged class.

*Monterey. Beautiful old Northern California city on the Pacific coast that represents the opposite of life in Tortilla Flat. Monterey reflects a social and economic status to which the paisanos never can aspire, but one whose values occasionally infiltrate the residents of Tortilla Flat causing them the anxiety of living with a liminal mentality of wanting what they cannot have and having what they do not want. This place may also be understood ironically, for its history suggests that the ancestors of Tortilla Flat once belonged to Monterey.

Danny's house. One of the two houses in Tortilla Flat that Danny inherits after the war. Ownership of two houses transforms Danny from a wandering homeless rogue into a respectable member of his community. With the rise in his social status comes privilege and responsibility. He rents one house to his friends, but they fail to pay rent, and then the house is burned to the ground due to their neglect. Five homeless friends and some dogs eventually move in with Danny in his second house. The locus of the novel, then, focuses on the interior of this place where these friends interact in tender brutality with one another. Their struggles reflect John Steinbeck's view of human life as a struggle for daily survival, grasping at fleeting pleasure while responding with instinctive insights to the greater bourgeois society beyond the barriers of their paisano barrio.

Danny's friends live in poverty, finding or stealing food, drinking away their time and what money they come by. Set against this poverty, the gang nonetheless feels security and enjoys brotherhood since they have a roof over their heads. Danny's house becomes the headquarters from which they launch numerous adventures in the author's naturalistic parody of errant knights. In his preface to the novel, Steinbeck says that "Danny's house was not unlike the Round Table, and Danny's friends were not unlike the knights of it."

— *Kenneth Hada*

THE TOWER

Author: William Butler Yeats (1865-1939)

First published: 1928

Type of work: Poetry

After returning to County Sligo, the ancestral home of his mother's family, William Butler Yeats resided in Thoor Ballylee, the "tower" of the title, while he wrote many of the poems in this collection. The literal landscape of Sligo and the imaginative and mythological terrain of his poetic vision intertwine in these poems to form a "place" based on actual geographic features.

*Byzantium. Capital city of the Byzantine Empire and Holy City of Eastern Christianity; renamed Constantinople in the fourth century and now called Istanbul. For William Butler Yeats, Byzantium represents the origins of artistic endeavor and functions as a link to the great achievements of classical civilizations. Yeats presents it as a symbolic home for the creative imagination and as a refuge from the responsibilities of his public persona.

Conversely, without naming it as Ireland, Yeats sets "Byzantium" in contrast to a land he calls "no country for old men." This version of the contemporary world is marked by its teeming fertility, populated by "fish, flesh, or fowl" driven by "sensual music," and is an uncomfortable domain for "an aged man," as the poet characterizes himself.

*Ben Bulben (Benbulbin). Mountain rising above Yeats's home in County Sligo, where, in "Under Ben Bulben," from his *Last Poems*, he depicted the setting of his gravestone. Within "The Tower" it is Yeats's figure for the natural world in the larger sense and also the specific region that encompasses his local community.

Ancestral houses. The term Yeats employs in the first section of "Meditations in Time of Civil War" to describe the gracious, affluent lifestyles of the Anglo-Irish aristocracy, which represented for him a standard of cultural accomplishment. In accordance with his amalgam of actual and imagined locations in *The Tower*, these "flowering lawns," where "life overflows without ambitious pains," were cast at a remove from his depiction in later sections ("My House," "My Table") of the stone structures and wood furnishings that formed the literal and symbolic elements of his home.

— *Leon Lewis*

THE TOWER OF LONDON

Author: William Harrison Ainsworth (1805-1882)
Type of work: Novel
Type of plot: Historical

Time of plot: Sixteenth century
First published: 1840

This novel is set almost entirely within the Tower of London during the brief sixteenth century struggle between Mary Tudor and Lady Jane Grey for England's crown. It endeavors to portray, as accurately as possible, life within the Tower of London during the Tudor period, laced with gothic melodrama.

*Tower of London. Historic castle on the River Thames is the principal setting of the novel. W. Harrison Ainsworth wrote *The Tower of London* as much for polemical purposes as for entertainment. He had, he noted, for many years hoped to make the setting the "groundwork for a Romance," but he was also concerned by the neglect of the fabric of the buildings, their inaccessibility to the general public and also by the mutilation of the structure as a whole. Part of the book's intention is to describe those parts of the Tower of London that were not open to the public at the time, hence the novel's elaborate descriptions of individual buildings.

Another part of the novel's intention, however, was to urge the authorities to take better care of the Tower of London. Ainsworth's particular bugbear was the Grand Store House, constructed by William of Orange, which is mentioned several times in the novel, always unfavorably, and which fortuitously burned down while the novel was being written. The tripartite structure of Ainsworth's novel was intended to mirror the complex's triple purpose as palace, prison, and fortress, and the novel rarely moves outside the confines of the Tower. Whenever it does, the action is brief, and the exterior places are not described.

The narrative strand that focuses on Lady Jane Grey's brief reign, after she is placed on the throne by her ambitious father-in-law, the duke of Northumberland, shows the Tower of London functioning as palace, with the business of the realm carried out in its public rooms and in private meetings. Jane is shown in her private apartments and visiting the chapel. Her movements within the building are invariably circumscribed by her rank and the need for her safety. Similarly, Mary, once she takes control of the government, turns the Tower into her palace, favoring it, albeit temporarily, over Whitehall.

Throughout Jane's brief reign, the Tower is not only a palace but also a place of sanctuary. It is not made explicit at first, but the implication is that Jane is secure on her throne only so long as she remains within the Tower. Outside, her safety cannot be guaranteed, and her claim to rule the country is suspect. Mary and her followers naturally recognize this and it is vital to their interests that the Tower be taken. Thus, some of the most dramatic action in the novel involves the storming of the Tower by Mary's followers and scenes of hand-to-hand fighting through its courts and greens. The Tower is most clearly seen to function as a fortress in the narrative strand that focuses on Mary's accession to the throne.

Ainsworth's most vivid description and storytelling, however, is reserved for the Tower as prison, and it is clear that it is this function that most grips his imagination. His novel's third narrative strand involves a young squire, Cuthbert Cholmondeley, who has come to the Tower in the retinue of Lord Guilford Dudley, Jane Grey's husband. By falling in love with the beautiful but mysterious young woman named Cicely, he incurs the wrath of the jailer Lawrence Nightgall, who also loves Cicely and intends to marry her, though she despises him. As jailer, Nightgall has access to all manner of hidden passages in the fabric of the Tower—whether these are real or imagined, Ainsworth does not say—and he imprisons first Cholmondeley and then Cicely, in secret rooms, hoping to kill the former and wed the latter. However, others are also aware of the Tower's secret passages, which are variously used by courtiers plotting treason and by rescuers of Queen Jane. Indeed, given the passages' alleged secrecy, the volume of traffic underground is perhaps the most remarkable part of the novel.

In his more sober moments, Ainsworth also paints a vivid and rather more accurate portrait of life for noble prisoners within the Tower. He depicts assorted lords and Queen Jane and Lady Elizabeth imprisoned in the Tower, in reasonable comfort, with frequent descriptions of the rooms being prepared for them, but also less important prisoners lodging with various members of the Tower community in their own homes.

— *Maureen Speller*

THE TOWN

Author: William Faulkner (1897-1962)
Type of work: Novel
Type of plot: Psychological realism

Time of plot: 1909-1927
First published: 1957

The town of this novel's title is William Faulkner's Jefferson, in his fictional Yoknapatawpha County, Mississippi, that he modeled on his hometown, Oxford, Mississippi. Jefferson's landscapes and buildings thus tend to resemble those of the real Oxford during the early twentieth century. As a small town in the American South, Jefferson contains all the expected religious, legal, business, and social entities.

Jefferson. Mississippi town that is home to aristocrats of the unreconstructed Old South, whose family names include the Compsons, de Spains, Sartorises, and Stevenses. The preserved culture and society of the old land-based, medieval class system survived in the American South well into the middle of the twentieth century. The town is the old order of an agrarian, white, Protestant social construct that has outlived its time and its use in the modern world.

Jefferson is also home to the poor white trash who come to populate it, personified by the members of the Snopes family whose numbers are endless. The new social order brought to town by the Snopeses causes the eventual collapse of the old, aristocratic order as the Baptist, illiterate, dirty, and immoral Snopeses take over Jefferson, first with their large numbers and later politically. Gradually, they take control of local businesses, become deacons and preachers in the churches, and get jobs as school teachers. Finally, one of them even maneuvers himself into being appointed president of the bank.

Water tower. Ever-present symbol of Jefferson's town's hypocrisy. Standing on a ridge high above the town, the water in the tower contains pieces of stolen brass that Flem Snopes has taken from the city power plant where he works. Everyone in town knows the stolen pieces are there. Whenever they drink a glass of water, they can taste the brass—yet no one will remove the brass to expose Snopes and thereby bring scandal to the community.

Snopes photograph studio. Another symbol of the town's hypocrisy. Montgomery Ward Snopes opens a photography studio where the town ladies go for free sittings. When it is revealed that Snopes is actually running a pornographic "magic lantern" show in the basement of the building, town officials arrest him on trumped up charges of bootlegging whiskey instead of what he is actually doing—showing sex films imported from Europe. The town cannot accept or acknowledge that its very own ladies have been in a porn store, even if they may have done so unknowingly.

Stevens's office. Rented rooms serving as offices for the lawyer Gavin Stevens. There, Gavin, amid his legal books and treatises on justice and morality and even religion, struggles with moral questions as the old order around him collapses in the face of encroaching Snopesism. In fact, it is there that he abets the growing influence of the Snopes clan. Moreover, in this office, Eula Varner Snopes offers her body to him twice. Although Gavin declines, the old order is further besmirched and weakened.

Cemetery. Burial place for Eula Snopes after her suicide. After Eula is driven to her suicide and is buried by ministers of the town who want to pretend that she is not an adulteress because she is, after all, the wife of the president of the bank, the cemetery becomes yet another setting for hypocrisy. Gavin chooses a Bible verse for Eula's tombstone with the reassuring text, "A virtuous woman is a crown to her husband; her children rise and call her blessed.

— *Carl Singleton*

THE TRAGEDY OF TRAGEDIES: Or, The Life and Death of Tom Thumb the Great

Author: Henry Fielding (1707-1754)
Type of work: Drama
Type of plot: Farce

Time of plot: Age of chivalry
First performed: 1731; first published, 1731

This play about the adventures of a midget capable of winning the hearts of all the women in King Arthur's court and defeating giants and scurrilous rebels in battle is at once a parody of the Romance tradition in literature and an indictment of modern political intrigue. Henry Fielding relies on readers' knowledge of Arthurian tradition to dramatize the petty intrigues that plagued the English court during his own time. The contrast of large and small, dramatized by the physical sizes of the major characters in the play, suggests a dichotomy between the grandeur of those in high positions who spend their time and talent nurturing petty jealousies and maneuvering for favor by undermining those in authority.

King Arthur's Court. The public and private rooms in the legendary King Arthur's castle are the settings for most action in this play. Through a series of scenes in which characters move on and off stage quickly, Fielding illustrates the petty jealousies that drive many in authority to carry out policies that affect the future of the state. Fielding uses the setting as a means of calling into question the social values espoused by the writers of Arthurian romance.

Knights and ladies of the court use Arthur's main hall and the various bedchambers and hallways of the castle as sites for plotting to eliminate rivals either for love or for political power. No character is exempt from the dramatist's satiric, even savage, wit: King Arthur himself is unfaithful to his beloved wife (here called Dollallolla), and only Tom Thumb—a dwarf in physical stature— demonstrates the high moral character expected from a knight of Arthur's Round Table.

Plain outside the court. Site of the battle between the forces of Tom Thumb and those of his archenemy, Lord Grizzle. The battle scene parodies those found in works such as Homer's *The Iliad*, Vergil's *Aeneid*, and other epic poems, as well as many found in traditional Arthurian romances. Fielding uses the scene to highlight the ludicrous nature of the Romance tradition.

— *Laurence W. Mazzeno*

THE TRAGIC MUSE

Author: Henry James (1843-1916)
Type of work: Novel
Type of plot: Social realism

Time of plot: 1880's
First published: serial, 1889-1890; book, 1890

Late nineteenth century Paris and London, both familiar to Henry James, are the two principal settings of this novel. Although London, as homeland, represents a life of conventional public service, Paris, strongly associated with artistic freedom, inspires devotion to the private life of art.

*****Paris.** France's capital is the setting of the first few chapters of the novel and several subsequent chapters. British visitors to this many-faceted city find much to delight or disgust them. For Nick Dormer, Paris represents the world of art, the freedom of creative expression, and the aesthetic life. He finds art and beauty in the museums, on the streets, and in the churches and squares, and the city's atmosphere provides stimulus and inspiration. An elixir to Nick and to Miriam Rooth, an aspiring actress, Paris is threatening to respectable philistines such as Nick's mother and Julia Dallow, his future fiancé. When faced with the choice of walking through Paris at night, "a huge market for sensations," or sitting at a café across from a church, Julia opts for the café because it is more respectable. The British tourists traditionally stay in hotels and sightsee on the Right Bank of the Seine River, but at the end of the novel when Nick returns to Paris as a committed artist, he visits "a new Paris," "a Paris of studios and studies and models" on the Left Bank. Paris encourages the development of the private man, the artist, rather than the public man, the statesman, in Nick Dormer.

*****Notre Dame.** Cathedral on the Ile de la Cité in the heart of Paris. For Nick, this magnificent cathedral, built over the course of several hundred years, represents the beautiful, a work of art that is "done," completed. James presents the cathedral as a work of art rather than as a religious institution and likens the exterior of the cathedral to a "huge dusky vessel," "a ship of stone, with its flying buttresses thrown forth like an array of mighty oars." It is the catalyst that inspires Nick to tell Gabriel Nash, an aesthete, of his desire to become a painter.

*****Théâtre Français** (tay-ah-tra frahn-say). Now called the Comédie-Française, the national theater, located near the Palais Royal in the heart of Paris. A box seat in this theater becomes Miriam Rooth's acting school as she

and her mother attend the theater nightly. A second step in her schooling is admission to the *foyer des artistes*, the room backstage where the players can meet select members of the audience between acts. Peter Sherringham escorts her to this room, which, like a temple, is filled with pictures and relics of past thespians. Ironically, Peter proposes to Miriam here, asking her to sacrifice her career. After refusing, Miriam is admitted to a famous actress's dressing room. The description of the stairs and hall as austere, "monastic," and conventlike reveal the devotion and possible hardships on the way to success as an actress. The dressing room is success itself—"an inner sanctuary," which appears "royal." The descriptions of the various parts of the theater reflect Miriam's progress from inexperienced to consummate actress.

*****London.** Great Britain's capital city is the place to which the British visitors in Paris return to work out their destinies. Under the influence of family and friends in England, Nick dutifully proposes to Julia and runs for Parliament, temporarily ensuring the financial security of his mother and sisters, then resigns to pursue his painting. In a London theater, Miriam Rooth establishes herself as a successful actress. Nick's studio, on the fictional Rosedale Road, and Miriam's home, the fictional Balaklava Place, represent the world of artistic exploration and bohemian life in London while Julia's elegant apartment on the fictional Great Stanhope Street exemplifies the elegant lifestyle of the British upper class.

Harsh. Fictional location of Julia Dallow's estate in England. There, Nick and Julia row to an island in the lake where, in a small replica of a temple dedicated to Vesta, Nick turns his back on art and proposes to Julia, professing his intention to run for Parliament and become a public man, thus bowing to the wishes of family and friends. Associated with the private and public hearth, this vestal temple is an appropriate place for

Nick to dedicate himself to a private home and family and to public service.

Abbey. Ruined old church in Beauclere, the fictional English hometown of Mr. Carteret, Nick's benefactor and his late father's best friend. Nick's changing perception of this old, ruined abbey mirrors his changing attitude toward his career. After he has won a seat in Parliament, Nick visits Beauclere and associates the abbey with incompleteness, in contrast with Notre Dame, and with images of religious and English history, confirming his patriotic decision to serve his country. On a later visit, when Nick has decided to resign his seat in Parliament and pursue a career in art, he sees only the abbey's beauty.

— *Elizabeth A. Hait*

THE TRAVELS OF LAO TS'AN

Author: Liu Ê (Liu T'ieh-yün, 1857-1909)
Type of work: Novel
Type of plot: Social realism

Time of plot: 1895-1900
First transcribed: Lao Ts'an youji, serialized 1904-1907 (English translation, 1952; revised, 1990)

This story is set in China's western Shantung province, where the author spent many years as a government advisor. His protagonist, Lao Ts'an, is an itinerant Chinese physician whose name might be translated as "Wanderer." The action takes place in administrative centers associated with historical figures whom the author praises or satirizes. Most of scenes are set in the inns in which Lao Ts'an stays and the halls of Ch'ing (Manchu) dynasty officials.

Inns. True to his name, Lao Ts'an moves to a series of inns of varying quality. These lodgings are spartan, but differ in cleanliness and service. Walls surrounding the inns allows animals and carts to be kept inside. Interior buildings include the owners' residences, kitchen areas, and guest rooms. Rooms are furnished simply with wooden tables, chairs, and benches. Important fixtures are heated brick beds called *kangs* that are also used for sitting. Travelers bring their own bedding and towels; the inns provide hot water for washing and drinking. Doorways and windows usually have curtains (*lientzu*) for privacy. In the summer these are light, but in winter they are heavy padded cotton to keep warmth inside. To supplement the modest heat radiating through the *kangs*, rooms have charcoal braziers. Some inns serve meals, but more often guests have food brought in from outside restaurants. Lao Ts'an's preference for such lodgings is a marker of his modesty and upright character.

Government offices. Lao Ts'an visits a number of different *yamen* or magistrate's offices located near centers of walled cities, within their own walled compounds, which contain linked courtyards that are hierarchically arranged. Buildings typically include the officials' living quarters, courtrooms and halls for business, small garden areas, offices for staff, and siderooms for bailiffs and runners. The grandeur of a *yamen* reflects the importance of the official who resides there. Some of the novel's action occurs in the halls where magistrates take evidence in their roles as judges. Lao Ts'an's skills lead some officials to ask him to reside in the better rooms available at the *yamen*, but his refusal to accept the offers is another indication of his probity.

*Shantung. Province in North China about the size of Mexico with a population of around thirty-five million people at the time in which this book is set. During the Ch'ing (Manchu) dynasty Shantung was arranged in an administrative hierarchy of 6 circuits (*tao*), 13 prefectures (*fu*), and 151 districts (*hsien*), all of which were walled cities. Dozens of Shantung places are mentioned in the novel, including several prefectures, districts, market towns, and villages to which Lao Ts'an pays short visits.

*Tengchoufu (TENG-choh-few). Important prefectural-level city on the north shore of the Shantung peninsula in which the novel opens. Better known as Chefoo or as Yentai, it was a major port for people traveling to Manchuria and had been a treaty port permitting foreign residence since 1863. It had a population of around seventy thousand people at the time. The narrative in the first chapter is intended as political allegory that takes place in well-known seaside locations. Later, this entire sequence is revealed to have been Lao Ts'an's dream.

*Tsinanfu (TSEEN-ahn-few). Provincial capital of Shantung; a walled city famous for its lakes and springs. Lao Ts'an passes through Tsinanfu as the novel opens and visits the city's famous sites in chapters 2 through 4.

*Ts'aochoufu (TSOW-choh-few). Southernmost prefecture in Shantung that is the setting for much of chapters 5 through 8. A walled city of some fifty thousand residents, Ts'aochoufu was in a poor region that was often threatened by Yellow River flooding and was the site of early disturbances linked to the Boxer Uprising (1899-1901). Liu Ê's novel uses the city to satirize a Manchu official who served there as a magistrate.

Peach Blossom Mountain. Imaginary mountain in the real Shantung district of Feicheng, which is the setting of chapters 8 through 12. Liu Ê uses the mountain to introduce his personal interest in a syncretic religio-philosophical doctrine most commonly known as the T'ai-chou school. It is the only completely fictional location in his novel.

*Ch'ihohsien (CHEE-hoh-seen). Small district-level administrative city on the Yellow River that was subject of frequent serious flooding. Liu Ê sets the action in chapters 12 through 18 there. He used Ch'ihohsien because a second Manchu official who was his real-life enemy served there. Like Liu Ê, the fictional protagonist, Lao Ts'an, is an expert in flood control, so the setting provides a site in which he can use his skills.

— *David D. Buck*

TREASURE ISLAND

Author: Robert Louis Stevenson (1850-1894)
Type of work: Novel
Type of plot: Adventure

Time of plot: Mid-eighteenth century
First published: serial, 1881-1882; book, 1883

This classic adventure story is narrated primarily by a young English boy, Jim Hawkins, a member of a treasure-hunting expedition to the West Indies. Because Robert Louis Stevenson had no personal knowledge of that region, his use of places in this novel should be seen as the product of imagination tailored to the interest of young readers.

Admiral Benbow Inn. Public inn owned by Jim Hawkins's parents near **Black Hill Cove**, an isolated and sheltered bay on Devon's north coast, along the road to Bristol, that is an ideal place for smugglers to come ashore. Tucked between somber hills and the rocky cove, up whose cliffs the surf roars during storms, the inn is remote from even the nearest hamlet, **Kitt's Hole**, and conveys an atmosphere of unrelieved loneliness and foreboding. The novel opens with a menacing figure appearing at the inn and demanding a room. Later unmasked as the pirate captain Billy Bones, he long overstays his welcome and so tyrannizes the inn that other guests leave, and Jim's father weakens and dies an early death. Having chosen the Benbow Inn because of its isolation, Bones lives in daily fear of being discovered by fellow pirates; after they finally appear, he dies of apoplexy, and Jim and his mother flee the inn before the other pirates return—but not before they open his sea-chest and find a map of Treasure Island. Despite the fear Jim experiences at the inn, he later dreams of returning there while he is experiencing even worse dangers on Treasure Island.

Admiral Benbow Inn is aptly named after a late seventeenth century English admiral, John Benbow, who won renown for fighting pirates in the West Indies and for his heroic death in action against the French after the captains serving under him mutinied.

***Bristol.** Busy port city in southwestern England where the expedition of the *Hispaniola* begins and ends. Bristol is also the home of the crafty one-legged pirate Long John Silver, who signs on for the voyage as ship's cook. Silver owns a tavern in Bristol called the **Spy-glass.** While waiting for the *Hispaniola* to sail, he befriends Jim, accompanies him around Bristol's docks and teaches him about ships and the sea. To Jim, Bristol is an exciting portal to the world outside, and he says though he "had lived by the shore all my life, I seemed never to have been near the sea till then."

Hispaniola. Ship on which Jim and his companions sail from England to Treasure Island and back. Apart from the fact that the *Hispaniola* is a sturdy two-hundred-ton schooner that sails well and initially has a crew of about twenty men, Stevenson describes little about the ship and even less about its voyages across the Atlantic, thereby avoiding details of navigation with which he was not familiar. Nevertheless, he makes the ship the setting for several of the novel's most thrilling moments. Even before its voyage begins, the captain expresses concern about the trustworthiness of the crew— which has been assembled by Squire Trelawney—so Jim's companions "garrison" the after part of the ship in case trouble develops.

A key moment at sea occurs when Jim innocently climbs inside a large apple barrel on deck and overhears the crew plotting mutiny. The mutiny itself occurs ashore, after the ship anchors off Treasure Island, and the mutineers seize the ship only after the captain's party go ashore to hole up in an old stockade. From that point, the ship becomes a kind of albatross; it is almost useless to the mutineers, who cannot navigate it, and is of limited use to the captain's party because of their small numbers. The latter choose to take their chances ashore, confident that a relief ship will eventually find them. Meanwhile, the mutineers plunder the ship's stores, get drunk, and fight among themselves. Their recklessness later allows Jim to retake the ship single-handedly and even work it around to the opposite side of the island, where he beaches it and kills a mutineer in a desperate fight in the ship's rigging.

Treasure Island. Small, uninhabited island, located in or near the West Indies—the classic center of pirate activity. The novel's plot is driven by a map of the island revealing where a pirate named Captain Flint buried the fabulous treasure that Jim and his companions cross the Atlantic to find. Indeed, Stevenson created the map before he wrote the novel around it.

About nine miles long and five miles wide, the island is "like a fat dragon standing up," with fine, nearly land-locked harbors at each end. Names of the island's features make it resemble a ship: Three prominent hills, spread out in a line, are called Fore-mast. Main-mast (also called Spy-glass), and Mizzen-mast. Other features include Haulbowline Head, Captain Kidd's anchorage, and Skeleton Island in the south harbor.

Although the map itself provides exact latitude and longitude, Jim never reveals the island's exact location to readers because "there is still treasure not yet lifted." The general direction that the *Hispaniola* sails to reach the island and remarks at the end of Jim's narrative about the "nearest port in Spanish America," where there are "shore boats full of Negroes and Mexican Indians," suggest that the island is in the Caribbean Sea off Mexico. However, few real islands exist in that region, and the fact that Jim finds a castaway who has been alone on Treasure Island for three years suggests that the island is distant from shipping lanes. It is thus probably best to dismiss questions about the island's location and accept it as a wholly imaginary creation. Indeed, before embarking on the expedition, Jim spends hours poring over the map of the island and fantasizing about the "savages" and "dangerous animals" he will find there. What he does find is unrealistic topography and flora and fauna uncharacteristic of the West Indies. Apart from its hot climate, the island could be located almost anywhere.

Shortly after the *Hispaniola* reaches Treasure Island, its crew members separate into mutinous and loyalist parties, and the balance of the narrative traces their skirmishes and maneuverings around the island. The loyalists under Captain Smollett take possession of a well-fortified stockade built by Flint's men over a freshwater spring, while the mutineers weaken themselves by camping in a feverish swamp.

— *R. Kent Rasmussen*

A TREE GROWS IN BROOKLYN

Author: Betty Smith (1896-1972)
Type of work: Novel
Type of plot: Bildungsroman

Time of plot: Early twentieth century
First published: 1943

Time and place are important forces shaping the young Francie Nolan and the many other characters who people this novel. The graphic depiction of sights and sounds realistically re-creates an environment that stifles many. In the case of Francie, however, it strengthens her into an independent, strong-minded young woman.

*Brooklyn. Borough of New York City that in the early twentieth century was filled with immigrant and second-generation Irish, Poles, Jews, and Italians. In this story, Brooklyn comprises neighborhoods of more than one social level, though poor, working people predominate. There are shabby tenements with residents whose lives are spent in sweatshops and other low-paying jobs. There are old houses owned by artisans, craftsmen, and storekeepers, many of whom are second- and third-generation Americans. Most of the schools are overcrowded and dismal, although Francie finds one that is not. There are stores of all kinds—bakeries, groceries, pawnshops, Chinese laundries, spice shops—places where an imaginative child can experience some of the wonders of a world different from her own. The daily life of the inhabitants of this diverse district offers a panorama of the likely, the improbable, and the possible, an education for the receptive heart and mind of a curious child like Francie.

Nolan flat. Four so-called railroad rooms (one leading into the next) on the third floor of a tenement in Williamsburg. The family must share a bath down the hallway with two other families. This is the third home Katie and Johnny Nolan have had in their seven-year marriage, and it includes a tree growing near the fire escape. The tree provides a leafy bower for Francie during the summer Saturdays as she sits with her books and peppermint candies, reading and watching the tenants in the nearby buildings go about their evening routines.

Aside from the tree, which is Francie's private sanctuary, the flat also has a piano, left over from the previous tenant. Thus music lessons become an enrichment of Francie and her brother Neeley's lives. There are other redeeming qualities to this flat on Grand Street, and the Nolans make it a good home for many years. Francie's father accurately predicts that it will be his last home; he dies while still in his thirties and before the birth of his second daughter Laurie.

Francie's schools. There are two elementary schools that Francie attends. The first is a dismal, ugly place built to accommodate one thousand pupils but actually crowded with three thousand. The pupils, first- and second-generation children of immigrants, are brutalized by one another and by their teachers. Corporal punishment, while against the law, is practiced freely and with impunity. Disease and head lice are rampant. Still, this is Francie's first school, and it is here she learns to read and write. She also learns a hard fact of life: that some of the fortunate ones will be favored by teachers and become their "pets," while some unfortunate ones will not. Francie is destined to be one of the unfortunate ones as long as she attends this school.

The second school she attends, in a different district, is vastly different from the first one in its nurturing atmosphere. The teachers are more agreeable, the number of students is small enough to allow each pupil some individuality, and the building itself has a much more welcoming ambience. Discovered by Francie on one of her Saturday walks, she asks her father to find a way for her to transfer to the school. Though it means walking forty-eight blocks each day (twelve blocks each way four times a day), Francie feels fortunate to be able to attend the school, and she thrives there.

McGarrity's saloon. Establishment in which Johnny Nolan spends time drinking and where, after his death, his son Neeley works. Looked upon by many of its patrons' wives as a place of disrepute and dereliction, the saloon becomes for Katie Nolan and her children a deliverance when the owner McGarrity provides employment for the children and a needed source of income after Johnny's death.

— *Jane L. Ball*

THE TREE OF MAN

Author: Patrick White (1912-1990)
Type of work: Novel
Type of plot: Parable

Time of plot: Twentieth century
First published: 1955

Patrick White's goal in writing this novel was "to discover the extraordinary behind the ordinary, the mystery and poetry" of human existence. If his characters and their lives were to be outwardly mundane, then it follows that place should be ordinary as well—neither a great city nor an exotic landscape. So White chose the monotonous Australian bush west of the metropolitan city of Sydney. There his characters seek "the extraordinary" through experiencing the land's natural forces: storm, flood, drought, and fire.

Bush. Australian term for wilderness area that also has connotations that make the bush a fearful place on one hand and a spiritual place on the other. As the novel opens, the central character, Stan Parker, walks into the virgin bushland awed by the "simplicity of true grandeur" where the silence was "immense." From the novel's beginning, then, the bush assumes religious dimensions comparable to a cathedral. It continues to be treated in this way throughout the work, and at its end, Stan's grandson undergoes a similar revelation as he walks through the bush.

A crucial passage of *The Tree of Man* describes a powerful storm that strikes the area and the flood that follows. Such unpredictable weather characterizes Australia, where bush regions suffer drought for years then heavy rains flood the parched earth. The raging water heightens the drab landscape and figures as a pivotal experience in Parker's quest for understanding. Like so many elements in the novel, the deluge carries religious significance and brings to mind the biblical flood.

Parker farm. Farm that Stan and his wife, Amy, build for half a century. It begins with Stan's clearing of a space in the bush and building a simple hut. Soon, he marries Amy, with whom he has two children. Over the years, their farm expands as more of the scrub and trees are cleared away. The crude hut evolves into a rambling house, typical of those in the Australian countryside, and serviceable farm buildings appear. Paths become roads, and more settlers arrive to develop similar properties. As the years pass, the Parkers create a most ordinary settlement, of a type that White himself knew well. On his return to Australia after serving in World War II, he lived in an area called Castle Hill on a farm closely resembling the Parkers' place.

Glastonbury. Grand country house that a wealthy Sydney family builds on land near the Parker farm. There, they and their society friends from the city spend holidays imitating the ways of British aristocracy. Amy, who works in the kitchen at the great house, finds the place fascinating, a welcome release from her humdrum farming life. However, when a bush fire destroys Glastonbury, Amy realizes that it was all merely a fantasy and no real part of her life. The country estate had violated the sanctity of the bush.

During the nineteenth and early twentieth centuries successful Australians developed a fondness for country houses patterned after the stately homes that dot the English countryside. In fact, White, who came from a wealthy family, spent part of his childhood in such a house in the New England region of Australia.

Duralgai. Village that arises near the Parker farm. It consists first of a general store and a post office, but gradually grows into a typical Australian country town, with dusty streets and buildings with verandas to protect people from the torrid sun.

*****Sydney.** Australia's most cosmopolitan city, which lies not far from the Parker farm, plays a minor but significant role in the narrative. It represents the spiritual vacuum that White saw in Australian society. To develop this theme, White moves the Parkers' two children into Sydney. The daughter, Thelma, marries a lawyer and devotes herself to middle-class pretensions, while the son, Ray, turns to gambling and crime. When Stan and Amy venture into the city, they are never comfortable in what they consider an artificial and destructive environment.

— *Robert L. Ross*

THE TREE OF THE FOLKUNGS

Author: Verner von Heidenstam (1859-1940)
Type of work: Novel
Type of plot: Historical

Time of plot: Eleventh and thirteenth centuries
First published: Folkungaträdet, 1905-1907 (English translation, 1925)

Set in East Gothland and Svealand in eastern Sweden, this novel relies on both imaginary and historical locales to relate the history of the medieval Folkungs dynasty—a story of racial, economic, political, and religious unions and conflicts, which—according to Verner von Heidenstam, created the vital core of the modern Swedish nation and culture. The setting of the novel functions as an organic extension of Heidenstam's stylistic shift toward an east-Nordic narrative tradition and a distinctly Swedish regional and nationalistic point of view, which defy the artistic authority of the dominant west-Nordic saga tradition.

Folketuna farm (FOL-keh-too-nah). Fictional farm in East Gothland that is associated with the eleventh century origins of the powerful Folkung family—a bleak union between the Swedish peasant, former Viking, and greedy robber Folke Filbyter and the daughter of Jorgrimme, a Finnish dwarf and magician. Although the richest farm in the region, Folketuna's appearance, a symbolic reflection of its owner's crude and ignoble character, presents a stark contrast to the noble and well-kept farm of Ulv Ulvsson that is the seat of an old aristocratic Swedish family, whose symbol is a centuries-old linden tree. Representative of the clash between the desire for material profit and questionable morality on one hand, and pure Swedish blood and respectable wisdom on the other, the opposition between the two farms turns also into the spiritual battleground on which Christianity meets and defeats Nordic paganism.

Bellbo estate. Seat of Earl Birger, the most powerful of the Folkungs, each of whose sons, Valdemar and Magnus, becomes a ruler of Sweden in the thirteenth century. This locale stands out as a portrayal of a peculiar merger in space and time of medieval Christianity. The second part of the novel, "The Bellbo Heritage," opens on a Wednesday during Holy Week when pagan spring customs were still practiced. This is further elaborated on by the symbolic fusion between native and foreign traditions, between Sweden's ancient heroic past, signaled by the sacred sword Gråne, and the Christian chivalric code. The sword of the saga hero Holmger, previously preserved at the convent of Sko, is the prize for the winner of the Bellbo tournament, which is arranged in the "foreign fashion," as the narrative points out.

*****Uppsala** (oop-SAH-lah). Sweden's medieval capital that is the stage upon which pagan Nordic religion and state government, supported by Blot Sven, clash violently with the Christianity of King Inge. As Uppsala is the site of both the temple of the Nordic gods, with the sacrificial grove, and the Thing-mound, where the King, Lawmen, and franklins (freeholders) meet annually to discuss and pass laws and elect, if necessary, a new king, Uppsala gives expression of Heidenstam's ethic of heroic resignation. This ethic is most noticeably felt in the author's realization that good and evil must necessarily coexist as well as in the paradox, which heavily underlies both parts of the novel, that evil is the frequent outcome of a genuine desire to do good. Thus, in the second part of the novel, Uppsala finds its symbolic parallel in the great forest of Tiveden, the realm of the god of strife Ti, where Magnus Ladulås defeats the army of his brother Valdemar, the rightful king, and takes the throne of Sweden in an effort to restore law and order to the country.

*****East Gothland** and **Svealand.** Regions in southeastern and eastern Sweden that, on one hand, help delineate an image of medieval Europe and Sweden's important position within it and, on the other hand, mark the core of Sweden as a modern sovereign Nordic nation. East Gothland and Svealand represent "home" and "native land" and are compared in the narrative with Micklegarth, or Constantinople, the seat of the Byzantine emperor. Courageous and loyal, Folke Filbyter's two elder sons are among the emperor's body guards (upon their return home, they join King Inge's guards).

Two centuries later, heroism and loyalty again underscore a chivalric devotion to earthly and divine peace and order and earn Sweden a distinguished place among Scandinavian and European Christian nations. These qualities are in unison with Heidenstam's cultural nationalism, based on his conviction that Sweden's living past is indispensable for Sweden's living present, for the natural growth of the nation and its culture.

— *Miglena I. Ivanova*

THE TRIAL

Author: Franz Kafka (1883-1924)
Type of work: Novel
Type of plot: Allegory
Time of plot: Twentieth century

First published: Der Prozess, 1925 (English translation, 1937; restored German edition, 1982; new English translation, 1998)

The sense of place in this novel provides a link between Joseph K.'s internal struggle to comprehend the obscure workings of the law under which he is condemned, and his physical pursuit of acquittal. Franz Kafka reinforces the apparent absurdity of Joseph K.'s situation, as a man accused of, and executed for, an unspecified crime, by setting the narrative in vague and unusual locations.

City. Kafka's urban setting for *The Trial* reinforces the ordinary quality of protagonist Joseph K.'s life. K. lives and works as anyone else might in a large, industrialized city. The urban setting also emphasizes the arbitrary nature of his trial, as K. appears to be an ordinary citizen picked at random to face charges for an unspecified crime.

Frau Grubach's boardinghouse. Residence of K., in which Kafka sets much of the novel, thereby creating a sense of personal invasion. One morning, while he is still in bed, K. discovers that he is under arrest. Two guards of the court have been sent to deliver the message; however, they give no information about the crime for which he is charged. His arrest is sudden and inexplicable, and because it occurs in his bedroom, the proceedings against him exhibit a confusing and invasive quality. They do not correspond to any rational system of justice. The law condemns Joseph K. in his bedroom in the opening chapter, and it returns for him there at the novel's conclusion to execute its sentence.

Court. Building to which K. goes, using the address given to him for his initial hearing. There he finds a dilapidated apartment complex, in whose cramped and overheated attic the court that has accused him meets. This unlikely setting for a court of law emphasizes the nightmarish nature of K.'s trial, while also creating questions about the legitimacy of the proceedings. The locations of other court offices in the upper rooms of buildings also suggest the transcendence of the court and its procedures. K. has difficulty breathing the air in the court, as though it exists at a level beyond, or above, normal life.

Junk room. Small storage closet in the bank building in which K. works. In one of the most unusual scenes in the novel, K. confronts a functionary of the court in the process of punishing the same two court guards who earlier had informed him of his arrest. The method of administering punishment, in this case by flogging, and the location of the punishment in a junk room of a bank building, augment the irrational quality of K.'s trial.

Huld's house. Home of a lawyer whose counsel K. seeks on the advice of his uncle, an old friend of Huld. Huld receives K. in his bedroom, where he is bedridden by illness. Just as the court meets in the attics of apartment buildings, so lawyers hold office hours in their bedrooms, further complicating the nature of the judicial proceedings throughout the novel and adding an increasing surreality to the events of the narrative.

Titorelli's bedroom. Small, oddly furnished attic bedroom in which Titorelli, a painter, lives and works—another example of the prominent role bedrooms play in the novel. Titorelli's bed stands in front of a door leading out of his bedroom. Titorelli explains to K. that through his doorway, officials of the court enter, often while he is sleeping. Titorelli, like many characters in the novel, lives at the mercy of the court.

Cathedral. Large, ornate church in the city where K. meets a priest who tells him a parable about the law. Rather than providing some measure of comfort for K., the priest complicates matters further by giving him only a cryptic description of the court and its procedures. K.'s discussion with the priest adds a metaphysical quality to his efforts to justify himself against the allegations of the court. Just as those to whom he turns throughout the novel for assistance can provide no substantive help, so the church can provide only parables, whose meanings are open to indistinct and conflicting interpretations.

Stone quarry. Located outside the city, the quarry is K.'s final destination, the site of his execution. The quarry provides an appropriate setting for K.'s execution, lending a sacrificial quality to the event. Executioners position him on a rectangular stone block, and their behavior during and after the execution resembles a religious ritual, as they stare into K.'s eyes at the moment of his death.

— *Philip Bader*

TRISTRAM

Author: Edwin Arlington Robinson (1869-1935)
Type of work: Poetry
Type of plot: Arthurian romance

Time of plot: Arthurian period
First published: 1927

This book treats the Tristram and Isolt strand of Arthurian legend in two hundred pages of ardent, passionate poetry, breaking the story into ten sections. Enclosed within scenes involving "the other Isolt"—Isolt of the white hands, on the coast of Brittany—the major portion of the poetic narrative focuses on the doomed passion of Tristram of Lyonesse and Isolt of Ireland, who fall in love on the ship bringing Isolt to Cornwall, where she is to marry King Mark.

*Brittany. Historical region of France that projects into the sea between the Bay of Biscay and the English Channel. In the opening and closing moments of Edwin Arlington Robinson's narrative, Isolt of the white hands, daughter of King Howel, gazes over a blank, bleak ocean view to the north. Waiting for Tristram in the beginning, she sees only white birds flying. At the poem's end, after Tristram's death, she again looks north to white waves, a "phantom" sky, sea foam, white birds, and white sunlight, a world bleached of all warmth and color. However, in section 5, Tristram and Isolt of the white hands spend a two-year interlude in Brittany in sunlit gardens away from the chilly seascape, a brief respite for "the other Isolt."

*Tintagel Castle. Castle of King Mark on the coast of Cornwall which some legends claim was the birthplace of King Arthur. This site probably never actually witnessed all the scenes that Arthurian legends have placed there; however, the castle is real and still exists. It is a romantic and dramatic setting for love, forbidden or otherwise. A key scene early in Robinson's poem is not located, strictly speaking, in the castle at all, but rather on a steep stone exterior palace staircase down to the sea, on which Tristram and Isolt of Ireland stand poised in the cold, misty moonlight above the noisy waves pounding a rocky shore—halfway between King Mark's palace and the ocean, halfway between heaven and hell. The intensity of the scene, to which Tristram returns often in memory, evokes a similar powerful image of place from Robinson's often anthologized poem, "Eros Turannos," in which love is described as being "like a stairway to the sea/ Where down the blind are driven." After Tristram leaves Tintagel, he finds himself in a silken, snaky trap—a house belonging to the jealous Queen Morgan: a dim room, a red window, low light. As soon as he is able to escape, he returns to Brittany.

Joyous Gard. Seaside castle of Sir Lancelot. When Gawaine arrives from Camelot to take Tristram back to England, the road leads eventually to Joyous Gard. There, Tristram and Isolt of Ireland enjoy a brief idyll, a time together that is, for once, not cold, not dark, not starlit. Instead the sea is bright with summer, a small forest displays new leaves and "laughing trees"; it is a scene of "precarious content" until Mark's men capture Isolt and take her back to Cornwall, where Mark, seeing her spirit and life force broken, allows her to see Tristram again. It is a brief coda, however, as on a day of dead calm sea, Andred, Tristram's "lizard" cousin, creeps up on the lovers and murders Tristram.

— *Nan C. L. Scott*

THE TRIUMPH OF DEATH

Author: Gabriele D'Annunzio (1863-1938)
Type of work: Novel
Type of plot: Psychological realism

Time of plot: Nineteenth century
First published: Il trionfo della morte, 1894 (English translation, 1896)

Above all else, this novel is a chronicle of restlessness. Its various settings are backdrops to the ever-increasing desperation of Giorgio and his mistress, Ippolita, to be somewhere else. Their changing aspects reflect the thought processes that lead them to the realization that their real destination is "Anywhere out of the World!"—from the phrase that Gabriele d'Annunzio's idol Charles Baudelaire borrowed from Thomas Hood's "The Bridge of Sighs" to make the title of one of his most famous prose poems.

*****Rome.** Italy's capital city, in which the novel begins with lovers Giorgio and Ippolita meeting for the first time in the Via del Babuino. The city is immediately established as a point of departure; the story then hurries on to a point, two years after their first meeting, when they are consulting a Baedeker travel guide for inspiration. No sooner have they left the city, however, than they begin to immerse themselves in their memories of it. It becomes part and parcel of their existential predicament that wherever they are, they will soon yearn to be elsewhere. They find it hard to select a destination, and in the early phases of the novel they are often sidetracked. There is a sense in which Rome remains the center of their conceptual universe no matter where they are, but they cannot be content to remain or return there. Perhaps, for Giorgio at least, Rome is symbolic of life itself; he finds it impossible to leave the city in any meaningful sense, even though he does not want to be there.

Villa Cesarini. House in Albano, not far from Lake Nemi, at which Giorgio and Ippolita stay while on their first excursion. Their mail catches up with them there, bringing them news from other places, renewing their restlessness and drawing them back to Rome.

*****Guardiagrele** (gwahr-dyah-GRAY-lay). Town in Chieti Province in which Giorgio was born and where various members of his divided family still live. He returns there in response to a call of duty, while Ippolita visits her own family in Milan. Guardiagrele lies on the lower slopes of the Majella mountain, overlooking the valley of the river Foro. The cold remoteness of the surrounding peaks underscores Giorgio's alienation from various members of his family and the world.

Hermitage. House at San Vito on Italy's Adriatic coastline, situated on a plateau that rises precipitately above the sea. Vasto Point, Mount Gargano, and the Treniti Islands are visible in one direction, Cape Moro and Cape Ortona in the other. Giorgio rents the house in order to begin a "new life" with Ippolita. When the life in question proves unsatisfactory, the promontory that extends from the plateau provides the launching pad from which Giorgio and Ippolita leap to their deaths.

The changing aspects of the distant city of Ortona—brilliantly white at first, but bathed, when the lovers look in that direction for the last time, in the gaudily problematic light of a fireworks display—mirror some of the extremes of Giorgio's moods. The Hermitage does provide a temporary haven from the lovers' existential malaise, but they find it hard to accommodate themselves to local ways. Giorgio becomes briefly fascinated with the local fishermen of the Trabocco and allows himself to be lulled into a stupor by the stifling warmth of the climate, but the respite thus gained cannot last. The addition of a piano to the house's sparse facilities provides a further measure of relief, but the echoes of Richard Wagner's music that it enables the lovers to conjure up only serve to feed Giorgio's malaise.

*Castalbordino.** Site of a shrine in the province of L'Aquila at which the Virgin Mary is supposed to have appeared in 1527. When Giorgio and Ippolita visit in the course of an excursion from the Hermitage, they discover a vast crowd in which the maimed, the mad, and the miserable jostle one another, competing for space with animalistic fervor as they implore the Virgin Mary (the Madonna) to grant them release from their suffering. This spectacle raises Giorgio's distaste for the world and its ways to a new intensity.

— *Brian Stableford*

TROILUS AND CRESSIDA

Author: William Shakespeare (1564-1616)
Type of work: Drama
Type of plot: Tragedy

Time of plot: Antiquity
First performed: 1601-1602; first published, 1609

Set in the ancient Troy of Homer's epic, this play's scenes alternate between the city of Troy itself and the camp of the besieging Greeks outside the city, with the final scene playing out on a battlefield. Dialogue and actions make evident the differences in these two cultures locked in war over Helen, who draws out their ideals of behavior.

*Troy.** Ancient city in Asia Minor that is ruled by King Priam. Faced with an unrelenting siege by the more powerful Greeks, the Trojans debate the wisdom of continuing their resistance. Troilus, who loves the Greek woman Cressida, represents the Trojans, who idealize love as integral to chivalrous behavior. Hector, a reasonable man epitomizing Troy's best values and strengths, urges his brothers to abandon the war as neither justified nor worth the cost.

Greek camp. Military encampment outside Troy, which the Greeks have been besieging for seven years. In contrast to the idealistic Trojans, the Greeks, who are soldiers, not courtiers, are pragmatic and ego-

centered—differences reflected in the play's two centers. Lack of progress in the siege has demoralized the Greek leaders, whom Agamemnon, the overall commander, tries to hearten by declaring that the long siege has been a test of Greek stamina. Ulysses argues that the problems of the Greeks lie in a lack of order and discipline, not in Trojan strength. Rather than debate their motive for war, the leaders urge their greatest hero, Achilles, to fight.

Battlefield. The two sides meet with the strength initially on the Trojan side. The Greek victory spells the end of Troy and its chivalric code as well.

— *Bernadette Flynn Low*

TROILUS AND CRISEYDE

Author: Geoffrey Chaucer (c. 1343-1400)
Type of work: Poetry
Type of plot: Love

Time of plot: Antiquity
First transcribed: c. 1382

Although Geoffrey Chaucer knew Giovanni Boccaccio's Il Filostrato *(c. 1335), his own treatment of the love affair of Troilus and Criseyde differs markedly. Chaucer uses the scene of ancient Troy in its last days as an opportunity to comment on the England of his own day. Medieval tradition attributed Troy's fall to its excessive sensuality. As such, Troy provided the ideal foil for the Lancastrian court in which Chaucer had to function.*

*__Troy.__ Ancient city-state on the coast of Asia Minor. Although Troy was an actual historical place, Chaucer's description of it bears no resemblance to the city Homer described in *The Iliad* (c. 800 B.C.E.; English translation, 1616) or to anything even remotely like the real city. It is, instead, the very type of a prospering, sensual city that easily corresponds to the court of England's King Edward III. However, this is not to say that Chaucer intends specific correspondences between the characters of his poem and English persons he actually knew. Still, his wife Philippa and her sister Katherine Swynford likely had love affairs with John of Gaunt, the king's third son and Chaucer's patron. The great innovation of *Troilus and Criseyde* is that it combines ancient locations with courtly love formulas to convey a definite political message. The kind of love allowed within the context of the court necessarily produces only instability and unhappiness.

Criseyde is not Helen, but the Trojans would willingly send her to the Greeks to ransom their hero Antenor. Pandarus functions, as his name implies, to satisfy the sudden lust of Troilus and to attempt to find a protector for his niece Criseyde. In the world of Chaucer's poem, all the characters do evil things from either neutral motives or simply for self-preservation.

Criseyde's father Kalkas deserts Troy for the Greek side based on his own prophecy of the city's doom. He leaves Criseyde behind, however palatially housed, and she soon acquires the protection of Hektor, the king's son. It is easy to see the role that class conflict plays here and to think of the challenge posed to the aristocracy by the Peasants' Revolt of 1381. What is clear is that Chaucer saw the complicated political nature of humanity with a timeless eye, and that love has always been the mistress of war.

— *Robert J. Forman*

THE TROJAN WOMEN

Author: Euripides (c. 485-c. 406 B.C.E.)
Type of work: Drama
Type of plot: Tragedy

Time of plot: Antiquity
First performed: Trōiades, 415 B.C.E.

The city of Troy, recently captured by the Greeks after a ten-year siege, is both the location and the subject of this play. This collective tragedy affects all the citizens of Troy. Only the women and children survive as the play begins.

*__Troy.__ Ancient city on the coast of Asia Minor that according to tradition was destroyed by the Greeks. In Euripides' play, the city's breached walls—which were originally built by Poseidon—symbolize the city's fate, and also serve as the backdrop throughout the play. Encamped before the walls, the captured Trojan women mourn their dead. From these walls they depart for slavery in Greece. Andromache's son, Astyanax, is hurled to

his death from the walls, and his grandmother, Queen Hecuba, buries him here before she herself departs in slavery. The collapse of the walls themselves in a conflagration caused by the Greeks symbolizes, at the end of the play, the final end of Troy itself.

__Achilles' tomb.__ Located on the plain outside Troy, the burial place of the Greek hero Achilles lies offstage in this play. Although the Greeks' greatest warrior is dead, he requires his share of Trojan plunder. During the play Hecuba learns that the Greeks have sacrificed her daughter, Polyxena, as a gift to the dead Achilles.

***Greece.** Homeland of Troy's hated conquerers and the destination of all the surviving women of Troy, including Hecuba, Andromache, and Cassandra. The crimes of the Greeks in this play, especially the murder of Astyanax, distort the natural tendency of Euripides' Greek audience to identify with their homeland and encourage them to sympathize instead with the conquered Trojans.

— *Thomas J. Sienkewicz*

TROPIC OF CANCER

Author: Henry Miller (1891-1980)
Type of work: Novel
Type of plot: Psychological realism

Time of plot: Early 1930's
First published: 1934

This novel offers a comic, if often shockingly naturalistic, portrait of Paris during its lean years, after such writers as F. Scott Fitzgerald, Ernest Hemingway, and other members of the "Lost Generation" had briefly made it their home. At the same time the city is also a mirror for its narrator, a struggling writer who has no possessions and no hopes but who has discovered that he is "the happiest man alive."

***Paris.** French capital city to which the narrator has moved with the hope of becoming a writer. *Tropic of Cancer* is a largely autobiographical account of Henry Miller's life and experiences in the south-central Parisian quarter of Montparnasse, from his arrival early in 1930 through 1932. Although Miller appears as himself, or at least a version of himself, his wife June is portrayed as Mona and his good friend Alfred Perlès as Carl. Colorful journalist Wambly Bald becomes the obsessive womanizer Van Norden. As the novel's narrator, Miller is not consistent in his treatment of Paris; he portrays it from different viewpoints as his mood changes and as his acceptance of circumstances grows. Initially, he presents Paris as a symbol of everything he finds wrong with life-denying modern civilization: a "huge organism diseased in every part." Some neighborhoods he describes as literal garbage heaps. Later, in the spring sun, the city looks different, and the narrator grows more content.

As a down-and-out writer, the narrator often has no place to stay; at such times, the streets of Paris become his refuge. Popular sidewalk cafés such as the Dôme, the Rotonde, and the Coupole provide him with vantage points from which he observes the city's fascinating street life, hoping for the appearance of an acquaintance who may treat him to a drink or a meal.

Apartments. Parisian homes of the friends of the narrator, who is obsessed with shelter and food. He sleeps wherever someone will give him space on a floor or in a hall. After some thought, he devises a scheme whereby he eats a meal with each of seven friends once a week. What he sees in their abodes provides him with further material for his indictment of society. The apartment of one friend is strikingly sterile: "There is not a crumb of dirt anywhere, nor a chair misplaced." Boris and Tania's apartment is squalid but equally repugnant. At one point the narrator is taken in by a group of Russians, but their heavy food, their habit of sharing meals with worm-ridden dogs, and their poor hygiene drive the suddenly fastidious American away. For a while he stays with an Indian named Nanantatee, but the man's hypocrisy and meanness lead to the narrator's labeling him Mister Nonentity.

Miss Hamilton's brothel. Brothel to which the narrator is asked to accompany another Indian man, a naïve disciple of Mohandas Gandhi. In one of the novel's comic high points, the Indian shocks the brothel's otherwise worldly employees by mistaking the function of the bidet. *Tropic of Cancer* was outspokenly explicit for its day, and much of its content involves the prostitutes of Paris.

***Seine River** (sayn). Major French stream flowing

through Paris that serves the narrator as a metaphor for everything flowing and in flux. Like Paris and its teeming streets, the Seine's character changes as the narrator learns to accept his fate. Looking at it once, he sees "mud and desolation, street lamps drowning, men and women choking to death, the bridges covered with houses, slaughterhouses of love." Later he characterizes the river as a "great artery," and later still feels it flowing through him.

*Dijon (dee-ZHAHN). French city southeast of Paris where the narrator teaches English at a *lycée* (school) after he loses the proofreading job that Carl gets for him in Paris. His new position involves terrible meals and a dingy room but no pay. It is winter, so bitterly cold that toilets freeze, and the narrator feels like a prisoner in the spiritless institution. Dijon itself strikes him as a dirty hole.

— *Grove Koger*

TROPIC OF CAPRICORN

Author: Henry Miller (1891-1980)
Type of work: Novel
Type of plot: Autobiographical

Time of plot: c. 1900-1928
First published: 1939

Annihilation of contradictions for self-discovery is the key in this autobiographical fantasy. Miller's wondrous sense of place on the physical and spiritual planes elevates his odyssey out of the seedy and resplendent streets of New York to encompass the world around him and the "universes within universes" inside him: unique, alike, transcendent of and composed of time and space. The discovery of the self is the only great adventure. Place in the novel symbolizes alienation, detachment, and modern horror, but deep within is the inestimable value of a life that is lived, truly lived, and that such a life, the only one worth having, can only originate from within after all other modes have been destroyed.

*New York City. City that represents the contradiction of opposites that must be annihilated for the self to emerge, and the spiritual and physical settings of the novel, ultimately, become the symbols and instruments imperative to crush and rebuild the false, imposed dream of society into the truthful vision of the artist. New York is a huge tomb, and among the human ants and human lice his "microcosmic life" is a reflection of the "outer chaos."

Henry's friends serve as dimensions of Henry himself that must be abandoned or transformed, and his long walks through New York's streets and stores (Bloomingdale's is an emblem of sickness and emptiness) become inner philosophical meditations on sex, death, religion, racism, and politics. He constructs spiritual universes within spiritual universes that harbor galaxies of doubts, fears, hopes, denials, and affirmations that explode and reform through annihilation and rebirth.

Cosmodemonic Telegraph Company. New York City company for which Henry works, hiring and firing messengers and other exploited workers. The company is heartless and inefficient, and mirrors, as does Henry's job, the degradation imposed by the city on those who work simply to survive. The company, like the city and America, is a Darwinian jungle. Henry resists and plays Robin Hood, the mark of his defiant nature, evident since his childhood in Brooklyn.

*Brooklyn. Borough of New York City in which Miller spent his childhood. His childhood in Brooklyn, vividly recalled, represents the only period until now where everything was clear and honest, except for school which made everything obtuse. His descriptions of Brooklyn, the clear reminiscences of sexual initiation, killing, stealing, friendship, and loyalty, symbolize the belief that one loses oneself as an adult, one becomes separate but not an individual.

*America. For Henry, America is a contradiction of pacifism and cannibalism. Outwardly, it seems to be a "beautiful honeycomb," inwardly, however, it is a "slaughterhouse." America degrades and humiliates all voyagers; it is a "cesspool of the spirit in which everything is sucked down and drained away to everlasting shit," and into the sewer he journeys, the mythic labyrinth in which the minotaur of the self must be encountered and made one with the hero through mutual destruction.

His introduction to literature and deep thinking in his early twenties opens up new sexual worlds—the "Land of Fuck" and "Realm of the Cunt"—glorious and yet unsatisfactory worlds, likened to Dante's purgatory, but capable of regeneration, like the world of his childhood, now lost, unlike America where the destruction is complete, annihilating, permanently apocalyptic.

In this section of the novel, "The Interlude," most of the setting is within Henry, his soul leaving its body and roaming, traveling through time and space with no restrictions save time and space (paradox upon paradox);

his astral projections become allegorical and metaphysical representations of human existence from its earliest forms to the present, the creation and destruction of life, hatred and love, compassion and cruelty, all the contradictions that must be annihilated in order for the self to materialize, to truly be at one with the universe. The ultimate realization of this quest will be Woman, and once she is found, boundaries will dissolve and everything will belong. Life is love, he asserts, not God. In the end, dying and reborn, leaving America for France, he begins to live, realizing that the one way to accept life absolutely is to be wide awake without writing or talking about it. Such is the plight and the triumph of the artist, Miller acknowledges, continuing the paradoxes to the conclusion, which is merely another beginning.

— *Erskine Carter*

TROUT FISHING IN AMERICA

Author: Richard Brautigan (1935-1984)
Type of work: Novel
Type of plot: Picaresque

Time of plot: Fall, 1960, through fall, 1961, with flashbacks to the 1940's
First published: 1967

Set in the western United States, this novel concerns itself not so much with trout fishing as the lost wilderness of the West. Trout streams are the hallmark of this largely destroyed legacy. In one chapter, a stream becomes an outdoor stairway, and in another a stream is sold in pieces as scrap in a wrecking yard. These illusory or wrecked streams carry the hopes of American individualism and innocence. Although often whimsical, the book laments the passing of the American wilderness and offers hope only for the power of the imagination.

*Washington Park. Public park in San Francisco, California, that is meticulously described in the first pages of the novel. The park is named after George Washington, one of the Founders of America. Within the park is a statue of another Founder, Benjamin Franklin, whose autobiography and aphorisms are famous for their optimism. The statue's four-sided base has the word "welcome" on each side. The park, however, is not filled with optimistic Americans opening their arms to strangers. Rather, winos hang around waiting for sandwiches to be distributed to them. The narrator reflects on the gap between the literary America represented by Franklin, and the actuality of the park. While average Americans hurry past on their errands, the narrator

wastes time with the winos, including a man named "Trout Fishing in America Shorty," who is confined to a wheelchair. The narrator recalls that it was one of his stepfathers, a drunk, who first told him about fishing for trout and about the great beauty of trout. If any Americans still appreciate the beauty and romance of nature, they are the bums, drifters, and assorted poor who have no place in the society around them, which views nature as a commodity.

The book's winos—including a boy who is a Kool-Aid wino—enjoy one advantage over more productive members of society: They still have imaginations. They talk with passion about improbable and hypothetical things, including how to train and maintain a flea circus.

In the American West of this novel, the frontier is closed, and the only escape from an oppressive society lies inward. This path, however, is ultimately self-destructive.

*American West. Richard Brautigan's story follows the emotional journey of the narrator, who progresses from the satire of the first pages toward a sad, noble embrace of life's transiency in the end. The book also moves from the specificity of the first chapter toward more generalized descriptions of the motels, roads, and bars of the poor in the American West. In this sense, the America of *Trout Fishing in America* is as much a quality as a place.

The book is also an excursion into the American pastoral literary tradition, and allusions to such works as Henry David Thoreau's *Walden* (1854) and the nature stories of Ernest Hemingway are frequent. "Trout Fishing in America" is also the name of a person, as represented by the wino in a wheelchair named Trout Fishing in America Shorty. This character is the satiric opposite of the type of woodland hero that has been a staple of American mythology from the nineteenth century books of James Fenimore Cooper to twentieth century films of John Wayne. The wino is Brautigan's comment on the end of the myth of the American West. One of the book's many verbal tricks, in fact, is simple repetition of the phrase "trout fishing in America" to a point at which it becomes an ironic, meaningless mantra.

The novel's surrealism, whimsicality, and critical stance toward materialism have endeared it to many members of the counterculture. The book's comic appeal to the imagination, however, is very strongly undercut by its consistent pessimism about the mechanistic destruction not only of the environment but also of the human aspiration for freedom and happiness.

— *Eric Howard*

A TRUE HISTORY

Author: Lucian (c. 120-after 180)
Type of work: Short fiction
Type of plot: Satire

Time of plot: Second century
First transcribed: Alēthōn diēgēmatōn, second century (English translation, 1634)

A fantastic sea voyage that parodies the outrageous lies of poets, historians, and philosophers, this satire takes readers on a surreal "odyssey" and resembles modern science fiction. Its main episodes occur on the Moon, inside a whale, and on the islands of the dead. Lucian makes it clear from the outset that every detail is invented. Throughout, his voyagers are analogous to readers, and their encounters with strange places and creatures form an allegory of the process of making meaning.

Sea. This work's voyage takes place over a boundless ocean, which lies beyond the Strait of Gibraltar. The sea is the realm of the unknown beyond the Mediterranean, a realm where fantastic creatures dwell in all sorts of imagined locations. Drawing on the tradition of Homer's *Odyssey* (c. 800 B.C.E.), Lucian uses the sea as a symbol of the unpredictability of human fortune and of sudden, unexpected turns of events. The sea also represents the literary text, as the sailors in the ship become analogous to the readers, striving to make sense of what they encounter in this fantastic narrative.

*Moon. The first full episode of the story occurs on the Moon, when the ship is whisked up to the heavens in a whirlwind. After a battle between the Sun and the Moon, in which both entities clearly stand for warring nations down on Earth, Endymion, the king of the Moon, takes the narrator and his crew on a tour of the lunar landscape, which is populated by bizarre life-forms. This appears to be Lucian's parody of Greek ideas about the dead, which included the notion that souls of departed humans spent time on the Moon. Thus the Moon is both a strange, yet oddly familiar, otherworld—much in the mode of modern science fiction—and an abode of the dead.

Whale. Upon their return to the sea, and the land of the living, the voyagers are promptly swallowed by a huge whale, inside which whole communities of beings live. The travelers spend several months in the company of an old man and his son, who have cultivated a farm in the whale's stomach. The whale appears to be a parody of Plato's Cave, where men live in intellectual darkness until they find their way out to the sun, through philosophical enlightenment. Once again, the voyagers get caught up in a war before escaping back to the sea by burning a hole in the whale's side.

Islands of the Dead. The third major episode takes the sailors to a group of islands lying far across the ocean. It turns out, after some initial confusion on the part of both the voyagers and readers, that these islands are the mythical Isles of the Blessed and the Damned. Both places afford Lucian the chance to parody all sorts of nonsense which was circulating about the afterlife, promulgated by philosophers, poets, and other notorious "liars." So, for instance, the city on the Isle of the Blessed, which has buildings of gold and an emerald wall and is surrounded by a river of perfume, is an elaborate pastiche of the Greek tradition of Utopia: the ideal city, where everyone lives in luxurious and harmonious

equality. The city is populated by heroes of mythology and historical personages, including Homer, who again offer ample opportunity for satirical comment. The Isle of the Damned is also described, again drawing upon the long tradition of accounts of Tartarus and Hades.

Other Continent. After a few minor episodes, including a visit to Lucian's version of the land of the Sirens, the ship is wrecked in a storm and the travelers struggle ashore on what is mysteriously termed the "Other Continent," at which point the narrator breaks off his story. The Other Continent may be the land at the end of the ocean, of which the Greeks had only a vague notion—that is to say, a place which is so radically different that it defies description. Alternatively, it may be the land from which the voyagers originally set out—their own land which they now fail to recognize, after the journey of philosophical and psychic enlightenment they have endured.

In terms of the symbolism of reading and making meaning, the Other Continent is the as yet unencountered literary work, which readers will have to explore and interpret. After passing through the initiation of Lucian's parodic satire, however, readers are now better prepared for this task.

— *David Larmour*

TUNG-CHOU LIEH-KUO CHIH

Author: Feng Menglong (1574?-1645?)
Type of work: Novel
Type of plot: Historical

Time of plot: 770-220 B.C.E.
First published: Xin Lieguo Zhi, Ming edition, after 1627; C'ing edition, after 1644

East central China, along the Huang He (Yellow) River in the north and Chang Jiang (Yangtze) River in the south, provides the setting for the vast military and political battles fought among powerful warlords during the rise and fall of China's eastern Zhou (Chou) Dynasty, which is the subject of this historical epic. Their walled cities serve as bases of power for the feuding lords, and the regions they dominate give name and strength to their noble houses. Places are constantly fought over, and the final unification of the whole region under a single emperor provides a final closure.

*Xi'an (shee-AN). Walled city on the right bank of the Wei river, about eighty miles west from its confluence with the Huang He. The old capital of what later became known as the western Zhou Dynasty. From this

city, the Zhou ruled their vast domain by granting their vassals hereditary rights to rule the lands adjacent to their individual fortified towns. This inadvertently led to the foundation of new local states on the Zhou lands.

The epic dramatizes the fall of Xi'an to a coalition of neighboring lords and "barbarians," which all non-ethnic Chinese of the region were called, in 770 B.C.E. The story turns the destruction of Xi'an into a moral lesson. Xi'an's magnificent lighthouse fails to summon loyal defenders, because the last king turned on its light merely to entertain his favorite concubine. After the city's destruction, it loses importance until the new Qin (Ch'in) Dynasty builds its capital there at the end of the epic. Thus, narrative closure comes when power returns to the place from which foolish human behavior had driven it five centuries earlier.

Luoyang (lew-oh-YANG). Capital of the eastern Zhou, who move there after the fall of Xi'an. Roughly two hundred miles east of Xi'an and on the southern bank of the Huang He, the new location provides more safety from raiders and lies in the fertile river plain, with floods presenting a major natural danger. As the eastern Zhou gradually lose real power, their capital also loses importance and splendor.

Qi (kee). Duchy based in the current province of Shandong, beginning two hundred miles southeast of present-day Beijing. There, the Huang He River flows into Bo Hai Bay at the northern tip of the Yellow Sea. The Dai Shan Mountains rise over the river plains. In the novel, Qi is the first duchy to eclipse the central power of the king of Zhou. Crafty treaties and alliances with its neighboring states help Qi to defend itself from the rising power to its southwest.

Chu. State located in the present provinces of Hubei and Henan (Hunan) between the rivers Huang He and Chang Jiang. In the novel, its inhabitants are regarded as half-barbarian and fierce. Through politics and warfare, Chu increases its area of control until all smaller fiefdoms along the Han River are conquered, and its power reaches into the fierce Huashang mountains.

Jiangsu Province. Area of the kingdom of Wu, which rose in the southeast along the coast of the Yellow Sea, and defeated the Chu. Ironically, Wu falls to the Yueh, conquerors out of the present Zhejiang Province, south of modern Shanghai. The novel's moral reading of history takes delight in the historical fact that the place of the conquerors from Zhejiang later becomes part of an invigorated state of Chu.

Warring states. The feudal system of allocating land not only to great lords of the Zhou Dynasty but also to the ministers and warriors of the lords themselves leads to the creation of smaller and smaller fiefdoms. A large number of local hereditary potentates are created, each of whom rules a domain of his own. This disintegration leads to the division of the large state of Jin, which splits into the three states of Zhao, Wei, and Han in today's province of Shanxi. During this period of the warring states, from 403 to 221 B.C.E., what the Chinese considered their homeland is divided into seven powerful states fighting and scheming against one another.

Qin (keen). Westernmost Chinese kingdom whose streams and forbidding mountains create a stronghold from which large armies can issue forth into the plains of the Huang He bordering the state to the east. Qin expanded by conquering the non-Chinese people to its west. The novel closes when the king of Qin defeats all six rival states and proclaims himself Shi Huangdi, or First Emperor of the new Qin Dynasty. During his subsequent reign, he would build the Great Wall of China.

— *R. C. Lutz*

THE TURN OF THE SCREW

Author: Henry James (1843-1916)
Type of work: Novella
Type of plot: Ghost

Time of plot: Mid-nineteenth century
First published: 1898

The setting of this ghost story is a country house in England, at which events transpire that may be interpreted as a subtle but powerful moral allegory, in which the estate represents a type of Garden of Eden and in which Evil enters to entrap two children who represent archetypal male and female innocents.

Bly. Country house in Essex to which an unnamed young governess, the daughter of a clergyman, is sent to look after two orphaned children whose wealthy uncle lives in London. The large house has two extensive floors, two towers, and grounds that include a pathway to a lake—elements characteristic of residences in gothic stories.

The house is managed by Mrs. Grose, an illiterate but talkative housekeeper, who oversees at least two maids and two servants. The governess has her own room, in which the child Flora has a bed. Flora's brother, Miles, has a bedroom across the hall. In the schoolroom and nursery, the governess instructs her charges and also listens to Miles at the piano. A winding staircase has a casement window at its landing. Among other downstairs rooms is a dining room with a large window. Several rooms are empty.

Strange sounds that the governess hears in the house make her increasingly aware that apparitions are present that only she seems to see. On one occasion, while she happens to be thinking of her absent employer, the children's uncle in London, she looks up at one of Bly's towers and sees, or believes she sees, the ghost of Peter Quint, who in life was the uncle's valet. Drunken and vicious, he was also the lover of Miss Jessel, the former governess who also is now dead. Miss Jessel appears frequently to the governess and to the children, who refuse to admit the appearances. The governess suspects the children of seeking out the ghosts but can prove nothing.

Lake. Body of water on the estate where the governess, accompanied by Mrs. Grose, finds Flora playing with a mast on a tiny wooden boat. When the apparition of Miss Jessel appears by the child, Flora turns on the governess viciously and the latter faints. Each ghostly sighting causes the governess to jump to various conclusions, accurate or otherwise, depending on one's evaluation of her psychological makeup.

The first appearances of the two evil ghosts, Mr. Quint and Miss Jessel, occur respectively on a tower and beside a lake, locations that could signify male and female sexuality, respectively. At the time of Miss Jessel's appearance, Flora, who is being watched by the governess, is engaged in a game involving joining together two pieces of wood, a game that could also have sexual overtones to the governess.

Harley Street. Fashionable London street that later became famous as a region of well-to-do physicians' offices. The children's uncle lives on Harley Street, where he interviews the governess twice before hiring her. She is impressed by him and grows enamored.

— *Robert L. Gale*

TWELFTH NIGHT: Or, What You Will

Author: William Shakespeare (1564-1616)
Type of work: Drama
Type of plot: Comedy

Time of plot: Sixteenth century
First performed: c. 1600-1602; first published, 1623

The Adriatic coast region of Illyria is significant to the theme of malaise caused by the fickle moodiness of love and the folly of self-love in this play. The port is a perfect setting for disparate characters to reach by misadventure—such as the shipwreck that brings Viola and Sebastian to it—and to experience the instability and volatility of passion and truth.

*****Illyria.** Region on the east shore of the Adriatic Sea, between Italy and Greece. Its history is marked by waves of conquering invaders, from early Slavs to Ottoman Turks. In William Shakespeare's time, Illyria—still part of the Ottoman Empire—was a group of city-states controlled by Venice. In the play, Illyria is distinctly Italianate, making for an atmosphere that is congenial to romance, with the seacoast providing an apt setting for plot conveniences of shipwreck, separated twins (Viola and Sebastian), and exotic adventures. At Illyria, fantasies and dreams are realized, and lessons are learned. There Viola is transformed from a woman to a man to

"Orsino's mistress," and there she is finally able to live in an earthly Elysium.

Duke's palace. Site of romantic sentimentality. The duke revels in wordplay and music, which feed his passion. The palace is also a site of ambiguous sexual identity, as shown by Viola's disguise as Cesario.

House of Olivia. House modeled on the English system of servants and retainers with prescribed duties. On one hand, there is the mourning figure of Olivia, and the humorless, austere, proud figure of her steward, Malvolio, the epitome of all puritans. On the other, there are Fabian and Maria, Olivia's servants, and the faithful old retainer, Feste—a well-educated clown. Olivia at-

tempts to live a cloistered life, but Sir Toby Belch and Sir Andrew Aguecheek, the two rowdy rioters, are unaffected by Olivia's sadness over her dead brother.

In a room within this house, Malvolio is confined indarkness and cruelly mocked and tormented by a disguised Feste, at the instigation of Sir Toby and Maria.

Olivia's orchard. Scene of Malvolio's gulling by Maria's faked letter. One of the comic highlights of the play comes from Malvolio's strange cross-gartering and absurd posturings as Olivia's would-be lover. However, the real point of the comedy is character revelation.

— *Keith Garebian*

THE TWELVE

Author: Aleksandr Blok (1880-1921)
Type of work: Poetry
Type of plot: Ballad

Time of plot: 1917
First published: Dvenadtsat', 1918 (English translation, 1920)

Aleksandr Blok's most famous poem depicts the Russian Revolution of 1917 as he saw and experienced it in the capital city. Though often hailed as the great poem of the revolution, it has also been criticized by the opponents as a distorted view of the revolution.

*Petrograd. Russian city in which the Bolshevik Revolution of 1917 started, when the city was known as St. Petersburg. Blok places the action of his ballad in the streets of the city during a blizzard at night. Twelve revolutionaries march through the almost deserted streets, chanting and yelling revolutionary slogans. They are rowdies, mistreating the bystanders, robbing and burning homes. Blok emphasizes their proletarian background by having them wear convict attire. They are looked upon with fear, suspicion, and hatred by their traditional enemies on the sidewalks—an old lady, a bourgeois, a writer, a priest, and two fur-coated ladies—all representing the old world that is crumbling in that winter night. The observers stand, as if nailed to the ground, while the revolutionaries move ahead, signaling progress.

The poem reaches a climax by having an apparition of Jesus Christ appear in front of the twelve. Blok himself was not sure why Christ appears. Is he leading or confronting them? If he is leading them, why is he facing them and why are they shooting at him? Despite many rejections of this symbol on the part of the critics and readers and despite Blok's own misgivings, there is no question that, by using clear symbols such as the number twelve (perhaps representing Christ's twelve Apostles), Blok wanted to express his acceptance of the revolution as necessary, hoping that it would bring about badly needed reforms. He would soon change his mind just before he died in 1921, but *The Twelve* remains artistically the best-known literary work about the Bolshevik Revolution.

— *Vasa D. Mihailovich*

TWENTY THOUSAND LEAGUES UNDER THE SEA

Author: Jules Verne (1828-1905)
Type of work: Novel
Type of plot: Science fiction

Time of plot: 1866-1867
First published: Vingt mille lieues sous les mers, 1869-1870 (English translation, 1873)

A master of fantastic voyage stories, Jules Verne based this novel on his two great loves—ships and the sea. It is a tale of going to the sea in ships, its primary vessels being a U.S. naval frigate and the mysterious submarine of Captain Nemo. Verne's descriptions of shipboard life reflect his own love of sailing, a passion he shared with a brother who served in the French navy. This novel is also a tale of the high seas, the "living infinite" on the millions of square miles of water that cover seven-tenths of the earth.

USS *Abraham Lincoln.* American naval frigate sent to investigate reports of a mysterious sea monster that is destroying warships on the high seas. Under Commodore Farragut—named after Civil War naval hero David G. Farragut—the *Abraham Lincoln* encounters not the sea monster it expects when it leaves New York but a mechanical wonder the likes of which did not exist in the civilized world. The encounter between the conventional warship and the exceptional submarine occurs only after the former's long and exhausting search of the Atlantic and Pacific Oceans, two hundred miles off Japan, where the *Nautilus* sinks the *Abraham Lincoln*. The *Nautilus* takes aboard three of the frigate's survivors: French scientist Pierre Aronnax, his servant Conseil, and Ned Land, an expert harpooner.

Verne's love of the sixteenth president of the United States is evidenced in his choice of name for this novel's frigate. Lincoln is also honored in the sequel to this novel, *The Mysterious Island* (1875), as the name of a Pacific island.

Nautilus. Submarine on which most of the novel is set. Verne's love of ships and technology is evident in his descriptions of the technologically marvelous *Nautilus*. He knew the kinds of keels that could be manufactured in France, the kinds of shafts that could be cast in London, the screws that could be forged in Glasgow, the instruments that could be invented in New York City, the powerful engines that could be devised in Prussia, and the steel battering rams that could be forged in Sweden. From his store of mechanical lore, he invented the novel's submarine. Verne also had knowledge of the battle of the American ironclad warships,

the *Monitor* and the *Merrimack*, during the U.S. Civil War.

Astounding for its time, the *Nautilus* is a submersible metal ship 232 feet long and 26 feet wide with a displacement of 1,500 tons of water. It possesses all the amenities of civilized life, including a twelve-thousand-volume library, an art museum, a collection of natural specimens, and even a pipe organ. It cost more than one million U.S. dollars to build—an amount that only a wealthy outlaw-prince, such as its Captain Nemo (a name meaning "no one") could afford to pay.

The world does not hear of this ship before it begins its reign of terror on the seas during the late 1860's because its parts had been secretly obtained and assembled on a desert island. This "Sailor" (for *Nautilus* is simply the Greek word for "sailor") can turn a wilderness into a garden. Once again Verne returns to his familiar theme of technology having the ability to free humankind from imprisonment in space—be it on earth, over or under the seas, or in the air.

*Oceans. Nemo takes his uninvited guests on a tour of the world's seas. To most people, the oceans are a watery wilderness, as hostile as the primordial oceans in the Bible's Book of Genesis. To Captain Nemo, however, the watery desert is the "Living Infinite," from which he obtains fuel for his ship, food for his crew, seaweed for his cigars, textiles for his clothing, and forbidden treasures from pearls, sunken ships, and the lost civilization of Atlantis. He has accumulated wealth enough "to pay the national debt of France."

Aronnax and his cohorts are prisoners, but their prison is an elegant one. They sail under the South Pole (an impossibility in the real world), explore Plato's legendary Atlantis, and navigate an unknown submarine passage under the Isthmus of Suez (where the Suez was being constructed at the time this novel is set). They experience high adventure—hunting with air guns in submarine forests, escaping attack by headhunters in New Guinea, and struggling with a notorious maelstrom off the coast of Norway, until they escape from Nemo's grasp and return to normal society.

— *C. George Fry*

THE TWO GENTLEMEN OF VERONA

Author: William Shakespeare (1564-1616)
Type of work: Drama
Type of plot: Comedy

Time of plot: Sixteenth century
First performed: c. 1594-1595; first published, 1623

Three distinct and shifting settings—Verona, Milan, and a forest—provide Valentine and Proteus, this play's two main characters, with new experiences that test their romantic relationships, which become entangled in the cities and, eventually, untangle in the forest.

*****Verona.** City in northern Italy in which William Shakespeare also set *Romeo and Juliet* (1595-1596). The Verona of *The Two Gentlemen of Verona* is a highly fictionalized place, a locale of relative innocence. There, Valentine and Proteus enjoy a firm and uncomplicated friendship until Proteus is sent by his father to Milan.

Tensions among the characters in Verona are mild and ordinary, features of fairly uneventful domestic life: Valentine disagrees with Proteus about the relative merits of love and travel; Julia at first does not to know what to make of Proteus's offers of affection; Antonio, Proteus's father, disapproves of his son's devotion to love; and Proteus objects to his father's command that he join Valentine in Milan. None of these conflicts is particularly significant. They all resemble the conflict between the buffoon Launce and his dog Crab, who refuses to weep upon his master's departure from home. Contrasted to Milan and the forest, Verona is a place of domestic tranquillity.

*****Milan.** Major northern Italian city, which, like Verona, is highly fictionalized in the play. In Milan, the two young gentlemen of Verona finally encounter serious problems in their lives. Valentine falls in love with Silvia, but her father, the Duke, wishes her to marry a wealthy but unpleasant character named Thurio.

When Proteus arrives in Milan, his life is also changed, for once he meets Silvia he abandons not only his professed love for Julia but also his lifelong friendship with Valentine. After a Machiavellian maneuver through which he secures the banishment of Valentine from Milan, Proteus manipulates both the duke and Thurio into giving him access to Silvia, who, however, remains impervious to his solicitations and deaf to his false claims that both Julia and Valentine have died.

It is as though the change of location from Verona to Milan has brought about alterations in the characters of both Valentine, who has become a lover, and Proteus, who has become an unscrupulous and deceitful scoundrel. The two main female characters, Julia and Silvia, are also forced to respond to changes in their lovers' status by resorting to drastic measures, including leaving their home cities.

Forest. Just as Verona is an abode of simplicity and inexperience and Milan is a locale in which Valentine and Proteus encounter challenges, the forest turns out to be the realm in which reconciliation becomes possible. Although this reconciliation eventually emerges from chaotic confusion, it proves surprisingly comprehensive, as the duke even pardons outlaws who have been terrorizing the area. Valentine forgives Proteus for his treachery although he is aware that his old friend was on the verge, a few minutes earlier, of raping Silvia. Julia, who in her disguise has witnessed Proteus's unconscionable behavior, also forgives him as he suddenly experiences a revival of his love for her.

Thus the natural environment of the forest contrasts favorably with the world of the city, in which human schemes so often work against human happiness. The duke's greedy disregard for his daughter's love for Valentine, Proteus's selfishness with respect to Valentine, Silvia, and Julia, and Thurio's self-centered conviction that he is entitled to marry Silvia all come to naught in the forest, where the true virtue of Valentine, Silvia, and Julia emerges and prevails.

— *Robert W. Haynes*

THE TWO NOBLE KINSMEN

Authors: William Shakespeare (1564-1616) and John
  Fletcher (1579-1625)
Type of work: Drama

Type of plot: Tragicomedy
Time of plot: Antiquity
First performed: c. 1612-1613; first published, 1634

Borrowing much of its plot and many of its places and characters from Geoffrey Chaucer's Knight's Tale, *which is itself largely a retelling of Boccaccio's* The Book of Theseus, *the authors of this play adapt the old story for a London audience.*

Athens. Ancient Greek city that is the scene of much of the play's action, Athens is ruled by Duke Theseus, whose marriage to the Amazon leader Hippolyta is interrupted by three royal widows who ask Theseus to avenge their husbands by attacking Creon, the tyrant of Thebes. Several significant events also occur in the countryside outside the city, the most significant of which are the fight between Palamon and Arcite, their discovery by Theseus and his entourage, and the tournament between the two Thebans for the hand of Emily.

Athens is also the location of a temple containing shrines to Mars, Venus, and Diana. In contrast to the depiction of these shrines in other writers' renditions of this story, these shrines are all located within a single temple.

Thebes (theebz). Greek city against which Theseus is persuaded to lead an army. His army overthrows Creon and captures Palamon and Arcite, who are members of the Theban royal family. From their Athens prison, the two noble kinsmen see the beautiful Emilia, sister-in-law of Theseus, and fall in love with her. Their rivalry for her affection drives the rest of the story.

— *Robert W. Haynes*

THE TWO TOWERS

Author: J. R. R. Tolkien (1892-1973)
Type of work: Novel
Type of plot: Fantasy

Time of plot: The Third Age in a remote legendary past
First published: 1954

In this second volume of J. R. R. Tolkien's The Lord of the Rings *trilogy, new places emerge as the divided fellowship moves east to the Riddermark of Rohan, Fangorn Forest, and Isengard and west to the barren Emyn Muil, near Mordor, a fitting emblem for the environmental abuse wrought by Sauron.*

East of the river. An Orc ambush has captured Merry and Pippin, and a remorseful Boromir has died trying to protect them. Aragorn, Gimli, and Legolas (human, dwarf, and elf) commit Boromir's body to the river and head southwest, following the Orc trail in the hope of rescuing the young Hobbits. Their route crosses into empty grasslands, territory given to the Rohirrhim by Gondor. Meanwhile Merry and Pippin escape during a fight between the Orcs and a band of the Riders of Rohan and slip into **Fangorn Forest**. There, in an ancient, almost stiflingly dense woods, they meet Treebeard the Ent, a giant "shepherd" of the trees.

The long-lived Ents rarely concern themselves with human power struggles; however, Saruman, an evil wizard who occupies a tower near the forest, has allowed his Orc workers to chop down trees, partly to feed the furnaces of his war ambitions and partly out of utter indifference to nature. Treebeard agrees to help the Hobbits, gathers other Ents, and, with Merry and Pippin on his shoulders, leads a march upon Isengard followed by furious "huorns," who may be degenerate Ents or angry animate trees, a green army intent upon payback.

Gandalf, who is not dead, finds Aragorn, Gimli, and Legolas, and they ride across the plains of Rohan to Edoras, where Theoden reigns in a primitive yet dignified palace which suggests the world of "Beowulf," a simpler and younger civilization than that of Gondor. Roused to action, Theoden, his Riders, Aragorn, Gimli, and Legolas gallop from the Golden Hall to Helm's Deep, a fortress from which the horselords are mounting a defense against Saruman's troops. Gandalf departs to seek other help, and after a night of graphic battle, he brings aid to the outnumbered Rohirrhim in the form of Huorns.

The company proceeds to Isengard, where Saruman's tower is now surrounded by flood and rubble. Merry and Pippin, perched on a pile of debris, greet their friends and offer them bacon, beer, and pipe tobacco. The allies now plan to march to Gondor's assistance by way of Edoras, but Gandalf counsels Theoden to muster his troops in Dunharrow, a hidden fastness in the hills, while he and Pippin ride ahead to Minas Tirith.

West of the river. Frodo and Sam, trailed by Gollum, wander through the **Emyn Muil**, a barren range of hills that demonstrates the harsh terrain of the Dark Lord's lands. They capture Gollum, who is temporarily tamed by a promise to the One Ring, which he covets. He leads the Hobbits through the Dead Marshes, the site of a long-ago battle, where graves of humans and elves have been swallowed by quagmires and fens. Crawling through the festering swamp, they approach the Black Gate, a heavily fortified entrance to the land of **Mordor**. They shelter in the shadow of a mound of slag, choking on fumes from a land hopelessly defiled by Sauron, where "neither spring nor summer would ever come again," a place "fire-blasted and poison stained." Gollum suggests a "secret" way into Mordor, and the three follow the Mountains of Shadow south, where they encounter a guerrilla band of Men of Gondor, who maintain an outpost in a cave behind a waterfall in Ithilien, once "the garden of Gondor" and still possessing "a dishevelled dryad loveliness."

The company captain Faramir lets Frodo and Sam go forward, but he warns them that the Pass of Cirith (Keareth) Urgol, Gollum's destination, has an evil reputation. Rejoining Gollum, the Hobbits slip past Minas Tirith's evil twin city, Minas Morgul, amid fields of noisome, toxic flowers and ascend a steep mountain pass. However, Gollum has twisted his vow and is taking them to the cavern of a giant spider Shelob, hoping that once she has devoured Frodo, he may find the Ring among the bones. Shelob stings Frodo; Sam, believing his master dead, wounds and repels the spider and accepts the burden of the Ring. Orcs from a guard tower just beyond the pass approach; as Sam uses the Ring to become invisible, he learns that Shelob stings not to kill but to immobilize "fresh meat." Frodo is not dead, but the Orcs carry the unconscious Hobbit into the tower as Sam beats desperately on its brazen door.

— *Nan C. L. Scott*

TWO WOMEN

Author: Alberto Moravia (1907-1990)
Type of work: Novel
Type of plot: Social realism

Time of plot: 1943-1944
First published: La ciociara, 1957 (English translation, 1958)

This novel focuses on a widowed shopkeeper and her gentle and naïve daughter who flee Rome during World War II to seek shelter and safety in a poor mountainous region south of the city. In the countryside they discover that the war has followed them and experience increasing hardships and degradation until they are able finally to return to their home as Allied troops advance up the boot of Italy.

*Rome. Capital and largest city in Italy. Cesira goes there from her girlhood home in the mountainous region of Ciociaria after her marriage to a much older husband who owns both a small shop and an apartment in Trastevere in Vicolo del Cinque. The city forces Cesira to adapt to a different way of life from her rural upbringing and provides Alberto Moravia with a base against which he can later contrast the experiences of Cesira and her daughter in the country.

After the death of her husband, Cesira is content with her small shop, her tidy flat, and raising her teenage daughter. When the war comes she initially prospers by selling black market goods she acquires from peasant farmers outside Rome. In spite of all the changes in her life, Cesira remains very much the same person she has always been until she confronts the war at first hand in the mountains after fleeing Rome to return to her family home at Vallecorsa with her daughter, Rosetta.

Sant'Eufemia. Small village high in the mountains where Cesira and Rosetta take what they believe will be only temporary lodgings in a crude lean-to with a peasant family. There, amid the ramshackle huts and rude life of the peasants, Cesira rediscovers the customs of her childhood, and her daughter is subjected for the first time to the hardships of country living, with its attendant poverty, isolation, and fears.

Moravia uses the nine months of the women's stay at Sant'Eufemia to introduce readers to the degradation of rural Italian life, far from the comforts of Rome. As their stay lengthens, the women are gradually exposed to the realities of a shooting war and the German occupation of Italy, as they wait for Italy's liberation by British and American armies. Moravia also uses this period in their lives to present to his readers the violence and humiliation of the occupation.

Fondi. Town closest to Sant'Eufemia. It provides a contrast between the relative prosperity of life on the lower plain, with its amenities, and the poverty and misfortune of peasants living in the mountains. This contrast is a consistent theme among postwar Italian novelists, especially those like Moravia who espouse socialist solutions to the problems of modern Italian society. Fondi is also the place where the women first encounter the Allied troops and receive food, shelter, clothing, and finally transportation to their initial destination, Cesira's family home at Vallecorsa.

Vallecorsa. Cesira's original home. When the women eventually reach the village, it is deserted and all of its houses are boarded up because the occupants, including Cesira's own family, have fled approaching military action. Throughout the novel Cesira assures Rosetta that her village will be a place of safety and sustenance. Instead, they arrive at the village at the lowest ebb of their fortunes, and there, in the local church, Rosetta is raped by French Moroccan soldiers. Afterward, Rosetta changes. Gone is her innocence and sweetness; she becomes hedonistic in her pursuit of the scarce goods, food, clothing, and pleasure, long denied her by the ravages of the war. For Moravia, Rosetta becomes emblematic of the postwar generation. At first devastated by her daughter's rape and the subsequent transformation it makes in her, Cesira becomes angered by Rosetta's behavior and her abandonment of what she perceives is a proper way of life. Eventually, however, she realizes that she must accept her daughter as she is despite everything that has happened to both of them. This recognition provides for the epiphany with which the novel closes.

— *Charles L. P. Silet*

TYPEE

Author: Herman Melville (1819-1891)
Type of work: Novel
Type of plot: Adventure

Time of plot: Mid-nineteenth century
First published: 1846

Set in the Marquesas Islands of the Central Pacific, this novel, based on Herman Melville's adventures on these same tropical isles, established his reputation as a chronicler of sea adventures and an observer of exotic lands and their peoples. Melville's detailed descriptions of the tropical landscape do much to tease the popular taste for tropical flora, while underscoring the ruggedness of the terrain and the wildness of the vegetation, suggesting that these islands are not the pristine, placid paradises dreamed of in romantic imaginations.

Dolly. Whaling vessel that carries the narrator to the Marquesas Islands. Before arriving there, the ship and its crew spend six months at sea in pursuit of sperm whales. Though Melville's descriptions of life on this ship are minuscule in comparison to his lavish depictions of the islands, these matters are important because they explain why the narrator and his cohort Toby decide to jump ship. It is also through these descriptions that the author chronicles injustices suffered by sailors and thus sets into motion one of his concerns in this and in later narratives: reform of oppressive and intrusive Western institutions.

*Nukuheva** (noo-koo-HEE-vah). Largest and most important of the **Marquesas Islands**. Approximately twenty miles in length and nearly as broad, Nukuheva (now generally rendered Nuku Hiva) is large enough to boast three good harbors and is consequently the place where foreign ships first land. As the *Dolly* enters the harbor, the crew finds that the French have occupied the island and are maintaining control with several warships and soldiers. However, despite this familiar Western presence, the narrator is still overcome by the exotic scenery as he describes the terrain of the island from the vantage point of the *Dolly*. What he finds most remarkable are the swelling heights of the surrounding hills and mountains rising from the placid, blue waters of the bay. After the narrator and Toby decide to jump ship and explore the island, their journey takes them deeper into the interior of this beautiful but forbidding landscape, where they eventually will enter the valley of the Typee, a fearsome tribe whose very name in the Marquesan language connotes cannibalistic practices.

Valley of the Happar. Valley on the island of Nukuheva that is populated by the supposedly peaceful Happar tribe. As the narrator and Toby plan their escape from the *Dolly* and venture into the interior of the island, they debate whether to enter the valley of the Happar or the valley of the Typee.

Valley of the Typee. Nukuheva valley that the narrator and Toby eventually enter after an arduous descent down rugged precipices and through areas overgrown with dense, suffocating vegetation. As he enters this valley, the narrator is struck by its immense and startling beauty, especially in contrast to the harsh landscape over which he had recently traversed. His wonder is tempered by his fear of the Typee; however, he soon learns that the Typee are not as fearsome and violent as he had feared. In fact, they seem to be a peace-loving people who greet him and his companion with much hospitality. Soon after the men enter the valley, Toby disappears, leaving the narrator alone to calculate his chances for survival among these strange but seemingly friendly people. Over the course of his four-month stay among the Typee, the narrator describes their dwellings and chronicles their daily practices, including their bathing habits and their dressing rituals. He also falls in love with Fayaway, a young woman whose breath-taking beauty he describes in surprisingly graphic detail. By including such a detailed, almost anthropological account of the domestic life of the Typee, Melville does much to humanize these Polynesian people and sets the groundwork for his critiques of the intrusive practices of Western merchants and missionaries.

— *R. Allen Alexander, Jr.*

ULYSSES

Author: James Joyce (1882-1941)
Type of work: Novel
Type of plot: Epic

Time of plot: June 16, 1904
First published: 1922

This novel, which one critic called the "most conscientiously topographical novel ever written," traces the movements of its protagonists, Leopold Bloom and Stephen Dedalus, through the streets of Dublin, Ireland, on a single day, June 16, 1904.

*Dublin. Ireland's capital city and principal east coast port on the Irish Sea, through which a young Irish writer and teacher named Stephen Dedalus (whom Joyce introduced in *A Portrait of the Artist as a Young Man* in 1914) and the Jewish advertising salesman Leopold Bloom wander until they eventually meet. The novel explores streets, shops, public houses, and countless other places found along their routes.

In 1904, Dublin is a city with a population of about three hundred thousand people. Ireland is still under the rule of Great Britain, whose local governor lives in a regal house in Dublin's Phoenix Park and governs from Dublin Castle. The city as a whole is a complex mix, with both wretched slums and lingering remnants of eighteenth century elegance. More than twenty thousand families live in one-room tenement apartments, many of which house four or more people. Dublin is also a city with an interesting history of Anglo-Irish literary and cultural activity and a kind of urban energy that tends to countermand James Joyce's estimate of psychological "paralysis." Dublin provided Joyce with the raw material for a cosmos built on patient attention to the minute particulars of city life. The dense texture of metropolitan detail in *Ulysses* complements and offers paths into the psychological substance of the novel's characters.

Many chapters depict the protagonists as well as multiple groups of people traveling routes across the landscape of Dublin. Throughout the book, the substance of the city is solidified by the landmarks and streets that are mentioned, ranging from well-known places such as Mountjoy Square, Grafton Street, and Phoenix Park, to a diversity of shops, pubs, tramcar stops, and quays.

*Sandycove. Suburb southeast of Dublin now known as Dun Laoghlaire, in which Dedalus, in one of the versions of the narrative consciousness (along with Leopold and Molly Bloom) that operates in the novel, is living as the novel opens. Dedalus shares rooms with the medical student Buck Mulligan in Martello Tower, built on the Dublin coast as one of seventy-four similar defensive constructions erected in anticipation of a French invasion. (The tower was later converted into the James Joyce Tower Museum.)

*Dalkey Avenue. Sandycove street on which the Clifton School, at which Joyce taught briefly as a young man, stands, and the location, near the Martello Tower, of the unnamed school from which Stephen is about to resign when the story begins.

*Sandymount. Beach several miles up the coast from Sandycove, along which Dedalus walks past the decaying house of his uncle Richie Goulding in the chapter that concludes the first section of the novel. Later in the novel, Bloom is entranced by the sight of Gertie MacDowell and her friends on the same beach.

Eccles Street (EH-clees). North Dublin street on which Leopold Bloom lives with his wife, Molly, at number 7. Their home is a worn-down but still genteel, three-story house. As Bloom begins his wanderings on June 16, 1904, he crosses to the "bright side" (southwest) of Eccles Street, then walks to Dorset Street, notices the sun near the steeple of St. George's church on Temple Street and passes St. Joseph's National School, on the way to the Dlugacz butcher shop. These accurate and very specific details establish the factual ground for an inventive series of imaginative devices that Joyce uses to create the reality of the lives of the inhabitants of Dublin.

Toward the end of the novel, Bloom finds Dedalus passed out in Dublin's red-light district and walks back to his house with him. Dedalus declines Bloom's offer of hospitality. Bloom then retires with his wife, whose soliloquy concludes the novel. Her recollective re-creation of her past with Bloom, as well as her life before, is anchored by a reflection on a moment in their courtship, when she and Bloom were together on Howth Reach, overlooking the sea north of Dublin, and by her thoughts of her girlhood and first love in Gibraltar, also near the ocean.

Sir John Rogerson's Quay. Dublin street that runs along the south bank of the River Liffey, the channel that carries the waters of the Irish Sea through the city and beyond to the west. Joyce would put much more emphasis on the Liffey in *Finnegan's Wake* (1939), in which the river spirit is incarnated in the character of Anna Livia Plurabelle, than he does in *Ulysses*. However, in this novel, Bloom proceeds south, passing a series of streets in the inner city, before picking up a letter at the Westland Row post office.

Bloom's path through the city continues in the next section as he takes a taxicab along Great Brunswick Street (now Pearse street), noting various prominent buildings (the Ancient Concert Rooms; St. Mark's Church; the Queen's Theatre) before his cab crosses O'Connell Bridge, where its passengers see the statue of the huge "cloaked Liberator's form." The cab then continues through North Dublin, across the Royal Canal until it arrives at Glasnevin Cemetery for the funeral of Paddy Dignam, an old friend of Bloom who died suddenly of a stroke. Dublin's waterways carry some suggestion of the rivers of Hades in this section.

Evening Telegraph. Newspaper located in an office on North Prince Street, where both Bloom and Stephen go on errands. From there, Bloom walks back across the Liffey and down Grafton Street, passing such notable Dublin landmarks as the Irish Parliament building (now the Bank of Ireland), the offices of the *Irish Times*, and various small shops, before stopping at Davy Byrne's "moral pub." (The pub now advertises its appearance in *Ulysses* and displays a plaque containing Joyce's semi-ironic description.) From the pub, he continues on to the National Library in Kildare Street.

Mabbot Street. Red-light district of Dublin (now considerably transformed by slum clearance), where Bella Cohen's brothel is situated (on what is now Corporation Street). There, Stephen passes out in the gutter and is rescued by Bloom, who looks for a cab near the Amiens Street Station (now the Connolly Station). Eventually Stephen and Bloom walk back to Bloom's home, on a course that Joyce describes with precision, street by street.

Homeric world. As a parallel to the episodes in Dublin, Joyce used Homer's *The Odyssey* (c. 800 B.C.E.) to amplify the narrative action of his own novel. Among other complementary sites, Paddy Dignam's funeral is likened to Odysseus's trip to Hades; the newspaper office is like Homer's Cave of the Winds, the editor similar to Aeolus, god of wind; Bloom's assault in Barney Kiernan's pub recalls the attack of the Cyclops in *The Odyssey*; the visit to the brothel resembles the Circe episode; and Bloom's return to his home is like the Penelope section (as emphasized by Molly's concluding soliloquy), after Odysseus finally returns to Ithaca.

— *Leon Lewis*

THE UNBEARABLE BASSINGTON

Author: Saki (Hector Hugh Munro, 1870-1916)
Type of work: Novel
Type of plot: Satire

Time of plot: Early twentieth century
First published: 1912

Various English houses as well as places of entertainment for the rich and well established are only vaguely sketched in this novel, but all of them are more than sufficiently made clear as places for the frivolous, ingrown, often boring, and essentially vicious life that Saki satirizes. The civilization and comfort of England is contrasted, almost violently, with the West African colony where Comus Bassington is exiled after he destroys his marriage chances.

Bassington house. London home of Francesca Bassington, whose house is hers only until Emmeline Chetrof marries. Thus, it is not truly a home, and its very impermanence drives Francesca's actions and suggests the shallowness of the society in which she lives. Francesca's only visitors seem to be her son and her brother—one more indication that the house will disappear. The furnishings that Francesca prizes she has acquired mostly by chance; her "delicious bronze Fremiet" she buys with winnings from horse racing; some Dresden figurines are given to her by an admirer; other Dresden figurines she acquires with bridge winnings. There are other things she values, in part because they come from marvelous, mysterious places, but above all because they are somehow connected with her own history. Her prize possession, the "Van der Meulen" painting, turns out to be a fake.

*****London.** Great Britain's chief city, in which almost all the action in the novel takes place. The people inhabiting Saki's London are strictly upper middle class, with an occasional member of the lower aristocracy. Francesca plays bridge with her female friends at various houses, especially Serena Golackly's, all of which are clearly in the West End of London, where the upper classes live. Besides bridge, the main purpose of these parties is gossip, of a petty and nasty sort.

Elaine's garden-park. Place where Elaine entertains both Comus and Youghal. With its roses, "emerald turf," and brilliantly plumed pheasants, the park functions as a kind of Garden of Eden. All should be well.

But Comus foolishly shows himself at his worst, just when he should be at his best, a small, self-destructive, selfish Adam who demands that Elaine give him a silver bread-and-butter dish which is a family heirloom.

Keriway farm. Place outside London where Elaine pays an accidental visit to Tom Keriway. The farm presents the ambiguities of the natural world against those of the city world. Keriway, too, has an Eden, and Elaine believes it is a real Eden. However, he himself points out its violence and, at the same time, its dullness. Like virtually all the places in the novel, the farm, too, disappoints.

African colony. Unnamed tropical British colony where Comus is sent and dies. With all its faults, the colony appears to be somehow superior to the superficial English world of the rest of the novel, though Saki is not making a clear anticolonial statement. At the same time, Africa is hot, humid, and dangerous—the very opposite of the well-furnished, comfortable houses of upper-middle-class life back in England. However, it is also the only place in the novel containing people of other races and other classes. Comus Bassington sees and envies the African children at play, something he would have hardly noticed back home. Indeed, the only glimpse of children in England is at the public school that the young Comus attends and at which casual cruelty is the ruling principle. Human violence and emptiness is not the point here. The finally irony is that Comus does not fit in—and that this place will kill him.

— *L. L. Lee*

THE UNBEARABLE LIGHTNESS OF BEING

Author: Milan Kundera (1929-   )
Type of work: Novel
Type of plot: Political

Time of plot: 1960's and 1970's
First published: Nesnesitelná lehkost bytí, 1984
(English translation, 1984)

Blending elements of Magical Realism, structural experimentation, and Old World romanticism, Milan Kundera's novel stands as one of the few late twentieth century novels to combine marked stylistic innovations with an enthralling story. Set against the backdrop of the Soviet invasion of Czechoslovakia in 1968, the novel explores how two lovers turn to each other for more personal forms of fulfillment in an environment in which they have been systematically stripped of their political and social freedoms.

***Prague.** Capital city of Czechoslovakia and home of Tomas, a successful surgeon and one of the novel's two protagonists, and the primary setting. At the beginning of the narrative Tomas welcomes a young waitress named Tereza, whom he met in a small provincial town some months before, into his flat on the presumption that she has moved to Prague to find work. Later he realizes that she has actually come to Prague to pursue a romantic relationship with him and that finding a job there is a mere pretense to gain access into his life. Although Prague promises greater financial and cultural opportunities for Tereza than her provincial home, her main goal is to win the love of Tomas.

In Tereza's mind, location is inconsequential—she must live with Tomas, and feels that her love for him will flourish no matter where it may take them. By the time she reaches Prague it has already taken her from her home and family, but Tereza is unmoved by the loss. A fatalist to the end, she believes from the first time she sees Tomas that he is her destiny. She sacrifices everything she knows in order to be a part of his life.

Kundera's choice of Prague as the novel's main setting provides him with a landscape for commentary on the challenges of everyday life in a Soviet satellite nation during the final years of the Cold War. According to the narrator, the people of postwar Prague have an "inferiority complex" because, unlike other European cities, theirs was almost completely spared the physical ravages of World War II. Most of Prague's historical architecture remained intact, and Prague was not forced to restore them after the war. Ironically, whereas most European cities enjoyed a renaissance as they rebuilt, Prague grew stylistically and spiritually stagnant. In this sense, the Soviet occupation seemed the fitting capstone to a process of moral and aesthetic bankruptcy that had been developing for decades.

***Zurich.** Swiss city to which Tomas and Tereza flee after the Soviets invade Czechoslovakia. An intellectual who has gone on record as a critic of communism, Tomas fears reprisals in Czechoslovakia. In Zurich, a colleague finds a position for him as a surgeon in a large, prestigious clinic. However, Tereza feels estranged by the anonymity of the cosmopolitan Swiss city. As her relationship with Tomas strengthens, she gradually convinces him that the sense of freedom they both feel outside the Iron Curtain is merely illusory and that their isolation from their native culture and way of life will damage them far more than the threats of communist ideologues. She urges him to return with her to Prague.

Although he becomes emotionally committed to Tereza, Tomas has a history of womanizing. In Prague, Tomas has sexual encounters with several women, and Tereza assumes that moving to a strange foreign city will end his affairs. However, Tomas manages illicit affairs in Zurich as well. When Tereza realizes that simply moving away from Czechoslovakia will not stop her lover's infidelities, the idea of living in a place where she is isolated from her friends and family and is dependent on Tomas for emotional support loses its appeal.

By the middle of the novel Tomas and Tereza return to Prague, having found that Western Europe holds little of the happiness and fulfillment it once promised. Despite holding a wealth of professional and cultural opportunities for both Tomas and Tereza, Zurich paradoxically affords neither a strong sense of personal growth or freedom.

Collective farm. Spartan collective farm in the Czechoslovakian countryside in which the final chapters of the novel are set. Because of his record of opposition to communist totalitarianism, Tomas is not permitted to resume work in Prague as a physician. After three years of working there as a window washer, he tires of living in the city that has rejected him. He and Tereza eventually take jobs on a collective farm, where they resign themselves to a simple existence herding cattle.

A few years later, both Tomas and Tereza are killed in an automobile accident. However, their demise is not characterized as tragic. Their decision to capitulate to a complacent, nameless existence on the collective farm rather than remain in Prague and actively resist Soviet oppression suggests that, at least figuratively speaking, Tomas and Tereza "died" long before any accident claimed their lives. However both were content to do so, seeing their personal commitment to each other as far more significant than any obligations to a state no longer sympathetic to the needs, dreams, or desires of its individual citizens.

— *Gregory D. Horn*

UNCLE SILAS: A Tale of Bartram-Haugh

Author: Joseph Sheridan Le Fanu (1814-1873)
Type of work: Novel
Type of plot: Gothic

Time of plot: Nineteenth century
First published: 1864

This novel's subtitle, "A Tale of Bartram-Haugh," is a reference to the secluded Irish estate that dominates its events. A dark and brooding environment, Bartram-Haugh is an archetypal Gothic dwelling that crystallizes the moral corruption of its tenant, Silas Ruthyn.

Bartram-Haugh. Sprawling estate in Derbyshire, a locale in the Irish countryside. For decades, it has been the home of Silas Ruthyn, Maud Ruthyn's ruined uncle, and its decrepit condition is clearly intended to symbolize aspects of Silas's character. Upon her arrival Maud notes palatial architectural features that have eroded over time and the growth of moss and vegetation around the doorways, all of which give the place "a forlorn character of desertion and decay, contrasting most awfully with the grandeur of its proportions and richness of its architecture." Like Silas, who is deeply in debt, the estate has seen more prosperous days. When Maud apprises the reader that "the actual decay of the house had been prevented by my dear father," who has regularly loaned money to his financially irresponsible brother, she establishes the importance of the family fortune she has inherited to her Uncle Silas.

The nature of Bartram-Haugh's dilapidation is also significant. Maud notes a courtyard "tufted over with grass" and a carved balustrade around the courtyard "discoloured with lichens." The rarely visited estate is slowly being reclaimed by the natural world outside its once well-kept borders. This encroaching wildness suggests Silas's own predatory scheme to dispose of his niece in order to steal her inheritance. Huge trees in the courtyard felled by a recent storm telegraph Silas's intentions to the reader: they "lay with their upturned roots, and their yellow foliage still flickering on the sprays that were to bloom no more . . ." Their general look suggests violent destruction of life.

Maud sees these subtleties of the estate's disrepair mostly on the morning of her second day at Bartram-Haugh, having overlooked them the night of her arrival. Bartram-Haugh seems perpetually dark and shadowy, and its most telling details are often not easily discerned—just as Silas's true motives are concealed from Maud by his affectation of avuncular devotion.

Bartram-Haugh is a classic gloomy gothic setting. As a writer, Joseph Sheridan Le Fanu was conscious of gothic tradition in literature, which was almost a century old at the time he wrote *Uncle Silas*. In one scene, Maud muses that Bartram-Haugh "was plainly one of those great structures in which you might easily lose yourself, and with a pleasing terror it reminded me of that delightful old abbey in Mrs. Radcliffe's romance, among whose silent staircases, dim passages, and long suites of lordly, but forsaken chambers . . . the family of La Mote secured a gloomy asylum." Anne Radcliffe, author of *The Mysteries of Udolpho* (1794), *The Romance of the Forest* (1791)—to which Maud alludes—and other gothic fictions, specialized in tales of heroines trapped in castles, and pursued through darkened halls and passageways. To Maud, the dark arches and the long corridors and galleries that stretch away "in dust and silence" are the stuff of sensational stories in which the menace to heroine is later revealed to have been more imagined than actual. But here, the menace is genuine. The estate is so large and unexplored that Maud will later be persuaded that she has been taken to another location when in fact she has been delivered back to an unfamiliar part of the house, where Silas committed a murder decades before. The intricacies of Silas's devious plan to eliminate his niece mirror the labyrinthine layout of Bartram-Haugh.

Knowl. Estate where Maud lives up to her relocation to Bartram-Haugh. In contrast to Bartram-Haugh, which is described as "the repeated scene of all sorts of scandals, and of one great crime," Knowl is a place of "affectionate associations, and kind looks and voice" for Maud. Knowl, her childhood home, symbolizes a world of innocence and purity that the inexperienced Maud leaves behind when she agrees to become Silas's ward at Bartram-Haugh.

— *Stefan Dziemianowicz*

UNCLE TOM'S CABIN: Or, Life Among the Lowly

Author: Harriet Beecher Stowe (1811-1896)
Type of work: Novel
Type of plot: Social realism

Time of plot: Mid-nineteenth century
First published: 1852

Locations shift constantly in this novel, which traces the divergent journeys of two slaves from the Shelby farm in Kentucky. While one slave escapes north to freedom, the other is sold south to his eventual death. These parallel plots focus on the horrors of slavery, particularly as it disrupts family life.

*****Kentucky.** South-central U.S. state that provides the setting for the first third of the novel. Kentucky is an appropriate location for slaves hoping to escape because it is separated from free territory only by the Ohio River. Harriet Beecher Stowe also felt comfortable describing this area since she spent a number of years living in nearby Cincinnati, Ohio.

Shelby farm. Kentucky farm on which two slaves, Uncle Tom and Eliza Harris, reside. Eliza's husband, George Harris, also a slave, lives nearby. As the narrative makes clear, Eliza and Tom both enjoy relatively pleasant lives on the Shelby farm; however, when financial problems threaten Mr. Shelby, he makes the decision to sell two of his slaves, Tom and Eliza's young son, Harry. Mrs. Shelby is the first of many principled women who speak out against the moral evil of slavery in the way that it breaks families apart. Stowe illustrates the perils facing slave families as Eliza decides to run away to protect her child, and Tom opts to stay and be sold, sacrificing himself to protect his family and the other slave families on the Shelby farm from a similar fate.

The narrative returns periodically to the Shelby farm to follow the fate of the Shelby family and of Tom's wife, Aunt Chloe. By the end of the novel, Mr. Shelby's son, George, after seeing Tom's brutal fate, frees all the Shelby slaves; therefore, Tom's bitter end does effect change, at least in one home.

Uncle Tom's cabin. Cabin on the Shelby farm in which the slave known as Uncle Tom lives until he is sold and forced to leave behind his wife and family, demonstrating that slaves can never have a true home.

*****Ohio River.** First of several bodies of water that play an important role in the novel. This river forms the border between Kentucky and Ohio, and hence between slavery and freedom. Here, Eliza makes her dramatic journey across ice floes to the free state of Ohio, illustrating the risks that a mother will make for her child and underlining the importance of family; Stowe uses this dramatic scene to engender sympathy for her imperiled slave heroine and to show how motherhood transcends race and social circumstances.

*****Ohio.** Free state to which Eliza flees from Kentucky. She finds refuge, first at the home of Senator and Mrs. Bird and then at the Quaker settlement, where she is reunited with her husband, George. Both these places represent model homes where family members act on moral principle. Senator Bird, although he has recently voted in favor of the Fugitive Slave Law, cannot bring himself to turn in Eliza. Instead, his wife persuades him to act not according to political expediency but moral principle, and he furthers Eliza's escape.

Words and actions are also one at the Quaker settlement, a model of perfect domesticity, both in its actual physical arrangement as well as its moral order. The group's actions and principles coincide as they harbor and aid fugitive slaves under the moral guidance of another strong woman, Rachel Halliday.

*****Mississippi River.** Another of the novel's important rivers, which marks yet another boundary. Aboard the steamship *La Belle Rivière* (the name of a real steamship on which Stowe's brother Charles Beecher had traveled when he worked in New Orleans), Tom journeys farther and farther away from his home and family. At the same time, as a novelist, Stowe ventures away from her own firsthand experience. The river also marks the boundary between sections of the novel as Tom gains his second owner, Augustine St. Clare, after rescuing St. Clare's young daughter Eva from drowning in the river.

*****New Orleans.** Louisiana city in which the St. Clare family home is located. Stowe describes the house as an ancient mansion, built in a mixture of styles. The St. Clare home's confusion of styles and exoticism stand in stark contrast to the ordered simplicity of the Quaker settlement in Ohio. The eccentricity and disorder of the place illustrate the disarray in which slavery leaves families, both black and white. Significantly, the St. Clare family also lacks a strong female moral center as Marie St. Clare devotes her attention to her own invalidism. While both Marie's daughter, Eva, and her cousin-in-law, Miss Ophelia, try to make up for this lack, neither has control over the household.

*****Red River.** Tributary of the Mississippi that forms part of the Texas-Oklahoma border and flows through Arkansas to Louisiana. The third important river in the novel, it marks yet another boundary between Tom's old life and his new one. After the death of St. Clare, Tom is sold to Simon Legree and transported on a small boat to Legree's farm.

Legree plantation. Louisiana cotton plantation on the Red River that becomes Tom's final home and illustrates how far his lot has fallen since leaving his Kentucky home. It is run-down, with some windows boarded up. At Legree's home, the veneer is wholly lifted from slavery, and its brutal ugliness stands fully revealed as Tom meets his fate. Significantly, Legree has only the memory of his dead mother to urge him toward better behavior, and another slave, Cassy, manipulates that memory to her advantage.

*****Lake Huron.** Another important body of water that serves as the boundary between freedom and slavery, Canada and the United States, for the Harris family.

*****Montreal.** Capital of Quebec, Canada, where the Harris family eventually settles, illustrating that the United States is not able to provide a safe and suitable home for escaped slaves.

*****Liberia.** West African republic settled largely by freed American slaves who began migrating there in the 1820's. The Harris family eventually migrates there. This final destination for the Harris family seems to suggest that no room remains for former slaves on the American continent. Tom dies in slavery and the other major slave characters settle elsewhere.

— *Sharon L. Gravett*

UNCLE VANYA

Author: Anton Chekhov (1860-1904)
Type of work: Drama
Type of plot: Impressionistic realism

Time of plot: Nineteenth century
First published: Dyadya Vanya, 1897 (English translation, 1914); first performed, 1899

Set on a farm in provincial Ukraine during the waning years of the Russian monarchy, this play highlights the impermanence and fragility of human beings. Anton Chekhov's characters confront their unfulfilled dreams and unrequited passions in ways that reveal the humor and tragedy of their situations as they struggle to find meaning in their tedious routines and in their romantic pursuits.

*Ukraine. Russian province (now an independent country) that borders the north coast of the Black Sea. The relationship between Vanya and Professor Serebriakóv mirrors the relationship between provincial Ukraine and Russia. During Chekhov's lifetime and well into the twentieth century, Russia exploited Ukraine's rich agricultural and natural resources to feed and fuel other regions and provinces. Similarly, Professor Serebriakóv exploits the labor of Vanya and Sónya in order to maintain his life and career in Moscow.

Serebriakóv farm. Farm in Ukraine from which Serebriakóv derives the wealth on which he has built his social position in Moscow. Chekhov provides an increasingly intimate portrait of the Serebriakóv family and the forces that begin to erode the relationships between family members as each act penetrates deeper into the family's history and deeper into the interior of the farm. A crisis between Vanya and the professor divides the household. In the play's second act, Yelena says that there is "something terribly wrong going on in this house." As tensions grow stronger among the characters, the farm becomes a microcosm of society in general. "You know perfectly well it's not crime and criminals that are destroying the world," Yelena explains to Vanya in the second act. "It's petty little emotions like envy . . . that end up with good people hating one another."

Garden. Garden adjacent to the farmhouse and just off the veranda. Gardens, and natural settings in general, are common elements in Chekhov's drama as symbols of the order and beauty of the natural world, providing contrasts to the chaotic lives of his characters. The garden in the play's first act sets the changing lives of the Serebriakóv family against the passive uniformity of nature and suggests an imbalance among family members. Sonya's defense of Ástrov's passion for reforestation emphasizes this imbalance when she explains that people who live in lush natural settings "spend less energy trying to combat nature, so the people themselves are kinder and gentler."

— Philip Bader

UNDER FIRE: The Story of a Squad

Author: Henri Barbusse (1873-1935)
Type of work: Novel
Type of plot: Political

Time of plot: 1914-1915
First published: Le Feu: Journal d'une escouade, 1916 (English translation, 1917)

This novel about the gritty realities of the lives of ordinary soldiers in the midst of war is one of the earliest to be written by a veteran soldier—one who had endured the hardships and horrors he described. Set on the Western Front of World War I, the novel follows the day-to-day activities of several French enlisted men, whose wretched existence Henri Barbusse sees as a microcosm of the contradictions present in the French capitalistic system. While the struggle to drive back the German invaders from France continues, so also does the class struggle, with all its tensions, pessimism, and despair.

Western Front. The novel is set somewhere along the scar of World War I trenches that stretched across northern France, southeast to the Vosges, and south to the Swiss border—a 550-mile-long fortified line with barbed wire, machine guns, and heavy artillery. In his dedication, Barbusse places the action in the valley of the Ourcq, in the department of Seine-et-Marne. However, he realizes that precision of location along a battlefront is not as important as the precision of experience of those who actually do the fighting—as he himself had done during the war.

The men of Barbusse's squad live not *on* the earth but *in* the earth, in the midst of a vast and "water-logged desert" on which convoys of troops have traced deep ruts that glisten in the weak morning light "like steel rails." The soldiers dig trenches into these desolate fields, defenses that are carpeted with slime that makes sticky sounds with each step and reeks of the night's human excretions. In this part of the world the men are "buried deep" in an everlasting battlefield.

The real home of Barbusse and his fellow soldiers is the home of the trenches whose tranquility is constantly broken by sounds of the methodical destruction of human life.

Barbusse never lets readers forget his main theme: that those who fight for the liberation of the country also must fight for their own liberation. That the fundamental difference between human beings is the unpardonable division between those who profit and those who sacrifice. Location in battle cannot be divorced from location in society, and all the blood spilled on the soil of the country counts for naught unless it leads to an uplifting of the people of the world.

Behind-the lines. Barbusse's soldiers are occasionally granted leaves that permit them to go to such towns as Cauchin-l-abbé, Villers-l'abbaye, Vanveldes, Argoval—all invented names—to rest and recuperate and regain their sense of life as they once lived it. In such places, the men may again find themselves in the company of women, relate to domestic animals, and worry about such mundane things as having enough money to pay for wine. There, they try to recapture their humanity, sort out details about one another's lives, share photographs and letters, and arrange their collections of small personal items which they have accumulated and lug around with their standard military equipment.

Paris. Some soldiers are lucky enough to enjoy their leave in France's capital city, where they can walk down the boulevard de la République, the nails in their boots ringing on the pavement. They can see a great city rich in femininity, beautiful cafés, and beautiful clothes. At the same time, however, common soldiers can find shame in the misery from which they come, and to which they must return. Paris is the supreme reminder of a world thrilled by commercial profit and money. There, rich people become richer, and tranquil people live in perfect homes and enjoy being served in cafés. Paris is the most egregious example of the nation's inequities.

— *Wm. Laird Kleine-Ahlbrandt*

UNDER MILK WOOD: A Play for Voices

Author: Dylan Thomas (1914-1953)
Type of work: Drama
Type of plot: Domestic realism

Time of plot: Indeterminate
First performed: public reading, 1953; radio play, 1954; first published, 1954; first staged, 1956

Dylan Thomas's mythical Welsh fishing village of Llareggub provides an ideal location for his loving, but often teasingly humorous, picture of a range of village characters. Although such stereotypes as a henpecked husband and a village drunk might be found in any village, Llareggub under Milk Wood gives Thomas's characters their particularly Welsh flavor and accounts for such qualities as their passion for music and poetry, as well as their unusual names.

Llareggub (yah-REH-guhb). Small fishing village on the coast of Wales. Despite the name's Welsh appearance, it is actually a typical Thomas joke—"bugger all," spelled backward. The phrase is a vulgar colloquialism which means "nothing" or "worthless" in British English—Thomas's way of suggesting that the play's actions be taken lightly.

Thomas seems to have modeled the village on the real Welsh coastal village of Laugharne, where he lived for many years. Despite his joking name for Llareggub, his play treats the village with love. The Milk Wood trees on the hills above it, its streets and lanes (Goosegog Lane, Coronation Street), its River Dewi—all such details suggest Thomas's interest in making a realistic, if sometimes comic, territory for his characters, themselves sometimes comic, to inhabit. Although village life may be universal, characters such as Organ Morgan, with his passion for the composer Johann Sebastian Bach, and the Reverend Eli Jenkins, whose passion is poetry, bear the stereotypes of the Welsh character.

Like the people who live there, Llareggub is defined by the sea. Its pub is the Sailors Arms; retired Captain Cat lives in Schooner House; and always in the background of the play's action is the bay itself, bobbing with its fleet of fishing boats.

Milk Wood. Wooded area in the hills above Llareggub. To Thomas, Milk Wood is a place of wonder and love. To old Mary Ann Sailors, humble in her faith, it is God's garden, the proof of Eden, a heaven on earth, and her belief is that Llareggub is the Chosen Land. To the restless, night-haunted village boys and girls it is the bridal bed of secret love. To the Reverend Eli Jenkins it is a sermon in green, wind-shaken leaves on the innocence and goodness of humanity.

— *Ann D. Garbett*

UNDER THE GREENWOOD TREE

Author: Thomas Hardy (1840-1928)
Type of work: Novel
Type of plot: Pastoral

Time of plot: Nineteenth century
First published: 1872

This pastoral novel is set in Thomas Hardy's home region of Dorset in southern England, which it calls by the ancient Saxon name Wessex. The story follows Dick Dewy through the course of one year, both as a member of the Mellstock church choir and as a young man in love. It is it filled with local folk, their music, and a close look at nature's heaths, woods, and meadows. Age-old customs connected with this rural life and its seasonal activities include Christmas caroling, bee-smoking, apple-picking, and nutting.

Tranter Dewey's cottage. This sociable and comfortable English home of Davy's father, who works as a tranter, or a carter, is modeled on Hardy's own long, low cottage with a hipped roof made of thatch. It is here the Mellstock choir readies for caroling on Christmas Eve and also where they discuss their imminent ouster from service at the local church. Later in the spring, they meet here to discuss strategy for a visit to the vicar. Readers watch as the members of the choir fortify themselves for the uncomfortable interview by eating a rasher of bacon and drinking cider.

Vicarage study. Office of Mr. Maybold, the village vicar, that is the setting for the most comic scene of the novel. The men march to the vicar's study to request a dignified farewell for their choir. Grandfather William exemplifies the country people's discomfort with the unfamiliar as he is startled at discovering springs in the vicar's chair seat. Tranter Dewey in his enthusiasm backs the vicar into a corner, and the scene is capped by a tableau of the other members of the choir, looking in at the door.

The vicar's study is also the setting for the saddest scene in the story, in which Maybold watches from his window as a boy leaves to deliver his sad letter to Fancy Day, the new schoolmistress. With the vicar looking on, the boy fights briefly with another boy who coincidentally carries a similar letter to the vicar from Fancy. Such crisscrossing of messengers or letters is developed in later Hardy novels to illustrate the workings of fate.

Mellstock Church. Village church in which three scenes take place. First, the carolers stop at the church at midnight to fortify themselves with hot mead and bread and cheese. They sit in the gallery and wonder at Davy's absence. They later find him under a tree by Fancy's window.

The church's gallery provides Christmas Day seating for the choir. In this early novel, Hardy practices the authorial bird's-eye view that he frequently uses in his later works. From this vantage point, the members of the choir watch the clerk chewing tobacco, young women reading, lovers touching fingers through a knothole, and a farm wife counting her money. Later, after the choir is disbanded, readers observe their discomfort as they take seats with their wives in the nave of the church, out of their familiar place, feeling "abashed." Hardy's own father and grandfather had played stringed instruments in church and for local festivals, and he intended for his novels to capture this earlier time in the lives of country folk.

Schoolhouse. Village school in which Fancy Day is the new mistress. On Christmas Eve, Davy first sees Fancy, framed in an upper window of the schoolhouse. Although the building and the tree outside it provide the setting for his growing love for Fancy, it is in the open air, when they are riding together in his cart and while he is in the woods gathering hazelnuts, that he announces his love and she accepts.

Geoffrey Day's house. Woodland cottage that is the home of Fancy's father. The cottage provides rustic comedy in the introduction of an eccentric wife who has doubles of every piece of furniture and who fusses over the table settings. The cottage is also the backdrop for two tense developments: Mr. Day's initial rejection of Davy, and rival farmer Shiner's confident wooing of Fancy under Davy's nose at the bee-smoking. However, in the final chapter, Fancy dresses here for her wedding and then returns here for the outdoor feast under the enormous, ancient tree in her father's yard. In this venerable tree, hundreds of birds have been born, rabbits have nibbled at its bark, and countless moles and earthworms have crept among its roots. This ageless and vital emblem of fertility now also embraces the wedding guests beneath its branches: oldsters telling stories, the young dancing and singing, the musicians, and Davy and Fancy, the happy newlyweds.

— *Marie J. K. Brenner*

UNDER THE VOLCANO

Author: Malcolm Lowry (1909-1957)
Type of work: Novel
Type of plot: Psychological realism

Time of plot: November 1, 1938, and November 1, 1939
First published: 1947

Set in Mexico on the Day of the Dead, this novel traces the disintegration of one man, alcoholic British consul Geoffrey Firmin, against the backdrop of a civilization on the brink of war. Firmin's disintegration depends on his time and place: the lush, haunted, contradictory landscape that is Mexico.

*Mexico. North American country whose tortured history—conquest and enslavement, revolution and unrest—serves as backdrop to the consul's tragedy. The Mexico through which Geoffrey Firmin walks (or stumbles) is a surreal landscape of ruined gardens and stinging insects, where vultures perch in washbasins and thieves clutch bloodied coins stolen from the dead but Geoffrey recognizes it as a mirror of his private hell.

Quauhnahuac (kwah-NAH-wehk). Fictional Mexican town that is Malcolm Lowry's nightmarish vision of Cuernavaca, a real city south of Mexico City. "Quauhnahuac" is, in fact, its original Nahuatl name, which means "among the trees." The Nahuatl name refers to the forest that surrounds Quauhnahuac, a forest through which the characters wander in the book's final chapter and which is linked to Dante's dark wood. Lowry in fact conceived *Under the Volcano* as a part of a modern *Divine Comedy* he planned to write. Mexico for him was Hell, just as the northern wilds of British Columbia, Canada, dreamed of but never attained as a refuge for the consul and his wife Yvonne, was an earthly paradise.

Many landmarks in Quauhnahuac have thematic significance. Jacques Laruelle's house, owned by Geoffrey's friend and Yvonne's former lover, recurs in several scenes, highlighting the consul's fatal flaw: He cannot fully love and forgive Yvonne or himself. Another thematic marker is the *cine* (cinema), with a looming poster advertising a film about an artist with a murderer's hands. The reference to murderer's hands may point to the mysterious guilt the consul bears for a World War I incident that happened when he was an officer onboard a British ship. In that incident, German prisoners of war were said to have been burned alive in the ship's furnaces. Jacques Laruelle, contemplating a different war, identifies the murderous hands with Germany itself. The biblical imagery of Adam and Eve exiled from the garden is clear and resonates with Geoffrey's own fall.

Barranca. Deep cleft or ravine that runs through Quauhnahuac, encircling the city from beneath just as the volcanoes shadow it from above. While the volcanoes symbolize the "striving upward" of humanity toward the divine, the barranca is a dark abyss suggesting the entrance to Hell, a waterless River Styx. In chapter 3, Geoffrey tells Yvonne of his returning home to find their cat dead, its body thrown into the barranca, a foreshadowing of his own death, in which his body is flung down the ravine alongside the dog, which follows him like a familiar throughout the book.

Farolito. Cantina, or bar, where the consul is drawn into the fatal web of coincidence that leads to his death. "Farolito" is Spanish for lighthouse yet the bar is a dark, sordid place, and the consul is led deep into a series of ever darker rooms for his degrading encounter with the prostitute María. Here the consul finds the lost letters Yvonne has written him; here, also, he is mistaken for a spy and shot by the corrupt local police.

— *Kathryn Kulpa*

UNDER THE YOKE

Author: Ivan Vazov (1850-1921)
Type of work: Novel
Type of plot: Historical

Time of plot: 1875-1876
First published: Pod igoto, serial, 1889-1890; book, 1893 (English translation, 1893)

This historical novel fictionalizes the real experience of the author's own town in the 1876 Bulgarian uprising against the Turks. Although certain names and other details are changed, the situations and events described therein are true. The novel captures the cycles of brutality that finally unite Bulgarians against their Turkish oppressors in the failed uprising, which, because of the brutality with which it was put down, moved Russia's Czar Alexander III to declare war on Turkey. At the same time, the novel captures much of the rugged beauty of Bulgaria and the love of the Bulgarians for their homeland.

Byala Cherkva (BYAH-lah). Fictional Bulgarian town in which the principal action takes place. Located in the Strema Valley or valley of roses, in the mountains of the Balkan Peninsula, it is a prosperous town with many merchants and has its own school. It is also the location of the *konak*, the Turkish governor's residence, a constant reminder to the Bulgarians that they are under the rule of Muslims who despise Bulgarians, most of whom are Orthodox Christians, as infidels. At first the wealthy members of the merchant class prefer to accommodate the Turks, but a random act of rebellion and the Turks' response to it lead the merchants to join the rebels in a doomed uprising. Yet afterward the merchants prefer to purchase their own safety by abject surrender of all weapons and any suspected individuals, rather than become another razed village. The town is heavily based upon Ivan Vazov's own hometown of Sopot.

Mill. Old mill building, located just beyond the main part of Byala Cherkva, on the Old River that is the site of the murder of two Turks. This act by a passing revolutionary is the spark that sets off the action of the novel. When the Turks' hastily buried bodies are discovered by the authorities as a result of a dog's obsessive pawing at the spot, the Turks then brutalize and kill a respected member of the community. This so outrages the previously apathetic merchants that they join with the rebels in the doomed uprising. At the end of the novel, Vazov brings the story full circle by having the protagonists cornered and captured at the mill, where the Turks kill them, mutilate their bodies, and place their heads on pikes as gruesome warnings to others who would raise their hand against Turkish rule.

Monastery. Center of Eastern Orthodox religious activity in the valley. Although the monastery is initially a lively center of activity, by the time of the novel it is run down, with only a few monks still living in it, including the half-wit Mooncho, who chatters obsessively. It is also the home of Deacon Vikenti, a historical rebel leader who provides shelter for the protagonist when he is in danger of being discovered by the Turks after the murder at the mill. At the close of the novel, Mooncho's grief-stricken curse against Muhammad and the sultan of Turkey leads to his being seized and hanged as a traitor by the Turks.

Klissoura (klih-SEW-rah). Village in which the first major insurrection begins and in which many important rebels stay or visit. When the uprising finally begins, it is tragically premature and is rapidly crushed by the Turks with extreme brutality. The entire village is put to the torch and its inhabitants massacred and scattered.

Zli-Dol (TSLIH-dol). Mountain outcropping overlooking the valley on which the rebels place improvised cannons made from hollowed-out cherry tree trunks bound with metal bands. However, these cannons prove useless—the first one bursts during its first and only firing—and they play no real military role in the uprising.

Altunovo (ahlt-ah-NOH-vo). Village in which Ognyanov hides. Here he is concealed in a house that is hosting a traditional wedding, which Vazov describes in some detail.

Rahmanlari (ra-HMAN-la-ree). Turkish village nearest Klissoura where several hundred Turks, mostly ill-disciplined mercenary irregulars or *bashi-bazouk*, gather to attack Klissoura and crush the rebellion.

— *Leigh Husband Kimmel*

UNDER TWO FLAGS

Author: Ouida (Marie Louise de la Ramée, 1839-1908)
Type of work: Novel
Type of plot: Sentimental

Time of plot: Mid-nineteenth century
First published: 1867

In this novel, Bertie Cecil, a British army officer dishonored by false accusations of forgery and larceny, flees London for Algeria and a career in the French foreign legion. The unforgiving desert environment and harsh military life he encounters in North Africa purges him of the irresponsibility and recklessness that drove him into exile and toughens his moral fiber, which is the hallmark of a true gentleman and soldier.

Household. London barracks of the 1st Life Guards, a British military unit that serves the government in a largely decorative capacity. Although the Life Guards are a military brigade, its members are mostly the pampered sons of royalty. Great camaraderie and fellowship exists within the ranks, but discipline is lax. The men spend most of their time indulging the vices of the privileged class: drinking, smoking, gambling, racing horses, and attending balls and parties. Life in the Household is characterized by dissipation and ennui.

Royallieu. Country estate of the Viscount Royallieu, and home of the Cecil family, to which the protagonist,

Bertie Cecil, belongs. The estate is located in the Melton countryside of central England. The estate's expansive grounds are well stocked with game for hunting, and its manor house is magnificently outfitted with servants, cooks, and grooms who cater to its distinguished visitors. Though its banquet halls, decorative paintings, and costly furnishings bespeak the luxury of wealth, in truth its luxury has been purchased at the cost of the future. Members of the Cecil family no longer have enough money to sustain the magnificence of their estate. Nevertheless the proud viscount refuses to change his spendthrift ways or sell part of the estate to subsidize his profligate sons. Royallieu embodies the unrealistic expectations of its idle-rich owner and represents the prodigality of the wealthy society the Cecil family keeps.

*Algeria. Country in North Africa whose native people are at war with the occupying French forces. Algeria is an exotic locale, bustling with commerce brought to it by visitors from many nations. Although different cultures mix in its streets, they do not assimilate, with the result that its markets and cafés are full of sound and color, at the very least energetic but often cacophonous.

There is great romance to the Algerian setting. The customs of the local people, alien to the European legionnaires, enhance the country's mystique. There is also a rough natural beauty to the desert landscape, as well as an omnipresent sense of danger. Outsiders in a hostile country, the legionnaires know that each day may be their last. Even as this binds the legionnaires into a close fraternity, it fosters an almost hedonistic live-for-today attitude, which the soldiers express through debauchery and stealing from the local people.

The glorious past of Algeria intensifies the brooding sense of mortality that hangs over the present. The country was once part of the vast North African lands of Solomon, Hannibal, and Cleopatra. Now, hostelries, dry goods stores, and gambling dens profane sites where holy mosques and monuments to gods once stood. Against the backdrop of Algeria's past, the decadent present seems but an inconsequential moment. It is only part of the passing show of history that inevitably consigns civilizations, no matter how magnificent, to the tomb.

The varying circumstances of the Algerian setting dictate a type of military life different from that in England. As Bertie's groom observes, the foreign legion is not preoccupied with fashion, protocol, and the small details of military etiquette that have driven true soldiers out of the service in England. It cares only that its recruits are able to rise to the occasion swiftly and efficiently in a combat situation, when lives hang in the balance.

The complexity and paradoxes of Algeria are an appropriate backdrop for Bertie's adventures. The country's chaos and heterogeneity resonate with the paradoxes of his character: He is a man of honor wrongly disgraced for secretly upholding the honor of another. As an expatriate soldier whose unwavering principles have earned respect from both the Europeans in the legion and the native Moors, he is proof that there are common denominators that join the East and West, even if assimilation of the cultures is not possible.

— *Stefan Dziemianowicz*

UNDER WESTERN EYES

Author: Joseph Conrad (Jósef Teodor Konrad Nałęcz Korzeniowski, 1857-1924)
Type of work: Novel

Type of plot: Psychological realism
Time of plot: Early twentieth century
First published: 1911

This novel of revolutionary intrigue and psychological guilt is set in two contrasting cities: St. Petersburg, Russia, which is the seat of a repressive government, and Geneva, Switzerland, which can accommodate all political philosophies because it has none of its own.

St. Petersburg. Capital of Russia and center of its brutally despotic government. In the opening sections of the novel the main character, Razumov, finds himself in settings which illustrate the range and variety of Russian life during the early years of the twentieth century. These range from the slovenly stables and eating-houses of the poor, drunken peasantry to the elaborately decorated, gilded palaces of the nobility. The difference between the extreme misery and poverty of the lower classes and the arrogance and wealth of the aristocracy is displayed most clearly in the contrast between their dwellings and furnishings. When Razumov becomes involved with the revolutionary Haldin, he also becomes well acquainted with the offices of the Russian secret police, that organization totally dedicated to the repression and, if possible, elimination of all expressions of freedom and individual liberty. In a sense, the Russian locations in the novel present a sort of physical argument in favor of revolution.

Razumov's dwelling. Modest set of rooms in a Russian apartment building. There is an outer room with a couch, table, and similar furnishings and an inner room with a bed. As described by Joseph Conrad, the apartment is small, sparsely furnished but functional; it is a reasonably comfortable place for a student such as Razumov to live and work. In the novel, its major importance is to serve as the physical setting where the terrorist Haldin intrudes to draw Razumov into his revolutionary circle. The decisions made in this unremarkable apartment set the story in motion.

Geneva. City in Switzerland traditionally known for its hospitality to exiles and revolutionaries. Its major physical feature is its lake ringed by mountains. Aside from the unnamed narrator, all the characters in the novel are exiles from the repressive Russian regime, living and plotting in the section of Geneva known as "Little Russia." Conrad's descriptions of the city are ironic and less than favorable; while it provides protection for the homeless, it is a city of "deplorable banality," which appears more beautiful than it actually is. The underlying cause, Conrad implies, is the famous tolerance of Geneva itself, which accommodates any and all philosophies.

Nathalie Haldin's apartment. Thoroughly middle-class apartment in a good but modest hotel in Geneva, where Nathalie lives with her mother. It is here that the mother and sister of the executed revolutionary live and, through their meetings with Razumov and others, learn the facts about his death. Conrad is slight on the physical descriptions, since the important point is what happens to the people inside these rooms.

Château Borel. Ugly, decrepit mansion on the outskirts of Geneva. The château is the home of the terrorist conspirator Madame de S——, whose dubious reputation is known to all Europeans of a certain political affiliation. Like the revolutionaries within its walls, the château is a grimy, run-down place, not at all respectable and in the end not really serious. It is filled with a wild assortment of characters who preach strange doctrines.

Cosmopolitan Hotel. Geneva home of Peter Ivanovitch, escaped Russian political prisoner and revolutionary. Like the Château Borel, this is a nest of revolutionaries intent on the violent overthrow of Russia. The conspirators' appearance and conduct and the disorderly confusion of their surroundings are repellent; however, the danger and threat of violence are real.

— *Michael Witkoski*

THE UNDERDOGS

Author: Mariano Azuela (1873-1952)
Type of work: Novel
Type of plot: Historical

Time of plot: 1914-1915
First published: Los de abajo, serial, 1915; book, 1916 (English translation, 1929)

A fictionalized account of the Mexican Revolution, this novel is set primarily in the north-central Mexican state of Zacatecas, in which ranchos, village cantinas, and town squares become centers of upheaval and turmoil as the revolutionaries, led by Demetrio Macías, a modest Indian and supporter of the revolutionary leader Pancho Villa, battle the Federalists for political control.

*Limón (lee-MOHN). Rural village in Zacatecas in which the novel begins and ends. In the opening pages, Federalists raid Demetrio's humble home, kill his dog, threaten his wife, and burn his fields. Demetrio flees to the mountainside and calls for his fellow revolutionaries to join him. Severe contrasts in the landscape symbolize the rugged nature and simple beauty of country life. The steep slopes, giant rocks, and dry branches of the river canyon contrast sharply with the delicate San Juan roses that dot the landscape. The rebels are outnumbered five hundred to twenty but because they have a more intimate connection with their surroundings, they force the Federalists to retreat.

At the end of the novel, Demetrio, who has risen in rank from chief to general, returns to Limón and briefly rejoins his wife and son, whom he hardly recognizes after his absence. Although Demetrio, too, has gone through many changes, the village landscape remains unchanged. When his wife asks him why he continues to fight in the revolution, he throws a stone against the mountainside and watches it slowly roll down. Like the tumbling stone, Demetrio is propelled, beyond his will, by the momentum of the revolution. The novel's cyclical structure denies a sense of progress that signifies the defeated aims of the revolution. Demetrio dies, rifle in hand, at the same ravine in which he won his first victory.

Camila's ranch. Tiny ranch owned by the Indian woman Camila, who tends Demetrio's wounds as he and his men recover from their battle with Federalists at Limón. Demetrio falls in love with Camila, whose ranch comes to symbolize the simplicity, honesty, and integrity for which he longs.

Vacant mansion. Abandoned home of a wealthy Federalist who has fled in advance of the rebels, who ransack the house. Filled with expensive books, carpets, furniture, and artwork, the mansion contrasts sharply with the houses of the revolutionaries, whose greed for material wealth combines with their brash, often violent behavior, to depict the seedy underside of the revolution.

*Moyahua (moy-AH-huah). Small Mexican town in the state of Zacatecas, where the rebels raid the home of a landowning Federalist, Don Mónico. In many ways, this raid parallels that of the Federalists on Demetrio's home in the first chapter. Although the revolutionaries want to ransack Don Mónico's house, Demetrio forbids such action. An idealist, he feels that such material pursuits distract the rebels from the true cause of their revolution. Moreover, if the wealth simply changes hands from the Federalists to the rebels, then corruption will not be defeated, and the revolution will be in vain. Instead of looting the house, Demetrio runs Don Mónico and his family off their property and has the house burned to the ground. Ironically, Demetrio and his men then spend the night in a dingy building that is used as a garbage heap.

*Juchipila (hoo-chee-PEE-la). Zacatecas village at the base of a high hill in which Pancho Villa won his first victory in 1910. When Demetrio and his men enter this village, he finds that the villagers no longer want to support the rebels. The town stands for both the promise and the failure of the revolution.

*El Paso. Texas border town to which the pretentious Federalist-turned-rebel Cervantes escapes. In a letter he tries to encourage fellow rebel Venancio to join him and start a new life. His flight marks his abandonment of the revolutionary cause.

*La Bufa (BOO-fah). Mountain near the city of Zacatecas where Demetrio leads a brave charge against the Federalists. His leadership earns him the rank of general.

— *Corinne Andersen*

UNDINE

Author: Friedrich de la Motte-Fouqué (1777-1843)
Type of work: Novel
Type of plot: Symbolism

Time of plot: Middle Ages
First published: 1811 (English translation, 1818)

Elemental spirits of Teutonic mythology, undines are associated with lakes and rivers. The principal watercourse featured in this novel is the Danube River. A passage from past to future, and from wilderness to civilization, the river is symbolically embodied in its descent from southwestern Germany's heavily forested mountains to the agricultural plain and Vienna—although it flows thereafter into the Black Sea. The river's symbolic embodiment is the king of the water-spirits, Undine's father.

Fisherman's hut. Hut in which the knight Sir Huldbrand meets and eventually marries the water spirit Undine; situated between the wild forest and the lake that provides his living. By virtue of her adoption by the fisherman, Undine is already removed from her true place, but while she and Huldbrand remain there, she is still connected to the lake and the various streams that feed into it. Of all the dwellings featured in the story, this is the one which best preserves a symbolic balance between nature and culture; however, the precariousness of that balance is reflected in hectic weather and unruly surges of the streams. Furthermore, it represents a state of being that has already been surpassed. It is significant that when Bertalda tries to return to the hut, she cannot make her way through the Black Valley; she has to be rescued by Huldbrand and returned to the relative safety of Ringstetten.

*Vienna. "Imperial city" to which Huldbrand initially takes his bride. The city is not immediately identified as Vienna—the Austrian capital of the so-called Holy Roman Empire in the era in which the story is set—nor is the river on which it stands clearly identified as the Danube. Friedrich de la Motte-Fouqué's decision to situate the story more specifically appears to have been made when he was partway through writing it.

In the novel, the city lies on the far side of the forest from the fisherman's hut. Although Huldbrand and Undine are entertained there by the duke and duchess, neither of them really belongs there—nor, indeed, does Bertalda, who is the fisherman's daughter, rather than the duke's. The names Vienna and Danube are not used in the story until Huldbrand and Bertalda, having become close again, decide to take a trip downriver from Ringstetten. They never actually reach the city, however, because Huldbrand breaks the condition imposed upon his marriage to Undine, which results in her being carried away by—and dissolved into—the river. The implication of the decision to visit Vienna after

Bertalda's attempt to return to the fisherman's hut has been thwarted is that it is in great cities, far more than in isolated havens such as Ringstetten, that civilized folk really belong.

Castle of Ringstetten. Huldbrand's home, situated in the mountains of Swabia, in close proximity to the stormy wilderness but strongly fortified against it. It has a natural fountain in the center of its courtyard that supplies the castle with water until Undine—fearing that the fountain will serve as a conduit for her meddlesome uncle Kühleborn—has it sealed up, symbolically reinforcing the castle's isolation from its surroundings. It is in the castle that Huldbrand marries, fatefully, for the second time; he is buried in a nearby hamlet, to whose churchyard all his ancestors had been consigned. The stream that springs up to bathe his tomb—a new incarnation of Undine—is thus permitted to avoid the castle itself.

Black Valley. Depression in the mountains not far from Ringstetten, named for the gloom cast upon its depths by the shadow of the pine forest on its slopes. It is there that Bertalda gets lost while trying to find her way back to her "true" home and is nearly destroyed by the elemental forces. Kühleborn's interference is, however, counterproductive, prompting the rescue that brings Huldbrand and Bertalda together. This location re-emphasizes the depth and darkness of the gulf that separates humans from nature; even the stream flowing through the valley is black, with none of Undine's symbolic beauty. Not only is it not a homely place, but it is not even a route through which one might safely pass in trying to reach home. No matter how nostalgic Undine may seem, therefore, it is no lament for a lost Golden Age. On the contrary, it is a celebration of the triumph of civilization over the wilderness, and of human artifice and ingenuity over the wayward and treacherous elements.

— *Brian Stableford*

THE UNFORTUNATE TRAVELLER: Or, The Life of Jack Wilton

Author: Thomas Nashe (1567-1601)
Type of work: Novel
Type of plot: Picaresque

Time of plot: Mid-sixteenth century
First published: 1594

This fictional travel narrative utilizes a variety of historical places to satirize people, beliefs, and political, social, and religious movements that Thomas Nashe viewed as antithetical to the conservative values of his native England in the late sixteenth century.

*Rome. Italy's chief city and the center of the Roman Catholic Church. The novel's lengthy section on Jack Wilton's adventures in Rome provide Nashe with ample opportunity for satire, including Jack's comment that if he were to memorize half the miracles he has heard there about martyrs' tombs and relics brought from Jerusalem, he would be considered the "monstrost liar that ever came in print." Nashe's primary target here is the Roman Catholic Church, from which the Church of England had severed its ties earlier in the sixteenth century.

Rome's Jews do not escape Nashe's vituperative bent in the Rome section, either. This is evident in the character of the Jewish physician who buys Jack from another Jew under whose control Jack has fallen. A Jewish doctor—who not coincidentally is also the pope's physician—plans to dissect Jack in a public anatomy demonstration for his own pleasure and profit.

*Münster. City in western Germany that, as a center of Anabaptism in the sixteenth century, is another target of Nashe's satire because it represents the Puritan reform movement that was beginning to threaten Anglicanism. Anabaptists—who were Puritans opposed to infant baptism—briefly controlled Münster. The novel provides a detailed description of Anabaptist soldiers, including one wearing a skullcap that had served him and his ancestors as a chamber pot for two hundred years. Nashe's conservative fear of the changes Puritanism portended is also reflected in his derisive remarks about the Puritans' "false glittering glass of invention."

*Wittenberg. Another German city important in Nashe's satire is the place where Martin Luther posted his theses that launched the Reformation movement, of which Puritanism was a significant part. Nashe describes scholars at the University of Wittenberg as representing "hooded hypocrisy." He generally describes residents of the city as "hot-livered drunkards," whose "boozing houses" are better constructed than their churches. Nashe's obvious implication is that the Protestant Reformation was a result of the superficiality of the religion professed by Luther and like-minded people. Nashe generally dismisses the "learned" in Wittenberg as "gross plodders." To Nashe, the only people who possessed any wit were those special few who completely agreed with him in all matters political, social, and religious.

*Venice and *Florence. Italian cities that Nashe focuses on to satirize the romantic love tradition generated by Petrarch and other writers of the Italian Renaissance. Venice and Florence are cities long connected to the love idealism by Dante, Boccaccio, and others. Jack's journey to these cities with the earl of Surrey are ostensibly to celebrate Surrey's love for Geraldine, his ideal woman—who happens to be from Florence. In Venice they encounter a beautiful young woman imprisoned by a jealous husband; Surrey recites impassioned Petrarchian love sonnets to her, despite his supposed dedication to Geraldine. As the imprisoned wife becomes Wilton's paramour, Nashe points up the ridiculousness of the romance. Further evidence of such excessive romantic silliness is Surrey's victory in a competition with other knightly lovers in Florence, which he achieves not by military prowess but through the outlandishness of his attire and his bribery of the judges. Clearly, to Nashe, Italy's romantic love tradition—like Catholicism, Judaism, the Protestant Reformation, and Puritanism—was created elsewhere and imposed upon the pragmatic English to their detriment.

— *John L. Grigsby*

THE UNNAMABLE

Author: Samuel Beckett (1906-1989)
Type of work: Novel
Type of plot: Absurdist

Time of plot: Mid-twentieth century
First published: L'Innommable, 1953 (English translation, 1958)

A monologue, spoken by an "unnamable" man uncertain of his own existence or even of the existence of an external reality, this absurdist novel has no recognizable geographical location but exists only in endless words and combinations of thought and stories. Tormented by his sense that certainty does not exist, by his inability to establish his own identity and to live in time and space, the narrator spins out a river of language. Shockingly, his narration proves to be nothing more than a long rationalization created by an infinitely rationalizing mind—the only substance in the novel.

Ideal room. Perhaps the most frequent reference to place in the novel alludes to a room that the narrator wishes for, in contrast to the room in which he perceives himself to be. His "ideal" room would be doorless, even windowless, with nothing but its six surfaces. It could be dark black. To the narrator, the room would be "home," a home that he would "find a way to explore." The narrator has trouble with motion, however, and has no idea how he might get around in his ideal space to do his exploration. He would like to put himself in the room: a "solid lump, in the middle, or in a corner, well propped up on three sides."

Narrator's habitat. The narrator speaks of existing in what can only be described as space with no boundaries. He speaks of feeling "no place, no place around me" and conveys the sense that there is "no end" to him. His sense of a lack of "end" is not to be understood that he has a body that is in some sense huge or infinite. He seems to have no sense of limits. His experience of self is an existence in endless time and space. Nevertheless, he has memories of the sea under his window and a rowboat, as well as a river, a bay, stars, beacons, lights of buoys, and the mountain burning.

The narrator's meandering among these memories of disparate places cannot be taken at face value because soon he denies their validity. For example, he says that he could just as easily be in a forest, "caught in a thicket, or wandering round in circles." So the narrative goes, round and round in intricate circles of denial and assertion. Such is the nature of the monologue, never to allow for any certainty, always to be on the brink of discovery and a fall into doubt and uncertainty.

The reason for these uncertainties is that the self is always changing, remaking itself continuously, much like the stream of conscious and unconscious thought. In an essay on Marcel Proust, Beckett wrote that the individual "is the seat of a constant process of decantation, decantation from the vessel containing the fluid of future time, sluggish, pale and monochrome, to the vessel containing the fluid of past time, agitated and multicolored by the phenomena of its hours." Although written about Proust, it is clear that he might as well be describing his own perspective on the individual.

— *Richard Damashek*

THE UNVANQUISHED

Author: William Faulkner (1897-1962)
Type of work: Novel
Type of plot: Bildungsroman

Time of plot: 1860's-1870's
First published: 1938

While the characters and actions of this novel are clearly a product of their setting in William Faulkner's imaginary world of Yoknapatawpha County, Mississippi, during the Civil War, the novel transcends the bounds of place and time to develop universal themes of honor and courage.

Yoknapatawpha County (YOK-nuh-puh-TAW-fuh). Fictional county in northeastern Mississippi created by Faulkner and used as the primary setting for most of his fiction, including *The Unvanquished*. The name of the county and its southern boundary, the Yoknapatawpha River, is an earlier spelling of the actual Yocona River. Yoknapatawpha County is similar to, though larger than, Lafayette County in northeastern Mississippi, where Faulkner lived most of his life. In addition to the Yoknapatawpha River, Faulkner's county is bounded by the Tallahatchie River to the north, hill country to the east, and thick woods and hills to the west. The terrain of this rural county contributes to the success of the protagonist Bayard Sartoris, his slave companion Ringo, and Bayard's grandmother Rosa Millard ("Granny") in their scheme to get and sell Union Army mules. On the other hand, when Bayard, Ringo, and Uncle Buck McCaslin turn into pursuers circling the county in search of Grumby, Granny's murderer, they too are handicapped by the terrain even though they know it well. Centered in the heart of the Confederacy, Yoknapatawpha County also functions as a microcosm of the South during the Civil War and Reconstruction.

Sartoris plantation. Large plantation located in Yoknapatawpha County about four miles north of Jefferson. With its mansion, slave cabins, and farm buildings, Sartoris is initially an idyllic place for the young Bayard, whose limited knowledge of the ongoing Civil War is demonstrated in the imaginary battles he and Ringo fight. The plantation, and consequently life as Bayard knows it, changes rapidly, however, with the burning of the Sartoris mansion by Yankee soldiers and the family's moving into one of the slave cabins. Although John Sartoris rebuilds the family mansion after the war, the innocence of Bayard's youth vanishes with the original house.

Jefferson. Seat of Yoknapatawpha County. Similar in many respects to Oxford, Jefferson is arguably not Oxford but rather a composite of several small northern Mississippi towns that Faulkner knew well, including Oxford, Faulkner's home for many years; New Albany, his birthplace; Pontotoc; Holly Springs; Batesville; and Ripley. Several times the action of the novel moves from the Sartoris plantation to Jefferson, the most crucial oc-

curring at the end of the novel, when Bayard courageously decides to face his father's killer unarmed, despite pressure from the townspeople to seek revenge. With his actions Bayard clearly rejects the town's and the South's values of violence and vengeance.

*Vicksburg. Mississippi river town that was the site of a major defeat of Confederate forces on July 4, 1863. More significant for the novel is the imaginary Vicksburg that Bayard and Ringo create with a handful of wood chips, a small trench dug with a hoe, and buckets of water. Only vaguely aware of the reasons for and the cruel consequences of the real war that is about to envelop them, they play their war games until the slave Loosh destroys their Vicksburg with a quick sweep of his hand. The destruction of their play world predicts both the fall of the Confederacy and the initiation of the children into a world of violence and evil.

Hawkhurst. Plantation of the Hawk family, located in northeastern Alabama approximately one hundred miles from Jefferson. After the Sartoris mansion has been burned, Granny, Bayard, and Ringo travel to Hawkhurst to visit relatives, only to find the destruction of Sartoris replicated. More disastrous in Bayard's view is the demolition of the nearby railroad, a symbol for Bayard of the war itself. Though Bayard recognizes the total loss, he decides that the train (the war) is not really gone as long as people are around to remember it.

*Oxford. Site of the University of Mississippi, located about forty miles from Jefferson. By including Oxford in his imaginary world, Faulkner precludes complete identification of his fictional Jefferson with Oxford and also creates a physical distancing of Bayard from his family, which reflects his moving beyond their values and beliefs.

*Memphis. City in southwest Tennessee, just over the Mississippi border. Granny views Memphis as a place of potential refuge when law and order seem to be breaking down in Yoknapatawpha County, but an attempt to reach it is quickly foiled by Union troops. Later Memphis, with its size, provides a feasible location for Ab Snopes to sell the Union Army their own mules taken from them by Granny's trickery.

— *Verbie Lovorn Prevost*

U.S.A.

Author: John Dos Passos (1896-1970)
Type of work: Novel
Type of plot: Historical

Time of plot: 1900-1935
First published: 1937: *The 42nd Parallel*, 1930; *1919*, 1932; *The Big Money*, 1936

John Dos Passos's narrative—along with its characters—speeds through dozens of settings in this rich, kaleidoscopic trilogy, but most settings have only momentary importance as Dos Passos paints a riotous portrait of America itself. Although the most often noted literary innovations in the trilogy are its "newsreel" and "camera eye" segments, Dos Passos's most powerful technique involving place is an implied ironic comparison between the "real" America and the America of the popular romantic imagination. America is an example of a country built from an idea, that is, the Romantic philosophy of the late eighteenth century that exalted the dignity of the common man, but there are vast differences between the nation and the philosophy. The novel chronicles a second American Revolution, one in which common people struggle toward the pursuit of happiness.

*United States. The United States of America of Dos Passos's trilogy is an ironic analogue to the free country of popular history, illustrating the difference between what America should be and what America is. Popular histories tend to view the United States as a promised land open to all, a country built by and for immigrants, a country in which all people are equal. Dos Passos's realism shows an America in which a working person who falls ill or is injured loses everything, and in which attempts to improve the lot of workers are seen as dangerous, "foreign" influences. It is also an America in which dissent is often met with immediate arrest; labor union organizers are imprisoned and deported, framed by the police, and even executed; men can be jailed for the crime of being unemployed; and a woman (Margaret Sanger) can be jailed for teaching other women about birth control.

The America of the trilogy is an isolationist, xenophobic nation, filling rapidly with a flood of European immigrants, ready to exploit the strength of their bodies in its mines and mills, but fearful of the radical ideas (Marxism, socialism, and anarchism) they bring with them from a rebellious continent. Everywhere the landscape is the same: Big companies owned by the rich use the poor as if they were parts of a machine. Workers who speak out, or who wear themselves out through overwork, are replaced. The reality of America as portrayed by Dos Passos contrasts sharply with the idea of America as envisioned by the nation's Founders or as imagined by average citizens.

*Goldfield. Nevada mining town where labor organizer Fainy "Mac" McCreary works for a socialist newspaper, the *Nevada Workman*. There is no romantic Wild West here; rather, the town is the scene of one of the great "free speech" fights that erupted between mine workers and owners throughout the West in the early years of the twentieth century. Although free speech is guaranteed to every citizen by the Bill of Rights, Mac and the other members of the Industrial Workers of the World (IWW) are frequently jailed for voicing unpopular ideas about the need for workers to organize to secure for themselves fundamental human rights. The sites of strikes or struggles between management and labor are the famous "battles" of Dos Passos's second American Revolution.

Mac's bookstore. Mexico City shop that illustrates how easily even a class rebel like Mac McCreary can slip into the comfortable life of the petty bourgeoisie. Mac owns the store, but Concha, the Mexican woman with whom he cohabits, actually runs it, leaving him little to do besides read and discuss politics with his cronies. The bookstore is a microcosm of capitalism at work, and it has made him—without his even realizing it—a small-time caricature of the capitalists he professes to hate. The small bit of money he has invested in the business allows him to exploit Concha, who here represents three groups that have historically been exploited in America: foreigners, the poor, and women. Mac himself lives on the labor of others, and when the bookstore fails and he is forced to flee, he discards the unfortunate

Concha in the same way that wealthier capitalists discard superfluous workers.

Ocean City. Largely undeveloped Maryland coastal town where young J. Ward Moorehouse begins his career working for Colonel Wedgewood's Ocean City Improvement and Realty Company. Ocean City is the dark side of the American Dream, a place where promised easy money never materializes.

*San Juan Hill. Site of an 1898 battle in Cuba during the Spanish-American War in which future president Theodore Roosevelt was involved. One of the most persistent false images in American history is that of Roosevelt charging up the hill on horseback at the head of his volunteer troop of "Rough Riders." As he does throughout *U.S.A.*, Dos Passos strips away the legend to reveal the truth: that Roosevelt ascended the hill on foot (only a fool would lead a cavalry charge up a hill) and that the hill had already been captured by U.S. Army regulars advancing up its opposite side. Because the legend is so firmly enshrined in the American imagination, the implied ironic analogue in Dos Passos's description seems inescapable.

*Bingham. Utah mining center that is the site of a bitter labor battle between the IWW and the Utah Copper Company in 1912. IWW organizers, including the legendary Joe Hill, win shorter hours and higher wages for the downtrodden miners. For Dos Passos and his characters, the names of strikes resonate in the same way that the names of battles might resonate for a soldier. Names such as Bingham, Goldfield, Lawrenceville, and Coeur d'Alene become part of a working-class hero's "service record."

— *Craig A. Milliman*

UTOPIA

Author: Sir Thomas More (1478-1535)
Type of work: Novel
Type of plot: Social morality

Time of plot: Reign of Henry VII of England
First published: 1516

Through the invention of an island located roughly at the antipodes of England, Thomas More not only wrote a telling satire on the social and religious state of Europe but also created the most famous ideal world in the history of literature.

*Antwerp. Flanders city (now part of Belgium) in which More's novel opens. In 1515 More was part of a diplomatic mission sent by England's King Henry VIII to Flanders, where he spent many months. While there, he met many of Europe's leading intellectuals, with many of whom he had already enjoyed a lively correspondence. One of these was Peter Giles, the town clerk of Antwerp. More uses his diplomatic mission, and in particular a visit he paid to Giles, as the starting point for his story. Other than a passing reference to attending a service at a cathedral, More makes no attempt to describe Antwerp; however, it is there that he is introduced to Raphael Hythloday, a philosophical traveler who has returned from Utopia. Hythloday's story is then told through a frame.

By anchoring his story to the events of a real embassy and real people, such as Giles, More gives his book plausibility, which is further enhanced by his making Hythloday a member of the explorer Amerigo Vespucci's crew. Vespucci's highly fanciful account of his voyages to the New World had been published widely only a few years earlier and contributed greatly to the European perception of the Americas as a land of strange peoples and creatures. So successful was More in making his book look like a true account that he was accused by a contemporary critic of having merely written down what someone else told him.

*London. England's capital city figures only peripherally in *Utopia*; however, More—through Hythloday—makes a number of pointed references to people and places in London, in particular the head of England's church, the archbishop of Canterbury. Although at pains to praise the intelligence and wisdom of the archbishop, Hythloday uses a debate about social and legal issues as a way of illustrating deficiencies in the English way of doing things.

Utopia. Far-off island adjacent to a larger landmass, somewhat like England in relation to the continent of Europe, which Hythloday reaches by a long, roundabout route and a series of strange adventures after being left behind in the New World by Vespucci. Hythloday's adventures serve to hide the exact location of Utopia, but it is possible to place it in the Western Hemisphere—on the other side of the globe from England. More places Utopia both physically and symbolically opposite to England.

The name *Utopia* is a Greek word, which contains a pun: In Greek, the name could be either *U-topia*, meaning "no place," or *Eu-topia*, meaning "better-place." Renowned not only as one of the most learned men of his day but also as a great wit, More almost certainly intended the pun. He describes his book as a comedy, and though not a comedy in the modern sense, it is clearly a work whose details are intended to amuse, one that uses a lightness of touch as a way to deflect the consequences of his criticism of religious and political institutions, which were, at the time, supposedly above criticism.

The novel is divided into two parts. The first records a conversation between More and Hythloday that introduces Utopia; the second is a discourse by Hythloday on the institutions and practices of Utopia. This latter is the main focus of the novel. More's intent in questioning the social and political institutions of his own country is served by presenting the ideal social and political institutions of Utopia. The nature of the location, therefore, enters only peripherally into the second part of the novel. It is more closely described in the earlier dialogue, when it becomes clear how well ordered the country is.

What makes Utopia "utopian" is how rational everything is, such as the treatment of criminals and the Utopians' relations with neighboring states. Utopia maintains its own peace in the face of ceaselessly warring neighbors through a Machiavellian mixture of alliances and corruption. The utopian ideal contains a healthy dose of reality: Their marriage practices require brides and grooms to be revealed naked to one another before their betrothals. The layout of Utopia is also rational; the ordered patterns of cities and towns—their roads and farms—clearly reflect the sensible way in which the country is run and contrast noticeably with the disordered pattern of towns and cities in the real world of England. While More is careful not to make the landscape seem artificially regular and contrived, he uses the shape of his imaginary island as a mirror for the sensible ordering of this ideal world that makes Utopia such a sane and happy land.

— *Paul Kincaid*

V

V.

Author: Thomas Pynchon (1937-   )
Type of work: Novel
Type of plot: Satire

Time of plot: 1898-1956
First published: 1963

In interrelated episodes, this novel explores states of mind as parallels to locations in place and time while including the United States, the Mediterranean, and Africa in its geographic sweep. Presented with a mix of surrealism and historical accuracy, these locales offer lessons about opposing states of mind, including decadence and reconstruction, paranoia and dissociation, and the urges for life and for death. The mysterious and terrifying title character represents the nexus at which these states intersect, just as the sides of a street appear to intersect at the vanishing point or as lines on a map meet at the poles.

*New York City.** During the 1950's, Benny Profane goes wherever events lead him. He spends time in Manhattan hanging out with a group of nihilistic bohemians who call themselves the Whole Sick Crew. One member of this group attempts suicide, another has an abortion; none seems undamaged or fully capable. They drink heavily, ride New York's subways endlessly, and hang out at the V-Note, a jazz club on Third Avenue, and the Rusty Spoon, a bar on the outskirts of Greenwich Village. At the urging of a woman who is something of a girlfriend, Profane occasionally makes forays into the job market, for example working briefly as a volunteer hunting albino alligators in the city sewers.

Profane's instincts win against his attempts at making a life for himself, however. With seemingly nothing better to do, he tags along when Herbert Stencil, who is obsessed with finding V., goes to Malta to investigate a tenuous lead about her presence there.

*Malta.** Island republic on the Mediterranean Sea, south of Sicily, that has historically occupied a strategic position on sea-lanes, and thus became the object of a long siege during World War II, in which it suffered constant attacks from Italian and German bombers. Amid this incredible ruin, V. appears as a woman dressed as a priest. Trapped under some rubble after a bombing, V. is disassembled by the children to whom she preaches her gospel of despair and death. The children remove her false eye, teeth, and other body parts, in a nightmarish reflection of what mechanized war is doing to human beings and their souls on Malta (or perhaps of what mechanized people and souls have created in World War II). Malta, midway between Europe and Africa, also stands as the intersection of the rational, mechanistic mentality symbolized by Europe and the irrational, corporeal mentality symbolized by Africa. Malta also symbolizes the confluence of opposites in that it is essentially a barren stone outcropping in the middle of a fertile sea.

One chapter of the novel is devoted to the story of a Maltese man who witnesses the siege and the agony of V. Additionally, the Mediterranean region figures in the experiences of Profane while he is in the Navy, before his days with the Whole Sick Crew. After World War II, it appears that the United States is reprising the historical role played by other empires that occupied the Mediterranean earlier in history. The novel leaves unresolved questions such as whether the whereabouts of a loser such as Profane and the rise and fall of empires are predetermined or matters of human volition.

*Africa.** One chapter follows British colonialists engaging in a spy mission laced with slapstick and menace. Traveling across North Africa, V. assumes various disguises while apparently keeping a godlike watch on the antics of the spies, who seem less like conquerors than bumbling, murderous tourists.

*South-West Africa. Mandated territory (now independent Namibia) administered by the neighboring Union of South Africa after World War I. There, V.'s malignant presence is felt during the 1920's, where a castle full of Europeans closes its gates to the outside while an African rebellion is put down. This small war,

as one of the castle's residents remarks with pleasure, recalls the horrors of the savagely suppressed Herero rebellion during the colony's German period in 1904. The collective insanity of the Herero genocide and the decadent civilization represented by the castle are explicitly analogized as precursors to the Jewish Holocaust and World War II.

— *Eric Howard*

THE VAGABOND

Author: Colette (Sidonie-Gabrielle Colette, 1873-1954)
Type of work: Novel
Type of plot: Psychological realism

Time of plot: Early twentieth century
First published: La Vagabonde, 1911 (English translation, 1954)

This novel focuses on its heroine's ambivalent view of herself and the world. The music-hall mime Renée Néré is torn between self-denigration and her desire for self-determination and freedom. Her ambivalence is manifest in Colette's settings for the novel, which include sections of Paris and their social implications, Paris music halls and Renée's dressing rooms, provincial France, and Renée's apartment. In these places Renée often hides and defends herself—or asserts her independence.

*Paris. Sections of the city that are seen most in *The Vagabond* include Renée's apartment on the avenue du Ternes quarter, near the Arc de Triomphe; Montmartre, the legendary center of bohemianism and artistic activity; and the Bois de Boulogne and residential areas surrounding it. The Bois de Boulogne, a vast wooded area on the west side of Paris, is traditionally a place to which the wealthy and the bourgeoisie go to see and be seen.

Renée's work as a dancer and mime in Parisian "café-concerts" where the mostly male audiences can smoke, drink, and enjoy the shows, is set mainly in the Empyrée-Clichy, on the southern border of the Montmartre area. In these theaters, Renée spends a good deal of time in her dressing rooms. She also finds a certain excitement in looking through theater curtains from the backstage to watch the audiences.

Occasionally, for relaxation, Renée and her friends frequent the cafés on the hill of Montmartre. But Renée does not really feel comfortable there because the neighborhood is too seedy and rough.

Dressing rooms. The rooms in which Renée prepares for her performances are important refuges that shelter her from the outside world and the people who pursue her. Her dressing rooms are surrounded by those of her colleagues, who form a comforting family for her. At her dressing tables, Renée makes up her face, creating the theatrical masks that offer another means of hiding and escape. However, her makeup work also requires her frequently to consider herself in mirrors, in which she finds the reflections of an aging, lonely woman frightening.

Renée's Empyrée-Clichy dressing room is the scene of her first meeting with a very important character, Maxime "Max" Dufferein-Chautel, the wealthy man who invades Renée's dressing room, her home, and her life in pursuit of her love.

Renée's apartment. Home of Renée located in the west-central part of Paris—between the theater in bohemian Montmartre, where she most often works, and the exclusive Bois de Boulogne area, where Max lives. This intermediate location represents the choices that Renée eventually faces, when she must choose between the freedom her career gives her and the tempting upper-class comfort offered by the adoring but domineering Max.

Renée is generally happier at the theater than in her apartment, but the apartment provides her with a refuge in which she can hide from responsibility. There, she is usually alone. However, there she also contemplates herself in mirrors, wondering exactly who she is. Her attitude toward her solitude is ambivalent—sometimes she feels lonely, but at other moments she savors the freedom that comes with being alone.

A focal point of Renée's apartment is the salon in which she receives visitors, including Max who besieges her. This room contains a divan, on which Renée physically and emotionally resists Max's pursuit until—roughly midway through the novel—he finally conquers her. Renée succumbs because Max succeeds in exciting her sexually, to her surprise, joy, and eventual dismay. This seduction and Renée's subsequent sensual rebirth (her name means "reborn" in French) comes to constitute the center of her struggle between commitment to Max and her freedom.

***Provincial France.** In the last third of the novel, Renée leaves both Paris and Max to tour the country with two acting friends. Her tour is circular: from Paris to the east, then to the south, the west, and back to Paris (and Max). She misses Max, but in the city of Avignon, in southeastern France, she experiences a revelation of sorts. At Avignon's railway station, she happens to buy beautiful roses, and an aesthetic epiphany sets her head to spin. This little crisis culminates in Nîmes, south of Avignon, where she strolls through a garden ecstatically absorbing the flowers, the warm air, and the beauty of an approaching storm. There, Renée comes to understand that such an experience is God-given—and given only to vagabonds and the solitary. Real joy, real freedom, and genuine identity are found, she sees, in rootlessness and wandering—no matter where, no matter what. Renée now begins to consider how to break off with Max, having chosen freedom and thus refused the confinement of marriage to Max.

— Gordon Walters

VANITY FAIR

Author: William Makepeace Thackeray (1811-1863)
Type of work: Novel
Type of plot: Social satire

Time of plot: Early nineteenth century
First published: serial, 1847-1848; book, 1848

This panoramic exploration of nineteenth century hypocrisy and greed follows the complex careers of insipid but wealthy Amelia Sedley and orphaned but resourceful Rebecca Sharp. The novel develops their various reversals and advances as their paths cross from London to Brussels, finally ending in Pumpernickel and a second marriage for each of them. Vanity Fair, with its shams and hypocrisies, is the constant background, no matter where the action occurs.

Vanity Fair. Place on the way to the Celestial City that John Bunyan created in *The Pilgrim's Progress* (1678, 1684), which represents the destructive temptations of the world. For Thackeray, "Vanity Fair" is likewise the place where lusts and pleasures are bought and sold, but for him the moral dimension of the threat of damnation is minimized. His Vanity Fair is mildly amusing and satirical; his characters are like puppets, jockeying for social position and money. His novel has no hero or heroine, but only his panoramic view of various versions of Vanity Fair, all filled with snobbery and acquisitiveness.

Miss Pinkerton's Minerva House Academy. Girls' school in which the wealthy Amelia Sedley and her orphaned friend, Rebecca Sharp, are trained. The importance of position and money is immediately obvious in the academy, for Amelia is polished with husband-acquiring skills, while the orphan Rebecca must earn her keep by teaching French, and she must also soon become a governess in the household of the wealthy Lord Pitt Crawley. The social contrast between the two students is also made obvious in parallel scenes at Dr. Swishtail's School, whose male students include the wealthy and snobbish George Osborne and the modest grocer's son, William Dobbin.

*Vauxhall. Pleasure gardens in London that represent Vanity Fair in microcosm, with their love of display, dark walkways, and matchmaking. There, Amelia plans a party and includes her brother Jos Sedley, a perfect counterpart to Vauxhall itself, foolishly vain and pleasure-seeking. Becky works hard to charm Jos in the hope of escaping from having to work for her living, but Jos's overindulgence in punch and his friend George's snobbery prevent her from snaring him.

Great Gaunt Street. London street on which stands the gloomy home of Lord Pitt Crawley, to whom Becky reports for work as a governess. Crawley finds Becky attractive, and she vows to make good use of all opportunities to advance herself in his home. His house, though grand with family portraits, is ruled over by no handsome baronet, but by a dirty, vulgar, and lewd old man. However, his country home, **Queen's Crawley**, proves to be a fertile ground for the shrewd Becky. She wins the affections of those who count in the household, especially wealthy old Miss Crawley, whose fortune and ill health make her everyone's focus. This wretched family is driven by greed, jealousy, and snobbery, and its members' very names reflect their vain, empty, selfish lives: "Rawdon" and the other "Pitts" of "Gaunt" Street and Queen's "Crawley."

*Park Lane. Home in London's Mayfair district of Miss Crawley, to which Becky is called to care for the wealthy, ailing, old woman. Comic but disgusting scenes follow those in the country home, as the rivals for Miss Crawley's fortune gather. Also on the scene are both Lord Pitt and his son Rawdon, rivals for Becky, each setting up in his own room adjacent to the sickroom and waiting for Becky, who regularly "comforts" them with news of the invalid's health.

At this house the old satyr, Lord Pitt Crawley, gets on his knees and proposes marriage to Becky, only days after his second wife dies. Becky tearfully declines, regretting her recent hasty and secret wedding to his son. This unfeeling and mercenary approach to both death and marriage is later echoed in the old man's death scene at Queen's Crawley. The butler's daughter had hoped to become his third wife, but while he is dying, she ravages the house's cupboards, leaving a fellow servant to make faces at the impotent and whimpering lord on his death-

bed. In both of these scenes, readers are shown that the residents of Vanity Fair make no foolish pretense to respect or to decency in love or death; instead, this acquisitive society values self-promotion at all costs.

*Brussels. Belgian city that represents a continental version of Vanity Fair. Brussels is located on the fringes of the great Waterloo battlefield, whose fighting remains totally offstage as Thackeray focuses on the civilian hangers-on and their social life in the weeks before the battle. There, the cowardly Jos Sedley, on leave from India, postures in his mustache and military dress, and Becky triumphs at a ball given on the eve of battle. All the characters are seen in a pointless and mindless pursuit of pleasure, while Napoleon's dangerous military threat is ignored. Meanwhile, Amelia suffers from her husband's flirtations with Becky, and Jos swaggers like a fat child. As an afterthought, Thackeray closes chapter 32 with a single battlefield scene: George lying face down, dead with a bullet through his heart.

*Curzon Street. Street in London's fashionable Mayfair district where Becky and Rawdon settle after they have become adept at living well on nothing. There, Becky plots to secure the needed connections to realize her ambition of being presented at court before Vanity Fair's supreme representative of self-indulgent dandyism, King George IV. She works tirelessly to become the vogue in London and to maintain her fashionable address and entertainment schedule.

Becky's court appearance secures her the conquest of the Marquis of Steyne and an invitation to his house in Gaunt Square, adjacent to the very house where Becky first goes as a governess. Although she now has no more real security or money than she did when she set out as a governess from this same street, she prides herself on belonging to Vanity Fair. When Rawdon is arrested and held in a sponging house by bailiffs for his ever-mounting debts, Becky pretends to have no money to rescue him and, instead, uses his absence from home as an opportunity to entertain Lord Steyne. The great discovery scene that follows is one of the novel's most memorable. Becky, covered with jewels and her arms coiled with bracelets, is in the arms of Lord Steyne. Rawdon enters and flings a diamond at the earl, scarring him for life. When he discovers that Becky did have money, he leaves her for good. Becky, fallen from her greatest heights in Vanity Fair, then becomes shabbily bohemian.

Pumpernickel. Small German duchy that is another microcosm of Vanity Fair and provides Becky with a second chance to snare Jos Sedley and his wealth which had escaped her at Vauxhall in the opening chapters. There, she also performs her single generous action. In a crucial awakening scene, she shows Amelia a love letter the faithless George sent to her on the eve of the Battle of Waterloo, in which he was killed. The letter enables Amelia finally to stop cherishing her false sentiments for her dead husband and wed the loving William Dobbin.

Ever resourceful, Becky also fastens herself on Jos, who then mysteriously declines, leaving his widow with a large insurance settlement. Now Becky can leave behind the low gaming tables of Europe to which she had resorted and return to England's provincial spas of Cheltenham and Bath where the novelist leaves her, still with a great deal of charm. Her final appearance is at a literal fair, suggesting that she will always be bargaining.

— *Marie J. K. Brenner*

VATHEK: An Arabian Tale

Author: William Beckford (1760-1844)
Type of work: Novel
Type of plot: Gothic

Time of plot: The past
First published: English translation, 1786; original French edition, 1787 as *Vathek*

This novel is set in a fantastic landscape borrowed from The Arabian Nights *in which everything is extravagantly exaggerated—especially the impossibly opulent palaces in which fabulous rich and powerful monarchs seek new sensations to excite their jaded palates.*

Palace of Alkoremmi. Vathek's own palace, situated on a hill above the city of Samarah (Sāmarrā), situated upriver from Baghdad on the Tigris, in what is now Iraq. To the edifice constructed by his father Motassem, whose tower has eleven thousand steps, Vathek has added five new wings, each intended to gratify one of the five senses: the Eternal or Unsatiating Banquet; the Temple of Melody, or the Nectar of the Soul; the Delight of the Eyes, or the Support of Memory; the Palace of Perfumes, also known as the Incentive to Pleasure; and the Retreat of Joy, or the Dangerous. These perfect incarnations of refined sensation cannot, however, prevent his determination to exceed their limits.

Mountain of the Four Fountains. Place at which the demoniac Giaour, Vathek's tempter, arrives after rolling like a ball across the plain of Catoul. The Giaour eventually falls into a chasm etched out by a cataract descending from the mountain, and it is to this chasm that Vathek brings his unsuccessful sacrifice of fifty children, hoping to buy admission to the black portal of the realm of Eblis, which he has glimpsed in its depths.

Valley of Fakreddin. Refuge that Vathek finds when he is lost in the wilderness en route to the stream of Rocnabad (from which he drank delectably in his youth). Emir Fakreddin's palace is a stone building with nine domes and nine bronze portals, whose advertised purpose is to offer asylum to pilgrims and safe repose to travelers. Although not as luxurious as the palace of Alkoremmi, it is well appointed. It stands within sight of the domes of Shadukiam and Ambreabad, the abodes of the peries (Persian fairies). The principal symbol of virtue in the text is the group of lofty crags to which the good Genius brings Gulchenrouz and the sacrificed children.

Ruins of Istakar. Ancient mountain city to which Vathek brings Nouronihar. Roofless watchtowers, too numerous to count, are arranged around an immense palace fronted by four colossal statues representing chimerical hybrids of leopard and griffin. The towers tumble when the mountain splits to reveal the entrance to the underworld through which Vathek is allowed to pass.

Realm of Eblis. Although roofed by a vaulted ceiling, the subterranean world to which Vathek and Nouronihar descend is a vast plain decorated with seemingly infinite arcades and colonnades. Its pavements are strewn with gold dust and odorous saffron and studded with censers in which ambergris and aloe-wood burn. Heavily laden tables set between the columns and troops of lasciviously dancing genies recall Vathek's own experiments in extravagance, but the agonized shades of the damned are not so pleasing to the eye. Eblis, enthroned on a globe of fire set within a vast tabernacle, generously offers Vathek the sole use of the fortress of Aherman (Ahriman, a Zoroastrian demon) and the halls of Argenk, but these seemingly infinite and interminably gloomy apartments have no power to relieve the torment of one who has exhausted his capacity for pleasure and hope. Endless corridors and multitudinous rooms do not signify power and wealth in Eblis's realm but serve instead to emphasize the awful loneliness of the human heart and the futility of hedonistic worldly ambition.

— *Brian Stableford*

THE VICAR OF WAKEFIELD

Author: Oliver Goldsmith (1728 or 1730-1774)
Type of work: Novel
Type of plot: Domestic realism

Time of plot: Eighteenth century
First published: 1766

Settings for this novel reflect the dichotomies between rural and urban, past and present, and simplicity and luxury that dominate Oliver Goldsmith's fiction. However, one of his purposes in this novel is to demonstrate that a country cottage is no more certain a refuge from evil than either the "town" of London, with all its vices, or the dangerous road that leads there.

Wakefield. English town in which the vicar, Dr. Primrose, settles after losing his fortune. Its locale is never named, but to Primrose it is more than a place where there is a cure available and a farm that he can manage—it is a refuge, where he can keep his family safe from the world.

Although Primrose's new home is clearly in England, Goldsmith's description of it probably draws upon his childhood memories of Lissoy, Ireland, which was undoubtedly also the model for the town celebrated in his meditative poem *The Deserted Village* (1770). In *The Vicar of Wakefield*, the hero comments on the fact that the farmers still hold to the old ways and live by the old virtues. They work hard, live frugally, go to church on the Lord's Day, and find their pleasure in the traditional festivals that every season brings. However, when the vicar returns home one evening, he sees his house on fire and his family in danger and realizes that no place on Earth is truly safe. Moreover, though the local villagers are mostly virtuous people, the vicar's neighbor and landlord, wealthy Squire Thornhill, has all the vices of "the town," that is, London.

"The town" (London). Eighteenth century term for London, the center of English society, luxury, and pleasure. It is a place of great appeal but of even greater peril.

After the vicar's son George is dissuaded from applying for a job in a London boarding school, he tries to become a writer, but fails, then becomes a dependent of Squire Thornhill, only to be used and finally abandoned. The evils associated with the town can also invade the country, exemplified by Squire Thornhill's success in bringing his easy manners and easier morality into the vicar's cottage, where he seduces the vicar's susceptible daughter Olivia, who he carries off to London in his coach. Because he is wealthy, there is little that the Primroses can do to set matters right.

Road. Path leading away from the vicar's cottage. The road is not the biblical narrow way of the virtuous but the broad path that leads toward town and temptation. When the vicar's son Moses takes the road to a village fair, he is cheated out of his horse; when Olivia steps into the coach, she forfeits her virtue; and when George reaches London, he finds only disappointment and betrayal. At the same time, however, the vicar's venture onto the road ends with his finding and rescuing Olivia. Moreover, the same road brings back Mr. Burchell—who turns out to be Squire Thornhill's uncle, the virtuous Sir William Thornhill—thus assuring that good will be rewarded and evil punished.

Arnold country house. Estate visited by the vicar

while he is on the road looking for Olivia. He is invited to the house by a well-dressed man who is actually the butler; however, when the Arnolds arrive with their niece Arabella Wilmot, George's former fiancé, they invite the vicar to stay on. He appreciates the beauty of the country house, its impressive facade, its elegantly decorated rooms, and its magnificent grounds and gardens. However, he assumes that because of his own carelessness, his children can never become part of the world the estate represents.

Village gaol. Jail in which the vicar is briefly held prisoner. The gaol consists of one large common room and a number of cells, in which the prisoners sleep on straw with only their garments for covers. Because the vicar utilizes his imprisonment there as a heaven-sent opportunity and betters the lives of the other prisoners, for him the gaol symbolizes not defeat and disgrace but spiritual triumph.

— *Rosemary M. Canfield Reisman*

VICTORY: An Island Tale

Author: Joseph Conrad (Jósef Teodor Konrad Nałęcz Korzeniowski, 1857-1924)

Type of work: Novel

Type of plot: Psychological realism

Time of plot: Early twentieth century

First published: 1915

This novel's plot unfolds on two minor islands in eastern Asia's vast Malaysian archipelago, seemingly tropical paradises but in reality places to which the six major characters bring ugliness and destruction, both to themselves and others. Only a minor character, the Chinese servant Wang is able to adapt to the simple joys of island life on its own terms.

Samburan (sahm-BEWR-ahn). Also known as Round Island, one of the thousands of small islands in the Malaysian archipelago, on which Baron Axel Heyst establishes the center of his Tropical Belt Coal Company. At its height, his company has offices in London and Amsterdam. After the death of Heyst's partner, the only person remaining in Heyst's house is his Chinese servant, Wang. On the side of the island opposite the house is a native village.

Although Heyst finds island life fascinating, he is generally disenchanted with it, even though he rarely feels lonely. He often sits in the main room of his house, under a picture of his father—a misanthrope and famous writer—and reflects.

Into this deserted wilderness Heyst brings Alma (whom he renames Lena), a women he has rescued from an obsessive-compulsive hotel owner at the nearest civilized island, three days journey by boat. In his sitting room, Heyst assures Lena that nothing can break in on them there.

Schomberg's Hotel. Hotel in Sourabaya owned by Wilhelm Schomberg, who is obsessed with controlling Lena, one of the eighteen women in his hotel concert hall. Desperate to escape the hotel, Lena persuades Heyst to take her with him after a concert.

Other residents of the hotel include two very suspicious characters, Mr. Jones and Martin Ricardo, who gamble in the hotel's shabby gaming room. These desperadoes brag to Schomberg about their adventures in Bangkok, Manila, Colombia, Venezuela, and Nicaragua. When these men tell Schomberg they intend to stay at the hotel for a month, he shows displeasure and is threatened by Jones. Nevertheless, Schomberg persuades the men to attempt to retrieve Lena and get revenge on Heyst by telling them a false story about a fortune that Heyst has hidden on the island.

Wang's hut. Walled quarters of Heyst's servant Wang, who retires to his hut at night and contentedly tends his vegetable garden by day. Heyst never enters the hut or its grounds. After Wang takes a village woman for a wife, she never emerges from this island of sanity, except to flee with Wang to her home village on the opposite side of the island when the desperadoes land on the island. The path to the woman's village is strewn with logs on the trail as a warning to the outside world to keep away.

Heyst's house. After Lena is shot by the invading desperadoes, Heyst takes her to his bed to die as his house catches fire. There Heyst apparently chooses to die with Lena, who is happy finally to be loved and free from Schomberg. Heyst, too, is finally free from a life of scorn. The lovers are both reduced to ashes, but ashes are as pure as their love. The island, too, is now purified from the influx of civilization. In this there may be victory.

— *Irwin Halfond*

THE VILLAGE

Author: Ivan Alexeyevich Bunin (1870-1953)
Type of work: Novel
Type of plot: Social criticism

Time of plot: Early twentieth century
First published: Derevnya, 1910 (English translation, 1923)

This highly controversial work offers an unsparing portrayal of a Russian village, not as the idealized home of deferential peasants who meekly live in harmony with their beloved gentry, but as a place of appalling brutality. The villagers are distinguished from their animals chiefly by their greater capacity for cunning in devising ways to harm and brutalize their fellows. It is a place teetering on the brink of a social catastrophe, a place ripe for social upheaval.

Durnovka (door-NOF-kah). Fictional Russian village in which the novel is set. Its name might be translated into English literally as "Evil Town" or "Illville," and Ivan Bunin clearly intends it to represent all that he regards as being wrong with Russian rural society in the last days of the czars. Durnovka is probably based to some degree upon the real village of Ognyovka, where Bunin himself lived. It is a generic peasant village of the period but also a symbol of all Russia, of all that Bunin perceives as being wrong with Russia at the time.

Standing in a deep ravine, the village has thirty peasant cottages on one side of its gorge and the tiny manor house on the other side. The manor is not held by exalted princes or gentlefolk of the sort one finds in books by Leo Tolstoy or Ivan Turgenev, but by a man named Tikhon Ilich Krasov, whose own grandfather was a freed serf. Tikhon Ilich is himself little more than a *kulak*—a wealthy peasant of the sort who, two decades later, would be murdered by the thousands in the collectivization campaigns of Soviet dictator Joseph Stalin. His manor house is little more than a well-built farmhouse, originally an outlier manor for a landlord who had a number of holdings and his primary seat elsewhere. The village's peasant cottages are equally unimpressive, small wooden shacks of appalling squalor. Many of them, such as that of Siery, are quite literally falling apart, missing parts of their roofs. Yet people continue to dwell in them, unwilling or unable to put them back in repair.

Black suburb. Tikhon's birthplace; an outlying part of a nearby unnamed town, to which Tikhon's grandfather had originally moved after obtaining his freedom and leaving Durnovka, only to be arrested subsequently and imprisoned for a rash of church thefts. The town also contains the fair, an open market for the area's villages, at which homely goods such as brooms and kettles are sold alongside agricultural produce and animals. There is also a cemetery, the haunt of the town's prostitutes, who are described as so hungry that, if paid in bread for their services, they gobble down every crumb as they lie under their customers. Bunin uses these scenes to show that the evils and brutalization of Russian life are not peculiar only to the one tiny village but are symptomatic of the entire culture.

*Voronezh (vor-on-EHZH). City on the Don River, about four hundred miles south of Moscow, in which Tikhon Ilich's brother Kuzma becomes a writer. Here Kuzma visits the grave of Koltzov, a local composer and poet, and in rapture at finally encountering the "culture" he longs for, scrawls a semiliterate epitaph upon Koltzov's tombstone. Here also Kuzma reads many famous Russian writers and talks with people of some learning, although he often misunderstands much of what he obtains. He ultimately publishes a book of his writings; however, many of his acquaintances believe that he has plagiarized them from newspapers.

Kazakovo (kah-zah-KO-vo). Village to which Kuzma travels to purchase an orchard. There he meets a number of broken-down and brutalized peasants and comes to decide that he is not really interested in owning an orchard.

Ulyanovka (ool-yah-NOF-kah). Home village of Rodka. It is also the location of the post office, to which Kuzma travels several times while he is keeping Durnovka for his brother. It is a slightly larger village than Durnovka, with more amenities, but the people are equally brutalized and willing to live in appalling squalor.

— *Leigh Husband Kimmel*

VILLETTE

Author: Charlotte Brontë (1816-1855)
Type of work: Novel
Type of plot: Bildungsroman

Time of plot: Nineteenth century
First published: 1853

The geographical and plot material for this novel derived from Charlotte Brontë's own two-year stay in Brussels, Belgium. Although the imaginary city of Villette is described as a great capital, a sense of enclosure is predominant both physically and in relationships.

Villette. Capital city of the fictional country of Labassecour. With a name that literally means "little city," Villette is not large; students walk out to the surrounding countryside before breakfast from the city center. The city is divided into two main parts: the Basse-Ville, the lower city, and the Haute-Ville, the upper city. The lower city contains the older, run-down areas. Here Dr. John goes on his philanthropic medical visits, and here is situated the rue des Mages, on which the house of Madame Walravens and other dependents of Monsieur Paul stands.

The upper city is the fashionable area in which the royal palaces, galleries, museums, and society meeting places are located. In one of the art galleries, the exhibition of a painting occasions an argument between Lucy and Monsieur Paul. At one of the theaters, she attends a concert also attended by the king and queen. Later, she spends the night enjoying a festival of lights and fireworks. It would be true to say that Lucy belongs to neither of these worlds, low or high.

Bretton. Old cathedral town in England. Lucy's godmother's family have lived here on St. Ann's Street for generations; in fact, her family name is also Bretton. Her son, John Graham, lives there with her. On one of Lucy's visits she meets Polly Home, a little girl.

Lucy's home. Situated fifty miles north of London, the place is never named or described. After her parents' death, she lives in the same place as companion to Miss Marchmont, an invalid. "Two hot rooms" become Lucy's world for a while until Miss Marchmont's death. Almost destitute, Lucy feels guided to go to London. There, Lucy stays near St. Paul's Cathedral and is captivated by the energy of London, the commercial and financial center of Great Britain. It emboldens her to sail for Europe.

Pensionnat de Demoiselles (pan-see-OHN-ah deh deh-MWAH-zay). Girls' school run by Madame Beck on the rue Fossette, five minutes walk from Villette's city center. On Lucy's nighttime arrival in Villette, she providentially stumbles straight to it and is offered a place there, first as governess to Madame Beck's children, then as one of four regular teachers. The school consists of a former convent plus some extensions, large enough for twenty boarders, the teachers, six servants, and Madame Beck's family. There are also one hundred day students. Madame Beck knows everything that goes on at the school, a picture similar to the girls' school portrayed in Brontë's first novel, *The Professor* (1857). The discipline is not too strict, and there is plenty of food and exercise in the large garden, in contrast to the Lowood School of her second novel, *Jane Eyre* (1847). There is a neighboring boys' school, as in *The Professor*, where Monsieur Paul also teaches.

La Terrasse (lah teh-RAHS). Villette House leased by Lucy's godmother, to which Lucy is taken in a state of nervous collapse by the school's physician, Dr. John, who turns out to be Graham Bretton. It is a small country house just outside the city limits, a mile or so from the Porte de Crécy. The interior is done in English fashion with many paintings and furnishings from the house in Bretton. Lucy stays there until fully recovered and then visits for a while.

Hôtel Crécy (oh-TEL KRAY-see). Grand hotel on the rue Crécy where Count de Bassompierre has his apartments on the second floor. De Bassompierre turns out to be Polly's father, now elevated through marriage to the country's aristocracy. He has also inherited Ginevra as his niece, thus completing the English network of friends that Lucy finally rejects in favor of Monsieur Paul.

Faubourg Clotilde (FOH-bur kloh-TEELD). Monsieur Paul rents a space to enable Lucy to start her own little school. At the end of the novel she is also able to rent the house next door as a "pensionnat" or boarding facility for the school.

— *David Barratt*

THE VIOLENT BEAR IT AWAY

Author: Flannery O'Connor (1925-1964)
Type of work: Novel
Type of plot: Psychological realism

Time of plot: 1952
First published: 1960

Within a setting of almost biblical simplicity—the country and the city—Flannery O'Connor tells the tale of a family cursed, or perhaps mysteriously blessed, with a powerful religious calling. The oldest member of the family is a self-proclaimed prophet living in a remote cabin in Tennessee with his great-nephew. He rescues the boy from his uncle, claiming that the Lord has told him to "fly with the orphan boy to the farthest part of the backwoods and raise him up to justify his Redemption."

Powderhead. Tiny settlement somewhere in rural Tennessee—perhaps east of Nashville—where the boy, Francis Marion Tarwater, has spent nearly all of his fourteen years living with his great-uncle. There they live as if in another century, literally prophets in the wilderness, in a two-story shack surrounded by woods and corn fields, plowing with a mule and selling homemade liquor from their still. After his great-uncle dies, Tarwater gets drunk and burns the cabin and the old man's body, instead of burying him as he has promised. He then escapes to the city, a place he views with distrust.

The imaginary Powderhead is a primal, magical realm, isolated from the modern world both literally and symbolically. The old man's cabin is inaccessible by car; like holy ground, it must be approached on foot. While Powderhead proves a paradise of sorts for the young Bishop Rayber, a city child who has "never caught a fish or walked on roads that were not paved," its

thorns bar his entrance when he returns as an adult. With its thickly enclosing woods, thorn bushes, and blackberry brambles, Powderhead is alternately oppressive and edenic. The old man's remote cabin, like his religious vision, has a haunting power that draws both nephew and great-nephew back after they have left it.

City. Large unnamed southeastern city—possibly modeled on Atlanta, Georgia—that is home to about 75,000 people, including Tarwater's uncle, the schoolteacher George Rayber, and Rayber's mentally challenged son, Bishop. When Tarwater first visits the city with the old man, he sees it as an evil place where strangers pass by with ducked heads and muttered words, as if "hastening away from the Lord God Almighty." After the old man dies, Tarwater returns to the city, turning up on the schoolteacher's doorstep. Though curious about city life, he shows no interest in giving up his country ways; he refuses to wear the new clothes his uncle buys him and finds a terrible hunger growing in him that city food, mere "shavings out of a cardboard box," cannot fill.

The city is seen as a dead place with no connections to God or the natural world; its packaged products cannot nourish the soul. Each night, Tarwater walks through the city streets with his uncle as if waiting for something to reveal itself to him. The city, he has been told, is where prophets must go to share the visions they receive in the wilderness. Tarwater claims to scorn his great-uncle's belief, but one night, he slips out after hours to visit a Pentecostal tabernacle, with blue and yellow windows "like the eyes of some biblical beast," where a child evangelist is preaching. Rayber follows him and finds him there. The boy claims "I only gone to spit on it," but he is clearly shaken.

Cherokee Lodge. Country motel thirty miles from Powderhead where George Rayber takes Tarwater and his son, Bishop, ostensibly for a fishing trip. The lodge is a green and white converted warehouse, one half of which rests on land and the other half perches on stilts above a small lake, where the novel's key scene takes place. Rayber's initial plan in bringing the boy to the lodge is to take him to Powderhead and make him face the site of his great-uncle's death, hoping that the shock of that return will end his obsession. While fishing with Tarwater on the lake, Rayber confesses that he once tried to drown his son but could not bring himself to do it. Later, Tarwater takes Bishop out on the lake in a boat and drowns him—but first baptizes him, thus fulfilling the task the old man has set for him.

— *Kathryn Kulpa*

THE VIOLENT LAND

Author: Jorge Amado (1912-2001)
Type of work: Novel
Type of plot: Social realism

Time of plot: Late nineteenth century
First published: Terras do sem fin, 1942 (English translation, 1945)

This story of conflict over the control of northeastern Brazil's cacao industry takes place amid the steaming jungles and rough frontier communities of the southern part of the state of Bahia. There, human lust, greed, and anger grow as lushly as the cacao trees that flourish in the region's soil, as the novel portrays a world in which either death or good fortune may lie around the next turn in a backcountry trail. In the midst of what often seems merely mindless disorder, however, there are influences at work that will eventually claim the area for civilization.

*Sequeiro Grande (see-KAY-roh GRAHN-day). Forest region of prime cacao-growing land in northeastern Brazil. In his foreword to the English translation of the novel, Jorge Amado describes his own boyhood in the area and states that his portrait of the land and its inhabitants is a true one. He also states that the story contains the very "roots" of his being and means more to him than any of his other books. In his novel, the Sequeiro Grande is sought by both the Horacio and Badaró families, whose plantations are located on opposite sides of the region's still-unclaimed interior. The forest is likened to a lovely young virgin whose appeal far transcends that of mere money, which makes the narrative both a story

about a love triangle and a chronicle of economic conflict. The novel's conception of male sexual drive as the engine of economic expansion is mirrored in its treatments of love relationships, which are similarly envisaged as dramas of a man's need to possess, control, and exploit the woman he desires.

Horacio plantation (oh-RAH-see-oh). Home of Colonel Horacio da Silveira and his wife, Ester. Important units of social organization on the Brazilian frontier, plantations are depicted in the novel as both outposts of civilization and feudal kingdoms reflecting their owners' personalities. Although Colonel Horacio's fields are worked by poorly paid laborers under the supervision of armed foremen, he is sufficiently responsive to the needs of his "retainers" to command their loyalty when conflict with the Badarós threatens.

While the colonel tames his land, his wife attempts to domesticate him by providing a sophisticated social life and imported cultural influences; if only partially successful in rounding off some of the colonel's rough edges, her efforts prefigure what the narrative sees as the eventual triumph of civilizing influences.

Badaró plantation (bah-dah-ROH). Home of brothers Sinhô and Juca Badaró and their sister Don'Ana. Like Colonel Horacio, the Badaró brothers are lords of their feudal plantation, with Sinhô's appreciation of European art and reluctance to use violence offering a more civilized alternative to Juca's propensity to violence. Although the Badaró estate is destroyed in a final battle with Horacio's forces, this is the final act of lawlessness in a narrative that concludes with the coming of law and order to the region.

Ilhéus (ihl-YAY-ahs). Major city of southern Bahia. Ilhéus is another location of conflict between incoming civilization and frontier anarchy, a thriving commercial center which at the beginning of the novel is dominated by a corrupt political establishment that sanctions chicanery in the courts and assassinations in the streets. The city's gradual evolution toward social order is symbolized by the pope's appointment of its first bishop, and the subsequent festivities that celebrate this notable event as a major advance on the road of progress.

Ferradas (fay-RAH-das). Town founded as a service center for Colonel Horacio's nearby plantation, and very much under his control. While Ilhéus develops into a dynamic and growing community, Ferradas remains a bandit's den whose failure to transcend its origins as a frontier outpost symbolizes its unworthiness to benefit from progress.

Tabocas (tah-BOH-kahs). Town between Ilhéus and Ferradas that prospers despite Colonel Horacio's proximity. Policed by an officer who manages to do his job properly while remaining on good terms with the colonel, Tabocas tolerates those partial to the Badaró clan, so long as they do not try for municipal office. As a consequence of this relatively enlightened attitude, the community is distinguished by great commercial prosperity, as well as the schools and churches that Ilhéus has previously established and Ferradas will never manage to create.

— *Paul Stuewe*

THE VIRGINIAN: A Horseman of the Plains

Author: Owen Wister (1860-1938)
Type of work: Novel
Type of plot: Western

Time of plot: Late nineteenth century
First published: 1902

This novel portrays life in expansive Wyoming during the period between 1874 and 1890, a time when the American cowboy and other elements that once represented the wild western frontier, such as the buffalo, the antelope, and open grazing lands, were rapidly disappearing.

Medicine Bow. Wyoming town in and around which the novel is set, during the latter part of the nineteenth century. The setting depicts a romantic scene with spectacular landscapes, including wide rangelands, impressive rock formations and colors, and vast distances. The reader is left with a sense of endless space in a wild, almost hostile environment. The scenery conveys the rugged image of courageous men who choose to be more attached to their horses and six-shooters than to the constraints demanded by marriage and a family.

Owen Wister notes that during the late nineteenth century the town of Medicine Bow consisted of twenty-nine buildings, including a general store, a saloon, a feed stable, two dining houses, a train depot, and a few houses. There were only two ranches that occupied the vast surroundings, one owned by Judge Henry and the other by Sam Balaam. A river running through their land provided a natural boundary of separation.

With the cattle boom of the late 1870's and early 1880's, Medicine Bow was quickly changing, as was the West in general. Medicine Bow became the largest cattle shipping point along the Union Pacific Railroad, shipping an average of two hundred head per day. In order to herd the cattle, roads were built. To raise and breed the cattle, fences were erected along the roads and other locations on the once-open range. The cattle business brought many changes to the pristine conditions that had existed there. The streets of Medicine Bow, as well as the open range in general, became littered with tin cans and other garbage. The West was changing, becoming more like the East, where the Virginian and the other major characters in the novel had originally lived. They moved West hoping to escape the decadent conditions that were prevalent in the East. Unfortunately, the same conditions were also rapidly developing in the West.

*Wyoming. Frontier state that in the early 1870's was almost entirely open rangeland, covered with long sequences of prairie grass and fertile land. The vastness was only occasionally interrupted by canyons and rivers, but it was not split up by roads, settlements, or fences. Wyoming was a new land, the unknown, and stood in sharp contrast to the American East. The title of "cowboy" implied an attitude and a lifestyle that were representative of the land. There was virtually no evidence that in only a few years the western frontier would become a mere memory.

Sunk Creek Ranch. Located more than two hundred miles from Medicine Bow, Sunk Creek is the location of Judge Henry's cattle ranch, where the Virginian becomes the foreman and demonstrates to other cowhands that a cowboy should live by the honor code of the old West. Sunk Creek represents a site of transition from the plains horseman to barbed wire, farming, and development. Here, as well as at Medicine Bow, Wister challenges his readers to be and do the best at all times, no matter what the circumstances, particularly during times of transition and development.

Bear Creek. Small Wyoming town in which Molly Wood, an easterner, takes up residence in order to teach school. Bear Creek symbolizes a place of selfless acts, tolerance, and love. It is where Molly devotes much of her time to teaching frontier children, who need her love and nurturing care. It is also where Molly patiently nurses the Virginian back to health after he is shot. Bear Creek represents one of the last places in America where true American virtues exist. The land, Molly, and the Virginian all symbolize those vanishing qualities.

— *Alvin K. Benson*

THE VIRGINIANS: A Tale of the Last Century

Author: William Makepeace Thackeray (1811-1863)
Type of work: Novel
Type of plot: Historical

Time of plot: Late eighteenth century
First published: serial, 1857-1859; book, 1858-1859

This novel is a sequel to The History of Henry Esmond, Esquire *(1852), in which an English gentleman seeks and finds his fortune in colonial America.* The Virginians *describes the return of his grandsons to England as the not entirely welcome guests of the disputatious Esmond family. As George and Harry Warrington are invited to country estates when in favor, shunted off to less palatial homes when merely tolerated, and exiled to modest apartments when in disgrace, their residences function as exact indicators of the extent to which their relations, and society in general, are willing to accept them.*

Castlewood House (England). Ancestral seat of the Esmond family, located in south-central England about one hundred miles west of London. At the beginning of the narrative, the colonials George and Harry Warrington look on their English relations with awe and respect; they have been deeply affected by their parents' nostalgic reminiscences of Castlewood House and have even memorized the estate's location on the map. After George is thought to have died in General Braddock's defeat by the French in the Pennsylvania campaign of 1755, Harry travels to England for the first time and cannot help but feel that he is returning to a place to which he belongs—one that constitutes an important part of his heritage.

Over the years, the English branch of the clan has declined to the point that only wealthy relatives who will contribute materially to Castlewood House's upkeep are welcome. What little income the mismanaged estate does produce is quickly frittered away by its improvident owner, Lord Castlewood, whose passion for horse racing, gambling, and card-playing has left him deeply in debt. The contrast between Castlewood House in England, the home of a prestigious family but in most other respects a drain on society, and Castlewood House in Virginia, a humbler but far more productive property, symbolizes the novel's characteristic view of the relationship between a mother country that has lost its moral authority and a colony that retains many worthwhile traditional values.

Since Harry is initially assumed to be a poor relation, it is only after the size of his parents' property and his status as its heir become known that he is suddenly received with open arms. Lord Castlewood, desperately in need of funds to keep the family solvent, now introduces Harry to the estate's liveliest and most profitable venue, its card room, where even Sundays are devoted to the rituals of gaming and the family chaplain spends more time at the card table than in church. Although certainly amusing as a satiric portrait of upper-class fads and fancies, the card-room scenes also suggest that English society has adopted rituals which reflect its blind pursuit of monetary gain. Thus, Harry's eventual loss of all of his assets to Lord Castlewood and other aristocratic gamblers means that he is no longer welcome in their homes and must now rely on his intrinsic merits to make his way in the world.

Castlewood House (Virginia). Site of the Virginia estate of the American branch of the Esmonds. Although most of the novel's plot is set elsewhere, this property plays an important role in the consciousness of its leading characters. George and Harry Warrington have frequent occasion to remember their birthplace's comfort and graciousness, whereas their venal English relations are more inclined to picture it as an abundant source of money ripe for the plucking. Throughout, Castlewood House in Virginia represents a place of prosperity and possibility that contrasts with its English equivalent's moral as well as economic impoverishment.

Lambert home. Country estate of Colonel, later General, Martin Lambert, his wife, and their two daughters in Oakhurst, England. When Harry Warrington suffers a highway accident outside their door, the Lamberts care for him and in the process provide a welcome alternative to what Harry has so far experienced among the English upper classes. The Lamberts' interest in Harry's well-being is not motivated by thoughts of pecuniary gain, but arises from a genuine concern for him as a person who is in need of their assistance. The Lamberts and their simple, unaffected approach to life, which is reflected in their unpretentious but comfortable and efficiently run home, represent those traditional English values that the novel sees as threatened by the unprincipled greed of Lord Castlewood and his cronies.

Lambert apartment. London residence of the Lambert family—a place as pleasant and welcoming as their country house. It is here that George and Harry fall in love with the Lamberts' daughters amid further scenes of what the narrative pictures as a nurturing family life.

*Bailiff's house.** Cursitor Street, London, jail in which Harry is imprisoned for debt after gambling losses and injudicious purchases on credit. That his relatives sanction his incarceration in this bleak, friendless institution underlines how completely they have abandoned him. It is only the reappearance of his brother, George—held captive by the French but finally ransomed—that rescues Harry from his plight. His brother's blood, at least, proves to be thicker than water.

*London.** Capital of Great Britain and center of English social and cultural life, and the background to approximately half of the narrative. As in many of William Makepeace Thackeray's other novels, notably *Vanity Fair* (1848), London is viewed as a vital, complex, and rather dangerous place, in which high artistic achievement and highway robbery are equally likely to occur.

*Tunbridge Wells.** Resort community for the upper classes about fifty miles southeast of London. The rise and fall of social reputation is the common currency of life at "The Wells," where rumors of Harry's wealth have preceded him and he is much sought after by marriageable young women and their monstrously ambitious mothers. The town's obsession with superficial values is portrayed as a more concentrated case of what is wrong with English society in general.

— *Paul Stuewe*

VOLPONE: Or, The Fox

Author: Ben Jonson (1573-1637)
Type of work: Drama
Type of plot: Social satire

Time of plot: Sixteenth century
First performed: 1605; first published, 1607

The principal setting of Ben Jonson's play is Venice, whose ornate and colorful architecture, canals, and gondolas connote wealthy decadence, perversion, and thriving criminality.

Volpone's house (vohl-POH-nay). Home of the Venetian magnifico, whose name means "fox." With an outer gallery or waiting room for dupes and a dazzling treasure cache, piles of gold, plate, and jewels hidden behind the rear-stage curtain, Volpone's house is a handy location for storing the rich gifts of solicitous visitors. When guests are present, the drawn curtains hide this shrine to wealth, and the foxlike Volpone stretches out on his sickbed in gown, furs, and nightcap, as his servant, Mosca, ushers in the assorted base creatures.

Hiding places are important to this set, for Bonario must observe Volpone's revelation of ardent passion unseen, just as Voltore must overhear Mosca and Corbaccio. Curtains close around Volpone on his couch as Mosca at a desk inventories the supposed inheritance of hopefuls.

Corvino's house (kohr-VEE-noh). Home of a Venetian merchant, near St. Mark's Place. The location attracts pickpockets, con artists, and schemers of every stripe. Corvino's wife Cecelia looks down from a balcony, which opens into a room in Corvino's house where he chides her. In front of the house, Mosca and a servant erect a stage for a medicine vendor to display his wares, and a disguised Volpone mounts the platform and haggles over high-priced quackery.

— *Andrew Macdonald and Gina Macdonald*

VOLUPTÉ

Author: Charles-Augustin Sainte-Beuve (1804-1869)
Type of work: Novel
Type of plot: Psychological realism

Time of plot: Early nineteenth century
First published: 1834 (English translation, 1995)

A pivotal text, Volupté *is the last echo of the Jean-Jacques Rousseau-inspired cult of sensibility and the departure point of a tradition that culminated in the Symbolist movement. Within its pages sensibility evolves—or decays—into sensuality (the closest translation of* volupté *that English can offer), which reconstructs perception so as to transform French landscapes, the buildings they contain, and the weather that disturbs them into allegorical representations of the irrational element of the human psyche.*

La Gastine (lah gas-TEEN). Isolated farmhouse in a remote part of the northern French region of Brittany; a calculatedly unostentatious one-story edifice set in a fertile plain interrupted by beech trees. It is the home of the Greneuc family, whose daughter, Amélie, Amaury might have married had he been so inclined; it symbolizes the quiet desolation of conventional rural existence.

Château de Couaën (SHAH-toh deh kwah-EH[N]). House about six miles distance from La Gastine, set in more precipitous country near a barren coast. It is equally remote, but even more ancient and forbidding, having served in bygone eras as a fortress. Its tower and ramparts survive, but only two of its floors remain in use, the upper one serving as the marquis' study, library, and bedroom. The garret is now a rat-infested granary. The château plays host to futile secret gatherings of the antirevolutionary French nobility. Madame Couaën's room is, however, exceptional; when Amaury first enters it, everything—polished antique furniture, porcelain, Irish crystal—seems to be shining.

Saint-Pierre-de-Mer (sahn-pyehr-de-mer). Mountain chapel overlooking a boulder-strewn bay, maintained by Madame Couaën—who contrasts the wild landscape in which it is set with her native Ireland. The ruins of a stone watch tower stand on the edge of the cliff, where the marquis decides to raise and keep a lighthouse after his wife's death. Amaury's obsession with the imagery of water begins at Saint-Pierre; once he has been there he continually thinks of human emotions in terms of their analogy with bodies of water, afflicted by tides and waves. When Amaury imagines the souls of the Couaëns as an allegorical painting whose centerpiece is a calm but misty lake fed by streams overflowing into waterfalls, he is echoing Madame Couaën's contradictory response to Saint-Pierre. It is significant that when Amaury first sets out for America, the tempestuous ocean drives his ship back to the Portuguese shore.

Madame de Couaën's childhood home (deh kwah-EH[N]). House situated a mile from Kildare on Ireland's Curragh River, idealized in Amaury's imagination on the basis of her description. The library's arched windows are surrounded by honeysuckle and roses; boxed myrtles and potted carnations decorate the terraced lawn. When the Couaëns' doomed son Arthur makes a little garden in the woods he calls it "Kildare."

Vacquerie's house (VAK-ehr-ee). Country house situated about one mile from the Château de Couaën; although it is surrounded by woodland, reached by sinuous paths, it is an intrusion of modernity; its facilities include a Barbary organ, an opticon, and a microscope.

Druid Island. Islet off the Breton coast, reputedly a sacred site of Druid religion, now pockmarked by the ruins of a Christian monastery. Amaury imagines himself living there alone, but finds it intimidating at night.

*Paris. France's capital city, on whose outskirts Amaury and the Couaëns always remain. They initially stay in a small religious community run by Madame de Cursy near Val-de-Grâce (whose famous convent became a military hospital), and later in Auteuil. Paris seems to Amaury to be ostentatious and feverish; his peregrinations aggravate his sensuality, except for his excursions to the Jardin des Plantes to hear the Chevalier de Lamarck expound his theory of evolution—whose worldview seems to him stark and dolorous. During later visits much of Amaury's time is spent visiting the marquis at the Sainte-Pélagie prison and the hospice at Passy. He eventually finds solace, however, in a library of religious works on the rue des Maçons-Sorbonne. During Amaury's brief flirtation with the idea of volunteering for military service, he and Captain Remi avidly trace the progress of one of Napoleon Bonaparte's campaigns on a map; however, when Amaury leaves Paris it is to go to an unidentified seminary, and then—after a final pilgrimage to Couaën—to America. When he finally achieves peace of mind he envisages himself in a calm sea, approaching the bank.

— Brian Stableford

THE VOYAGE OUT

Author: Virginia Woolf (1882-1941)
Type of work: Novel
Type of plot: Psychological realism

Time of plot: Early twentieth century
First published: 1915

The fictional town of Santa Marina and idealized images of London city life provide the backdrop for this novel's critique of the socially prescriptive behavior of Victorian culture. The tourist life at a Santa Marina hotel contrasted with Rachel Vinrace's freedom at the Villa San Gervasios characterize the nature-versus-nurture controversy at the center of this novel.

*London. Great Britain's capital city serves as a contrast to Santa Marina, which is represented by its "primitiveness." The novel opens as Helen and Ridley Ambrose hurry along the Embankment, a walkway along the River Thames, in order to board a ship to Santa Marina. The Thames symbolizes the strength of British commerce, culture, and colonization. Also mentioned in the novel are Richmond, a comfortable suburb south of London, where Rachel lives with her aunts, and Bloomsbury, a London neighborhood characterized by the intellectuals and bohemians who live there.

Euphrosyne (yew-FROH-seen). Ship owned by Willoughby Vinrace on which Rachel and others travel to Santa Marina. On this ship Rachel is expected to function as hostess for her father, signaling the beginning of her feminine education. The characters on the *Euphrosyne* form a microcosm of English society, which includes the servants, the middle class (Ambroses), the political elite (the Dalloways), and an eccentric scholar (Pepper). These types are also found among the English tourists at the Santa Marina hotel and together they represent an idealization of England as culturally sophisticated. On the ship the travelers discuss cultural and political activities in London. For instance, the sea reminds them of the British Royal Navy, a symbol of patriotism in postcolonial Great Britain. The voyage is also reminiscent of mythologized western sea voyages embarking on discoveries not only of new territories but also of human strengths and foibles; Rachel becomes the focus of this voyage. In this sense, the *Euphrosyne* sets the stage for Rachel's self-discovery and self-realization. Euphrosyne, a word which means joy, was one of the three Graces, Greek goddesses who presided over social events, and is thus significant to Rachel's socialization.

Santa Marina. Fictional South American town where most of the action takes place. In this exotic setting Rachel might discover herself free from the usual Victorian restrictions for women. However, because the English tourists transport their class and gender expectations to the natural, unpretentious Santa Marina setting, Rachel does not escape the restrictions of Victorian society. The hotel that houses the English tourists and the Villa San Gervasio, where Rachel stays with the Ambroses, symbolize her struggle to find herself. Exoticized and romanticized through its picturesque mountains, dusty villages, and astonishing vistas, the landscape is depicted in an impressionistic manner which implies a freedom of vision, allowing Rachel the opportunity to develop free from the Victorian standards represented by the hotel guests. The tropical heat, cool water, and glorious lighting symbolize a fearful sensuality that directs Rachel toward self-discovery.

River. Several English tourists, including Rachel and her soon-to-be fiancé Terence Hewet, take an excursion upriver to explore remote inland villages. On the trip they pass into an edenic landscape with brilliant flora, eerie lighting, and mysterious animals. In this setting Rachel and Terence lose their inhibitions and fears about each other and about marriage and declare their love for each other. This primordial river setting enhances the contrast between the Santa Marina landscape and the urbane setting of the hotel. As the group makes its way into the heart of the jungle, its members demonstrate their snobbish attitudes about the indigenous people and their culture. Their judgmental opinions serve to criticize British colonialism and suggest shallow humanitarian values at the center of Victorian society. After this surreal voyage on the river, Rachel obtains confirmation of her entrance into society, represented by her marriage proposal. However, she suddenly falls ill and dies at the moment her socialization is complete. Ironically the marriage proposal both literally and figuratively eradicates her identity.

— *Kathryn N. Benzel*

WAITING FOR GODOT

Author: Samuel Beckett (1906-1989)
Type of work: Drama
Type of plot: Absurdist

Time of plot: Indeterminate
First published: 1952; first performed, 1953 as *En attendant Godot* (English translation, 1954)

This play about two tramps waiting for the arrival of a mysterious entity, identified only as "Godot," could be set almost anywhere. The spare simplicity of its set and its lack of specific locales exemplifies Samuel Beckett's minimalist aesthetic and gives the plight of his characters a timeless universality.

Country road. Unnamed road, alongside which Vladimir and Estragon await the arrival of Godot. No clues are given to identify the location, whose terrain is a flat and unbroken plain to the distant horizon. In a ditch nearby, Estragon has spent the night, despite beatings by an unknown "they." In effect, the road stretches to and from nowhere in particular, although Pozzo says he is leading his servant, Lucky, down the road to a fair. Pozzo's claim that he owns the land is not necessarily true. Although Vladimir refers to past experiences together atop the Eiffel Tower in Paris and grape-picking "in the Macon country," Estragon claims that he has never been in Macon country and has "puked [his] puke of a life away here . . . in the Cackon country." None of these claims is verifiable.

Despite Beckett's insistence that productions of his plays should always adhere to his specifications, the austere set he intended for this play has occasionally been radically altered by stage designers. For example, the set of the 1988 Broadway production of *Waiting for Godot* designed by Tony Walton was a stretch of Nevada highway, cluttered with debris and abandoned car parts.

Tree. Sole landmark by the road that helps direct Vladimir and Estragon to where they are to meet Godot. The scraggly tree is bare in the play's first act. Although no other trees can be seen, Vladimir and Estragon are uncertain that this is the correct tree by which they should be waiting. Indeed, they think it might not be a tree at all, but rather a shrub or a bush. Vladimir suggests that it might be a willow but admits that he does not know. He also suggests that the tree may be dead. However, when the second act opens there are four or five leaves on the tree, proving that the tree is alive and that an indeterminable length of time has passed.

Beckett reportedly told a biographer that *Waiting for Godot* was inspired by Kaspar David Friedrich's painting *Two Men Observing the Moon*, in which such a tree figures prominently.

Low mound. Slight slope of land on which Estragon sits at the beginning of the play, struggling to remove his boot. This is the only other feature of the landscape mentioned in the stage directions.

— *William Hutchings*

A WALK ON THE WILD SIDE

Author: Nelson Algren (Nelson Ahlgren Abraham, 1909-1981)
Type of work: Novel

Type of plot: Picaresque
Time of plot: 1930's
First published: 1956

This novel is a quintessential Depression-era story that presents the wildly humorous as well as sad experiences of Dove Linkhorn. The pattern of his travels and his adventures, the ups and downs of his station in life, is cast in the ancient tradition of the picaresque novel dating back to Miguel de Cervantes' famous picaro, Don Quixote. That tradition typically involves travel, and Dove moves from Texas's Rio Grande Valley to New Orleans.

Arroyo. Town in southern Texas's Rio Grande Valley where Dove begins his adventures. His father, Fitz Linkhorn, originally went there in the early twentieth century from Virginia. The valley orange trees scented the air and yielded an abundance of fruit each year. Cotton crops were equally bountiful, and oil was soon discovered in the area. Within a year, however, the oil dried up and the crops failed. As a result of these problems, Dove leaves on his travels, but at the end of the novel, he returns to Arroyo, blind, defeated, and no longer the innocent young man who originally left the place.

*Houston. Large southeastern Texas city to which Dove first goes after leaving Arroyo. From there he moves from one hobo camp to another in the Rio Grande Valley, living with and learning from men who have been dispossessed of jobs and homes by the Depression. The starkness of the hobo camps educates Dove in the realities of the Depression-era world. In each "hobo jungle," he learns a new lesson of life, just as traditional picaresque heroes always do.

*New Orleans. Louisiana's major city, where Dove arrives at the height of the Depression. As a city of the Old South, to which the Civil War and Reconstruction had already brought dire economic changes, New Orleans is a particularly impoverished place in the 1930's.

Nevertheless, its diverse shops, restaurants, and fascinating people make it appealing to Dove. The various neighborhoods in which he lives and works—mainly in the French Quarter and Perdido Street—are mostly slums, inhabited by poor whites and African Americans struggling to eke out meager existences doing whatever is required of them. Despite its problems, New Orleans is a place in which people have fun. For Dove, it is a place that always seems to be "rocking."

Algren portrays New Orleans as place filled with corrupt businessmen and politicians. Not only is the corruption tolerated by politicians and the clergy, it is even encouraged by some of them. Houses of prostitution and other establishments that would be forbidden in other cities operate openly.

Dove takes on a variety of jobs: coffee salesman; door-to-door con man, condom maker, and salesman; Watkins Products salesman; and finally actor in a fake show in which he pretends to deflower "virgins" in a brothel. These jobs reflect the New Orleans of 1931 and its decayed, impoverished state at the time. They also reflect the standard elements of the picaresque novel in which innocent and ignorant protagonists learn about life from their difficult encounters in unusual places.

— *W. Kenneth Holditch*

THE WANDERER

Author: Alain-Fournier (Henri-Alain Fournier, 1886-1914)
Type of work: Novel
Type of plot: Psychological

Time of plot: Nineteenth century
First published: Le Grand Meaulnes, 1913 (English translation, 1928)

In this novel a search for a mysterious French estate that Augustin Meaulnes discovers and then loses is symbolic of his desire for the beautiful but seemingly unattainable Yvonne de Galais and for a perfect, idealized love.

Sainte-Agathe. French village where Francois Seurel spends most of his childhood. His parents are the village schoolteachers and the family lives in the buildings of the secondary school, which is at the far end of the village, bounded by a road, gardens, and meadows. The schoolhouse is large and much of it remains unused. For Seurel, it is the only world he knows, as a disability has kept him from exploring the countryside with the other village boys. This changes with the arrival of Augustin Meaulnes, who encourages him to become more independent. Even at this stage, Seurel's knowledge of the village does not extend beyond its main streets. When he and Meaulnes are obliged to enter a quarter known as the Petits-Coins, Seurel knows only one street in the area, that which leads to his mother's dressmaker. Places beyond the village are little more than names allied to the method of transport needed to reach them. Seurel and Meaulnes, who come from some distance away, have little awareness of the area's geography, which is why they cannot identify the mysterious domain visited by Meaulnes.

French countryside. The landscape beyond the village is rural, a mixture of fields and woods. In winter, when the reader is first introduced to the area, it is bleak and deserted. In fact, Meaulnes is almost literally in the dark as most of his journey to and from the domain occurs either in the late afternoon or at night. Emphasis is placed on the emptiness and the difficulty of traveling; it is an inward-turning landscape. The summer landscape consists of green woodland, clear streams, and dusty roads, where people hunt and swim, cycle or walk, an outward-looking landscape. It is significant that while Meaulnes first discovered the lost domain in the depths of winter, it is only relocated in the height of summer.

Les Sablonnières (lay sah-blawn-NYEHR). Estate of the de Galais family, comprising a house, outbuildings, and gardens, built around a courtyard, mirroring the layout of the school at Sainte-Agathe. Augustin Meaulnes discovers it when he becomes hopelessly lost in the country lanes beyond Saint-Agathe. His first view of the estate is of the spire of a turret rising above the trees, and Meaulnes assumes that it is an abandoned manor house. Closer inspection reveals that while the outbuildings and garden are run-down and derelict, the main house is nonetheless still inhabited and, unusually for winter, preparing for a festival. The freedom afforded by the festival enables Meaulnes to explore the entire domain and to meet Yvonne de Galais, the daughter of the house. When Meaulnes finally returns to Les Sablonnières to propose marriage to Yvonne de Galais, he finds that the estate is much smaller, the land having been sold to pay debts incurred by Frantz de Galais.

*Paris. Capital of France to which Meaulnes goes in his quest to find Yvonne de Galais after finishing his schooling at Sainte-Agathe. There he looks for an address given to him by Yvonne's brother. The house he finds is closed up, and he does not see her. Meaulnes later returns to Paris to locate Valentine Blondeau, Frantz's fiancé, who lives close to Notre-Dame.

Le Vieux-Nançay (luh vyuh-nawn-SAY). Village that Seurel describes as his favorite place in the world; however, his description concentrates on one building: the shop kept by his uncle at the edge of the town. Also, although Seurel only discovers this after Meaulnes has left, the village is close to Meaulnes's mysterious domain.

La Ferté d'Angillon (lah fer-TAY DAHN-yohn). Small village where Augustin Meaulnes lives with his widowed mother. Seurel visits it for the first time as an adult, having cycled from Sainte-Agathe, and his description of it is notable for including details of the village itself, rather than concentrating on the house's interiors.

Saint-Benoist-des-Champs (sah[n]-ben-wahst-day-SHAN). Hamlet whose school stands isolated at the crossroads, this is where Seurel is appointed schoolmaster. It is also within an hour's walk of Les Sablonnières, where Seurel visits Yvonne de Galais regularly. After her death, he lives at the domain and walks to the school.

— *Maureen Speller*

THE WANDERING JEW

Author: Eugène Sue (1804-1857)
Type of work: Novel
Type of plot: Melodrama

Time of plot: 1831-1832
First published: Le Juif errant, 1844-1845 (English translation, 1868)

As with most successful novels originally published in installments, The Wandering Jew *ranges far and wide— here, within the city of Paris—although the heirs to the Rennepont fortune must initially make their way there from various distant parts. The plague-ridden city swallows and ultimately devours all but one of them, who is permitted to withdraw, without a fortune, to a rural refuge with a handful of other survivors.*

***Paris.** France's capital city, the focal point of the novel, is minutely defined as the Red Room in number 3, rue Saint François, the house where the heirs to the fortune are instructed to assemble on February 13, 1832, and then reassemble on June 1. It is near the rue Saint-Gervais and the rue Doré in the Marais district.

Other significant settings in the novel are numerous but would be tightly clustered if plotted on a map. In the rue du Milieu-des-Ursins, off the quai Napoleon near rue Landry, Rodin serves as secretary to the abbé d'Aigrigny. The Baudouin house, where Dagobert's wife Agricola and Mother Bunch live, is in the rue Brise-Miche, near the Church of Saint-Méry. The sumptuous Saint-Dizier town house, in which Adrienne is introduced, is number 7, rue de Babylone. The Comte de Montbron lives at 7, place Vendôme. Baleiner's asylum, where Adrienne is confined, is next door to St. Mary's Convent, where Rose and Blanche are secreted; the convent's gardens look out on to the boulevard de l'Hôpital.

Mother Arsène's shop, where Rodin rents the rooms where he keeps his picture inscribed "Sara Papa," is 4, rue Clovis, in Montagne St. Geneviève. Djalma is established by the treacherous Faringhea in a house in the rue Blanche. After her release from the asylum Adrienne takes up residence in the rue d'Anjou. The Jesuits' retreat, which becomes a highly significant setting in the late phases of the plot, is at the end of the rue Vaugirard. Marshal Simon lives in the rue des Trois-Frères. The temporary hospital where Morok dies of rabies and the cholera epidemic claims the lives of Rose and Blanche is in the rue de Mont-Blanc. Saint-Colombe's house, where Adrienne and Djalma perish, is in the rue de Richelieu.

Famous Parisian landmarks used as backdrops for important scenes include the Champs-Elysées, the Porte-Saint-Martin theater, and the square of Nôtre-Dame, where the cholera masquerade takes place. The Wandering Jew looks down on the city from the crest of Montmartre, where—unknown to Sue—the famous basilica of Sacré-Coeur was later to be constructed. The abbey of St. John where Herodias experiences her vision does not appear to be in Paris, although she was there earlier; its actual location is not specified.

Möckern (mewk-ehrn). German village two miles northwest of Leipzig. The site of a French defeat in the Napoleonic Wars, it is a significant choice for the location of the **White Falcon**, the inn in which Morok attacks Dagobert, Rose, and Blanche in the novel's opening chapters, eventually contriving to have them imprisoned in Leipzig.

***Batavia** (bah-TAY-vee-ah). Major port on the island of Java (now part of Indonesia). Although a native of India (his father was king of the hill state of Mundi), Djalma is living there when he narrowly escapes death at the hands of the strangler—who then retreats to the ruins of Tchandi, about nine miles to the west. Djalma is imprisoned in Batavia before setting sail for France.

Château de Cardoville (shah-TOH deh car-doh-VEEL). Adrienne's family home, situated on the cliffs of Picardy, not far from Saint Valery. Rodin visits it before the *Black Eagle* goes down within sight of it; Rose, Blanche, and Djalma are among the survivors who are brought there.

***Plessis** (PLEH-see). Town near Paris where François Hardy's ill-fated factory is situated. The village of Villiers, where conspiracies are hatched against him, is close by.

*Bering Strait. Stretch of ocean that separates Siberia from Alaska, serving in this novel as the symbolically loaded venue at which the Wandering Jew and Herodias signal to each other from opposite shores before the Wandering Jew wends his weary way to Paris from the Siberian cape.

Springwater Farm. Rural retreat, near the village of Saint-Aubin in the Sologne region of France's Loire valley, to which Gabriel and the other survivors of the plot's attrition eventually retire.

— *Brian Stableford*

THE WAPSHOT CHRONICLE

Author: John Cheever (1912-1982)

Type of work: Novel

Type of plot: Social realism

Time of plot: 1890's-1950's

First published: 1957

This novel is an account of an old New England family in the fictitious town of St. Botolphs, John Cheever's recreation of an inland port that had been a commercial center during the great days of sailing fleets. By the midtwentieth century, the town is reduced to a minor manufacturing location and tourist site. For the Wapshot family, however, it is home ground, a comforting and familiar place where every feature of topography and nearly every shop and street has resonance and meaning. The Wapshots' forays into the world beyond are a kind of displacement where they are generally uneasy and uncertain, separated from the support of a world which defines their values and validates their character.

St. Botolphs. Small Massachusetts town with a distinguished past that has been experiencing an economic, intellectual, and spiritual decline since the middle of the nineteenth century. The town is emblematic of the shift in emphasis from New England to other regions of the United States in postcolonial times. Cheever models St. Botolphs on the classic arrangement of many towns in areas around Boston, with a central square that is the focus of social and commercial life, and other characteristic geographic features like a hill rising above the square, a river running from the hills toward the coast, and farmlands stretching toward the mountains in the north.

Aside from the descriptive details which evoke the terrain, Cheever uses references to the way the scents of the location—particularly the aroma of various bodies and courses of water—contribute to the psychological atmosphere of the narrative, and to the moods of the characters. Captain Leander Wapshot is exhilarated by the "brine-smelling summer days" as he sails toward the bay beyond Boston harbor. The festival commemorating Independence Day is darkened by the dark, raw smell of mud. Mrs. Wapshot is touched by melancholy, epitomized by her taste for the smell of orange rinds and wood smoke.

Wapshot house. St. Botolphs home of the Wapshot family, a large house beside the river on land that was part of a farm in earlier days. This house and other individual homes and shops have acquired a distinctive identity through a local oral tradition and are like landmarks in an internalized map of the mind that long-term residents instinctively understand and relate to. Across the river, which is like a national boundary, families who speak Italian are regarded as foreigners and treated as a lesser species.

Travertine. Small market town, four miles from St. Botolphs, on the main road to Boston. Travertine is the commercial component of the social matrix, a complement to the church, meetinghouse, and elegant domains of St. Botolphs, where the Wapshots and their neighbors acquire provisions and regularly see the members of the community with whom they might not interact otherwise.

*Boston. Capital of Massachusetts and central city of New England, a powerful presence affecting everyone in the area but not a constant part of the lives of the Wapshots. It is the beginning of the outer world which to the inhabitants of the novel is a scattered and uncertain place, lacking the comforting features of the familiar.

Nangasakit. Resort town on the Atlantic coast, with small bungalows for visitors, modest houses for residents, the standard attractions of a tourist economy, and the appeal of the coastal waters and the topography of the beaches and dunes.

Langeley. Settlement with a post office and a general store on the fringes of the wilderness north of Boston toward New Hampshire and French Canada, where the Wapshot men fish in ponds deep in the woods. Moses Wapshot thinks that the landscape is enthralling, but Cheever calls it an ugly and treacherous place. Langeley affords the men opportunities to be without women, in a place where their absence is conspicuous.

*Washington, D.C., and **New York City.* Distant metropolitan areas to which Moses and Coverly Wap-shot venture to establish themselves as independent men. They are never comfortable in these urban centers, however, and meet an array of unfathomable and strange characters. Coverly is stationed for a while in Honolulu, and then posted to a rocket base called Remsen Park somewhere in the Northeast. Moses spends some time at Clear Haven, an opulent mansion in the suburbs near New York City, where he is involved with a vulpine family of wealthy predators. These settings are essentially isolated islands in vague terrain, where the central characters in the novel find themselves contending with forces and social patterns that highlight, by contrast, the mores and historic verities that have accrued to St. Botolphs through two centuries of settlement.

— *Leon Lewis*

THE WAPSHOT SCANDAL

Author: John Cheever (1912-1982)
Type of work: Novel
Type of plot: Social satire

Time of plot: Early 1960's
First published: 1964

This novel continues the story of brothers Moses and Coverley Wapshot begun in The Wapshot Chronicle, *taking them from their young manhood in the decade following World War II through the turbulent and transitional times of the 1960's. As was the case in the first novel, John Cheever uses the Wapshot's ancestral New England home as an oasis of integrity in a chaotic world. Nearly every other location in the novel is presented, by contrast, as evidence of a decline in the quality of life. The sense of loss that pervades the narrative is built on a loving portrait of a vanishing community that Cheever eulogizes in his vision of an almost mythic New England town.*

St. Botolphs. Massachusetts town, introduced in *The Wapshot Chronicle* as an old river town, that becomes in *The Wapshot Scandal* a seat of virtue and value in a corrupting, debased world. Cheever recapitulates his presentation of the town in the first pages of the second book, beginning with the square in the town's center and then moving out to show the shops and homes which, in their individual characteristics, exemplify the positive attributes that Cheever admires.

In spite of the inevitable pressures wrought by changing economic conditions, the town is still a place of decorum and relative tranquillity. Its comparative insularity, which makes it seem quaint and old-fashioned, affords a place of refuge to its inhabitants, so that Coverly Wapshot exclaims on its "pathos and beauty" after re-turning from the outside world. He regards his aunt Honora's bizarre behavior as one of the "eccentric niceties" of the village.

At the book's close, Cheever steps out of the omniscient authority of the narrative to compose an envoi to his real/fictional setting, admitting "I love this water and its shores; love it absurdly as if I could marry the view." The novel is his paean to a place that he feared was soon to be lost forever. On the last page of the novel, Cheever regretfully states about St. Botolphs, "I will never come back" and adds, "if I do there will be nothing left . . . there will really be nothing at all."

Talifer. Newly developed suburb near Boston that is the site of a missile research and development facility and a planned tract of homes for most of the people working at the complex. Coverly is employed there (until he loses his security clearance) and lives with his wife Betsey and young son in a nondescript mixed neighborhood, in which no one speaks to neighbors.

As Cheever conceives Talifer, it is an emblem of scientific heartlessness, cold and mechanistic, and inhabited by people who seem like robots, drones, and drudges. Its computer programmers and technicians are as eccentric as the residents of St. Botolphs, but their quirks tend to be antisocial, unfriendly, coarse, and often embarrassing. The sameness of the insubstantial houses that makes them seem to smell of shirt cardboard is set against distant mountains, which are the products of natural forces. Much of Cheever's satire of contemporary America is built on Talifer's repulsiveness.

*Rome. Capital city of Italy in which the worst of the rest of the world is objectified. In spite of its reputation as the "eternal city," Rome is used by Cheever to stand for non-American ugliness. When Moses Wapshot's wife Melissa visits Rome on an adulterous tryst, she experiences "Roman Blues"; when Honora is in Rome she

is swindled and confused; Melissa's paramour Emile experiences a "suspension of conscience" in Naples when he participates in an auction of sexual favors. The Italian landscape exemplifies for Cheever a mood which he describes as "autumn in a European city with war forever in the air."

Proxmire Manor. Upscale suburb on three leafy hills north of New York City that Cheever contrasts with nearby Parthenia.

Parthenia. Ramshackle small town on the outskirts of New York City where the tradespeople who work for residents of Proxmire's opulent mansions live. While Proxmire has "palatial" shopping centers, Parthenia's few remaining stores are mostly deserted. Parthenia's streets are dirty and dangerous. Whereas Proxmire is "handsome and comfortable," Parthenia is a forecast of a future for once-thriving rural communities (like St. Botolphs) which had functioned as vital places where the local railroad station had "the rich aura of arrivals" prior to their current demise.

— *Leon Lewis*

WAR AND PEACE

Author: Leo Tolstoy (1828-1910)
Type of work: Novel
Type of plot: Historical

Time of plot: 1805-1813
First published: Voyna i mir, 1865-1869 (English translation, 1886)

Leo Tolstoy's monumental classic of Russian literature follows three Russian noble families through the epic crisis of the Napoleonic Wars. The wide-ranging novel covers both Russian and Western European events and touches upon almost every aspect of human existence. However, Tolstoy intended the book as merely the beginning of an even longer work that would have carried the protagonists through Russia's unsuccessful 1825 December Revolution.

*St. Petersburg. Capital of Imperial Russia amid whose high society Tolstoy introduces his novel's major players through the mechanism of a formal party. In many ways Tolstoy portrays St. Petersburg as an empty place, of people who only pretend to live—a view in line with a long tradition in Russian literature that St. Petersburg is an unnatural city in which reality is at best tenuous. Even while central Russia is being invaded by

Napoleon's French army and Moscow is endangered, rounds of parties and social activities continue unabated in St. Petersburg, although there is much talk about war and self-sacrifice.

St. Petersburg is also the place where Pierre Bolkonsky is initiated into the mysteries of Freemasonry, an experience that he finds profoundly meaningful. He later becomes disillusioned when his fellow Masons do not want to get their hands dirty with real social reform work and reject his suggestions for a world shadow government that would advise and reshape the world's governments in accordance with Christian principles.

*Moscow. Traditional capital of Russia. Here the Rostovs live, closer to what Tolstoy regards as the real heart of Russia than the glittering stone palaces of St. Petersburg. Although Moscow is no longer the official seat of the imperial Russian government during the period in which the novel is set, its citadel known as the Kremlin still retains important cultural and ceremonial roles. Czar Alexander visits the Kremlin, leading to a near-riot among a mob of people gathered to adore him.

Because of Moscow's deep cultural significance, it becomes the primary target of Napoleon's thrust to conquer Russia. However, Napoleon's taking of the Kremlin proves to be a hollow victory, for his forces arrive after the residents of the city have already fled after setting fire to the wooden buildings to deny the French any profit from their invasion.

Bleak Hills. Estate of Prince Nikolai Andreivich Bolkonsky. The hills are a microcosm of rural Russia, where the prince lives as the master of his domain, with everything precisely ordered in accordance with his will. However, his comfortable certainty is soon swept away by Napoleon's invasion. In Bleak Hills the old prince's son Andrei sees his wife die giving birth and is tormented by guilt at his inability to relieve her suffering. When Napoleon's armies approach, the peasants panic and refuse to help their landlord's family flee to Moscow, and the old prince dies of apoplexy amid the ensuing chaos.

*Branau (BRAH-now). Battle site where Nikolai Rostov is stationed. When he publicly reports a fellow hussar for theft, he is accused of lying and in turn calls his colonel a liar. Although Rostov comes to agree that his public denunciation has compromised the regiment's honor, he refuses to apologize to the colonel.

*Vienna. Capital of the Holy Roman Empire (later of Austria). General Kutuzov falls back to it, burning his bridges along the way, in a desperate attempt to consolidate his forces and hold Napoleon's forces back. During this retreat Nikolai Rostov comes under fire for the first time, an incident Tolstoy uses to show the chaos and insanity of battle.

*Austerlitz. Battle at which Prince Andrei Bolkonsky is badly wounded. Here Tolstoy shows the fog of battle. Although "fog" is usually a metaphor in military jargon for the confused state of communications and intelligence during intense combat, here it is a literal fog into which the Russian and Austrian soldiers charge. Amid this confusion, Andrei grabs a fallen flag and urges his soldiers into a heroic charge against the French, but few follow and he is hit by enemy fire. He is then captured by Napoleon, whom he idolizes in a confused way.

*Tilsit (TIHL-siht). East Prussian town (now a Russian town called Sovetsk) where Napoleon and Czar Alexander meet under truce. Nikolai Rostov is first horrified by the upstart Corsican's presumption of equality with the divine-right monarch of Russia, then confused as to how their sudden profession of friendship can be reconciled with the pile of amputated limbs in Denisov's infirmary.

*Borodino (bo-ro-DEE-no). Battle site about seventy miles west of Moscow where the Russians try to stop Napoleon's invasion. Here Tolstoy combines the historical and the fictional, both passing judgment upon the performance of Napoleon and General Kutuzov, and further developing the characters of Prince Andrei and Pierre.

*Tarutino (tah-roo-TEE-no). Battle site at which the Russians rout the French. Here Tolstoy shows Napoleon as the prisoner of the blind panic of his own army, while he fancies himself in command. Paradoxically, Pierre finds a strange freedom in being a prisoner of war, bereft of distractions such as titles and conveniences, reduced to his essential humanity.

— *Leigh Husband Kimmel*

THE WAR OF THE WORLDS

Author: H. G. Wells (1866-1946)
Type of work: Novel
Type of plot: Science fiction

Time of plot: Late nineteenth century
First published: 1898

This story of a Martian invasion of the safe and comfortable counties around London allows H. G. Wells to explore two familiar themes in his work. He suggests, at a time when Darwin was still a controversial figure, that the Victorian gentleman may not be the high point of evolution. At the same time, a popular strand of alarmist invasion stories had made these counties an imaginary battlefield.

***Horsell Common.** Rough, wooded landscape in Woking, on the edge of one of London's dormitory towns, where the first Martian cylinder comes down. It is a hint of wildness close to the heart of Victorian domesticity where the narrator and his fellows first have to come to terms with the nature of the invasion. The narrator, who writes about science, maintains a dispassionate voice, observing, reporting, and rarely judging, so the reader gets a clear record of how the Martians emerge from their cylinder, which is dug into a sandy pit. This pit is at first an amphitheater for the observers and later a trench within which the attackers prepare their weapons.

Fleeing the destruction, the narrator embarks on a zig-zag odyssey through the suburbs southwest of London, an area which highlights the destructive threat of the Martians by being supposedly safest and most prosperous.

***Weybridge.** Prosperous Surrey town on the River Thames where the narrator witnesses the first of the Martian war machines to be destroyed by a lucky artillery shot. This victory, however, is offset by the appearance of the curate, a weak and cowardly figure who is used to represent some of the worst aspects of human character.

***London.** Great Britain's capital city. The narrator's own eyewitness account of the invasion cannot encompass the whole picture that Wells wants to present, so he interpolates the story of the narrator's cousin in London, who is also a man of science and hence a dispassionate reporter. At first, away from the fighting and getting only confused and intermittent reports of what is happening in Surrey, the reader is given an image of a great Victorian city enjoying its wealth, power, and confidence. When reports do come through, the people initially behave well, but this confidence is quickly broken when London itself comes under attack. In the exodus from the city that then follows, kaleidoscopic scenes of panic, cruelty, greed, selfishness, and violence are presented. This image is set against that of heroism presented by the gunboat which manages to destroy two of the Martian war machines before being destroyed itself.

***Sheen.** Suburb of London. By this stage, the comfortable little towns on the outskirts of London have become ruined and depopulated, the very image of Victorian success laid low. It is in Sheen that the narrator and the curate become trapped in the cellar of a house when a Martian cylinder lands beside them. This allows, for the first time, close and prolonged observation of the Martians, during which the reader learns, for example, that they are using captured humans for food. However, this is contrasted with the final breakdown of the relationship between the narrator and the curate, as the latter tries to gorge on their small but carefully hoarded food supply.

***Putney Hill.** Suburb of London. After escaping from the ruined house, the narrator's journey takes him on along the south bank of the Thames toward London. It is on Putney Hill, at this point a landscape not unlike Horsell Common, that he meets again with the artilleryman with whom he had escaped from Woking. The narrator's odyssey has seen a gradual stripping away of the veneer of civilization, and the artilleryman now presents a fantasy of guerrilla warfare, of collaboration with the invaders, and of a new but far more primitive human society. It becomes clear that the artilleryman cannot even live up to the crude ideals of his new society: Victorian society, it is implied, is barely a step away from savagery. Meanwhile it is the narrator, the man of science, who is thus somewhat outside society, who goes on to London to discover the Martians killed by bacteria.

— *Paul Kincaid*

THE WARDEN

Author: Anthony Trollope (1815-1882)
Type of work: Novel
Type of plot: Social realism

Time of plot: Mid-nineteenth century
First published: 1855

This novel is set primarily in the fictional English cathedral town of Barchester, which provides the ecclesiastical location for the events involving the Warden, Mr. Harding, who finds himself the center of the conflict among the various forces of religious reform in mid-Victorian England.

Barchester. English town that Anthony Trollope based on the cathedral city of Salisbury in the west of England, as the locale for his novel about various ecclesiastical tensions and reforms and their cultural, economic, political, as well as religious implications. The mid-nineteenth century was a period of fervent upheaval in Victorian society, and the privileges and wealth of such institutions as the Church of England came under scrutiny. Barchester, because it is a community largely religious in character, with its religious buildings, political intrigue, and ethical dilemmas, provides a perfect place in which to explore those reforms and their effect on the guilty and the innocent—especially the warden, Mr. Harding.

Barchester Cathedral. Seat of the bishop of Barchester. The close, the building complex surrounding the cathedral, provides the main physical setting for the novel. The magnificent Gothic church and attached collateral structures and the remunerative livings that go with them present the target for both Trollope's satire and the reformer's jibes. Trollope describes the close and its occupants, as he does throughout the entire novel, in often contradictory ways. On one hand, the buildings and their occupants are unquestionably examples of a church rich in money and privilege, but they also represent a tradition rich in architectural beauty and in spiritual value. It is the tension between these conflicting views that proves the fuel for Trollope's narrative.

Hiram's hospital. Barchester hospital of which Mr. Harding is warden. It is a venerable institution devoted to the maintenance of twelve indigent old men of Barchester that is supported by an ancient beneficence, the bulk of whose income goes to the warden rather than to the old men. The hospital and its sinecure thus become a perfect target for the reformers, and especially after the hospital's financial arrangements come under attack by reforming zealots backed by the national newspaper, *The Jupiter*—Trollope's name for *The Times of London*. The physical location of the warden's residence on the close surrounding the cathedral points to its central place, both literally and symbolically, in Trollope's satirical look at Victorian religious institutions. Here, Harding and his unmarried daughter live in quiet comfort, unaware of the furor that is about to erupt. Harding goes about his rounds doing what good he can for his charges unaware of the discrepancy in the distribution of the founder's money. The somnambulant hospital grounds mirrors this lack of awareness.

Plumstead Episopi. Home of Archdeacon Grantly. Trollope's penchant for evocative names is clear in his calling this rather grand, overblown example of the Church of England's system of patronage, "Plumstead." As its name suggests, it is a "plum" of a place and is accompanied by a substantial salary. Although Grantly works hard at his job and is not a target of the reformers' crusade, his living and style of life provides another example of ecclesiastical excess which is satirized in the novel.

*Westminster Abbey. One of London's most famous landmarks, an eleventh century Gothic church that has been the site of most royal coronations and is the burial place of many of England's greatest figures. During an interlude near the end of the novel, Harding spends a contemplative afternoon at the abbey, where he wanders around the church sorting out the various options open to him concerning his position as warden. In the sanctity of the church, he makes up his mind about his fate. The abbey is an island of solitude in the sea of commercial London and therefore suited to Harding's character and temperament. It becomes the perfect place, away from all of the turmoil of Barchester, where he can make his unpopular but principled decision to leave his position.

— *Charles L. P. Silet*

WASHINGTON SQUARE

Author: Henry James (1843-1916)
Type of work: Novel
Type of plot: Psychological realism

Time of plot: c. 1850
First published: 1880

Most of this novel takes place in New York City. Although it focuses on the psychologies of its major characters, its delineations of place help express the qualities of its main character, Catherine Sloper.

*Washington Square. Fashionable neighborhood at the southern end of New York City's Manhattan borough that sits near the transition between the narrow, helter-skelter streets with quaint names of the original colonial settlement and the carefully planned grid of streets and avenues with numbers for names above the island's Fourth Street. Henry James himself was born near Washington Square.

Catherine's father, Dr. Austin Sloper, first lived near city hall in the older part of Manhattan, which by the time in which the novel is set was becoming commercialized and unfashionable. Dr. Sloper's late wife came from a neighborhood even farther south—the Battery. After her death, Dr. Sloper moves with his sister, Mrs. Penniman, and Catherine, to Washington Square itself. The novel provides a vivid picture of the Slopers' house: its front and back parlors; the doctor's study or library; Catherine's bedroom at the back, on the third floor; and Mrs. Penniman's bedroom on the same floor at the front of the house.

In the novel, the contrast between Washington Square and the city around it helps James to communicate the contrast between his central character, Catherine, and the world around her. Even though Dr. Sloper owns the house, readers are likely to see it as attuned to Catherine. She is a large, sensitive, intelligent, shy, guileless woman; her calm and steady character is at the heart of the novel. Moreover, she leaves Washington Square by herself only once, when she makes a desperate walk to Duane Street. As she is surrounded by her father, her aunt, and her would-be lover, Morris Townsend, so Washington Square itself is portrayed as an oasis of "established repose" in the midst of a "long, shrill city."

*New York City. Contrasts between Washington Square and New York City as a whole are furthered by other references to places in New York. Mrs. Montgomery's small house, not nearly so grand as Catherine's, is several blocks east on Second Avenue. Mrs. Penniman meets Townsend in lower-class or desolate neighborhoods: at an oyster saloon west of Washington Square on Seventh Avenue and at a street corner where they see vacant lots and unpaved streets. Mrs. Almond lives uptown on an embryonic street that has a number for its name.

New York is not only busy, it is changing: Old parts are torn down, and new houses and businesses spring up as new numbered streets are developed. Mrs. Montgomery's house is gone by the time the story is told. One enterprising young businessman remarks that he will buy a new house every five years to move north with the cutting edge of the bustling city. Amid all this activity Catherine remains still, an emblem of her constancy, her stability. Once she considers moving to a smaller brownstone house farther north, but decides to remain in Washington Square, which hardly changes itself.

*United States. Not only does the busy world of New York surround the calm of Washington Square, but readers also get hints of the energies of the nation beyond that city's boundaries. Townsend says he will go to New Orleans to buy cotton. He writes Catherine from Philadelphia.

*Europe. The Old World continent has two functions in this novel. Townsend's wanderings take him to Europe: He has been to Paris and London, and he knows some Spanish. Later, Catherine learns that Townsend has married a European woman.

European scenes also help to bring the conflict between Catherine and her father to a climax. In an attempt to make Catherine forget Townsend, Dr. Sloper takes her on a Grand Tour of Europe. They travel in Italy, Switzerland, and England. James tells his readers little about specific places, stating only that the relics of ancient civilizations make no impression on Catherine, with one exception. About halfway through the tour, Catherine and Dr. Sloper walk to a remote valley in the

Alps, where her father confronts her. When she refuses to give up Townsend, she thinks that her father might strangle her. Readers worry that Catherine's father might leave her behind. This scene, the closest the novel comes to exhibiting violence, is in an appropriately wild natural region thousands of miles from the quiet of Washington Square, Catherine's usual setting.

— *George Soule*

THE WASPS

Author: Aristophanes (c. 450-c. 385 B.C.E.)
Type of work: Drama
Type of plot: Satire

Time of plot: Fifth century B.C.E.
First performed: Sphēkes, 422 B.C.E. (English translation, 1812)

As is typical of all classical Greek drama, the action in this play occurs in public spaces—here a street in Athens in front of the house of Bdelycleon. The location is important because the play is concerned with the political situation in Athens, and since there is no faster means of disseminating information, all political news and attitudes must be obtained on the street or in the marketplace. By placing the action in a public street, Aristophanes invited identification with, and participation from, his contemporary audiences.

Athens street. Street scene outside the home of Bdelycleon (whose name means "Cleon hater"), where two slaves stand guard. They explain that their master is holding his old father, Philocleon ("Cleon lover"), captive inside the house to keep him from joining the other old jurors who follow the philosophy of the ruling tyrant Cleon by daily sentencing anyone brought before them, especially political prisoners. A chorus of old jurors, resembling wasps because of the way they "sting the accused," come to call for their colleague. The house is covered with a net, and although Philocleon attempts to escape by chewing through the net, he is restrained. To placate his father, Bdelycleon stages a mock trial of a dog. The dog, accused of stealing cheese, is tried in front of the house in much the same manner as all Athenian trials were staged outdoors and open to the public.

House of Bdelycleon (DEH-lih-klee-on). As a final gesture in changing the attitudes of his father, Bdelycleon takes him inside his house to introduce him to elite society. The audience does not see this indoor scene, but listens instead to the chorus of Wasps, being told about how the old man is insulting everyone inside. Soon Philocleon returns outdoors—to the proper location for action in a Greek play—with a young woman entertainer and challenges his old colleagues to a dance contest as the play ends.

— *August W. Staub*

THE WASTE LAND

Author: T. S. Eliot (1888-1965)
Type of work: Poetry

First published: 1922

This poem contrasts ancient and modern places to present a picture of the decline of civilization. Society in the ancient world, represented by centers of civilization including Jerusalem, Athens, Alexandria, Carthage, and Phoenicia, was sustained by religion and connections to history and tradition. In contrast, the modern world, represented by London and Europe, embodies the lack of connection to religion, tradition, or cultural heritage.

*London. Great Britain's capital city, a place cloaked in brown fog, is populated by people who walk in circles without connection to anything or anyone. The walk from London Bridge down King William Street leads past a church to the financial district, which for Eliot represents spiritual and cultural emptiness. Although the street, named after William the Conqueror, the first king of England, and the church carry important names in England's rich history and religious experience, the citizens take no note of them. Other scenes convey this spiritual emptiness: a tawdry sexual encounter between a clerk and a secretary in her shabby apartment and a conversation in a saloon involving an anxious pregnant woman concerned about how to deal with a pregnancy by another man now that her lover is returning from a tour of duty in the army.

*London Bridge. Historic bridge over the River Thames; a transcendental symbol of all that is good and promising in contemporary life, London Bridge leads to the city of the dead, to the loss of possibility and meaningful spiritual life.

*River Thames (tehmz). England's greatest river symbolizes a more romantic and joyful past and, in its present polluted condition, the spiritual emptiness of modern life. An elaboration of this symbolism comes in the reference to the Leman, the Swiss name for Lake Geneva, where Eliot was convalescing while writing this poem. Through the connection of watery sites, Eliot identifies with the biblical psalmist lamenting the spiritual desolation of the exiled Jews in Babylon.

*Europe. Selected sites in Europe also convey a sense of lack of roots or connection to the past. The references to the Starnberger See and the Hofgarten convey a sense of nostalgia for an earlier, more innocent time.

*Ganga. The water references to the Ganges, India's sacred river, and the dark clouds over Himavant, the Himalayan Mountains, symbolize the potential for spiritual renewal.

— *Richard Damashek*

WATCH ON THE RHINE

Author: Lillian Hellman (1905-1984)
Type of work: Drama
Type of plot: Melodrama

Time of plot: Late spring, 1940
First performed: 1941; first published, 1941

Set in the early days of World War II, this play juxtaposes the societal values of suburban Washington, D.C., with the harsh political realities affecting those living under the oppressive thumb of fascism in Europe. To the antifascist German Kurt Muller and his American wife, Sara Farrelly, home means very different things. Yet each seeks to find solace, in completely different ways, by returning home, and both want safety and peace for their families.

Farrelly country house. Suburban home of the distinguished Farrelly family, located outside Washington, D.C. The house's living room is the setting for most of the action in the play, literally and figuratively. The play's stage directions reveal that the room holds furniture from several different generations, "all people of taste." It is a busy room, with "too many things in it." Here people gather, argue, and get on with the business of life. The room represents prosperity and political connectedness, as well as Fanny's well-decorated life,

including her concern with appearances. It offers a closed view of the world she once shared with her late husband. For Sara it represents her former life, a life she sought to escape but now returns to as a kind of safety net with her family. The terrace off the living room is a place the family members and their guests go to breathe freely in the open air; it represents the winds of change that are to come.

*Rhine River. European river that flows north, from Switzerland, through Germany and the Netherlands, to the North Sea. The play's title is symbolic of the river's course, as it passes through countries that were "on watch" as fascism was spreading across Europe in the late 1930's and early 1940's. The Rhine stands as a tangible symbol of the danger facing Europe. Kurt Muller returns to Germany, continuing his own "watch on the Rhine," as his American relatives rest in their naïveté in the Farrelly home.

*Germany.** Kurt Muller's homeland, which he hopes to defend against the spread of fascism, and the place to which he returns for refuge in the end.

— *Kathleen Schongar*

WAVERLEY: Or, 'Tis Sixty Years Since

Author: Sir Walter Scott (1771-1832)
Type of work: Novel
Type of plot: Historical

Time of plot: 1745
First published: 1814

As in most of Sir Walter Scott's historical novels, this novel uses a wide variety of fictional and real places to symbolize and dramatize its themes and conflicts. The young English officer Edward Waverley's attempts to define himself and his loyalties as he is caught up in the Scottish Jacobite uprising of 1745 are given force and color by the English and Scottish scenes in which he is placed.

Tully-Veolan (TUHL-ee vee-OHL-uhn). Ancient Scottish manor house and estate in Perthshire north of Edinburgh which is the home of the Bradwardines. Scott used a number of real Scottish houses as the basis for his description of Tully-Veolan. This manor house is of central importance throughout *Waverley*. The house is Edward Waverley's first real introduction to Scotland, and it is a romantic and enchanting place that appeals strongly to his naïvely romantic temperament.

Tully-Veolan is eventually revealed as a very complex place and as a virtual symbol of Scotland itself. It has strong associations with poetry, romance, history, sentimental Jacobitism, and beauty but is also a place in which madness, weakness, violence, provincialism, and an ineffectual and feudal nostalgia exist. Tully-Veolan's virtual identification with Scotland as a whole is further evident when, after the crushing defeat of the Scottish Jacobites at the Battle of Culloden, it is the desolation of Tully-Veolan that Scott describes and Waverley sees. When Tully-Veolan is rebuilt and returned to Baron Bradwardine by the English colonel Talbut, Scott is symbolically pointing out the value and importance of the union of Scotland and England, as opposed to the violent destructiveness of the Jacobite uprising.

Waverley-Honour. English estate of the Waverley family at which Edward Waverley is reared. Early in the novel, Waverley-Honour symbolizes Waverley's rather dubious but influential upbringing in which the chivalric romances in the Waverley-Honour library and his uncle and aunt's nostalgic Jacobitism play major roles. At Waverley-Honour, Waverley is given an education that prepares him to be seduced by the romance and chivalry of Scotland. The Englishness of Waverley-Honour, however, reminds readers, and eventually Waverley himself, of Waverley's own essential Englishness. When Waverley finally discovers who he really is, Waverley-Honour becomes the symbol of that maturity. When Waverley marries Rose Bradwardine and unites Waverley-Honour and Tully-Veolan, he is symbolically uniting England and Scotland.

Glennaquoich (glihn-uh-KWOYK). Ancient Scottish highland estate of Fergus and Flora Mac Ivor at which Waverley sees the manners of the Scottish Highlands in all of their seductive romance, chivalry, and poetry. At Glennaquoich, Waverley finds in Fergus a chieftain seemingly straight out of his early reading, in Flora a beautiful woman who seems the embodiment of Scottish minstrelsy, and in everything about the place, a colorful way of life that contrasts strongly with life in more prosaic England. Eventually, however, Glennaquoich is revealed as a center of intrigue, fanaticism, and arbitrary power and as a symbol for a kind of Scottish romanticism that is out of touch with the modern world.

Edinburgh (ehd-en-BUR-uh). Traditional capital city of Scotland. In *Waverley* Edinburgh is captured by the Jacobite army of Charles Stuart, and Scott uses the city as a way of revealing both the strengths and weaknesses of the Jacobite cause. On one hand, life in Jacobite Edinburgh seems gay, chivalric, courtly, and charming. When Waverley meets Charles Stuart at Edinburgh's Holyrood Palace, he is overwhelmed by the romantic appeal of the Pretender and the palace; however, Scott shows that intrigue and politics are everywhere in Jacobite Edinburgh. Furthermore, although Edinburgh is captured by the Jacobites, Edinburgh Castle remains armed and in English hands. This raises serious questions about the realism of Jacobite hopes even at the height of the rebellion. These questions are intensified when Waverley sees the Jacobite army marching out of Edinburgh and realizes that although it is impressive in its best units and leaders, it is ragtag and ill prepared in other respects.

Preston. Battlefield near Edinburgh that is the scene of the greatest military victory of the Jacobites in their 1745 uprising. With remarkable sweep, power, and energy, Scott describes the field of battle and the battle itself. The symbolic importance of Preston is that it is at the same time a place of Jacobite triumph and of great personal doubt for Edward Waverley. As Waverley watches the scene of battle, he finds his conflicted loyalties toward Scotland and England more conflicted than ever.

Carlisle Castle (kahr-lil). Gloomy Gothic fortress in the north of England where Fergus Mac Ivor is tried and executed for treason. Waverley's last meeting with the condemned Fergus takes place here, and the dark and forbidding castle as described by Scott perfectly underscores and symbolizes the sadness of Fergus's fate, the harsh reality of English justice, and the remorseful regret of Waverley for his lost friend.

— *Phillip B. Anderson*

THE WAVES

Author: Virginia Woolf (1882-1941)
Type of work: Novel
Type of plot: Psychological realism

Time of plot: 1920's
First published: 1931

Although much of this novel occurs as the flow of thought in the consciousness of the book's main characters, its ostensible geographical settings are the English Midlands and London, which is an emblem of British life and the symbolic center of the cultural and social elements the characters represent. As characters move through the city, singly or in groups, their observations about the flow of life in the great metropolis grow into a composite portrait of England itself. The spirit of place that Virginia Woolf evokes is as much the subject of the book as its characters, particularly in terms of Bernard, the prime authorial voice, who is both a representative modern urban man and an intellectual questor whose meditations and reflections are designed as inquiries about aspects of life in the British Empire.

London. Woolf was the child of a prominent family living in a London great house, and for her the city was at the center of civilization, albeit a civilization to which she brought profound questions and challenges. Landmarks such as Lords Cricket Ground, the National Gallery, Picadilly Circus, Trafalgar Square, and others are iconic places for the establishment that effectively ran the British Empire. These are not discussed in detail, however, because merely mentioning them suffices to evoke associations that contain epochs of historical meaning. Beyond these references, Woolf presents a portrait of a London which is enchanting. Although *Mrs. Dalloway* (1925) is regarded by many critics as Woolf's "London novel," the tableaus that recur throughout *The Waves* offer a rich depiction of a city pulsing with energy.

The flow of life in London's streets is at the heart of Woolf's method for developing the moods of the city, which in turn stand for the moods of the English people. There is a blending of judgmental distance and participatory enthusiasm in her descriptions.

***Midlands.** Central region of England. Whereas London provides a concrete ground for the narrative, the setting where the characters have reached maturity as adults, the countryside surrounding the city is the region of their origins and often operates as a metaphor for particular emotional states of being. In italicized prefaces to individual sections of the novel, the title motif stands for the passage of time. "Trees wave," "hay waves," "the brisk waves" and the like are typical phrases suggesting transition and alteration, while the concept of the garden as a controlled vision of awesome natural forces offers a contrast to the mechanized life of the city.

Elvedon. Semimystical place that Bernard claims he and Susan found in childhood, a magical land of fantasy and possibility glimpsed as a hazy apparition.

— *Leon Lewis*

THE WAY OF ALL FLESH

Author: Samuel Butler (1835-1902)
Type of work: Novel
Type of plot: Social realism

Time of plot: Nineteenth century
First published: 1903

Closely mirroring the environment in which Samuel Butler was raised, this novel tracks the life of Ernest Pontifex, who suffers the consequences of a strict and repressive upbringing. The Victorian home of the Pontifex family, especially clergyman Theobald Pontifex and his pious wife Christina, is central to the novel. This inhibiting and puritanical household shapes and thwarts the character of Ernest as he struggles to come into his own.

*England. All events in this novel take place in Victorian England, a powerful society which presided over a vast British Empire. Armed with an aggressive confidence and a puritanical morality, Victorian England is depicted in Butler's novel as both preposterous and dangerous and as having an especially dire effect on the young.

Battersby-on-the-Hill. Small English farming village that is based on Butler's own childhood home at Langar Rectory near Nottingham. Dominated by a large hilltop rectory, this clergyman's abode appears to be a cherished stronghold of Victorian family values, but it is here that Ernest is subjected to incidents in which his natural trust and affection is betrayed by his father, the rector Theobald Pontifex, and his slavishly devoted wife Christina. For Ernest, the rectory, which appears idyllic, is in reality the venue where his complacent, self-congratulatory parents subject him to relentless abuse. Battersby-on-the-Hill's name suggests the psychological and physical battering Ernest must endure at the hands of his parents.

Roughborough Grammar School. School that Ernest attends. Typical of the exclusive British public schools of its day and based on the Shrewsbury School, which Butler attended as a child, this school is presided over by Dr. Skinner, a character modeled on the headmaster who succeeded Butler's own grandfather. Seemingly a figure of unassailable moral rectitude, Dr. Skinner is portrayed as foolish, pedantic, and self-deluding. At Roughborough, whose name, like that of Ernest's home, is apt, Ernest struggles against an impervious educational system that seems to exist solely to dog him with demerits. His only safe haven is his kind Aunt Alethea, who has moved to the area to make his life bearable.

Emmanuel College. Fictionalized college of Cambridge University. Cambridge has an Emmanuel College, but Butler based this setting on St. John's College, Cambridge, which he attended himself. This setting is distinctive in that it is one of the few places in which Ernest finds himself truly happy. Cambridge University, located in the south of England and long renowned as one of the finest universities in England, is presented as a venue in which personal development and intellectual freedom are valued far more than in the rest of Victorian England. It is here, however, that Ernest comes under the baleful influence of his classmate Pryer, who persuades him to invest money unwisely in a venture called the College of Spiritual Pathology. It is at Cambridge that Ernest also becomes fervently religious and is ordained as a minister.

Ashpit Place. Small working-class street in London near Drury Lane Theater. A more raffish, fictional version of Heddon Street, in which Butler actually lived during this time of his life, it is in a boardinghouse here, run by the colorful and eccentric Mrs. Jupp, that Ernest attempts to convert and minister to the poor. However, Ernest fails to do anyone in the area any good and instead undermines his own faith in his vocation. After mistaking a respectable boarder for a prostitute, Ernest is sentenced to six months in jail.

Coldbath Fields. Prison to which Ernest is sentenced to six months of hard labor. Here he loses his religion, realizes he is nothing but an insufferable prig, and begins to sense a great chasm opening up between his past and his future.

*****Blackfriars Bridge Road.** Street on the south side of the River Thames near the public house known as the "Elephant and Castle," where Ernest and his wife, the former Pontifex housemaid Ellen, live above a shop where they sell old clothes and books. It is here that his two children are born and where his wife reverts to her old, alcoholic ways.

*****The Temple.** Set of courts and buildings in London by the Thames, with rooms originally intended for lawyers. Here Ernest finally lives as a contented bachelor and finds his true vocation writing iconoclastic books which question the conventional wisdom of the Victorian era.

— *Margaret Boe Birns*

THE WAY OF THE WORLD

Author: William Congreve (1670-1729)
Type of work: Drama
Type of plot: Comedy of manners

Time of plot: Seventeenth century
First performed: 1700; first published, 1700

This play is one of the quintessential English comedies of manners. As such, the setting, fashionable seventeenth century London, plays an important role in establishing the values and trends presented.

*****London.** Capital city of England that provides the world in which the play is set—a world of coffeehouses, periwigs, and elaborately formal dress. It is an upper-class world of gallants and fine ladies, as opposed to would-be gallants and merely attractive ladies. The world of trade and agriculture surrounds this world but is not a part of it except by way of contrast.

Chocolate-house. Setting for act 1. Such houses as Will's near Covent Garden and White's near St. James Park were the fashionable meeting places of young gallants and wits. Often gaming was associated with them.

*****St. James Park.** Large park in central London in whose fashionable Mall act 2 is set. The Mall was a long tract in St. James that was formerly used for playing pall-mall. It is often confused with Pall Mall, another park close by to the north.

Country. Although no scene in the play occurs in the country, the country is always in the background. Sir Wilful Witwoud is a country bumpkin who serves as the butt of ridicule for all. His half brother, Witwoud, has done all he can to eradicate traces of the country from his manners, dress, and speech but without success. No character in the play is associated in a positive way with the country. Millamant, perhaps the most regular character in the play, loathes the country.

— *Paul Varner*

THE WAY WE LIVE NOW

Author: Anthony Trollope (1815-1882)
Type of work: Novel
Type of plot: Social realism

Time of plot: 1873
First published: 1874-1875

No novel of Anthony Trollope's is more rooted in a precise geographical setting than this blistering attack upon the greed and corruption of public life in the England of the 1870's. While the novel also contains many references to a wider world, London remains the physical heart of the novel, and Trollope locates his characters in residences which clearly differentiate their rank, wealth, and fashionable standing, thus providing the reader with a social map of contemporary London life.

Melmotte house. Ostentatious London home of Augustus Melmotte, the celebrated swindler whose dealings form the central plot of the book, and his family, in Mayfair's Grosvenor Square, a highly fashionable area east of Hyde Park and north of Piccadilly. Melmotte's business offices, obscure and unobtrusive by contrast, are located on Abchurch Lane close to the Royal Exchange and Lombard Street in the business district of London. Melmotte also has business ties (necessarily vague and shady) with New York, Hamburg, Vienna, and Paris.

*****Welbeck Street.** Less-than-fashionable London neighborhood, on the north side of Oxford Street, that is home to Lady Carbury, a hack writer who supports herself by persuading editors to publish favorable reviews of her execrably bad books. Her daughter Hetta and her wastrel son, Sir Felix, live with her, but the latter spends most of his time at his club, the Bear Garden.

Bear Garden Club. Fashionable London club favored by Sir Felix Carbury that is the scene of much of the action of the novel, located off St. James Street, the traditional heart of London clubland.

*****Longstaffe house.** Home of Adolphus (Dolly) Longstaffe's family on London's Bruton Street, a highly fashionable address from which to participate in the London social "season." The London house is shut down for reasons of economy, and the family's enforced rustication at its Suffolk seat at Caversham is a source of intense mortification for Georgiana Longstaffe, Dolly's sister. Dolly's own country seat, at Pickering Park in Sussex, is instrumental in the cause of Melmotte's downfall.

*****Sackville Street.** London street north of Piccadilly that is described as the residence of Paul Montague, one of the book's two heroes, although a flawed one. Montague later seems to be living on Suffolk Street, off Pall Mall.

*****Islington.** Unfashionable London working-class area that is the location of the temporary lodgings of Paul's femme fatale, Mrs. Hurtle, whose exact address is not specified. Islington is also the scene of Sir Felix's attempted assault on Ruby Ruggles, and the location of the music hall which they had previously frequented on the City Road.

— *Gavin R. G. Hambly*

THE WEB AND THE ROCK

Author: Thomas Wolfe (1900-1938)
Type of work: Novel
Type of plot: Impressionistic realism

Time of plot: 1900-1928
First published: 1939

New York City and Libya Hill, North Carolina, both represent the "rock" and "web" of this novel's title. The novel is the story of George Webber mastering what makes a place his own personal rock and web. His earliest days are spent in Libya Hill, where he is subject to a web not of his choosing. As a young adult, he moves to New

York City, where he finds no web and a far-less-welcoming rock than Libya Hill. His transitions between Libya Hill and New York are facilitated by his experiences at college, and then on two separate trips to Europe.

Libya Hill. Small North Carolina town in which George is born and raised. It is a sharp, vivid place, where specific buildings are grounded. His uncle's hardware store is not a vague business in the town proper, but a particular store with certain wares, plate glass windows, and a location relative to other downtown landmarks. George's parents were divorced shortly after he was born, and after his mother's death, when George was eight, he moved in with his Aunt Maw in a small house in the backyard of his uncle's fancier home. George escapes this, however, by going to the front yard of his uncle's house. From there, he sees the townspeople, and he imagines other lives. In particular, he imagines the life of his father, who also lives in Libya Hill but whom he is not allowed to see. George imagines his father actively participating in the life of the town: going to the barbershop, greeting the other residents, and so forth, or he imagines Pennsylvania, where his father was born.

Libya Hill provides the first web-rock interface for George. His mother's family is rooted there, and Aunt Maw's stories bring those roots alive. His father is a bricklayer who built many of the town buildings, a physical demonstration of how Libya Hill is a stable touchstone. It is a small town in which most people are aware of, if not involved in, one another's business. For example, when George's parents divorce, the townspeople take sides, condemning either his father or his mother. Every person's place, physically and mentally, is known not only by that person, but by everyone else, who participate in keeping the person in his or her proper place.

George leaves Libya Hill at age sixteen, when he receives a small inheritance from his father, in order to attend college. During his schooling, George tries to move past the constraints of Libya Hill. The Russian writer Fyodor Dostoevski fires his imagination, but the old Libya Hill crowd at school mocks this kind of intellectual exploration—it might move George too much out of his place in their network. After graduating, George moves to New York City for the first time.

*New York City. George moves to New York City twice, and the novel ends with him planning a third period of residence there. At first he rooms with some old college buddies. His impressions of New York are nonspecific—towering buildings, rushing crowds, anonymous women—underscoring how difficult it is to get a hold on this particular rock. He does not work but lives on the dwindling inheritance from his father. While his university friendships are less stifling than his family ties in Libya Hill, he grows past these as well and replaces them with nothing. Adrift, George sets out for Europe.

On George's return voyage, he meets Esther Jack, beginning his most important relationship of the next few years. She is his mistress, his mentor, his muse. She also represents one who has made New York City her own, both as web and rock. Her hospitable homes, her job as a theatrical costume designer, her friends and family among artists and businessmen, connect her to what still seems dizzying and intimidating to George. Esther sets George up in a small studio apartment and visits him every day, cooking for him, encouraging him, and working on her own designs. George teaches composition and works on his own novel, and when he goes out, he moves within Esther's circles. He finishes his novel and, with Esther's support, sends it out to publishers. However, his core frustrations in New York have not lessened. He is still anonymous there; Esther mediates his attempts at making New York his own.

George finds being bound into Esther's world stultifying in turn. He breaks off their relationship and again flees to Europe. Once abroad, though, he haunts the mail service for her letters, demonstrating how he has finally begun to realize that he is connected with other people. During the Oktoberfest in Munich he is involved in a brawl. While recovering in the hospital, he does nothing but muse over the past decade or so of his life. Finally he acknowledges his newly found sense of self-worth, the lack of which had always led him to shelter behind others. Encouraged, George decides to return to New York, ready to establish his own web to secure him to its particular rock.

— *Clare Callaghan*

THE WELL OF LONELINESS

Author: Radclyffe Hall (1880-1943)
Type of work: Novel
Type of plot: Social realism

Time of plot: Early twentieth century
First published: 1928

The ancestral home of protagonist Stephen Gordon is by far the most significant place in this deliberately jumbled version of the life of author Marguerite Radclyffe-Hall. Morton Hall and the Malvern Hills countryside in England symbolize Stephen's great love of her father, Sir Philip Gordon, with whom she shares all the joys of the rambling estate.

Morton Hall. Located between Upton-on-Severn and the Malvern Hills in the British Midlands, Morton Hall is Stephen Gordon's home until her early twenties. This is where she has her first crush on a housemaid, Collins, at the age of seven, and where she falls in love at twenty-one with Angela Crossby, the duplicitous American wife of an English businessman. Both of these loves go unrequited.

Morton Hall also has symbolic significance for Stephen—the very feel of the soil, the old Georgian, red-brick house with circular windows, the stables and especially the horses, the schoolroom where she receives private tutoring in preparation for Oxford University, the two large lakes on the grounds, and the flora and fauna on the estate and around it. Even the love between her parents adds up to a definition of home for Stephen.

Battlefield. French battlefield on which Stephen ferries wounded French soldiers to the hospital as a volunteer ambulance driver during World War I, She thus proves that "sexual inverts" also can lead useful lives and contribute to society. This is the setting in which Stephen meets Mary Llewellyn, an innocent Welsh orphan and another volunteer, with whom Stephen is to have a long affair.

*****Paris.** Capital of France, where Stephen tries to jump-start her and Mary's social life to relieve Mary's boredom and loneliness. Now that Stephen has become a famous author, her demanding writing schedule has left Mary feeling neglected (in reality, Radclyffe Hall did not become famous until she was in her forties). Through Valerie Seymour, a wealthy American writer

engaged in multiple lesbian affairs, Stephen and Mary are introduced to Paris's homosexual society. In due course, they visit the seamy Parisian lesbian bars populated by unhappy misfits leading tortured lives—women drowning in alcohol, poverty, and self-loathing. Stephen contributes their lack of self-respect to social disapproval. In fact, it is to make this point forcefully that Hall omits mentioning the lively salons and cafés, equally familiar to her, where lesbians were less mortified and apologetic.

Paris is also the place where the youthful Canadian Martin Hallam, who, through neighbors in England, has met Stephen Gordon and innocently proposed marriage, now resurfaces. At that time, Stephen herself had not yet understood the underlying reason for her rejection of Martin, with whom she had shared a love of nature.

Martin Hallam now becomes romantically involved with Mary Llewellyn. Stephen decides to sacrifice herself for Mary's happiness after a bitter contest with Martin and after Stephen's deeply religious experience in a Montmartre church, in which she identifies with the crucified Christ (Hall was a voluntary convert to Catholicism). Thus, feigning an affair with Valerie Seymour, Stephen drives Mary into Hallam's arms and a conventional heterosexual future on his farm in British Columbia. This is the last of her renunciations, which had started with her giving up Morton Hall, her cherished family home.

35, rue Jacob. Paris apartment in which Stephen sets up a household with Mary, and they vow to weather the world's harsh judgment of their same-sex "marriage."

— Peter B. Heller

WESTWARD HO!

Author: Charles Kingsley (1819-1875)
Type of work: Novel
Type of plot: Historical

Time of plot: Late sixteenth century
First published: 1855

This novel dealing with epic naval struggles between England and Spain in the time of Queen Elizabeth I is set principally in the Devon countryside and in the West Indies.

*Bideford. English town in north Devon in which the novel's protagonist, naval hero Amyas Leigh, was born and to which he returns after each of his voyages. Bideford was an important port in southwest England during the time in which the novel is set. It slopes upward from the broad tidal river Torridge, which the town bridge, with its twenty-four arches, has spanned since the Middle Ages. The hills above the town are covered by oak woods, through which can be seen fern-fringed slate outcroppings. Below the town, the land flattens into salt marsh and sand dunes. Kingsley knew Bideford well, as part of the book was written in the Royal Hotel in the town. Bideford Bay, into which the Torridge flows, is one of the places in which Amyas likes to bathe. The bay protects the fertile alluvial fields from high tides. Clovelly, Will Cary's home, is at the western end of the bay. The westernmost headland is Hartland Point on which an abbey stood until the dissolution of the monasteries. This site is now the site of a minor stately home.

Burrough Court. Bideford home of the Leigh family; it nestles on a wind-swept down amid a ring of oaks. From the gray stone gateway is a view westward of a wide bay bounded to the south with purple cliffs. Lundy Isle is dimly visible out to sea. Below and to the right, the River Torridge flows westward to its estuary. On the other side of the river is Tapeley Park.

Stow house. Home of Sir Richard Greville, located near Moorwinstow (now Morwenstow) on the west coast between Bude and Hartland Point. The house is a huge, rambling building, part dwelling house, part castle, on the north side of a wooded valley.

*West Indies. New World archipelago stretching between the southern tip of Florida to the mainland of South America—the **Spanish Main**—that separates the Caribbean Sea from the Atlantic Ocean. At the time in which the novel is set, most of the islands and surrounding landmasses were Spanish colonies, which were subjected to English raids during time of war. The novel depicts the islands and the northern coast of South America as fragrant with flowers and filled with the sounds of insects, tree frogs, and birds. The shorelines are edged with palm trees, and there is fruit in abundance. Amyas makes his initial landfall on the southern side of the island of Barbados, where Bridgetown now stands.

*La Guayra (lah GWEE-ree-ah). Venezuelan port north of Caracas, at the foot of a mountain eight thousand feet high. The port itself is on a low black cliff crowned by a wall with a battery at either end. A few narrow streets of white houses run parallel to the sea, and behind it is the mountain wall. It is to this place that the new Spanish governor, Don Guzman, takes Rose Salterne, to whom he describes the town as the "loveliest place on earth, and the loveliest governor's house, in a forest of palms I shall only want a wife there to be in paradise." His house is approached up a zigzag path from a pebble beach, marked by white shell sand winding between the tall thorny cacti. It ends in a wicket gate. From here, a smooth turf walk passes through a pleasure garden of trees and bushes. The house is long and low with balconies along the upper story. The under part is mostly open to the wind.

*Orinoco River. Principal river of Venezuela in whose basin Amyas and his men wander for three years. The river and its tributaries run between green, flower-bespangled walls of forest with trees growing as much as two hundred feet tall and countless birds, insects, and monkeys. Rapids and islands dot the river. On one island, Amyas encounters the presumed Indian maiden Ayacanora, whom he eventually marries. Her village nearby is made up of palm-leaf houses, with hammocks slung between the trees.

*Smerwick Bay. Bay on Ireland's cliff-lined Kerry coast where the Spanish army gains a foothold during the Armada's invasion. The Spanish build a fort at the head of the bay. In a battle between Spanish and English forces, Amyas takes Don Guzman prisoner.

*Plymouth.** Major English port on the coast of Devon, on the east bank of the Tamar estuary. To the town's east is the Catwater, the estuary of the River Plym, from which the English fleet sails to face the Spanish Armada. Plymouth is also the home of Sir Francis Drake and John Hawkins. The famous lawn-bowling game that the English commanders play before the fleet sets sail takes place on a green behind Plymouth's Pelican Inn.

*Lundy.** Island off the north coast of Devon that is visible from the hills above Bideford on clear days. The granite cliff that forms the western side ends at the southern end, in a precipice three hundred feet high, topped by a pile of white rock covered with lichens. Below, Gull-rock is a roosting and nesting place for thousands of birds. The waves break across a sunken shelf of rock. The Shutter is a fang of rock projecting from the sea on which the Spanish ship *Catharina* is wrecked after Amyas pursues it and Don Guzman around the coast.

— *Pauline Morgan*

WHAT MAISIE KNEW

Author: Henry James (1843-1916)
Type of work: Novel
Type of plot: Psychological realism

Time of plot: 1890's
First published: 1897

This novel about Maisie Farange, a child of divorce, takes her on outings in England and France that provide her with insights that allow her to make sense of her parents' and stepparents' behavior. As the adults in the novel use Maisie as a cover for their illicit rendezvous, Maisie's own growing knowledge is a product of the settings in which her learning takes place.

*Kensington Gardens.** Great London park in which Maisie and her stepfather, Sir Claude, discover her mother, Ida, with another man known as the Captain. This scene is one of several in the novel in which the adult characters are discovered with their lovers in public places. Much of what Maisie "knows" about her parents' activities throughout the novel derives from visual observations. This scene enables readers to understand both how Maisie obtains her knowledge and how inadequately she interprets what she sees.

The scene is humorous in that, when Sir Claude and Maisie spot Ida at a distance, they speculate on which of several possible men her companion may be. Maisie herself does not find anything unusual in the situation and, when asked to sit with the Captain while her mother and stepfather argue, she is concerned mostly with trying to get the Captain to say he loves Ida. The outdoor public setting allows not only for the discovery to be made but also for the conversation between Maisie and the Captain to occur.

Exhibition. Carnival-like event in London that is the setting for another scene similar to that in Kensington Gardens. In this scene, Maisie's stepmother discovers Maisie's father with his mistress. Mrs. Beale takes Maisie to the event hoping to run into her own lover, Sir Claude, but instead sees her husband with the Countess. The exotic and chaotic setting, with crowds, noise, and diversions such as side shows, entices and frustrates Maisie as she and Mrs. Beale have no money to view the attractions. The crowded scene enables Sir Claude to slip away when he realizes that his lover has discovered her husband with another woman.

Countess's house. Home of Beale Farange's mistress. There Maisie's father renounces responsibility for her, trying to word the decision as if it were Maisie's. Having finally lost interest in his former wife, Ida, he no longer feels that he needs his daughter. Awed by the exotic decor of the countess's house, Maisie is inclined to sacrifice her father to its owner.

*Boulogne** (bew-LOHN). Coastal city in northern

France that Maisie visits with her stepfather, Sir Claude, and stepmother, Mrs. Beale. After losing interest in each other, her natural parents no longer need Maisie to argue over and leave her in her stepparents' care. The excuse given for living in this city, rather than staying in London or going on to Paris as Maisie dreams of doing, is that it is inexpensive. The novel ends with Maisie and Mrs. Wix, her governess, leaving Boulogne to return to London. In Boulogne, Maisie realizes that Sir Claude can never give up Mrs. Beale for her. Maisie is left to be raised by her governess, the only adult in the novel who values Maisie above a competing lover.

Schoolroom. Place in Maisie's mother's home where Maisie spends most of her time. The lack of decoration or attention given to this room in Ida's otherwise elaborately decorated home indicates her mother's lack of interest in either Maisie or her education. The room's most striking decoration is a picture of Ida's husband, Sir Claude, symbolic of Maisie's affection for this stepparent who shows an interest in her.

— *Joan Hope*

WHAT THE BUTLER SAW

Author: Joe Orton (1933-1967)
Type of work: Drama
Type of plot: Farce

Time of plot: 1960's
First performed: 1969; first published, 1969

The private psychiatric clinic in which this play takes place provides an appropriate setting for a farce in which allegations of madness recur frequently and even the most taboo Freudian impulses are blithely taken for granted.

Dr. Prentice's psychiatric clinic. Office of Dr. Prentice, a psychiatrist, that is the play's only set. Not part of England's National Health Service, this private clinic caters to wealthy patients who pay for their care and treatment. Doors exiting from Prentice's office lead to the clinic's wards, a dispensary, and a hall, and French windows open to a pleasant garden. The office itself is furnished with a desk, bookshelves, a sink, and a consulting couch with privacy curtains.

Within the office's walls, as Joe Orton's masterfully intricate plot unfolds, charges of madness and instances of mistaken identity abound, as Freudian taboos seem to be flouted (and flaunted) with blithe impunity. Allegations and misperceptions include double incest, necro-philia, male and female cross-dressing, Oedipus and Electra complexes, voyeurism, various fetishes, nymphomania, lesbianism, and rape. Late in the second act, when an alarm is pressed, a siren wails and metal bars drop over each of the doors, transforming the office into a literal cage (or jail) as the lights go out and the set is lighted only by the glare of a bloody sunset.

Once a number of the characters' crises are resolved, a skylight opens and Sergeant Match, a policeman, descends on a rope ladder. Weary, bleeding, drugged, and drunk, Orton's characters then climb the ladder to the blazing light above, resolving to get dressed and face the world with renewed respectability.

— *William Hutchings*

WHEN WE DEAD AWAKEN

Author: Henrik Ibsen (1828-1906)
Type of work: Drama
Type of plot: Psychological symbolism

Time of plot: Nineteenth century
First published: Naar vi døde vaagner, 1899; first performed, 1900

Henrik Ibsen's last play dramatizes the struggle of the artist to invest himself in life. The major male figures, an artist and a wealthy sportsman, personify the struggle Ibsen sees between art and life. The artist Rubek is so committed to his art that he destroys all who come close to him; in similar fashion, the sportsman Ulfheim's passion for living is seen as equally destructive of others. Ibsen uses the sense of place symbolically in the play. Stereotypes associated with seaside and mountaintop suggest the alternatives facing the artist: to rest contented with life, or to seek greatness by living through one's art.

Seaside resort. Spa on the coast of Norway where the play opens. The artist Rubek and Maia, his wife of four years, are there to rest from travel and to escape the fame Rubek has achieved through production of a sculptural masterpiece. Rubek discovers that he cannot retreat from his role as an artist. The presence at the spa of Irene, the woman who modeled for his masterpiece, helps him realize his destiny. At the same time, Rubek's wife becomes enamored with the sportsman Ulfheim, who invites her to hunt with him in the mountains. Restless by the seaside, she agrees to join him. Rubek, too, goes back into the mountains where he lived earlier.

Norwegian mountain resort. The final two acts of the play are set on a mountain. There Rubek is reminded that he promised both his wife and Irene that he would take them "up a high mountain" and show them "all the glory of the world." On the mountain, Rubek realizes that this is the symbolic journey the artist makes, but he finds he is unable to share this glory with either of them; his commitment is to his art, not to relationships with others. Maia leaves with Ulfheim to descend to the valley, suggesting that she is abandoning art for a life of pleasure. Irene stays with Rubek, and their death in an avalanche is less a catastrophe than an acknowledgment that the artist, as artist, cannot survive outside his art.

— *Laurence W. Mazzeno*

WHERE ANGELS FEAR TO TREAD

Author: E. M. Forster (1879-1970)
Type of work: Novel
Type of plot: Social realism

Time of plot: Early twentieth century
First published: 1905

Place is at the heart of this novel in which three English travelers in Italy shed their inhibitions and discover the joy of life.

Sawston. English town that is home to the conventional middle-class Herriton family. E. M. Forster modeled this dreary, repressive town on Tonbridge, Kent, southeast of London, where he himself had attended school. A gray place preoccupied with duty, respectability, and tradition, Sawston represents the worst of English repression of self and others.

When family friend Caroline Abbott later dreams of the Italian town Poggibonsi as a "joyless, straggling place, full of people who pretended," she recognizes it as Sawston. At the end of the novel, Philip Herriton's growth is evident in his decision to move from his hometown to London. (Forster also uses Sawston to symbolize English middle-class deadness in his second novel, *The Longest Journey,* 1907.)

*Tuscany. Region of west-central Italy along the Ligurian and Tyrrhenian Seas that includes the provinces of Firenze (Florence), Pisa, Livorno, and Siena. Forster's depiction of the Tuscan landscape draws on a long holiday he took there in 1901. Particularly close echoes of his travels come in his description of Philip and Harriet Herriton's tourist hardships in several cities while they are on their way to Monteriano. Harriet, to whom "foreigners are a filthy nation," embodies strong English chauvinism and is the only traveler unresponsive to the magic of Italy.

Monteriano (mahn-teh-ree-AHN-oh). Hill town in Tuscany modeled on San Gimignano southwest of Florence and northwest of Siena, which is one of the best preserved medieval towns in Italy. Forster invents a description of his fictionalized town for his characters' tour book, which characterizes Monteriano as a town with 4,800 inhabitants, a Siena gate, walls, a magnificent view from the fortress at sunset, and Giotto frescoes that earn it "one star." Later, the narrator's comment that the town's Piazza has "three great attractions—the Palazzo Publico, the Collegiate Church, and the Caffè Garibaldi: the intellect, the soul, and the body" recalls the model, San Gimignano, with its Palazzo del Populo and its Collegiate, a former cathedral. However, Forster also clearly elevates Monteriano into symbolizing a full, integrated life.

Monteriano's overall role in the novel resembles that of Florence in Forster's *A Room with a View* (1908). Both Italian settings overflow with the beauties of nature and Renaissance art, as well as passion and spontaneity, and both are enchanted places of transfiguration and liberation—almost Forster's version of the regenerative "green world" of Shakespearean comedy. In *A Room with a View*, Forster explicitly links these Italian locations by having two English tourists in Florence gossip about Monteriano as the site of an ill-fated Anglo-Italian marriage.

*****Poggibonsi** (po-jee-BON-see). Town east of San Gimignano and of its fictional counterpart Monteriano. In the novel, Monteriano is described as having thrown off Poggibonsi's rule in 1261—much as Lilia, Caroline, and Philip liberate themselves from the tyranny of English propriety.

House opposite the Volterra gate. Stuffy two-story house outside Monteriano in which Lilia spends her short married life with Gino. Confinement of Italian women to their homes leaves Lilia feeling alienated in the Italian culture that initially seemed her refuge from oppressive English norms.

Stella d'Italia. Hotel in which Philip, Caroline, and Harriet stay. Formerly a palace with Gothic windows, the hotel represents a guiding star on Caroline's and Philip's journeys to self-realization.

Collegiate Church of Santa Deodata. Monteriano's church, decorated with Giotto's frescoes of the death and burial of a patron saint of the Dark Ages who denied herself everything. In Monteriano, which simultaneously affirms art, nature, and passion while honestly embracing pain and death, Caroline and Philip question their modern, English abstention.

Caffè Garibaldi. Café in Monteriano where men enjoy freedom and camaraderie while their wives stay home or go to church. Forster depicts this café, where Philip and Gino cement their friendship, as the locus of male privilege in a patriarchal Latin culture, indicating that although England is generally more constrained, it nevertheless offers its women a freedom of movement alien to Italian custom.

Theater. Tiny garishly decorated building that houses Monteriano's opera. There Philip and Harriet confront Italian crudity, vitality, joy, and kindness at a performance of *Lucia di Lammermoor*, which, as an Italian opera based on a romance by Sir Walter Scott, harmoniously merges Italian and British cultures.

— *Margaret Bozenna Goscilo*

WHERE I'M CALLING FROM

Author: Raymond Carver (1938-1988)
Type of work: Short fiction

First published: 1988

This short story is set entirely within Frank Martin's alcoholic treatment center, to which the narrator goes to recover from his addiction to alcohol and where he experiences the first few days of withdrawal from alcohol.

Alcoholic treatment center. Fictional institution representative of a real alcohol recovery facility. Frank Martin's facility is central to the title and characterization of the story. The unnamed narrator, who has already spent a few days at the center when the story opens, describes the various events he has witnessed. For example, he has seen a man suffer seizures from alcohol withdrawal and fears he may experience the same physical reaction. The narrator spends most of his time listening to J. P., another recovering alcoholic at the center. J. P's dialogues reveal the downward spiral his life has taken because of his drinking.

"Where I'm Calling From" is one of many of Raymond Carver's stories about alcoholism. Like the problems J. P. and the narrator experience, many of the problems of Carver's other working-class characters are exacerbated because of alcoholism. At the end of the story, the narrator says that he will call his wife, from whom he is separated. He suspects that his estranged wife will ask where he is calling from, and he knows he will have to tell her. Where he is calling from represents both Frank Martin's institution and the narrator's psychological state of mind.

It is significant that the story ends on New Year's Day, a holiday in which resolutions are made. However, the narrator vows not to make any resolutions. Like the process of recovering from alcohol, the story is open-ended. The story shows a few days at the beginning of that process, which never ends for those recovering. As the symbolic significance of the title suggests, the story concerns the place from which the narrator calls, the psychology of the first few days of an alcoholic's recovery process.

— *Laurie Champion*

WHERE THE AIR IS CLEAR

Author: Carlos Fuentes (1928-   )
Type of work: Novel
Type of plot: Mythic

Time of plot: Early to mid-1950's
First published: La región más transparente, 1958
  (English translation, 1960)

This novel's mixture of historical and mythical qualities converge in a major urban setting from which the author extends the narrative to describe the human struggle to balance spiritual enlightenment with the costs and conflicts of modernization.

Mexico City. Mexico's capital city is the central location of the novel, providing a modern urban setting that contrasts with the country's primarily rural history. Carlos Fuentes uses the city as a protagonist to which the characters must react as much as they interact with one another. Against this emerging modern backdrop, the characters struggle to understand their individual destinies, and in a collective sense, they embody the new, rising, modern Mexico coming to terms with the fallout of its early twentieth century revolution. The urban setting poignantly displays Fuentes's cynical irony. The modern, postrevolutionary era does not provide equality nor justice. Remnants of classicism and political corruption abound.

The novel is framed with the question: "Here we abide. And what are we going to do about it? Where the air is clear." Only in an ironic sense is Mexico City a place where the air is, in fact, clear. The phrase suggests a fatalistic alliance with a place that is changing but whose inhabitants have not yet figured out their role in the changes. There is no optimistic assertion that a movement toward capitalism and a middle class will satisfy the needs of the populace. Instead, the phrase suggests the betrayal of the ideals of the revolution that now finds itself played out in the dramas of citizens caught up in the cultural shift taking place.

Historically, Mexico City was the center of the indigenous Aztec culture and thus signified mythical and spiritual values of the land. The novel plays off this mythical association to suggest a spiritual decline of the citizenry. It calls into question whether a people living in modern urban settings can remain true to historical and mythological roots that have created them.

Rural Mexico. In contrast to the urban setting of Mexico City, the novel implies a connection to several less urban settings. Many of the characters have roots in outlying areas, but have since migrated to the metropolitan area. The rural landscape is not simplistically viewed as an Eden, but it is associated with the mythical origins stemming from the Aztec culture. This culture, brutally interrupted by the Spanish Conquest, has been lost, but modern Mexicans seem almost subconsciously to act out some of the principal tenets of its system. For example, blood sacrifice and sun worship are ironically continued in modern urban settings in the forms of murder, rape, and sunbathing, suggesting a mythical connection to indigenous origins.

Acapulco. Port city on Mexico's Pacific coast where both American and Mexican tourists intermingle in rituals of sunbathing. In these scenes, characters try to avoid the stresses of urban life, and references to these settings show the few times when people gather in collective rituals of celebration. These moments contrast with the individual struggles prominent elsewhere in the novel.

Europe. Frequent references to the Old World continent are used collectively to suggest that Mexico is still struggling with the class issues of the Old World feudal system that presumed a romantic idealization of society.

One character, for example, says that it makes him laugh to live in a "culture Europe had its fill of more than a century ago." Aristocrats in Mexico still try to live out the values and privileges of a dying culture assumed to be alive in France and other European countries.

The novel also contains allusions to the Bolshevik Revolution in Russia whose attempted land and political reforms seem to parallel the ideals of the Mexican Revolution.

United States. The large and prosperous country to the north of Mexico is referred to collectively and usually negatively. The use of this place suggests a counter system in which capitalism is assumed to be thriving and whose economic benefits lure Mexicans north across the border. Frequently characters discuss the choice of leaving home for economic advancement at the cost of national identity and pride. Finally, the economic concerns squelch the true need of spiritual awareness that Fuentes's work demands. To play off the title phrase, the air is never clear in any place where materialism dominates.

— *Kenneth Hada*

THE WHITE DEVIL

Author: John Webster (c. 1577 to 1580-before 1634)
Type of work: Drama
Type of plot: Tragedy

Time of plot: Late sixteenth century
First performed: c. 1609-1612; first published, 1612

With its settings in the Italian cities of Rome and Padua, John Webster's play stresses the "Machiavellian" plots and counterplots associated with that country in English revenge tragedy.

Rome. Leading city of Italy, in which the first four acts of the play take place. During Webster's time, Rome was known for its political and moral complexities and corruption. The play's second act is set at midnight in an isolated Roman location where Duke Brachiano watches as a conjurer produces a dumb show that achieves an appropriately theatrical effect while also advancing the drama's plot. The setting of the third act assumes a more official air, as the characters Flamineo, Marcello, and Vittoria are brought to trial before Cardinal Monticelso in his palace.

House of the Convertites. Home for reformed prostitutes to which Vittoria is sent after she is condemned by Cardinal Monticelso. Here she is effectively imprisoned, with the additional punishment of being stripped of her reputation. There is dramatic irony in the fact that the virtuous Vittoria must serve her unjust sentence in a home for "fallen women" in what the playwright regards as one of the most corrupt cities in Christendom.

Vatican. Roman residence of the pope and the headquarters of the Roman Catholic Church. During the play the reigning pope, Gregory XIII, dies, and the College of

Cardinals assembles to elect his successor, who is none other than Cardinal Monticelso. The combination of the scene and the action reinforce the drama's theme of the moral hypocrisy of Vittoria's enemies and the pervasive corruption of Italy.

*Padua. City in northeast Italy, near Venice, to which Brachiano and Vittoria flee and get married after their escape from Rome. Although Padua at first seems a refuge from the treachery and deception of Rome, it proves to be equally corrupt, and the couple are murdered by their foes. In a land and time of utter moral depravity, no innocent persons or couples are safe.

— *Michael Witkoski*

WHITE-JACKET: Or, The World in a Man-of-War

Author: Herman Melville (1819-1891)
Type of work: Novel
Type of plot: Adventure

Time of plot: 1840's
First published: 1850

The subtitle to this novel, "The World in a Man-o-War," suggests that the novel's setting is a microcosm—a manifestation of life writ small. From beginning to end, the narrative is set within the confines of a U.S. naval frigate teeming with the contradictions of nineteenth century American life, from the democratic impulses and creative energies of its common sailors to the short-sighted tyranny and reactionary tendencies of its officers. Within the boundaries of this constricted environment, Herman Melville explores the tensions tearing at the heart of the fledgling United States, including the conflict between individual rights and the public welfare, and the undeniable hypocrisy of freedom for some juxtaposed with servitude for others.

USS *Neversink.* U.S. naval frigate that is the novel's primary setting. The narrator describes its crew and the vessel in great detail, delineating the various roles of the seamen and the functions of different parts of the ship. The narrator devotes entire chapters to character sketches, each of which not only delves into the psychological make-up of the individual described but also in some instances includes detailed descriptions of his physical labors, the tools of his trade, and his working environment. Through these character sketches, the narrator outlines the distinct hierarchical structure upon which life on the ship is based, an organizing principle that he decries as being fundamentally undemocratic and inhumane.

As the narrator works his way through the ship's colorful and diverse crew, he points out that each crew member has not only specific and limited duties but also a well-defined physical space in which to fulfill those responsibilities. Consequently, a seaman may typically work in only one part of the ship and have little or no knowledge of what goes on in other parts of the vessel.

The officers have free run of the entire ship and therefore know more than most, but they impose their own limits, preferring to remain among fellow officers rather than mixing with those beneath their rank. Common sailors, on the other hand, have no choice but to accept their boundaries, and thus their environment, already constricted by the physical limits of the ship on the perilous ocean, closes in on them even more, adding to the oppressive nature of their already limited freedoms.

The narrator also describes the relative monotony and somewhat domestic nature of daily life on board the naval vessel, thereby debunking the romantic misconception of sea adventures inspired in the popular imagination by Melville's contemporaries and, even to some extent, by Melville himself. Readers learn that a seaman's life is rarely about glorious battles and heroic escapades. A sailor is more likely to spend his days and nights cleaning the ship and washing clothes, sitting for hours on watch and staring off at a limitless horizon of sameness, drying out from the frequent storms and finding consolation only in his daily allotment of grog.

However, the narrator also points out that the common sailor overcomes the dehumanizing character of his lowly life through all sorts of creative outlets, including the performing arts and literary interests. This ship is full of coarse, weather-beaten men but also contains lively human minds devoted to the writing of poetry and the performances of plays, thus demonstrating that even in the midst of oppressive social structures and fearsome natural boundaries, humans still strive to make their voices heard. With that in mind, the narrator uses his own platform, his narrative, to voice his concerns regarding the injustices perpetrated upon American sailors, including most notably the deplorable practice of flogging.

Cape Horn. Treacherous stretch of water along the southern tip of South America through which the *Neversink* sails to cross from the Pacific Ocean to the Atlantic Ocean. The narrator rarely focuses on specific locales outside the boundaries of the ship, but he dedicates three chapters to his description of the cape, detailing many of its dangers, including unpredictable weather, violent currents, and icebergs from Antarctica.

— *R. Allen Alexander, Jr.*

WHO'S AFRAID OF VIRGINIA WOOLF?

Author: Edward Albee (1928-   )
Type of work: Drama
Type of plot: Absurdist

Time of plot: Mid-twentieth century
First performed: 1962; first published, 1962

This play, in which Edward Albee focuses on the sterility, cruelty, hypocrisy, and opportunism of the social elite, is set in the living room of a professor's house on the campus of a small college in the fictional New England town of New Carthage.

New Carthage. Fictional town named after a city from the ancient world. Carthage was destroyed forever when the Romans added salt to the soil, ensuring that nothing would grow there and that the place would become a wasteland. George and Martha's marriage is sterile—the only child they produce is an imaginary one—and nothing positive seems to come from their union. The play is a black comedy of vitriolic abuse and tart sleaziness, as it highlights licentious drink and sex, with the two couples descending into sadomasochistic games and behavior.

New Carthage has a symbolic significance in the play. Because it is a place dedicated to higher learning and hence to the progress of civilization, the name of New Carthage is particularly significant. The ancient city called Carthage, founded by the Phoenicians and later destroyed by the Romans, conjoins history and destruction ironically. George is a history professor, but according to Martha, he lacks ambition and so is stuck in a rut. Nick, who has been invited over for drinks with his mousey wife Honey, teaches biology, which implies that he belongs to a class of scientists who would reorder the world even at the price of rendering it mechanized and dehumanized. Therefore, there is an intellectual clash between the man of history and the man of science, along with other lacerating conflicts of a more personal nature. All outward signs of respectability and decorum disintegrate in a searing exposé of corruption.

George and Martha's home. Private residence on a campus in New Carthage, New England. Martha drunkenly calls the house "a dump" as she and George fumble in the dark after returning at 2 A.M. from a faculty party. However, the setting expresses the anarchic state of her marriage to George, as well as pointing to a larger failure. The set design of the original Broadway production showed a wrought-iron American eagle, an American flag turned upside down, and antique American furniture, along with bookshelves, a stereo set, and a bar. These props and furnishings fortify the symbolism of the names of Martha and George, the names of the first U.S. president and his wife. Albee seems to suggest that the foibles and flaws of the characters are signs of larger flaws in American society.

— *Keith Garebian*

WIDE SARGASSO SEA

Author: Jean Rhys (Ella Gwendolen Rees Williams, 1894-1979)

Type of work: Novel

Type of plot: Domestic realism

Time of plot: Late 1830's

First published: 1966

Set in the West Indies and England, Wide Sargasso Sea *retells Charlotte Brontë's novel* Jane Eyre *(1847) from the point of view of Rochester and his first wife. Its primary settings on Jamaica and one of the Windward Islands help make the reader understand and empathize with Antoinette/Bertha, who is depicted unsympathetically in* Jane Eyre.

England. Although only the brief third section of the novel actually takes place in England, the country's influence reverberates throughout. All the people in power are English: Antoinette's father, stepfather, stepbrother, and husband; Aunt Cora's husband; the island police; and the people in Spanish Town, Jamaica. Antoinette admires an English girl in a painting called "The Miller's Daughter" but identifies with Tia, an African American girl. Antoinette cannot believe that England is real, just as Christophine does not believe its reality because she has not seen it. Christophine prophetically calls it a "cold thief place." Even when Antoinette is taken to England, it seems real to her only once, when she is allowed to visit the countryside and see its grass, water, and trees. Otherwise she compares the house in which she is imprisoned to "cardboard" and thinks that she and her husband became lost on their way from the West Indies. For Antoinette, England is a cold place, and she is left longing for the passion and beauty of the West Indies.

West Indies. Island chain separating the Gulf of Mexico and the Caribbean from the Atlantic Ocean, colonized by European powers. Antoinette blames her lack of identity on having grown up there. Her husband mistrusts his bride because of her foreign ways and blames the islands for tricking him into a loveless marriage. In contrast to England, the West Indies are warm and seductive, with the power to make people behave irrationally. Antoinette's final desperate act is an attempt to return home.

Jamaica. Island in the West Indies taken from the Spanish by the British, who made fortunes using slaves to raise sugarcane. Since emancipation in 1834, many freed slaves have grown to hate their impoverished former masters. Antoinette's deceased father is a decadent, rich Englishman, her mother a beautiful young Creole from Martinique. After her father's death and emancipation, the former slaves poison Antoinette's mother's horse, call the women "white cockroaches," and burn their home. The English people in Jamaica scorn and gossip about the family.

Colibri. Jamaican estate where Antoinette spends her childhood. Like its row of royal palms which have been either cut down or have fallen, Antoinette is proud but lost. The warm, wrought iron handrail in front of Colibri comforts her, but the orchids in the overgrown garden seem like snakes and octopi. Despite the comforts of the isolating sea and mountains which surround Colibri, the stones which cannot be stolen or burned, and a big stick, her widowed mother's focus on her sickly younger brother makes Antoinette feel unloved. The beauty and returning wealth of the place frighten the wild girl and help bring about Colibri's destruction, just as Antoinette's beauty and inheritance destroy her.

Spanish Town. Town near Kingston where Antoinette lives with Aunt Cora after Colibri burns. The convent there, especially its cool stones and shadows, provides Antoinette some safety and security, though the threatening half-caste children and English people who gossip about her mother's insanity grieve Antoinette. In Spanish Town, Antoinette's mother marries Mr. Mason, just as Antoinette marries the groom arranged for her by Mr. Mason's son. Unlike her mother, who dances gaily at her wedding to a wealthy man, Antoinette does not want to marry the strange, young Englishman who Aunt Cora and Christophine believe is only after her inheritance.

Martinique (mahr-teen-EEK). French-ruled Windward Island near Antoinette's honeymoon island. A for-

mer slave of Antoinette's mother, Christophine is a strong woman feared by the indigenous population, of which she is a member, and is rumored to practice a form of magic called obeah. When Antoinette's marriage erodes, the servant offers to take her to Martinique. The English husband refuses out of fear that there she may find someone else and be happy. Martinique is an island of mystery, sexuality, and tolerance, a place the English despise and fear as they do both Christophine and Antoinette's mother.

Granbois (grahn-BWAH). Shabby white summer home inherited from Antoinette's mother, located on an unnamed Windward Island near Martinique, probably based on the island of Dominica, where Jean Rhys was raised. Granbois is the setting of Antoinette's disastrous honeymoon; she loves the place until her husband's betrayal makes her hate it. The bathing pool where she throws rocks at a crab is a happy place, contrasted to the pool at Colibri, where Tia mocks her and steals her clothes. In Granbois Antoinette shows some self-confidence, feels almost at home and safe except at night, when she dwells on insanity and death and compares herself to the moths that fly too close to the candle's flame and are burned to death. Antoinette's hus-

band is attracted to the beauty of Granbois yet feels that the place and its surroundings have a personal grudge against him. In contrast, the more realistic Antoinette asserts that Granbois is impartial and indifferent. He finds its colors too bright, its jungle hostile and threatening, and the perfume of its night-blooming flowers too sweet. He wants to conquer its wildness and penetrate the secret of its beauty but fails to do so, just as he fails with Antoinette. Instead, out of revenge, he decides to destroy her psychologically. Though he softens as they leave Granbois and pities the little white house struggling against the "black snake-like forest," he asserts that the dark forest always triumphs, just as he has triumphed over Antoinette. Not only have his greed, intolerance, and lack of love destroyed Antoinette, but also they have damaged him.

*Sargasso Sea. Region of the North Atlantic between the Caribbean Sea and the Azores islands in whose comparatively warm and calm waters large amounts of seaweed float. Although mentioned only in the title, the Sargasso Sea symbolizes Antoinette's rootlessness and her husband's feelings of being smothered and trapped by her.

— *Shelley A. Thrasher*

WIELAND: Or, The Transformation, an American Tale

Author: Charles Brockden Brown (1771-1810)
Type of work: Novel
Type of plot: Gothic

Time of plot: 1763-1776
First published: 1798

The events of the novel take place between 1763 and 1776 largely in the eastern Pennsylvania countryside on the Wieland farm situated on the Schuylkill River a few miles from Philadelphia. Occasionally, characters go from the farm to Philadelphia, and in the final chapter, Clara lives in Montpellier, a real city in France near the Mediterranean Sea.

Mettingen (MEHT-ihn-jehn). Fictional name of the Wieland's eastern Pennsylvania farm and later of Clara's house located on her share of the farm. Mettingen is also the name of a real city in Germany that is the Wielands' ancestral home. Charles Brockden Brown uses this site as part of an overview of American history, starting with the arrival of the Puritans and proceeding to

the Revolutionary War. In the Wieland family history, Brown creates parallels with American history including the escape from religious persecution in England, the resolve to spread the gospel in the new world, the material success of the settlers, and the subsequent abandonment of the religious mission and its replacement by private worship. Significantly, he locates the principal characters near Philadelphia (where the institutions of American democracy were born), in the late eighteenth century, and on a farm, suggesting the founding fathers' belief in agrarianism as the cornerstone of American society. Additionally, in the Wieland family history, Brown explores developments in intellectual history, as seventeenth century Puritan lives based entirely on faith clash with eighteenth century lives based on reason.

The life of Clara and Theodore's father is grounded in faith in God's plan. After he dies, the Wielands convert their father's temple from a place for the exercise of religious faith to a place wherein the rationalistic precepts of the Enlightenment are largely practiced, although Theodore retains some of his father's reliance on faith. Close to Philadelphia but isolated from its direct influences, the Wielands and Pleyels establish an eighteenth century utopian, pastoral society—an Enlightenment Garden of Eden safe from the sounds of war which echo in the background and safe from having their ideas tested until an outsider, Carwin, enters the garden. Whereas before Carwin's entrance, the isolation of Mettingen served as protection, after Carwin's appearance it serves to exacerbate the effects of his deception because the Wielands and Pleyels have no resources other than their own minds with which to respond to the addition to their society and to the events which occur after his arrival. The issues are whether the voice the characters hear has a supernatural source beyond the ken of humans or can be explained rationally, and whether Carwin is the embodiment of evil or is an inno-cent trickster. Neither faith nor reason serve the members of the utopian society well because, in either case, the minds of the individuals create "reality." The result is that the Garden of Eden is transformed into a scene of horror.

Clara's house. Scene of the events that transform Clara's life. The house is located by the river which flows through the land and is not quite a mile from Theodore's house. Furthermore, Clara names her house Mettingen. Living in separate houses, Clara and Theodore are even further isolated, with disastrous results. While they still enjoy the company of others, they both have time alone, time in which to allow their minds to shape the worlds in which they live. Like his father, Theodore builds his reality upon his faith that God works through him, causing him to kill his family. Clara wavers between a belief in the supernatural and a belief in rational explanations of events, causing her to interpret events in such a way as to blame Carwin for the deaths of her loved ones and the fate of Theodore.

***Montpellier** (mont-peh-LEEAY). French town in which Clara reunites with Pleyel and plans to spend the rest of her days. While Clara does not find complete peace here, she does find the stability that was absent in America, suggesting that Europe, with its traditions, provides more security than America with its emphasis on individualism. Both faith and reason as ways of knowing can lead to disaster in a political system which privileges the individual.

— *Michael A. Benzel*

THE WILD ASS'S SKIN

Author: Honoré de Balzac (1799-1850)
Type of work: Novel
Type of plot: Allegory

Time of plot: 1829-1831
First published: La Peau de chagrin, 1831 (English translation, 1896)

The fortunes and spiritual condition of the protagonist of this novel, Raphael de Valentin, are mapped by his movements through the city of Paris—and, in the end, by his desperate and futile flight from there to the country in search of revivification in fresh pastures. Paris is a symbol of the world, with all its traps and illusions.

Parisian gambling house. Located at 36 Palais Royal, this is the place where Raphael loses the last of his money, save for the three sous he gives to beggars on the quai Voltaire.

Parisian antique shop. The impossibly well-stocked treasure-house into which Raphael wanders from the quai Voltaire (having just been lost in contemplation of the Louvre, the towers of Notre-Dame and other similarly imposing edifices). Its wares include works of art from all over the world and from many different periods of history; each of its four galleries contains works more priceless than the last. The fateful piece of shagreen is mounted in significant opposition to a portrait of Jesus Christ painted by the fifteenth century old master who shared Raphael's name.

Hôtel de Saint-Quentin (oh-TEL deh sahn-ken-TA[N]). House in Paris's rue des Cordiers in which Raphael lodges before his seduction by luxury; he selects it for its nearness to the former residence of the philosopher Jean-Jacques Rousseau. His room is a dirty, narrow, yellow-walled garret with a sloping ceiling and gaps between loose roof tiles that expose the sky. There he works without respite on his two literary projects for three years, as if dedicated to a fast, although his dreams are of wealth and conspicuous consumption. After ten months he becomes enamored of the landlady's daughter Pauline, who reminds him of the heroine of Charles Perrault's conte "Peau d'Ane" ("Donkey-skin"; Honoré de Balzac's title is an ironic transfiguration of it). The point is carefully made that these are inapt surroundings for a man whose family name links him to Valencia and Valence, and to the throne of Byzantium.

*Rue Joubert (rew zhew-BEHR). Site of the house where Raphael and his friends eat, drink, philosophize, and womanize orgiastically.

Fedora's house. Luxurious establishment in the Faubourg Saint-Honoré, appropriate as the residence of a character who is explicitly identified as a symbol of "Society." It includes a Gothic boudoir and a gilded apartment in the style of King Louis XIV. The text observes that almost the whole of Paris separates it from the rue des Cordiers.

*Luxembourg Palace. Parisian palace built in the seventeenth century for Marie de Medici. In its celebrated gardens Raphael meets Fedora in order to visit the museum and the Jardin des Plantes located in its grounds, where he begins courting her in earnest.

*Rue de Varennes (rew deh VAHR-en). Parisian location of the munificent residence that Raphael buys and refurbishes with his newly acquired wealth. Its doors are mechanically connected so that they all open whenever Raphael turns the handle of one of them, enabling him always to pass unhindered through his little empire. However, he lives there as a virtual recluse, shunning the society of his fellows.

*Paris Opéra. Fulcrum of nineteenth century Parisian society, where everyone who is anyone is to be seen. It is, inevitably, there that Raphael meets Pauline again, having gone there to demonstrate his scorn for Fedora.

*Rue Saint-Lazare (rew sah[n]-lah-zar). Location of Pauline's new home, as the daughter of the newly discovered Baroness Gaudin.

*Aix-les-Bains (aks-lay-bayn). Town in southeastern France's Savoie region renowned for its hot sulfur springs; a favorite spot for health-seeking Frenchmen to "take the waters." Raphael's futile search for a cure embraces a remarkable profusion of images of water, commencing with the duck pond, fortuitously situated between the wine market and the Salpêtrière hospital, where he meets Monsieur Lavrille, the first of several scientists who assure him—mistakenly—that the fatal skin can be stretched by technological means. (The irony of the fact that Monsieur Spieghalter's house is in the rue de la Santé—"Health Street"—is noted in passing.) After the baths at Aix fail him, Raphael goes rowing on nearby Lake Bourget. After leaving Aix in the wake of the duel, he goes to a similar resort at Mont-Dore in the Auvergne, where he climbs the highest peak, the Pic de Sancy, before his brief reunion with Pauline. The last view the text offers of Pauline is an illusory glimpse of a quasi-elemental spirit on the river Loire, near Tours.

— *Brian Stableford*

THE WILD DUCK

Author: Henrik Ibsen (1828-1906)
Type of work: Drama
Type of plot: Social realism

Time of plot: Nineteenth century
First published: Vildanden, 1884 (English translation, 1891); first performed, 1885

This play is set in the homes of two different Norwegian families, whose vastly different financial circumstances are reflected in the different lighting used in the two sets. Exploring each place is a metaphor for exploring the inner-self. In creating place, Henrik Ibsen employs transcendental illusion: minimizing or denying reality. Ambiguity abounds. The Ekdals deny truth by not recognizing the source of their place. Place creates a screen against reality, a metaphor for escape, and a symbol of government forests.

Werle house. Home of the wealthy industrialist Haakon Werle in which the play opens. Shaded lamps in its rich study cast a greenish glow, giving the illusion of a forest or seascape setting. Werle's former partner, Old Ekdal, begs release from a locked office, symbolizing his earlier imprisonment. The dim study screens him and allows others to ignore him. A brilliant inner room and other chambers suggest depth of place and characters.

Ekdal house. Shabby home of the Ekdal family in which the play's second act is set at night. A single lamp in the set suggests Old Ekdal's poverty, stressing the contrast with Werle's brilliantly lighted home.

Old Ekdal spends most of his time in a garret, in which he keeps a curious assortment of animals. He pretends that the garret with its old Christmas trees is a forest like the one in which he hunted as a young man. The ambiguous attic place suggests freedom but is actually a prison to the animals. Although the family bases its life primarily on self-deception and illusion, the Ekdal home is a happy one.

When Gregers visits the house to see his friend Hjalmar Ekdal, he is appalled by its condition and vows to reveal the truth to the Ekdals. To that end, he rents a room in the house. When he smokes up the house, pours water into the stove, and makes the floor a "wet pigsty," the disaster symbolizes the family disruption caused by Gregers's revealing the truth. The subsequent darkness of the place symbolizes melancholy; darkness and sadness remain, despite a lighted lamp with no shade. Hedvig believes that in daylight (symbolizing truth and happiness) their place (family) will again be stable. When he threatens to leave, Gina says they need an attic place (illusion) for happiness. This attic place, however, later brings grief—not happiness. Gregers's closing metaphor for himself uses place: He is the thirteenth place at a table and a source of unrest.

— Anita Price Davis

THE WILD GEESE

Author: Mori Ōgai (Mori Rintaro; 1862-1922)
Type of work: Novel
Type of plot: Psychological realism

Time of plot: 1880
First published: Gan, 1911-1913 (English translation, 1959)

This novel infuses the real neighborhood surrounding old Tokyo University with a sense of nostalgia and romance in its loving and detailed descriptions of houses, shops, restaurants, and a landmark pond. Set in a time thirty years earlier than the novel's original publication, the place is remembered as it was before Japan began to modernize. The novel's characters avail themselves of the opportunities offered by a bustling metropolis to use the city's space for their own pleasures or to welcome romantic possibilities arising from chance meetings in this nostalgic, yet active, place.

Otama's house. Residence of the young woman named Otama, located on Tokyo's Muenzaka Slope. Otama's lover, the middle-aged moneylender Suezo, carefully chooses the house in which he sets up his young mistress. Situated above Tokyo University, the wooden house sits in a mixed neighborhood. With its carefully designed traditional front garden, granite doorway, and exquisite interior, it previously belonged to a wealthy merchant, whose death puts it on the market. In spite of the house's gloomy appearance and the noise emanating from a sewing school next door, it is in an out-of-the-way location that is appreciated by the careful Suezo. Suezo also buys the house for its investment potential, as its timber is of fine quality. The house is within easy walking distance from his own family home, so Suezo can visit Otama there on a daily basis.

Because Otama's traditional Japanese house lacks a bathroom of its own—as was quite common even for expensive houses of its time—Otama is free to travel to a public bathhouse. It is while returning home from the bathhouse one day that she encounters the medical student Okada, with whom she begins a flirtation. However, circumstances prevent them from developing a more serious romantic relationship.

*Shinobazu Pond (shee-noh-bah-zew). Pool of water in the middle of Tokyo's university district designed to give aesthetic pleasure to the neighborhood. A small shrine on an artificial wooden island at the center of the pond is visited by wild geese; however, students treat the place disrespectfully, and one day Okada accidentally kills a goose with a stone that he throws on a dare from a fellow student. Later they retrieve and cook the goose and get drunk, and Okada misses his opportunity to visit Otama's house while Suezo is away from the city.

Suezo's home (sew-eh-zoh). House that Suezo buys for his family on fashionable Ike-no-hata street after he becomes rich. Acquiring a stylish home is not enough for him, however; he also wants a mistress. After renting a house on his own street for Otama's impoverished father, he finds another house for Otama a somewhat greater distance away. When Suezo's wife learns of his affair, she takes revenge by neglecting their home. Its unkempt and run-down appearance consequently literally symbolizes the lack of domestic peace and happiness within the home, from which Suezo flees with increased frequency.

*Matsugen Restaurant (mah-tsew-jen). Noted real establishment on Ueno Square near Tokyo University. It still existed at the time of the novel's publication, and had not suffered from the fires that have historically plagued Tokyo, regularly destroying the fragile wooden houses designed to withstand frequent earthquakes. Suezo meets Otama and her father at this restaurant, where he formally proposes taking her as his mistress. The novel nostalgically reflects on the changes that had wrought havoc with the restaurant's surroundings since the period in which the story is set. For example, Shinobazu Pond was once splendidly visible from the restaurant, but later horse-racing and bicycle tracks were built around it, reflecting the fast pace of Japan's modernization and embracing of Western culture.

*Kamijo (kah-mee-joh). Boardinghouse in which Okada and the novel's narrator live as students. The social order of the place, which is run by a strict landlady, appears to be as old-fashioned as the building itself. The real Kamijo burned down, a historical event used in the novel to heighten the sense of a place lost forever.

— *R. C. Lutz*

THE WILD PALMS

Author: William Faulkner (1897-1962)
Type of work: Novel
Type of plot: Tragicomedy

Time of plot: 1927 and 1937
First published: 1939

Always an experimentalist, William Faulkner created in this novel an innovative narrative device: the juxtaposition of two seemingly disparate stories, "Wild Palms" and "Old Man." These stories are starkly different in tone, action, and characters. It is particularly in their settings that the stories vary, with "Old Man" cast against a violent background of nature and "Wild Palms" set against urban environments as well as in nature. "Old Man" relates the exploits of a convict temporarily released from prison during the famous 1927 Mississippi River flood to aid in fighting in rescue efforts. The other, "Wild Palms," is a love story between Harry Wilbourne and Charlotte Rittenmeyer.

Mississippi Gulf Coast. The first section of the "Wild Palms" part of the novel opens in a summer cottage on the beach in southern Mississippi. In the strong wind from the Gulf the characters constantly hear the rattling of the palm leaves along the shore. The setting is an appropriate backdrop for the tragic story that reaches its conclusion here.

New Orleans. Known as "the City that Care Forget," New Orleans is a Latin city, a contrast to much of the rest of the United States, where the Protestant work ethic is generally stronger. Harry Wilbourne grew up in that small-town, restrictive, impoverished environment, and the easy-going moral attitude of New Orleans serves to free him from the conventional life he has previously lived. Charlotte Rittenmeyer in a sense represents the city's sensual attitudes. Harry is an intern at Charity Hospital and lives in the quarters provided for him there. When he ventures downtown with his roommate Flint to attend a party in the French Quarter ("French Town" in the novel), he encounters an entirely new environment and a group of bohemians with a distinctively different slant on life.

Chicago. It is to Chicago that Harry and Charlotte flee after they have begun their affair and she has left her husband. This thriving northern city is markedly different from the slow and languid life of subtropical New Orleans, especially during the frigid winter months. The environment there, as in New Orleans and on the Gulf coast, is a crucial element in plot and character development. From Chicago, Harry and Charlotte move to a cottage in a vacation community which is mostly abandoned because it is autumn. Afterward, they return to Chicago.

Utah. Rocky Mountain state in which Harry accepts a position at a mining camp when life in Chicago becomes too difficult for him and Charlotte. At the mining camp, he looks after medical needs of miners. It is even colder there than in Chicago, and the intense isolation of the site further separates it from the lush, warm climate of New Orleans, from which they have fled. In the harsh environment of Utah, their relationship begins to unravel as they move toward their tragic ending.

Mississippi River. Many of the "Old Man" sections of *The Wild Palms* are set on or along the Mississippi River during its great flood of 1927. The tall convict and other prisoners are transported from Parchman to the Delta region of western Mississippi State, where they are assigned various tasks, including rescuing people trapped by the flood. The action of the "Old Man" section is set on the river, uncontrollable at floodtide and sweeping away all objects and people in its path. In southern Louisiana, the tall convict and his charges, a woman and her baby, survive as he works among the Acadians (known as Cajuns) until the flood ebbs and they can return north.

Parchman. Mississippi state penitentiary, which is a large cotton plantation that employs the inmates as laborers. The first part of the novel called "Old Man" is set within the prison, where the protagonist, known only as the "tall convict," is incarcerated. It is through Parchman that the two parts of the novel, "Old Man" and "Wild Palms," are connected. It is to the prison where the tall convict is confined that Harry Wilbourne will be sent after the death of Charlotte following the botched abortion he performs.

— *Kenneth W. Holditch*

WILHELM MEISTER'S APPRENTICESHIP

Author: Johann Wolfgang von Goethe (1749-1832)
Type of work: Novel
Type of plot: Bildungsroman

Time of plot: Late eighteenth century
First published: Wilhelm Meisters Lehrjahre, 1795-1796 (English translation, 1824)

As an account of personal development, this novel features varied locales appropriate to elements of its principal character's education; however, it presents them largely from the perspective of his evolving experience of life rather than from their historical or topographic reality. In early chapters covering Wilhelm's experiences as an aspiring actor and theatrical promoter, descriptions of places are almost as sparing as the directions for stage productions—perhaps reflecting the novel's origins as an account of the life of the theater. As the narrative progresses, places take on more complex, symbolic features.

Lothario's estate. Home of the nobleman Baron Lothario. Set in the German countryside, the estate is Wilhelm's initial point of contact with the social circle that will transform his life. Although the estate is that of a wealthy aristocratic family, the main structure is an irregular building in which symmetry and architectural style have been sacrificed to domestic comfort.

As a keen student of the visual arts and of architecture, Johann Wolfgang von Goethe was readily able to describe any sort of architecture, and thus his evocation of the baron's estate is precisely aimed at having the reader put aside notions of ostentation on the part of those characters who come from the aristocracy. Instead, the estate is to be taken as an index of the ethical and intellectual stature of its owners, who are not aristocrats in a traditional mold. In place of French-inspired formal gardens are domestic gardens that run right up to the buildings. Wilhelm's observations that there is a cheerful village nearby and that all the gardens and fields seem to be in very good condition reflect Goethe's interest in a range of domestic and agricultural issues during the time he served in an important administrative capacity within the court at his adopted home of Weimar, Germany.

The rustic exterior appearance of Lothario's castle and its tranquil setting initially conceal from Wilhelm that it is the seat of a secret society constituted from his immediate circle. Wilhelm observes that a whole side of the castle, including its ancient tower, remains inaccessible to him, but he is soon conducted through dark passageways into a converted chapel that serves as a home for the society. There he is inducted into the group in a ceremony that recalls the stagecraft of the novel's earlier episodes in the theater, except that instead of being illuminated by lamps, this stage is bathed in morning sunlight coming through a stained glass window. From this room Wilhelm emerges into the garden, observing nature anew with a recognition of how feeble his interest in the world outside himself had been. In this passage Goethe clarifies his sense of the need for a dynamic relationship between cultural experiences and those arising from the natural, organic world.

Hall of the Past. Magnificent hall, built by Lothario's now-deceased uncle, in which two of the novel's crucial concluding episodes take place. Wilhelm is taken there for the first time by Natalie, one of Lothario's two sisters. The hall is a temple consecrated, not to a religious faith, but rather to art and music. However, because it is also a mausoleum Wilhelm expects to find a somber and perhaps gruesome interior. Instead he encounters a world of bright light—another manifestation of the ethos of the secret society into which he has been received.

The hall is also the scene of a further trial of Wilhelm's character, the sudden death of his foster child, Mignon, who along with Wilhelm's natural son, Felix, has been in the care of Natalie. The fateful visit to the Hall of the Past, and the subsequent funeral there of Mignon, provide Goethe with opportunities to describe an imagined architecture and to speculate on how musical performance may be integrated into the experience of the beautifully designed interior.

Therese's house. Home of Therese, a friend of Natalie and one of the women whom Wilhelm loves.

Both women have homes that reflect their differing stations in life as well as the roles they play in the formation of Wilhelm's character. Therese's little house, painted red and white, is "amusing to look at" and though it has only a few fields, her extraordinary skill at managing fields and forests for others has gained her an excellent reputation as well as some prosperity. Therese personifies the worldly individual who thrives on physical activity and is at home in the natural world. Wilhelm's love for her arises from his intellectual appreciation of her character and worldly competence.

Natalie's house. Home of Natalie, Lothario's sister. Natalie, whom Wilhelm seems destined to marry, contrasts with Therese in being a more contemplative person whose dwelling is the most solemn and sacred place Wilhelm has ever seen. When he first visits it, he feels as though he is in a fantasy world. The nobility of the house corresponds to the nobility of its owner, and in fact Wilhelm had long been seeking this woman who had once come to his aid as he lay wounded and delirious following a woodland attack by brigands. Natalie is a redemptive figure allied more with realms of art and the spirit than with the natural world, and Wilhelm's love for her is from the heart.

— *Clyde S. McConnell*

WILHELM MEISTER'S TRAVELS

Author: Johann Wolfgang von Goethe (1749-1832)
Type of work: Novel
Type of plot: Philosophical
Time of plot: Early nineteenth century

First published: Wilhelm Meisters Wanderjahre: Oder, Die Entsagenden, 1821, 1829 (English translation, 1882)

Although this novel's title may seem to promise something akin to a travelogue, its locales are employed principally as a backdrop for the author's philosophical notions. Counter to a pronounced tendency in the Romantic art and literature of Johann Wolfgang von Goethe's time, neither Goethe nor his principal character is much concerned with the beauty of nature in its wild state, and the tenor of the novel is better evoked by an alternative translation of its German title, Wilhelm Meister's Journeyman Years: Or, The Renunciants.

Pedagogic Province (peh-duh-GAH-jihk). At almost precisely the halfway point of the novel, Wilhelm enters the Pedagogic Province, a region subdivided into sections according to the nature of the educational activity that is pursued in each. As with many of the locales in the novel, Goethe gives the Province only a schematic description that allows him to explore a range of philosophical ideas. In the case of the Pedagogic Province, Goethe's objective is in part to parody the ideas of two leading German educators whose writings reflected the contemporaneous theories of the French savant Jean-Jacques Rousseau.

Wilhelm's purpose in visiting the Pedagogic Province is to see his son, Felix, who is a pupil in a rigorous and somewhat implausible program that combines a hardworking farming life with the study of the fine arts and foreign languages. Passing first through the district for instrumental music—a pastoral settlement made up of cottages that are isolated in order to separate the practicing musicians—Wilhelm comes to the district of the visual arts. At first he perceives it as a solidly built town, but then he recognizes that it is an expansive and stately city.

Soon the scene changes to nighttime in an adjacent mountainous district, where a miner's festival is in progress amid tiny flames flickering in clefts and valleys. This passage is one of several in the novel that momentarily evoke a sense of the sublime, a category of aesthetic experience popularly associated with awesome, uncanny, or even frightening aspects of nature in the late eighteenth century. Such unexpected changes of tone, scale, and perspective, as well as discontinuities of time, are features of *Wilhelm Meister's Travels* that clearly set it apart from Goethe's earlier *Wilhelm Meister's Apprenticeship* (1795-1796). Scenes of life in the countryside, and in villages and towns, are features of both novels, but in the earlier work the physical setting and the social implications of agricultural and industrial labor are significant themes.

Italian Lake. The first of the many instances of "renunciation" promised by the book's German title is a condition that has been imposed upon Wilhelm by his philosophical mentors: that he not remain in any place more than three days at a time, and that he never travel less than one mile from his lodging before he stops. Thus, the discontinuous parts of the novel that narrate Wilhelm's travels are infused with a sense both of his separation from friends and family and of his displacement and restlessness. One notably poetic passage, set in a valley of northern Italy, briefly suspends this restlessness, even as it lends depth to the theme of renunciation.

Traveling to Italy in order to gather strength for the challenges that he is to face in bringing his "journeyman years" to a conclusion, Wilhelm meets a young painter in whose company he learns to see afresh the beauty of the natural world. Soon the pair is joined by two women whose own story of renunciation Wilhelm knows well, and in the span of several days spent together in boating and conversation, complex bonds of love spring up among the four. At the end of this brief idyll, on a moonlit night by the lakeshore, love must be simultaneously acknowledged and renounced in the stronger illumination of the characters' loyalty to their "society" of renunciants.

*American wilderness. In a writer so closely identified with mainstream European culture, it is more than a little surprising to find North America employed as an idealized social and geographic locale, yet a significant aspect of Goethe's concern in this late novel is the effect of the Industrial Revolution upon the social life and the landscape of Europe. In repeated, if somewhat generic, references to the relatively new American nation, Goethe speculates about the economic and political renewal that might follow from the resettlement of agricultural and industrial activity in America. These passages notably contrast with the emotional content of the novel, but they are just part of the overall fabric of disparate moods and literary forms that the work embraces.

— *Clyde S. McConnell*

WILLIAM TELL

Author: Friedrich Schiller (1759-1805)
Type of work: Drama
Type of plot: Historical

Time of plot: Fifteenth century
First performed: 1804; first published, 1804 as
    Wilhelm Tell (English translation, 1841)

Switzerland's Lake Lucerne and the snow-clad mountains that encircle it—which Friedrich Schiller himself never saw—are in the minds and hearts of Schiller's characters and are visible on stage in his play. The terrain is associated with a political freedom that the people of the flatlands do not enjoy. Complete with hunters, fishermen, and herdsmen, this is a tamed landscape that signifies the harmony of the Swiss with nature and the common effort necessary to meet the challenges it presents. The houses of citizens of the forest cantons represent all classes, and show how a tradition of private landholding has fostered courage, moral independence, and personal responsibility.

*Altdorf. Town in Switzerland's Uri canton on whose public square people are building a prison fortress under duress, and where William Tell is forced to shoot an apple off the top of his son's head with his bow. The fortress—along with the pole with the hat near the town, to which the Swiss are required to pay obeisance—represents the claim of the Austrian governor to rule this area. As a visual sign of how the citizens of the forest cantons later freed themselves through common action, the Swiss dismantle the building on stage to the sound of bells and an alpenhorn.

*Rutli Meadow. Forest clearing from which Lake Lucerne is visible, as are mountain glaciers in the background. Located between two of the forest cantons, this meadow is the scene for the solemn oath of mutual defense among the cantons of Uri, Schwyz, and Unterwalden, which became the nucleus of Switzerland. The Swiss consider the historic oath on this meadow to be the founding act of the modern Swiss Confederation. Every year, the Swiss restage Schiller's play on the actual meadow to commemorate their political union.

Baron von Attinghausen's mansion (AHT-tihng-how-zehn). Home of Werner, Baron von Attinghausen, Ulrich's uncle, the elderly leader of the Swiss nationalist movement. The mansion contains a Gothic hall, decorated with coats of arms and helmets that represent the old political order, when Swiss nobles swore allegiance directly to the Holy Roman emperor, not an Austrian governor. The baron cultivates the old local customs, which emphasize solidarity of rich and poor. His blessing on the uprising of the Swiss against Austria helps assure a bright future. His death in the play marks a new era in which a Swiss nobility is no longer needed and all Swiss are to be equal and free.

— *Julie D. Prandi*

THE WIND IN THE WILLOWS

Author: Kenneth Grahame (1859-1932)
Type of work: Novel
Type of plot: Allegory

Time of plot: Early twentieth century
First published: 1908

The main setting for this allegory of friendship is the river as it dominates the world of Rat, Mole, Badger, and Toad. These widely different characters live near its banks, and as it rushes past their beloved homes, uniting them in space, so it is the focus of their adventures and misadventures, uniting them in friendship.

River. Fictional river in England that flows to the sea past meadows, woods, and towns and which serves as the focus of the novel. The river, never named in the story, is modeled after the rivers of southern England well known to Kenneth Grahame throughout his life. It gurgles along its course between banks covered with rushes, flowers, reeds, and trees—silver birch, alder, and willow trees. As the novel progresses, it is the setting for Rat's patient tutelage of Mole, Mole's growing skill as a boatman, Otter's despair over the disappearance of his son, Toad's near-drowning following his escape from prison, and Rat and Mole's mystical encounter with Pan.

Riverbank. Rat's home, a multichambered hole in the muddy riverbank just above the water line. It is a marvel of cozy domesticity with its parlor where armchairs are pulled close to the fireside, its kitchen which supplies the food for the table and picnic baskets, and its bedrooms offering rest in their soft sheets and blankets.

Toad Hall. Toad's home, a large English country house with lawns sloping down to the river. In keeping with his bombastic character, Toad's home is a grandiose establishment. In addition to an imposing brick manor house it includes a banqueting hall, a coach house and stable-yard, and a boathouse. Toad, careless in so many ways, is equally careless in appreciating all that his home means to him. Only after he has lost it does he understand its value. To regain his home, Toad works on a battle plan devised by Badger, who knows of a secret tunnel leading from the river to the interior of the house.

Mr. Badger's home. Extensive series of stone-lined rooms connected by paved passages, and bolt holes underground in the Wild Wood. In the novel, Badger observes that when humans went away, their structures fell into ruins and were eventually engulfed by the forest, and the animals, who always remain, made use of what the people left behind to create secure and comfortable homes.

Mole End. Mole's home, a simple underground burrow in the meadow near the river, with sleeping bunks built into the parlor wall.

Pan Island. Small wooded island in the river. Here Rat and Mole, in their search for Otter's lost son, experience at sunrise the mystical presence of the god Pan, guardian of animals.

— *Beverly Haskell Lee*

WIND, SAND AND STARS

Author: Antoine de Saint-Exupéry (1900-1944)
Type of work: Novel
Type of plot: Autobiographical

Time of plot: 1920's and 1930's
First published: Terre des hommes, 1939 (English translation, 1939)

This strongly autobiographical and episodic novel recalls Antoine de Saint-Exupéry's experiences as a pioneering airline pilot and provides fresh and often poetical perspectives on the places he visits, as well as on the ways of nature and humankind that he observes as he experiences the majesty and dangers of flight, discovers his capacity to endure the rigors of the desert, and observes both the folly of war and the courage of those caught in its snare.

Airplane. After training as a pilot in the mid-1920's, the author carries mail and passengers over oceans and continents. During his first years as a pilot, he flies a small, single-engine craft whose guidance system is mainly his own eyes and ears. In this plane, he is always acutely aware of the engine and of the possibility that if it fails, he may plunge to his death. Piloting gives him an exhilarating feeling of power and motion. In his comparatively primitive plane, the pilot senses his interactions with its controls more powerfully than he does later in his career—after engineering advances automate many piloting functions. Meanwhile, he cannot take for granted the reliability of his plane's instrumentation. Within his cockpit, he experiences the violence of nature in new ways, for aloft there is no shelter from tornadoes, cyclones, and other extremes of weather, and even ordinary winds can be dangerous.

In compensation for the danger he faces in his plane, he enjoys new perspectives on the earth from vantage points thousands of feet above the planet's surface and rediscovers nature. In this way, mechanical advances can promote spiritual advances, as from his aircraft the pilot appreciates natural places that he may never see on the surface of the earth.

*****Sahara.** Immense desert that extends across the entire width of northern Africa that provides the setting for

much of the book. At least twice, aircraft malfunctions force the pilot down in the desert—once in Spanish colonial Africa on the western coast and once in the Libyan desert. His mishaps land him on a plateau with sides so steep as to make it inaccessible from the ground, leaving the pilot to suppose that he is the first person ever to stand on that location.

When the pilot and his mechanic, Prévot, go down in Libya, they do not know exactly where they are, beyond the fact that they are too far from the Mediterranean Sea to reach it on foot. They then begin walking eastward, across endless sand. After three days they see mirages— images that look like fortresses and patches of vegetation that turn out to be the shadows of cumulus clouds. Eventually, they return to their plane where they stave off thirst by capturing morning dew on parachute strips. The desert days are hot, but the nights are cold. When they again set forth on foot, they encounter Arabs who lead them to safety. Their desert experience teaches them that they have the courage and resourcefulness to survive hard conditions and that even this lonely and inhospitable place supports people who, though alien in speech, garb, and customs, possess great human kindness.

*****Barcelona.** Spanish port city near the Pyrenees, the mountains that separate France and Spain, that the pilot visits during the midst of the Spanish Civil War. From the air, the city's wartime damage looks minimal; however, on the ground the pilot sees the war's true devastation in the once-beautiful city, within which many people are still going about their daily business. He concludes that civil war is a "disease" afflicting the participants, whether communists, anarchists, or fascists.

***Madrid.** Spain's capital city, which to the author seems like a ship loaded with humanity that an enemy intends to sink. He witnesses a bombing of the city that kills and mutilates innocent civilians but also fortifies the citizens' will to endure.

***Andes.** South American mountain range where the pilot almost crashes during a strong downdraft near the coast of Argentina. From this experience he learns why some accidents occur in the mountains even when visi-

bility is not obstructed by fog or rain. However, he himself does not crash because a sudden reversal of the wind sends him back high into the air. Then a cyclonic wind blows him out to sea. In a matter of a few minutes, he is carried, against his will, high over mountains, through a deep valley, and out over a rough Atlantic Ocean. Such a struggle against the elements, he discovers, can temporarily rob a person even of sensation.

***Punta Arenas** (poon-tah ah-ray-nahs). Town in northern Chile on whose central square the pilot spends an evening observing people and musing about not only the solitariness he feels as a stranger but also about the isolation of human beings generally, of the difficulty of entering the world of any other person.

— *Robert P. Ellis*

WINESBURG, OHIO: A Group of Tales of Ohio Small Town Life

Author: Sherwood Anderson (1876-1941)
Type of work: Novel
Type of plot: Psychological realism

Time of plot: Late nineteenth century
First published: 1919

The stories in this book describe the loneliness and emptiness of life in a small midwestern American town at the end of the nineteenth century. Winesburg, in Sherwood Anderson's understated prose, becomes a microcosm for many of the country's spiritual ills.

Winesburg. Ohio village of some one thousand inhabitants. All two dozen stories in *Winesburg, Ohio* are set in Winesburg, a small town probably based on Clyde, Ohio, where Anderson lived as a young boy. One of the qualities that makes Winesburg a novel rather than a simple collection of stories is that the village setting is constant, and the same characters (especially the central character, George Willard) wander through it in different stories. In most editions of the novel, a map of the town's layout faces the title page and shows its two main roads, Main and Buckeye Streets, the railroad tracks, and the eight most important structures in the town, including the railroad station, the New Willard House hotel, the office of the *Winesburg Eagle*, and the fairground. Winesburg is like any small midwestern village: Surrounded by farms, it is the regional center of commercial and social life.

The stories concern several of the prominent citizens of the town, including two doctors (Reefy and Parcival), the Presbyterian minister (Reverend Curtis Hartman), and a schoolteacher (Kate Swift). Most of the characters in the stories are lonely, estranged from their fellow townspeople, and incapable of expressing their inner, often neurotic longings. Part of the "revolt from the village" movement in American letters at the beginning of the twentieth century—a literary movement which included poet Edgar Lee Masters (*Spoon River Anthology*, 1915) and novelist Sinclair Lewis (*Main Street*, 1920)—Anderson showed the isolation and frustration of small-town life. "I told the stories of repressed lives," Anderson later said about *Winesburg, Ohio*. Attacking one of the dominant myths of American culture, Anderson demonstrated that village life, far from being supportive and joyous, was marked by alienation and restlessness, the legacy of American puritanism and commercialism.

New Willard House. Winesburg hotel run by Tom and Elizabeth Willard. Shabby and disorderly, the New Willard House reflects the lives of its inhabitants. Elizabeth Willard has inherited the hotel from her father, but it is an unprofitable venture. She and her husband are estranged, but both pin their hopes on their young son George, the reporter for the *Winesburg Eagle* who wanders the village gathering stories for his paper. As a young girl in her father's hotel, Elizabeth had dreamed of escaping Winesburg and becoming an actress. In one of the last stories of *Winesburg, Ohio*, "Death," Elizabeth Willard has a brief affair with Dr. Reefy, but then she dies. Her death helps to free her son from this unhappy town.

Winesburg Eagle. Offices of the local newspaper. Located (according to the frontispiece map) at the main intersection of town, the newspaper office is the site of much traffic. People wander in to talk to George Willard, especially late at night, for George is often there, if not working, then thinking about his encounters with the various "grotesques" who inhabit his village. No one story is set in the office, but several end here. At the conclusion of "The Strength of God," for example, the Reverend Hartman spills out his religious epiphany to George "half incoherently"; at the end of "The Teacher," Kate Swift lets George Willard take her in his arms in this office—and then starts to beat on his face with her "sharp little fists."

Fairground. "At the upper end of the Fair Ground, in Winesburg," Anderson writes in the penultimate story, "Sophistication," "there is a half decayed old grandstand," and here George Willard and Helen White go late one fall evening. With Helen, George no longer feels the loneliness and isolation he has felt in town, and her presence renews him. "They kissed but that impulse did not last." Instead, mutual respect for each other grows; "they had for a moment taken hold of the thing that makes the mature life of men and women in the modern world possible." Several months later—and in the next, last story—George Willard leaves Winesburg, alone.

— *David Peck*

THE WINGS OF THE DOVE

Author: Henry James (1843-1916)
Type of work: Novel
Type of plot: Psychological realism

Time of plot: c. 1900
First published: 1902

Place has great symbolic import throughout Henry James's fiction. In this novel, as in many of James's works, Europe represents sophistication, decadence, and corruption, while America represents innocence, morality, and honesty. England serves as a transitional setting, representing all the elegance—and the social stratification—of the Old World, but providing a comparatively "safe" environment in which a young American woman is watched over by conservative guardians of society.

Lancaster Gate. Large London estate belonging to Mrs. Maud Lowder that symbolizes the vulgarity of wealth with power but without taste. Merton Densher describes the estate as immense but ostentatiously vulgar and, because Mrs. Lowder controls Kate's prospects for the future, a place much like a prison. The vulgarity of Lancaster Gate symbolizes the vulgarity of the position of Mrs. Lowder's niece, Kate Croy, as her ward. Kate must marry for money and position in order to inherit her aunt's fortune and fulfill her obligations to her impoverished family.

Matcham. Estate in England belonging to Lord Mark, one of Milly Theale's suitors. Clearly historic, the house is adorned with armor and tapestries. In contrast to the vulgar Lancaster Gate, Matcham is elegant, tasteful, and unostentatious, but its seamless elegance begins the seduction of Milly, whose innocent American eyes see it as if it were a highly idealized and romantic painting by the early eighteenth century painter Antoine Watteau. The estate symbolizes Milly's naïve perceptions of Great Britain and Europe.

*Venice. Famous northeastern Italian city made up, in large part, of islands and canals. To James's contemporary readers, Italy was an exotic land of sumptuous palaces, handsome noblemen, and a mysterious religion—Roman Catholicism—and Venice was an essential stop on the Grand Tour of Europe—the capstone of a young person's education. Sunny Italy was also a land where one might recover one's health, and where one might be seduced into letting one's passions have their way.

Far from the stifling formality of London society and the watchful eyes of Mrs. Lowder, Venice provides the atmosphere in which Merton Densher can seduce the naïve Milly, and in which Milly, trying to live life to the fullest while she knows she is dying, willingly gives in to her feelings for Densher. One of the most mysterious of Europe's cities, Henry James's Venice symbolizes the European decadence and corruption that test—and often destroy—his innocent heroines.

Palazzo Leporelli. Elegant old island mansion rented by the wealthy Milly during her stay in Venice. Modeled on the real Palazzo Barbaro, which was owned by friends of Henry James, the Palazzo Leporelli should be Milly's refuge, but instead it symbolizes her besieged state.

"Leporelli" suggests "lepers," whom society has traditionally shunned; however, Milly is pursued by Densher and Lord Mark precisely *because* she is physically ill. The "friends" who surround her are really her enemies, just as her rented house is surrounded by the sea.

*Alps. Europe's most famous range, the playground of the wealthy and, like Venice, an essential stop on the Grand Tour. Here Milly's American friend Susan Stringham secretly follows her to the rim of a deep abyss and spies her seated at its very edge. The abyss, which symbolizes death and the despair of the terminally ill Milly, is described in terms that ironically echo Satan's temptation of Christ: The world and its kingdoms are spread before Milly, but the temptation she must resist is suicide. Jesus turned his back on the world, knowing he would soon die, but Milly, who also knows she will soon die, instead embraces the world fully.

*Regent's Park. Large public park in London, into which Milly wanders by accident after meeting with her doctor, Sir Luke Strett. The park symbolizes real life because Milly has only seen it before from a distance while riding in her carriage. Now she sees the park as it really is, with its poorly kept grass, its dirty sheep, its loafers playing games, and its tired, anxious people. Here Milly decides to live to the fullest the short life she has remaining.

— *Craig A. Milliman*

THE WINTER OF OUR DISCONTENT

Author: John Steinbeck (1902-1968)
Type of work: Novel
Type of plot: Social realism

Time of plot: 1960
First published: 1961

Set in a middle-class Long Island town, this novel places a nation's loss of its moral moorings against the backdrop of its Puritan past. The protagonist struggles to reconcile his proud family history and his own Harvard education with the prosaic reality of his dreary and undistinguished life in a provincial town.

New Baytown. Harbor town on Long Island, New York, in which the novel is primarily set. New Baytown has deep connections to an old seafaring and whaling industry that had made the former fortune of the Hawley family, to which the protagonist, Ethan Allen Hawley, belongs. A Harvard graduate, Hawley works as a clerk at Marullo's Fruit and Fancy Groceries, a store his family once owned—one of the old-fashioned, neighborhood stores, where he waits on people individually, makes sandwiches for a bank teller across the street, and extends credit on occasion.

Hawley lives in his family's ancestral home, from which he walks two blocks every weekday down Elm Street that angles into High Street where he works.

Nearby, the old Bay Hotel is being leveled, to be replaced by a Woolworth store, the old giving way to the new. New Baytown is a charming town with tree-lined sidewalks where Mr. Baker, the banker, walks daily from his home on Maple Street to the First National Bank, with unequal steps observing the old childhood superstition that stepping on the cracks will break his mother's back.

Baker's father and Ethan's grandfather, Captain Hawley, had jointly owned the *Belle-Adair*, an exceptionally fine whaling ship that mysteriously burned—a fire Ethan suspects Baker's father of instigating for the insurance money.

*Harvard University. Cambridge, Massachusetts, university from which Ethan graduated. Although Ethan complains that his education is worthless in his present job, his use of language, literary quotations and allusions, and obvious love of the humanities, and the sophistication he gained at Harvard provide a contrast to the provinciality of New Baytown.

Old Harbor. Abandoned harbor near New Baytown that reflects the past that infuses the novel. Once protected by Whitsun Reef, the harbor now is filled with silt and sand and no longer fit for ships like those that once frequented it. While going to Old Harbor, Ethan reflects on the nautical lore that his grandfather taught him.

Located just off the edge of the harbor is Ethan's private and secret "Place," a tiny enclosure with a seaward view near the remnants of the Hawley dock. Within this womblike space Ethan escapes his mundane world, descending into a self-absorbed solipsism—a passive experience that he likens to a sheet being hung on the line to dry. While musing on what happens to him when he goes to his place, he rationalizes that it does not matter whether what happens there is good or bad as long as it is right for him—thus reflecting what John Steinbeck at the time saw as America's extreme emphasis on individualism.

At the end of the novel when Ethan goes to his private place to commit suicide after his son has been caught plagiarizing in a national essay-writing contest, he is spared by an epiphany. As he reaches into his pocket for razor blades, he finds instead a family talisman that his daughter placed there. Thanks to this discovery, a sense of familial responsibility and love returns to him, and he struggles against the rising tide, to leave his place to return home and return the talisman to his daughter.

Porlock Street. New Baytown neighborhood in which the most luxurious homes are located—houses with widow's walks on their roofs and exotic furniture and artifacts, many from China. By contrast, the Hawley and Baker houses on Elm Street are Early American, with peaked roofs and board siding, shaded by huge elms planted when the houses were built.

— *Barbara A. Heavilin*

THE WINTER'S TALE

Author: William Shakespeare (1564-1616)
Type of work: Drama
Type of plot: Tragicomedy

Time of plot: Legendary past
First performed: 1610-1611; first published, 1623

This play is set in largely mythical versions of Sicily and Bohemia. Because no stage directions have come down with the play, modern editors supply them. Time is both Chorus and a major theme in a cyclic movement within the three-part structure, with action in Sicily, Bohemia, and back to Sicily for the resolution after a lapse of sixteen years.

*Sicily. Island off the southern tip of the Italian peninsula in which the play opens, with Polixenes, the king of Bohemia, visiting his old friend Leontes, the king of Sicily. In Shakespeare's time, Sicily had a reputation for crimes of jealousy and revenge that Shakespeare used in this play by having Leontes turn against Polixenes when he suspects that his friend is having an affair with his wife. Leontes' Sicilian heritage—and the play's insightful analyses of a jealousy so intense that it is mad—puts in context his irrational behavior in rejecting his pregnant wife Hermione and their son Mamilius. Leontes consults the Greek oracle at Delphi and rejects its judgment against his delusions. Following his son's death, Leontes finally accepts his guilt and undertakes familiar Christian penances, performed with saintly sorrow. The final scene is in a chapel, in which the statue of the supposedly dead Hermione comes alive in a resurrection that restores lost ones, so that the sad tale for winter has a happy ending.

*Bohemia. Mountainous inland country that now forms part of the Czech Republic. The play alludes to Bohemia's having a seacoast, but it is accessible by water only on rivers. Known as a site of romantic adventure in Shakespeare's time, Bohemia is a place where a bear eats a man shipwrecked in a storm, shepherds care for an abandoned infant, and young love thrives. Shakespeare both moved the pastoral celebration of Arcadia from its southern location to a northern clime bathed in light and made it a realistic sheep-shearing. But the regeneration of this spring/summer festival is marred by the jealousy and wrath of Polixenes, the wronged friend of the opening. When all return to Sicily, where there was "winter/ In storm perpetual," calm and light come with forgiveness and the promise of fruitfulness in the marriage of Perdita and Florizel.

— *Velma Bourgeois Richmond*

WINTERSET

Author: Maxwell Anderson (1888-1959)
Type of work: Drama
Type of plot: Tragedy

Time of plot: Twentieth century
First performed: 1935; first published, 1935

This play takes its setting from the theme that within any urban area, there are pockets of extreme poverty where the disenfranchised eke out a drab, day-to-day existence. Even in the United States, a nation of golden promise, there are those who slip through the cracks in the social system and are further oppressed by a system of justice that favors the wealthy and the powerful.

Riverfront. Tenement house, nestled under a soaring bridge and surrounded by huts, which shelters street people and demonstrates that the streets of America are not paved with gold nor is America in fact the proverbial "land of milk and honey." The bridge span hovering over this depressed area symbolizes oppression, which shadows and darkens this neighborhood and its population. By specifying neither the city nor the state, the description of this place implies that both the scene and action could take place in any city or state.

Basement apartment. The ceiling of the apartment is covered with huge pipes and suggests some huge predator, a constrictor or perhaps an octopus, which somehow holds the inhabitants there and prevents them from escaping. The warm interior suggests a sanctuary when contrasted to the cold and sleet outside, but in reality, it is a trap disguised as a haven.

The interior and exterior scenes alternate throughout the drama. The oppressive and stifling exterior is equated with the exploitation of the weak and powerless. These human flotsam and jetsam attempt to eke out an honest but meager living. However, they are thwarted by the very laws designed to protect them. The law enforcement officer is not a friend but an oppressor. The interior trap suggests that hidden prejudices, such as anti-Semitism, rob individuals of opportunities and dignity until the only possibility left to them is a life of crime. In this world, the powerful and the criminal are protected, while the hopes and dreams of the innocent are murdered. This could happen in any city or state in America.

— *H. Alan Pickrell*

WISE BLOOD

Author: Flannery O'Connor (1925-1964)

Type of work: Novel

Type of plot: Psychological realism

Time of plot: Early twentieth century

First published: 1952

This novel's action takes place primarily in a fictional city in Alabama in which the protagonist, Hazel Motes, intends to found his Church Without Christ. The novel's urban landscape is an appropriately shabby backdrop for a citizenry who share Hazel's determination to believe in nothing.

Taulkinham. Imaginary Alabama city that is the setting for most of the action of *Wise Blood*; loosely modeled on Birmingham, Alabama. Hazel Motes decides to go to Taulkinham when he discovers, after leaving the Army, that none of his family remains in the family home in Eastrod, Tennessee. Taulkinham is filled with characters and locations that are rooted in the 1930's and 1940's. Its street preachers, movie promotions, car salesmen, prostitutes, and bumpkins can be found in any time or place, but Flannery O'Connor gives these a southern flavor.

Hazel's first evening in Taulkinham offers a good example of O'Connor's use of the city. As Hazel walks through the garish streets of the commercial district, O'Connor paints a picture of shoddy cheapness in direct contrast to the sky full of stars, which suggests the majestic beauty of God. Not surprisingly, the people of Taulkinham are ignoring the sky in favor of watching a man selling potato peelers.

The settings of Taulkinham—the prostitute Leora Watts's house; Hazel's rented room; Enoch Emery's room, in which even the pictures make him feel guilty; the used car lot; and the street corners on which Hazel preaches his depressing message of meaninglessness— all suggest the emptiness of Hazel's own vision (a vision that changes when his faith returns after he blinds himself).

A location of particular interest in the city is the museum from which Enoch Emery steals a mummy. The museum is a classical building and carved into its face is the Latin-styled inscription in which the letter *u* is replaced with *v*—MVSEVM. Enoch finds the word terrifying (he pronounces it *muvseevum*) and can hardly bring himself to say it aloud, as if it were a sacred word.

Appropriately enough, Enoch believes that the mummy he has stolen from such a holy place is the "new jesus," and he tries to persuade Hazel of its power.

O'Connor wrote as a committed Catholic surrounded by southern Protestantism, and as such she wanted to make her fiction represent those moments in which God's grace touches human souls. However, she also wanted to write about the world she and her readers knew. The result was her representation of places like Taulkinham, the secular city and its inhabitants. Although some readers have called O'Connor's people grotesques, she claimed they were simply realistic pictures of a world where people are more quickly drawn to street hawkers and fraudulent preachers than to matters of true faith. It is not surprising that when Hazel's landlady realizes he has wound barbed wire around his chest, evidently in penance, she tells him no one does such things any more, "like boiling in oil or being a saint or walling up cats."

Eastrod. Tennessee crossroads community in which Hazel Motes's family once lived. Hazel returns to Eastrod (which once was home to twenty-five people) when he gets out of the Army only to discover that both the town and his family's house have been abandoned. The general store is boarded up, the barn is in collapse, and Hazel's house is reduced to a "skeleton" and empty of everything but an old chifforobe (a combination dresser and wardrobe) his mother had once bought for thirty dollars. Later, on the train, Hazel dreams of the chifforobe, blending it with his mother's coffin in his dream. It is on this train that Hazel announces his loss of faith and his abandonment of his youthful plan to return to Eastrod and become a preacher like his grandfather.

— *Ann D. Garbett*

WIVES AND DAUGHTERS

Author: Elizabeth Gaskell (1810-1865)
Type of work: Novel
Type of plot: Domestic realism

Time of plot: Mid-nineteenth century
First published: serial, 1864-1866; book, 1866

This novel plays out provincial life in a country town of Hollingford and its surroundings. Everyday life is lived in a period of English society that ushers in social and scientific changes. Old aristocracy makes way for liberal social shifts. The feudal traditions of the past painfully make way for a new order. Hollingford is an extended Cranford (actual town in Cheshire County, West England) in a sense of community and social interactions in tremulous humanity facing a changing time.

Hollingford. English provincial town that provides the main setting in which country life and her central figures interact as their stories unfold. Molly Gibson, the central figure and moral fulcrum of the novel, lives her whole sheltered life in Hollingford, growing up in a single-parent home. Mr. Gibson, her father, a well-known and respected doctor, is usually seen making his rounds with house calls, up and down many dirt roads, from morning until evening. Although he is not a native of the town, his practice and domestic life are here. Molly Gibson herself is greatly attached to the town. However, her father, as a man of scientific and rational bent, has little patience and energy for the rustic and parochial manners and peculiarities of the locals. He lives there primarily for the sake of his daughter, for all she knows and is conversant with is in Hollingford. However, despite her familiarity with the town and its people, she is often susceptible to her own timidity and modesty because Hollingford is a small community of simple people.

Hollingford is representative of many English country towns with old but fading aristocracies; its leading citizens are the count and countess Cumnor. Other residents include figures such as the two Misses Browning, as typical of small English country towns. These women represent the past, frowning here and there with disapproval at change.

Hollingford is a rather dull and slow-paced place, in which the place of women is in the home, doing needle-work or reading pretty books and novels. Unlike the Cumnors, not all Hollingford people can go to London or other cosmopolitan centers for a change of air or season. Hollingford is a small community of country folks, with a few exceptions, whose cause for much talk, antic-ipation, and great preparation is an event at Cumnor Towers or an occasional ball.

Cumnor Towers. Official residence and estate of the count and countess Cumnor, who carry on the old traditions of noblesse oblige by periodically hosting balls for their neighbors to display their gentility and refinement. The count and countess live in waning gentility, and their daughter, Lady Harriet, is almost radical in her views; she represents a major change in the country's social and class structures.

Gibson home. Modest Hollingford home of Molly Gibson and her widowed father. Reared by her father, she is not completely free to show any sentimental or emotional feeling in this domestic space. With all of her existing unvoiced emotions, Molly has to endure the ways and whims of a new stepmother in this house, her private space. Mr. Gibson and his daughter have to adjust to his new wife's penchant for posh domesticity and her emulative taste of the aristocratic Cumnors' refinement. Mr. Gibson's forced silence in all of his wife's wishes and whims and his preoccupation with his medical duties leave little attention for Molly's innermost feelings and suffering. Eventually, this home becomes a prison to Molly.

Hamley Hall. Family home and estate of Squire Hamley, which represents an aspect of country society that contrasts strongly to that of the aristocracy. From an ancient family whose wealth depends on advantageous marriages, he is eccentric and cantankerous but at heart quite compassionate. He tries to uphold feudal traditions in a time of social change; Hamley Hall estate and its dwindling fortune represent the old feudal ways.

— Hanh N. Nguyen

THE WOMAN IN THE DUNES

Author: Kōbō Abe (1924-1993)
Type of work: Novel
Type of plot: Allegory

Time of plot: 1962
First published: Suna no onna, 1962 (English translation, 1964)

The continually shifting sand dunes of Japan's coastline that form the landscape of this novel serve a central symbolic function in stating Kōbō Abe's existential theme of human inability to come to terms with the changing nature of reality. The remote seaside village represents the human community, which the main character refuses to join.

Sand dunes. Coastal region in an unspecified part of Japan. At the beginning of the novel, the main character, Jumpei Niki, a science teacher and amateur entomologist, seeks to examine the sand dunes in a scientific manner, describing their physical properties and attempting to control them through rational strategies, clearly a defensive gesture to avoid confronting the existential reality of his situation. However, the sands quickly become a pervasive and unavoidable dimension of his existence, permeating his clothes, irritating his skin, and always present in his mouth. He finally comes to accept the presence of the sand dunes and to view them not as an enemy to be controlled but as a force to be worked with. At the novel's conclusion, he uses his knowledge of science in order to construct a trap to collect condensed water from the sands.

Abe spent his boyhood in Japanese-occupied Manchuria, whose desert landscapes made a strong impact on his consciousness. The constantly changing, windblown shapes of the desert sands came to symbolize to him the fluid and transitory nature of what people take to be "reality" in the everyday world. Abe's sand imagery in his novel presents an existential vision of reality that rejects any conceptualized and rationalized view of the world—the objective attitude of science, for example—that posits enduring and fixed absolutes through which human beings experience and manipulate nature. All that humans have is subjective human existence, which is experiential and ephemeral. Abe was influenced by European existentialism, and his point of view is consistent with his Japanese Buddhist heritage, which also posits the ever-changing nature of being as it truly is and rejects the false dualism of an absolute reality that is created under the illusion of ego consciousness.

Village and sand pit. Isolated coastal village at an unnamed location in Japan, where Niki takes a brief holiday from his job to look for insects common to the coastal sand dunes. He falls into a sand pit in which there is a small house and a lone woman. She sleeps during the day and toils at night in a vain effort to remove the always encroaching sands that threaten to engulf the pit and the entire village. Niki believes he is being held captive in order to force him to aid the woman in holding back the sands.

The isolated village and its shifting sand pits function as a surrealistic expression of the character's alienated existence. Abe was greatly influenced by the existential themes and surrealistic style of Franz Kafka, and this novel owes much to Kafka's work. His character Niki is an alienated and lonely man who is unmarried and has few friends. He is described at one point as a man who uses a psychological condom that protects him from any intimate emotional contact with others. In extreme paranoia, he refuses to aid the villagers in their efforts to hold back the sands and abuses the woman in the pit. Niki is a man who lives in psychological denial about the true conditions of his life. His refusal to join the community efforts to survive and his reluctance to establish a meaningful and supportive relationship with a partner clearly condemn him to a lonely and alienated existence. The novel's conclusion has Niki, after a vain attempt to escape the woman and the village, accepting his fate and joining in the daily communal efforts to combat the sands. He enters into a mutually supportive relationship with the woman and comes to live a peaceful life.

— *Thomas F. Barry*

THE WOMAN IN WHITE

Author: Wilkie Collins (1824-1889)
Type of work: Novel
Type of plot: Detective and mystery

Time of plot: 1850's
First published: 1860

Ancestral homes in various European countries provide the settings for all the ingredients of this mystery novel. Schools, churches, cemeteries, morgues, and asylums contribute to its eery mood.

Hampstead, on the Finchley-road. This lonely, isolated stretch of woods, near a crossroads leading to London, provides the first sighting of the woman in white by Walter Hartright, on the night before he leaves for Limmeridge House. In his conversation with her, she gives him the clues he needs months later to free Laura from the asylum after her husband has committed her.

Limmeridge House. Ancestral home on the Cumberland coast, with a view of Scotland, that belongs to Frederick Fairlie. Limmeridge House represents normalcy, security, and safety for Laura and her half sister Marian until Laura's marriage to Percival Glyde. Hartright is employed to live here and give art lessons to Laura and Marian Halcombe. Hartright's art lessons, happy days for the sisters, and an arranged marriage occur here. Limmeridge House is not a safe harbor during Laura's marriage until the death of Glyde and his accomplice Count Fosco. Then Limmeridge House again becomes Marian and Laura's home, as well as the home of her husband Walter Glyde and their son, the heir of Limmeridge House. The novel begins and ends at Limmeridge House.

Limmeridge School. School at which Laura Fairlie's mother taught; located near Limmeridge House. Eleven years later, the school that Laura and Anne Catherick attended is still used. This is also the scene of one of the students saying that he has seen, what he calls, the ghost of Anne.

Church and cemetery. Well-kept church, grounds, and cemetery in a valley near Limmeridge House is the location in which Anne is sighted at the grave of Mrs. Fairlie. The church is the setting of the marriage of Laura and Baron Percival Glyde; it is also where the fake grave of Laura is located.

Blackwater Park. Family estate of Sir Percival Glyde in Hampshire. Amid the rubble and decay of the house, one habitable wing of Glyde's ancestral home in an isolated area of Hampshire is where, after an extended stay of six months in Europe following Laura's wedding, Count Fosco and his wife accompany Glyde and Laura. The house and the grounds are where these two men plot murder, kidnapping, poisoning, lies, deceit, and violence against anyone who gets in the way of their obtaining Laura's money. The boathouse and lakefront are the scenes of several conversations between Laura and Anne. Marian arrives to stay there and finds a small dog nearly dead from a gunshot. She wishes that her first day at Blackwater Park had not been associated with death.

Vestry at Old Wilmington. Decaying, neglected vestry located in the abandoned old part of the town of Wilmington. The worm-eaten, decaying wooden vaults of the vestry contain marriage records of all who were married in the area. Glyde forges the record of his parents' marriage; Hartright uncovers this. Glyde breaks into the vestry, accidentally sets it on fire, and burns to death.

Asylum. Private asylum near London is where the wealthy gentry are permitted to incarcerate family members. Both Anne and Laura are committed to this asylum at different times. Glyde is responsible for both because he believes that they know and will tell society and their solicitor his secret.

*Dead-house. Paris morgue in which the unidentified body of international spy Count Fosco is placed for public viewing. His death ends the threats and conspiracy against Laura.

— *Anna Hollingsworth Hovater*

A WOMAN KILLED WITH KINDNESS

Author: Thomas Heywood (c. 1573-1641)
Type of work: Drama
Type of plot: Tragicomedy

Time of plot: Early seventeenth century
First performed: 1603; first published, 1607

Different meanings of "house," both as "dwelling" and as "lineage or kin," are central to the two plots of this play, which contains some of the most detailed stage directions in early modern English drama. The specific regional setting not only authenticates this portrait of the burgeoning English middle class but also enables Thomas Heywood to dramatize the fault lines in early modern ideologies of the family, civility, and private life.

***Yorkshire.** Historic county in northern England in which the play is set. Yorkshire and its inhabitants are usually described as bleak, independent, dour, and craggy. The play's regional setting, with Yorkshire's small, self-policing communities, middle-class marriages, religious underpinnings, and bumpkin servants, is typical of domestic tragedy dramas. Unlike other plays usually grouped with it, however, Heywood's experimental play is not based on any known contemporary scandal.

Frankford's house. Home of the provincial gentleman John Frankford. A large house and rural estate that is one of the finest in Yorkshire, Frankford's home symbolizes the confident wealth of this gentleman-farmer and his new marriage to his aristocratic wife, Anne. The house itself may be viewed as one of the principal presences in the play, a kingdom in which the husband is regent.

By using a comical array of servants, key social rituals, and unusually extensive stage directions, Heywood constructs a realistic portrait of household activity. The subversion of Frankford's marriage and middle-class values of hospitality is symbolized by his having to break into his own house at night, like a robber. He is barely prevented from killing his wife's lover by an anonymous maid, whom some critics have read as the domestic spirit of the house itself.

Mountford's estate. Neighboring estate of the provincial nobleman Sir Charles Mountford, in central Yorkshire, that has been in Mountford's family for three hundred years. After killing two men in a fight over a wager, Sir Charles is forced to spend his patrimony, descending into poverty and eventually prison in York Castle. The importance of house and land to his family's honor becomes apparent when Sir Charles opts to sacrifice his willing sister to an unhappy marriage and likely suicide rather than lose his property.

— Nicolas Pullin

A WOMAN'S LIFE

Author: Guy de Maupassant (1850-1893)
Type of work: Novel
Type of plot: Naturalism

Time of plot: Early nineteenth century
First published: Une Vie, 1883 (English translation, 1888)

Maupassant uses this novel to provide his readers with a vivid feel for life in rural France in the early nineteenth century. It depicts a spectrum of Norman country society—the petty land-owning nobility, an aristocracy of a higher degree, the peasants, the clergy. But the novel's real importance in terms of place focuses on the protagonist, Jeanne, and the ways in which her natural and material surroundings determine—or reflect—her happiness or misery.

***Normandy.** Largely agricultural region on western France's Atlantic coast in which the novel's fundamental settings—both literal and symbolic—are established in the opening chapter. In that chapter's very first image, seventeen-year-old Jeanne Le Perthuis des Vauds looks out over rainy Rouen, a major city in Normandy. She has just left a convent after spending five years within its walls absorbing a proper education. She awaits her father, who will take her home to the country again.

Walls are one key motif that appears early in the novel—the walls of the convent, the confines of the city. Indeed, Jeanne looks forward to returning to the family estate, Les Peuples, where she and her parents will spend the summer. The convent is thus constraint, while the beautiful countryside is the essence of freedom: sun, open pastures, trees and flowers, the seaside. The landscape seems to Jeanne to represent a bright, wide-open future.

Les Peuples (lay PUHP-luh). Perthuis family estate. Jeanne longs for—dreams of—freedom. Indeed, "dreams" may be the novel's key word. But ultimately, one might argue that Jeanne's dreams are her weakness. She expects life to conform to her fantasies of perfection—her dreams of a great passion, a handsome lover, the perfect marriage and family. She marries a local nobleman of low degree, Julien de Lamare. According to plan, Jeanne's parents give the newlyweds Les Peuples as their home.

Instead of fulfilling Jeanne's dream of freedom, her beloved Les Peuples becomes her prison. Her husband's infidelities, the deaths of her parents, Julien's murder, and her irresponsible son all beat Jeanne into submission. Her despair is represented physically by her self-confinement to her estate, by her subsequent taking of refuge in her house, and finally in her room. As Jeanne grows old, she questions the very meaning of life.

***Corsica.** Large French island in the Mediterranean Sea. On their honeymoon, during their brief initial happiness as a couple, Jeanne and Julien spend some time on Corsica, whose legendary mystique involves a rugged but beautiful mountainous terrain and a population given to violence, family feuds, and banditry. The romantic side of Jeanne's character is captivated by the island's landscape and the people she meets there. In fact, this ambience of wildness and brutality curiously inspires an awakening of sensuality in Jeanne—another moving manifestation of the kind of freedom she hoped for in her adolescence and early in her marriage. Late in her life, Jeanne will sadly look back on this time on the island with nostalgia for fragile happiness.

***Paris.** France's capital and leading city. After having been abandoned for years by Paul, her ne'er-do-well son, Jeanne summons the courage to look for him in Paris. However, she is thoroughly disoriented by the city, which she has not visited in decades. She is frightened by labyrinthine Paris's dark streets and alleys, the movement of the crowds, even by the busy cafés and restaurants that she cannot bring herself to enter. She sees people around her, especially in the chic Palais Royal area, laugh at her quaint, behind-the-times clothes and her nervous manner. Moreover, Jeanne finds that Paul has moved, leaving no new address. This experience in the city simply drives Jeanne back to her country home and further into her passivity, loneliness, and despair.

The novel's tragedy is Jeanne's repeated disappointment and disillusion, as she discovers, again and again, that reality is not as pretty as fantasy. In physical terms, Jeanne's tragic disillusion is manifested in the narrowing of her circle of activity. Jeanne's essential story is one of misfortune and loss of spirit. Only at the novel's arbitrarily happy and unconvincing ending, when Paul and his baby come to live with Jeanne in Normandy, does Jeanne come out of her shell.

— *Gordon Walters*

WOMEN BEWARE WOMEN

Author: Thomas Middleton (1580-1627)
Type of work: Drama
Type of plot: Tragedy

Time of plot: Early seventeenth century
First performed: c. 1621-1627; first published, 1657

This Jacobean drama is set in Italy, a background which, in tragedies of its period, implies luxury, vice, and violence. Within this framework, Thomas Middleton dispassionately and ironically records human—especially feminine—motivation and passion. Intertwined sexual and economic corruption—a recurrent theme in Middleton's drama—links three residences in seventeenth century Florence.

*Florence. City in the Tuscany region that was one of Italy's main centers of culture and political intrigue in the seventeenth century. The main plot's adulterous triangle derives from an actual Florentine scandal surrounding an unfaithful Venetian bride. Although Middleton's Venetian source sympathized with Bianca, Middleton himself does not blame her fall entirely on Florence's immorality. However, he does suggest living in an alien city whose inhabitants she describes as "all strangers to me, Not known but by their malice," made her more vulnerable to seduction.

Widow's house. Home to which Leantio, in the opening scene, brings his stolen Venetian bride, intending to hide the "treasure" of her beauty "under this plain roof." In the first striking use of upper- and lower-stage dynamics, a window in this house displays Bianca to the duke, below, riding to St. Mark's Temple. Soon afterward, Bianca despises both fidelity and the poverty of her mother-in-law's house.

Lady Livia's house. Home in a higher-class milieu, dominating the second and third acts, where both Bianca and her subplot counterpart, Isabella, are betrayed into sexual corruption by Livia. Here, in an even more dramatic counterpoint of upper- and lower-stage actions, Middleton has the duke rape Bianca in an alcove while, below them, Livia defeats the mother-in-law in a chess game that clearly parallels the sexual "game" upstairs. Here Livia also facilitates her brother's incestuous affair with their niece, while simultaneously promoting Isabella's loveless marriage to a lascivious idiot. Although fashionable, Livia's home resembles a house of prostitution.

Duke's court. Palatial and decadent setting for the play's last two acts, in which luxury, lust, and treachery prove fatal for six sinners. In the final scene, a masque celebrating the duke's marriage to Bianca ends in mass death, upheaving "the general peace of Florence."

— *Margaret Bozenna Goscilo*

THE WOMEN OF BREWSTER PLACE: A Novel in Seven Stories

Author: Gloria Naylor (1950-   )
Type of work: Novel
Type of plot: Social realism

Time of plot: 1930's-1960's
First published: 1982

The neighborhood in which this novel is set is as much a character as the humans who inhabit it. Brewster Place's history of gradual decline while doggedly clinging to its few remaining communal qualities is also the story of the women who live there.

Brewster Place. Neighborhood in a large, unnamed northern city, possibly New York, possibly Chicago. New York seems more likely since, aside from its being Gloria Naylor's hometown, there is mention in one episode that the state of "Maine ain't far" away. Chicago is also a possibility because one character, Etta Mae Johnson, went home to Brewster Place "with a broken nose she'd gotten in . . . St. Louis," suggesting the distance

between the two was not so great. However, the actual identity of the city is not explicitly revealed.

Brewster Place was originally conceived in the story as a way for crooked politicians and businessmen to resolve some of their personal concerns to their political and financial advantage. First Irish, then Mediterraneans, and finally African Americans came to inhabit the district. Though the neighborhood was relatively inviting at first, its streets and buildings were allowed to decline; its one through street was soon walled up to make a dead end, basically isolating the inhabitants from the rest of the city.

The dreariness of the gray tenement buildings, the oppressiveness of the wall, and the segregation make the women of Brewster Place racial, social, and economic victims. Yet they come together finally to tear down the wall, which increasingly seems a manifestation of their oppression, using "knives, plastic forks, spiked shoe heels, and even bare hands" to dismantle it. With this one symbolic act, they demonstrate their determination to change their lives for the better.

Miss Eva's house. Home of Miss Eva Turner in Asheville, North Carolina, which becomes a haven for Mattie Michael and her infant son Basil. Miss Eva literally takes in Mattie, who is wandering the streets of Asheville. She gives her a home, and when she dies, she leaves the house to Mattie. Mattie, having left her own family home in Tennessee, pregnant and disgraced, views Miss Eva's house as a mark of respectability and a promise of security for herself and Basil. However, she puts the house up as collateral for Basil's bail after he is arrested in the killing of a white man. Basil jumps bail, disappears, and both he and the house are lost forever. The house has been a sanctuary for Mattie for more than fifteen years; when she has to give it up and move away to settle in Brewster Place, she is not only bereft of her only child but of the only home she has known as an adult.

Canaan Baptist Church. Church near Brewster Place where Mattie Michael attends services and achieves the peace-of-mind she rarely experiences otherwise. Described as "a brooding, ashen giant," it is the place where her friend Etta Mae Johnson meets an itinerant preacher, who seduces her. Etta Mae's unrealistic hope when she first meets him is that somehow this "holy" man will be the one with whom she can finally settle down. The preacher's dynamic sermonizing and charismatic personal charm encourage Etta Mae's natural flirtatiousness. She ends up in a hotel with the not-so-holy preacher, a familiar and depressing scenario for Etta Mae. The church is a source of solace to Mattie, but after the episode with the preacher, it is mainly a reminder to Etta Mae of the futility of her hopes for a conventional future.

Alley. Brewster Place's three-hundred-foot-long, six-foot-wide strip adjacent to the hated wall. It is the place where the teenage males with no place to go hang out. They "reign" there "like dwarfed warrior kings," smoking marijuana, stealing, and generally terrorizing the vulnerable of Brewster Place. A dark and forbidding place, it is where the gang leader C. C. Baker and his cronies beat and rape the lesbian Lorraine and where she, out of her mind from the pain and trauma, murders Ben the janitor.

Rock Vale. Rural area in Tennessee's Rutherford County near the border with North Carolina. This is where the young Mattie Michael is "seduced" by a young man named Butch Fuller. The resulting pregnancy causes a breach with her father, and she leaves home, never to return.

— *Jane L. Ball*

THE WOMEN OF TRACHIS

Author: Sophocles (c. 496-406 B.C.E.)
Type of work: Drama
Type of plot: Tragedy

Time of plot: Antiquity
First performed: Trachinai, 435-429 B.C.E. (English translation, 1729)

The setting of this ancient Greek tragedy is simply the front of the house of Herakles at Trachis. However, the main character, Deianeira, the wife of Herakles, employs the Greek poetic technique of word-painting to create a picture of two river scenes: a battle between Herakles and the river god Acheloös and a crossing of another river by the centaur Nessus.

Herakles' house (HEHR-uh-kleez). Home of Herakles, for which Sophocles uses a set with dramatic effectiveness: When Deianeira learns that the robe she gave to Heracles as a love charm actually causes irrevocable pain and burning, she rushes into the house without saying a word. A few moments later her nurse emerges to report and lament Deianeira's suicide.

*Trachis (tray-KEHS). City on a high plain northwest of Thermopylae in the central Greek region of Locris. More remote and less bustling than the earlier homes of Herakles (Thebes and Mycenae), Trachis is where Herakles had hoped to retire in relative solitude.

*River Evenos. River in central Greece; it is not shown on stage, but in the prologue Deianeira reenacts an incident that occurred at the river years earlier, when Herakles took her home as his bride and came to the river. There, the centaur Nessus offered to ferry Deianeira across then return for Herakles. Instead, Nessus tried to molest Deianeira in midstream, and Herakles shot him from the shore with his bow. Between the description of this incident and that of Herakles' battle with a river god, images of rivers dominate this tragedy, pervading the mental, if not the physical setting.

— John R. Holmes

WONDERLAND

Author: Joyce Carol Oates (1938-   )
Type of work: Novel
Type of plot: Psychological realism

Time of plot: 1939-1971
First published: 1971

This novel is the life story of a man searching for a true identity and place of his own after beginning his life with a terrible trauma when, as a teenager, he becomes the sole survivor of his father's massacre of his family. Afterward, he lives in a series of dysfunctional families until he becomes a medical doctor and marries and starts his own family. Through these changes, he never fully develops a self-directed life of his own. Ultimately, it is only by saving his daughter, whose identity and life have been ground to nothingness, that his own life has a chance to begin.

Yewville. Town in New York's upstate Niagara County where Jesse Harte, one of six children, grows up in a small and crowded house built by his father, Willard, next to a gas station that he owned until it failed. The novel opens when Jesse is fourteen years old and his father turns the family house into a place of horror by shooting his pregnant wife and children, wounding Jesse, who escapes, and then shooting himself. When Jesse later returns to the house, which has a for-sale sign on it, he has no feelings about the murders, only the realization that he is still alive, a survivor. He later returns to Yewville to live with an aunt and uncle.

Vogel farm. Home of the orphaned Jesse's stern and unloving grandfather, where he is taken to live after recovering from his gunshot wound. The farm is located in a rural area outside Yewville, in a place where people live empty lives of "sleep, wake, and work." Grandfather Vogel keeps the shabby furnishings salvaged from Jesse's former home locked in his barn and refuses to let Jesse see any of them, thereby denying him tangible links to his past.

*Lockport. New York town to whose nearby Niagara School for Boys Jesse is sent by his aunt and uncle to board. At first, he lives in a dark red building enclosed by fences. However he is adopted by Dr. Pedersen, who lives in a three-story mansion on Locust Street in Lockport. Pedersen's house has a cavernous foyer and a beautiful music room, but what most impresses Jesse is that he has a room entirely his own for the first time in his life.

Pedersen, his wife, and son are grotesquely fat. Pedersen is a self-indulgent megalomaniac who tries to control everyone in his household. He makes Jesse become a serious student, dedicated to a career in medicine. After Jesse helps Pedersen's wife escape Pedersen's control, Pedersen disowns him, making him once again an orphan.

*Chicago.** City in which Jesse does his internship after earning a degree in medicine at the University of Michigan. During this period, he lives first in the basement of a three-story frame house but eventually moves to the top floor. There, he lives among slobs who linger in the hallways and with a dominating landlady. After several inconsequential relationships Jesse marries Helene Cady, the respectably boring daughter of a Nobel Prize-winning medical researcher, and with her moves into a small apartment in a four-story brownstone near his hospital.

Jesse and Helene lead separate lives together. Hospital work for Jesse is a blur of frenzied and impersonal activities. His intentions are to be an impersonal presence to do people good. Jesse's ability and hard work attract the notice of Dr. Perrault, a top surgeon who makes Jesse his assistant at his own clinic. Jesse now becomes Perrault's younger self, inheriting both his likes and dislikes, and still has no true personal life of his own. After Perrault retires, Jesse takes charge of the clinic.

*Winnetka.** Town in Illinois where the newly prosperous Jesse purchases a mansion near Lake Michigan. It has forty-eight windows and a huge living room that Jesse uses only to pace the floor nervously. What most concerns him is his young daughter, Shelley, who has run away with her dominating and sociopathic hippie boyfriend, Noel. He traces Shelley to Greenwich Village in New York City. The search proves fruitless.

*Toronto.** City in Canada's Ontario Province where Jesse finds his daughter in a derelict apartment on Yonge Street, where she is living with Noel and several other men. Shelley is sick and malnourished, and Jesse almost kills Noel but instead causes him to flee in fright. The novel ends with Shelley believing that her father is the devil come to take her home.

— *Irwin Halfond*

WOODCUTTERS

Author: Thomas Bernhard (1931-1989)
Type of work: Novel
Type of plot: Social realism

Time of plot: 1980's
First published: Holzfällen: Eine Erregung, 1984
(English translation, 1987)

A dinner party at a Viennese musician's apartment is the occasion for a monologue whose unnamed narrator has mostly harsh words for everyone, including himself. Although the narrator does not physically leave the apartment until the last few pages of the novel, his thoughts take the reader on a journey that encompasses both metropolitan and rural Austrian communities and sketch a vivid portrait of place by means of evocative personal recollections.

Auersberger apartment. Location of the dinner party in Vienna. The narrator's rage is directed primarily against the artistic pretensions of his hosts and their friends, which he detects in every aspect of their existence. Regardless of what they wear, what they eat, or what they say, he sees only sham and pretension in their efforts to impress their fellow guests. The narrator spends most of the evening sitting alone in an out-of-the-way corner, which gives him the opportunity to watch without being seen and also symbolizes his profound estrangement from this social gathering.

Although the narrator has something nasty to say about all who are at the dinner, he reserves his severest comments for those who represent three aspects of Viennese cultural life. His hosts are musicians; the guest of honor is an actor, and another severely denigrated guest is an author with whom the narrator once had an affair. In describing his deep dislike of these people, he does not stop with his contempt for their personalities, but goes on to justify his opinions by sketching a bleak picture of the cultural context of their individual art forms. Thus his hosts are the pathetic survivors of a moribund musical tradition, the actor is a pompous example of the theater's irrelevance to contemporary life, and the author is an all-too-typical representative of the mutual admiration society that stifles genuine literary talent. These exercises in sociological analysis of the places where culture is created greatly enrich the novel's already detailed portrait of Viennese social life.

*Vienna. Austria's capital, and the center of its cultural activity. The narrator thinks about Vienna so constantly and obsessively that one is always aware of the city's presence in the background of the novel, and many of his specific observations are closely identified with patterns of travel through Viennese streets and neighborhoods. These interior recollections of exterior environments are frequently repeated and meditated upon, so that an equivalence is set up between the places themselves and the narrator's thoughts about them. This in turn produces a map of his mental geography that literally charts his history and concerns, and is also a fascinating example of the interaction between public place and individual psychology.

*Kilb. Small Austrian town about fifty miles west of Vienna. Many of the narrator's remembrances are devoted to his deceased friend Joana, who has recently committed suicide in Kilb and whose funeral has been held there on the morning of the day of the dinner party. Although the hosts and other dinner guests disparage Kilb as a provincial backwater, the narrator defends it as a more authentic, and much less pretentious, place than the Vienna from which they come. His recollections of Kilb center around the local inn, where on previous visits to Joana he encountered a refreshingly relaxed and informal attitude to socializing that was the reverse of his Viennese experiences. An extended scene in which the attendees at Joana's funeral dine at the inn, and in the process give him further evidence of their pompousness and stupidity, is marked by the narrator's decision to leave their table and sit with some of Joana's local friends. As at the Auersberger's dinner party, the physical positioning of the narrator is indicative of his relationship with the supposed peers whose society he finds intolerable.

Maria Zaal. Fictional village in Austria's Styria region. The site of the Auersbergers' country retreat, which they have ruined by selling off small parcels of land on which cheap vacation homes have been built. For the narrator, this and their behavior at the inn at Kilb perfectly symbolize the Auersbergers' alienation from the Austrian countryside.

— *Paul Stuewe*

THE WOODLANDERS

Author: Thomas Hardy (1840-1928)
Type of work: Novel
Type of plot: Social realism

Time of plot: Nineteenth century
First published: serial, 1886-1887; book, 1887

A drama of human emotions in conflict, crystallized in an ill-made marriage that brings misery into the lives of all concerned, this play has an English country setting in which tensions between the past and present and between nature and society illuminate its central concerns.

Wessex. Fictional region of England in which Thomas Hardy set most of his major novels. It is situated east of the Cornish coast, between the River Thames and the English Channel. At the time in which this story is set it is still very much a rural setting.

Little Hintock. Wessex village so closely intertwined with the forest surrounding it that a traveler from a nearby town cannot locate it without the help of locals. In some spots the foliage is so dense that it obscures the road to the village, cutting it off from the outside world. The majority of Little Hintock's residents live in harmony with their natural setting. Many cut timber in the forests owned by George Melbury or help Giles Winterbourne press cider in the apple orchards. These are trades that villagers have plied for centuries, and Hardy depicts the village as largely untouched by the present and the many changes transforming the English countryside in the nineteenth century. The townspeople still follow many of the old customs and traditions, including a primitive Midsummer's Eve ritual, in which the unmarried village women try to use enchantments to conjure glimpses of their future husbands.

The village's isolation contributes to its simple, tranquil character. Little Hintock is what Hardy calls a sequestered spot "outside the gates of the world" where meditation is more common than action, and listlessness more common than meditation. However, even so harmonious a setting is not without its problems. The village is a place where grand and even Sophoclean dramas unfold because of the concentrated passions and interdependence of the villagers.

Little Hintock evokes a sense of the simple, uncomplicated past, and the dramas that unfold there are consequences of collisions between things from a simple past and those from a complicated present. For example, in an effort to redress an injustice George Melbury committed while a young man, he plans to engineer a marriage between his daughter Grace and Giles Winterbourne, son of the man he wronged. At the same time, Giles's fortunes are based precariously on an old land lease that the current landlord chooses not to renew.

Fitzpiers cottage. Modest village described as "boxlike and comparatively modern." In contrast to the wildness of the countryside, the cottage and its garden are exquisitely designed and maintained. The artificiality of the grounds suits Edgar Fitzpiers's nature as a modern, educated man, with a fondness for things from the European continent—which makes him out of step with other villagers. He considers himself superior to his rustic neighbors, and as a physician seems incapable of understanding them in any but cold, clinical terms. Shortly after moving to the village, he recommends cutting down a tree to cure a patient of his psychological fixation on it, inadvertently hastening the man's death and demonstrating his failure to appreciate the symbiotic relationship of the townspeople to their environment.

Melbury house. Comfortable middle-class household that was once the manor house in Little Hintock, but has since been supplanted by the house of Mrs. Charmond, whose adjoining estate is slowly absorbing it. The faded grandeur of the Melbury house suggests that the family's fortunes are declining, as are other aspects of the past that Melbury's woodcutting trade represents. Indeed, Melbury has sent his daughter Grace away to school in the hope that she might rise socially above her hometown origins, setting the stage for her relationship with the newly rich Mrs. Charmond upon her return to Little Hintock.

Hintock house. Manorial house on the outskirts of Little Hintock that is home to Mrs. Charmond. Though it rises picturesquely from a deep glen, it is damp and overgrown with ivy and vegetation. Notable for its "unfitness for modern lives of the fragility to which these have declined," it is one of several dwellings in town grander than the home of the average woodlander, and thus out of character for the natural setting. Similarly, its owner, a former stage actress, is out of place among the humble people of Little Hintock.

— *Stefan Dziemianowicz*

WORLD ENOUGH AND TIME

Author: Robert Penn Warren (1905-1989)
Type of work: Novel
Type of plot: Philosophical realism

Time of plot: 1801-1826
First published: 1950

Robert Penn Warren's plot derived from a series of real events known as "the Kentucky Tragedy," in which fatal love, vengeance, treachery, and betrayal had unfolded against the backdrop of shady Kentucky politics in the early nineteenth century. Warren clearly perceived that the events could be properly understood only in the environment where they occurred, the land of his own childhood, which he referred to as "this dark and bloody ground."

Frankfort. Kentucky city in which the crucial event of the novel occurs: the assassination of Colonel Cassius Fort, a prominent state politician. A young attorney, Jeremiah Beaumont, is avenging the earlier seduction and presumed slander of the woman who is now his wife. Beaumont's trial is also held in a Frankfort courtroom where, not surprisingly, he is convicted through perjury rather than evidence. Awaiting his public hanging, Beaumont is joined in his cell by his wife, Rachael, who wishes to share his fate.

Saul County. Fictional Kentucky county modeled on Simpson County of the real Kentucky tragedy. Rachael's family has retreated to rural Kentucky from the more favored regions of Virginia, after reversals of fortune. Suffering both emotional and cultural exile, they live in relative isolation, comforted by a few books salvaged from more favored times, including the romantic verse of Lord Byron.

La Grand'Bosse's refuge. This setting, somewhere in a southwest direction, totally departs from the historical record of "the Kentucky Tragedy" and has generally been regarded as the novel's least effective location, but it is essential to the development of Warren's own themes. His characters, unlike their real-life models, are rescued from their Frankfort prison and taken to the lair of a half-breed pirate, La Grand'Bosse. The outlaw refuge serves as a further means of Beaumont's enlightenment. Throughout the narrative he has spoken of "going west," sharing the American myth of the West as a land of escape. Now, as he fraternizes with the utter dregs of society, he sees the untamed territory as it is, a land of lawlessness, gracelessness, and even further treachery.

— *Allene Phy-Olsen*

THE WOULD-BE GENTLEMAN

Author: Molière (Jean-Baptiste Poquelin, 1622-1673)
Type of work: Drama
Type of plot: Comedy of manners

Time of plot: Seventeenth century
First performed: 1670; first published, 1671 as *Le Bourgeois Gentilhomme* (English translation, 1675)

Although Molière wrote hilarious comedies, he adhered to the classic "Aristotelian unities" that governed French drama until the nineteenth century. French tradition decreed that a play must be confined to a single action occurring in a single setting within a period lasting no longer than a single day. All the action in this play is confined to a single space representing the Parisian mansion of the wealthy Monsieur Jourdain (the "would-be gentleman") in the time of King Louis XIV (for whom the comedy-ballet was originally performed in 1670).

Jourdain mansion (zhohr-DAHN). Parisian home of Monsieur Jourdain, a rich tradesman. It is instructive to study the ingenuity with which France's greatest comic genius uses a single bare setting to present a complicated story that even includes five interludes performed by musicians, singers, and dancers. Foolishly enamored with the beautiful Marchioness Dorimène, Jourdain tries desperately to become a gentleman in the shortest possible time and spares no expense to attain his goal. His impulsive haste makes it possible for Molière to adhere to the Aristotelian unity-of-action dictum by confining all the events, including the subplot of the love affair between Cléonte and Lucile Jourdain, within a time frame of only a few hours. The bourgeois gentleman's foolishly impractical ambitions provide an excuse for the entrance of a variety of visitors in appropriate costumes, escalating to the hilarious climactic Fourth Interlude, in which the mufti, four dervishes, six Turkish dancers, six Turkish musicians, and other instrumentalists disguised as Turks perform a ceremony that transforms Jourdain into a *Mamamouchi.*

This ridiculous but likable tradesman's home is crucial to the drama because it is the only possible place in which such an extravagant assortment of characters could appear and such a strange—but logically ordered—progression of scenes could occur. Jourdain's house in Paris provides the mandatory Aristotelian unity of place because it is a magnet for all the characters who want to take advantage of the money that is pouring out of this would-be gentleman's pockets during the brief period of infatuation preceding his inevitable disillusionment.

— *Bill Delaney*

WOYZECK

Author: Georg Büchner (1813-1837)
Type of work: Drama
Type of plot: Psychological realism

Time of plot: Early nineteenth century
First published: 1879 (written, 1836; English translation, 1927); first performed, 1913

Georg Büchner's unfinished play takes place in an early nineteenth century German town and the surrounding countryside. Its settings often affect how its characters behave. In open-country scenes, for example, the military conscript Woyzeck feels threatened by mysterious powers beyond his control; when in town, he is often exploited or misused by other characters.

Open country. Woyzeck interprets natural phenomena like mushroom patterns or the blazing noontime sun as omens of a world about to be engulfed by some catastrophe. After he hears voices in the open country that instruct him to kill, he takes Marie to a spot outside the city in order to murder her. Feelings of foreboding overwhelm Marie as Woyzeck leads her in the evening to a spot near the lake.

Marie's room. Home of Woyzeck's mistress, Marie. Marie's bed, her son's bed, a dressing table, and a mirror represent aspects of her life. The room is also associated with her sexual desires, for it is where she consummates her affair with Woyzeck, where she stands at the window when admiring the Drum Major, and where she later submits to the latter's advances. The presence of Woyzeck's son in the room reminds her of her bond with Woyzeck. When her conscience is stricken with guilt about her sexual betrayal of Woyzeck, she is also in her room.

Fairgrounds. Festive, colorful place with tents, lights, and booths crowded with people. Monkeys dressed as soldiers and an astronomical horse on display invite audiences to contemplate the proximity of animal and human behavior. In this atmosphere, the usual rules of everyday life are suspended. While the Drum Major is powerfully attracted to Marie in this setting, the imperfectly civilized animals help point up the crucial role that "unidealized nature" plays in human behavior.

Tavern. Public hall in which drinking and whirling dancing couples heat up the atmosphere and provide increased likelihood that passion will overrun reason and even will. Men brag and show off, among them drunken artisans who make coarse speeches. Woyzeck challenges the Drum Major for Marie, and a fistfight ensues. The beat of the dance music is allied to Woyzeck's obsession with Marie's betrayal and his fury at the evidence it provides for the uncontrollable nature of human sexual urges in general.

— *Julie D. Prandi*

THE WRECK OF THE *DEUTSCHLAND*

Author: Gerard Manley Hopkins (1844-1889)   *First published:* 1918
Type of work: Poetry

This poem is Gerard Manley Hopkins's great lyric meditation on human suffering as a channel of God's mercy. In an important sense, therefore, the poem takes place in the mind and heart of the poet himself. His poem was inspired by an actual shipwreck, and details of the ship's route, and of activities on board, root his meditation in fact. However, the poem soars beyond fact as Hopkins imagines the event as a mystical interpretation of scripture.

*Deutschland.** Ship whose 1875 sinking caused the deaths of five Franciscan nuns to whom Hopkins dedicates this poem. Also the German-language name for Germany, "Deutschland" is, in Hopkins's words, "double a desperate name!" because it is both the ship on which the nuns perished and the country that passed the anti-Roman Catholic laws that expelled the nuns from their homeland and forced them to undertake their ill-fated voyage.

Hopkins's poem re-creates the sufferings of the ship's passengers after their ship struck a sandbar near the mouth of England's River Thames. He notes that the day after the death of the "tall nun"—December 8—was the Catholic feast day celebrating the conception of Mary without the stain of Original Sin, making her fit to be Christ's mother. Just as Mary physically gave birth to Christ, so the tall nun, calling out his name before she died, brought forth Christ in a "birth of a brain." The nun's faith, Hopkins imagines, served to "Startle" the other passengers—"the poor sheep" he calls them—back to Christ. Hopkins suggests that the site of the wreck is the Lord's harvest field. He rhetorically asks, "is the shipwrack then a harvest,/ does tempest carry the grain for thee?"

*Britain.** The poem ends with Hopkins's address to the tall nun, the "Dame, at our door/ Drowned," that she remember "English souls" still on their journey through life, that they might eventually attain the only true shelter, not a port or a political refuge, but a "heaven-haven." Just as he earlier surmised that the nun's call to Christ quickened the faith of those on the *Deutschland*, so he now prays that Christ will be resurrected in the hearts of those in Hopkins's own "rare—dear Britain."

*Tarpeian Rock** (tar-PEE-yahn). Famous cliff in Rome that made the ancient capital, in John Milton's

words, a "citadel." Immediately after referring to the tall nun as "The Simon Peter of a soul," Hopkins says she was "to the blast/ Tarpeian-fast." To Hopkins, the nun's faith made her like the rock, and like the Apostle Peter, whom Christ spoke of as the rock on which He would build His church, like the house Christ spoke of that resisted the blasts of storm because it was built on a rock.

*Gennesareth** (geh-NEHZ-eh-ret). Another name for the Sea of Galilee in the Holy Land's Jordan Valley. Sudden fierce storms often occur over it because of cold air masses from the north. Hopkins evokes an incident in the Gospels in which such a storm found Christ asleep in a boat on the lake, with his terrified disciples. Christ then calms the storm and takes note of the disciples' small faith. Hopkins evokes this incident to suggest that the men on the *Deutschland* were in the spiritual condition of the disciples in the boat, and to highlight by contrast the strong faith of the tall nun that—he expresses the hope or belief in stanza 31—was a source of comfort to them, bringing them back to Christ.

*Galilee.** Region in northern Palestine (now Israel) where Jesus began his ministry. Hopkins notes that God's mercy dates from the time of Christ's life in and around Galilee. That ministry culminated with His death on a cross, by which in Christian belief He redeemed humankind. As Hopkins puts it, Christ became "hero of Calvary," a reference to the hill outside Jerusalem where Jesus was crucified. However, as Divinity, Christ is not limited to time and place and, in Christian belief, is present in a special way wherever and whenever people say "yes" to Him: the main examples in Hopkins's poem being in the first part, Hopkins's own assent—"I did say yes"—and in the second part, the cry to Christ of the tall nun in 1875, off England's coast.

— *Jack V. Barbera*

WUTHERING HEIGHTS

Author: Emily Brontë (1818-1848)
Type of work: Novel
Type of plot: Love

Time of plot: 1757-1803
First published: 1847

The principal action in this novel is divided between two estates on England's desolate Yorkshire moors: Wuthering Heights, a prosperous farmhouse, and Thrushcross Grange, an upper-class manor house. In both locations, the nature of the houses directly parallels the nature of their inhabitants. Wuthering Heights, a place of stormy and passionate emotions, is the home of the wild and untamed lovers Catherine Earnshaw and Heathcliff. Similarly, Thrushcross Grange, a place of order and control, is home to the more civilized and refined Edgar and Isabella Linton.

*Yorkshire. Region comprising three English counties—North Yorkshire, West Yorkshire, and South Yorkshire—in northern central England. The properties of Wuthering Heights and Thrushcross Grange are located in this region of Yorkshire's lonely, wild, and sparsely populated moors. The moors are characterized by spacious, open grassland and the heather that grows abundantly throughout the region.

Wuthering Heights. Estate of the Earnshaw family located on England's Yorkshire moors. Wuthering Heights is described by Mr. Lockwood, a tenant at neighboring Thrushcross Grange, as desolate and the ideal home of a misanthropist. Lockwood explains that "wuthering" is a local word used to describe the tumultuous and stormy conditions that are common at Wuthering Heights. The house itself seems dark and forbidding, with a decidedly Gothic physical and spiritual atmosphere. Upon entering the gates of Wuthering Heights for the first time, Lockwood points out its general state of disrepair, especially noting the carvings of griffins at the threshold. Mr. Lockwood also observes that Heathcliff appears as a gentleman, in sharp contrast to the house itself, while the young Catherine Linton Heathcliff appears wild and untamed. He finds in time, though, that in reality the opposite is true.

As the novel progresses and the house passes from one owner to the next, in and out of the Earnshaw family, it is evident that the physical state of the house is somehow connected with the emotional state of its inhabitants. While the elder Mr. and Mrs. Earnshaw live, the house retains a more civilized feeling, but as first Hindley Earnshaw and then Heathcliff obtain ownership, the atmosphere of the house becomes darker and

more brooding. Like Heathcliff, the current master of the property, the house steadily deteriorates until the height of its disrepair is described by Mr. Lockwood, who has rented Thrushcross Grange near the end of Heathcliff's term of ownership.

*Liverpool. Major port city in western England. When Hindley and Catherine Earnshaw are young children, their father goes to Liverpool on business. He returns with a young and untamed boy, a homeless child he found in the streets of Liverpool and was unable to leave behind. No one in Liverpool knew who the homeless child was or where he came from, though he was thought by many in Liverpool to be a gypsy. The foundling boy is named for a former inhabitant of Wuthering Heights, Heathcliff, the name of the elder Earnshaws' dead infant son.

Gimmerton. Fictional village near Wuthering Heights and Thrushcross Grange. The village plays a minor, though integral, role in the novel. Heathcliff returns first to Gimmerton before he reappears at Wuthering Heights and Thrushcross Grange after his three-year absence. Near the end of the novel, when the young Catherine Linton and Ellen Dean are held hostage by Heathcliff at Wuthering Heights, the people of Gimmerton are enlisted to join in the search for them in the Yorkshire moors.

Thrushcross Grange. Home of the Linton family, the nearest neighboring estate to Wuthering Heights. In stark contrast to the dark and forbidding Wuthering Heights, the Grange is lighter and more orderly, a home filled with windows and fresh air. Even the willful and wild Catherine Earnshaw changes markedly when, as a girl, she stays for a few weeks at this location. The atmosphere of Thrushcross Grange does much to tame the formerly unrefined girl.

Like Wuthering Heights, Thrushcross Grange passes from the hands of the elder generation, Mr. and Mrs. Linton, to those of a younger generation, first to their son Edgar and later to his daughter Catherine. In the process, as opposed to Wuthering Heights, the atmosphere of the house becomes increasingly refined and civilized. Even the marriage of Edgar Linton of Thrushcross Grange and Wuthering Heights' Catherine Earnshaw does little to change the more civilized atmosphere of Thrushcross Grange. However, though Catherine's high spirits are held in check during the first days of her marriage to Edgar, the reappearance of Heathcliff does begin to affect the emotional state of all those who live at Thrushcross Grange. It is only when Thrushcross Grange falls into the hands of Heathcliff, who has gained ownership of the Heights through the marriage of his son Linton to young Catherine, that it begins to fall into a state of relative disrepair. It is this condition in which Mr. Lockwood finds Thrushcross Grange at the beginning of the novel.

By the end of the novel, young Catherine inherits Thrushcross Grange and Hareton Earnshaw inherits Wuthering Heights. The marriage of Catherine Linton Heathcliff and Hareton Earnshaw, then, unites the two houses in one well-matched and happy marriage. Finally, both the houses and the people who live in them can begin the process of physical and spiritual healing.

— *Kimberley H. Kidd*

X

XALA

Author: Ousmane Sembène (1923-   )
Type of work: Novel
Type of plot: Social realism

Time of plot: Early 1970's
First published: 1973 (English translation, 1976)

This cutting satire set in postcolonial Africa is set in Senegal's capital city, which like most African cities is marked by stark contrasts between the rich and the poor, the modern and the traditional, the elegant and the shabby. Ousmane Sembène uses these contrasts to construct a fable about the downfall of a once-humble teacher transformed into a successful businessman. In the process, the city's disparities emerge as an essential element of the narrative. Better known as a film director than as a novelist, Sembène adapted the novel from a film script; he tends to visualize settings in cinematic terms, then integrates the action into the backgrounds he establishes.

*Senegal.** Country located at the extreme western tip of West Africa, a humid tropical region in which agricultural productivity is limited and most people who live in rural areas are desperately poor. *Xala* generally ignores the areas of Senegal outside the capital city, Dakar, because it focuses on the new African elite, who remain in their comparatively prosperous urban enclaves and shun what they consider primitive and undesirable regions. At the same time, however, Sembène has the rest of the country in mind as he ridicules the protagonist and his associates whose greed and political maneuvering hinder the nation's development.

*Dakar.** Capital and leading port of Senegal, a cosmopolitan city whose roots go back to the earliest days of French colonization in the late eighteenth century. The beauty of this tropical coastal city does not escape Sembène, who draws vivid pictures of such natural phenomena as the bougainvillea hedges, flame trees, cloudless skies, and shimmering water.

Because the novel's major characters are from the upper class, most of the action takes place in official edifices and in the well-tended villas in which they live. Many of the structures are left over from the French colonial era and are European in design. Sembène underscores the ironic nature of the buildings by viewing these newly rich Africans as simply new versions of the French colonials displaced by independence movements.

When the novel's protagonist, the businessman El Hadji, becomes desperate about his impotence (the meaning of *xala*), he visits a famous seer to seek treatment, and another side of Dakar comes into focus. The modern El Hadji is forced to go into one of Dakar's outlying districts whose alleys are so sandy and narrow that he must leave his Mercedes automobile behind and walk through a shantytown full of jerry-built houses made of corrugated tin, cardboard, wood, and whatever other materials are available. He watches a long line of women returning from the communal water supply carrying plastic buckets on their heads. Brief glimpses, such as this one, of the many-sided Dakar tend to be cinematic, as though Sembène is conjuring up a scene that he will later put on film.

— *Robert L. Ross*

Y

THE YEARLING

Author: Marjorie Kinnan Rawlings (1896-1953)
Type of work: Novel
Type of plot: Regional

Time of plot: Late nineteenth century
First published: 1938

This novel is set in northeastern Florida, a region with bushy vegetation and thin forests that provide a harsh living for farming and raising livestock. The isolated setting reinforces the loneliness that young Jody Baxter feels but also provides him with an opportunity to grow to manhood by learning to understand nature's cycles and forces.

Baxter's Island. Farm of the Baxter family covering one hundred acres of Florida scrubland in the middle of a dry forest. Penny Baxter bought the land from the Forrester family, whose neighboring farm is called Forrester's Island. The Baxter farm is covered with hardwood trees and rich foliage, representing a place of refuge, an oasis in a harsh natural environment.

Marjorie Kinnan Rawlings, who lived in Cross Creek between the towns of Gainesville and Ocala, not far from the places her novel describes, admired the independence of the people who lived in Florida's backwoods. Her fictional Baxter evidently chose to farm on this land because of its isolation. Shunning city life, which makes "intrusions on the individual spirit," Penny settles on the Florida scrub because the "wild animals seemed less predatory to him than the people he had known." He learns to live in harmony with nature and to subsist on what his land has to offer. The challenge is great, however, because Baxter's Island is "ringed with hunger," and the family's survival is constantly threat-

ened by natural hazards, including harsh weather, predatory animals, and even the docile deer that Jody Baxter adopts as a pet—the "yearling" of the novel's title.

Ocklawaha River. Florida river that originates in several lakes near the center of the state and flows northward along the edge of what is now the Ocala National Forest before it joins the St. Johns River south of Palatka. Lined with cypress trees, swamp maples, and sable palms whose growth is dense enough to form a canopy above its channel, the river symbolizes the danger and beauty that humans must learn to respect, and understand.

After his mother shoots the yearling that has been destroying the freshly planted corn, Jody decides to run away from home. He heads for the river, on which he sets off in a dugout canoe. After several days without food, he is picked up by a river mail boat and returned home, ashamed and penitent.

Juniper Creek. Exceptionally clear stream fed by a spring that for Jody is a natural sanctuary.

— *Ginger Jones*

THE YEARS

Author: Virginia Woolf (1882-1941)
Type of work: Novel
Type of plot: Domestic realism

Time of plot: 1880-1937
First published: 1937

As its title suggests, this novel is primarily concerned with time rather than place. However, the passage of time is reflected and embodied in the characters' changes of addresses and countless journeys across London. Virginia Woolf's descriptions are continually preoccupied with the play of light on the skylines of the city, the orderly cyclic changes of the heavens contrasted with the progressively disordered landscape below.

***London.** Every major shift in date within the novel is introduced by a panoramic descriptive sequence that contrasts the capital with the surrounding countryside or more distant vistas, but the lists of landmarks cited undergo an unsteady evolution. The novel's opening, set in 1880, refers to shoppers in the city's West End, clubs in Piccadilly, Marble Arch and Apsley House, coupled with a derisory reference to the poorer areas of Bermondsey and Hoxton. The 1891 sequence begins with the great churches of St. Paul's and St. Martin's and also encompasses Parliament Square and the Law Courts; however, these are situated within a much broader frame of reference taking in the southern coast, the north of England, and Devonshire. The introduction to the 1907 chapters uses much broader brush-strokes, taking in whole districts at a time—Covent Garden, Hammersmith, Shoreditch, Wapping, and Mayfair—but is more narrowly confined to London.

This series of contexts serves to frame the residences of the various members of the Pargiter clan. In the midst of all their movements, however, one London location continually recurs, seemingly unchanging and always reminding the Pargiters of happier and more innocent days: Hyde Park, especially the Serpentine, the Round Pond, and nearby Kensington Gardens. Other London landmarks that recur—the National Gallery in Trafalgar Square, Parliament Square, and the Law Courts—are merely noted in passing, but the park is a place of refuge.

Pargiter homes. The first and most important residence of the various members of the Pargiter clan is a town house in Abercorn Terrace, to the west of Piccadilly. Its cluttered drawing room is dominated by a Dutch cabinet laden with blue china; its dining room has carved chairs and a fine sideboard; it is equipped with a night-nursery and schoolroom, and it has a pleasant back garden.

The first home with which this one is sharply contrasted is situated in a little street in the shadow of Westminster Abbey, where the colonel keeps his mistress, Mira; this reappears in the story at a much later date as a residence of family members now living in severely reduced circumstances. In the meantime, Eleanor and Sara move continually from one address to another, moving down the property-ladder all the while, even though the house in Abercorn Terrace is not actually sold until 1913. Browne Street, Hyams Place, Richmond Green, Ebury Street, and Milton Street provide addresses for a sequence of modest homes whose descriptions are scanty, except continually to emphasize the fact that they are not in Abercorn Terrace.

***Oxford.** University city where Edward is a student. Oxford provides several significant locations, but they are described only in vague terms. For example, readers are never told to which Oxford college Edward is attached, although "the Lodge" is a significant setting. The other significant Oxford location is a small house in Prestwich Terrace.

Wittering. Village in which Eleanor spends some time visiting Morris at his mother-in-law's house. There is an actual English village called Wittering in East Anglia, but the one in the novel is in Dorset; it too is described very vaguely, equipped with a Station Road and a High Street but little else.

***India.** Asian country that is one of many places mentioned in the story as locations briefly visited by Eleanor; others include the south of France and Greece. Uganda is also mentioned in passing, as is Germany—with whom Britain is at war for much of the novel—but in the same way that most of the addresses featured in the plot are negatively defined by their lack of resemblance to Abercorn Terrace, locations in continental Europe and beyond are only important in terms of their geographical and social distance from London. Given that the world at large is so nebulously conceived, it is hardly surprising that as the march of time draws the characters further and further away from the old night-nursery and private schoolroom, they gradually lose all sense of direction and belonging.

— *Brian Stableford*

THE YEMASSEE: A Romance of Carolina

Author: William Gilmore Simms (1806-1870)
Type of work: Novel
Type of plot: Adventure

Time of plot: Early eighteenth century
First published: 1835

This novel's events occur within a relatively narrow geographic scope: the settlements, forests, and swamps along the banks of the Pocota-ligo River in South Carolina. These wilderness settings are described in language that strives for a theatrical effect.

*Pocota-ligo council house. Meeting house in the town occupied by the Yemassee Indian tribe and the primary setting for fierce internal tribal conflict, as tribal leader Sanutee leads his people in a revolt against their own chiefs in order to forestall further treaties with the Carolinians and instigate a rebellion. European settlers named the town Pokitellico.

Blockhouse. Edifice built for the purposes of defense and one of several Carolinian forts. It is besieged by a Yemassee war band, accompanied by English pirate Richard Chorley. Thus, it is one of the primary settings for armed conflict between the low-country Carolinians and their Yemassee neighbors. The besieged blockhouse also offers one of the novel's most pronounced explorations of gender roles when a broken ladder separates the women and children in the upstairs section from the men in the downstairs section, and Granger's wife, described approvingly as almost masculine in her capacity for decisive action, is forced to defend the women and children trapped upstairs.

Pirate ship. Vessel belonging to the English pirate Chorley. At first merely mysterious, the ship becomes the visible symbol of the Spanish threat to the Carolina settlement, as well as Chorley's own threat to Bess Matthews, as it moves up and down the Pocota-ligo River.

Carolinian cabins. Mirroring the larger conflict building throughout the novel between the Yemassee Indians and the Carolinian settlers, personal homes are the settings for domestic conflicts. The domestic conflict in the Matthews cottage, while ostensibly centered on the conflict between the different generational and religious values of the old Puritan Reverend Matthews and his daughter Bess's suitor, Gabriel Harrison, also delineates the debate over the two visions of the future of the Na-

tive Americans, with Matthews arguing that the Yemassee have been safely domesticated and Harrison arguing that no such thing is possible, a position that Sanutee echoes repeatedly as well. Similarly, Hugh Grayson's arguments with his mother in the Grayson cabin attest to the supposedly natural superiority of born leaders like Harrison and the need to maintain proper order in society by following those leaders.

Sanutee's lodge. On the Yemassee side, in Sanutee's lodge, his wife Matiwan's futile attempts to reconcile the old Yemassee chief with their son Occonestoga, a drunken ally of the English settlers, help to clarify the bitter debate between those Yemassee wishing to find an accommodation with the Carolinians and those wishing to risk all in an attempt to push them out of Yemassee lands forever.

Forests and swamps. William Gilmore Simms saves his most stylized descriptions for wilderness scenes. The novel's most gothic settings are those involving the Yemassee themselves, an association between American Indians and dreadful terror that seems to echo early Puritan depictions of New World wilderness as desolate and hellish, inhabited by wild beasts and savages. In at least one scene, the Yemassee play the role of both victim and villain—the place just above the town of Pocota-ligo, where Occonestoga is carried after his capture by his fellow Yemassee and where his mother kills him to prevent his banishment from the Yemassee tribe and afterlife, is described as gloomy. A gust of wind obligingly sweeps through the scene, making the night grow even more theatrical. The novel's strongest pastoral depictions, by contrast, involve Bess Matthews in an oak grove, where she meets her beloved, Gabriel Harrison.

— *Michael T. Wilson*

YOU CAN'T GO HOME AGAIN

Author: Thomas Wolfe (1900-1938)
Type of work: Novel
Type of plot: Autobiographical

Time of plot: 1929-1936
First published: 1940

Filled with a mixture of fictional conversations and historical accounts, this strong autobiographical novel explores the search for personal meaning during the years of America's Great Depression and the rise of totalitarianism in Europe, with protagonist George Webber's life following the pattern set by Thomas Wolfe himself, as he moves from city to city and country to country.

Manhattan. Borough of New York City in which the novel opens, shortly after George Webber has published his first novel. During a Park Avenue party, Webber reveals his disgust with the emptiness of America's materialistic culture leading up to the Great Depression, and after obtaining the funds needed to become a full-time writer, he resigns his position at New York University to pursue a solitary literary career.

Libya Hill. North Carolina town modeled closely on Wolfe's hometown of Asheville that is Webber's birthplace and hometown. When he returns there to attend his mother's funeral, he comes to the realization that Libya Hill no longer furnishes him with any opportunities, that he cannot, in fact, go home again. Meanwhile, signs of America's faltering economy during the Great Depression are evident in the closing of the local bank, the Citizens Trust Company.

Brooklyn. New York City borough in which Webber, following Wolfe's own experience there, lives a spartan existence for four years, as he struggles to publish his second book. Brooklyn is full of dilapidated housing, seedy hot dog stands, broken-down roads, and dreary coffeehouses. During his residence there, Webber receives his only comfort from the company of his editor, Foxhall Edwards, who helps Webber cope with the mixed reviews that greet his first novel.

London. Webber goes to the capital of Great Britain in 1934, seeking fame and adventure and an escape from his monotonous life in Brooklyn. There, he rents a flat while trying to finish another novel. He hopes that the culture and civilization of the Old World will supply him with ample experiences to write about and the motivation to succeed. He lives on the third floor of a small London house that he shares with a doctor's office and a tailor shop; during the evenings, he has the entire place to himself. While in London, Webber meets the author Lloyd McHarg (modeled on F. Scott Fitzgerald), who calls Webber one of the leading young figures of the American literary scene. McHarg gives Webber incentive to go on with his writing.

Berlin. After a brief return to New York to deliver his second novel, Webber goes to Germany, which he visited several years earlier and came to regard as one of the great founts of European culture. In keeping with the theme that one can never truly return to the past, Webber encounters a Germany drastically altered by the rise of Adolf Hitler and Nazism. Although he still admires the natural beauty of Germany, he eventually concludes that Nazism is a manifestation of humankind's historical preoccupation with barbarism, cruelty, and hatred.

— *Robert D. Ubriaco, Jr.*

YOUMA: The Story of a West-Indian Slave

Author: Lafcadio Hearn (1850-1904)
Type of work: Novel
Type of plot: Psychological realism

Time of plot: 1840's
First published: 1890

This novel is set on the French West Indian colony of Martinique, where many French colonists lead nearly idyllic lives until the island's black slaves rise in rebellion and turn on their masters. One of the slave leaders urges the beautiful Youma to escape with him by boat to the free soil of nearby British-ruled Dominica, but she chooses loyalty to love and perishes with the French child for whom she is caring during the rebellion.

Saint Pierre (sah[n] pyehr). City on the West Indian island of Martinique, which is a French colony with a slave-based economy. Located fifteen miles from the cloud-crested volcano Mount Pelée, the town has a church, a convent and school, an army fort garrisoned by cowardly French soldiers, and homes of proud, conservative Frenchmen. Creole-speaking slaves work their masters' sugarcane fields that reach to Pelée's slopes, build zigzag roads through heavy forest growth up and down lush valleys, and toil as domestics in their masters' houses. Madame Peyronnette's mansion is on the Grande Rue, in the Quartier du Fort. Monsieur Desrivières's city residence is on the nearby rue de la Consolation.

Anse-Marine (ans-mar-een). Prosperous estate on the east coast, inherited by Monsieur Desrivière, that is spoiled and idle. Youma, tall and graceful, has her own room in his plantation house. She dresses in vividly colored robes for special occasions. The stalwart fieldworkers, their half-naked bodies glistening like polished bronze, toil and sing under the sweltering sun, while their overseer guards them from poisonous snakes. The overworked women sing in caravans as they go to market balancing head trays of cocoa, coffee, coconuts, mangoes, oranges, and bananas. Other slaves work at nearby sugar mills and wharfs. Their sixty-foot-long canoes transport barrels of rum and casks of sugar to larger vessels waiting beyond the surf.

On Sundays, Madame Peyronnette occasionally visits Anse-Marine, dispensing small silver coins to swarms of obedient black children, inspecting their feet for possible infection, and often scolding their neglectful mothers. A Roman Catholic priest visits on horseback from the neighboring village, instructs the children in the Creole catechism, and hears their prayers to "Bon-Dié" and "Zézou-Chri." Many evenings are livened by the telling and retelling of folktales by old retired slaves. One such story concerns a serpent that might bite a little girl, lost in the woods, but instead takes her to her mother. Mayotte, the child placed in Youma's care, often accompanies Youma to the river to bathe, admire the vivid surrounding vegetation, and play with little crawling creatures on the adjacent sandy beach.

De Kersaint mansion. The only two-storied residence on a cottage-lined Saint Pierre street. The imposing structure has a massive door, windows with heavy shutters banded by iron, beautifully furnished lower rooms, and stairs of pine with a mahogany balustrade. When the house is besieged during the slave rebellion, its upper rooms are filled with French refugees from a mob maddened by oppression and excited by fermented drink. Armed with cutlasses, bamboo pikes, and sand-filled bottles, the rebels kill the French refugees, set fire to the downstairs, and feed the engulfing flames with splintered stair rails and furniture, portraits, curtains, and mats. Soon the house is a "skeleton of stone . . . black-smoking to the stars."

Sea. When Youma and Gabriel rendezvous at the beach, Gabriel tells Youma that they can steal the master's boat and sail to freedom. However, the ocean is a danger-fraught avenue to freedom. Looking across the water, toward the "silhouette of Dominica towered against the amethystine day," Youma decides that liberty is a "shining apparition in the horizon," but not for her.

— *Robert L. Gale*

YVAIN: Or, The Knight with the Lion

Author: Chrétien de Troyes (c. 1150-c. 1190)
Type of work: Poetry
Type of plot: Arthurian romance

Time of plot: Sixth century
First transcribed: Yvain: Ou, Le Chevalier au lion, c. 1170 (English translation, c. 1300)

This poem is thought to be the fourth of the five romances by Chrétien de Troyes. As in Chrétien's other works, the focus here is on the legendary English king Arthur and the adventures of his knights. Localities serve not only to place events in the historical past, but also to view the inner workings of Yvain's mind. Place provides the work with a somewhat mythic quality that transcends time.

*Carlisle Castle (CAHR-lil). Castle of King Arthur where Calogrenant narrates the tale of his own disgrace. The knight Yvain wishes to avenge Calogrenant and decides to take on this task as a personal challenge. As with Chrétien's other romances, this castle represents chivalry and grandeur—a place at once mystical and real that still exists in the great border city between England and Scotland.

Spring. Yvain mortally wounds the knight who guards it. He returns later, only to find the maiden who saved him imprisoned there. It is a place of circumstances that defy logic and appeal to the imagination. It is a part of the world, yet it is enigmatic.

Forest. Sylvan location in which Yvain goes mad after breaking his promise to his beloved. The setting is analogous to Yvain's mind: Just as he exists in a state of madness here, the forest represents the instability of life and a mind that is not functioning properly. The deep woods also seem to reflect the inner workings of Yvain's mind. In the context of the work, a battle in the deep woods signifies the struggle between good and evil, or stability and madness, with the lion symbolizing the first image and the dragon, the latter. The honorable knight chooses to help the lion that repays him with much loyalty.

Tower. Setting of the "Dire Adventure," in which Yvain, with the help of his trusted companion the lion, vanquishes the two evil beings that guard the young women in the tower. The setting is of unknown origin.

— *Adriana C. Tomasino*

ZADIG: Or, The Book of Fate

Author: Voltaire (François-Marie Arouet, 1694-1778)
Type of work: Novel
Type of plot: Social satire

Time of plot: Antiquity
First published: Zadig: Ou, La Destinée, histoire orientale, 1748 (English translation, 1749)

An Eastern setting, which was very popular for both libertine and philosophical works during the eighteenth century, is especially suited to Voltaire's novel. The theme of the novel, a philosophical inquiry into destiny, is one of the major problems examined in oriental philosophy. This setting also distances the tale and provides a veil for Voltaire's satire and criticism of the French monarchy, French society, the Church, and his contemporaries.

***Babylon.** Capital of ancient Babylonia on the Euphrates River in Mesopotamia in which the novel begins and ends. Exotic and far removed from the reality of the France of Voltaire's time, Babylon provides Voltaire with a setting in which he can plunge his readers into a fantasy world of his own creation—one in which customs, beliefs, and the turn of events can be manipulated to illustrate his philosophical ideas. No longer in familiar territory, readers have no preset expectations of what can and will happen; they are free to indulge in the fictional fantasy and concentrate on the philosophical inquiry carried on in the novel. Babylon, its court, its King Moabdar, his courtiers, and his subjects thus combine to make an excellent vehicle for Voltaire's satire. Babylon also is an excellent setting for Voltaire's inquiry into destiny and how an individual should react to it. Controlled by a despotic king who often rules by whim, Babylon is a place where one's fortune can change very quickly, where good works do not necessarily bring reward, and where happiness and misfortune alternate with all too great a regularity.

***Egypt.** North African land to which Zadig escapes from Babylon that Voltaire uses to satirize judicial systems. Zadig, who has slain a man in self-defense while trying to help a woman, is condemned to be sold into

slavery. His camels are sold, the proceeds allocated to the city, and his money is divided among the inhabitants. Nevertheless, Voltaire praises the Egyptians for their humanity and their sense of justice.

Desert of Horeb. Biblical site of uncertain location—possibly the Sinai Peninsula—that is home of the tribe of Sétoc, the Arab merchant who buys Zadig. Here, Voltaire creates a number of incidents that illustrate the precariousness of an individual's fate. Zadig is highly respected by the tribe for his cleverness in trapping a dishonest Hebrew debtor and in abolishing the custom of widows burning themselves; however, priests who previously profited from jewels and other valuables of self-immolating widows regard Zadig as someone who should be eliminated. Though highly favored, Zadig finds himself accused of blasphemy and condemned to be burned. Destiny once again apparently decrees that good fortune and happiness are not to last for Zadig.

Balzora fair. Place where merchants from every corner of the earth are found. A discussion among the merchants at supper permits Voltaire to engage in a comparison of religious beliefs in various countries and to conclude that different beliefs that may appear to be in conflict are actually all based on belief in a Supreme Being.

*Syria. Country where Zadig's wanderings end. There he encounters Arbogad, the fisherman who was a cheese maker near Babylon, and other characters who recount tales illustrating the unpredictability of life. Syria is also the place where Zadig is reunited with Astarté, the queen of Babylon.

— *Shawncey Webb*

EL ZARCO, THE BANDIT

Author: Ignacio Manuel Altamirano (1834-1893)
Type of work: Novel
Type of plot: Historical

Time of plot: 1861-1863
First published: El zarco: Episodios de la vida mexicana en 1861-1863, 1901 (English translation, 1957)

Against the backdrop of the political and social unrest and criminal activity that plague Mexico after its independence, this novel centers on a single representative area. Embroidering on historical facts and personages, its action revolves around the behavior of diverse fictitious inhabitants whose lives are affected by the bandit known as El Zarco. Havoc, ruin, and death are visited on wrongdoers, and those who follow social convention and law are rewarded.

*Tierra caliente. Hot rural lowland region to the west and south of Mexico City where the novel is set. Because the primarily agricultural area is lightly populated and separated from urban areas by mountains, banditry is rampant.

*Yautepec (yow-teh-PEK). Pleasant and peaceful Mexican village with hard-working and honest people in the *tierra caliente* that is home to Doña Antonia, her daughter Manuela, and her goddaughter Pilar. Strongly traditional in its social conventions, the village is a symbol of that which is orderly and good in society. The villagers rightly fear the political disorganization, social unrest, and criminal activity that are beginning to encroach on their lives.

The novel's leading characters, Doña Antonia and her family, live in a typical Mexican home, in which the mother attempts to protect and appropriately socialize her resistant daughter. However, Manuela longs for the freedom and excitement that lie beyond the village. Her romantic fantasies about bandits combined with her lack of life experience eventually moves her to run off with the bandit. Her mother dies of grief.

The Indian blacksmith Nicolas and Pilar believe that they, as symbols of righteous convention, are meant for each other and plan to marry. At their wedding at the end of the novel, the village is the site of righteous retribution and the restoration of social order. Martin Sanchez, a prior victim of the bandits from a nearby ranch, gains official approval of his continued pursuit of the bandits, whom he recaptures at Yautepec during their attempt to murder Nicolas and kidnap Pilar. Sanchez executes the bandits, and Manuela dies of grief and shame on the spot.

Atlihuayan (ah-tlee-WAH-yan). Nearby sugar plantation that symbolizes stability and order in society. It is somewhat more secure from the bandits than the village because of the large number of able-bodied men it has to resist criminal forays. The plantation is home to Nicolas, Manuela's suitor. Nicolas symbolizes personal stability, order, and social equality, just as Atlihuayan itself does. Doña Antonia's delight that Nicolas is courting her daughter contrasts with Manuela's own immature distaste for her Indian suitor, and with Pilar's secret passion for him.

*Xochimancas (soh-chee-MAHN-kahs). Stronghold of El Zarco; a hacienda with rich soil, abundant water, and ideal climate for growing crops that has fallen into ruin during the occupation of El Zarco and, apparently, more than five hundred bandits. El Zarco takes Manuela to the place, which proves to be little better than a prison for her. There, she is forced to live with drunken, ragged women and unscrupulous bandits. Manuela's first experience of life outside conventions horrifies her, but she is trapped.

— *Debra D. Andrist*

THE ZOO STORY

Author: Edward Albee (1928-   )
Type of work: Drama
Type of plot: Absurdist

Time of plot: Late 1950's
First performed: 1959; first published, 1959

The stage setting of this play is restricted to a pair of benches in New York City's Central Park on a sunny Sunday afternoon; however, there are also important allusions to other locations.

*Central Park.** Large public park in central Manhattan represented in the play only by benches on opposite edges of the stage. The atmosphere initially seems pleasant as a man named Peter, seated at stage right, reads under a canopy of plants and the sky. The repose is broken when Jerry enters and insists on engaging Peter in conversation. Another pair of locations quickly becomes central to the unfolding events. Peter lives in a toney neighborhood east of the park, while Jerry resides in a shabby rooming house on Central Park West. These locations reflect the characters' vastly different lives and suggest fundamental incompatibilities.

On the surface, Central Park appears to occupy neutral ground, but through Jerry's monologues and interrogations, it emerges as symbols of New York City itself and the impersonality of modern urban life. People pass one another without comment or occupy benches and barely exchange glances. Jerry is determined to break through Peter's reserve and establish a human relationship.

Jerry's rooming house. Jerry describes his residence as a battle zone in which he contends with a neighbor's ill-tempered dog. At first, he had tried to placate the dog with hamburgers; later, he had tried to poison the dog. Eventually he and the dog had achieved an understanding; however, Peter cannot comprehend the implications of Jerry's tale.

Zoo. Location that remains off-stage yet uppermost in Jerry's mind. With its cages, the zoo is another symbol of the condition of modern people, constrained by conventionality, etiquette, and repressed emotions. When Peter fails to understand Jerry's dog story, Jerry surrenders his own life to illustrate the condition of debilitating isolation and to establish a profound human connection.

— *David W. Madden*

ZOOT SUIT

Author: Luis Miguel Valdez (1940-   )
Type of work: Drama
Type of plot: Historical

Time of plot: Early 1940's
First performed: 1978; first published, 1978

This play, the first Chicano play produced on Broadway, is based on a historical incident that occurred in Los Angeles in 1942, when hundreds of young Chicanos were arrested and one was tried for murder after a riotous clash with uniformed servicemen.

*Los Angeles.** Sprawling Southern California city in which the play is primarily set in 1942—a time when the city is preparing for war, divided by race, and filling up with military personnel getting ready to ship out to the Pacific. Tensions are high, the mood among military personnel is hyper-patriotic, and the city has no tolerance for anyone who appears to be an unpatriotic slackard. When hundreds of servicemen and party-going Mexican Americans accidentally clash, the result is a large-scale riot that results in hundreds of arrests, including one for murder.

The play's bilingual dialogue, flamboyant "zoot-suit" costuming, energetic dance hall settings, Latin rhythms, and references to Mexican cooking convey the strongly

Mexican flavor of Los Angeles. The play's experimental staging, echoing Chicano street theater, moves rapidly from set to set, from past to present, and from mainstream perspectives to Mexican American perspectives. Meanwhile, the play's master of ceremonies, El Pachuco, pulls everything together through his onstage narration.

Newsboys shout inflammatory headlines on city streets, describing armed zoot-suiters knifing and killing until stopped by the U.S. Navy and Marines and deservingly imprisoned. In one fight scene in an unnamed city bar, Anglo servicemen overpower and strip the Pachuco narrator.

Scenes in the play alternate rapidly among a police station, a courthouse, a jail, and a prison, and the homes, parties, dance halls, and city streets. Flashbacks merge past and present, as a zoot-suited "master of ceremonies" identified only as "El Pachuco"—a term for a street tough—wearing the colors of an Aztec god, narrates the onstage action, connecting the disparate settings and providing multiple interpretations of onstage reality.

At the end of the play, playing with the Mayan philosophy of multiple levels of existence, El Pachuco calls forth a series of vignettes representing alternative futures for the murder suspect, Henry Reyna: a supportive and united family scene in a family living room; a prison scene with Henry killed in a prison fight; a Korean War scene, with Henry dying heroically; a public political scene with Henry awarded a posthumous Congressional Medal of Honor; a family vignette of Henry as a father surrounded by several children; and a mythic Aztec scene, with Henry transformed into El Pachuco, a symbol of Chicano heritage and oppression.

Reyna house. Lower-middle class home of the family of Henry Reyna, who is arrested for murder during the riots. His family sits around a kitchen table, the mother cooking, the father sharing a first drink with his son, as the three youngsters prepare for a night out.

Dance hall. Scene of Reyna's farewell celebration before he is to ship out for the Pacific the next day. Bright colors, lively Latin music, zoot suits, and fast-paced dancing signify a nonmainstream culture. A minor scuffle with a rival gang pushes dancers into the streets, where gang territory and switchblades turn Reyna's brave attempt to end a one-sided conflict into police violence and mass arrests.

Sleepy Lagoon reservoir. Romantic spot in East Los Angeles where young couples meet, and near which the Mexican Americans, attracted by lively music of a birthday party, are mistakenly attacked. The Mexican American youths tell one story, the Anglo youths another.

Courtroom. Place in which Reyna is tried for murder. His trial is a legal farce. The deck is stacked against Mexican Americans, who are regarded as unpatriotic outsiders, and the judge prejudges Reyna's guilt. The trial itself creates the passion within the play. The boys of Reyna's gang are looked upon as social delinquents, as criminals, and even as foreigners. At no point during the proceedings are they or their attorney allowed a fair opportunity to present their case. The trial is presented in only two scenes of the first act, but it propels much of the conflict of the play.

— *Gina Macdonald*

ZORBA THE GREEK

Author: Nikos Kazantzakis (1883-1957)
Type of work: Novel
Type of plot: Psychological realism

Time of plot: Mid-twentieth century
First published: Vios kai politela tou Alexe Zormpa,
1946 (English translation, 1952)

Set on the island of Crete, this story of an unnamed narrator known as the Boss and the irrepressible Zorba dramatizes two conflicting views of life: the ascetic and the hedonistic. Devastated by separation from a close friend who has given up scholarship for soldiering, the Boss is taking tentative steps to become more active in society, although he clings desperately to his life as a writer. Zorba, on the other hand, approaches life with élan, *taking pleasure where he can and refusing to look too deeply for meaning in anything that happens to him or others. The events of this episodic novel seem mere pretenses for Kazantzakis to create conversations between his two protagonists about what gives life meaning. Eventually, both the narrator and Zorba tire of Crete and separate.*

Piraeus tavern. Place on Crete where the Boss meets Zorba. A chance encounter throws together the two protagonists, and readers immediately see the difference in their outlooks on life. Zorba is a reckless adventurer who travels where his heart takes him; the Boss is a sensitive thinker, afraid to strike out on his own. The location is important because it establishes a motif that is thematically central to the novel: the lure of the sea, a metaphor for the unknown that awaits every traveler through life.

The Boss's hut. Seaside shack in which the Boss and Zorba live as they work at mining lignite. While Zorba supervises the miners and works beside them, the Boss frequently remains at the hut writing a book about Buddha. At the end of each day, the two frequently converse about issues such as God, human immortality, the wisdom of activity versus contemplation, the place of women and family in men's lives, and other philosophical and moral issues.

Significantly, the hut is set beside the sea, a central symbol in the novel. Both Zorba and the Boss recognize the mystery posed by the sea, on which hundreds of generations of men have gone to seek adventure, fortune, and happiness. The warm breezes that blow north across the sea from Africa suggest both the source of human life and the life-giving forces of nature—concepts that the Boss struggles to understand.

Madame Hortense's hotel. Located in the village, Madame Hortense's hotel is a pivotal locale in the novel. Through the character of Madame Hortense, Kazant-

zakis displays the fate of women in the world, and her home is emblematic of the transient nature of male-female relationships. Once the mistress of men from many nations, she is now reduced to keeping house for travelers who pass through the village. At her death, the house is scavenged by other women who take away the mementos that signified her worth as a human being.

Village. Locale for the majority of the action in the novel. Here Zorba carries on a love affair with Madame Hortense, and the Boss meets the widow whose death at the hands of angry villagers causes him personal pain and leads him to question further the purpose of life. Like the inhabitants of Megalokastro, the village in Kazantzakis's *Freedom or Death* (1953), the citizens of this village display the values that characterize Crete itself: a proud sense of self-reliance based on isolation from other centers of civilization, a keen sense of family loyalty, and a zest for life that Zorba admires but the Boss mistrusts.

Monastery. Religious community that the Boss and Zorba visit at the invitation of Zacharias, a monk who has become disillusioned with life there. Within the walls of the monastery, they discover that monks ostensibly devoted to the service of God carry on lives characterized by petty jealousies, scandalous sexual behavior, acquisitiveness, and preferment based on favoritism rather than merit. With Zorba's help, Zacharias gains revenge on the monks by burning down the monastery.

— *Laurence W. Mazzeno*

ZULEIKA DOBSON: Or, An Oxford Love Story

Author: Max Beerbohm (1872-1956)
Type of work: Novel
Type of plot: Satire

Time of plot: Early twentieth century
First published: 1911

England's Oxford University in this novel represents a microcosm of upper-class life in England, within which the doomed love affair of two people who do not understand the nature of love is examined in satirical detail.

*Oxford. City that is home to one of England's great universities. Max Beerbohm was educated at public school and Oxford University, and his familiarity with the city and the establishment of which it was a part is clearly shown in *Zuleika Dobson*. As a city, Oxford is not described in much detail in the novel. General references to "the Corn" (Cornmarket Street), "the Broad" (Broad Street), and other landmarks assume that the reader is familiar with the city and satirize assumptions made in other novels about Oxford. Beerbohm exploits this vagueness when he inserts a fictional college into the genuine layout of the city and moves two streets without unduly disturbing its geography. However, even the "real" Oxford of his novel is somehow unreal, as the omniscient narrator recognizes when he describes the warden's landau moving "through those slums which connect Oxford with the world."

There is a constant emphasis on the world within the world: the university as a second city within the city; the college within the university; and, finally, at Judas College, the hidden quadrangle, the Salt Cellar, within the college itself. There is no world portrayed outside the city: The closest the reader comes to that is at Oxford railway station, which acts as a symbol of arrival and departure, or the river, which flows out of Oxford. All this is embedded within an iconic vision of Oxford, the "city of dreaming spires." This provides a neat geographical metaphor for the self-absorption shown in various ways by the primary characters, each of whom is too self-contained to be able to engage properly with the world at large.

Judas College. Fictional Oxford college that lies somewhere beyond Broad Street. Zuleika Dobson's connection to Oxford is through her grandfather, the warden of this college. Founded by Christopher Whitrid Knight, in the reign of Henry VI, its dedication to the disciple who betrayed Jesus could only belong to a fictional college. Most Oxford colleges have a reputation of one kind or another, and Beerbohm here implies that Judas is the least worthy of colleges. Like most colleges,

Judas is a self-contained world, but Beerbohm suggests that even by Oxford standards it is remote and cites an episode of its history when sixty armed men hid within Salt Cellar, its most secret quadrangle, for a month before their presence was betrayed by the warden of that time. The current warden of Judas is thoroughly unworldly and remains mostly aloof, even from the life of his own college.

Zuleika lives in the warden's lodgings during her stay at Oxford, further underlining her family's dislocation from the university, the town, and the town's residents. The reader sees her in her room, leading a fairy-tale existence in which she is waited on, hand and foot, by her maid, while all her possessions, however inappropriately, are ornamented with jewels. The duke of Dorset, a distinguished member of the college, chooses to live in ordinary lodgings in Broad Street, in the belief that this brings him into closer contact with the "town," but in truth, he is no closer to the townsfolk than he would be if he lived at the college, as he is waited on by the landlady, Mrs. Batch, and her daughter Katie, in exactly the same way as he would be looked after at the college. His contact with the city is limited to dealing with tradesmen. Otherwise the reader encounters him in the streets only in the company of other students.

*River Thames (tehmz). England's longest river, which runs through Oxford. The climax of the novel takes place on the Thames during rowing competitions. It is here that Oxford's students throw themselves into the river at the end of the final race, emulating the duke of Dorset, who has sworn to drown himself for love of Zuleika. The river provides a symbolic and literal means of escape from Oxford and, by extension, life itself, the two having been equated throughout the novel, particularly in a scene earlier in the novel, when the duke, temporarily "sent down" from Oxford, is accompanied to the railway station by a mock-funeral procession (a not-uncommon practice in Oxford until just after World War II).

— *Maureen Speller*

Cyclopedia

of

LITERARY

PLACES

TITLE INDEX

AUTHOR INDEX

PLACE INDEX

This index contains two kinds of entries. Most are primary entries, which are names of specific places, usually followed by the names of the states, provinces, or countries in which they are located. Secondary entries are those listed under the names of countries, states, and major cities. The names in both kinds of entries are boldfaced in the main text, but not all boldfaced terms are listed here. Primary entries include only the names of real places and major fictional places for which readers might reasonably be expected to search and exclude generic place names (e.g., bedrooms, gardens, houses, hotels). However, many generic names—as well as many names that appear as primary entries—can be found in lists of secondary entries.